Flower of the Deep Sleep

BY YUANA KAZUMI

VOLUME ONE

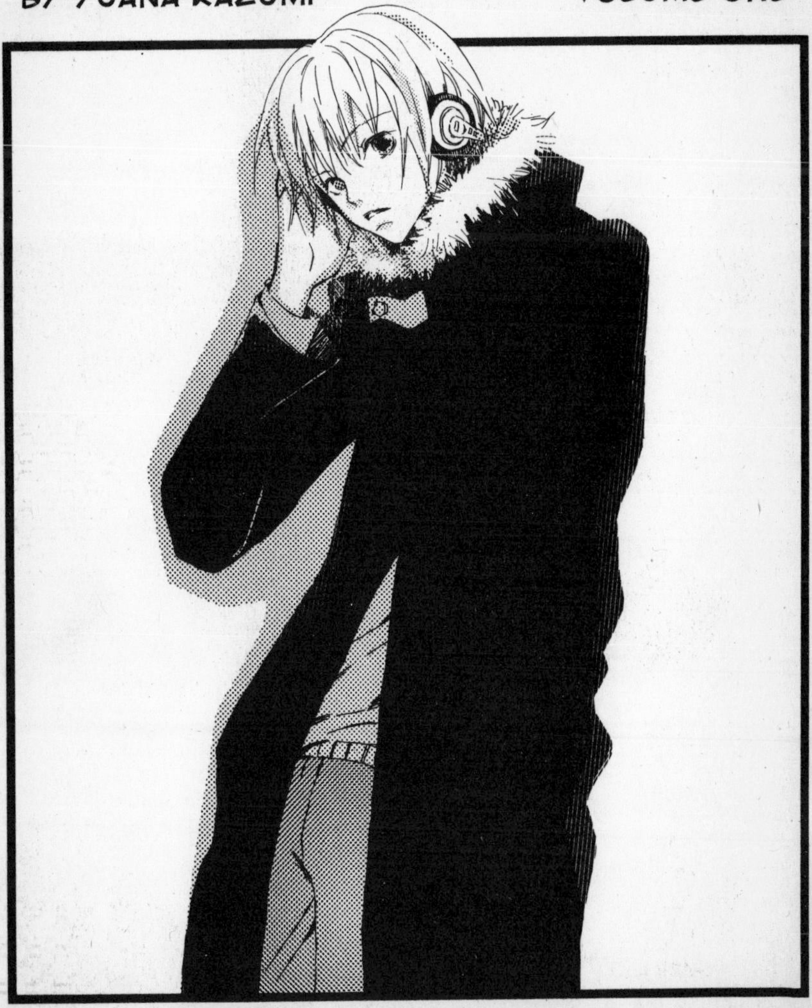

Flower of the Deep Sleep, Vol. One
created by Yuana Kazumi

Translation - Christine Schilling
English Adaptation - Judith Whitaker
Retouch and Lettering - Jose Macasocol, Jr.
Production Artist - John Lo
Copy Editor - Peter Ahlstrom
Graphic Designer - James Lee
Cover Design - Patrick Hook

Editor - Jodi Bryson
Digital Imaging Manager - Chris Buford
Pre-Press Manager - Antonio DePietro
Production Managers - Jennifer Miller and Mutsumi Miyazaki
Art Director - Matt Alford
Managing Editor - Jill Freshney
VP of Production - Ron Klamert
Editor-in-Chief - Mike Kiley
President and C.O.O. - John Parker
Publisher and C.E.O. - Stuart Levy

A  Manga

TOKYOPOP Inc.
5900 Wilshire Blvd. Suite 2000
Los Angeles, CA 90036

E-mail: info@TOKYOPOP.com
Come visit us online at www.TOKYOPOP.com

ISBN: 1-59532-271-X

First TOKYOPOP printing: January 2005
10 9 8 7 6 5 4 3 2 1
Printed in the USA

Flower of the Deep Sleep

VOLUME ONE

BY
YUANA KAZUMI

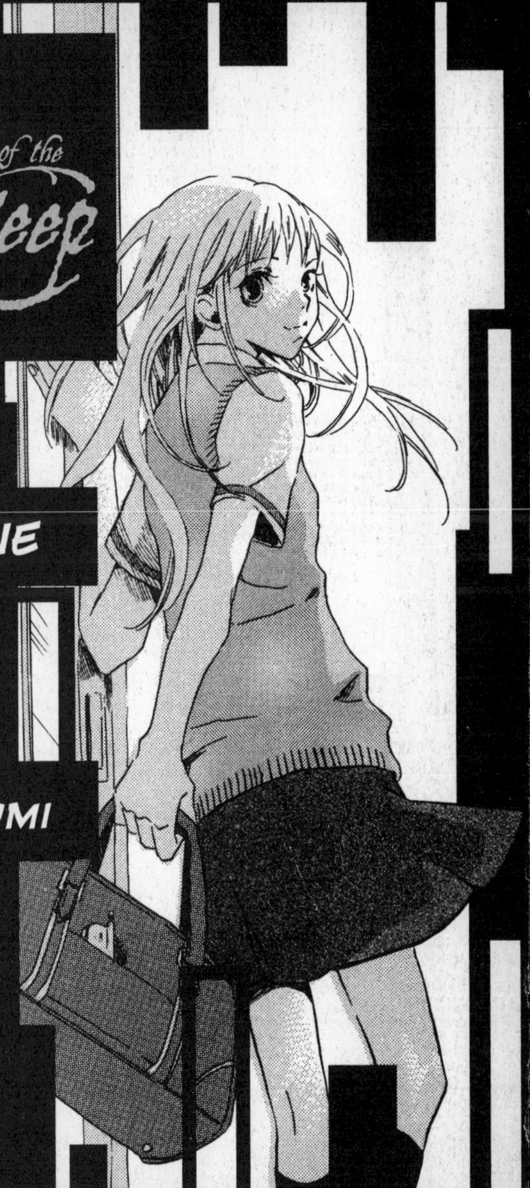

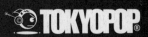

TOKYOPOP®

HAMBURG // LONDON // LOS ANGELES // TOKYO

CONTENTS

CHAPTER 1)
THE FIRST
NIGHT

-3-

CHAPTER 2)
THE SECOND
NIGHT

-47-

CHAPTER 3)
THE THIRD
NIGHT

-79-

CHAPTER 4)
THE FOURTH
NIGHT

-111-

CHAPTER 5)
THE FIFTH
NIGHT

-143-

AFTERWORD

-175-

CHAPTER 1 THE FIRST NIGHT

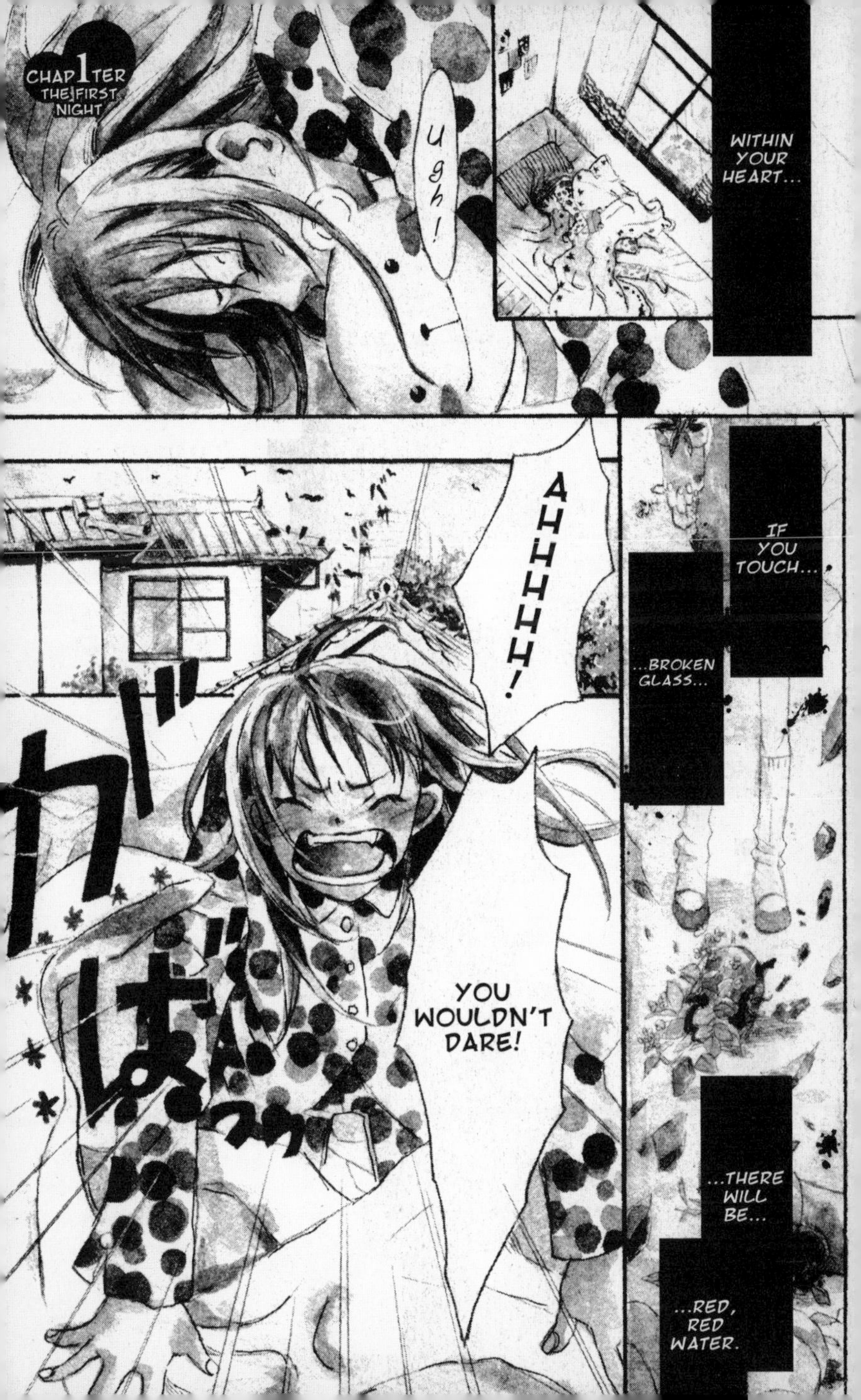
WITHIN YOUR HEART...
Ugh!
IF YOU TOUCH...
...BROKEN GLASS...
...THERE WILL BE...
...RED, RED WATER.
AHHHHHH!
YOU WOULDN'T DARE!

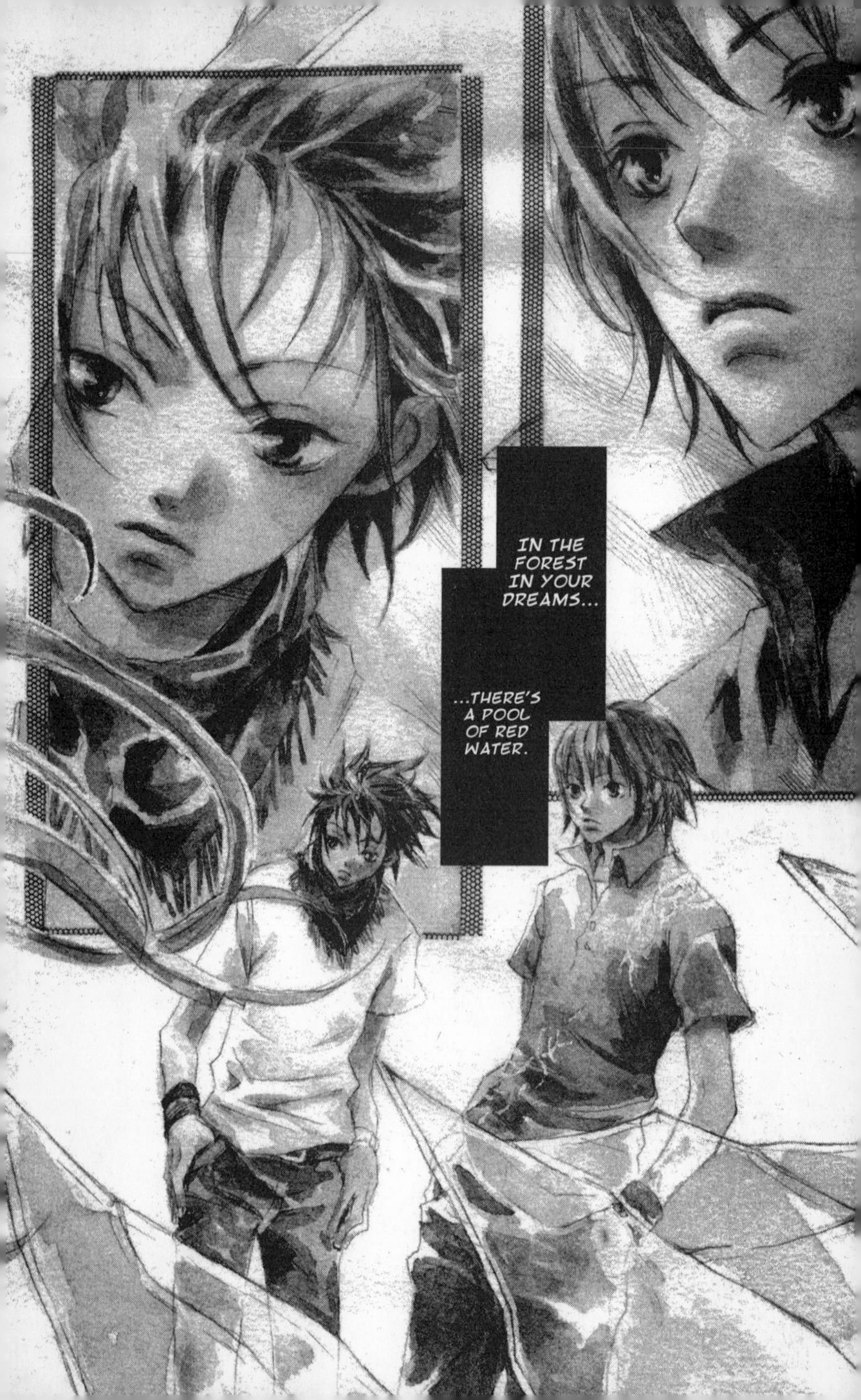
IN THE FOREST IN YOUR DREAMS...
...THERE'S A POOL OF RED WATER.

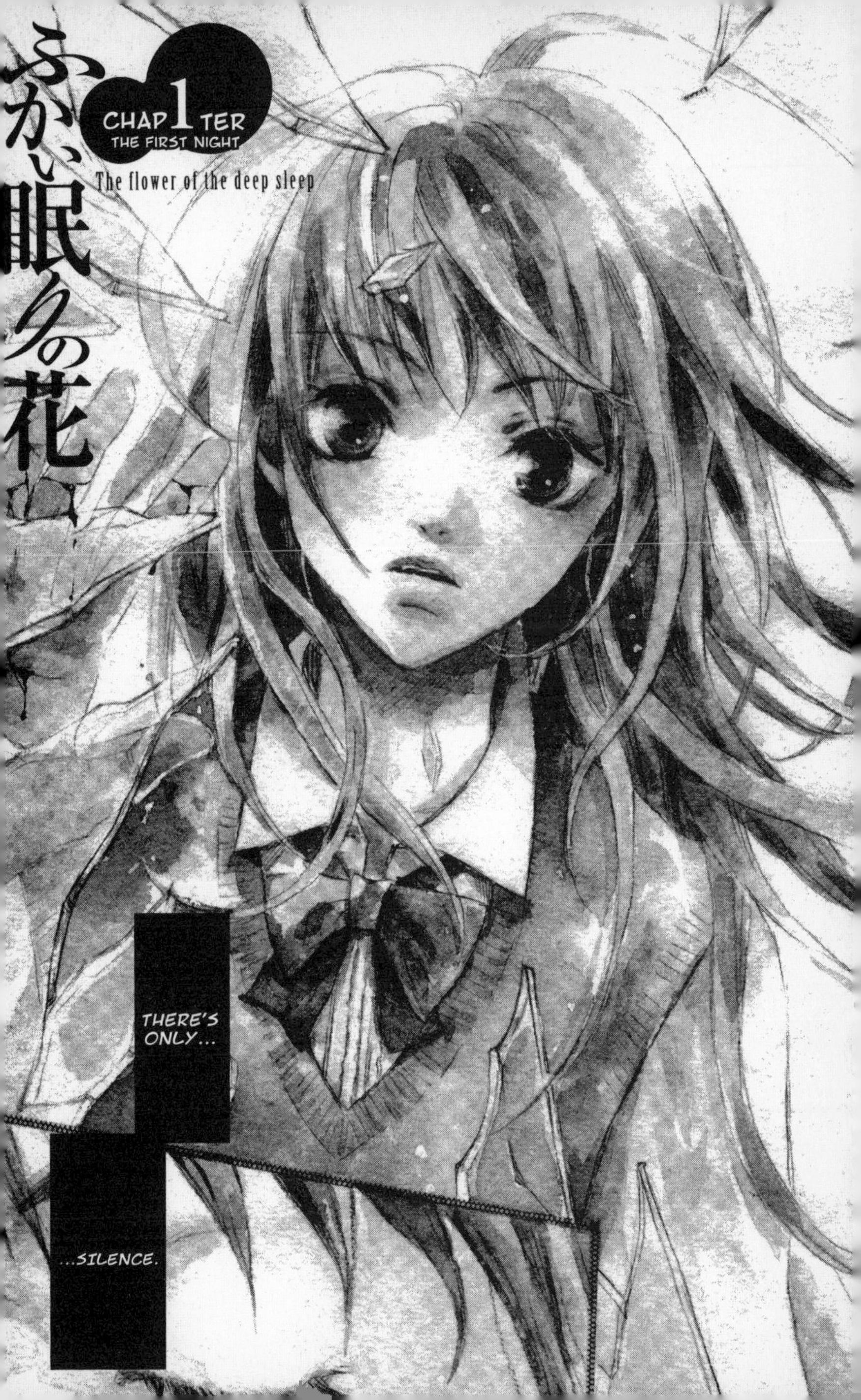
ふかい眠りの花
CHAP 1 TER
THE FIRST NIGHT
The flower of the deep sleep
THERE'S ONLY...
...SILENCE.

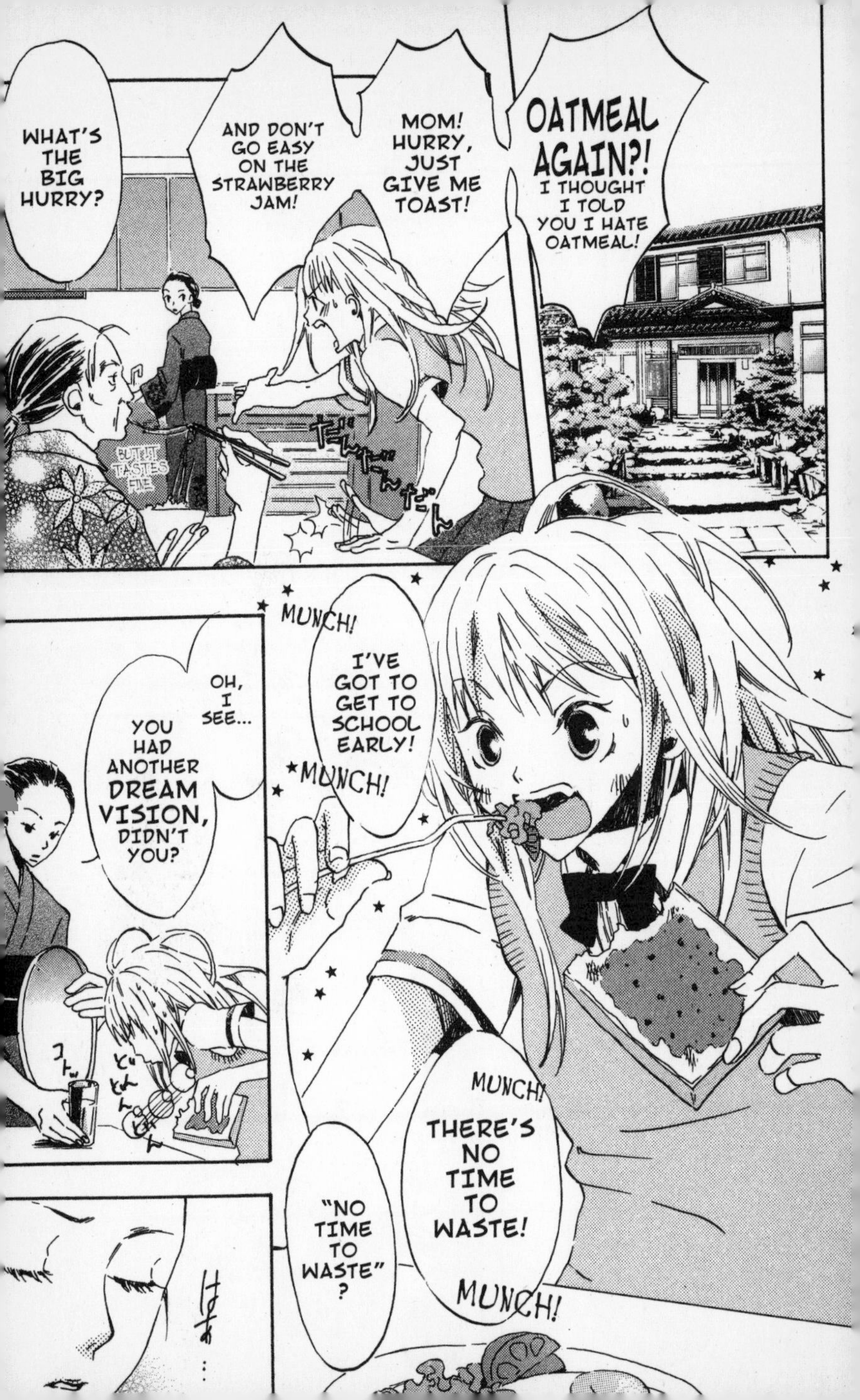

OATMEAL AGAIN?! I THOUGHT I TOLD YOU I HATE OATMEAL!
MOM! HURRY, JUST GIVE ME TOAST!
AND DON'T GO EASY ON THE STRAWBERRY JAM!
WHAT'S THE BIG HURRY?
BUT IT TASTES FINE
MUNCH!
I'VE GOT TO GET TO SCHOOL EARLY!
MUNCH!
MUNCH!
THERE'S NO TIME TO WASTE!
MUNCH!
OH, I SEE...
YOU HAD ANOTHER DREAM VISION, DIDN'T YOU?
"NO TIME TO WASTE"?

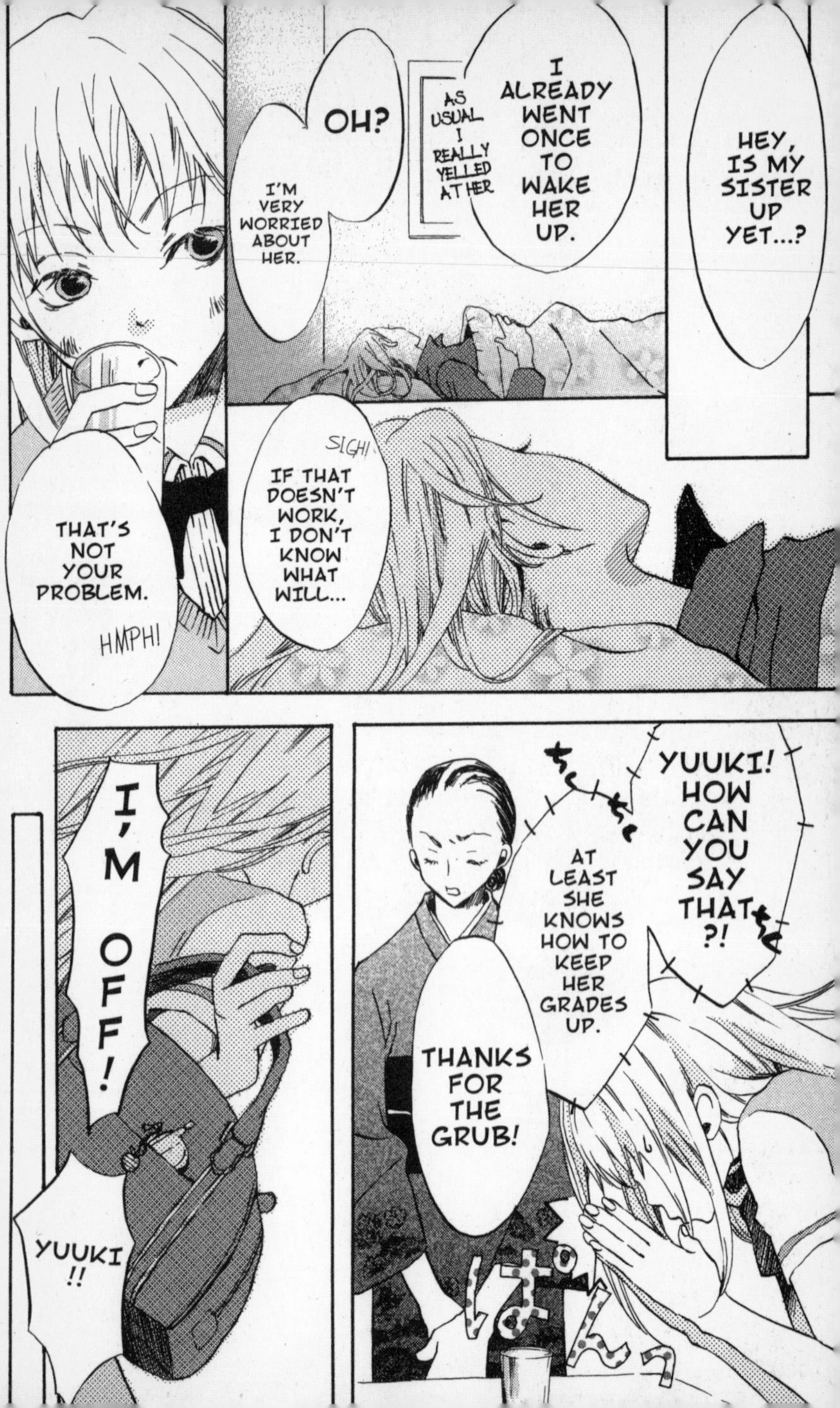
HEY, IS MY SISTER UP YET...?
I ALREADY WENT ONCE TO WAKE HER UP.
AS USUAL I REALLY YELLED AT HER
OH?
I'M VERY WORRIED ABOUT HER.
SIGH!
IF THAT DOESN'T WORK, I DON'T KNOW WHAT WILL...
THAT'S NOT YOUR PROBLEM.
HMPH!
YUUKI! HOW CAN YOU SAY THAT?!
AT LEAST SHE KNOWS HOW TO KEEP HER GRADES UP.
THANKS FOR THE GRUB!
I'M OFF!
YUUKI!!

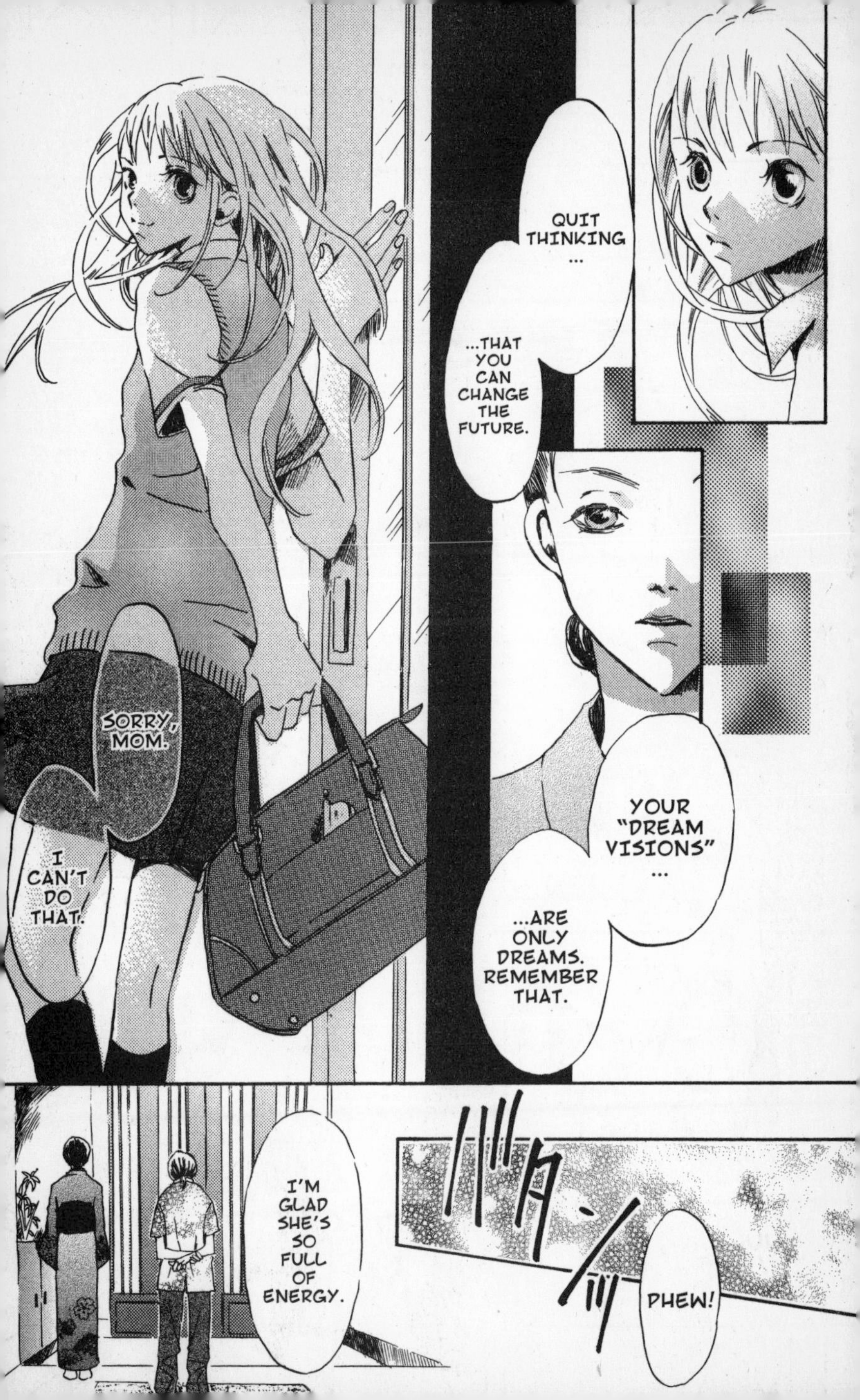
QUIT THINKING ...
...THAT YOU CAN CHANGE THE FUTURE.
YOUR "DREAM VISIONS" ...
...ARE ONLY DREAMS. REMEMBER THAT.
SORRY, MOM.
I CAN'T DO THAT.
PHEW!
I'M GLAD SHE'S SO FULL OF ENERGY.

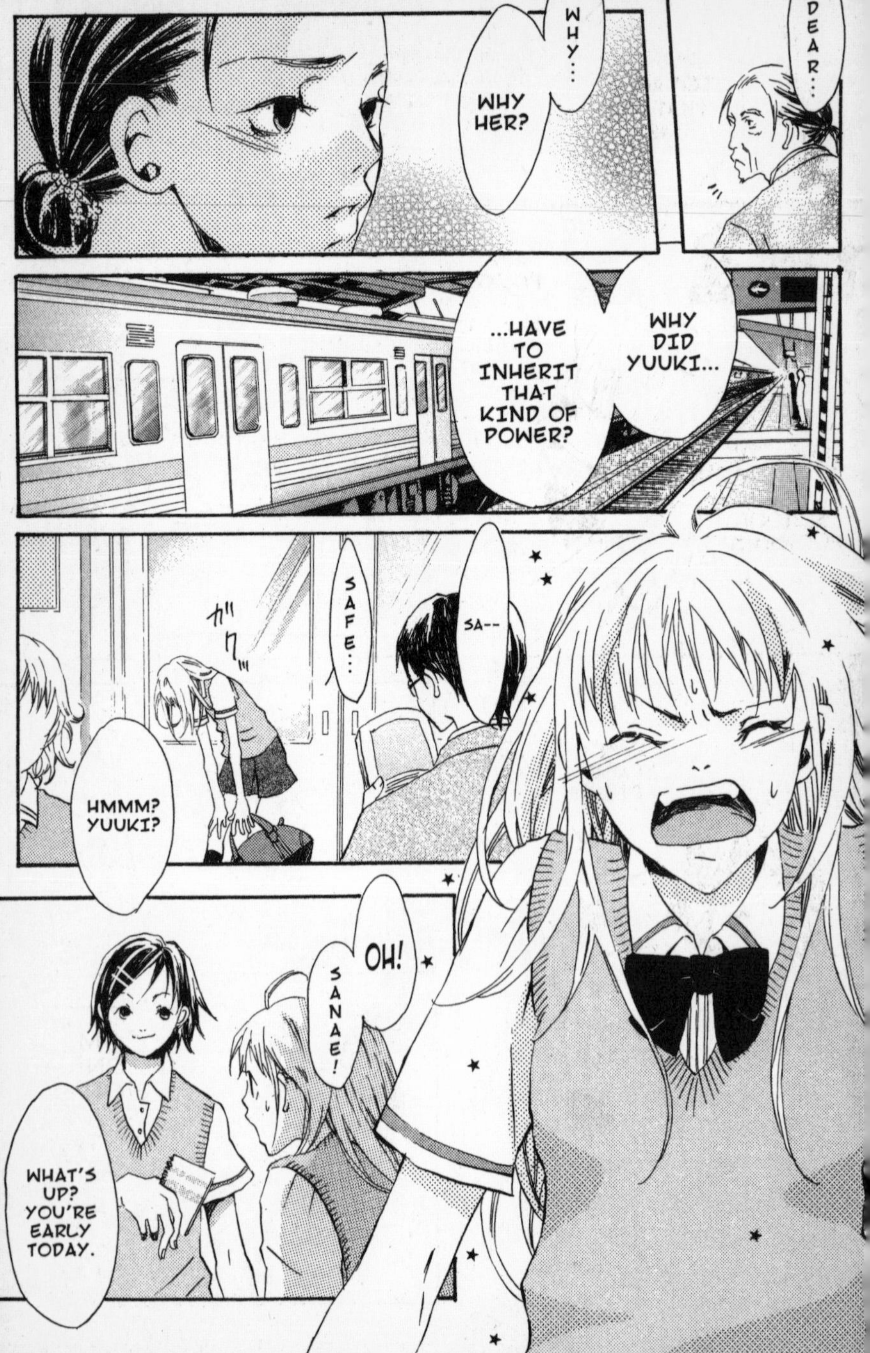
DEAR...
WHY... WHY HER?
WHY DID YUUKI...
...HAVE TO INHERIT THAT KIND OF POWER?
SA--
SAFE...
HMMM? YUUKI?
OH!
SANAE!
WHAT'S UP? YOU'RE EARLY TODAY.

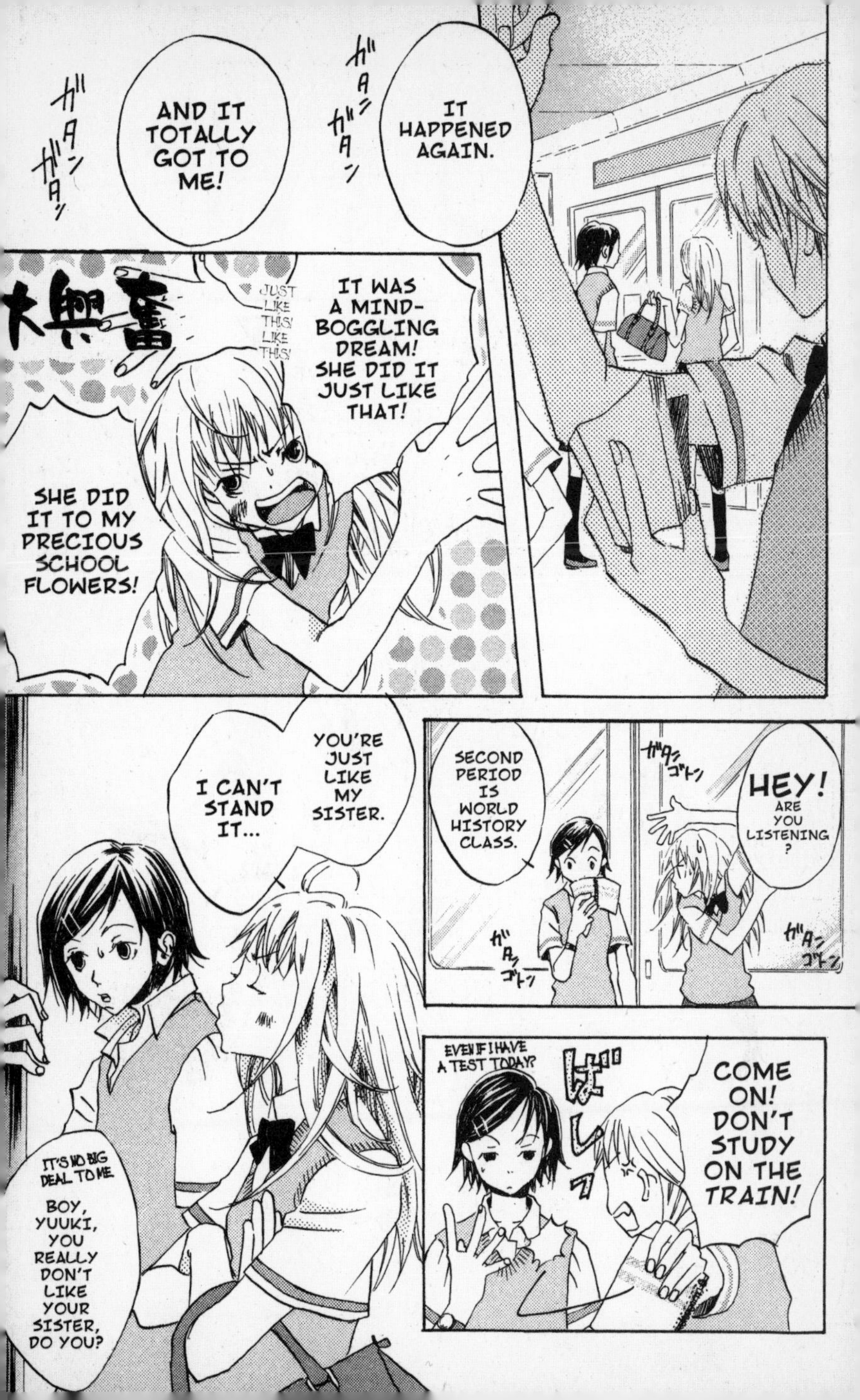
ガタン ガタン
IT HAPPENED AGAIN.
ガタン ガタン
AND IT TOTALLY GOT TO ME!
大興奮
IT WAS A MIND-BOGGLING DREAM! SHE DID IT JUST LIKE THAT!
JUST LIKE THIS! LIKE THIS!
SHE DID IT TO MY PRECIOUS SCHOOL FLOWERS!
HEY! ARE YOU LISTENING?
SECOND PERIOD IS WORLD HISTORY CLASS.
COME ON! DON'T STUDY ON THE TRAIN!
EVEN IF I HAVE A TEST TODAY?
YOU'RE JUST LIKE MY SISTER.
I CAN'T STAND IT...
BOY, YUUKI, YOU REALLY DON'T LIKE YOUR SISTER, DO YOU?
IT'S NO BIG DEAL TO ME

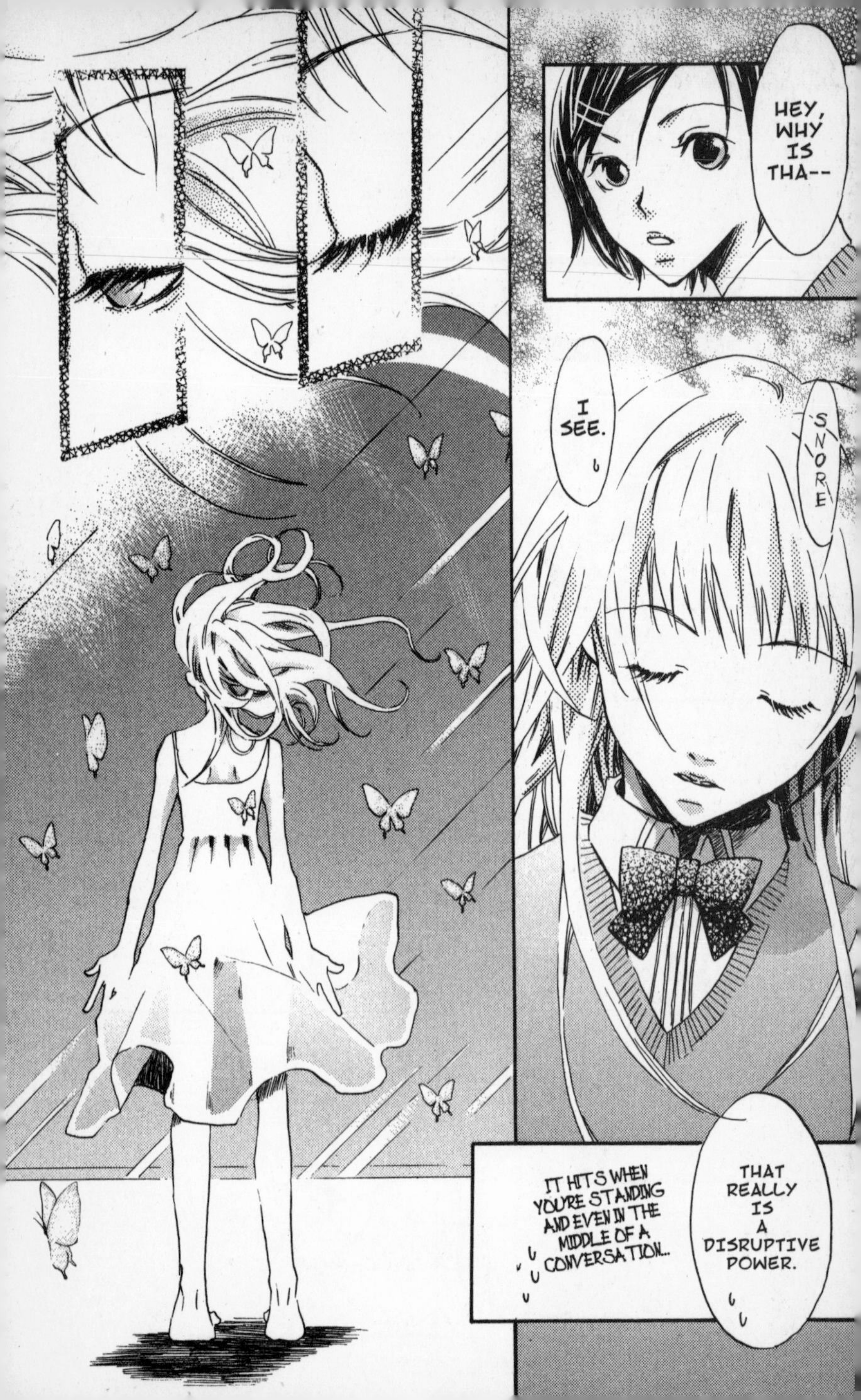
HEY, WHY IS THA--
I SEE.
SNORE
THAT REALLY IS A DISRUPTIVE POWER.
IT HITS WHEN YOU'RE STANDING AND EVEN IN THE MIDDLE OF A CONVERSATION...

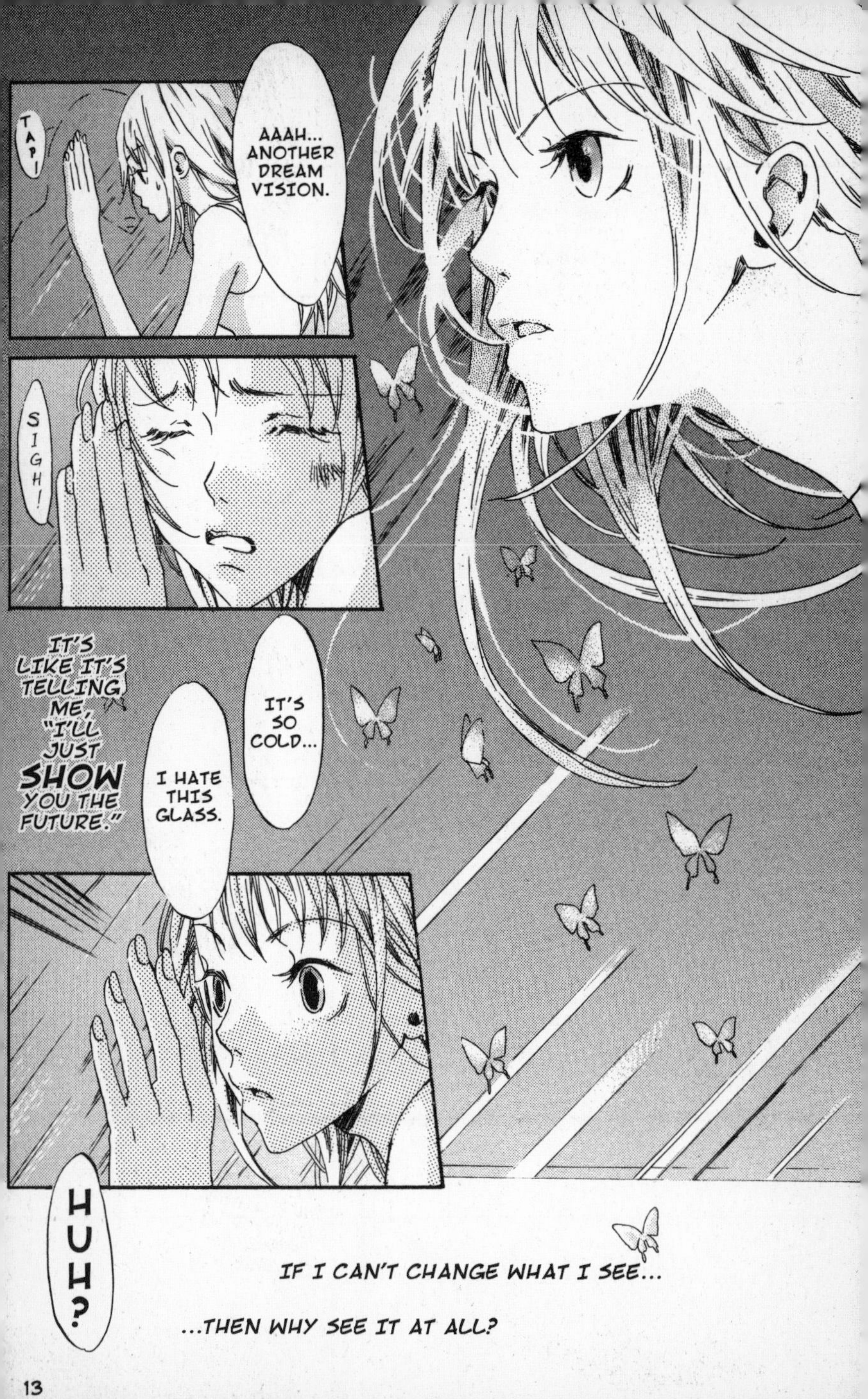
AAAH... ANOTHER DREAM VISION.
TAP!
SIGH!
IT'S SO COLD...
I HATE THIS GLASS.
IT'S LIKE IT'S TELLING ME, "I'LL JUST SHOW YOU THE FUTURE."
HUH?
IF I CAN'T CHANGE WHAT I SEE...
...THEN WHY SEE IT AT ALL?

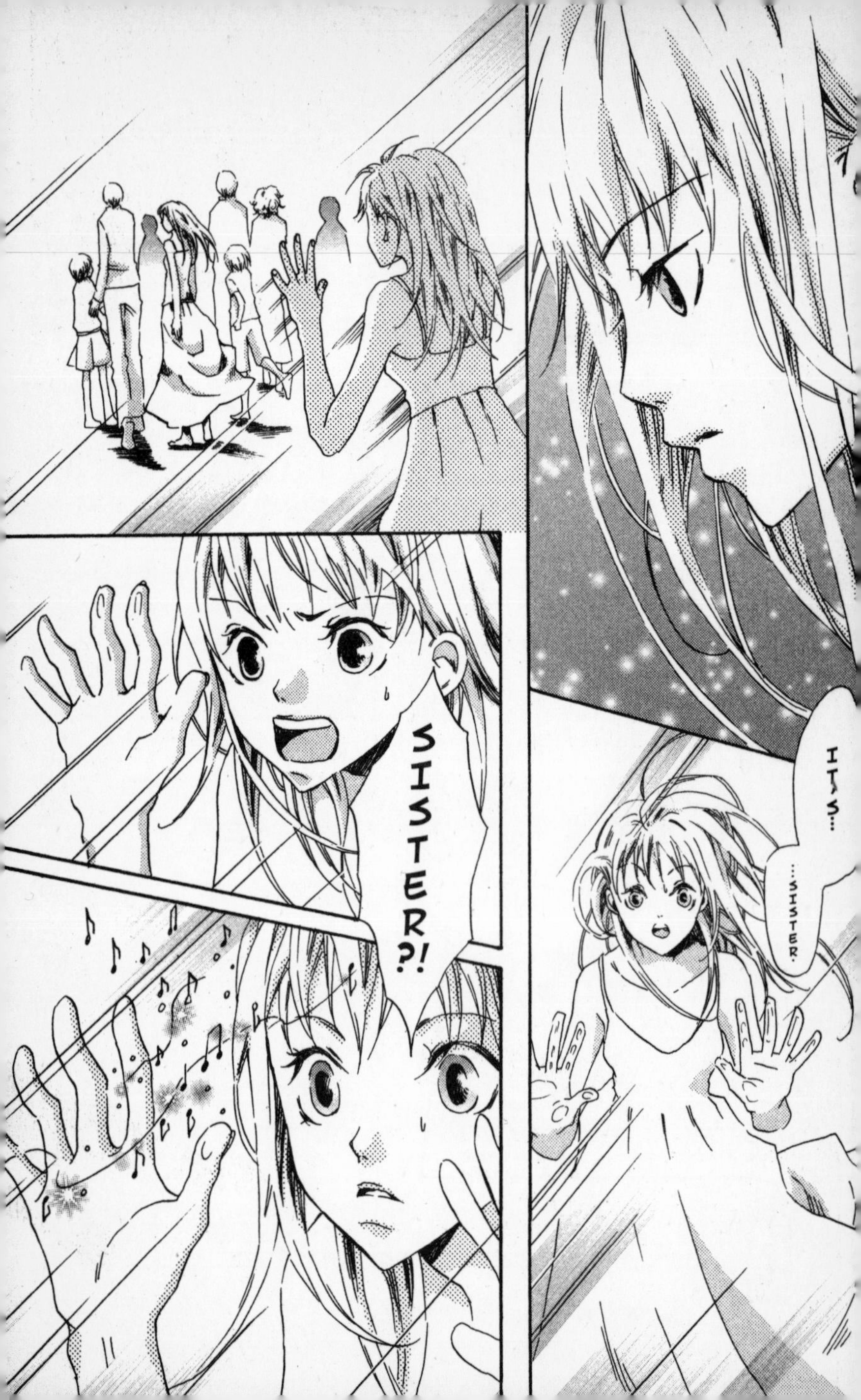
IT'S...
...SISTER.
SISTER?!

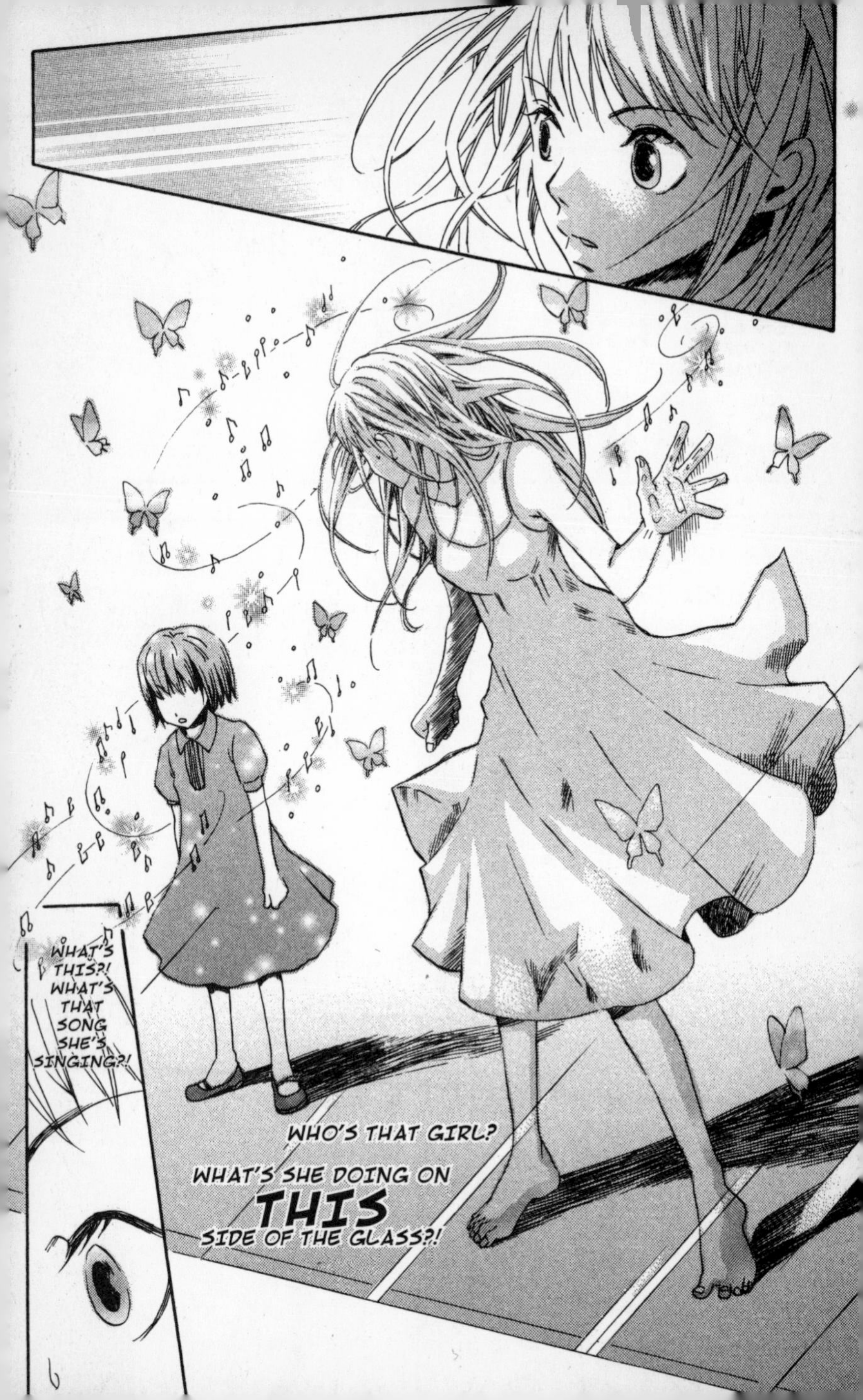
WHAT'S THIS?! WHAT'S THAT SONG SHE'S SINGING?!
WHO'S THAT GIRL?
WHAT'S SHE DOING ON THIS SIDE OF THE GLASS?!

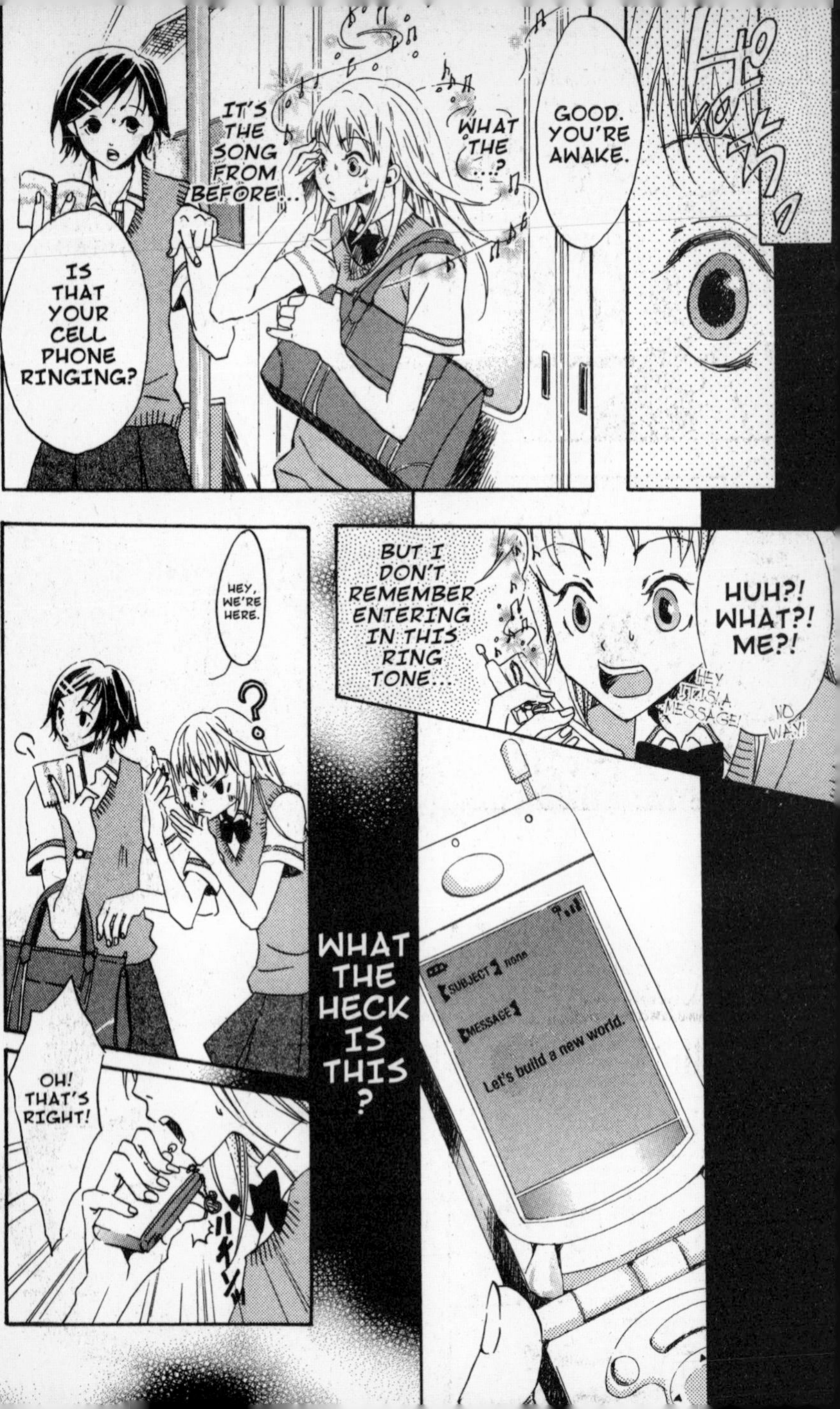
GOOD. YOU'RE AWAKE.
WHAT THE ...?
IT'S THE SONG FROM BEFORE...
IS THAT YOUR CELL PHONE RINGING?
HUH?! WHAT?! ME?!
HEY IT'S A MESSAGE!
NO WAY!
BUT I DON'T REMEMBER ENTERING IN THIS RING TONE...
HEY, WE'RE HERE.
【SUBJECT】 none
【MESSAGE】
Let's build a new world.
WHAT THE HECK IS THIS?
OH! THAT'S RIGHT!

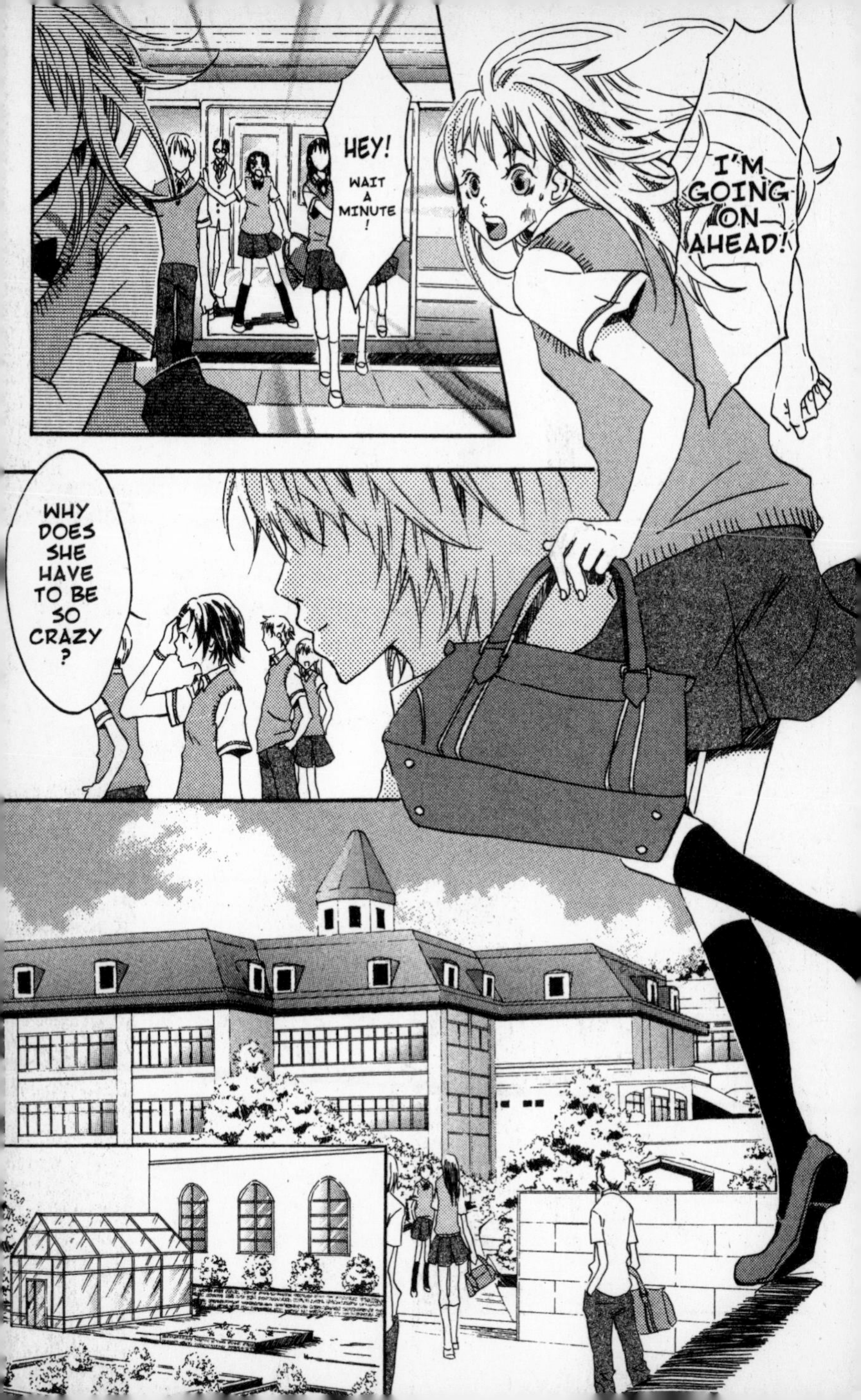
I'M GOING ON AHEAD!
HEY! WAIT A MINUTE!
WHY DOES SHE HAVE TO BE SO CRAZY?

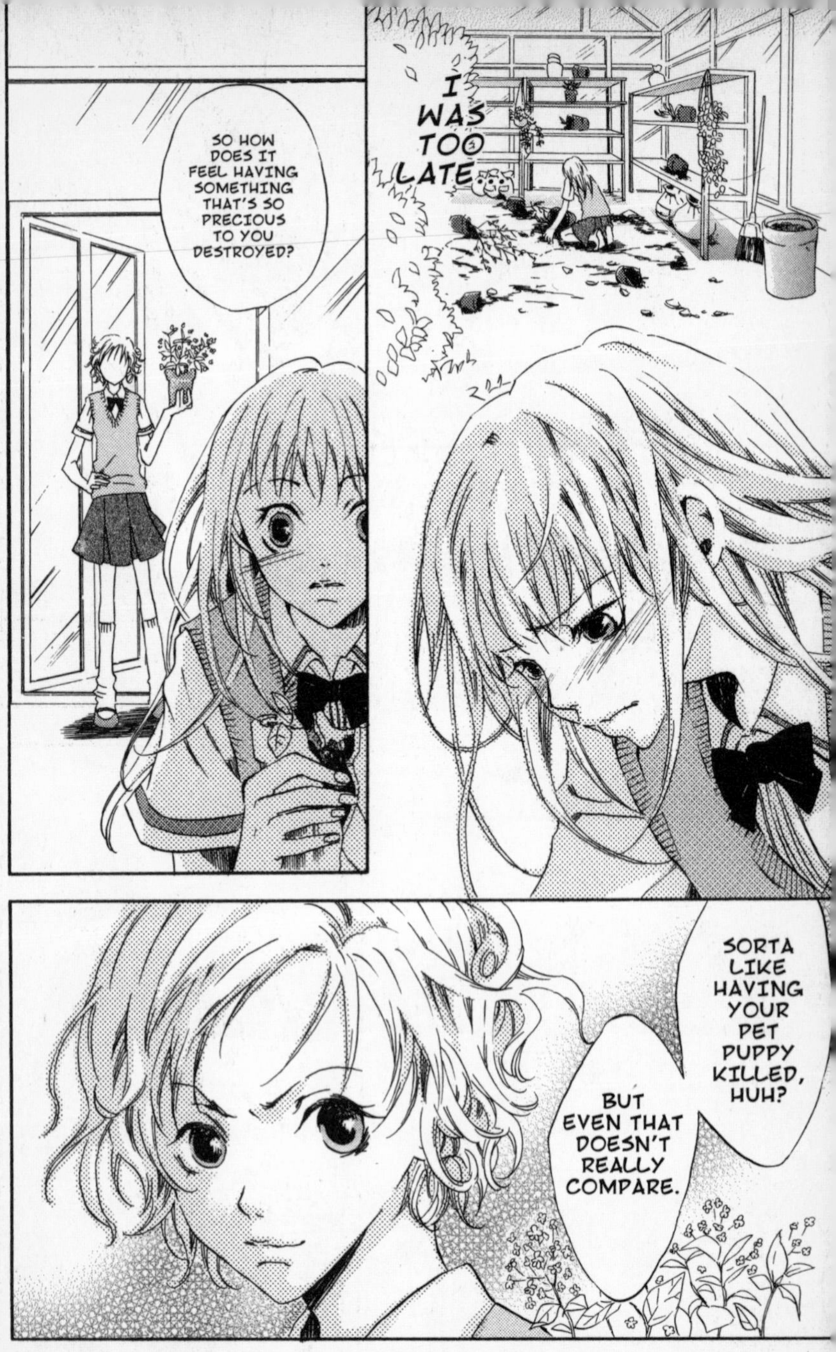
I WAS TOO LATE
SO HOW DOES IT FEEL HAVING SOMETHING THAT'S SO PRECIOUS TO YOU DESTROYED?
SORTA LIKE HAVING YOUR PET PUPPY KILLED, HUH?
BUT EVEN THAT DOESN'T REALLY COMPARE.

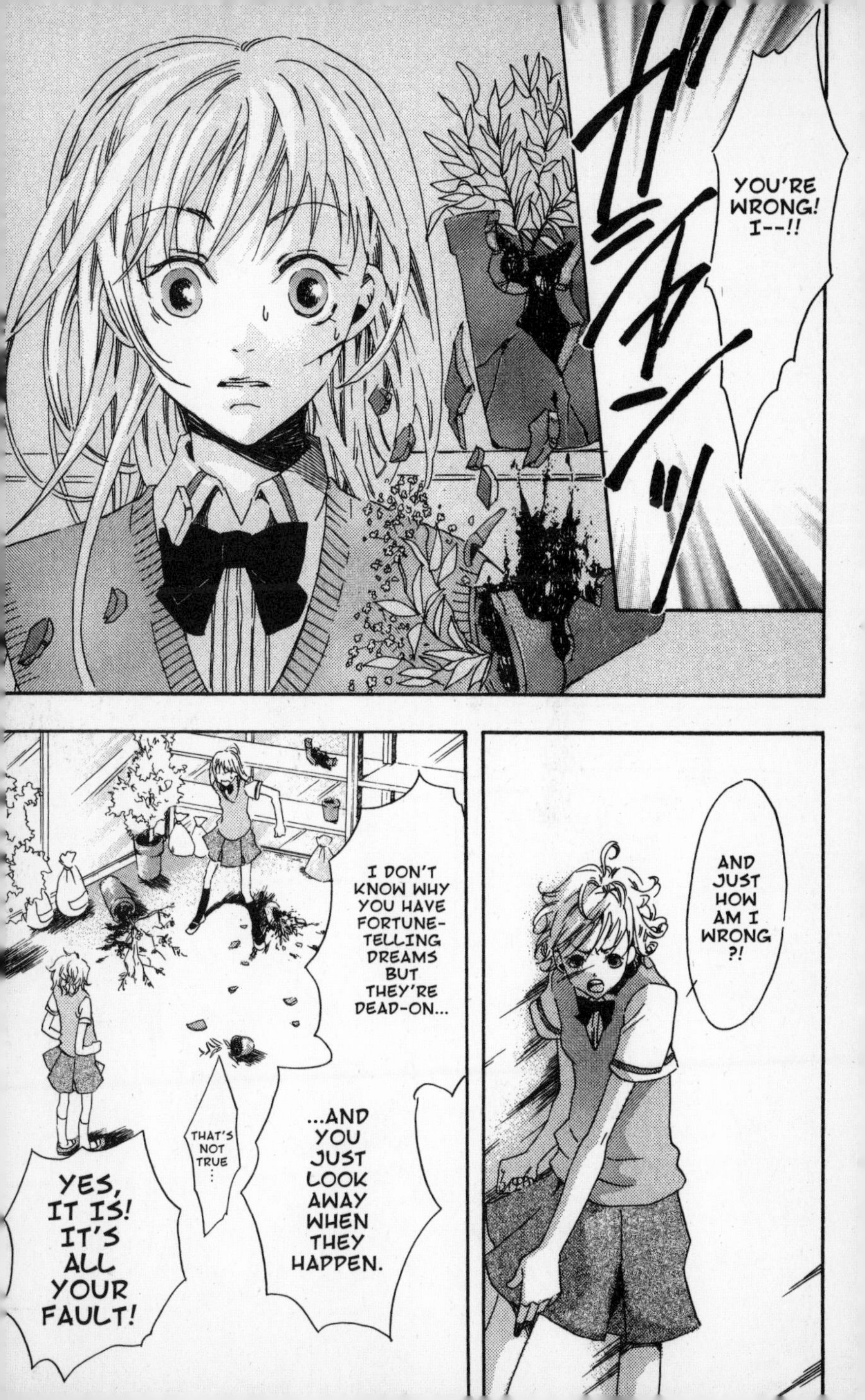
YOU'RE WRONG! I--!!
AND JUST HOW AM I WRONG?!
I DON'T KNOW WHY YOU HAVE FORTUNE-TELLING DREAMS BUT THEY'RE DEAD-ON...
...AND YOU JUST LOOK AWAY WHEN THEY HAPPEN.
THAT'S NOT TRUE...
YES, IT IS! IT'S ALL YOUR FAULT!

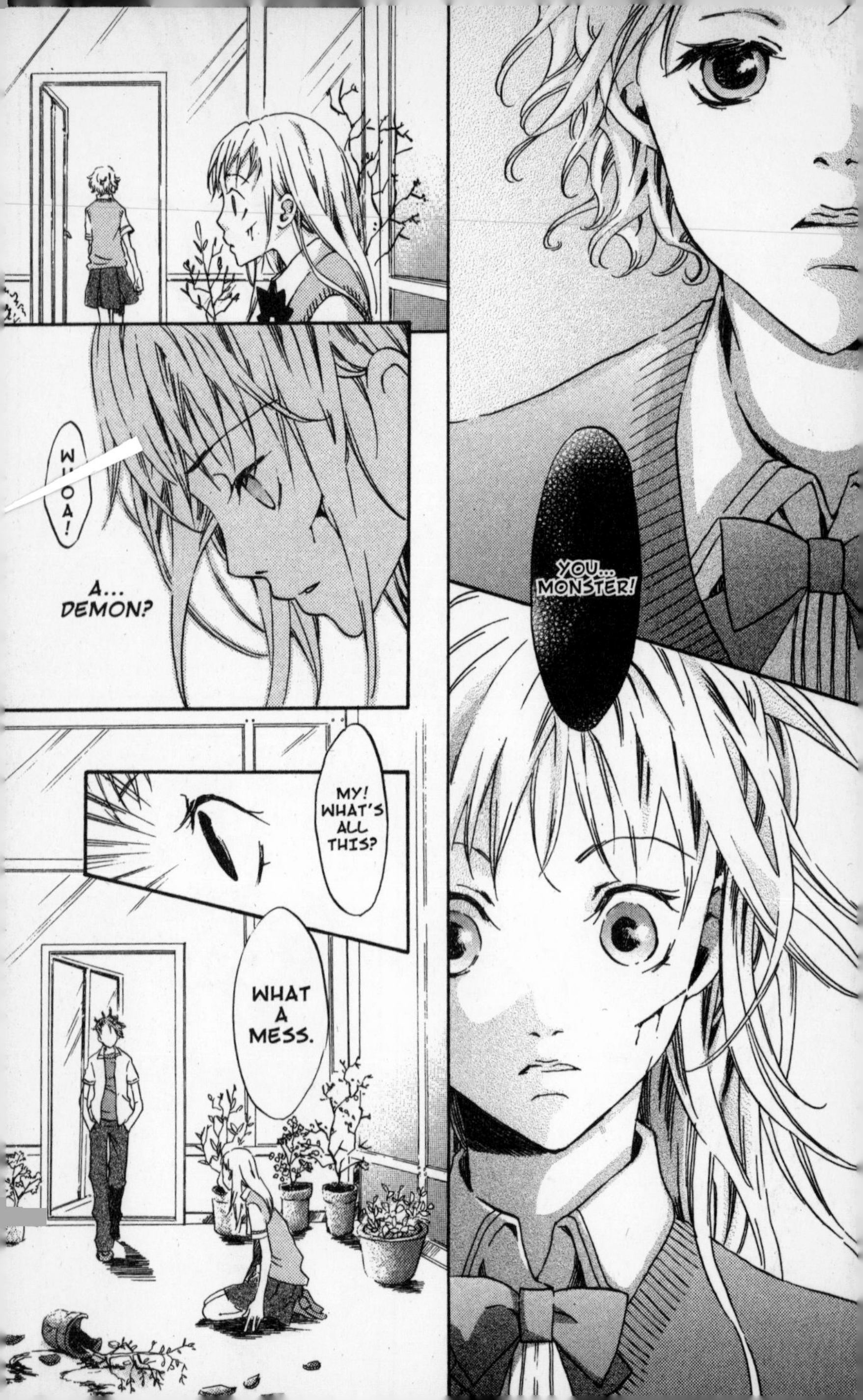
YOU... MONSTER!
WHOA!
A... DEMON?
MY! WHAT'S ALL THIS?
WHAT A MESS.

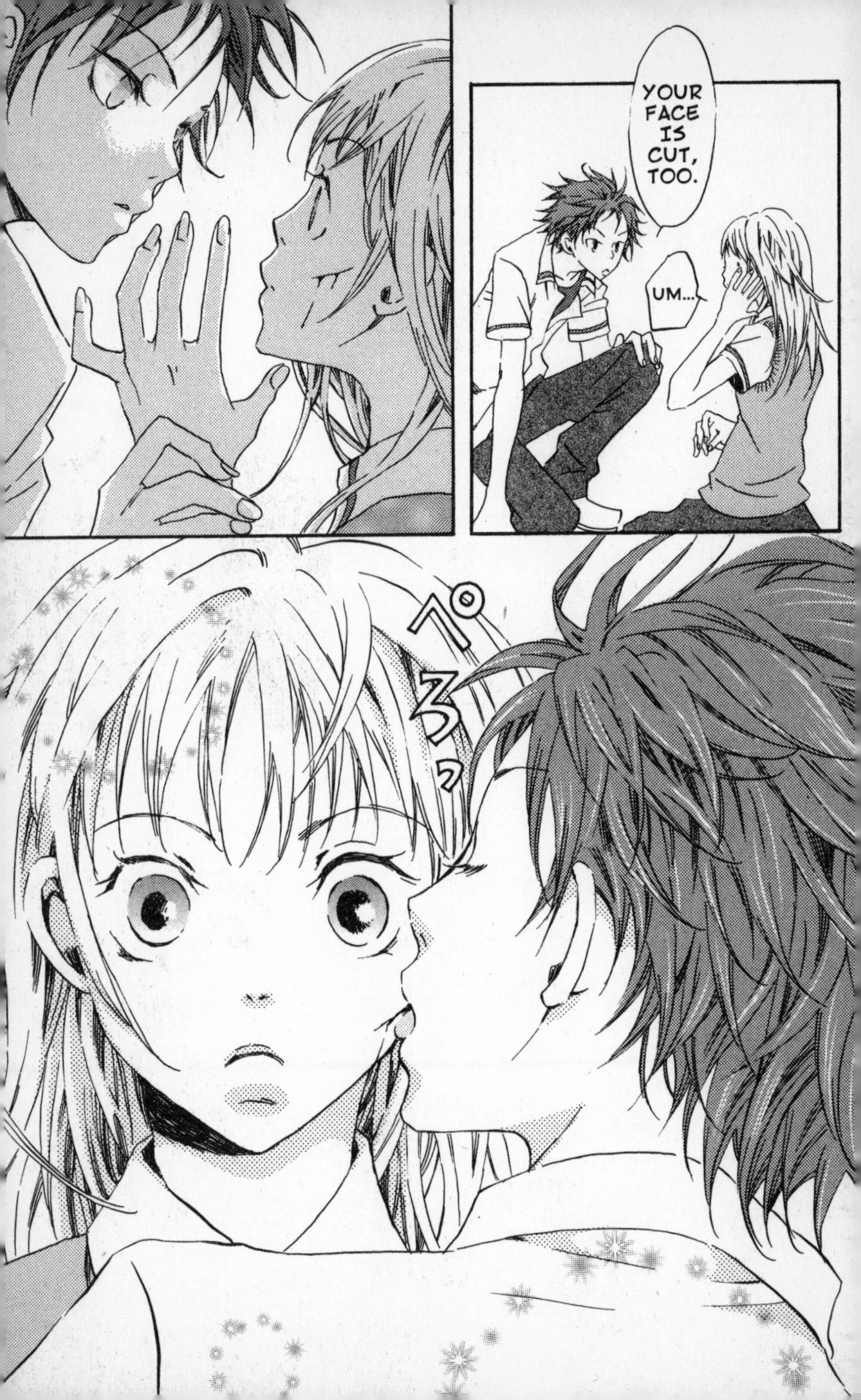
YOUR FACE IS CUT, TOO.
UM...
ぺろっ

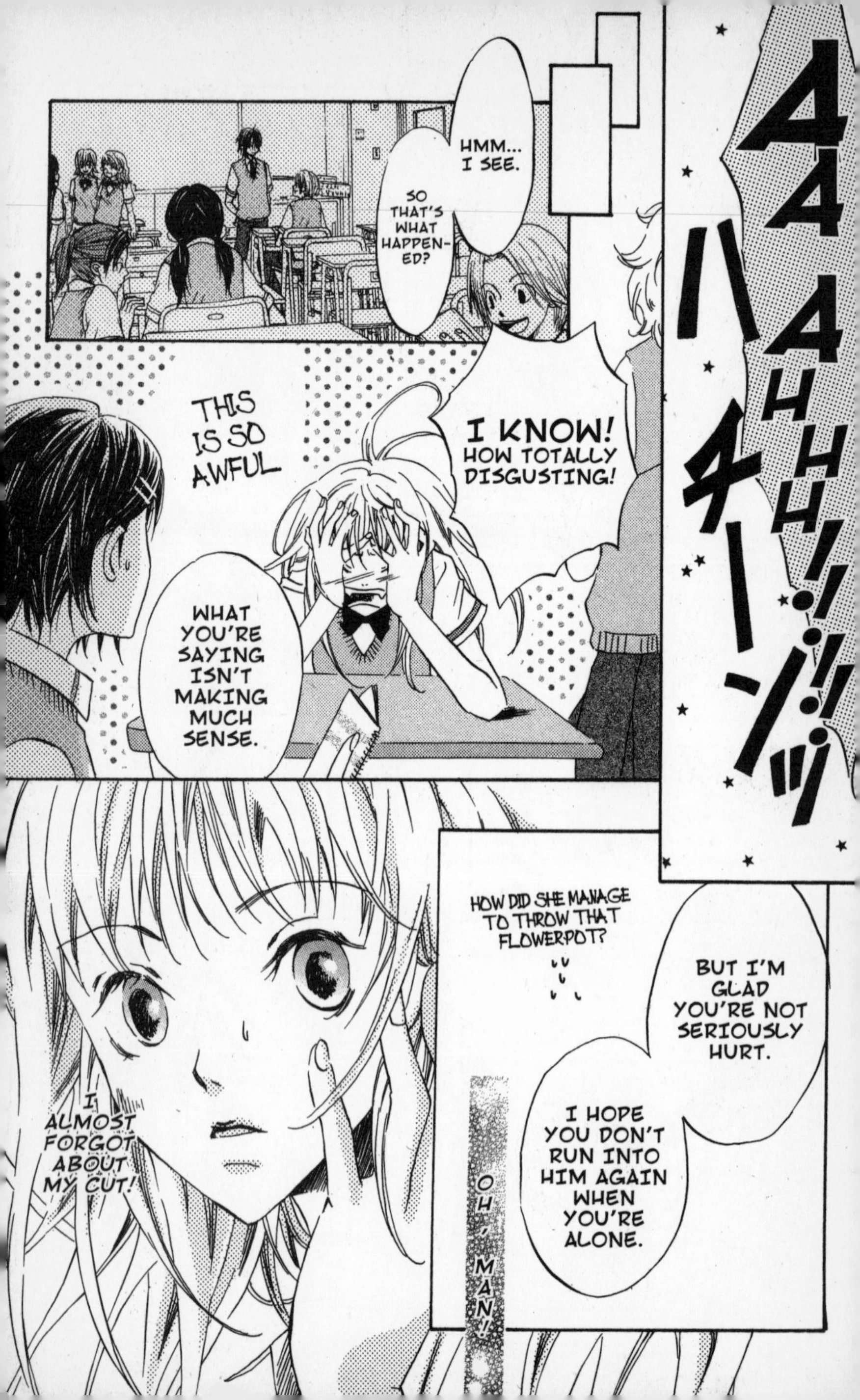
AAAHHHH!!!
HMM... I SEE.
SO THAT'S WHAT HAPPEN-ED?
I KNOW! HOW TOTALLY DISGUSTING!
THIS IS SO AWFUL
WHAT YOU'RE SAYING ISN'T MAKING MUCH SENSE.
HOW DID SHE MANAGE TO THROW THAT FLOWERPOT?
BUT I'M GLAD YOU'RE NOT SERIOUSLY HURT.
I HOPE YOU DON'T RUN INTO HIM AGAIN WHEN YOU'RE ALONE.
OH, MAN!
I ALMOST FORGOT ABOUT MY CUT!

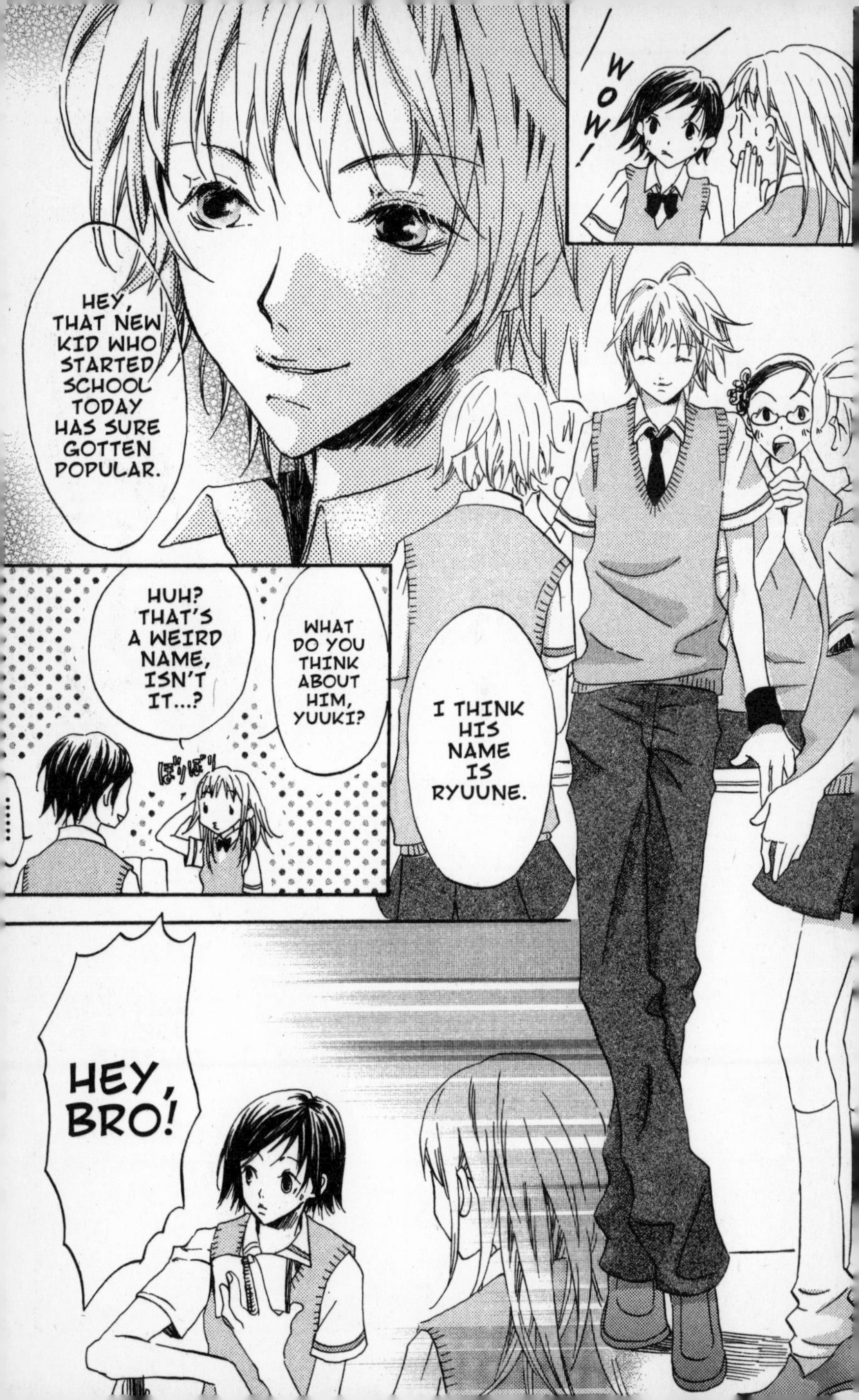
WOW!
HEY, THAT NEW KID WHO STARTED SCHOOL TODAY HAS SURE GOTTEN POPULAR.
I THINK HIS NAME IS RYUUNE.
WHAT DO YOU THINK ABOUT HIM, YUUKI?
HUH? THAT'S A WEIRD NAME, ISN'T IT...?
ぽりぽり
......
HEY, BRO!

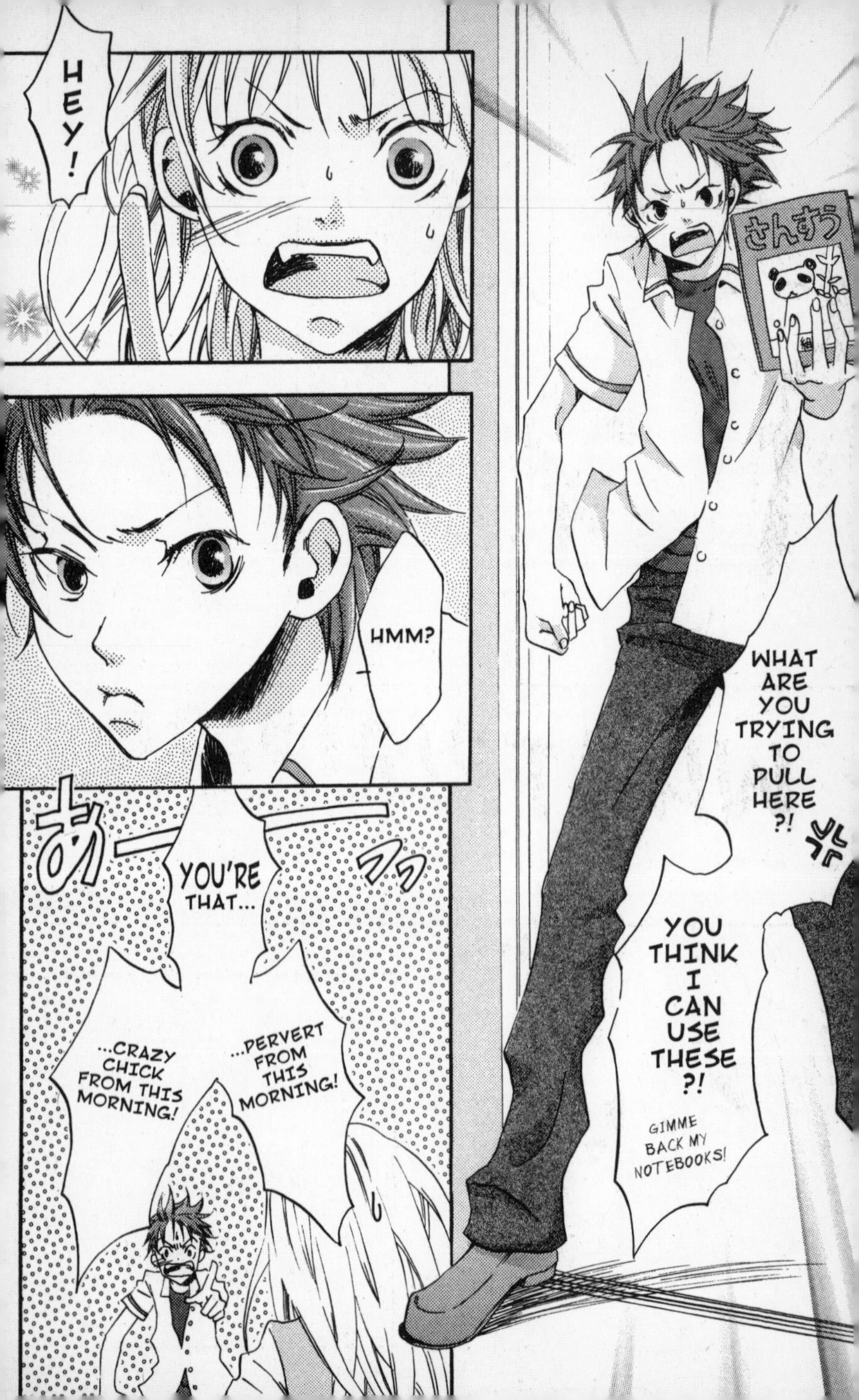
さんすう
WHAT ARE YOU TRYING TO PULL HERE?!
YOU THINK I CAN USE THESE?!
GIMME BACK MY NOTEBOOKS!
HEY!
HMM?
あーーっっ
YOU'RE THAT...
...PERVERT FROM THIS MORNING!
...CRAZY CHICK FROM THIS MORNING!

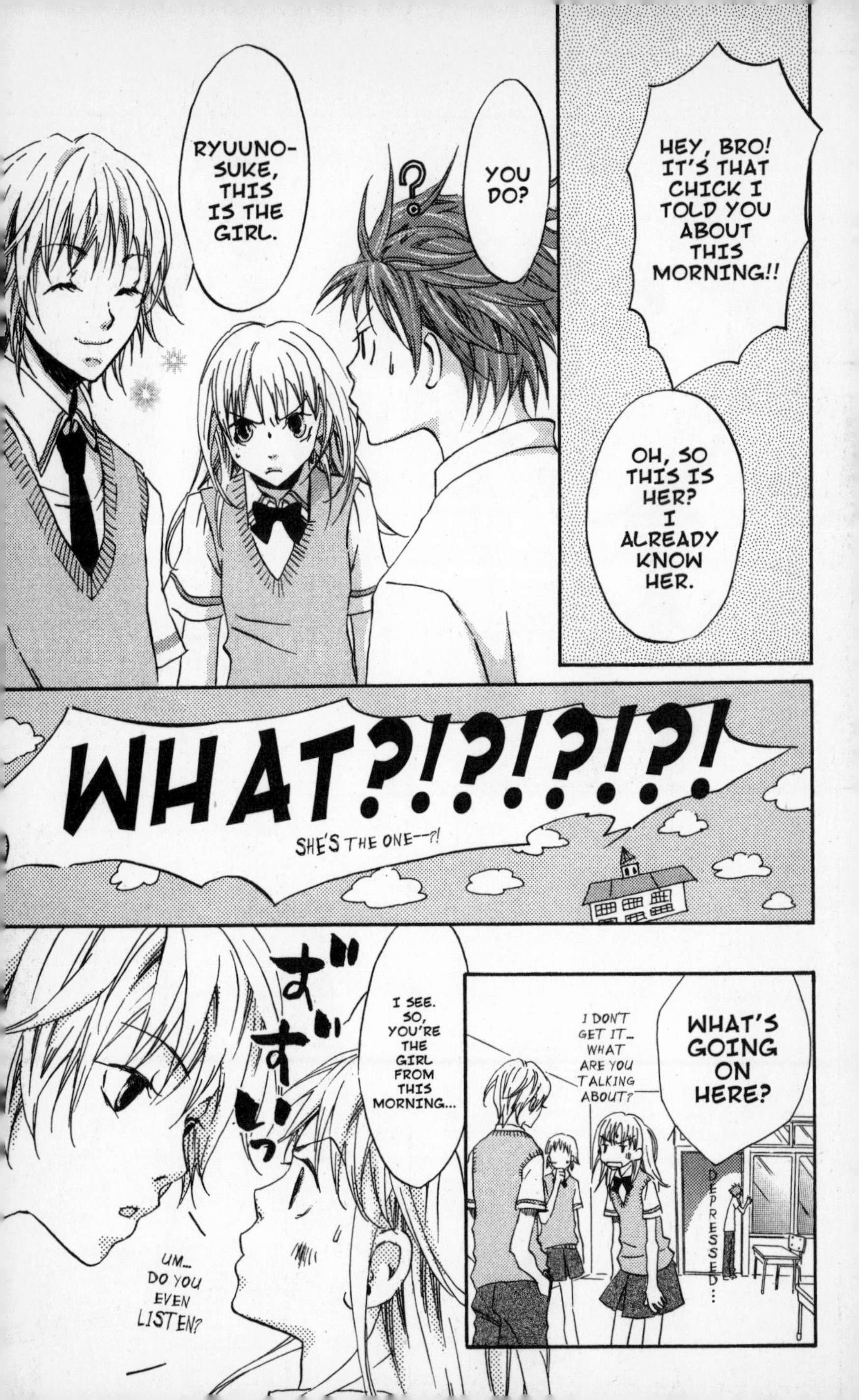
HEY, BRO! IT'S THAT CHICK I TOLD YOU ABOUT THIS MORNING!!
OH, SO THIS IS HER? I ALREADY KNOW HER.
YOU DO?
RYUUNO-SUKE, THIS IS THE GIRL.
WHAT?!?!?!?!
SHE'S THE ONE--?!
WHAT'S GOING ON HERE?
I DON'T GET IT.. WHAT ARE YOU TALKING ABOUT?
DEPRESSED...
ずずいっ
I SEE. SO, YOU'RE THE GIRL FROM THIS MORNING...
UM... DO YOU EVEN LISTEN?

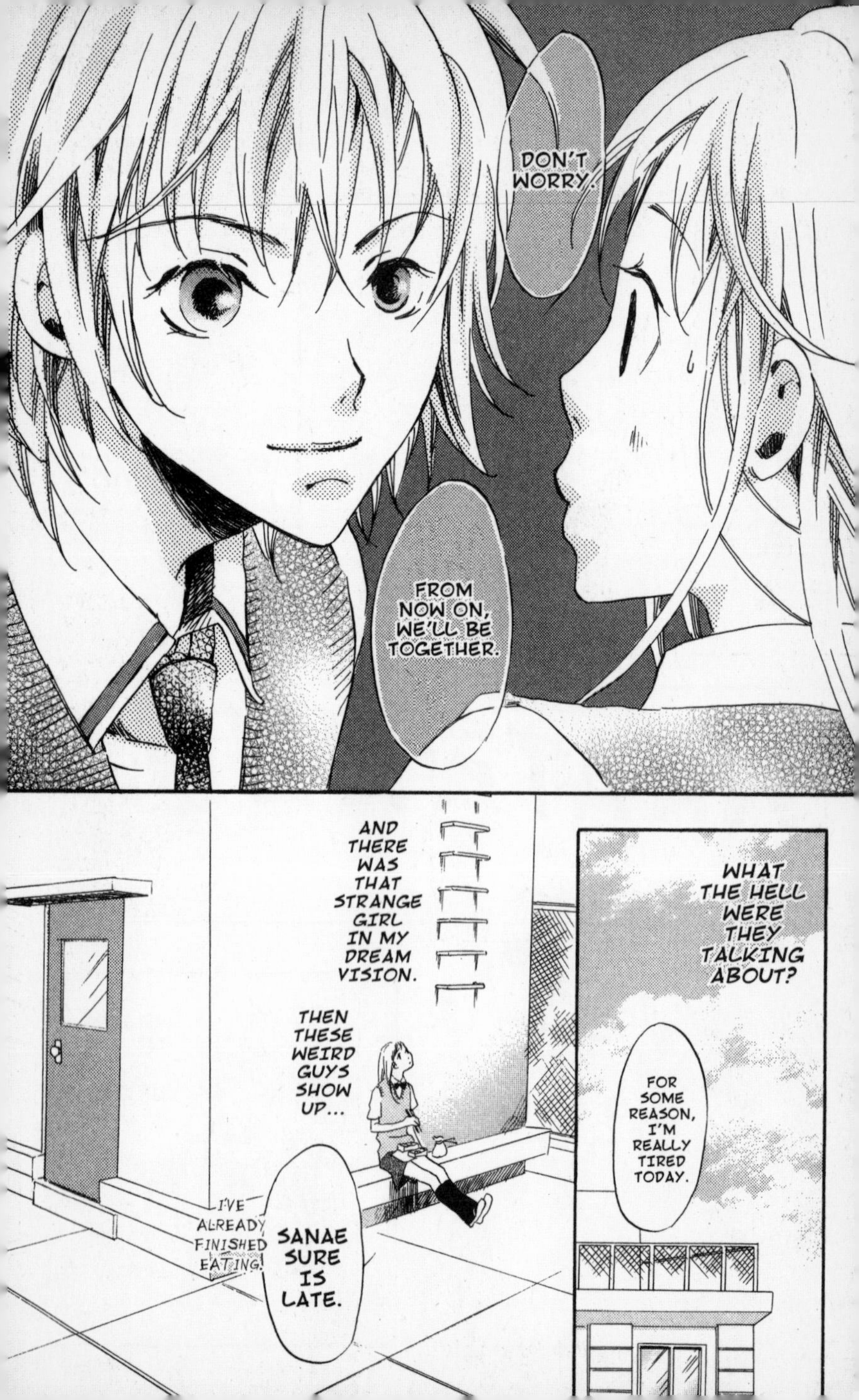
DON'T WORRY.
FROM NOW ON, WE'LL BE TOGETHER.
WHAT THE HELL WERE THEY TALKING ABOUT?
FOR SOME REASON, I'M REALLY TIRED TODAY.
AND THERE WAS THAT STRANGE GIRL IN MY DREAM VISION.
THEN THESE WEIRD GUYS SHOW UP...
SANAE SURE IS LATE.
I'VE ALREADY FINISHED EATING!

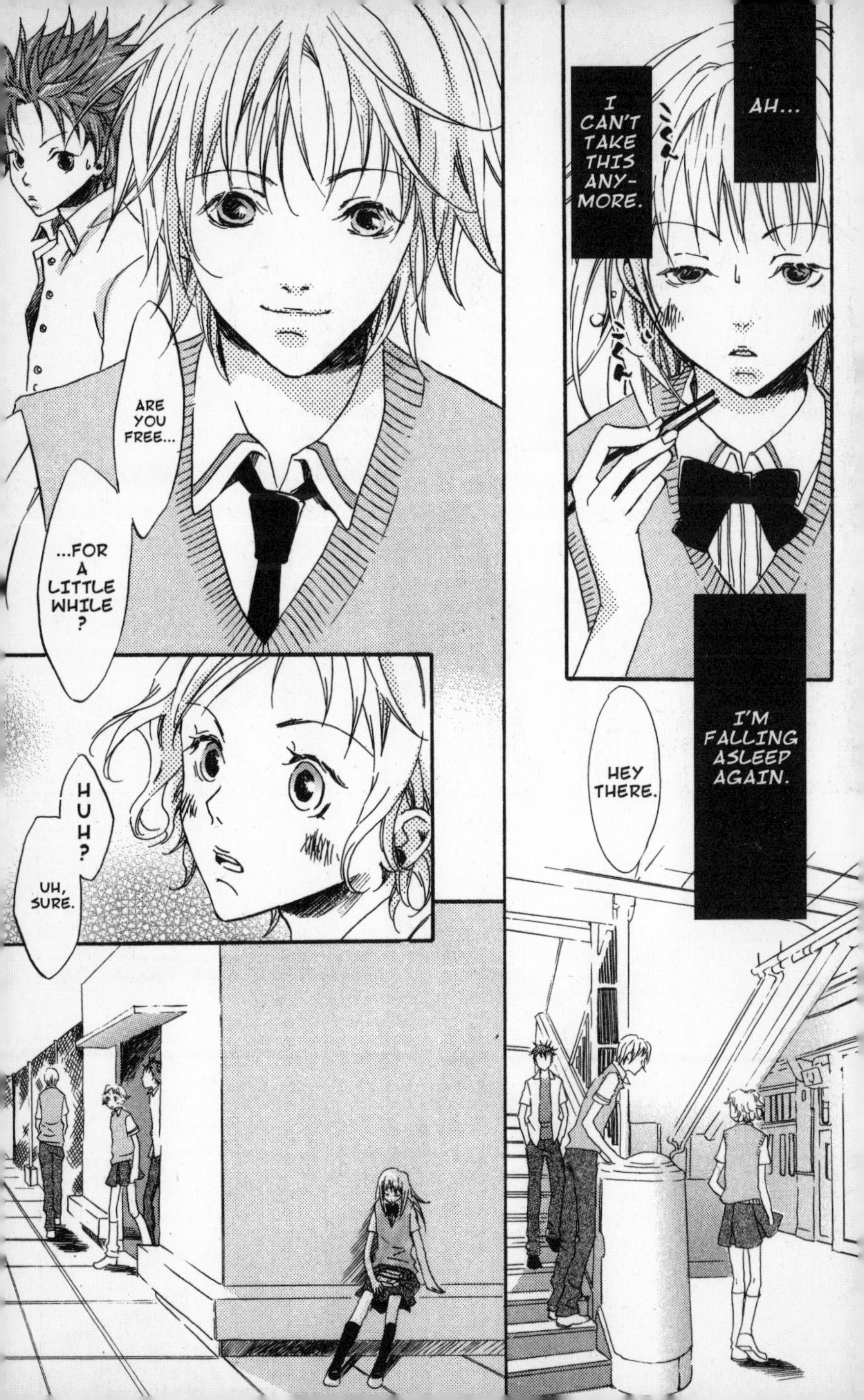
AH...
I CAN'T TAKE THIS ANYMORE.
I'M FALLING ASLEEP AGAIN.
HEY THERE.
ARE YOU FREE...
...FOR A LITTLE WHILE?
HUH?
UH, SURE.

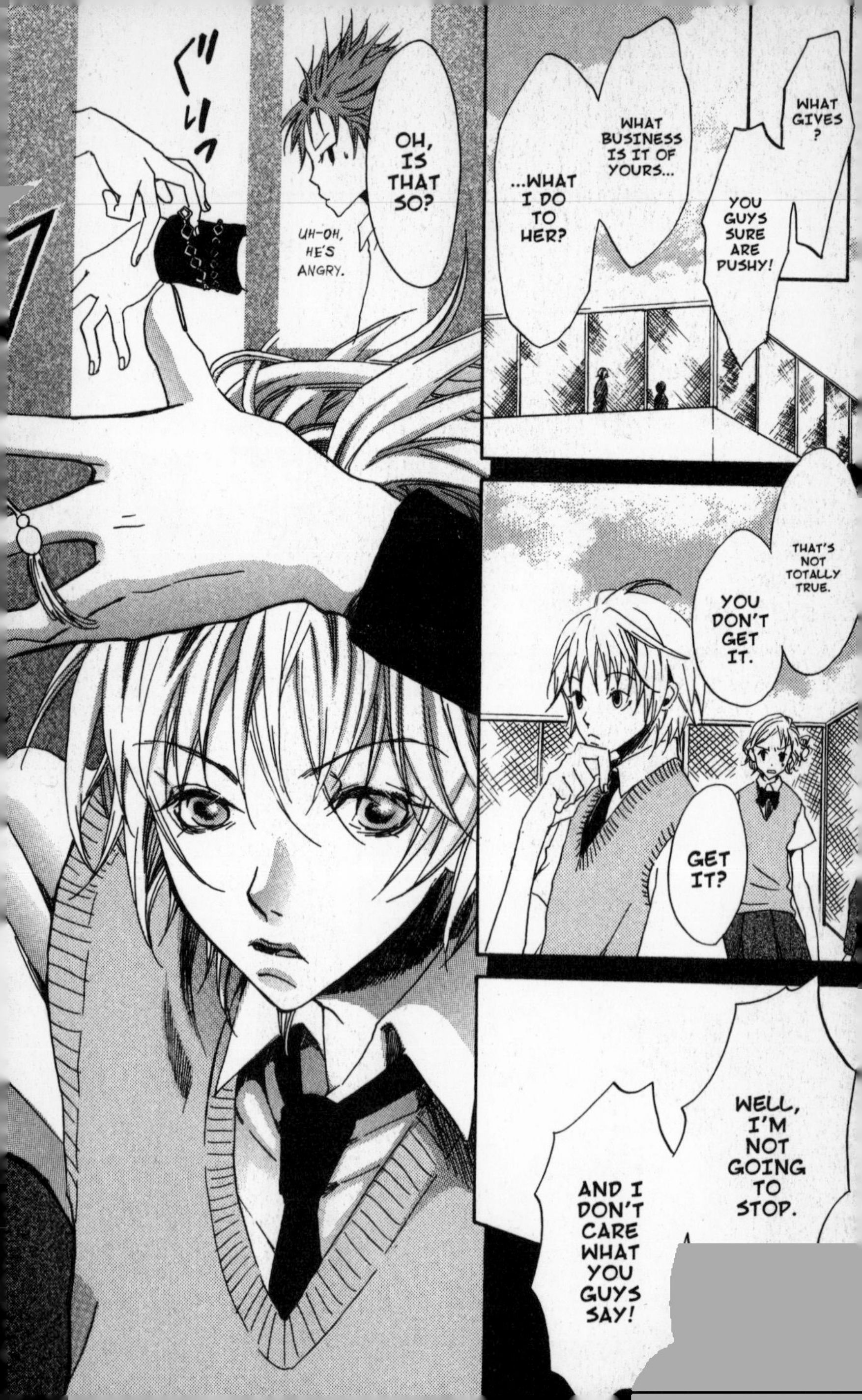
WHAT GIVES?
YOU GUYS SURE ARE PUSHY!
WHAT BUSINESS IS IT OF YOURS...
...WHAT I DO TO HER?
THAT'S NOT TOTALLY TRUE.
YOU DON'T GET IT.
GET IT?
WELL, I'M NOT GOING TO STOP.
AND I DON'T CARE WHAT YOU GUYS SAY!
OH, IS THAT SO?
UH-OH, HE'S ANGRY.
ぐいっ

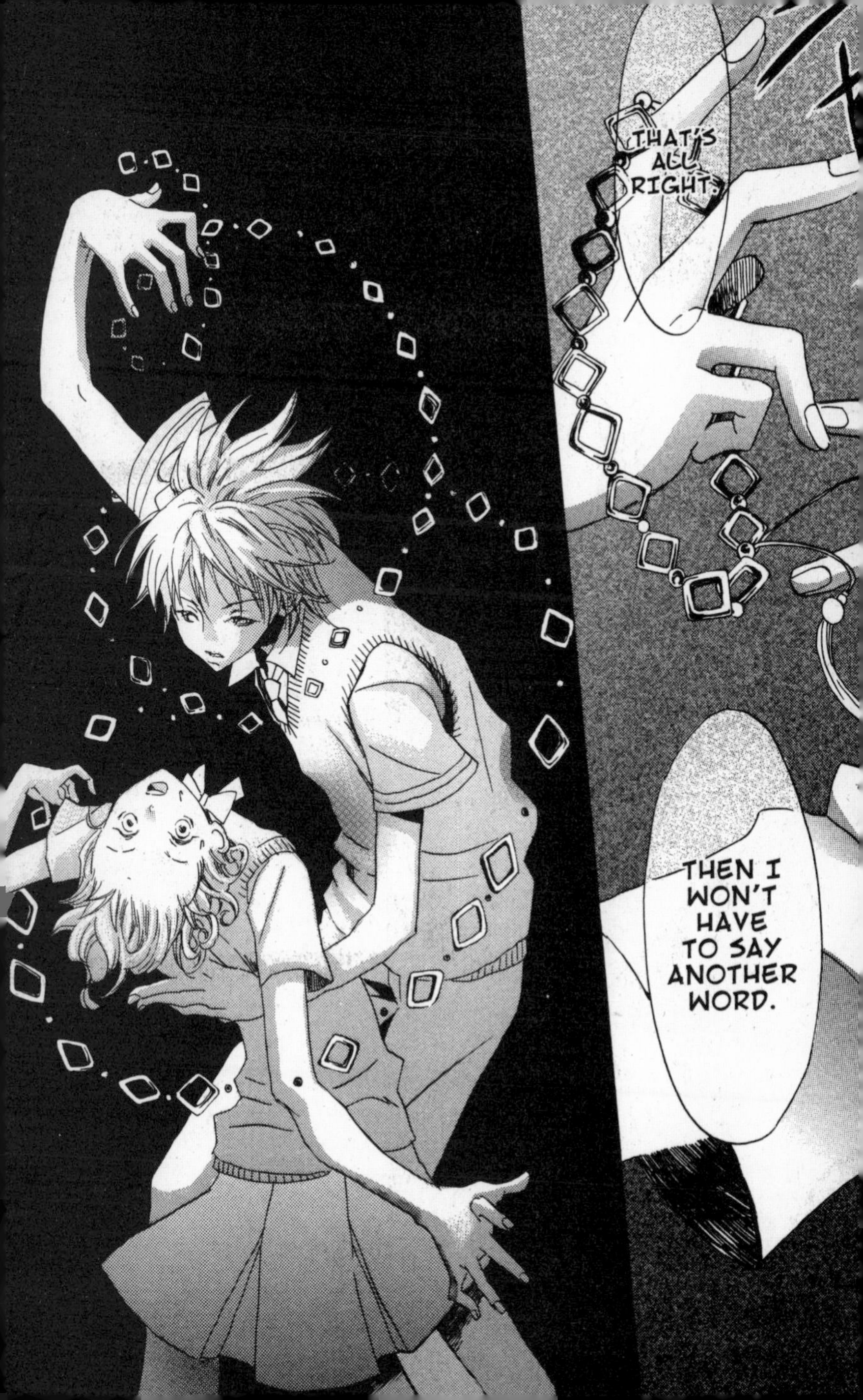
THAT'S ALL RIGHT.
THEN I WON'T HAVE TO SAY ANOTHER WORD.

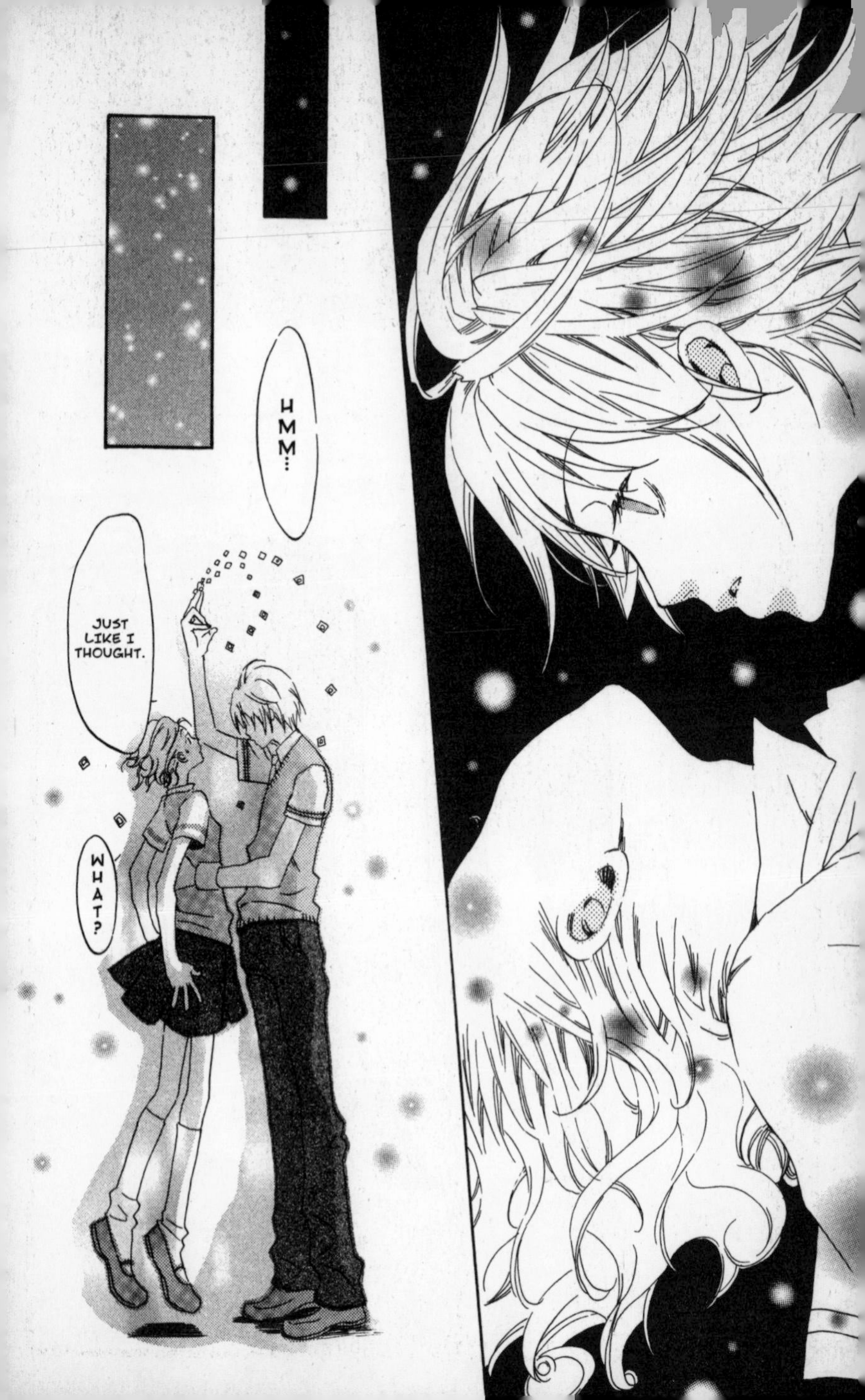
HMM...
JUST LIKE I THOUGHT.
WHAT?

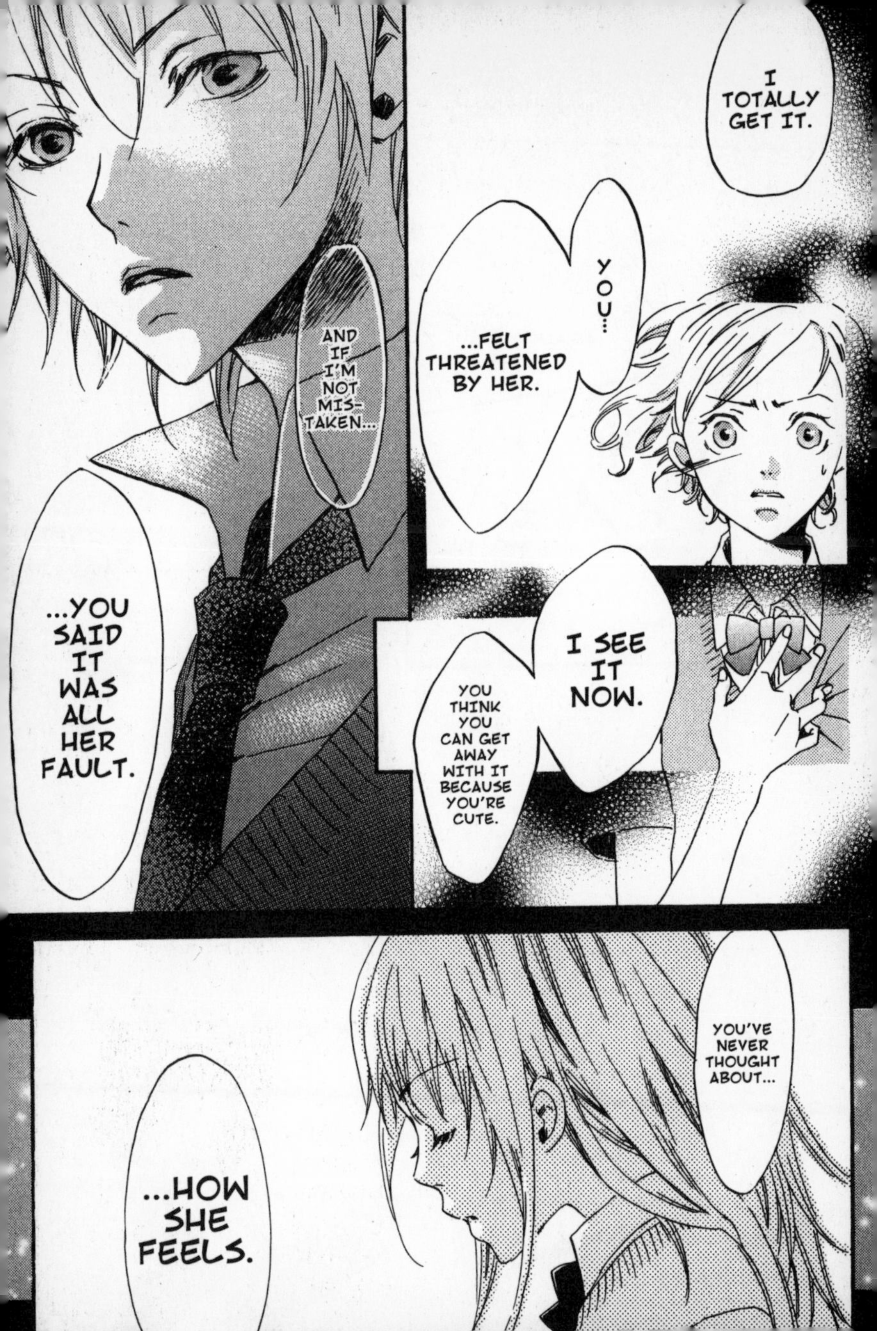
I TOTALLY GET IT.
YOU...
...FELT THREATENED BY HER.
I SEE IT NOW.
YOU THINK YOU CAN GET AWAY WITH IT BECAUSE YOU'RE CUTE.
AND IF I'M NOT MIS-TAKEN...
...YOU SAID IT WAS ALL HER FAULT.
YOU'VE NEVER THOUGHT ABOUT...
...HOW SHE FEELS.

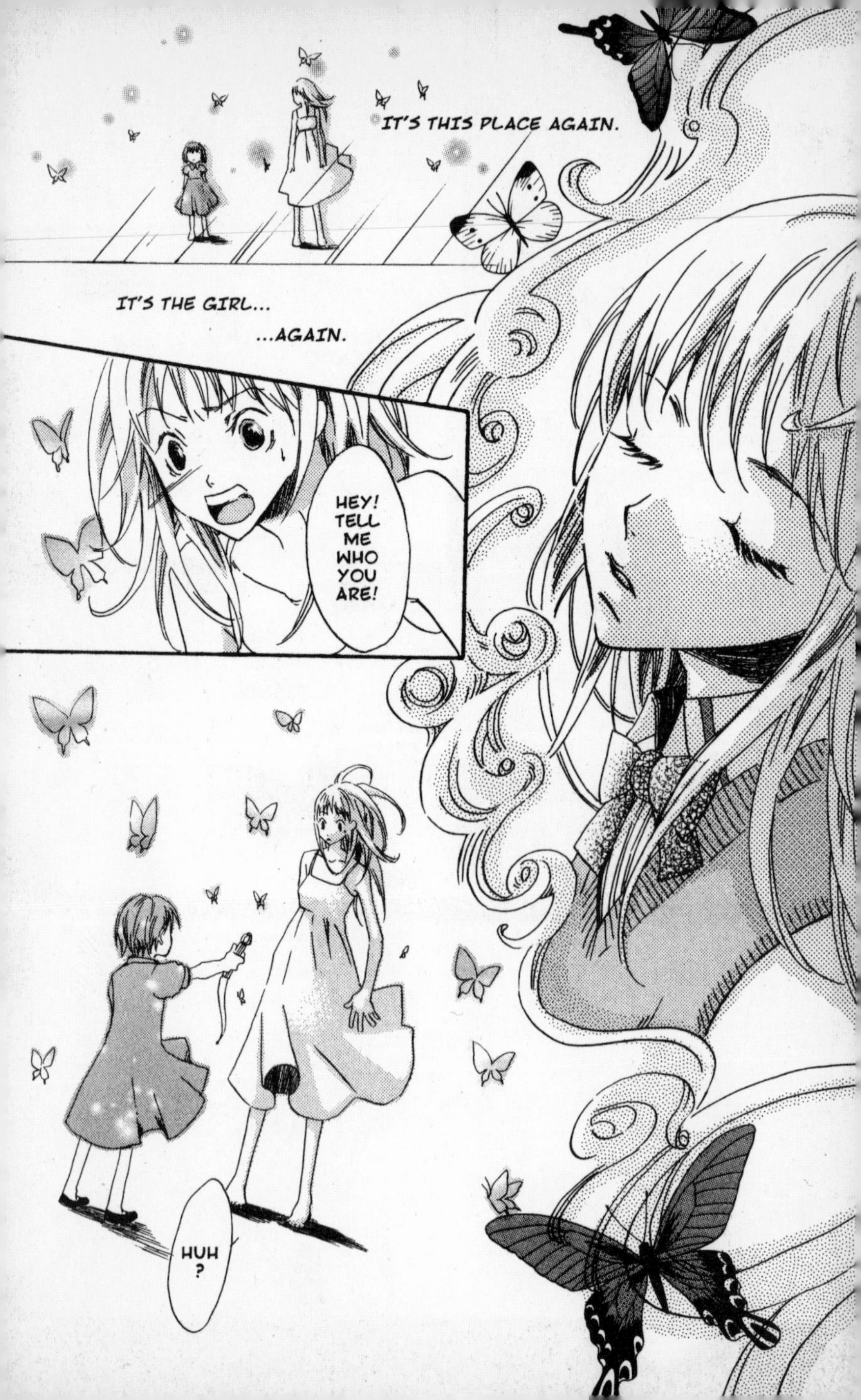
IT'S THIS PLACE AGAIN.
IT'S THE GIRL...
...AGAIN.
HEY! TELL ME WHO YOU ARE!
HUH?

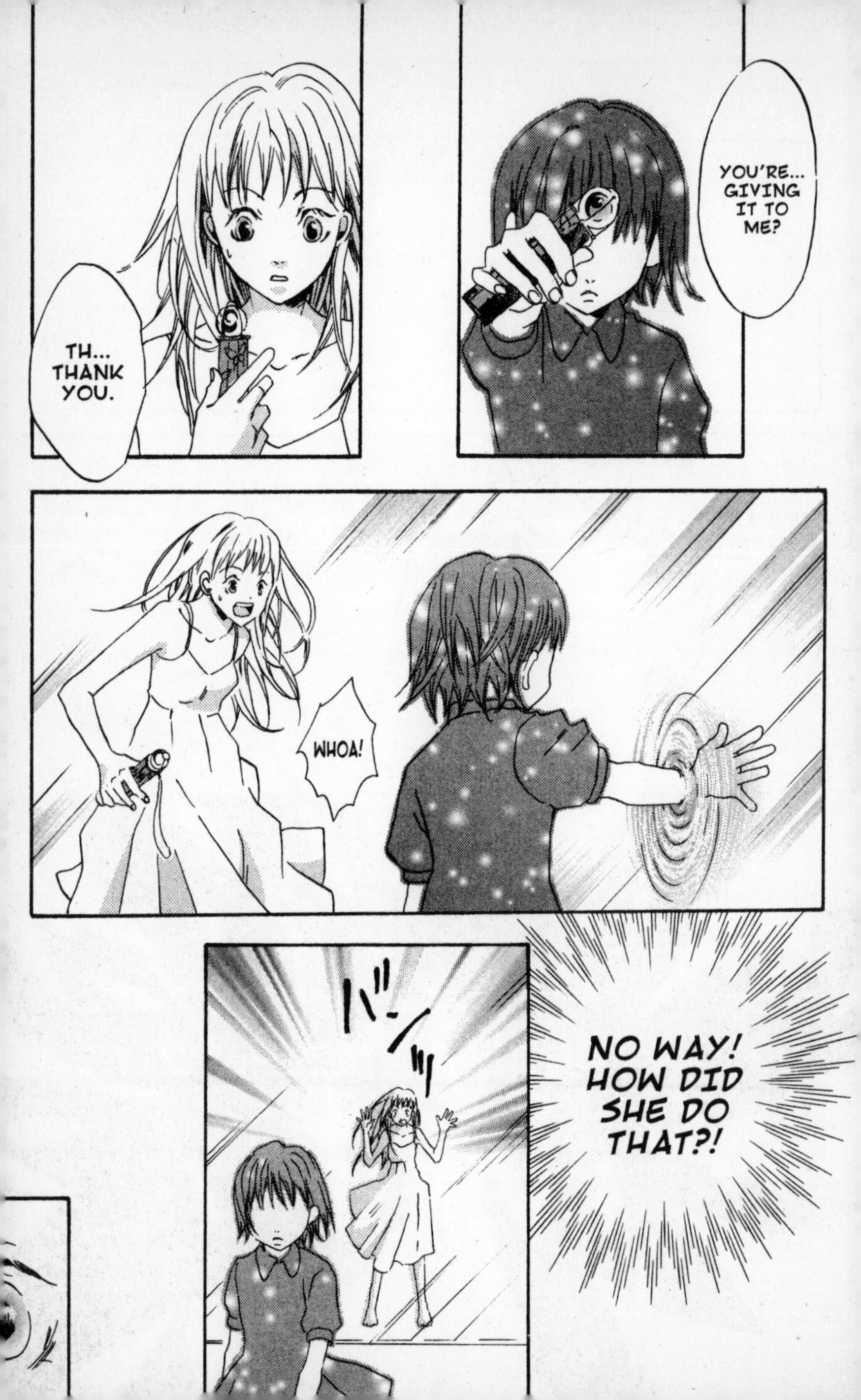
YOU'RE... GIVING IT TO ME?
TH... THANK YOU.
WHOA!
NO WAY! HOW DID SHE DO THAT?!

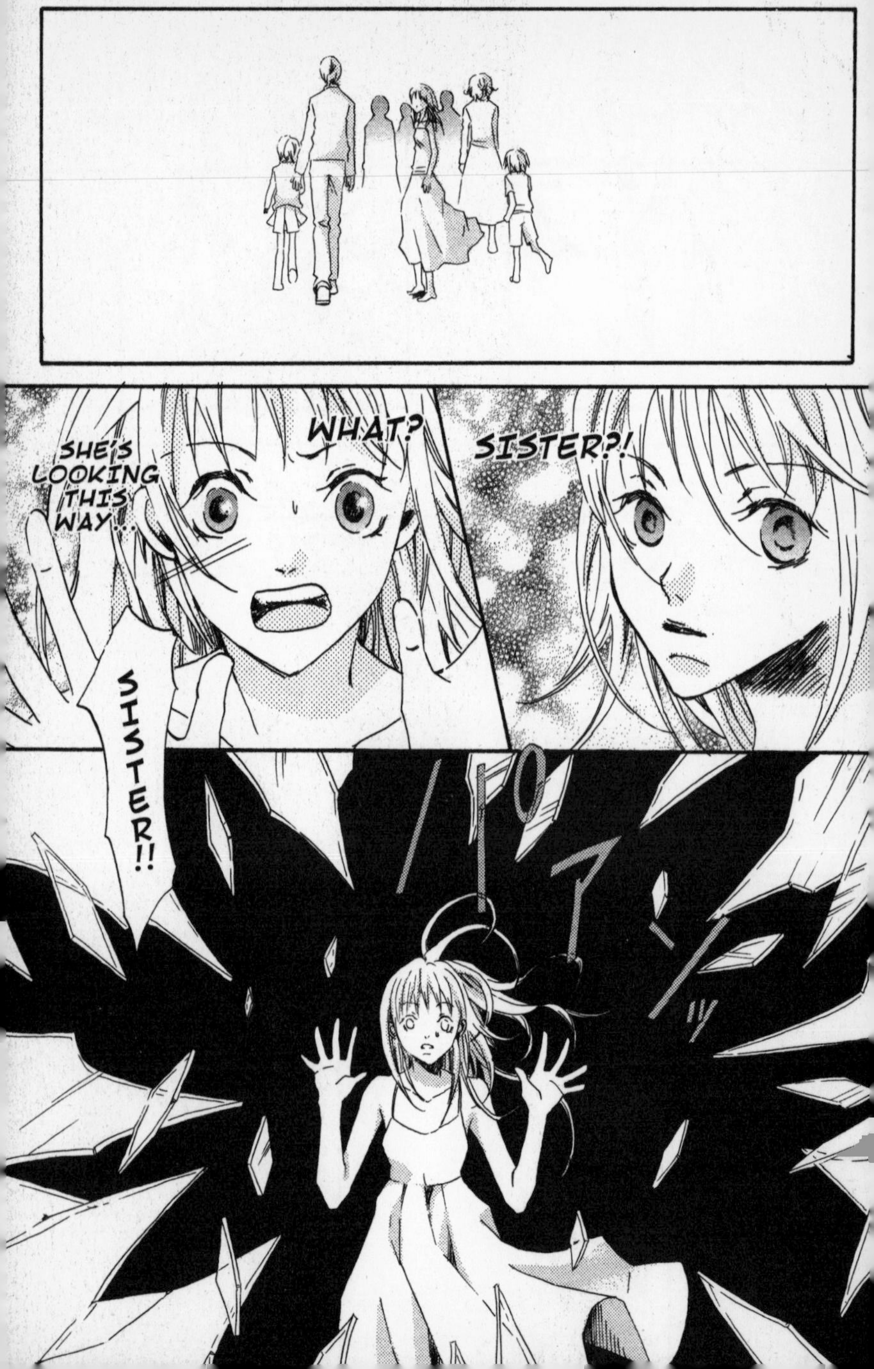
SISTER?!
WHAT?
SHE'S LOOKING THIS WAY...
SISTER!!

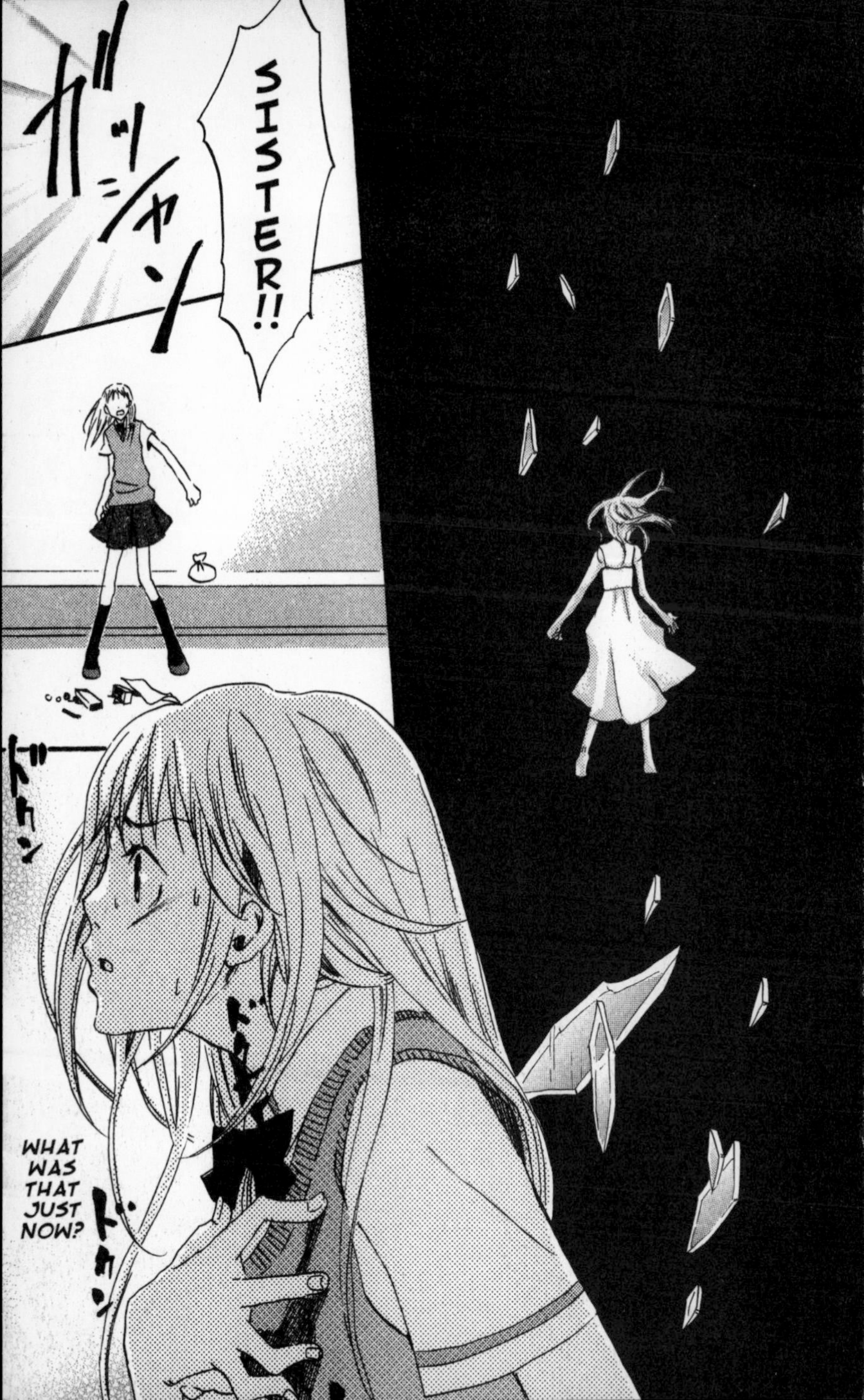
SISTER!!
ガッシャン
ドクン
WHAT WAS THAT JUST NOW?
ドクン

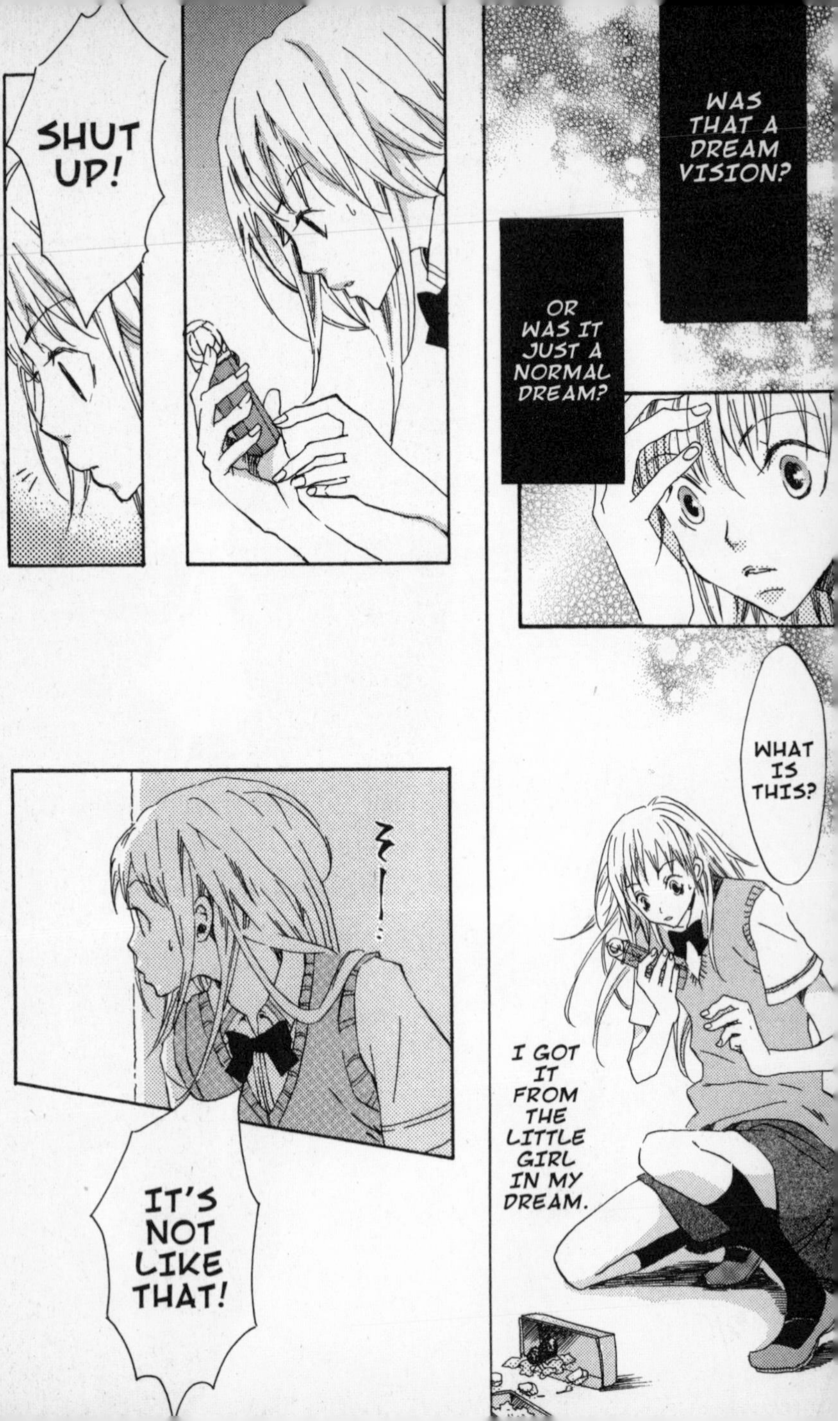
WAS THAT A DREAM VISION?
OR WAS IT JUST A NORMAL DREAM?
WHAT IS THIS?
I GOT IT FROM THE LITTLE GIRL IN MY DREAM.
SHUT UP!
IT'S NOT LIKE THAT!

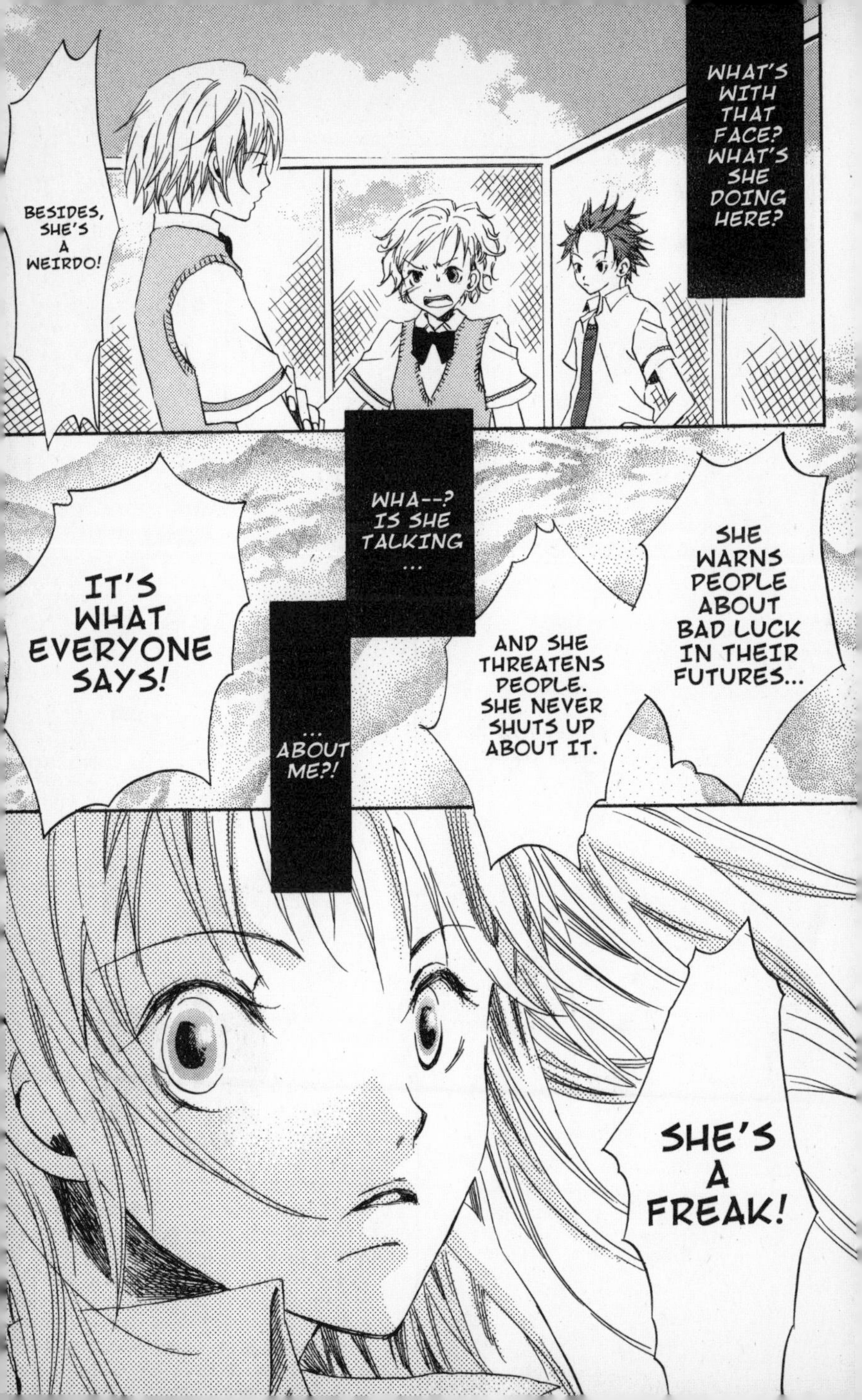
WHAT'S WITH THAT FACE? WHAT'S SHE DOING HERE?
BESIDES, SHE'S A WEIRDO!
SHE WARNS PEOPLE ABOUT BAD LUCK IN THEIR FUTURES...
AND SHE THREATENS PEOPLE. SHE NEVER SHUTS UP ABOUT IT.
WHA--? IS SHE TALKING ...
... ABOUT ME?!
IT'S WHAT EVERYONE SAYS!
SHE'S A FREAK!

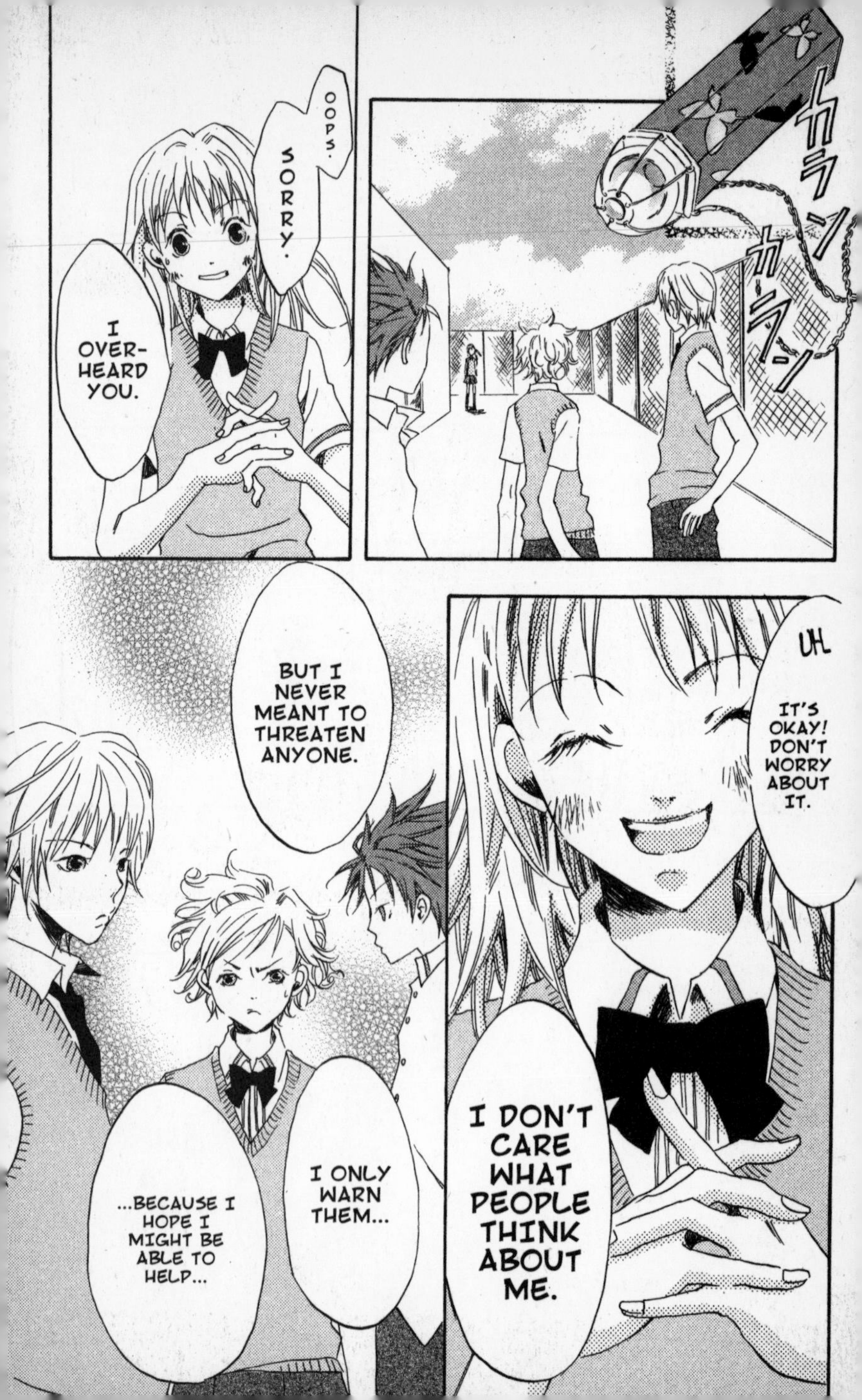
カラーン
カラーン
OOPS. SORRY.
I OVER-HEARD YOU.
UH
IT'S OKAY! DON'T WORRY ABOUT IT.
I DON'T CARE WHAT PEOPLE THINK ABOUT ME.
BUT I NEVER MEANT TO THREATEN ANYONE.
I ONLY WARN THEM...
...BECAUSE I HOPE I MIGHT BE ABLE TO HELP...

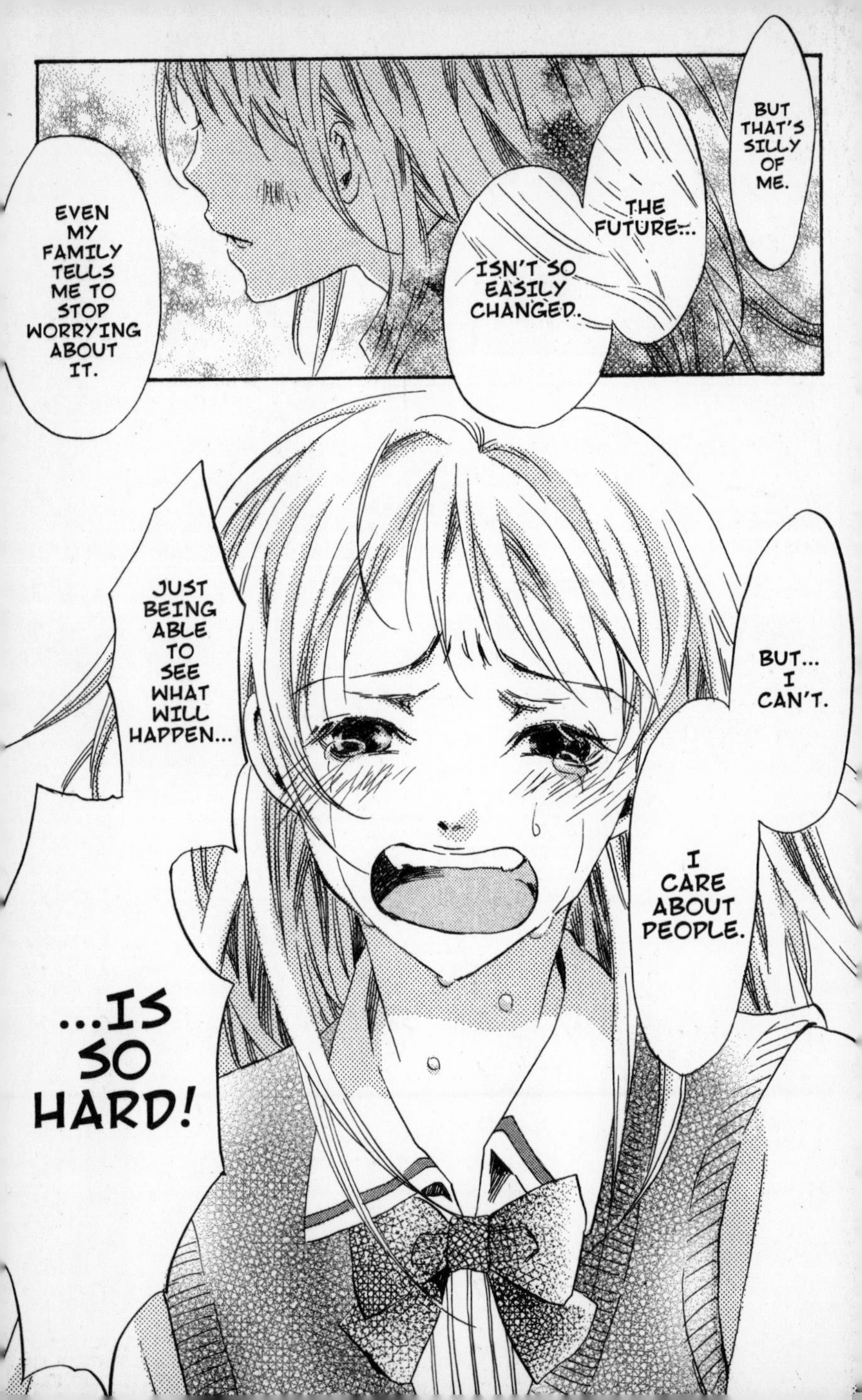
BUT THAT'S SILLY OF ME.
THE FUTURE...
ISN'T SO EASILY CHANGED.
EVEN MY FAMILY TELLS ME TO STOP WORRYING ABOUT IT.
BUT... I CAN'T.
I CARE ABOUT PEOPLE.
JUST BEING ABLE TO SEE WHAT WILL HAPPEN...
...IS SO HARD!

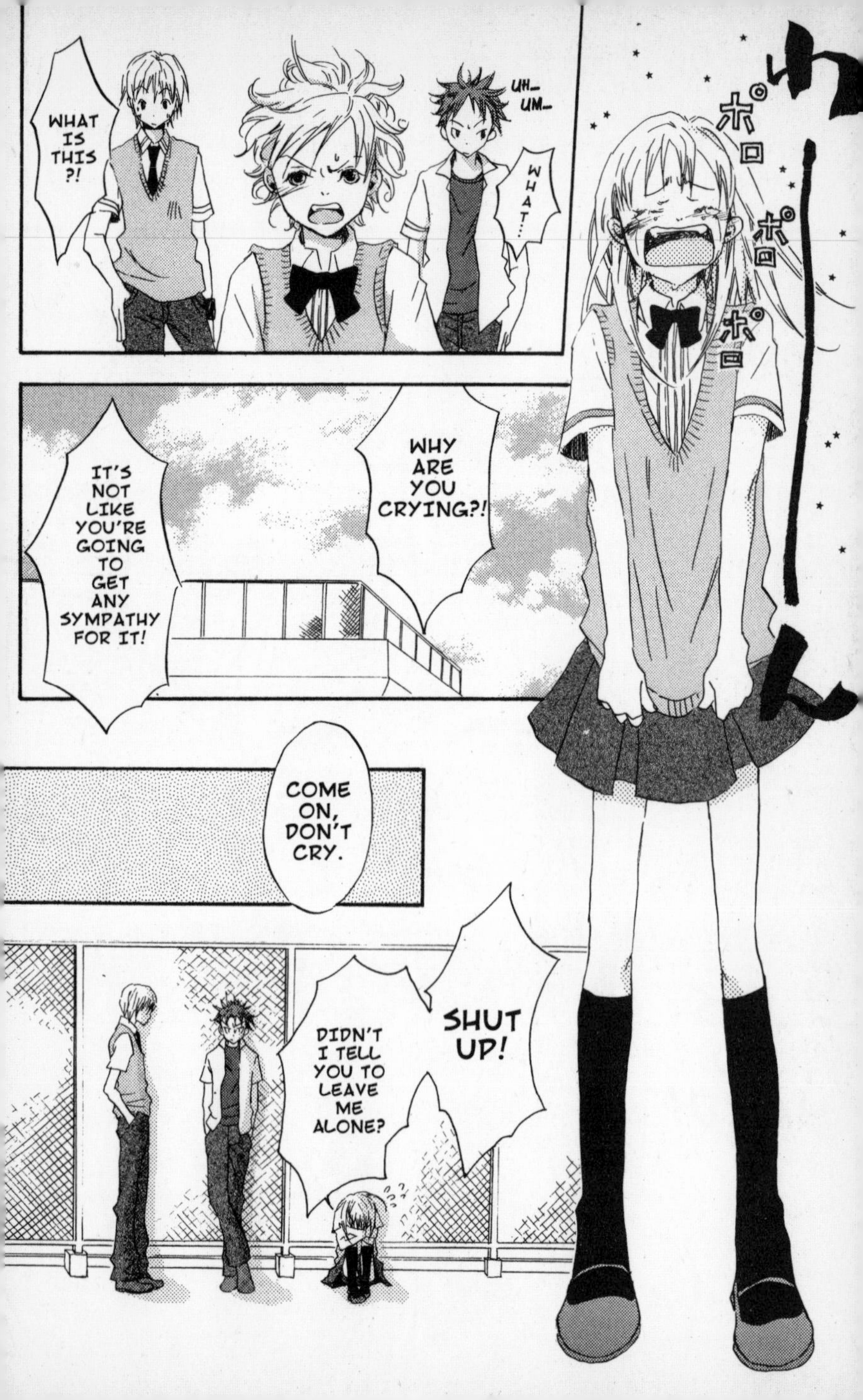
わーん
ポロ
ポロ
ポロ
UH— UM—
WHAT...
WHAT IS THIS?!
WHY ARE YOU CRYING?!
IT'S NOT LIKE YOU'RE GOING TO GET ANY SYMPATHY FOR IT!
COME ON, DON'T CRY.
SHUT UP!
DIDN'T I TELL YOU TO LEAVE ME ALONE?

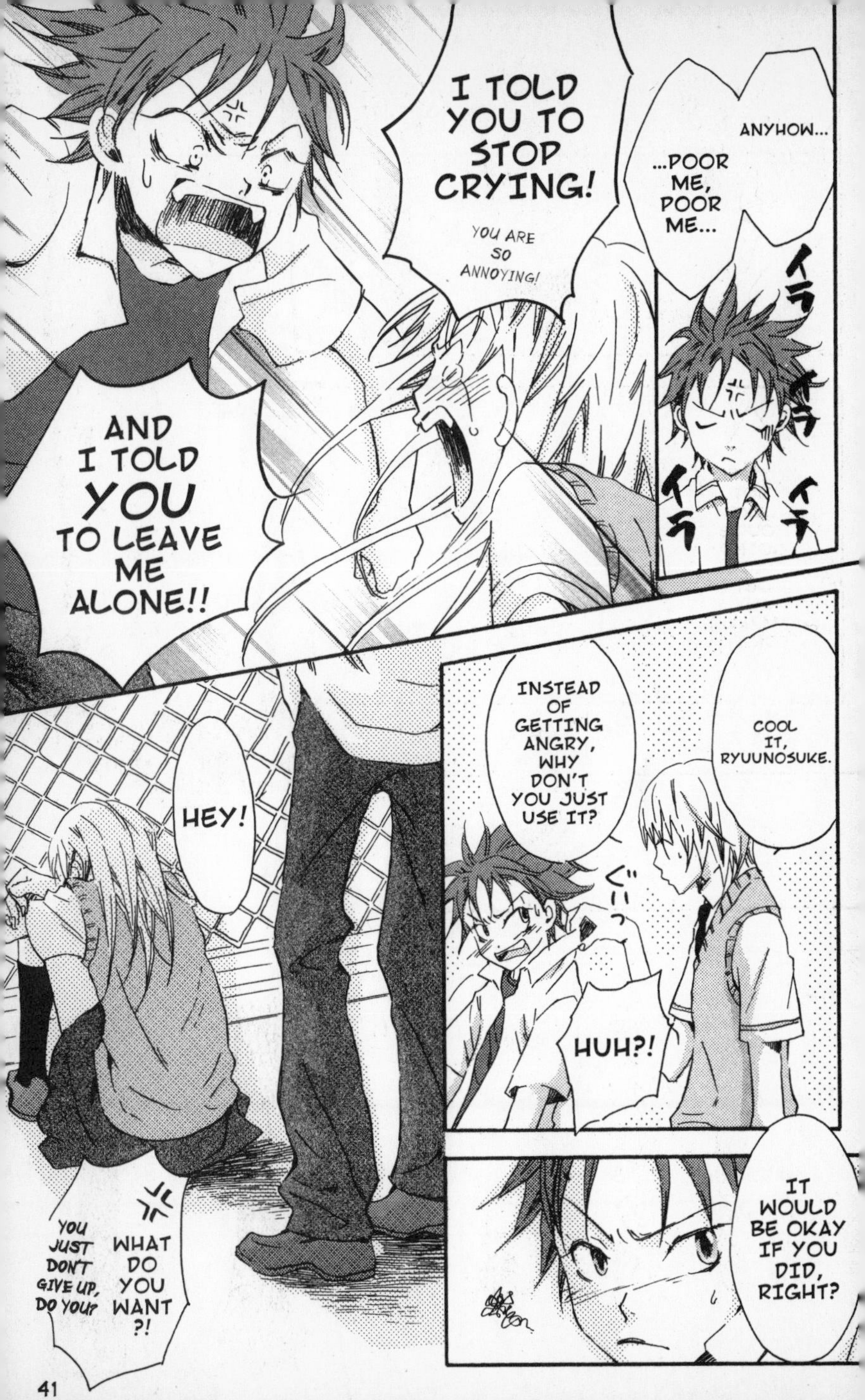
ANYHOW...
...POOR ME, POOR ME...
イラ イラ イラ イラ
I TOLD YOU TO STOP CRYING!
YOU ARE SO ANNOYING!
AND I TOLD YOU TO LEAVE ME ALONE!!
COOL IT, RYUUNOSUKE.
INSTEAD OF GETTING ANGRY, WHY DON'T YOU JUST USE IT?
ぐいっ
HUH?!
IT WOULD BE OKAY IF YOU DID, RIGHT?
HEY!
WHAT DO YOU WANT?!
YOU JUST DON'T GIVE UP, DO YOU?

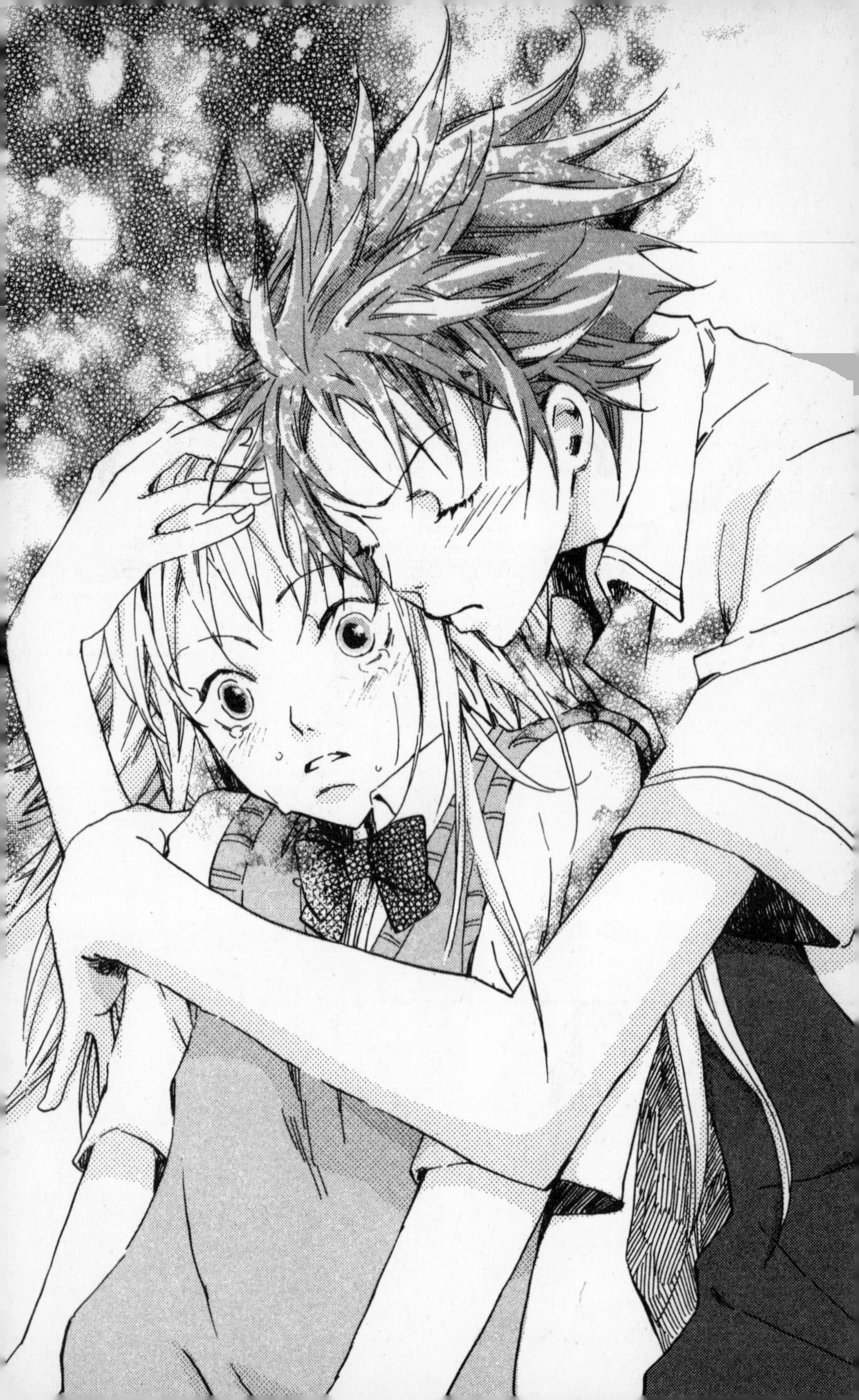

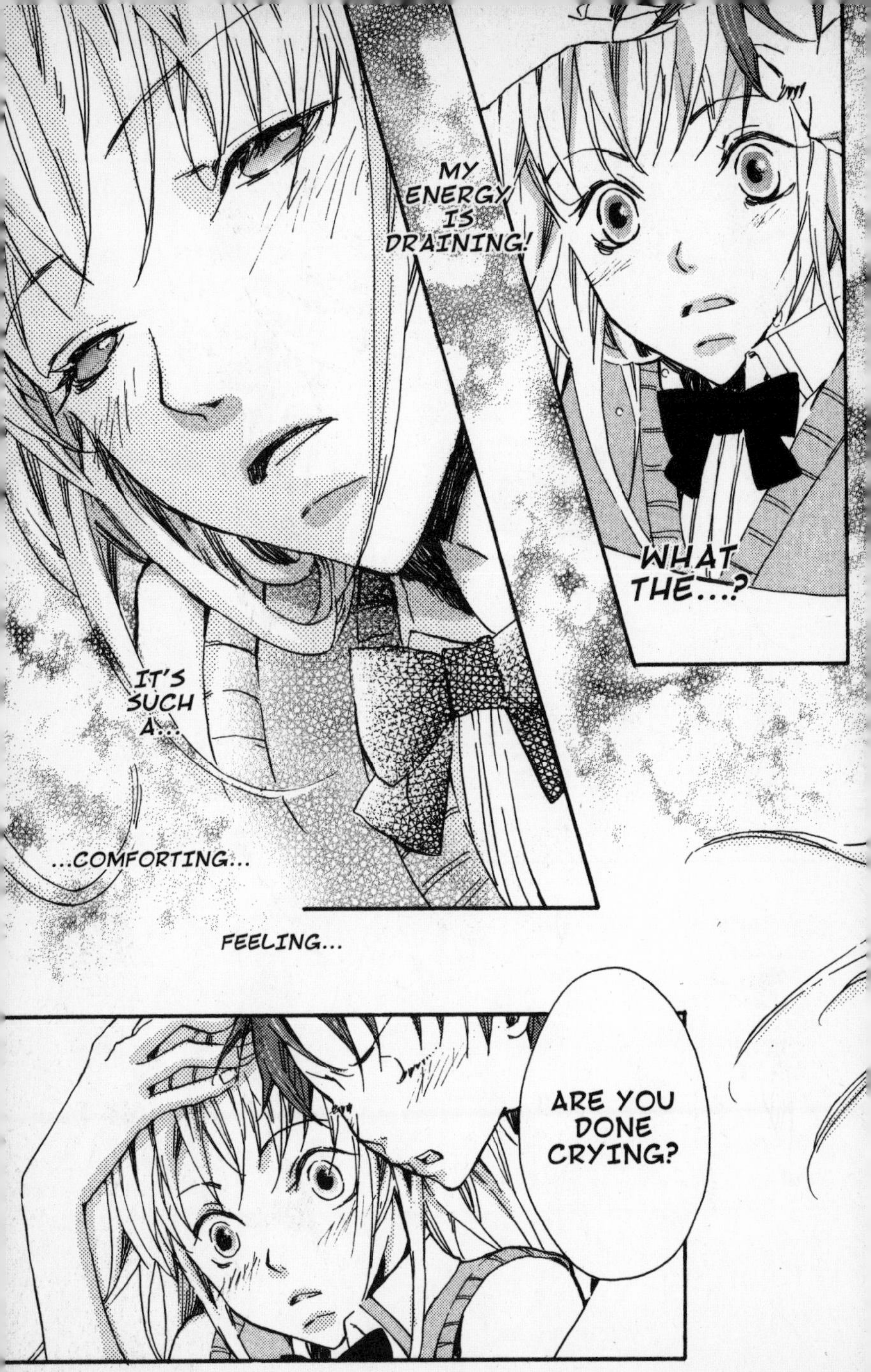
MY ENERGY IS DRAINING!
WHAT THE...?
IT'S SUCH A...
...COMFORTING...
FEELING...
ARE YOU DONE CRYING?

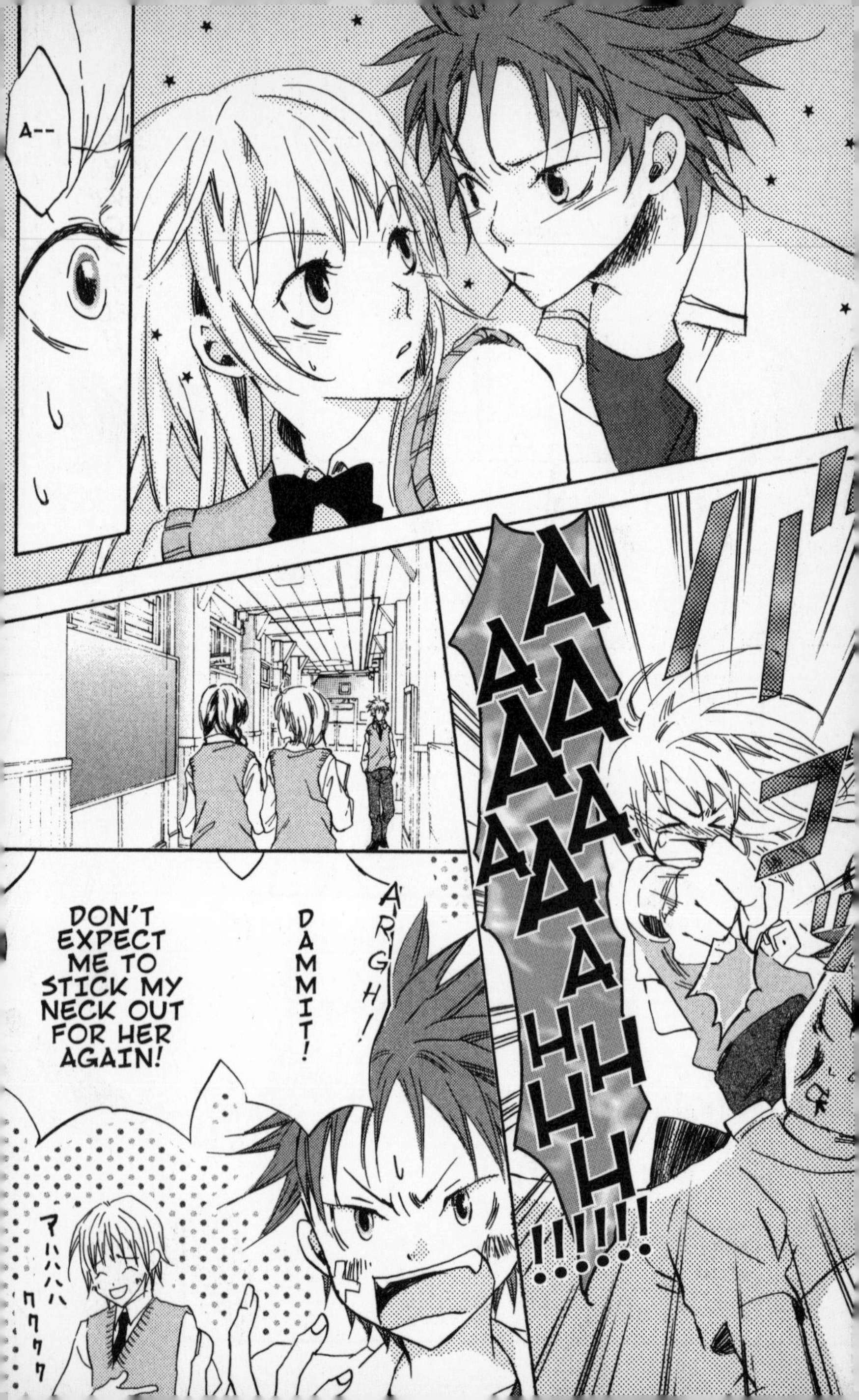
A--
AAAAAAAAHHHH!!!!!!
ARGH!
DAMMIT!
DON'T EXPECT ME TO STICK MY NECK OUT FOR HER AGAIN!
アハハハ
ククク

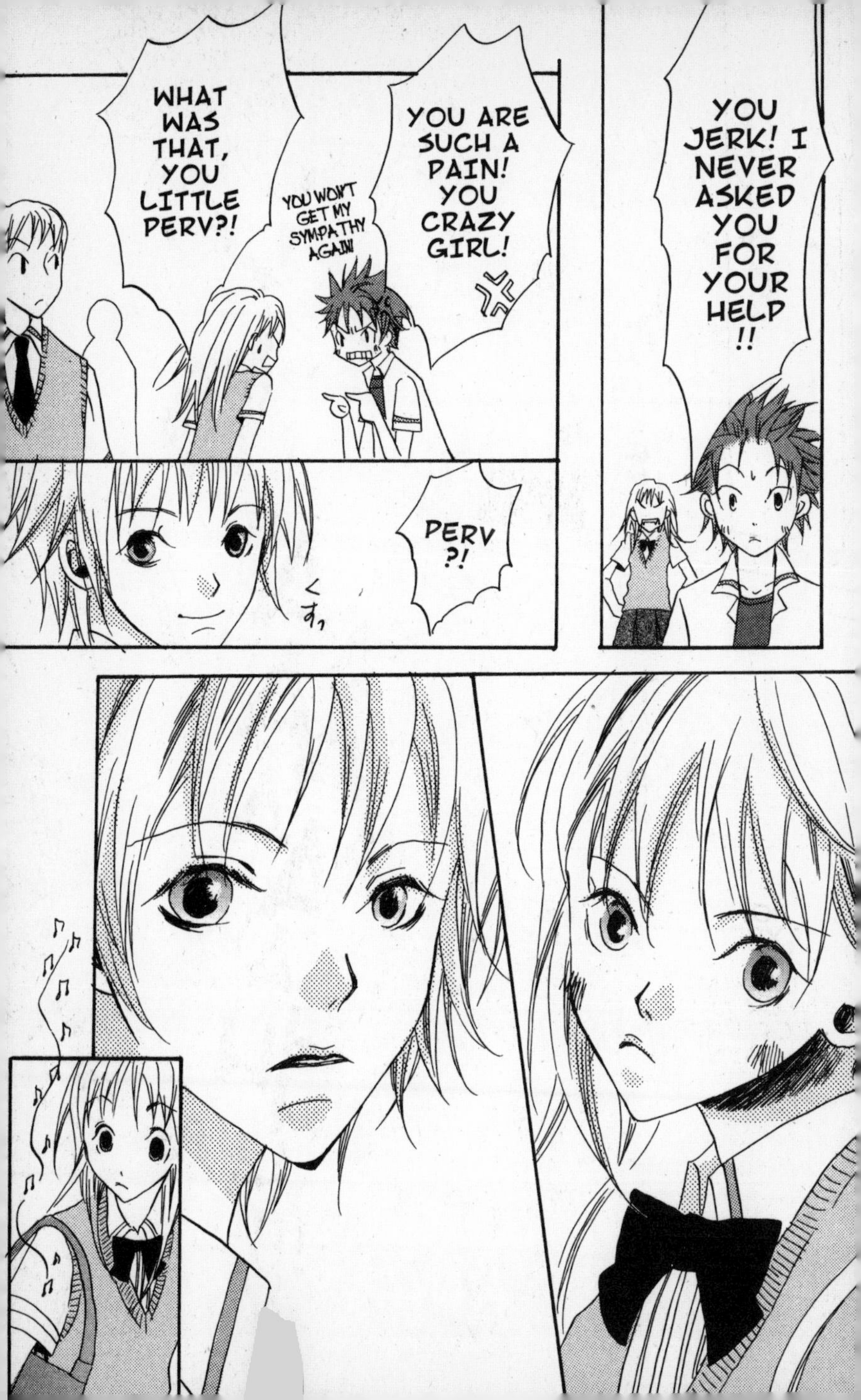
YOU JERK! I NEVER ASKED YOU FOR YOUR HELP!!
YOU ARE SUCH A PAIN! YOU CRAZY GIRL!
YOU WON'T GET MY SYMPATHY AGAIN!
WHAT WAS THAT, YOU LITTLE PERV?!
PERV?!
くすっ

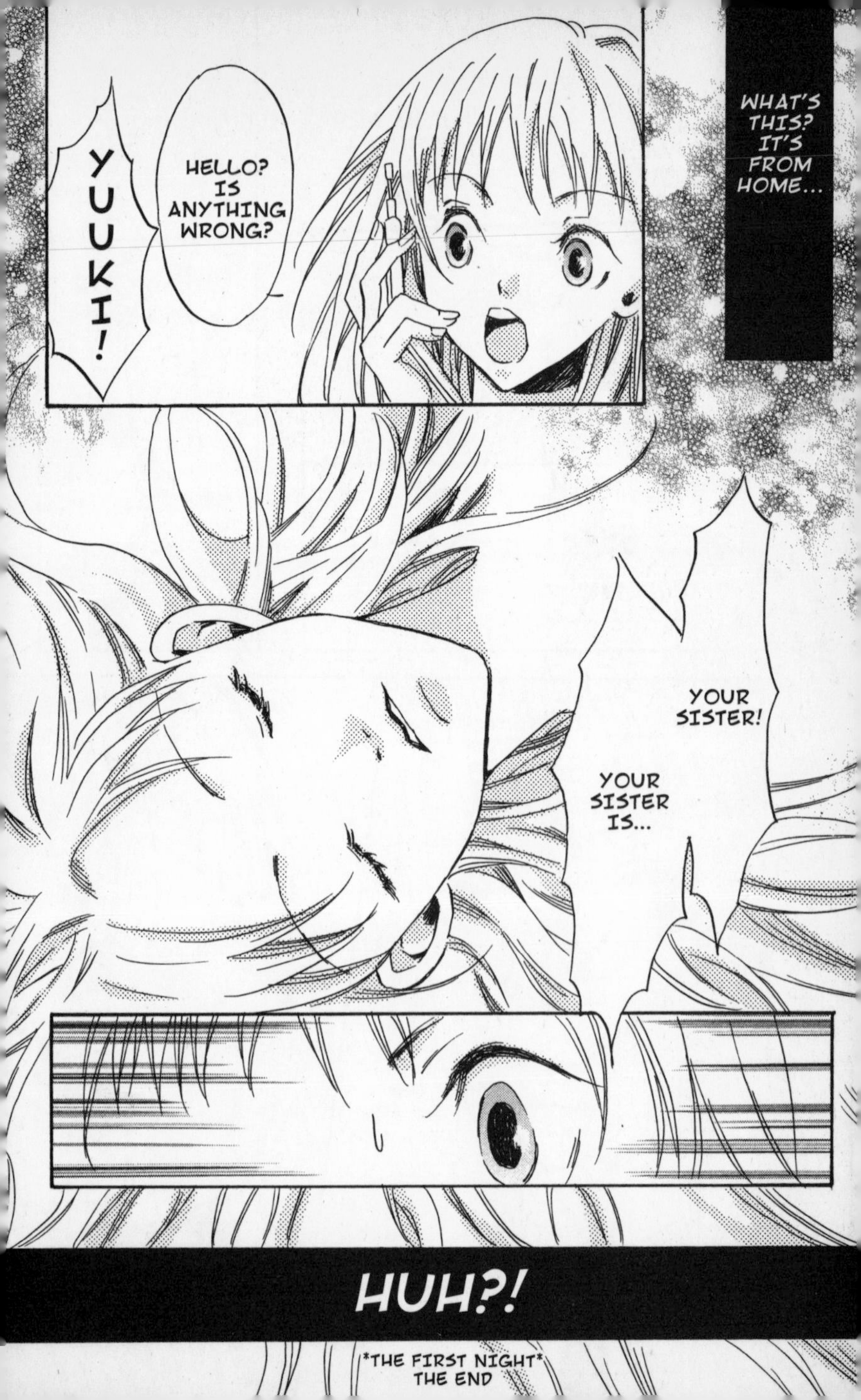
WHAT'S THIS? IT'S FROM HOME...
HELLO? IS ANYTHING WRONG?
YUUKI!
YOUR SISTER!
YOUR SISTER IS...
HUH?!
THE FIRST NIGHT THE END

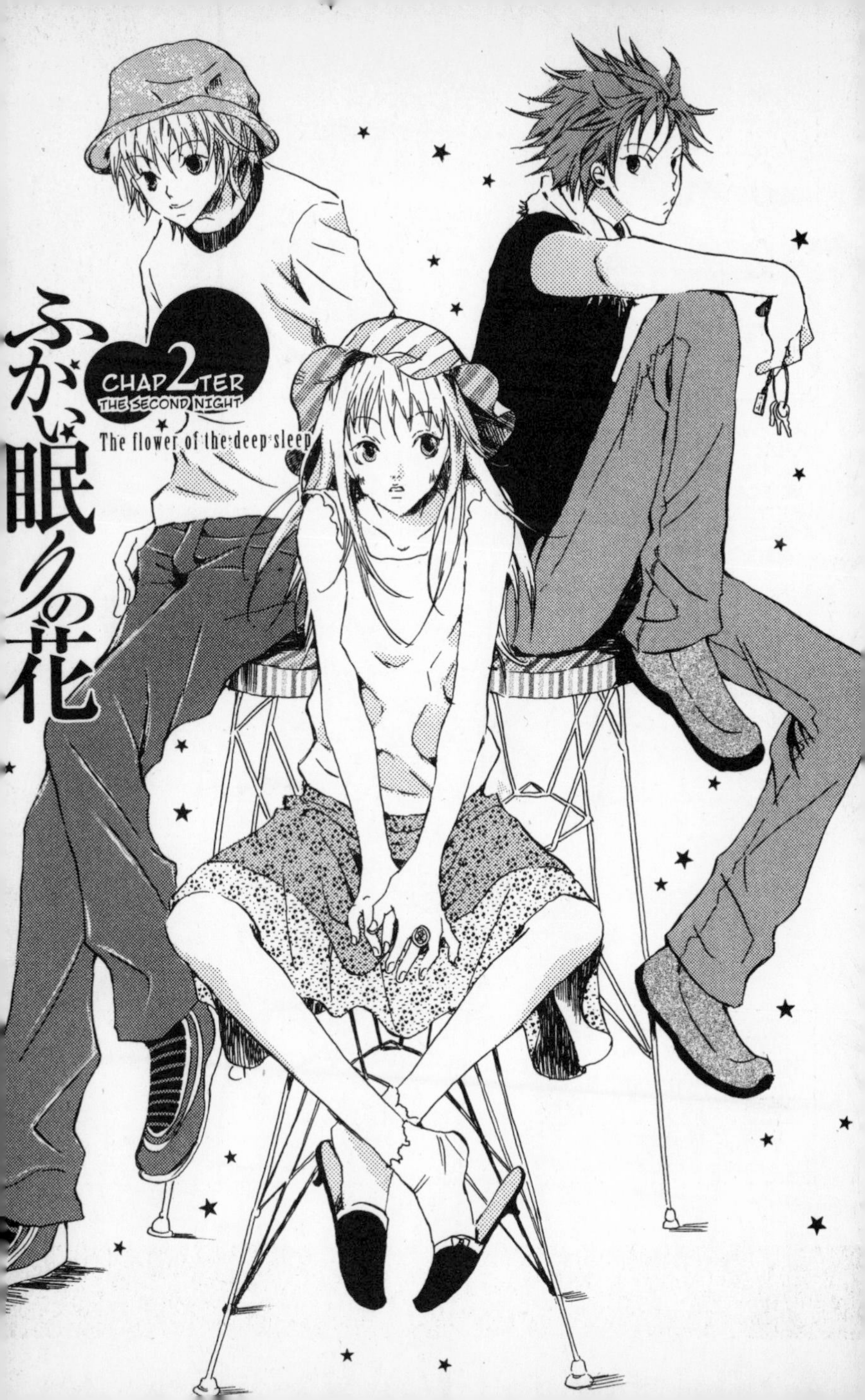
ふかい眠りの花
CHAP2TER
THE SECOND NIGHT
The flower of the deep sleep

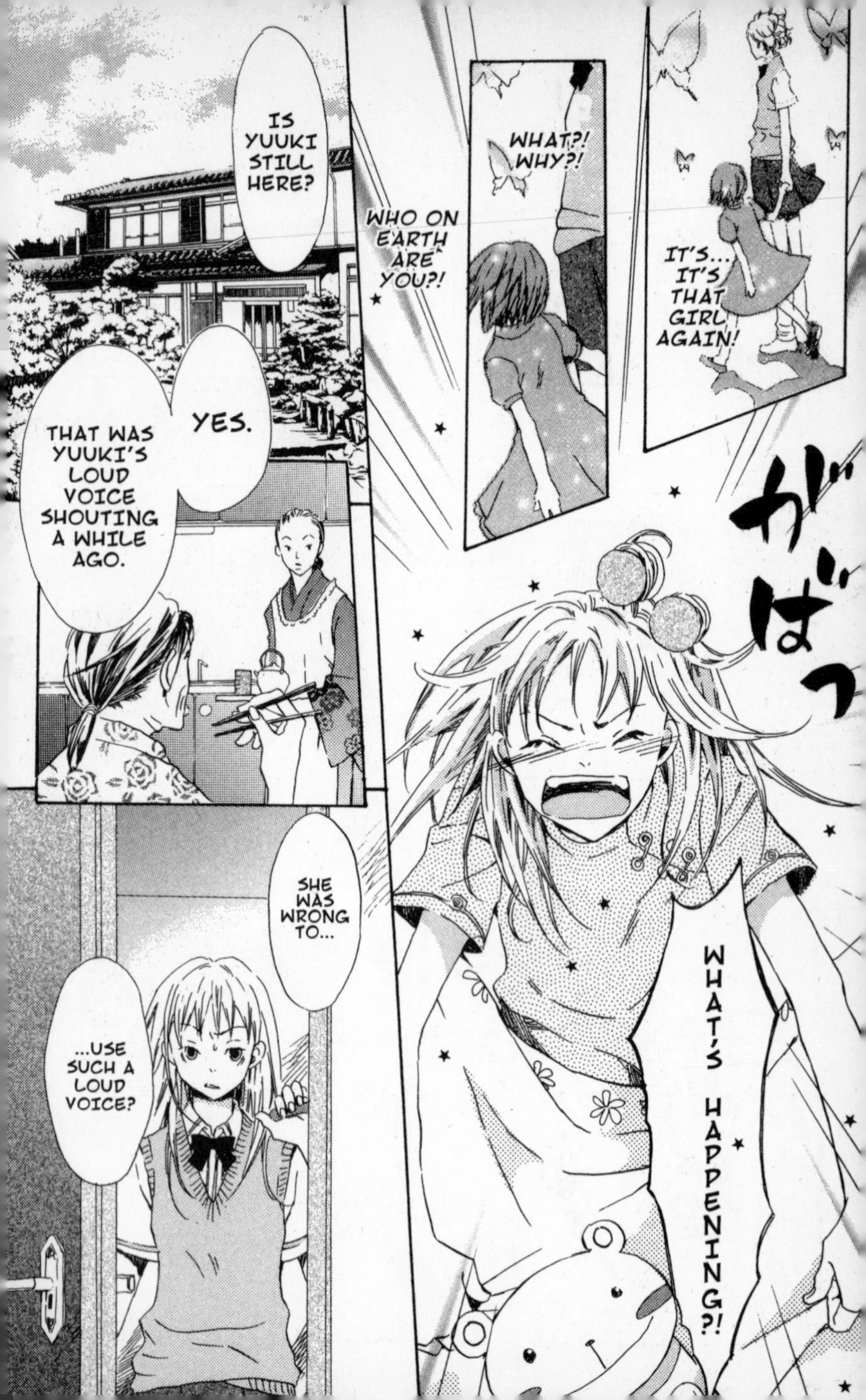
IT'S... IT'S THAT GIRL AGAIN!
WHAT?! WHY?!
WHO ON EARTH ARE YOU?!
がばっ
WHAT'S HAPPENING?!
IS YUUKI STILL HERE?
YES.
THAT WAS YUUKI'S LOUD VOICE SHOUTING A WHILE AGO.
SHE WAS WRONG TO...
...USE SUCH A LOUD VOICE?

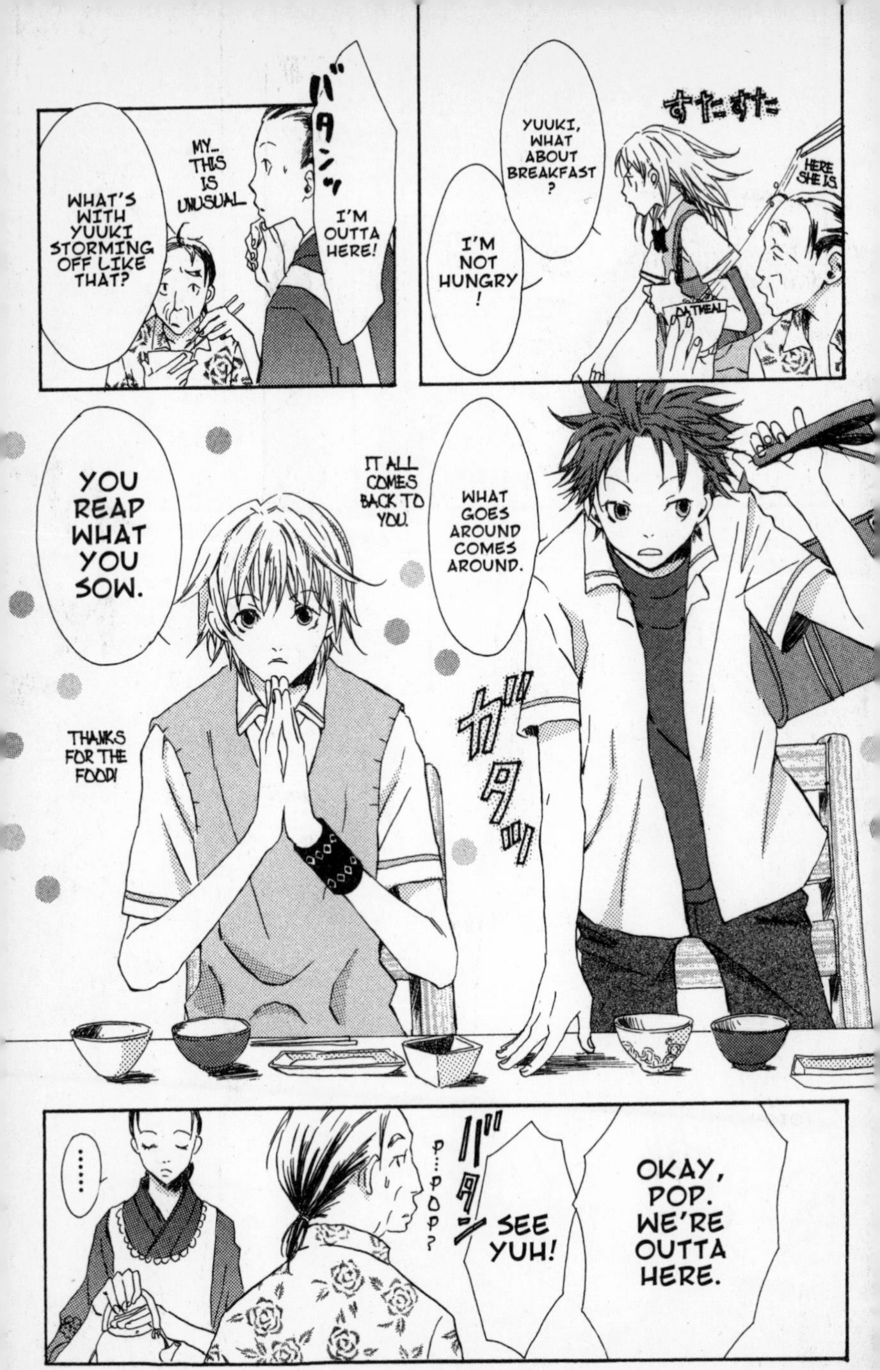
すたすた
HERE SHE IS.
YUUKI, WHAT ABOUT BREAKFAST?
I'M NOT HUNGRY!
OATMEAL
バタン
I'M OUTTA HERE!
MY.. THIS IS UNUSUAL
WHAT'S WITH YUUKI STORMING OFF LIKE THAT?
WHAT GOES AROUND COMES AROUND.
IT ALL COMES BACK TO YOU.
ガタッ
YOU REAP WHAT YOU SOW.
THANKS FOR THE FOOD!
OKAY, POP. WE'RE OUTTA HERE.
バタン
SEE YUH!
P...POP?
......

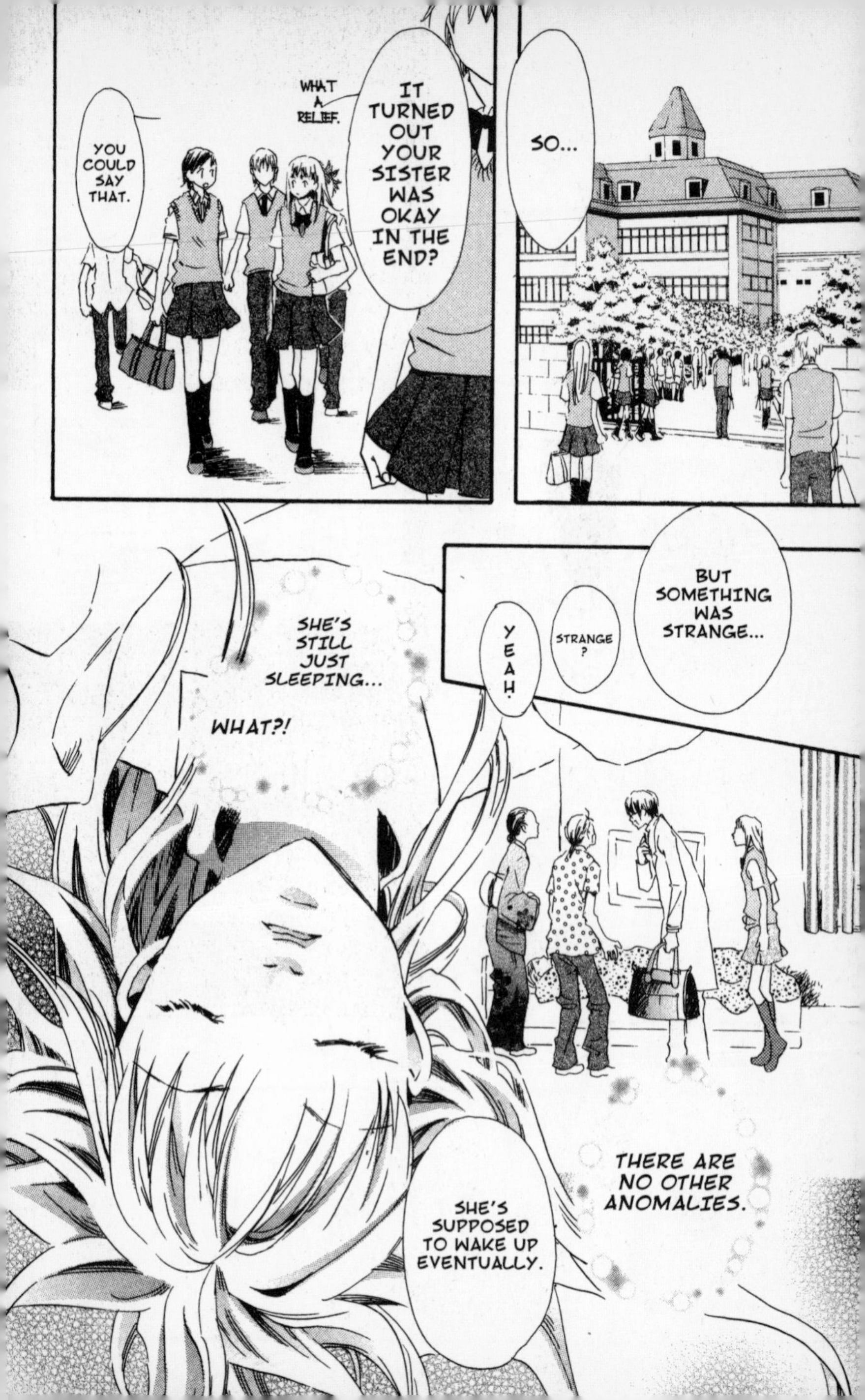
SO...
IT TURNED OUT YOUR SISTER WAS OKAY IN THE END?
WHAT A RELIEF.
YOU COULD SAY THAT.
BUT SOMETHING WAS STRANGE...
STRANGE?
YEAH.
SHE'S STILL JUST SLEEPING...
WHAT?!
THERE ARE NO OTHER ANOMALIES.
SHE'S SUPPOSED TO WAKE UP EVENTUALLY.

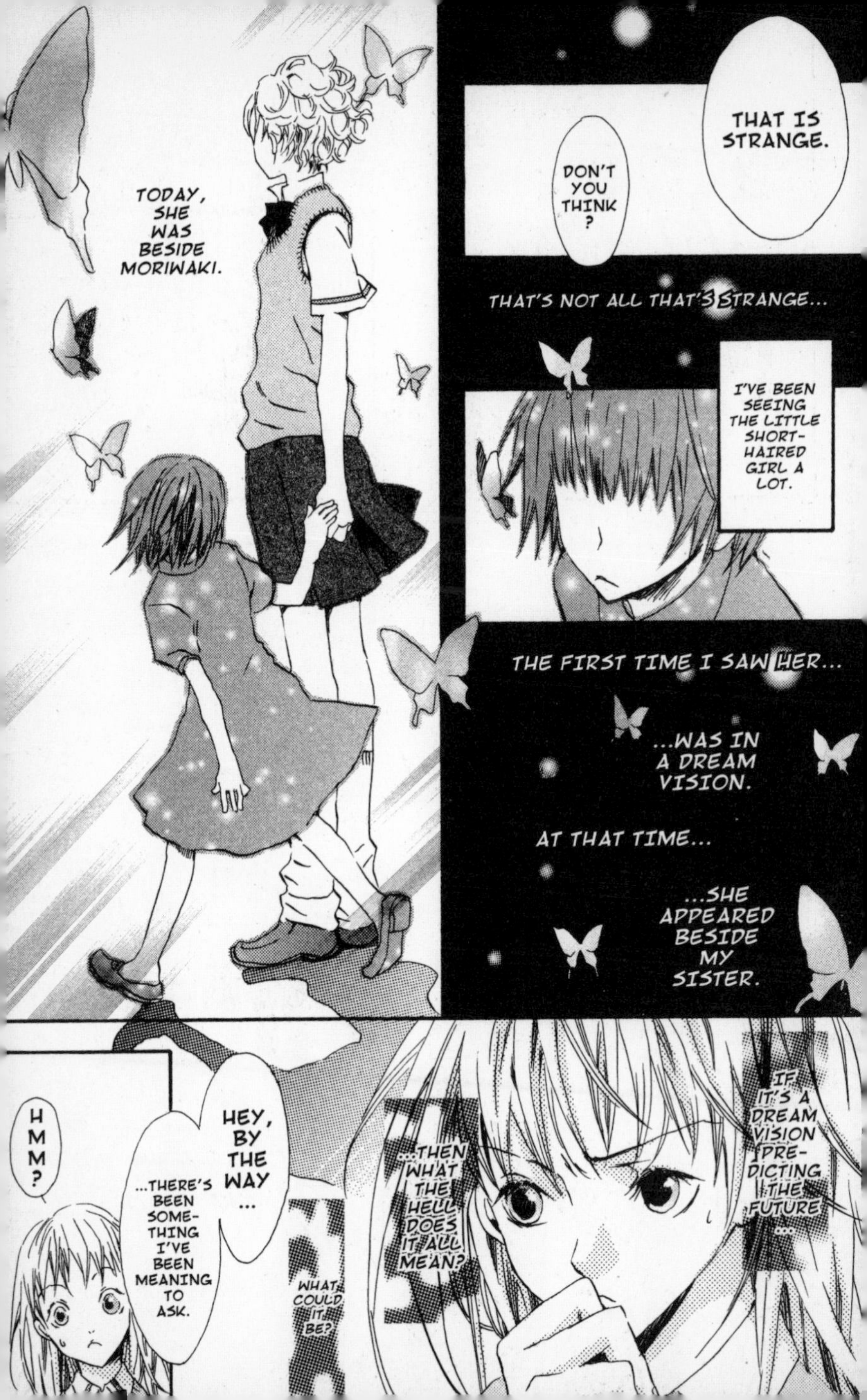
THAT IS STRANGE.
DON'T YOU THINK?
THAT'S NOT ALL THAT'S STRANGE...
I'VE BEEN SEEING THE LITTLE SHORT-HAIRED GIRL A LOT.
THE FIRST TIME I SAW HER...
...WAS IN A DREAM VISION.
AT THAT TIME...
...SHE APPEARED BESIDE MY SISTER.
TODAY, SHE WAS BESIDE MORIWAKI.
IF IT'S A DREAM VISION PREDICTING THE FUTURE...
...THEN WHAT THE HELL DOES IT ALL MEAN?
HEY, BY THE WAY...
...THERE'S BEEN SOMETHING I'VE BEEN MEANING TO ASK.
HMM?
WHAT COULD IT BE?

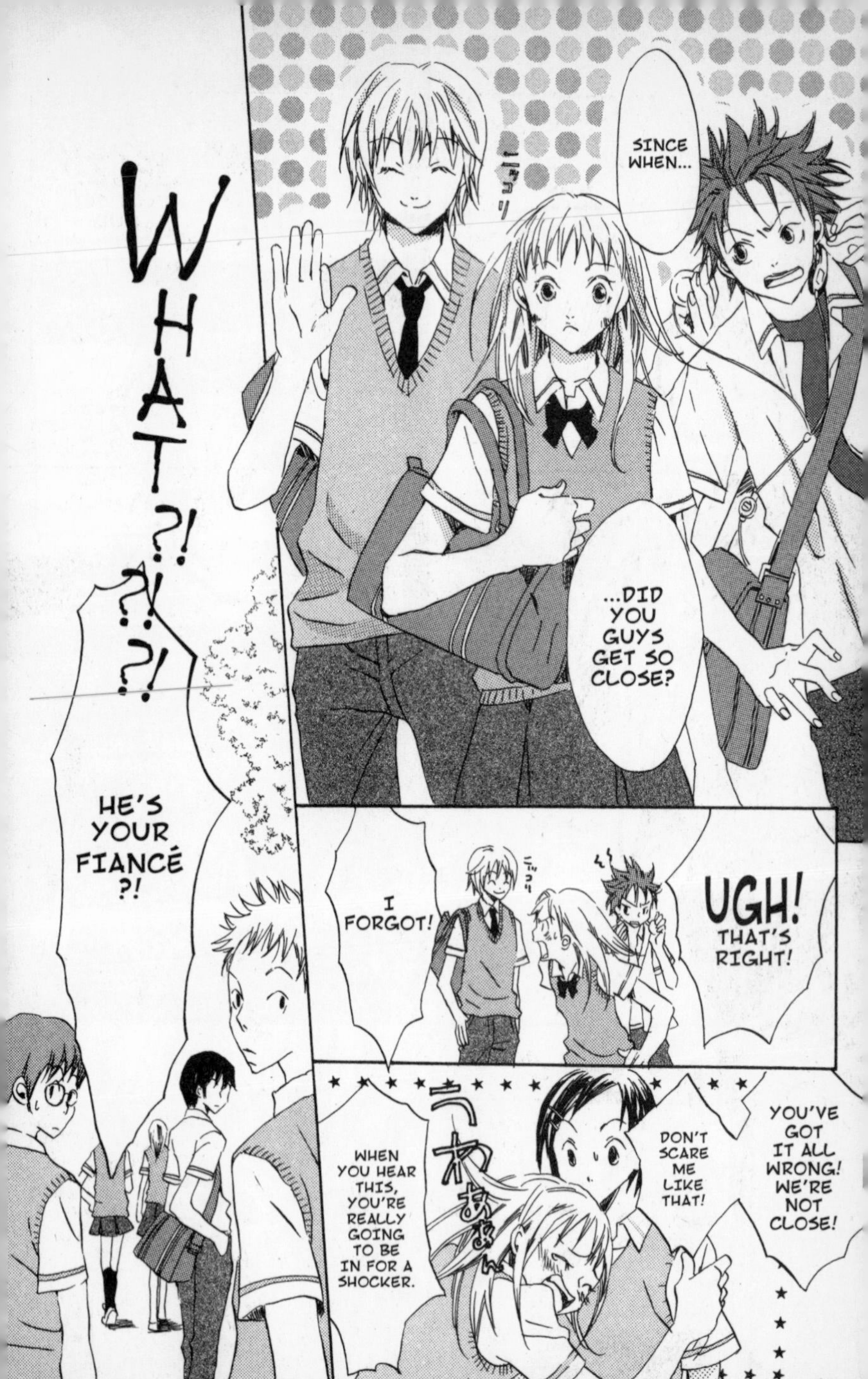
SINCE WHEN...
...DID YOU GUYS GET SO CLOSE?
UGH! THAT'S RIGHT!
I FORGOT!
YOU'VE GOT IT ALL WRONG! WE'RE NOT CLOSE!
DON'T SCARE ME LIKE THAT!
WHEN YOU HEAR THIS, YOU'RE REALLY GOING TO BE IN FOR A SHOCKER.
WHAT?!?!?!
HE'S YOUR FIANCÉ?!

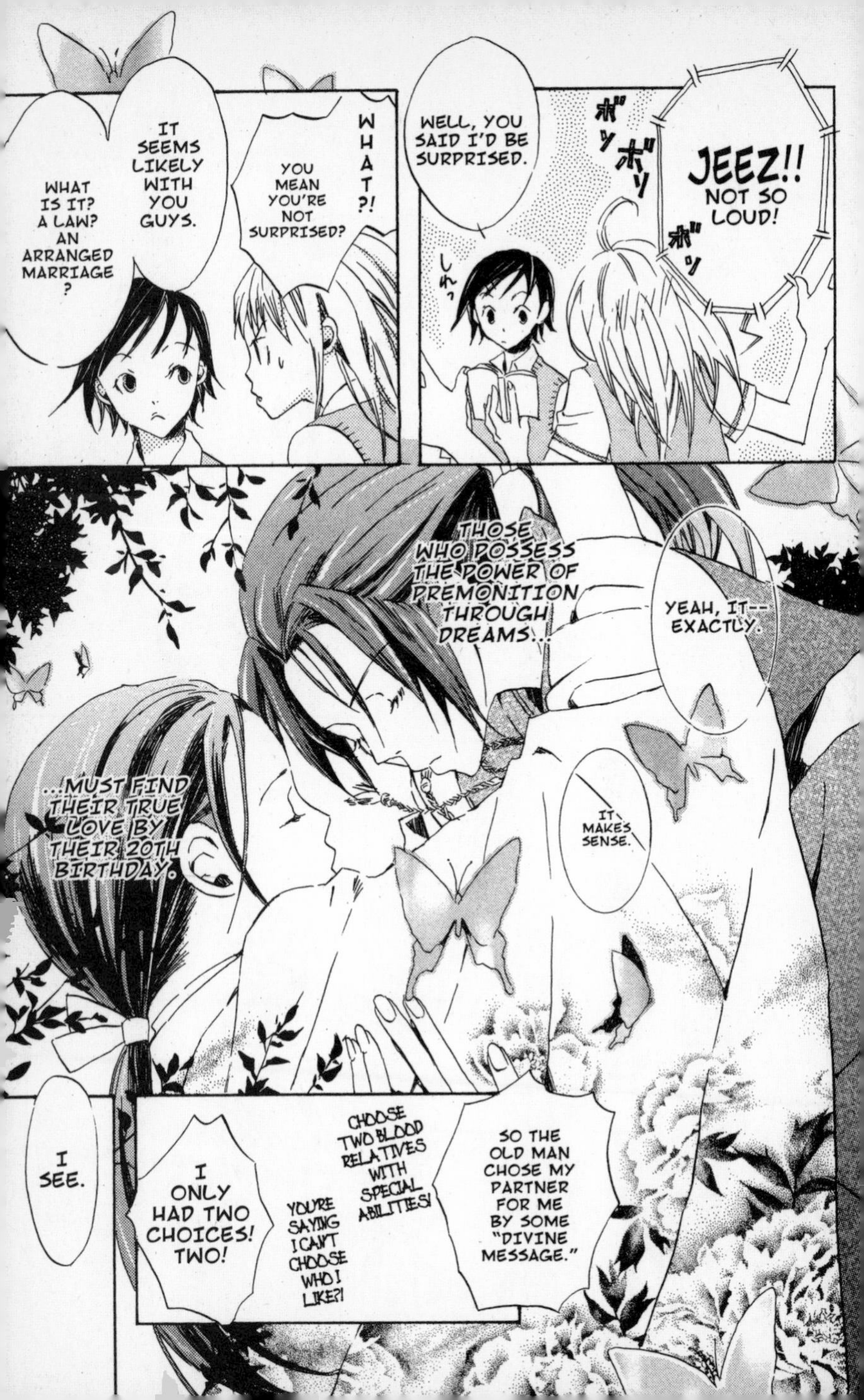
WHAT IS IT? A LAW? AN ARRANGED MARRIAGE?
IT SEEMS LIKELY WITH YOU GUYS.
WHAT?!
YOU MEAN YOU'RE NOT SURPRISED?
WELL, YOU SAID I'D BE SURPRISED.
しれっ
ボッ
ボッ
JEEZ!! NOT SO LOUD!
ボッ
THOSE WHO POSSESS THE POWER OF PREMONITION THROUGH DREAMS...
...MUST FIND THEIR TRUE LOVE BY THEIR 20TH BIRTHDAY.
YEAH, IT-- EXACTLY.
IT MAKES SENSE.
I SEE.
I ONLY HAD TWO CHOICES! TWO!
YOU'RE SAYING I CAN'T CHOOSE WHO I LIKE?!
CHOOSE TWO BLOOD RELATIVES WITH SPECIAL ABILITIES!
SO THE OLD MAN CHOSE MY PARTNER FOR ME BY SOME "DIVINE MESSAGE."

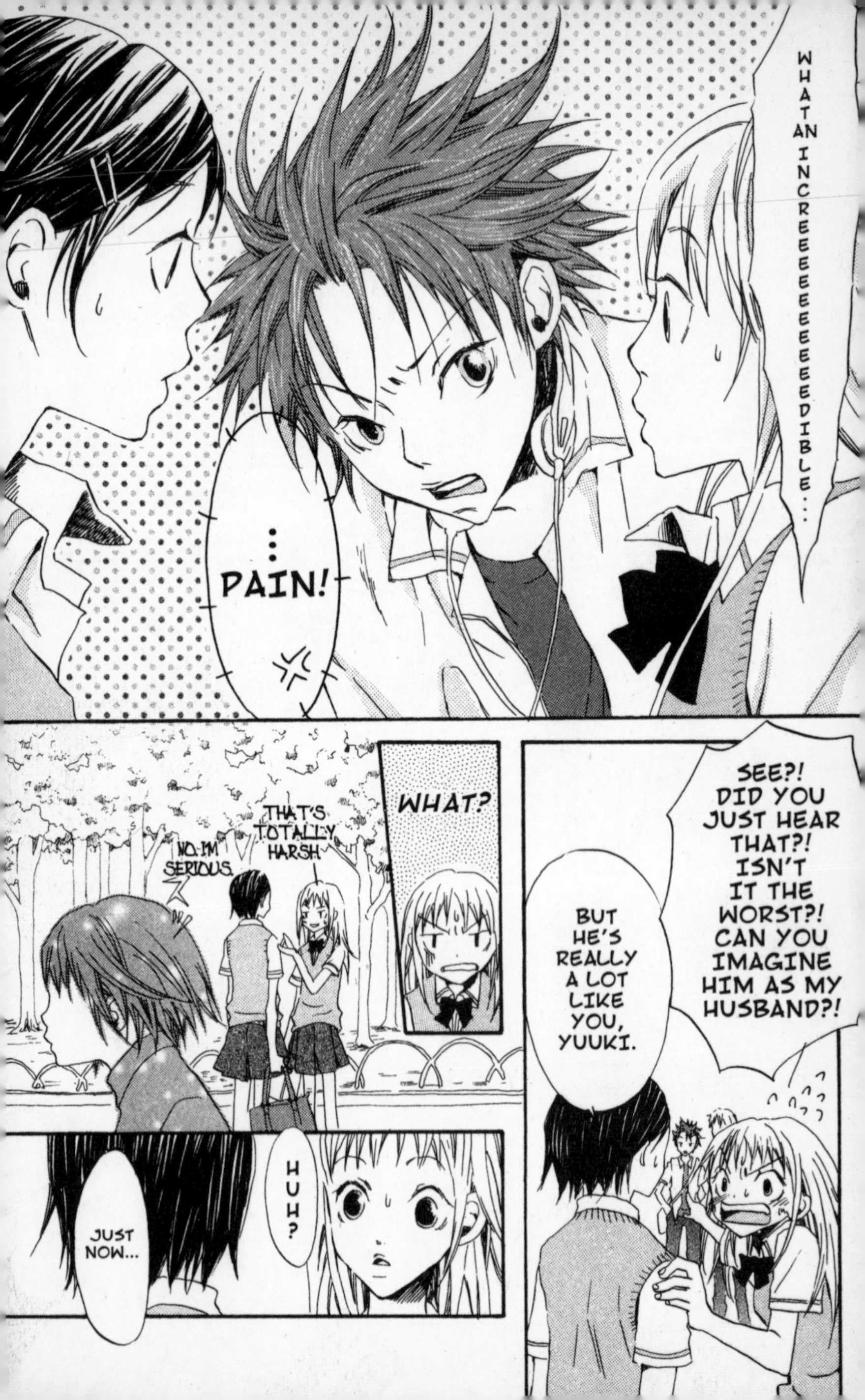

WHAT AN INCREEEEEEEEEEEDIBLE...
...PAIN!
SEE?! DID YOU JUST HEAR THAT?! ISN'T IT THE WORST?! CAN YOU IMAGINE HIM AS MY HUSBAND?!
BUT HE'S REALLY A LOT LIKE YOU, YUUKI.
WHAT?
THAT'S TOTALLY HARSH.
NO, I'M SERIOUS.
HUH?
JUST NOW...

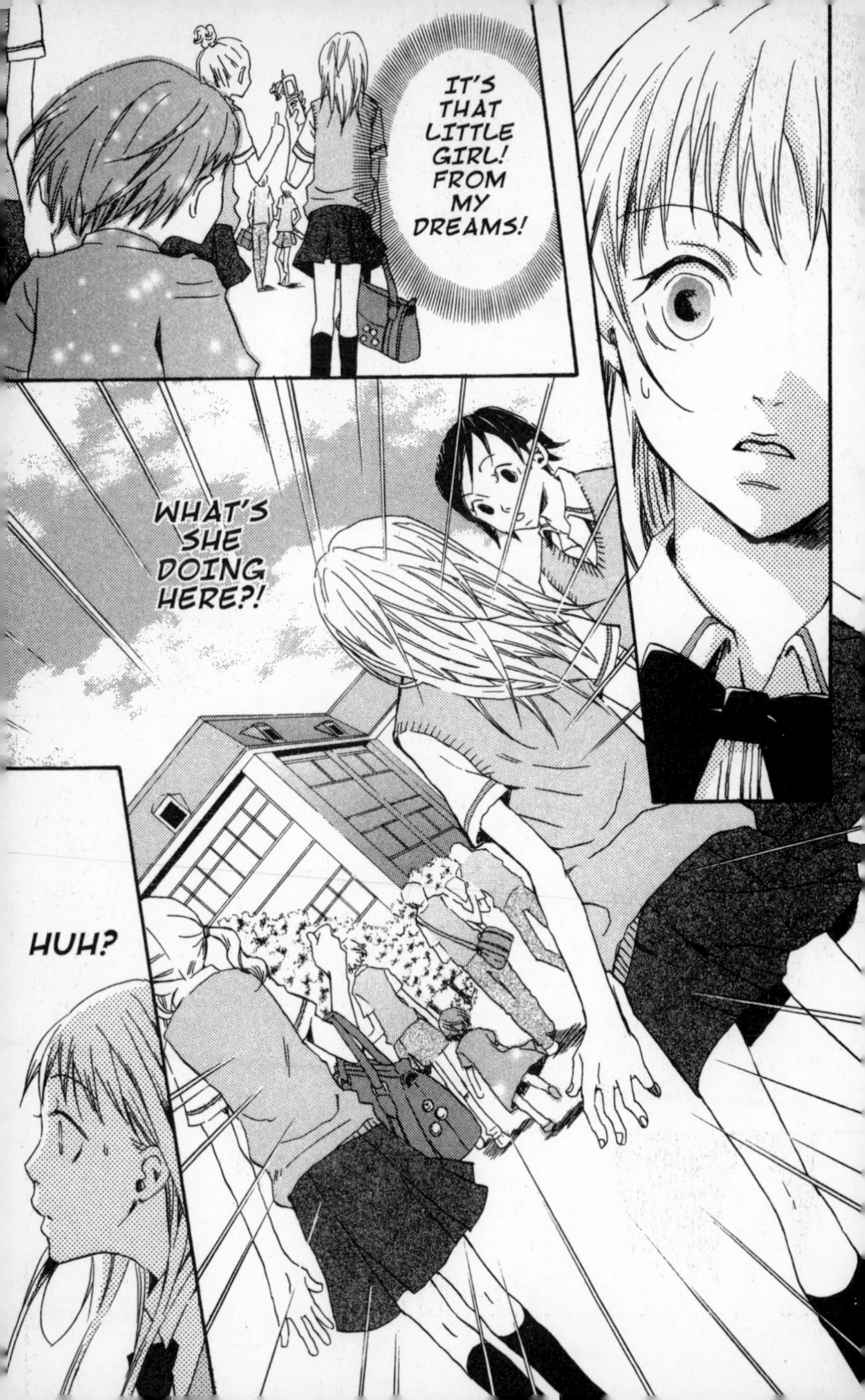
IT'S THAT LITTLE GIRL! FROM MY DREAMS!
WHAT'S SHE DOING HERE?!
HUH?

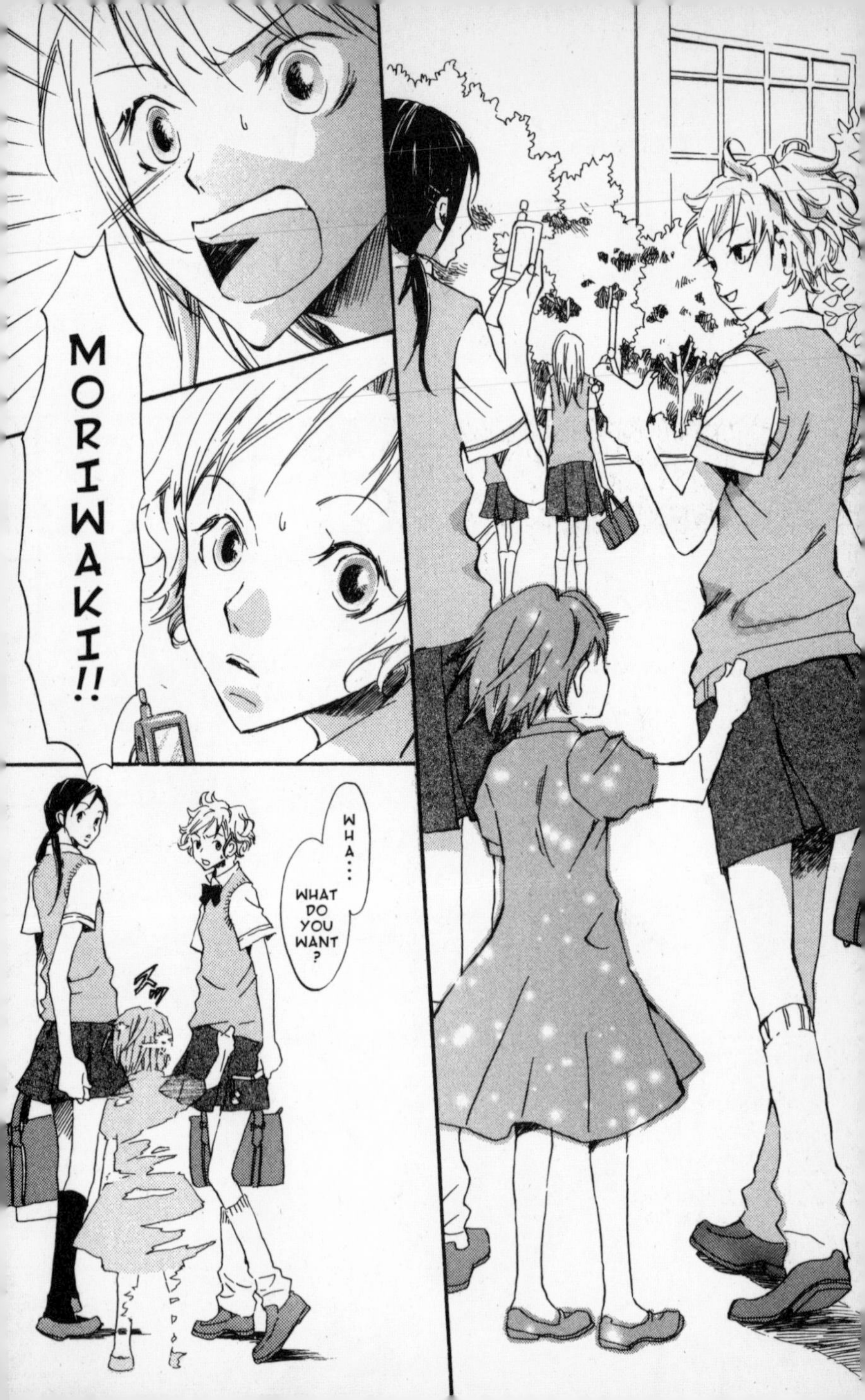
MORIWAKI!!
WHA... WHAT DO YOU WANT?

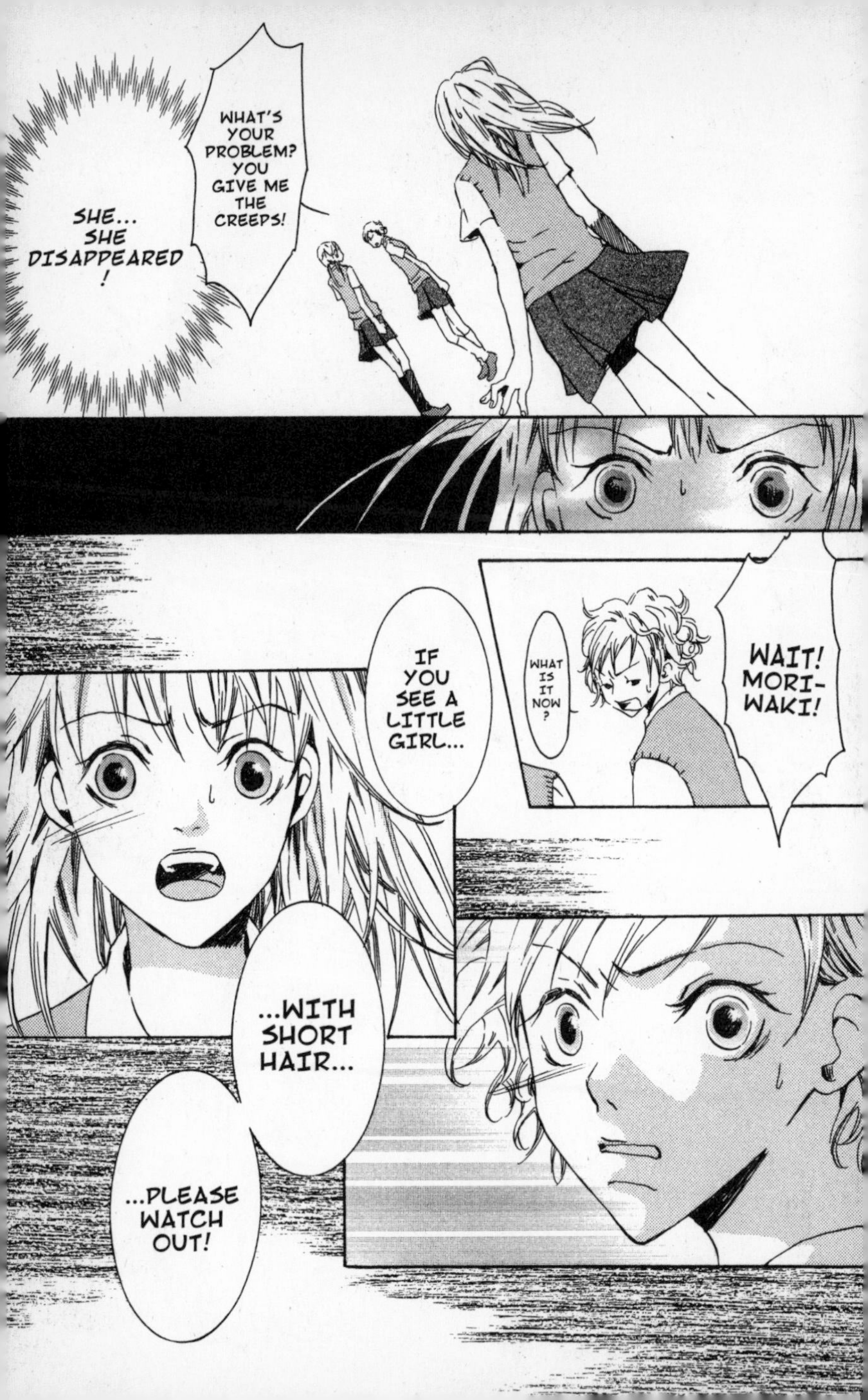
WHAT'S YOUR PROBLEM? YOU GIVE ME THE CREEPS!
SHE... SHE DISAPPEARED!
WAIT! MORI-WAKI!
WHAT IS IT NOW?
IF YOU SEE A LITTLE GIRL...
...WITH SHORT HAIR...
...PLEASE WATCH OUT!

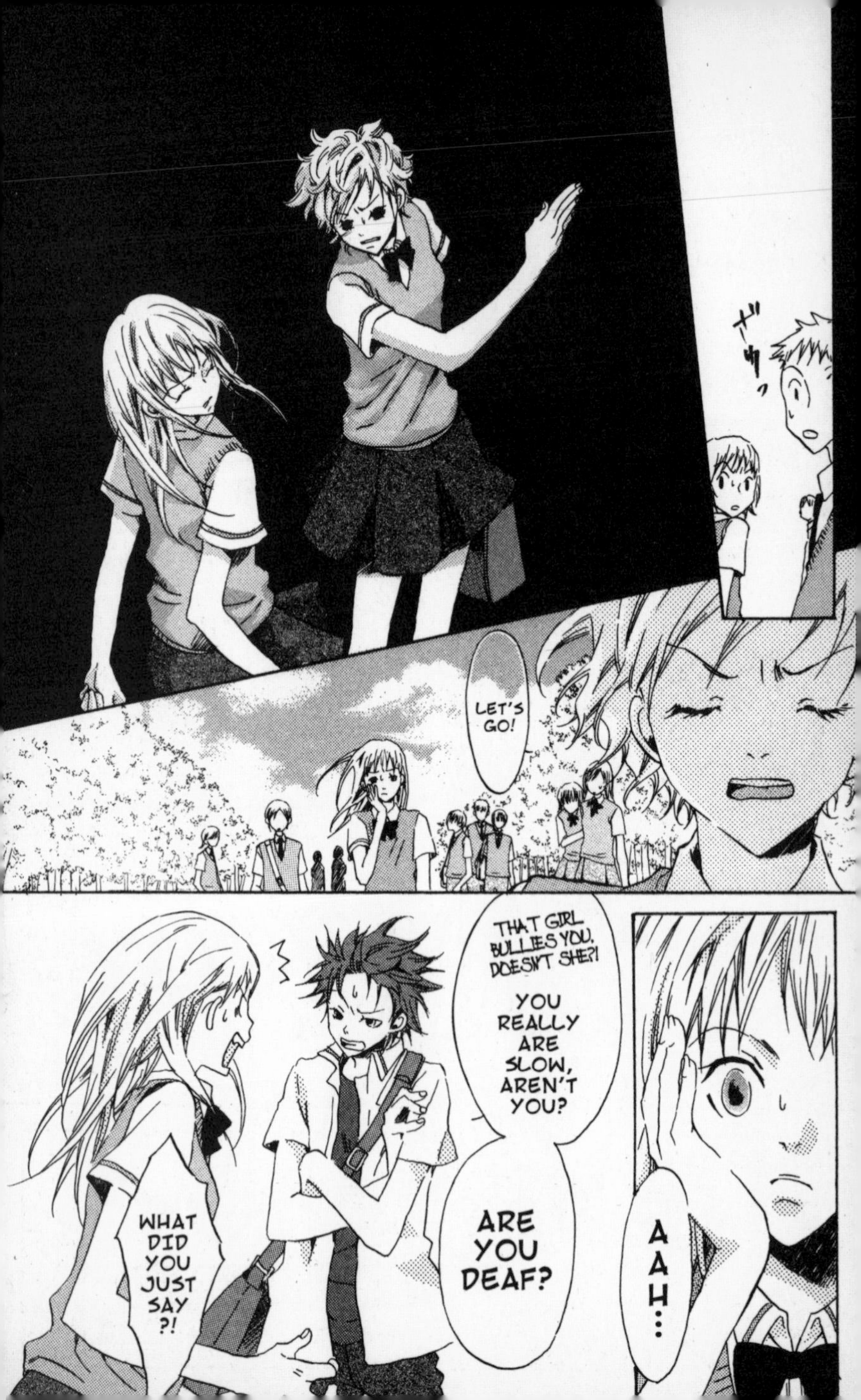
ザワッ
LET'S GO!
AAH...
THAT GIRL BULLIES YOU, DOESN'T SHE?!
YOU REALLY ARE SLOW, AREN'T YOU?
ARE YOU DEAF?
WHAT DID YOU JUST SAY?!

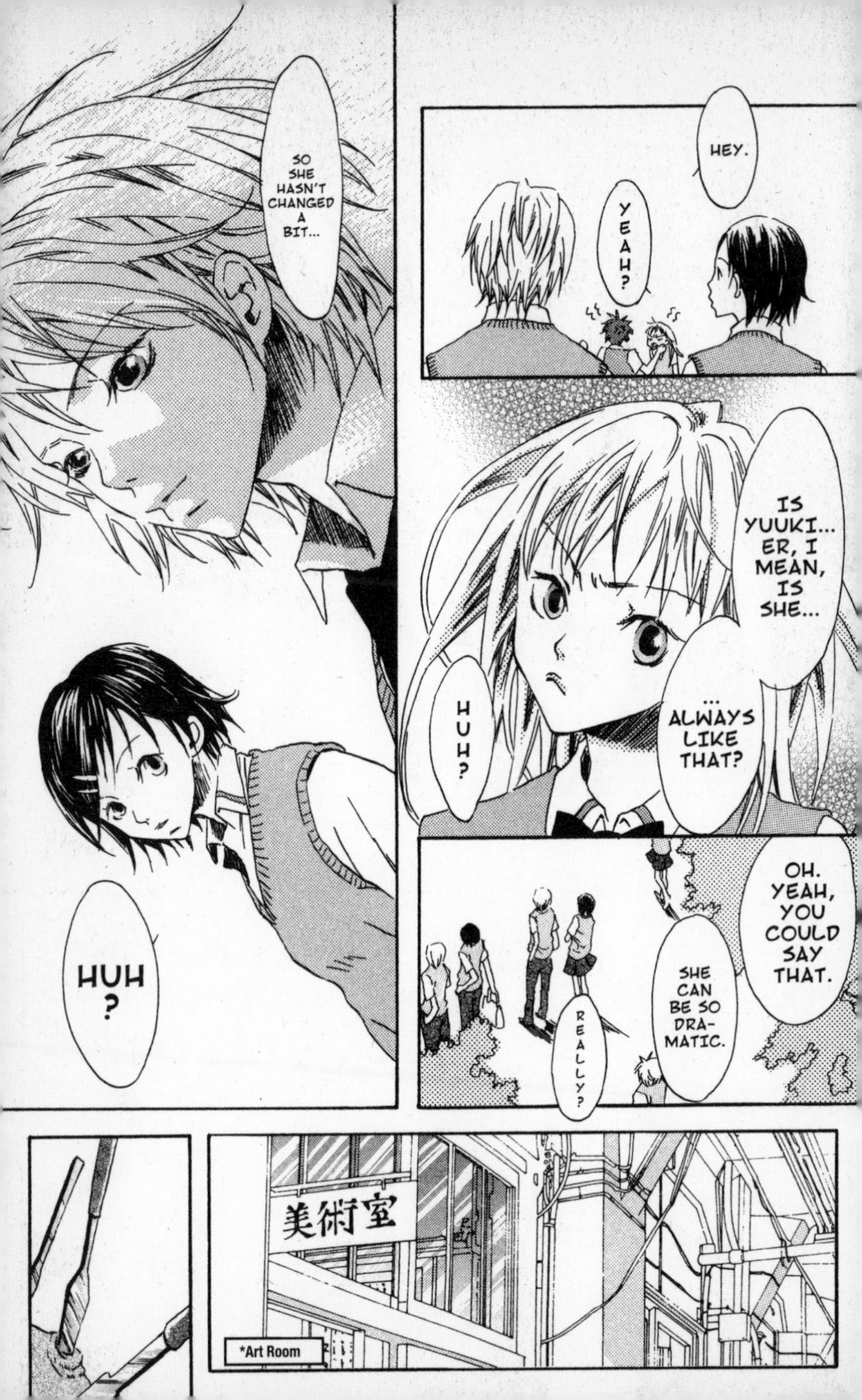
HEY.
YEAH?
IS YUUKI... ER, I MEAN, IS SHE...
...ALWAYS LIKE THAT?
HUH?
OH. YEAH, YOU COULD SAY THAT.
SHE CAN BE SO DRAMATIC.
REALLY?
SO SHE HASN'T CHANGED A BIT...
HUH?
美術室
*Art Room

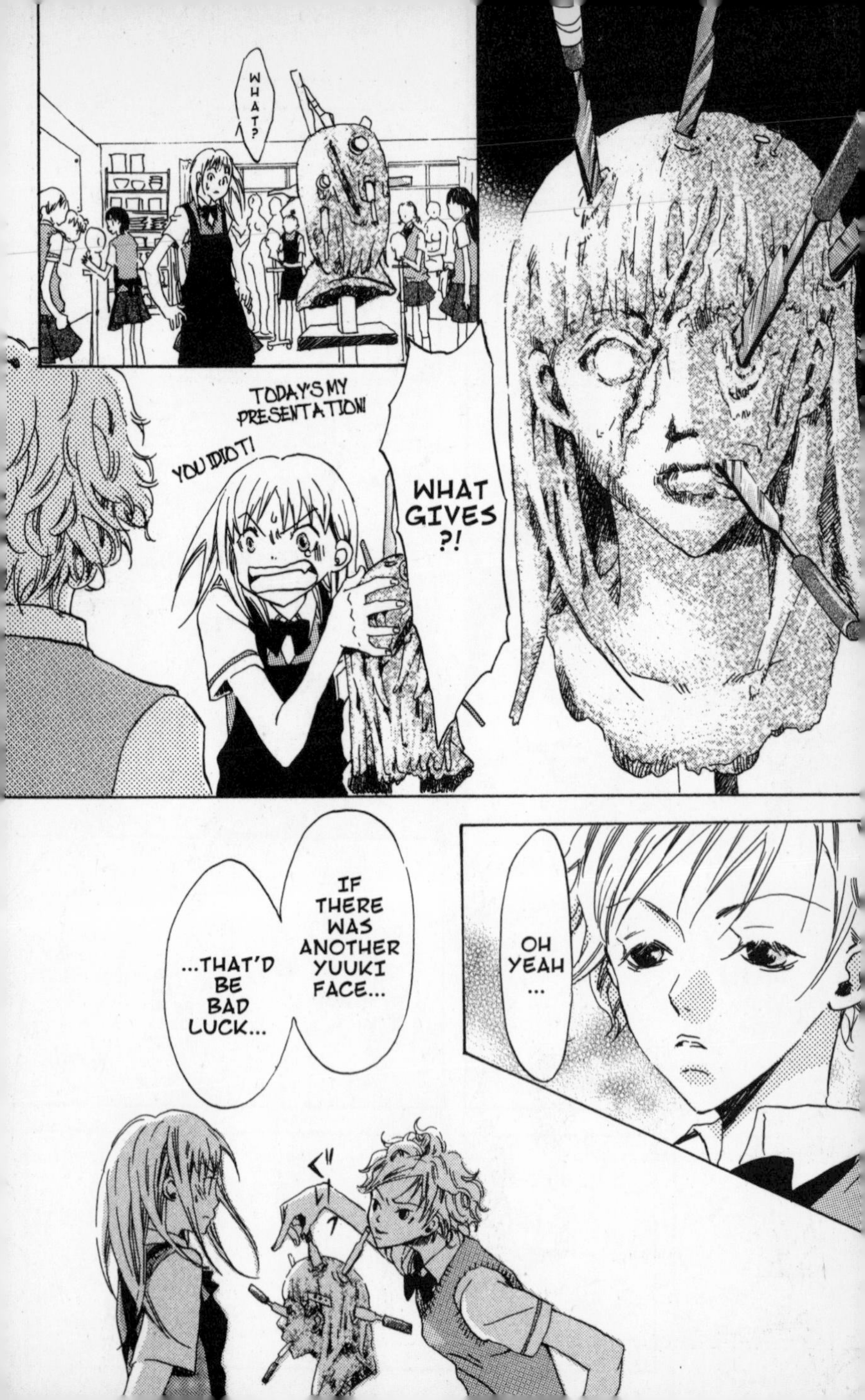
WHAT?
WHAT GIVES?!
TODAY'S MY PRESENTATION!
YOU IDIOT!
OH YEAH...
IF THERE WAS ANOTHER YUUKI FACE...
...THAT'D BE BAD LUCK...

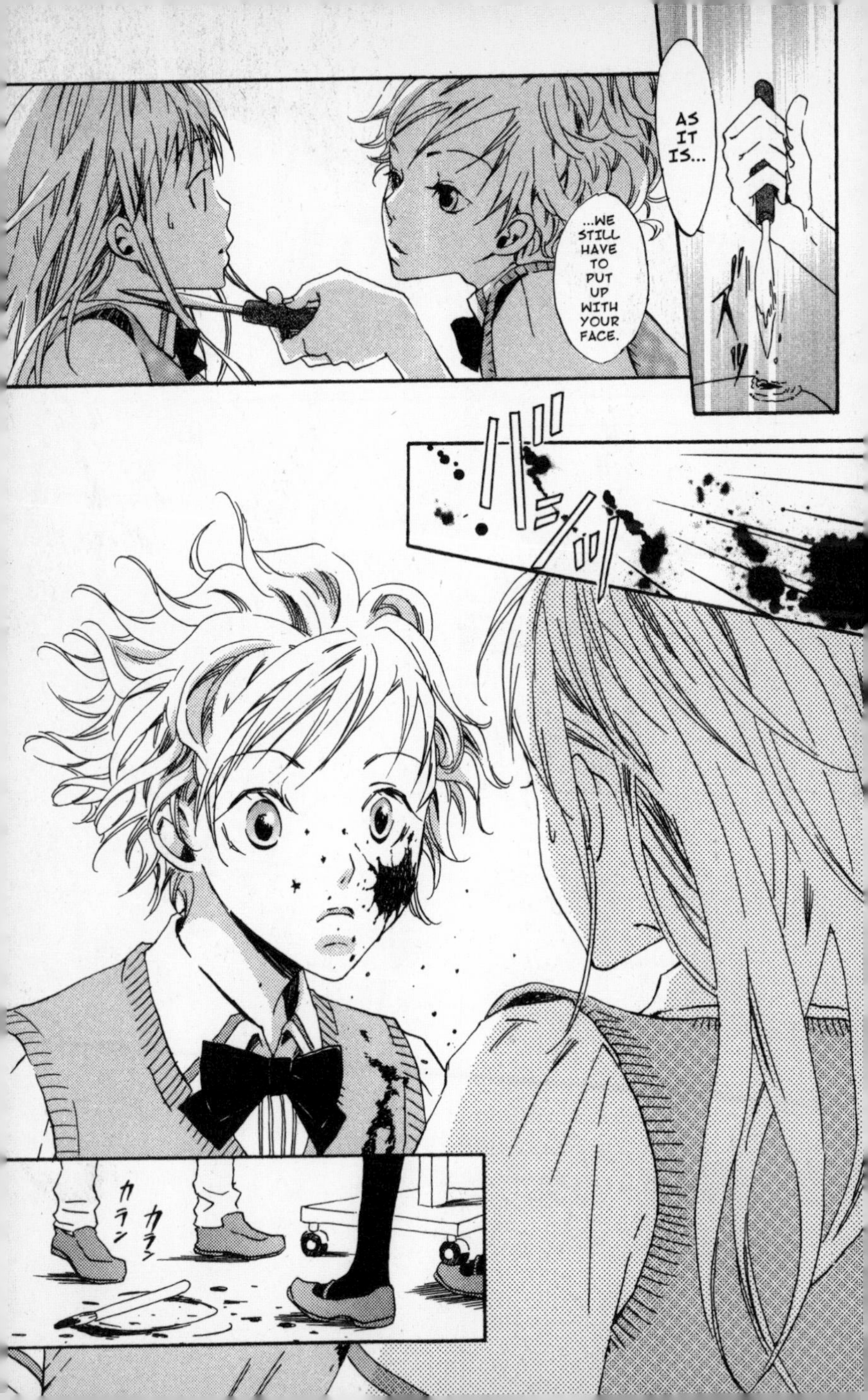
AS IT IS...
...WE STILL HAVE TO PUT UP WITH YOUR FACE.
カラン
カラン

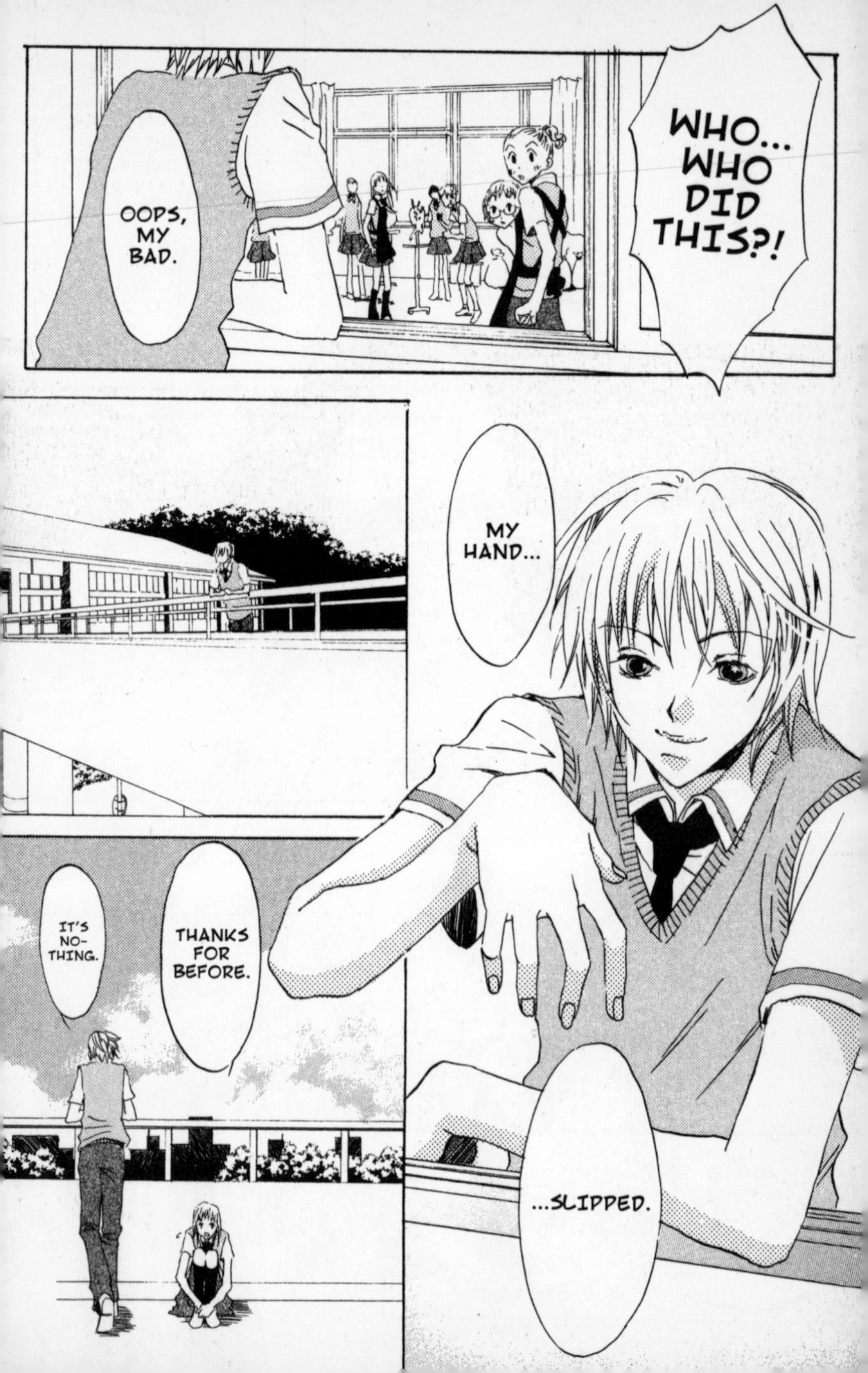
WHO... WHO DID THIS?!
OOPS, MY BAD.
MY HAND...
...SLIPPED.
THANKS FOR BEFORE.
IT'S NO-THING.

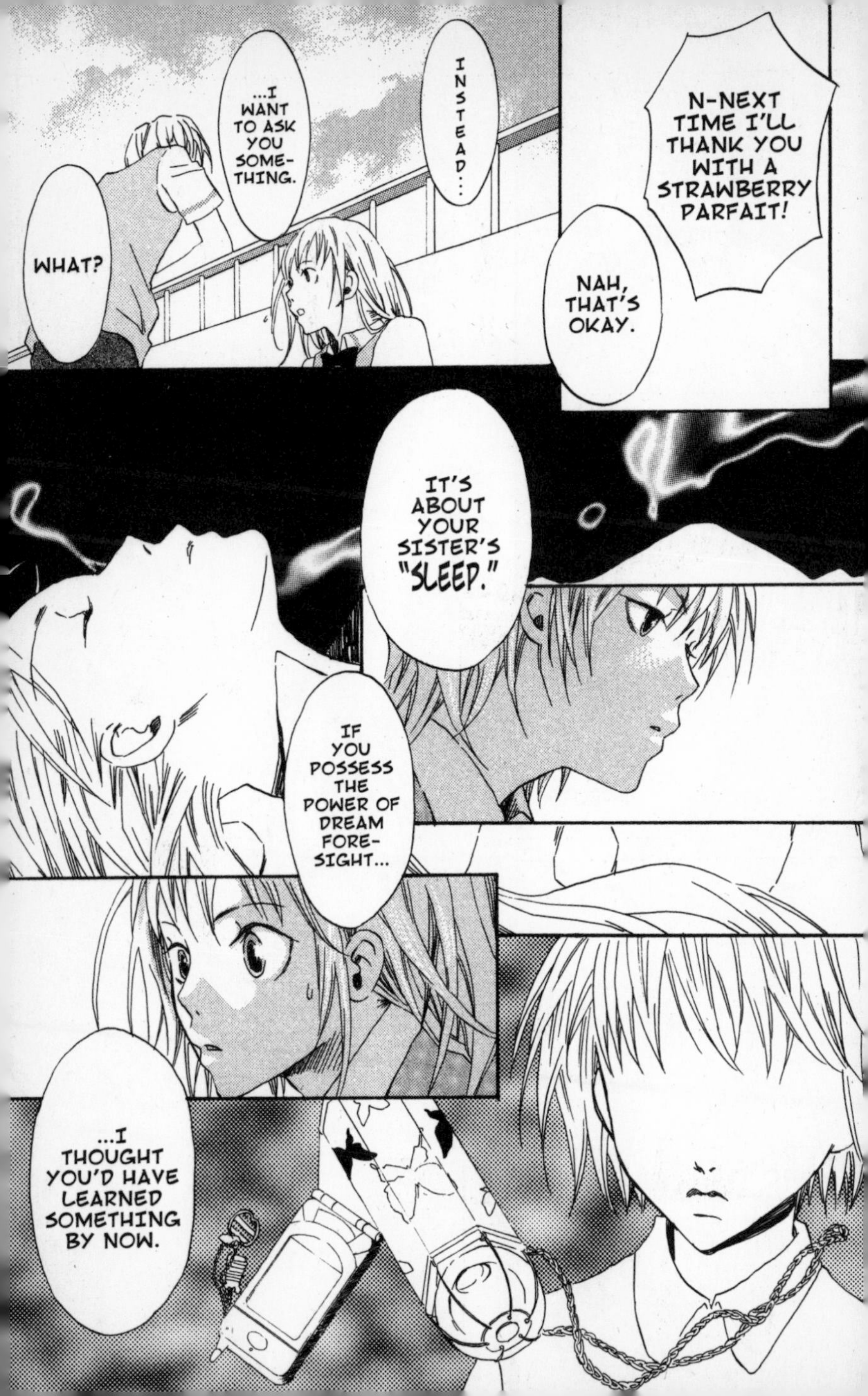
N-NEXT TIME I'LL THANK YOU WITH A STRAWBERRY PARFAIT!
NAH, THAT'S OKAY.
INSTEAD...
...I WANT TO ASK YOU SOMETHING.
WHAT?
IT'S ABOUT YOUR SISTER'S "SLEEP."
IF YOU POSSESS THE POWER OF DREAM FORESIGHT...
...I THOUGHT YOU'D HAVE LEARNED SOMETHING BY NOW.

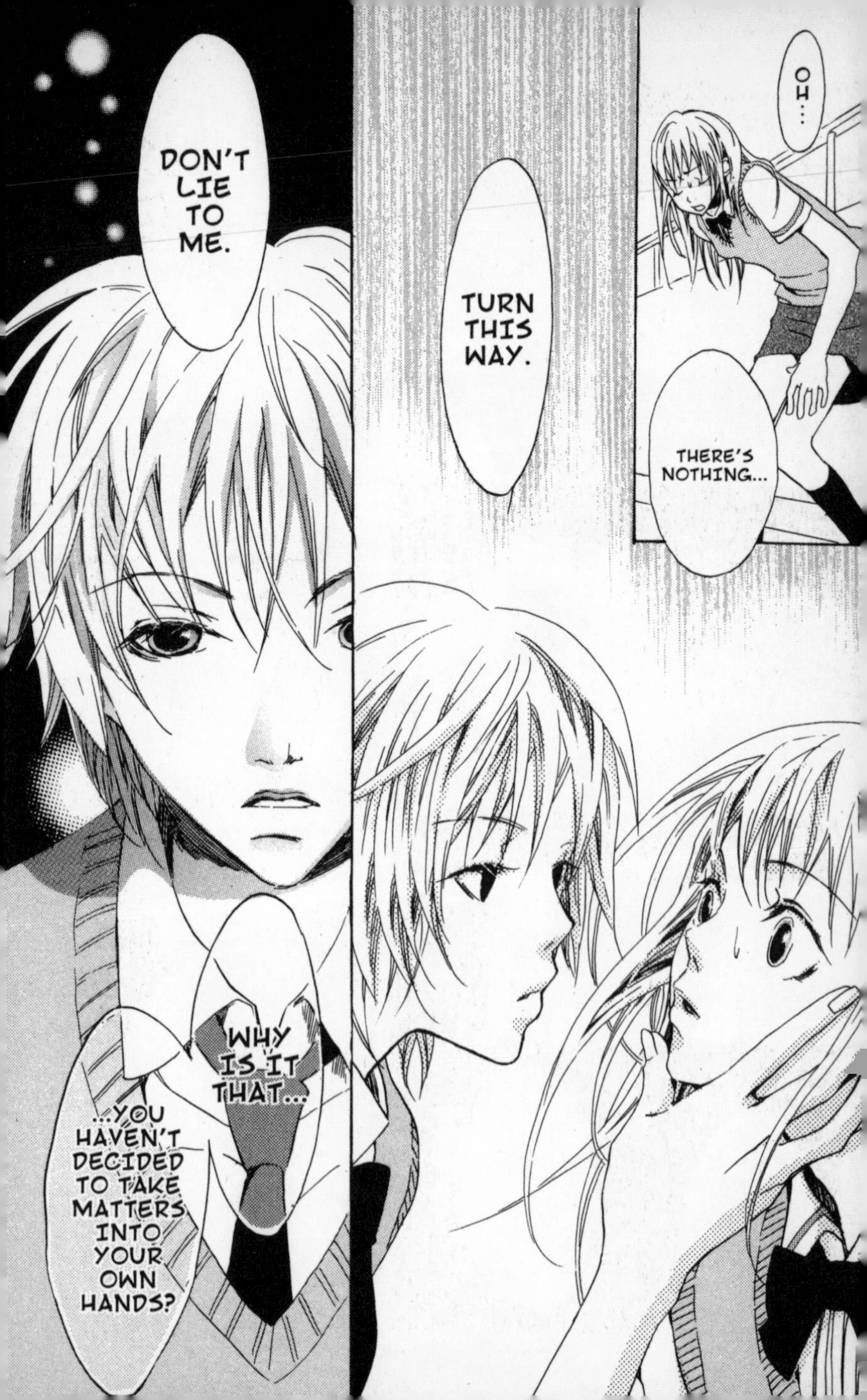
OH...
THERE'S NOTHING...
TURN THIS WAY.
DON'T LIE TO ME.
WHY IS IT THAT...
...YOU HAVEN'T DECIDED TO TAKE MATTERS INTO YOUR OWN HANDS?

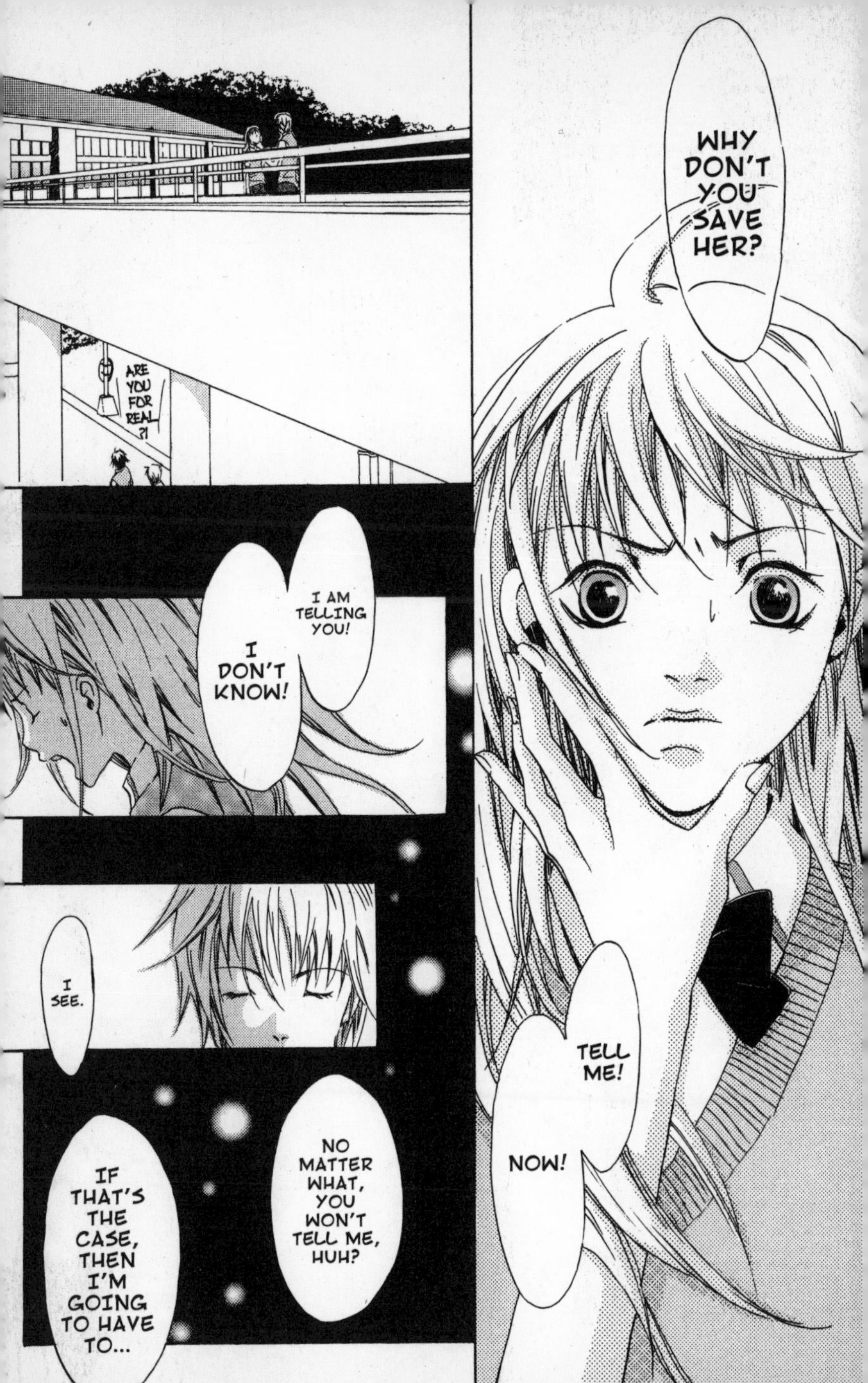
WHY DON'T YOU SAVE HER?
TELL ME!
NOW!
ARE YOU FOR REAL ?!
I AM TELLING YOU!
I DON'T KNOW!
I SEE.
NO MATTER WHAT, YOU WON'T TELL ME, HUH?
IF THAT'S THE CASE, THEN I'M GOING TO HAVE TO...

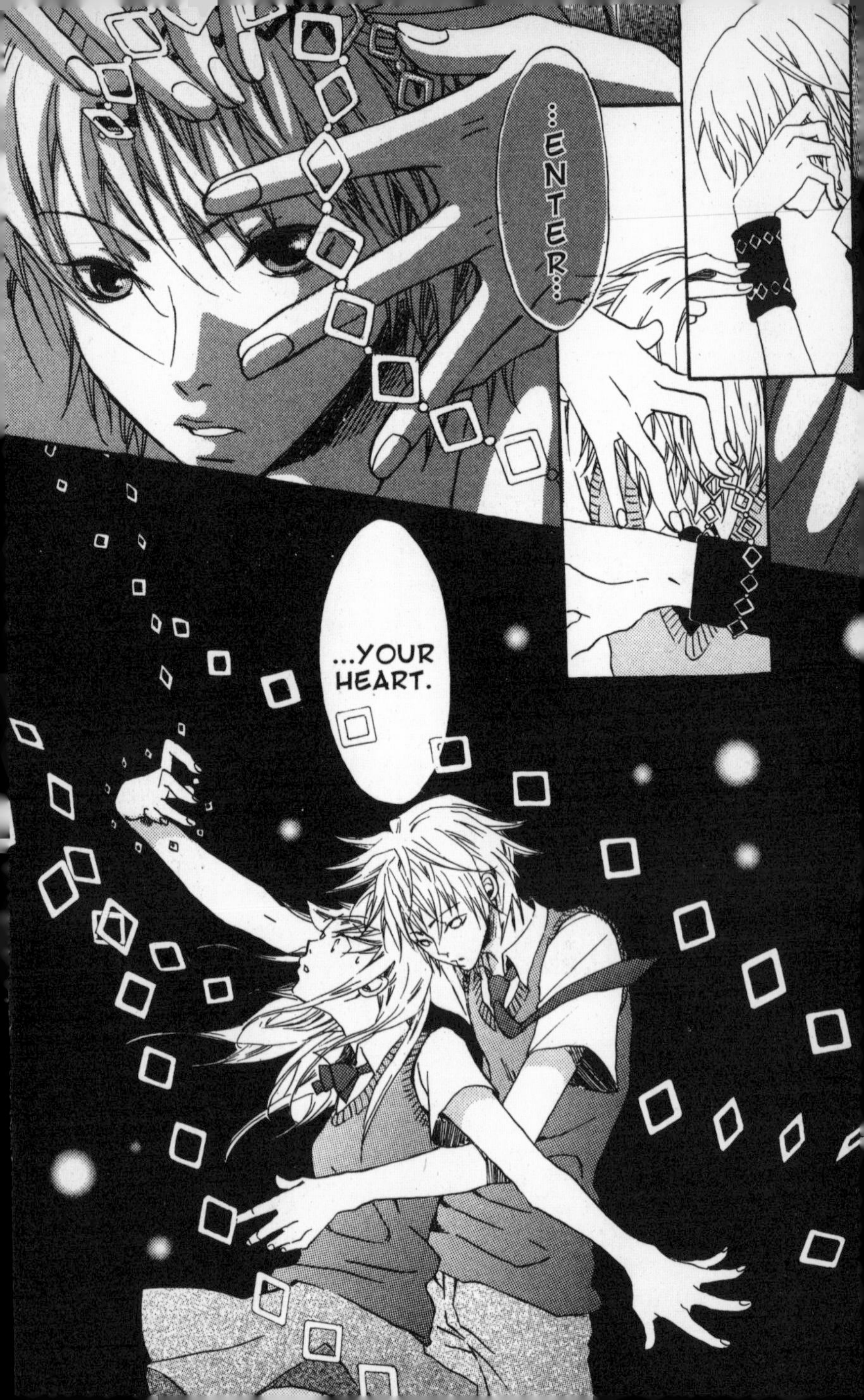
...ENTER...
...YOUR HEART.

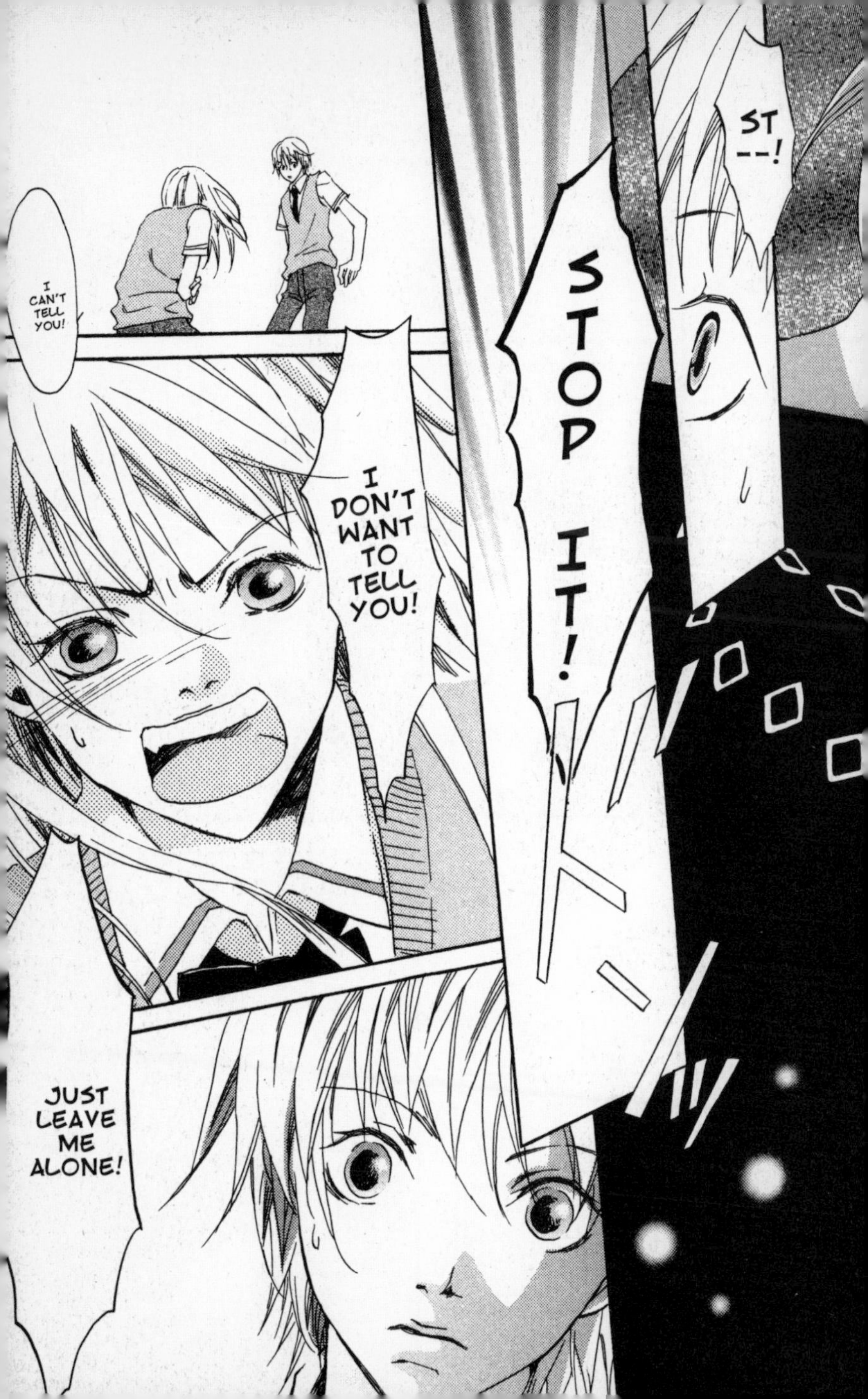
I CAN'T TELL YOU!
I DON'T WANT TO TELL YOU!
JUST LEAVE ME ALONE!
ST--!
STOP IT!

JINGLE

ジャラッ

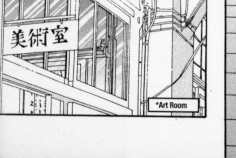

*Art Room

美術室

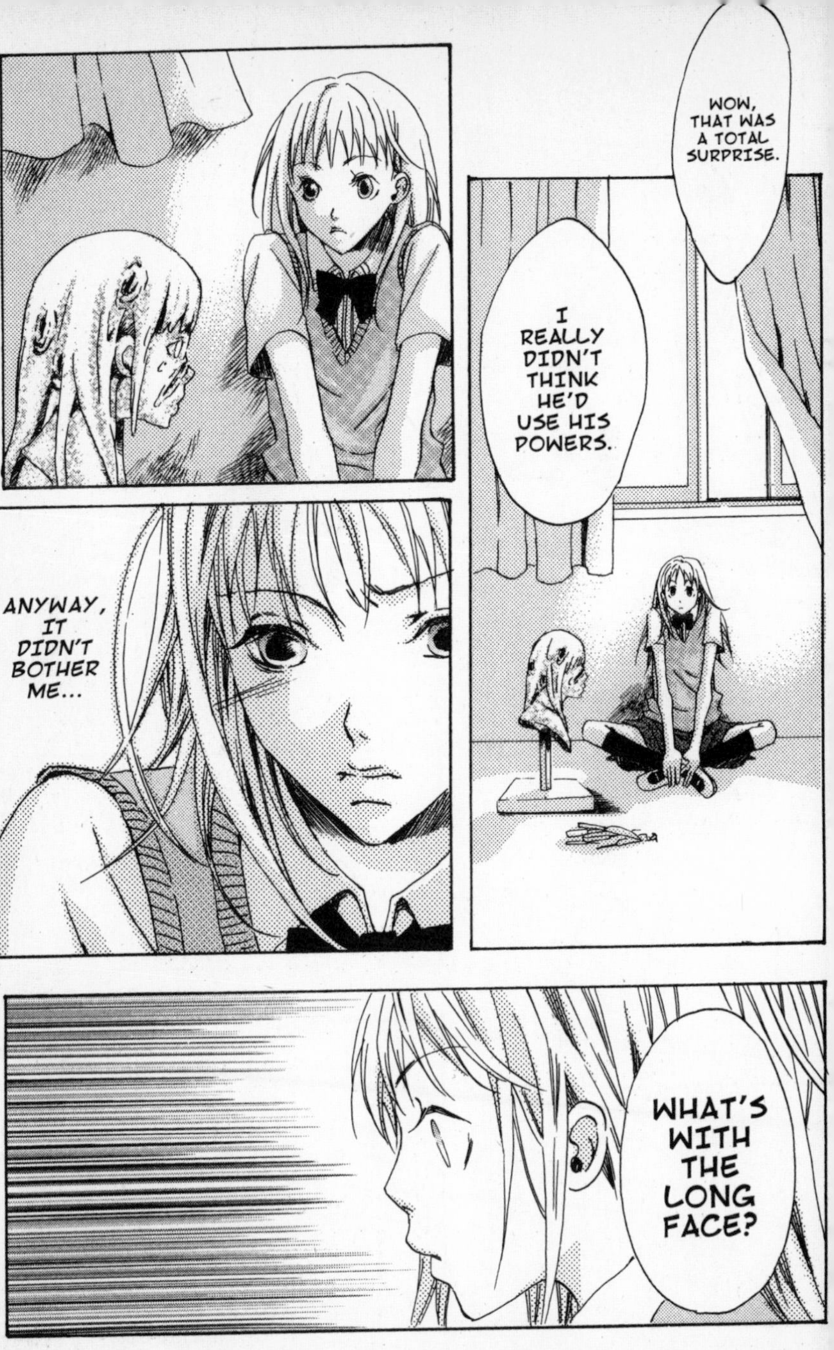
WOW, THAT WAS A TOTAL SURPRISE.
I REALLY DIDN'T THINK HE'D USE HIS POWERS.
ANYWAY, IT DIDN'T BOTHER ME...
WHAT'S WITH THE LONG FACE?

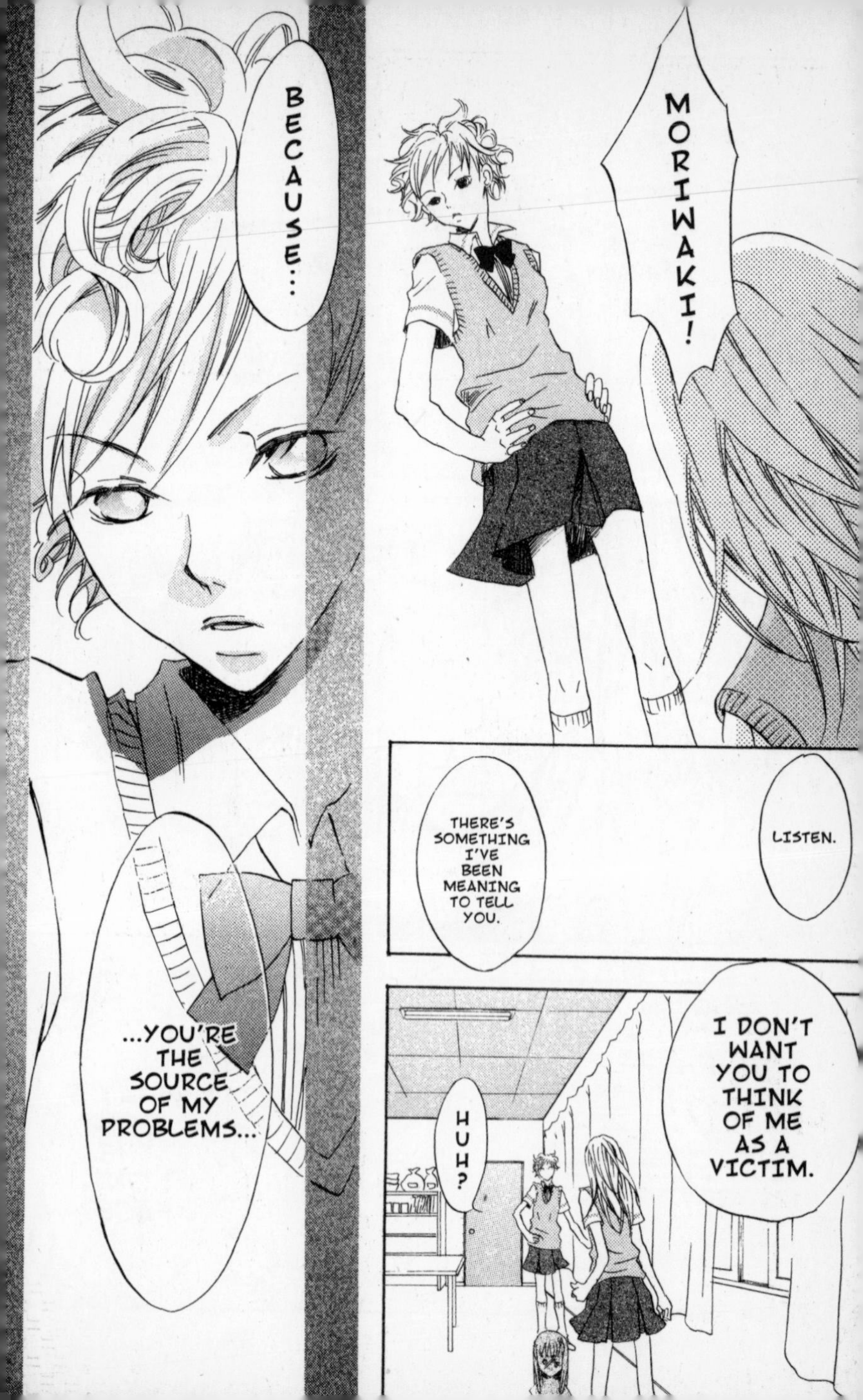
MORIWAKI!
LISTEN.
THERE'S SOMETHING I'VE BEEN MEANING TO TELL YOU.
I DON'T WANT YOU TO THINK OF ME AS A VICTIM.
HUH?
BECAUSE...
...YOU'RE THE SOURCE OF MY PROBLEMS...

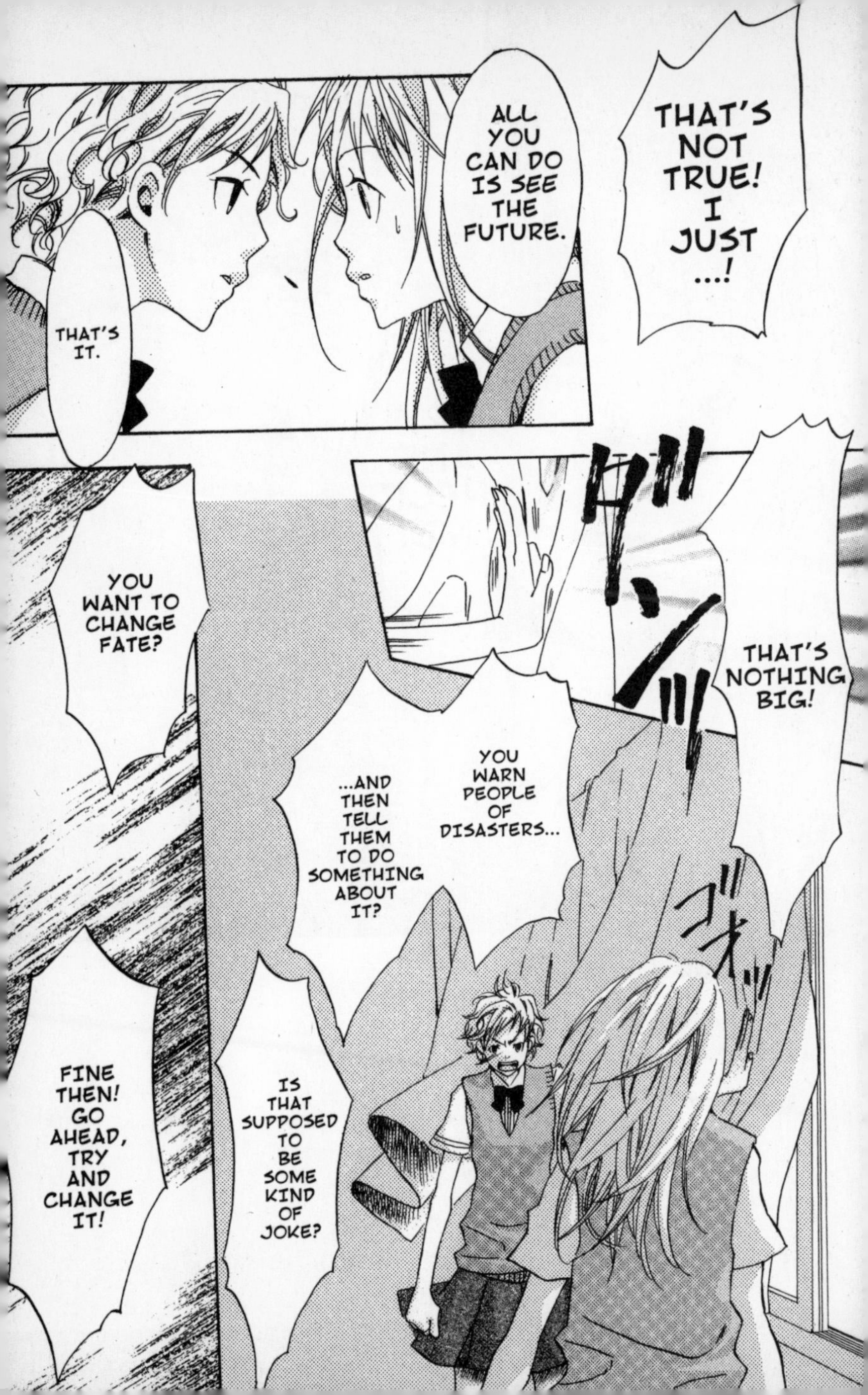
THAT'S NOT TRUE! I JUST ...!
ALL YOU CAN DO IS SEE THE FUTURE.
THAT'S IT.
ダンッ
THAT'S NOTHING BIG!
YOU WARN PEOPLE OF DISASTERS...
...AND THEN TELL THEM TO DO SOMETHING ABOUT IT?
YOU WANT TO CHANGE FATE?
ゴオッ
IS THAT SUPPOSED TO BE SOME KIND OF JOKE?
FINE THEN! GO AHEAD, TRY AND CHANGE IT!

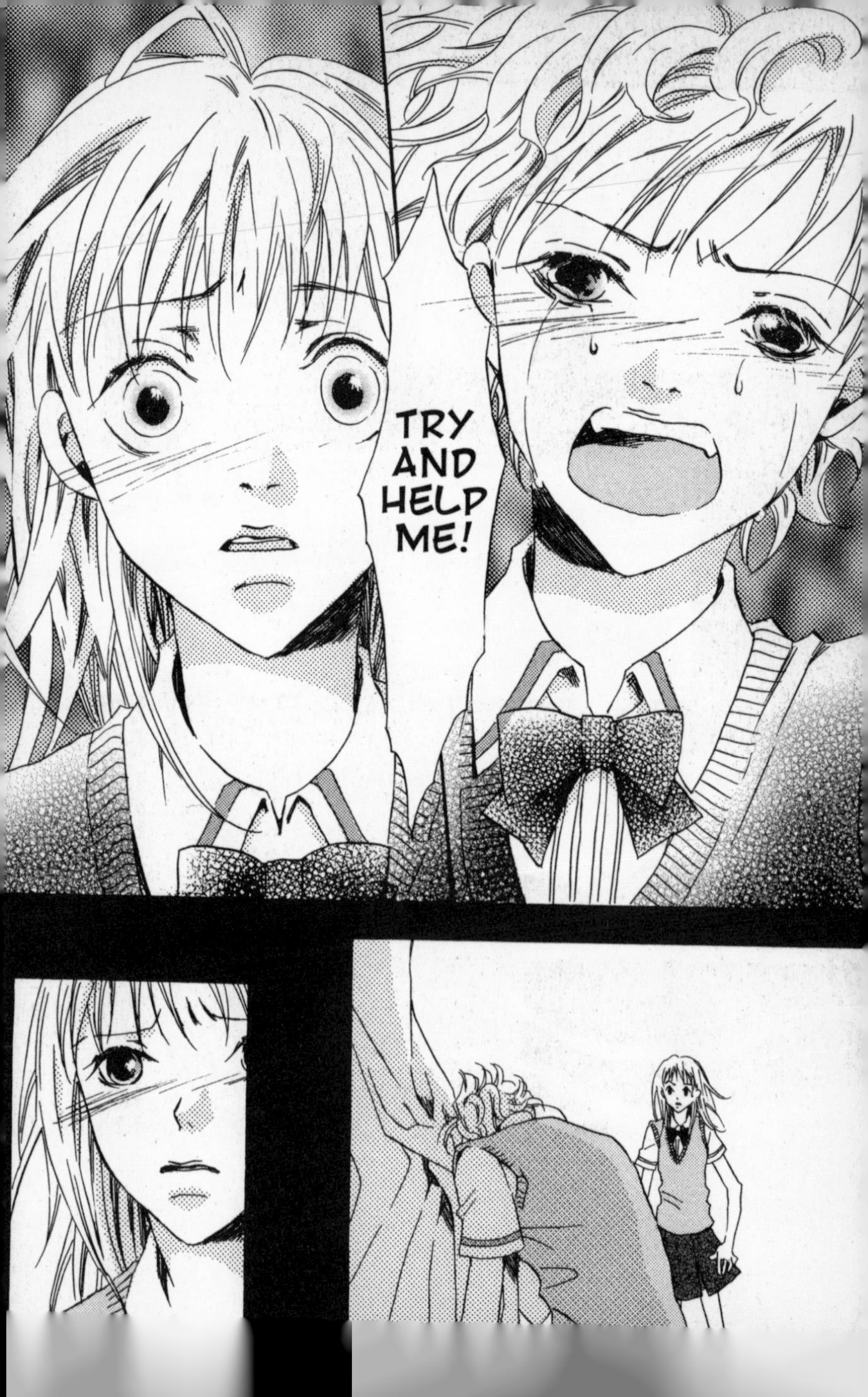
TRY AND HELP ME!

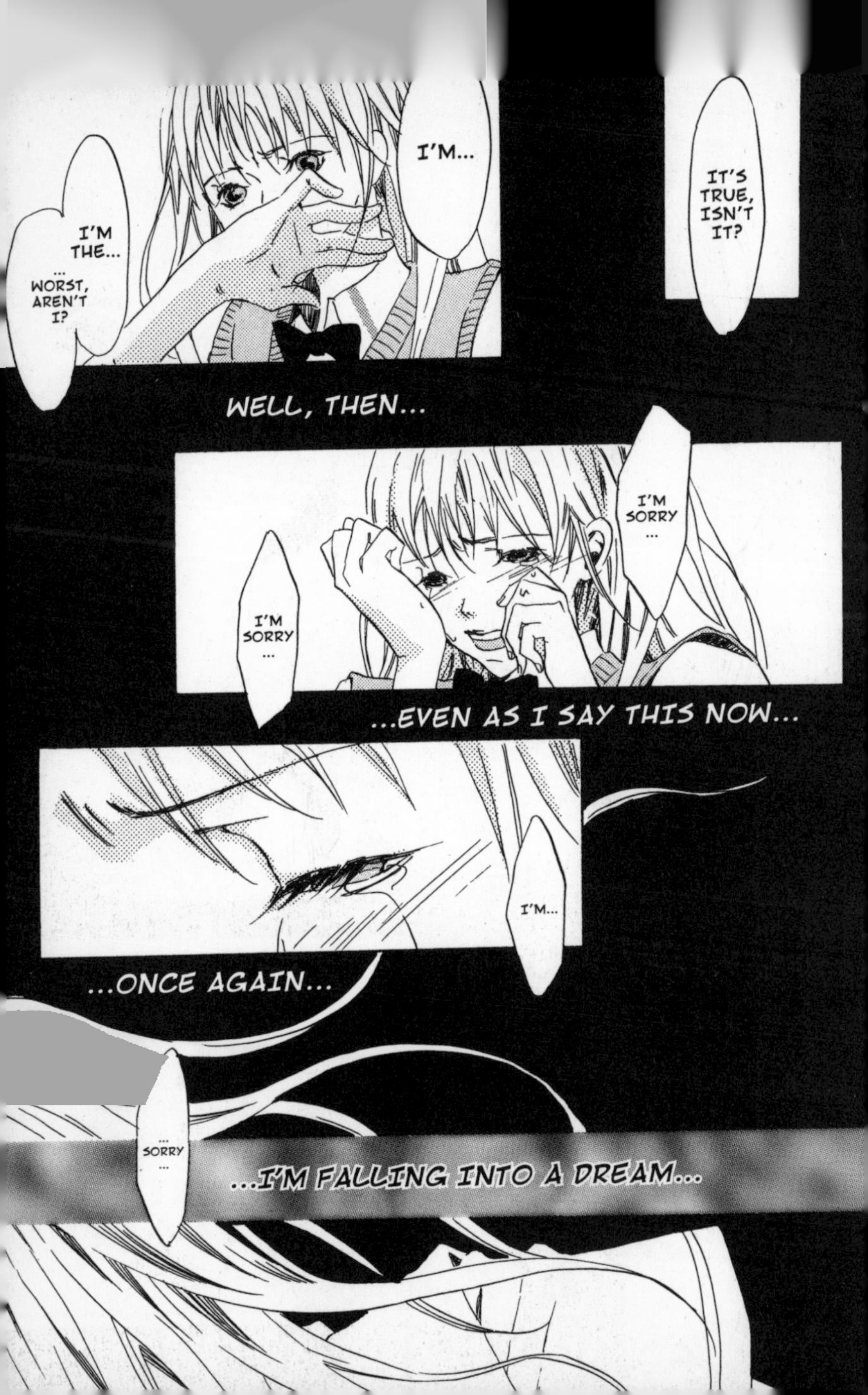
IT'S TRUE, ISN'T IT?
I'M...
I'M THE...
...WORST, AREN'T I?
WELL, THEN...
I'M SORRY...
I'M SORRY...
...EVEN AS I SAY THIS NOW...
I'M...
...ONCE AGAIN...
...SORRY...
...I'M FALLING INTO A DREAM...

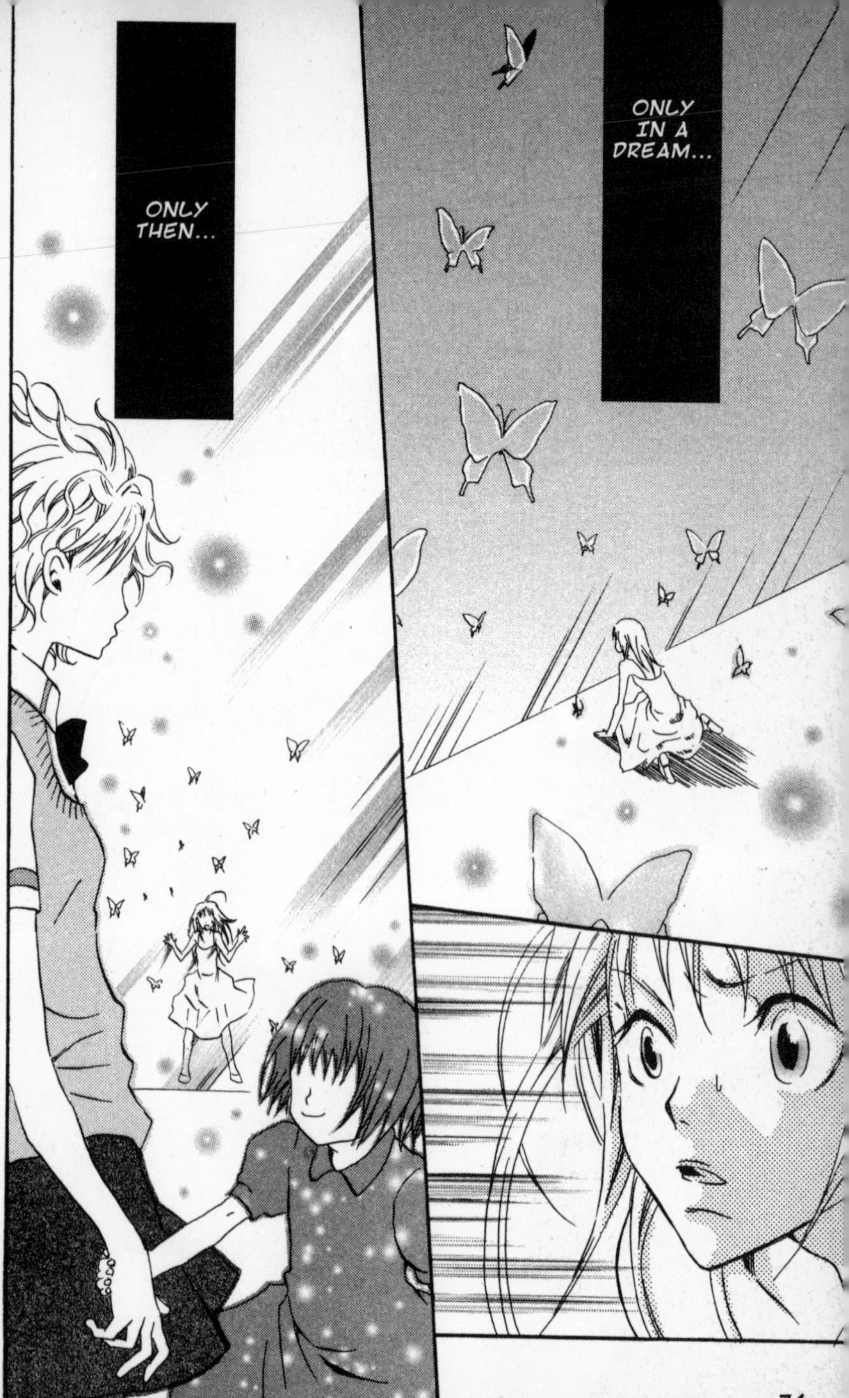
ONLY IN A DREAM...
ONLY THEN...

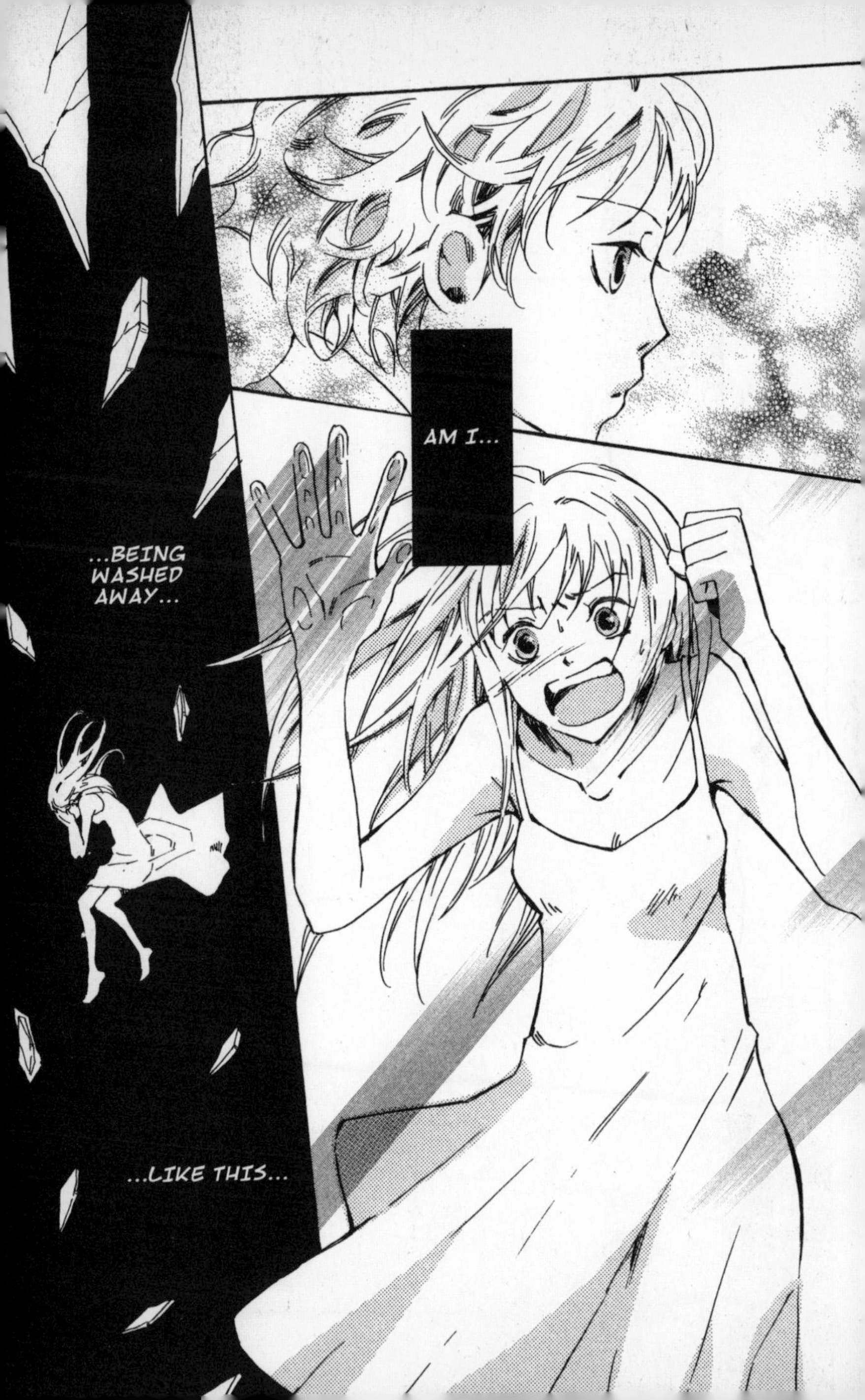
AM I...
...BEING WASHED AWAY...
...LIKE THIS...

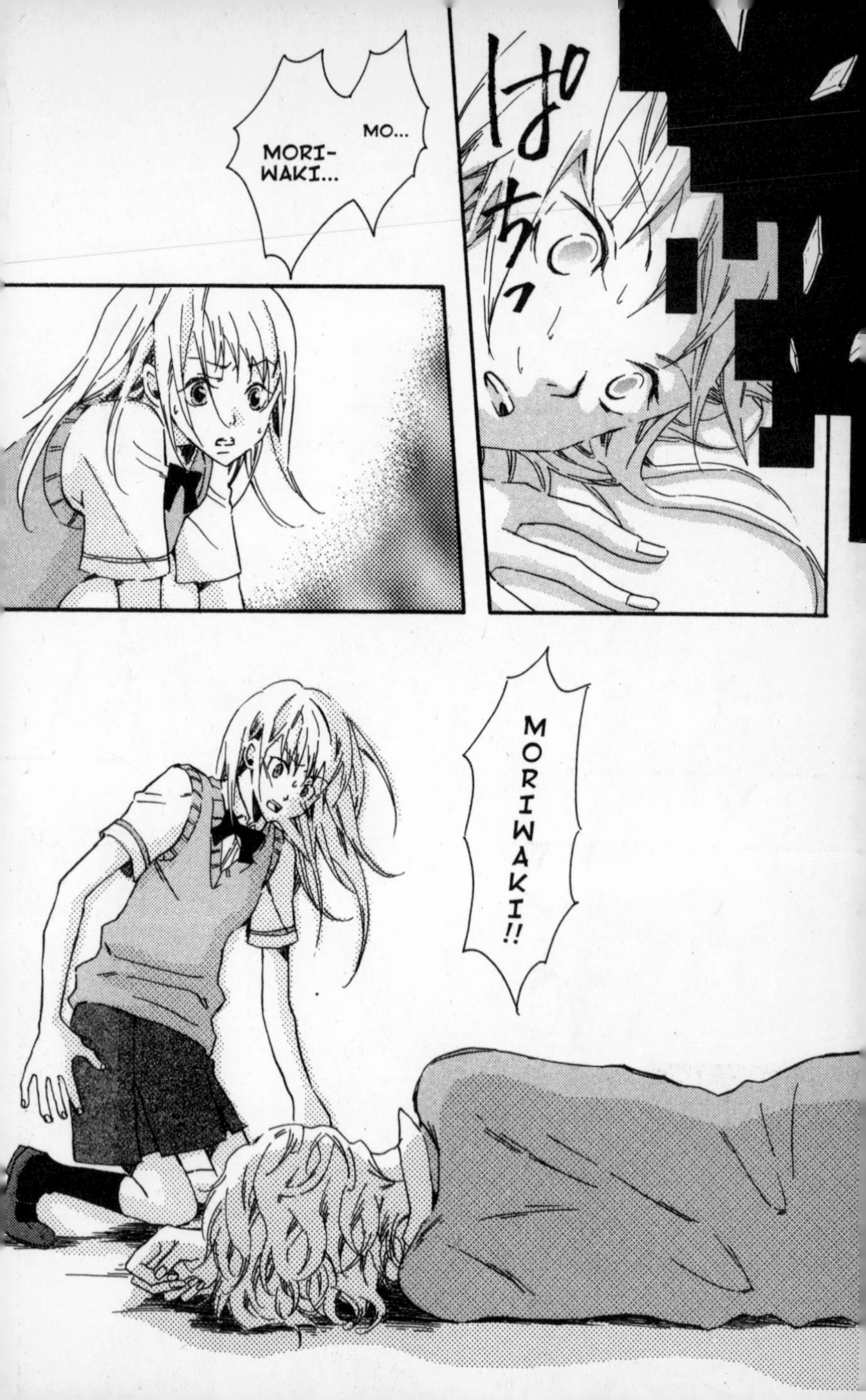
ぱちっ
MO... MORI-WAKI...
MORIWAKI!!

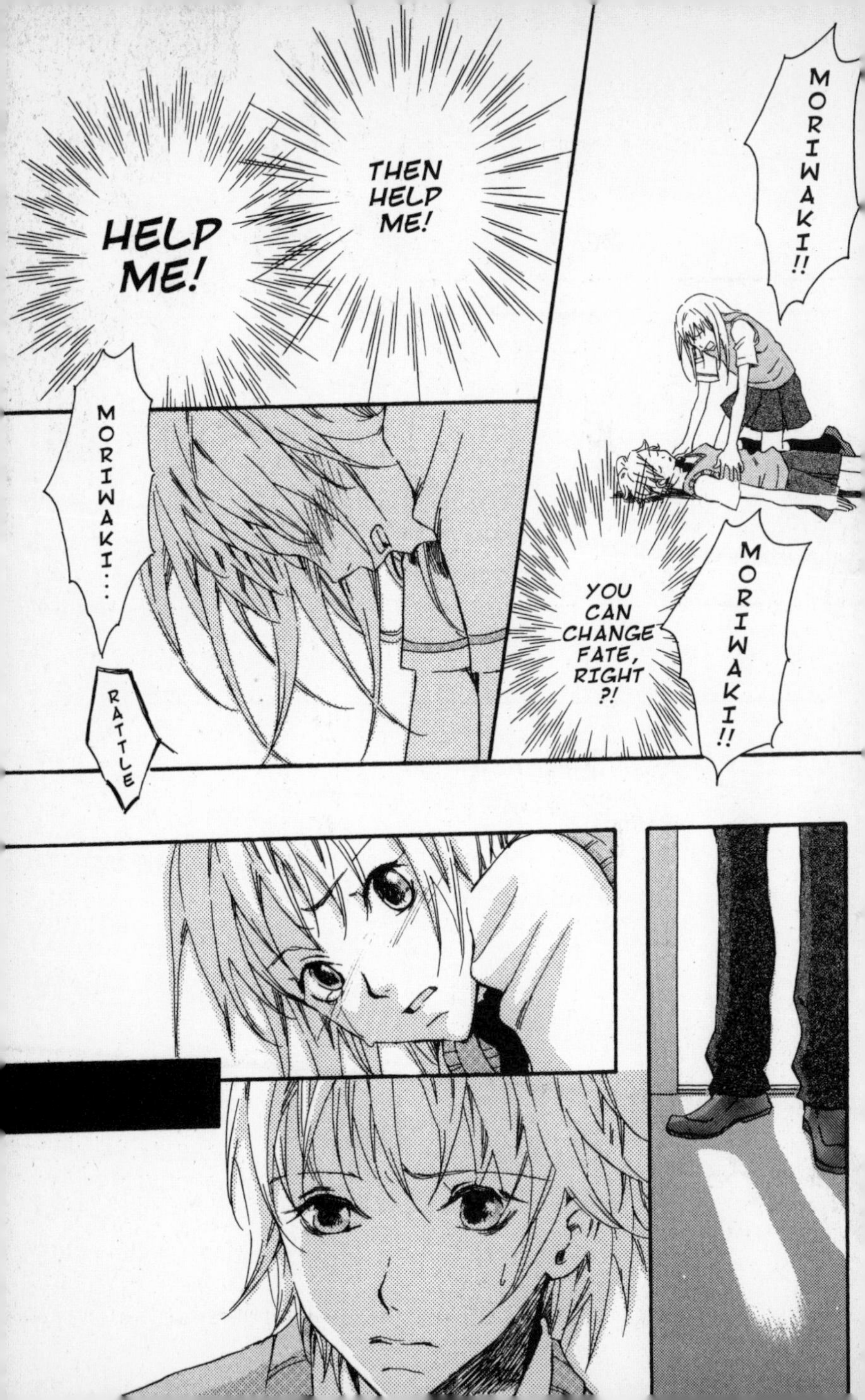
MORIWAKI!!
MORIWAKI!!
YOU CAN CHANGE FATE, RIGHT?!
THEN HELP ME!
HELP ME!
MORIWAKI...
RATTLE

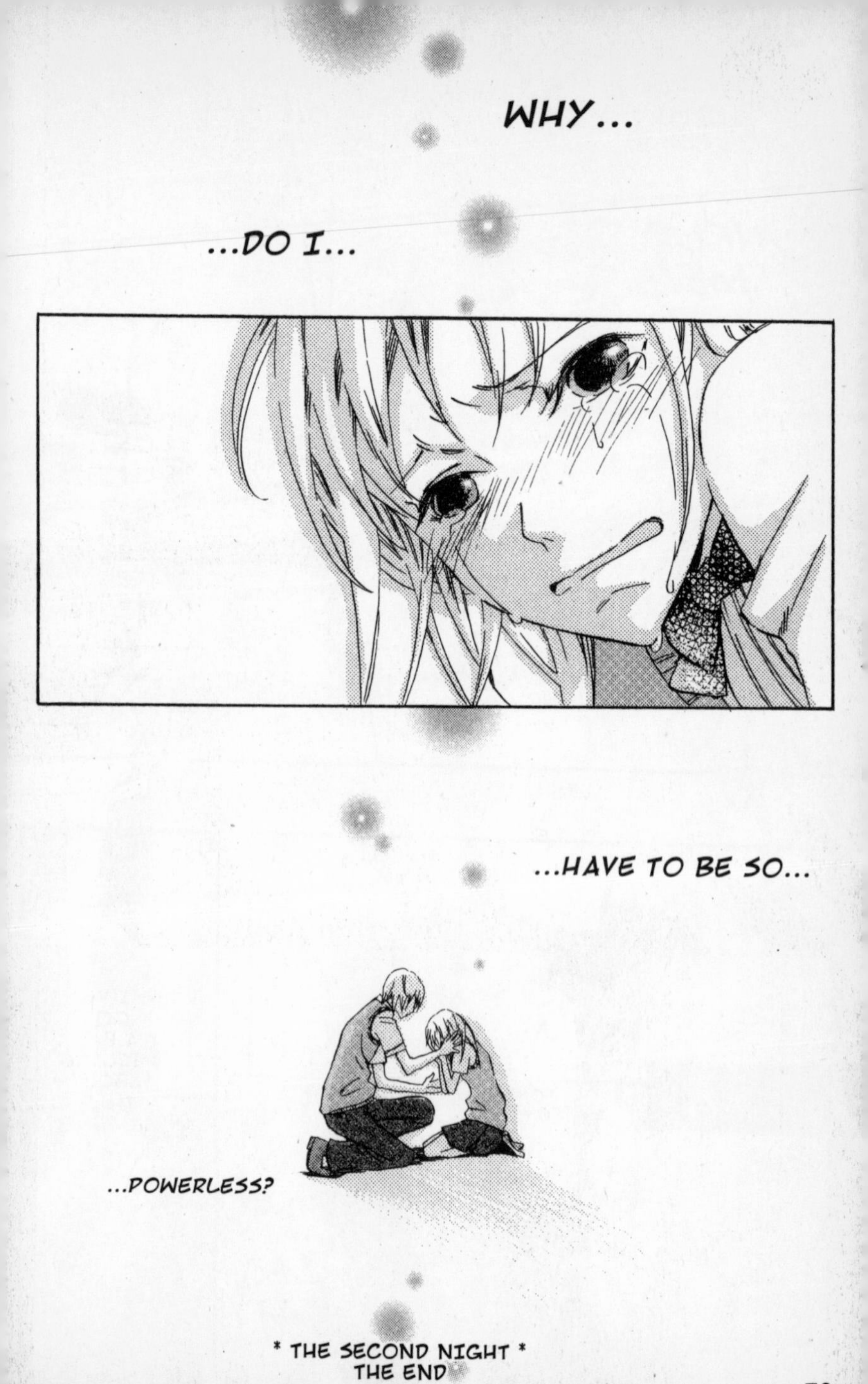
WHY...
...DO I...
...HAVE TO BE SO...
...POWERLESS?
* THE SECOND NIGHT *
THE END

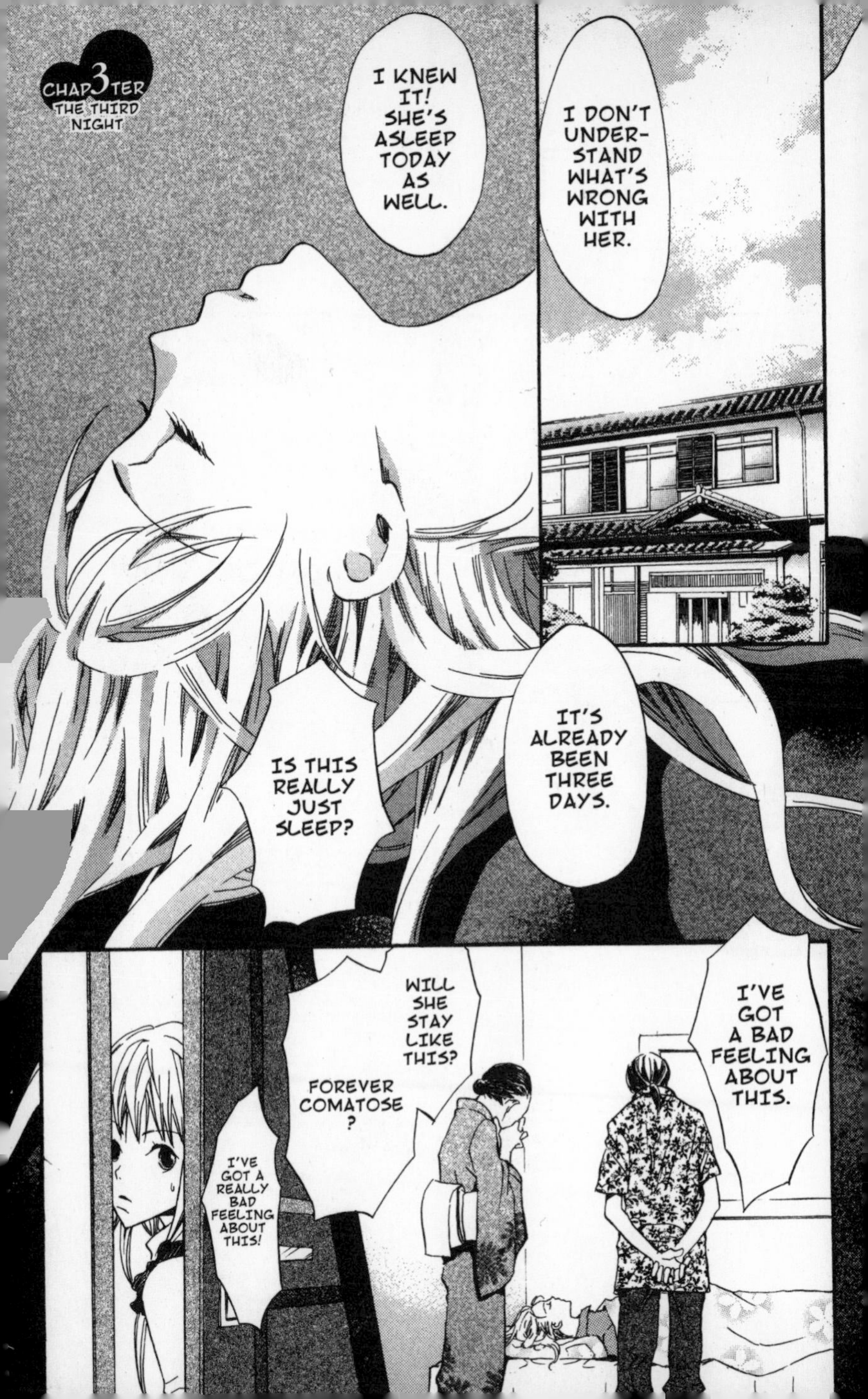
CHAP3TER THE THIRD NIGHT
I DON'T UNDER-STAND WHAT'S WRONG WITH HER.
I KNEW IT! SHE'S ASLEEP TODAY AS WELL.
IT'S ALREADY BEEN THREE DAYS.
IS THIS REALLY JUST SLEEP?
I'VE GOT A BAD FEELING ABOUT THIS.
WILL SHE STAY LIKE THIS?
FOREVER COMATOSE?
I'VE GOT A REALLY BAD FEELING ABOUT THIS!

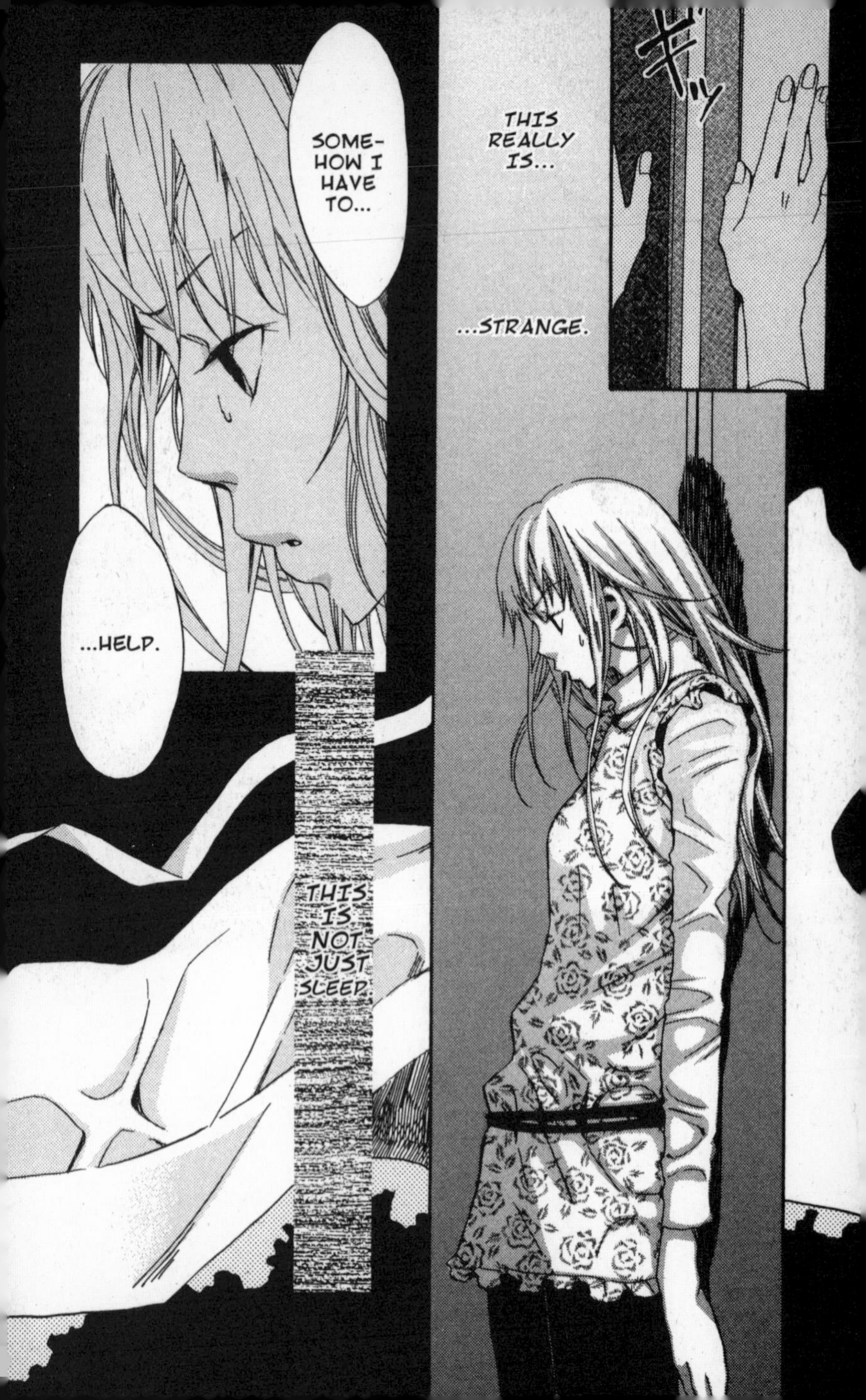
THIS REALLY IS...
...STRANGE.
SOME-HOW I HAVE TO...
...HELP.
THIS IS NOT JUST SLEEP.

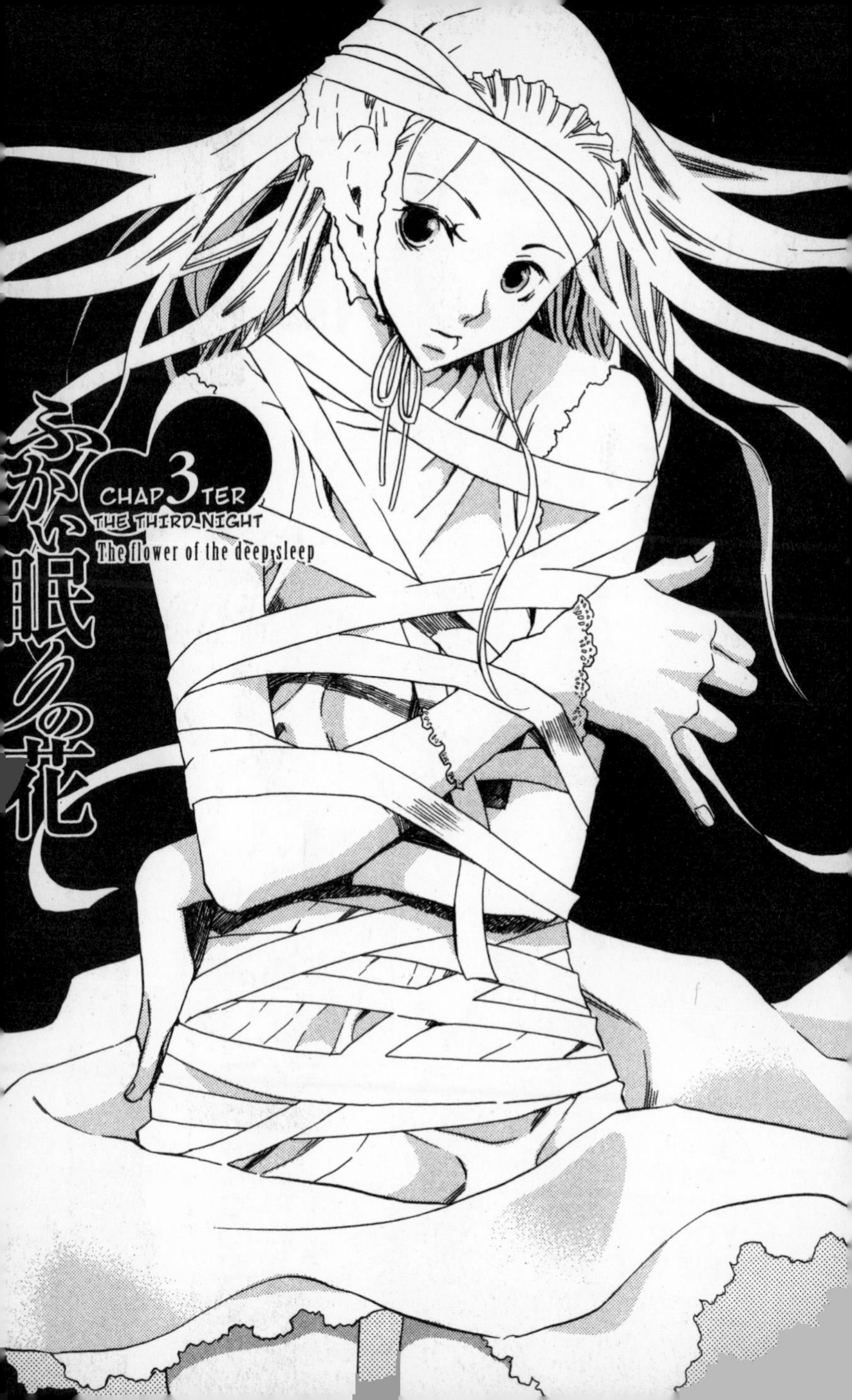
ふかい眠りの花
CHAP 3 TER
THE THIRD NIGHT
The flower of the deep sleep

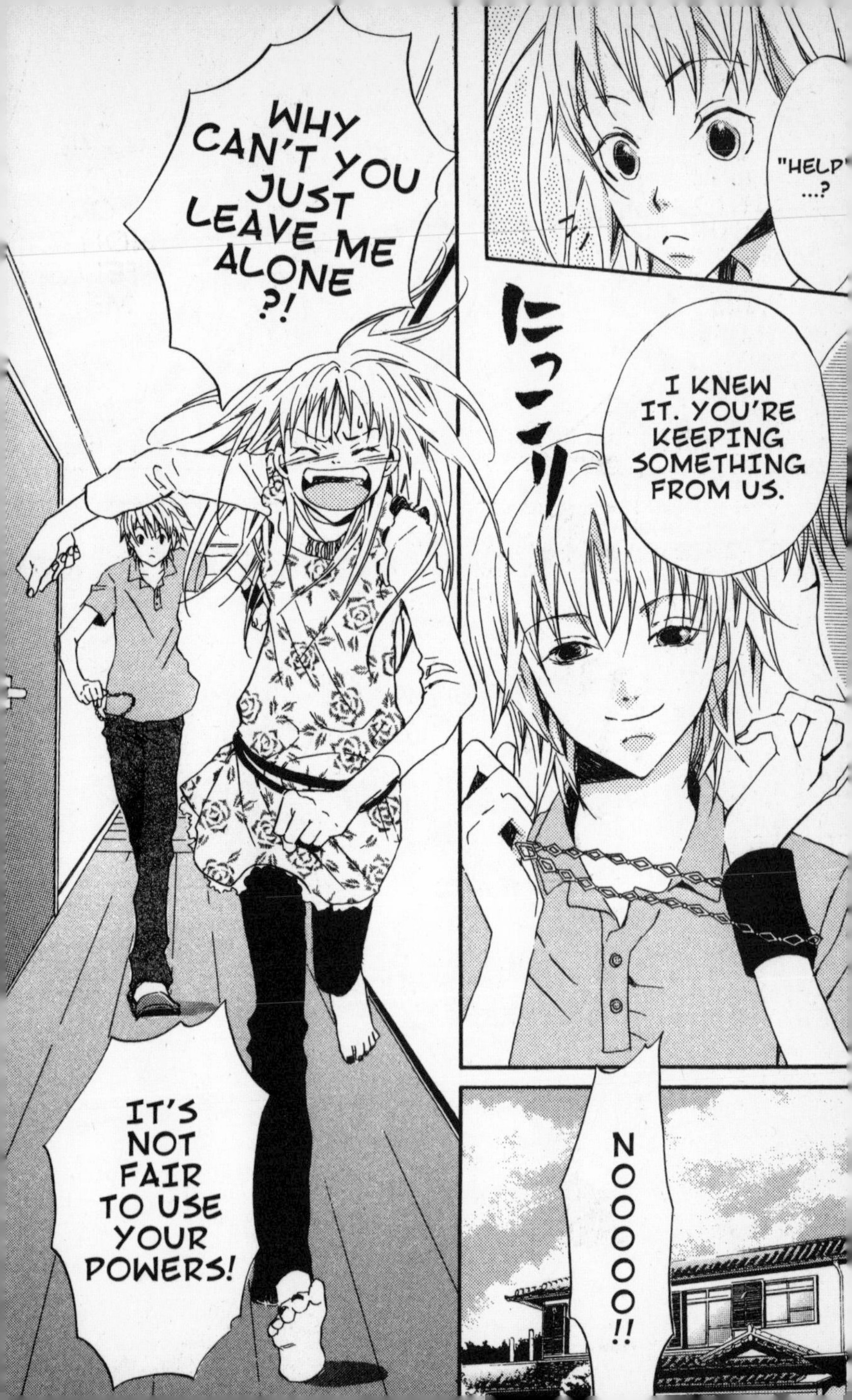
"HELP" ...?
にっこり
I KNEW IT. YOU'RE KEEPING SOMETHING FROM US.
NOOOOOO!!
WHY CAN'T YOU JUST LEAVE ME ALONE ?!
IT'S NOT FAIR TO USE YOUR POWERS!

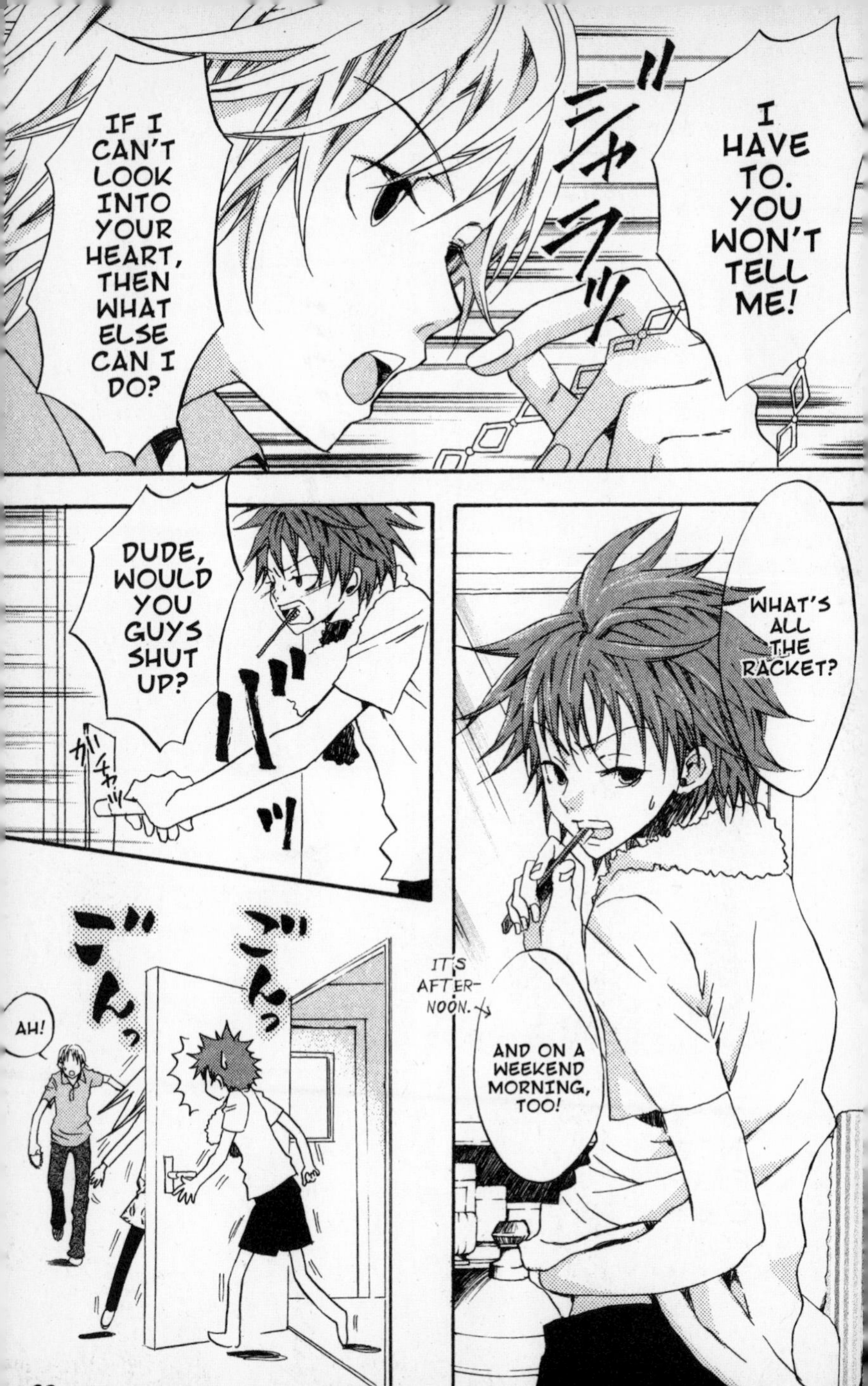
I HAVE TO. YOU WON'T TELL ME!
IF I CAN'T LOOK INTO YOUR HEART, THEN WHAT ELSE CAN I DO?
WHAT'S ALL THE RACKET?
IT'S AFTERNOON.
AND ON A WEEKEND MORNING, TOO!
DUDE, WOULD YOU GUYS SHUT UP?
ごんっ
ごんっ
AH!

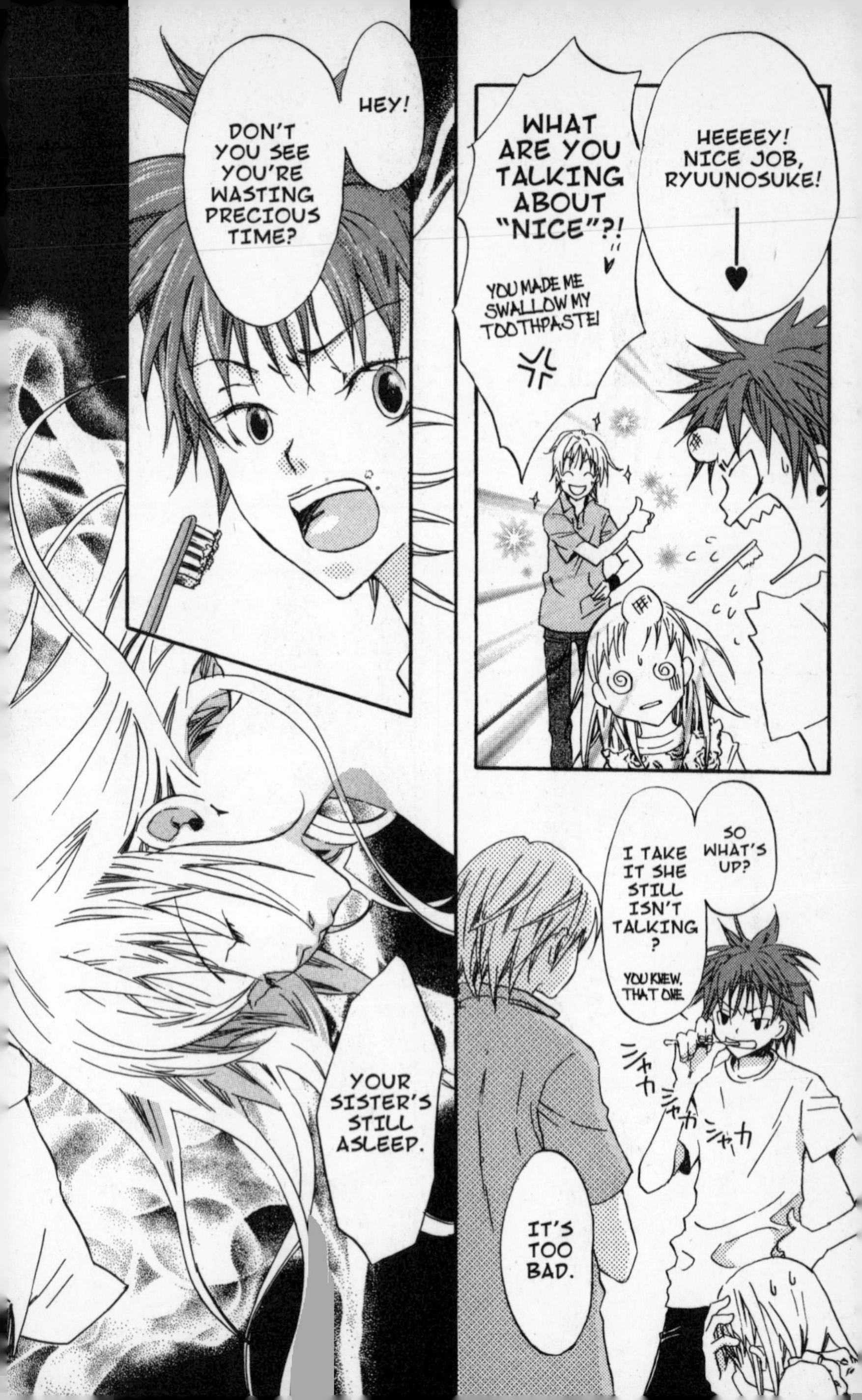
HEEEEY! NICE JOB, RYUUNOSUKE!
WHAT ARE YOU TALKING ABOUT "NICE"?!
YOU MADE ME SWALLOW MY TOOTHPASTE!
SO WHAT'S UP?
I TAKE IT SHE STILL ISN'T TALKING?
YOU KNEW, THAT ONE.
シャカ
シャカ
シャカ
IT'S TOO BAD.
HEY!
DON'T YOU SEE YOU'RE WASTING PRECIOUS TIME?
YOUR SISTER'S STILL ASLEEP.

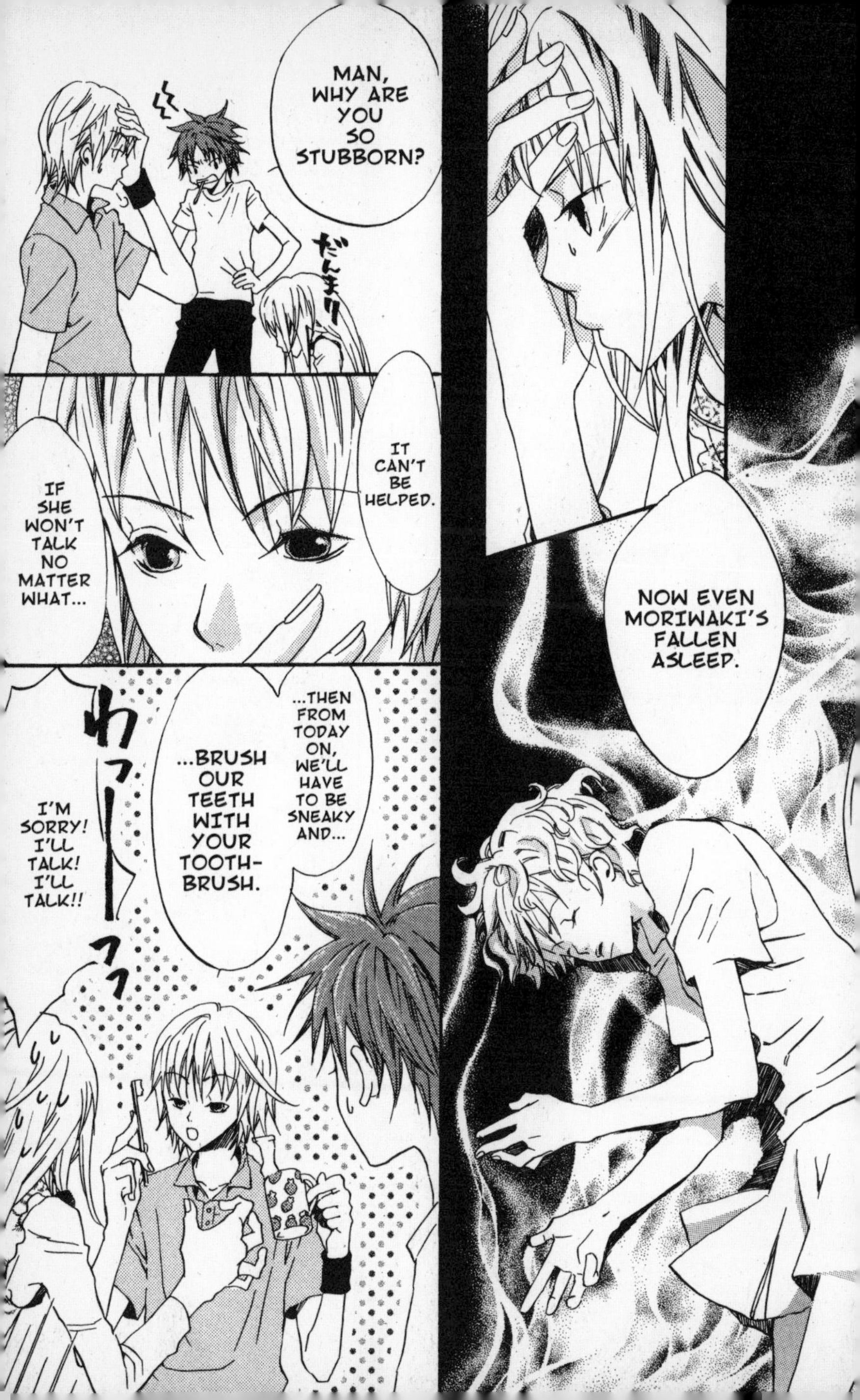
MAN, WHY ARE YOU SO STUBBORN?
だんまり
IT CAN'T BE HELPED.
IF SHE WON'T TALK NO MATTER WHAT...
...THEN FROM TODAY ON, WE'LL HAVE TO BE SNEAKY AND...
...BRUSH OUR TEETH WITH YOUR TOOTH-BRUSH.
わっーーっっ
I'M SORRY! I'LL TALK! I'LL TALK!!
NOW EVEN MORIWAKI'S FALLEN ASLEEP.

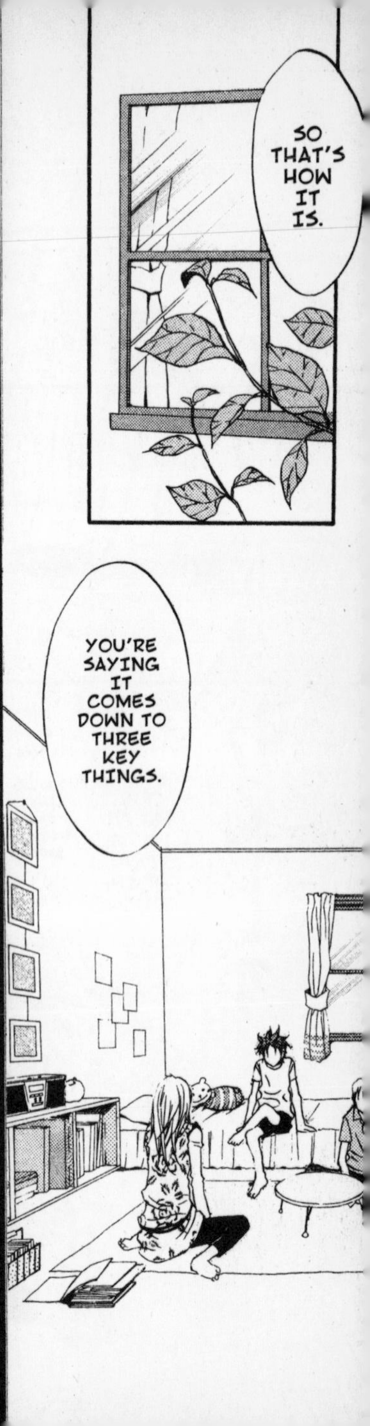
SO THAT'S HOW IT IS.
YOU'RE SAYING IT COMES DOWN TO THREE KEY THINGS.

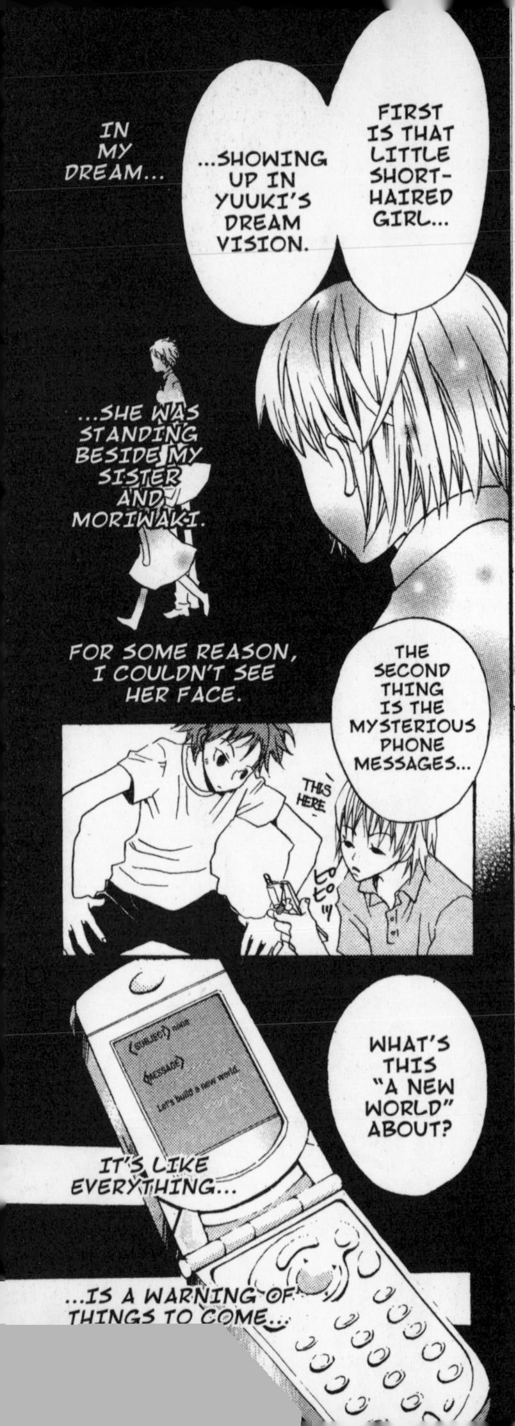
FIRST IS THAT LITTLE SHORT-HAIRED GIRL...
...SHOWING UP IN YUUKI'S DREAM VISION.
IN MY DREAM...
...SHE WAS STANDING BESIDE MY SISTER AND MORIWAKI.
FOR SOME REASON, I COULDN'T SEE HER FACE.
THE SECOND THING IS THE MYSTERIOUS PHONE MESSAGES...
THIS HERE
Let's build a new world.
WHAT'S THIS "A NEW WORLD" ABOUT?
IT'S LIKE EVERYTHING...
...IS A WARNING OF THINGS TO COME...

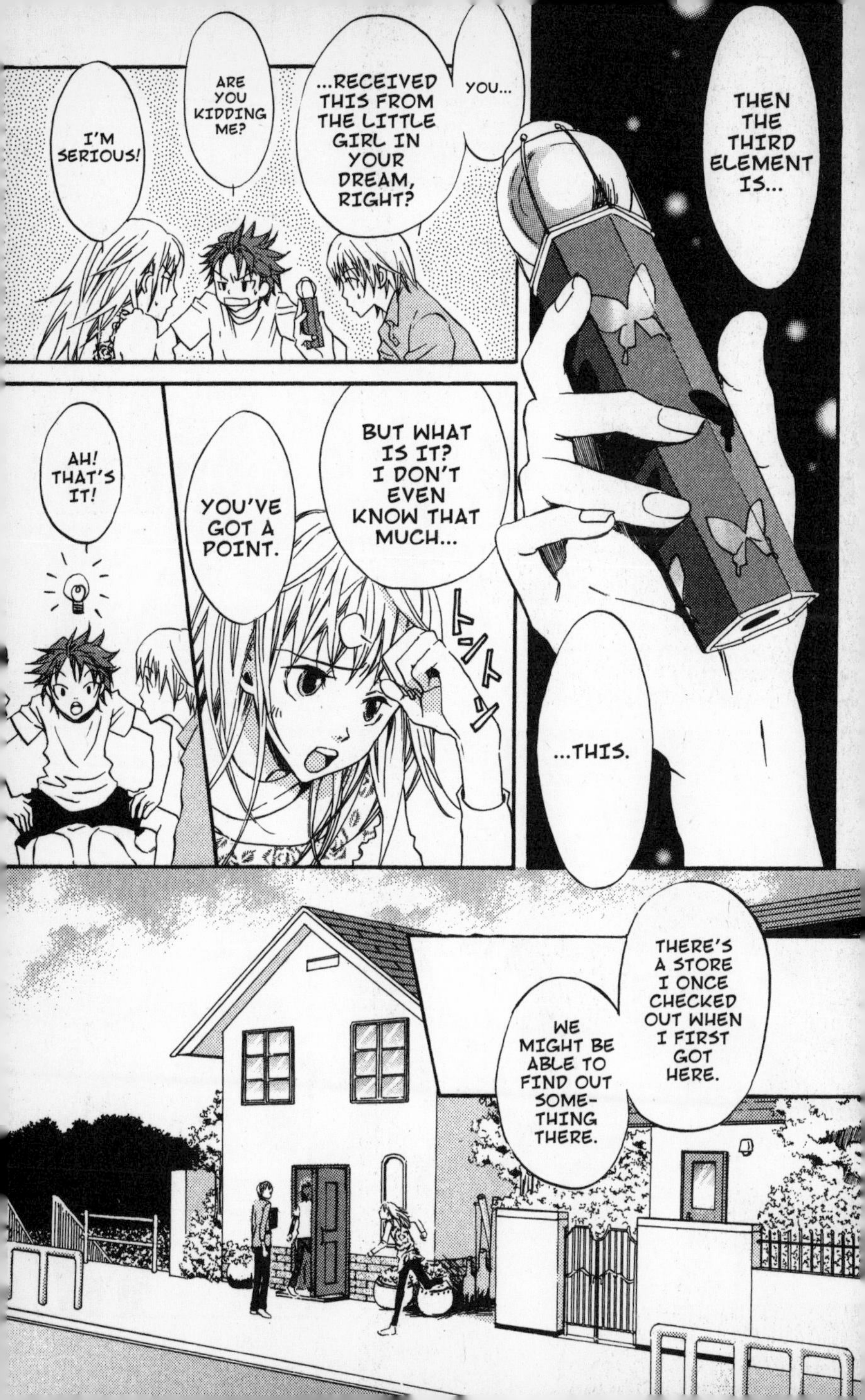
THEN THE THIRD ELEMENT IS...
...THIS.
YOU...
...RECEIVED THIS FROM THE LITTLE GIRL IN YOUR DREAM, RIGHT?
ARE YOU KIDDING ME?
I'M SERIOUS!
BUT WHAT IS IT? I DON'T EVEN KNOW THAT MUCH...
YOU'VE GOT A POINT.
AH! THAT'S IT!
THERE'S A STORE I ONCE CHECKED OUT WHEN I FIRST GOT HERE.
WE MIGHT BE ABLE TO FIND OUT SOME-THING THERE.

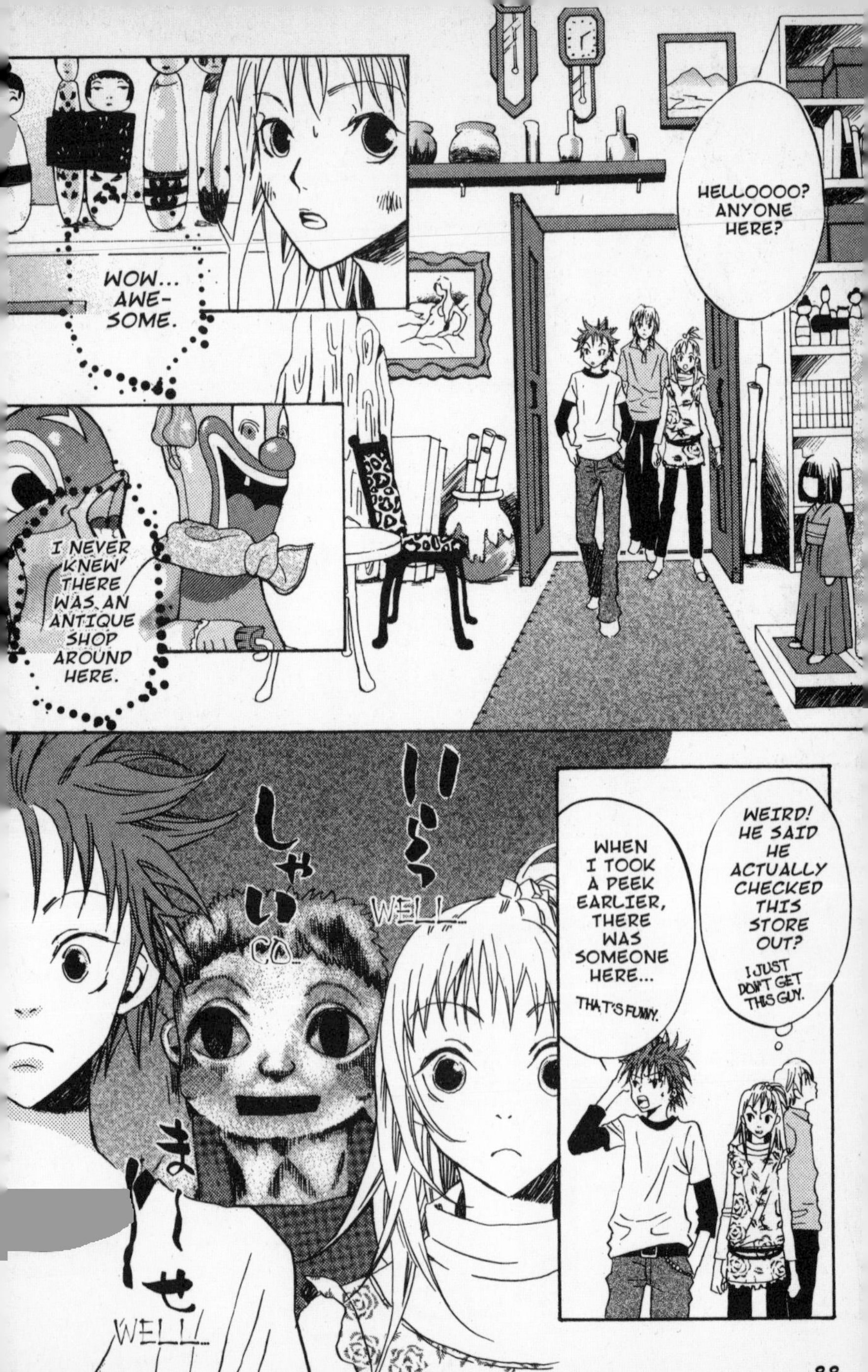
HELLOOOO? ANYONE HERE?
WOW... AWE-SOME.
I NEVER KNEW THERE WAS AN ANTIQUE SHOP AROUND HERE.
WHEN I TOOK A PEEK EARLIER, THERE WAS SOMEONE HERE...
THAT'S FUNNY.
WEIRD! HE SAID HE ACTUALLY CHECKED THIS STORE OUT?
I JUST DON'T GET THIS GUY.
いらっ
WELL...
しゃい
CO...
ませ
WELL...

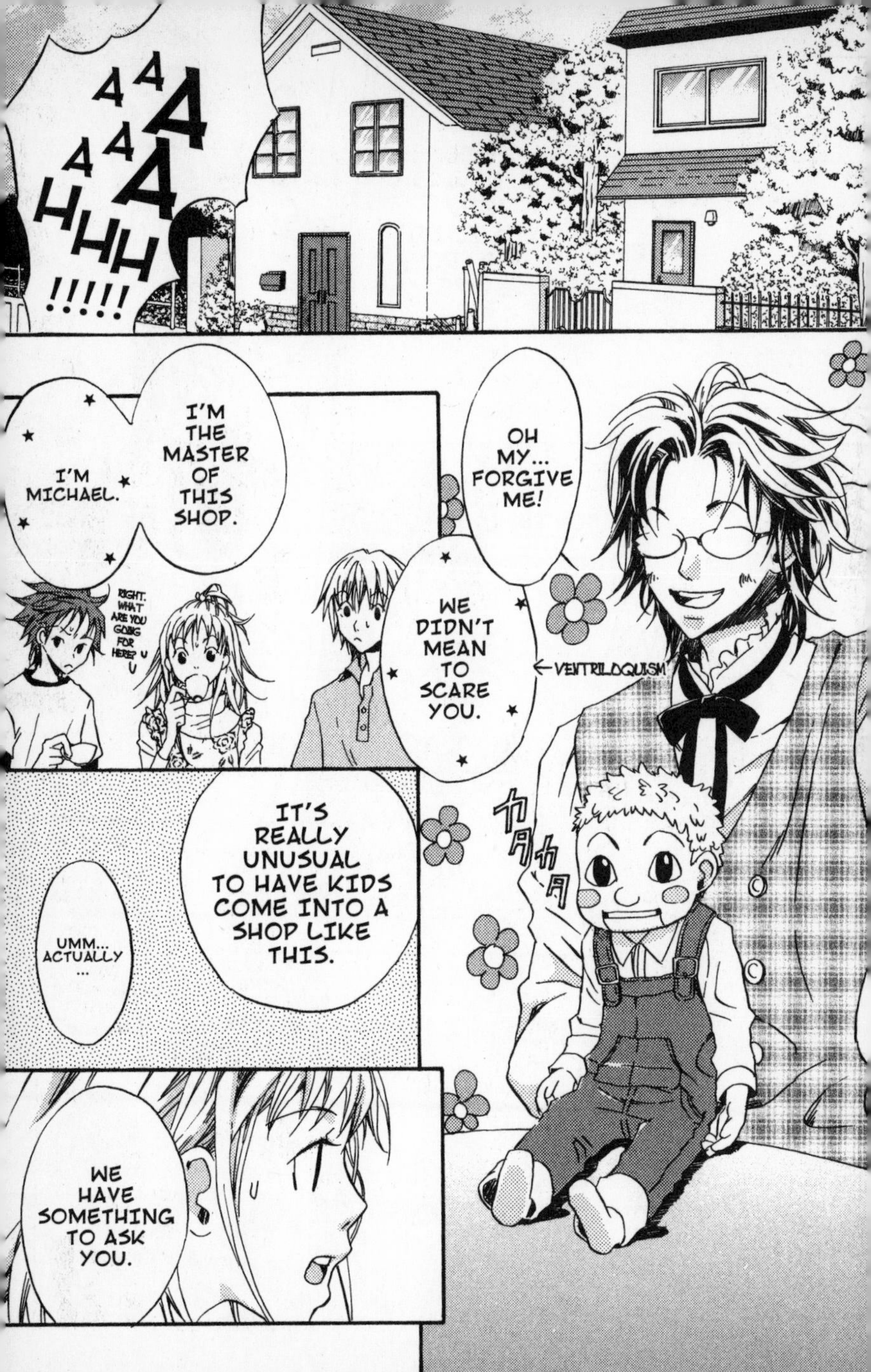
AAAAAHHH!!!!!
OH MY... FORGIVE ME!
WE DIDN'T MEAN TO SCARE YOU.
←VENTRILOQUISM
I'M THE MASTER OF THIS SHOP.
I'M MICHAEL.
RIGHT. WHAT ARE YOU GOING FOR HERE?
IT'S REALLY UNUSUAL TO HAVE KIDS COME INTO A SHOP LIKE THIS.
UMM... ACTUALLY ...
WE HAVE SOMETHING TO ASK YOU.

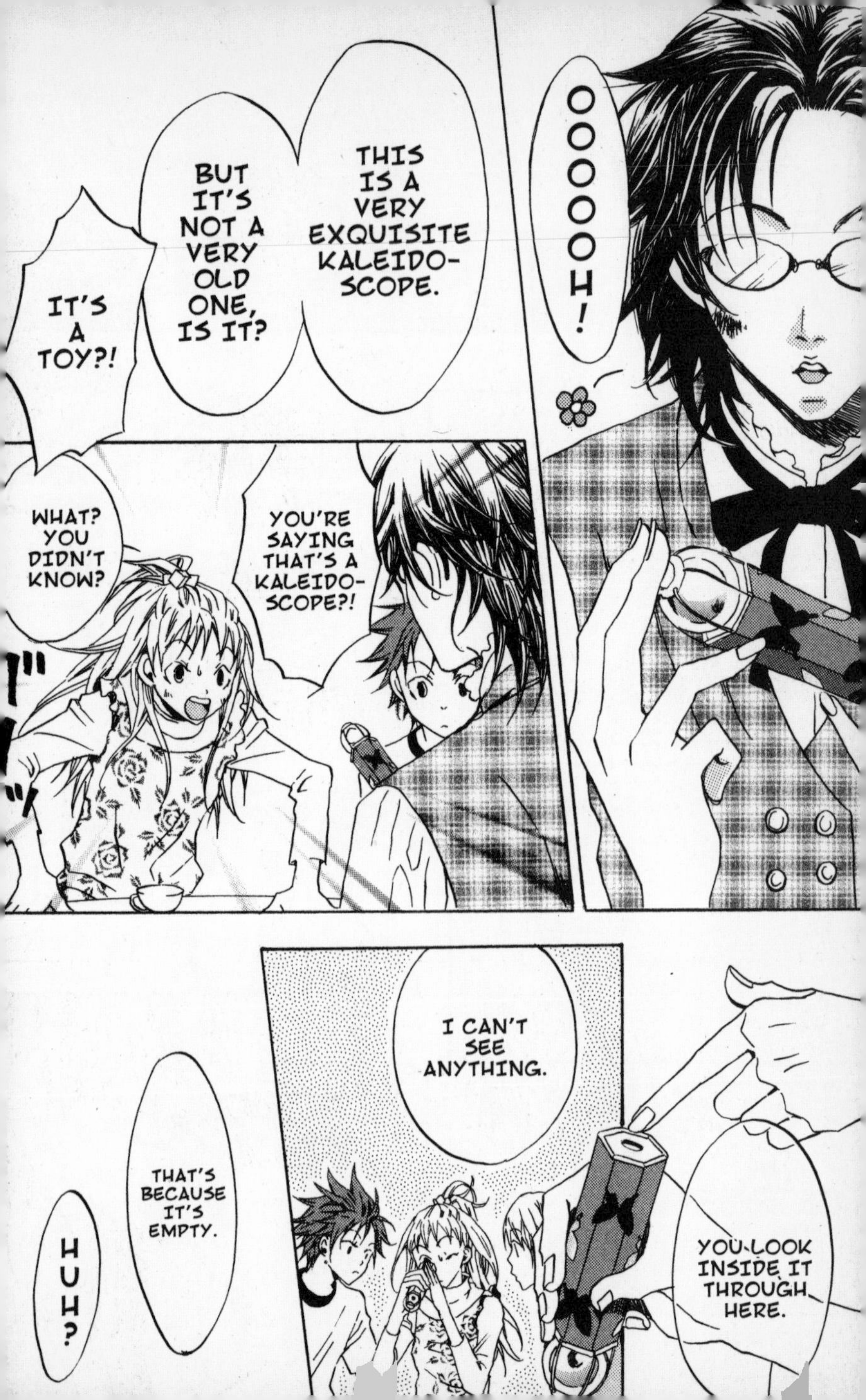
OOOOOOH!
THIS IS A VERY EXQUISITE KALEIDO-SCOPE.
BUT IT'S NOT A VERY OLD ONE, IS IT?
IT'S A TOY?!
YOU'RE SAYING THAT'S A KALEIDO-SCOPE?!
WHAT? YOU DIDN'T KNOW?
YOU LOOK INSIDE IT THROUGH HERE.
I CAN'T SEE ANYTHING.
THAT'S BECAUSE IT'S EMPTY.
HUH?

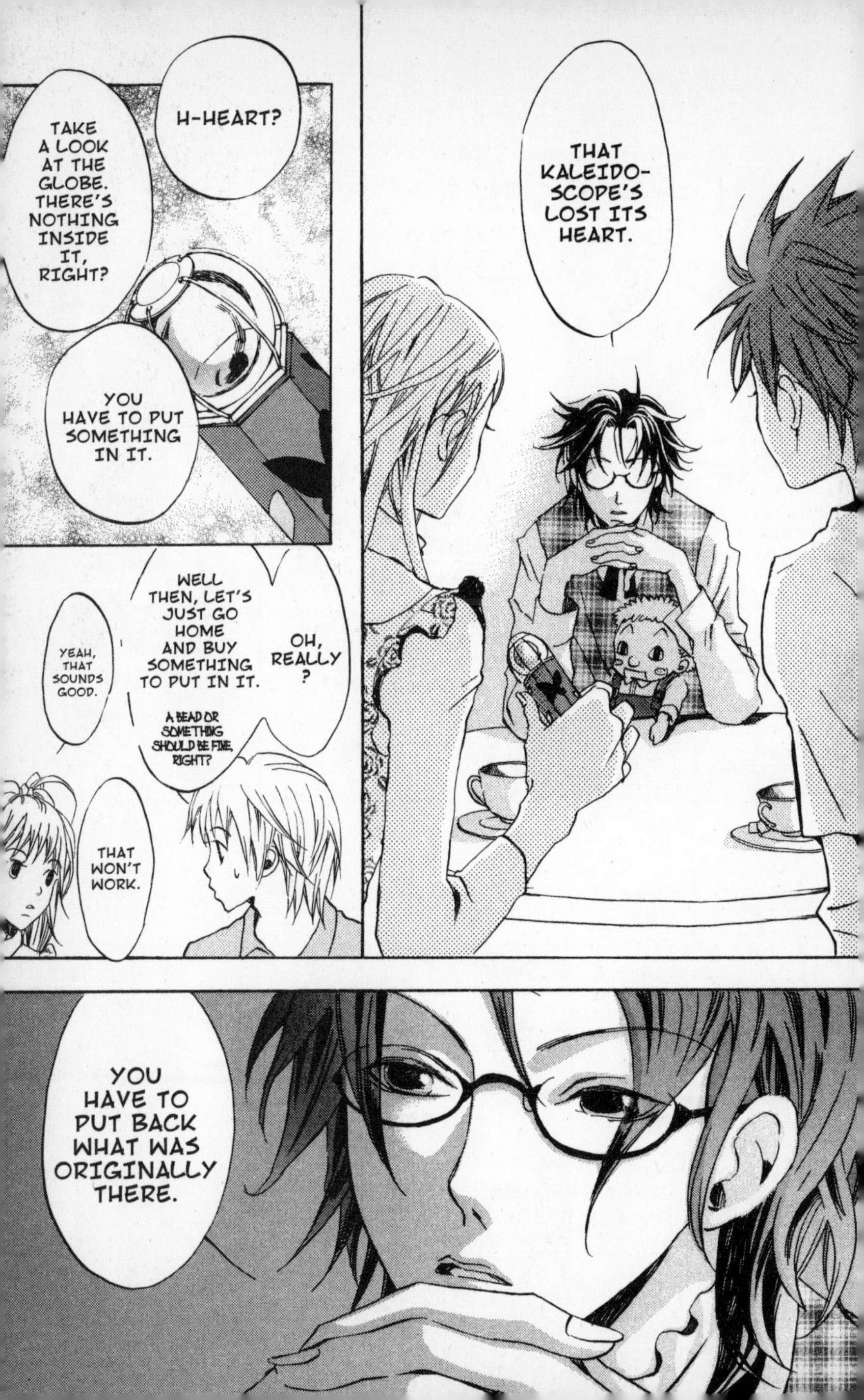

THAT KALEIDO-SCOPE'S LOST ITS HEART.
H-HEART?
TAKE A LOOK AT THE GLOBE. THERE'S NOTHING INSIDE IT, RIGHT?
YOU HAVE TO PUT SOMETHING IN IT.
OH, REALLY?
WELL THEN, LET'S JUST GO HOME AND BUY SOMETHING TO PUT IN IT.
A BEAD OR SOMETHING SHOULD BE FINE, RIGHT?
YEAH, THAT SOUNDS GOOD.
THAT WON'T WORK.
YOU HAVE TO PUT BACK WHAT WAS ORIGINALLY THERE.

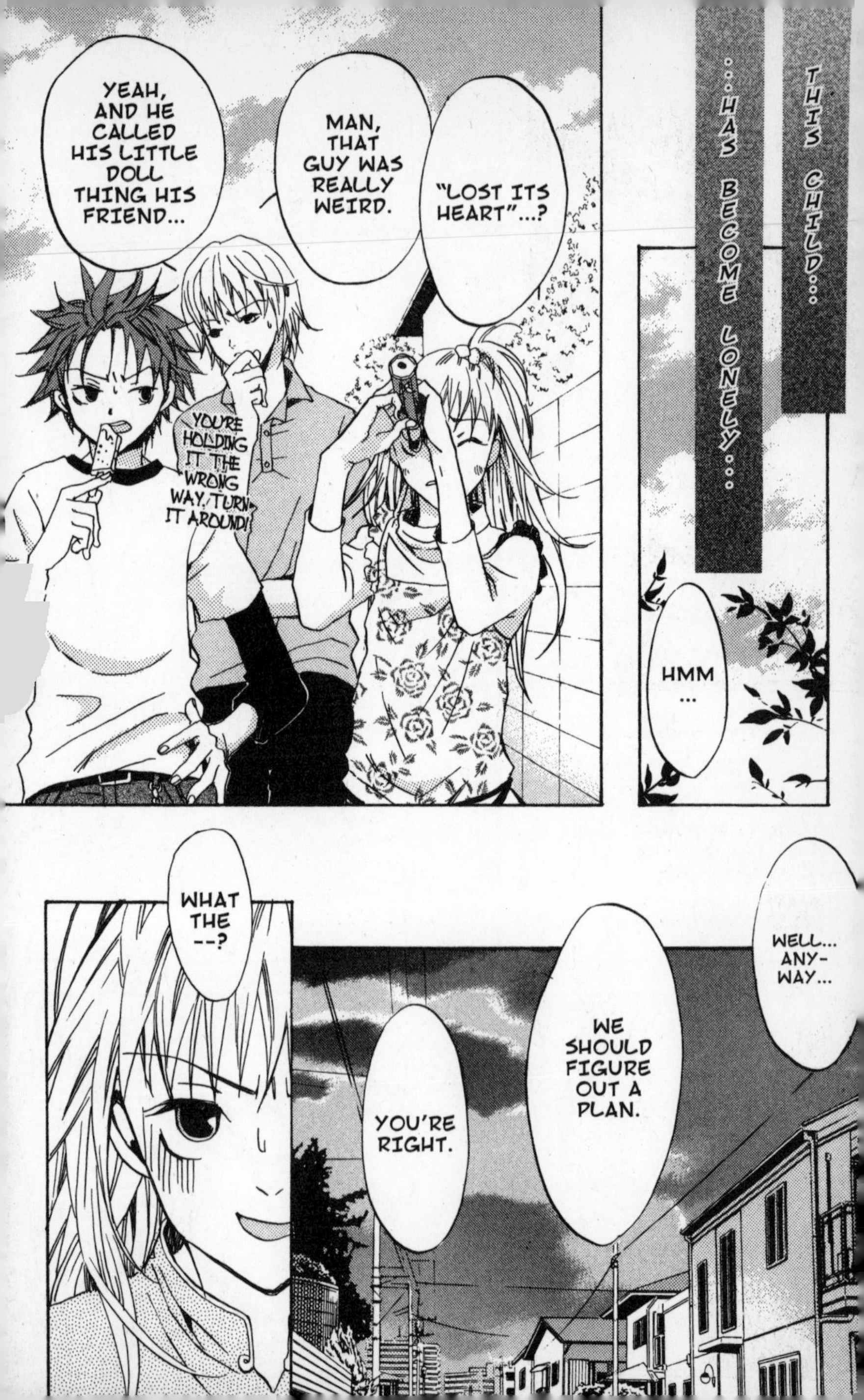
THIS CHILD...
...HAS BECOME LONELY...
HMM...
"LOST ITS HEART"...?
MAN, THAT GUY WAS REALLY WEIRD.
YEAH, AND HE CALLED HIS LITTLE DOLL THING HIS FRIEND...
YOU'RE HOLDING IT THE WRONG WAY. TURN IT AROUND!
WELL... ANY-WAY...
WE SHOULD FIGURE OUT A PLAN.
YOU'RE RIGHT.
WHAT THE --?

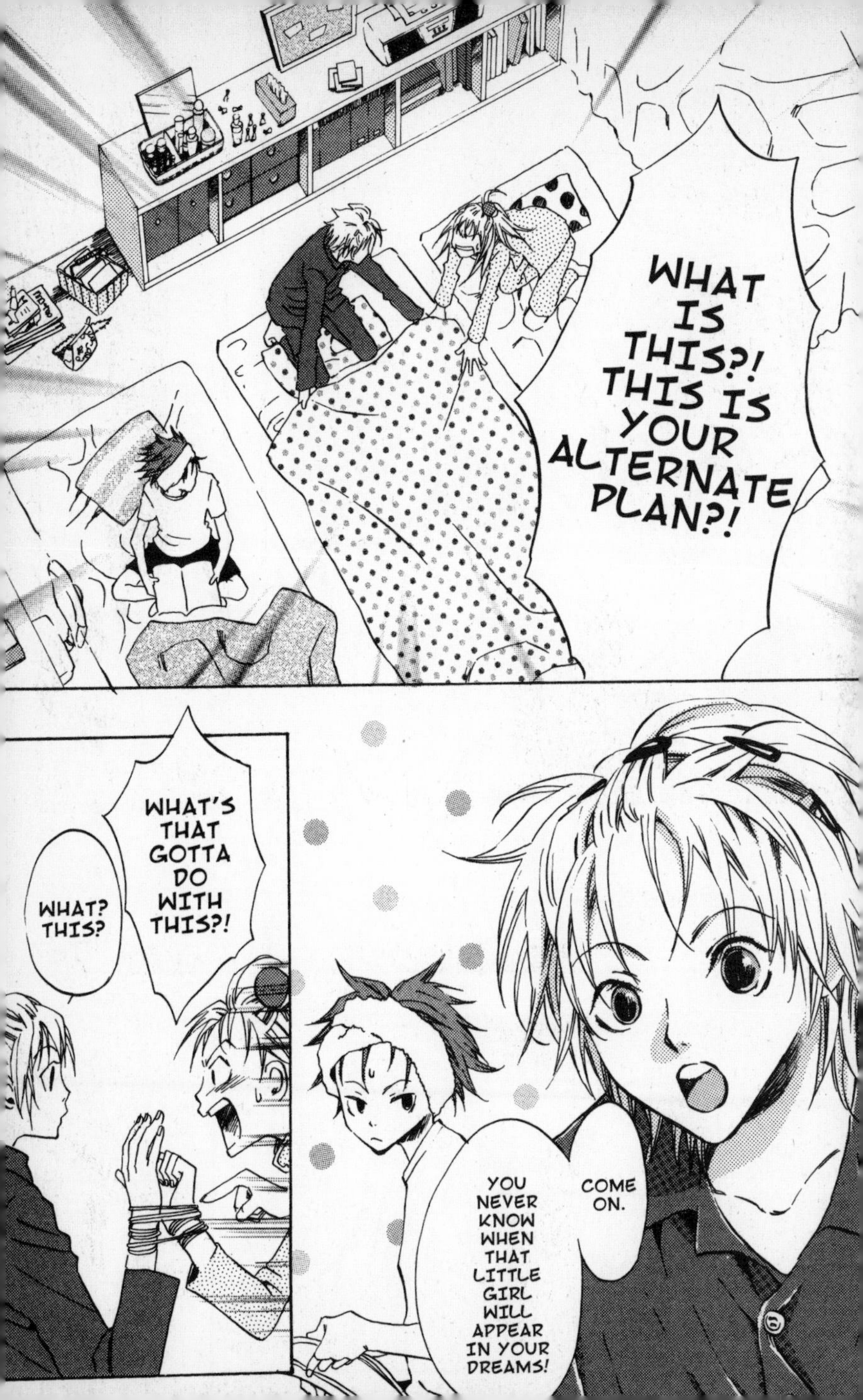
WHAT IS THIS?! THIS IS YOUR ALTERNATE PLAN?!
COME ON.
YOU NEVER KNOW WHEN THAT LITTLE GIRL WILL APPEAR IN YOUR DREAMS!
WHAT'S THAT GOTTA DO WITH THIS?!
WHAT? THIS?

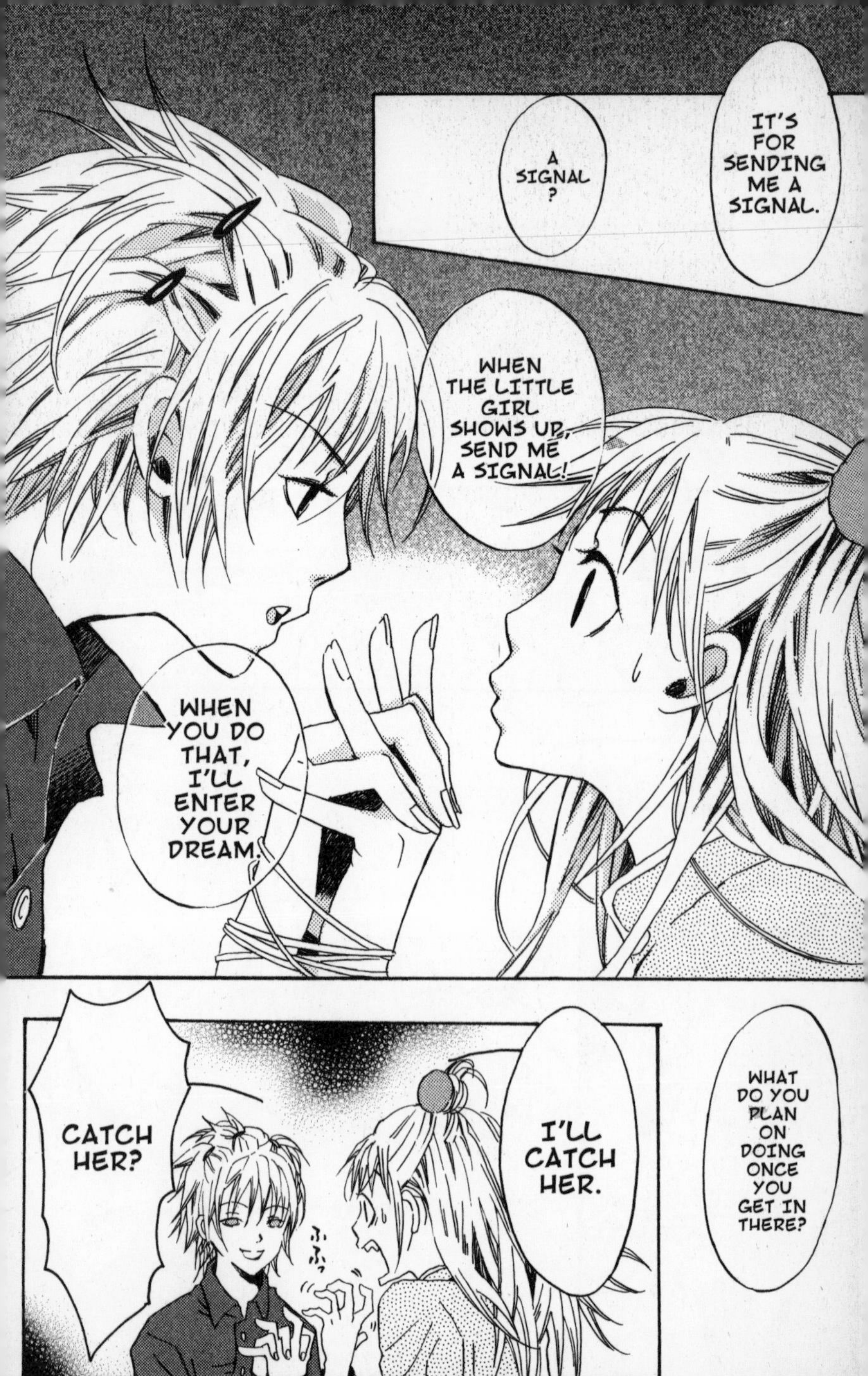
IT'S FOR SENDING ME A SIGNAL.
A SIGNAL?
WHEN THE LITTLE GIRL SHOWS UP, SEND ME A SIGNAL!
WHEN YOU DO THAT, I'LL ENTER YOUR DREAM.
WHAT DO YOU PLAN ON DOING ONCE YOU GET IN THERE?
I'LL CATCH HER.
ふふっ
CATCH HER?

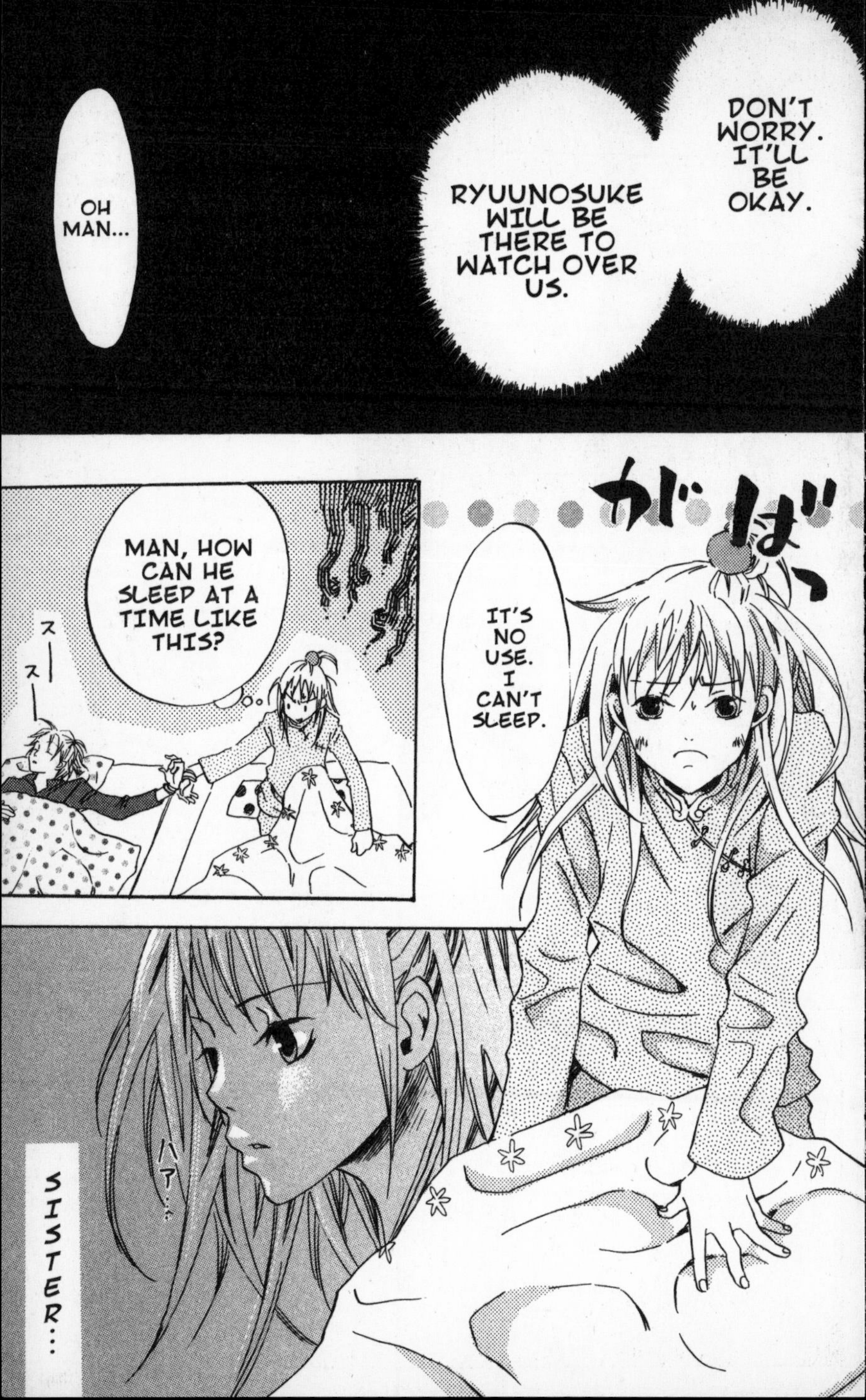

DON'T WORRY. IT'LL BE OKAY.
RYUUNOSUKE WILL BE THERE TO WATCH OVER US.
OH MAN...
がばっ
IT'S NO USE. I CAN'T SLEEP.
スースー
MAN, HOW CAN HE SLEEP AT A TIME LIKE THIS?
ハア…
SISTER...

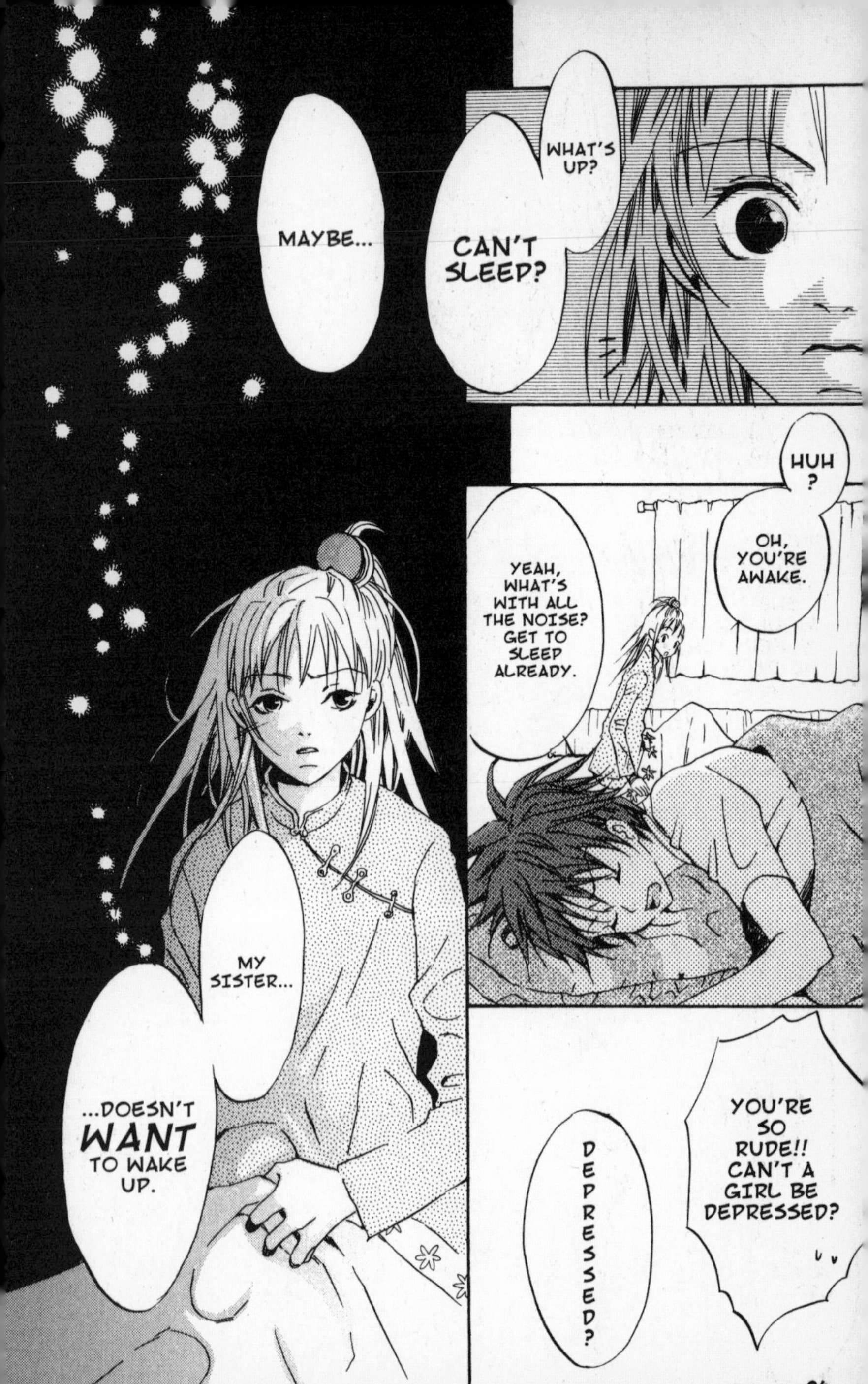
WHAT'S UP?
CAN'T SLEEP?
HUH?
OH, YOU'RE AWAKE.
YEAH, WHAT'S WITH ALL THE NOISE? GET TO SLEEP ALREADY.
YOU'RE SO RUDE!! CAN'T A GIRL BE DEPRESSED?
DEPRESSED?
MAYBE...
MY SISTER...
...DOESN'T WANT TO WAKE UP.

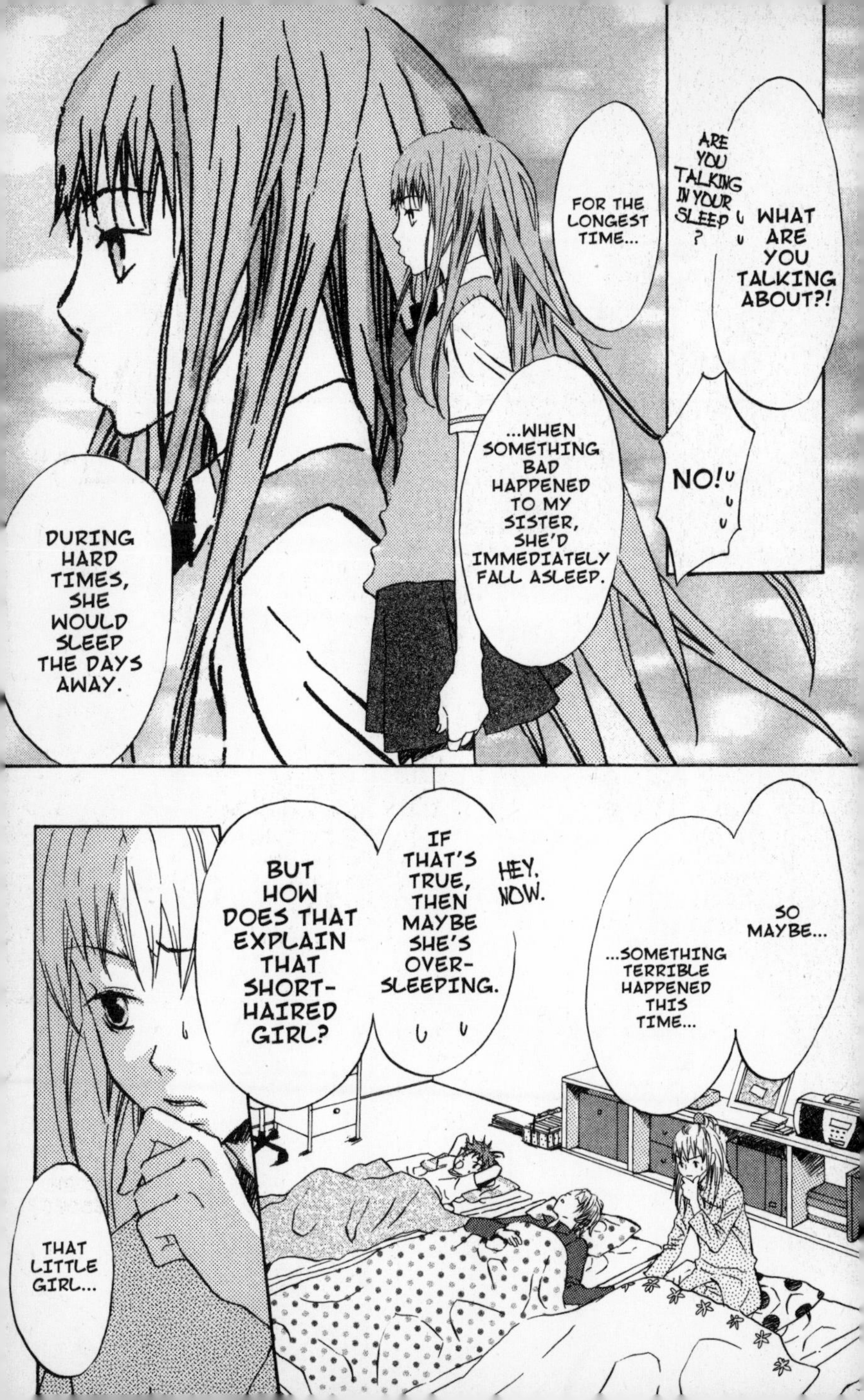
WHAT ARE YOU TALKING ABOUT?!
ARE YOU TALKING IN YOUR SLEEP?
NO!
FOR THE LONGEST TIME...
...WHEN SOMETHING BAD HAPPENED TO MY SISTER, SHE'D IMMEDIATELY FALL ASLEEP.
DURING HARD TIMES, SHE WOULD SLEEP THE DAYS AWAY.
SO MAYBE...
...SOMETHING TERRIBLE HAPPENED THIS TIME...
HEY. NOW.
IF THAT'S TRUE, THEN MAYBE SHE'S OVER-SLEEPING.
BUT HOW DOES THAT EXPLAIN THAT SHORT-HAIRED GIRL?
THAT LITTLE GIRL...

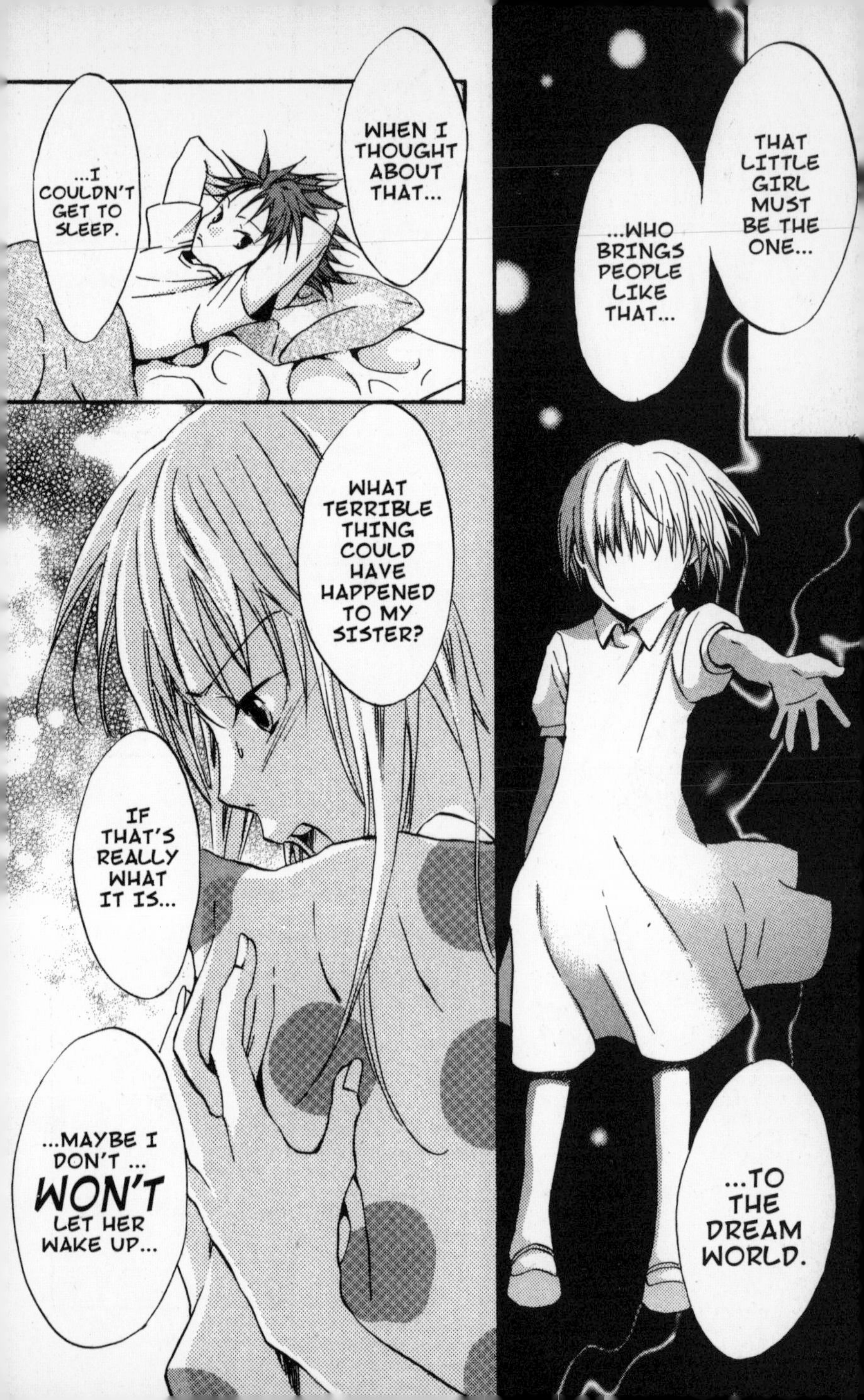
THAT LITTLE GIRL MUST BE THE ONE...
...WHO BRINGS PEOPLE LIKE THAT...
...TO THE DREAM WORLD.
WHEN I THOUGHT ABOUT THAT...
...I COULDN'T GET TO SLEEP.
WHAT TERRIBLE THING COULD HAVE HAPPENED TO MY SISTER?
IF THAT'S REALLY WHAT IT IS...
...MAYBE I DON'T ... WON'T LET HER WAKE UP...

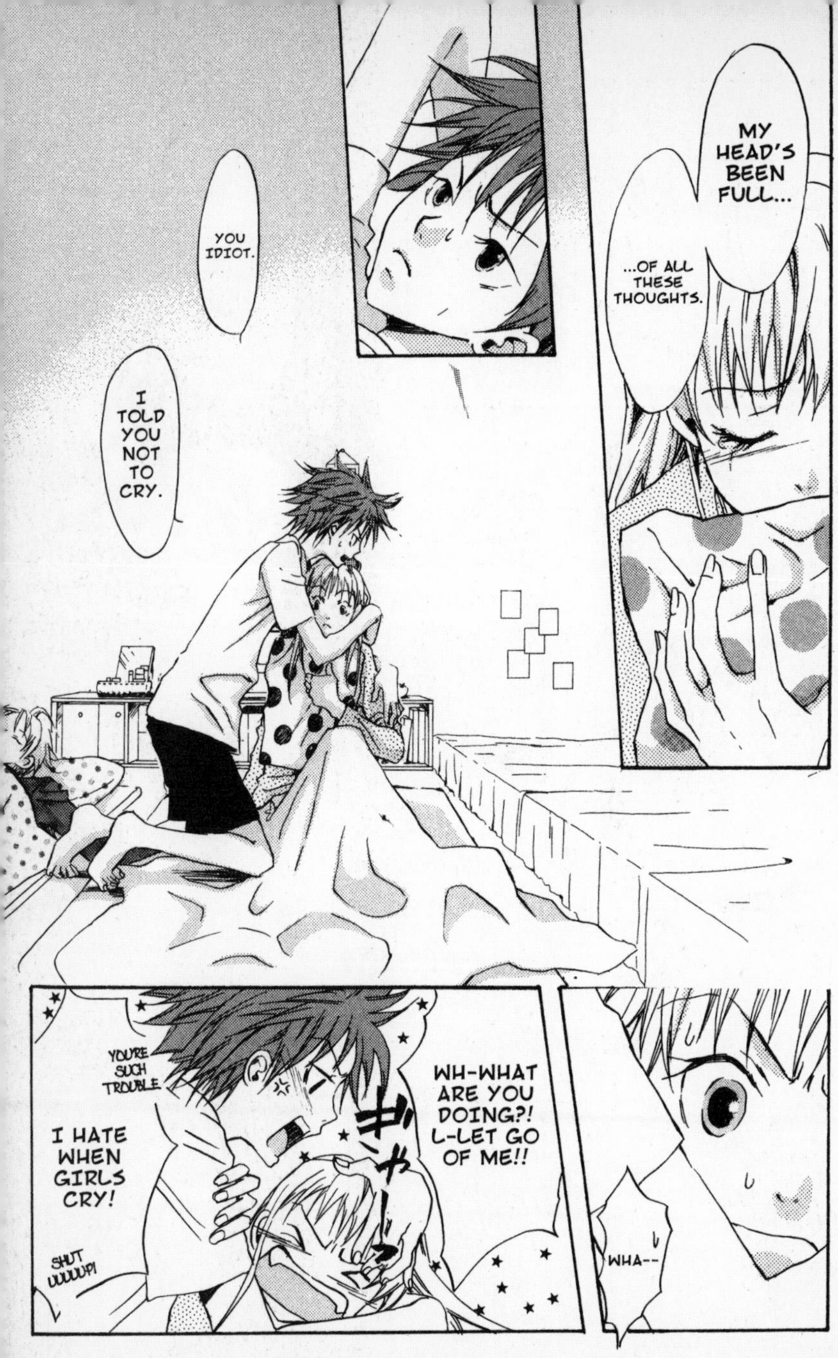
MY HEAD'S BEEN FULL...
...OF ALL THESE THOUGHTS.
YOU IDIOT.
I TOLD YOU NOT TO CRY.
WHA--
WH-WHAT ARE YOU DOING?! L-LET GO OF ME!!
YOU'RE SUCH TROUBLE
I HATE WHEN GIRLS CRY!
SHUT UUUUUP!

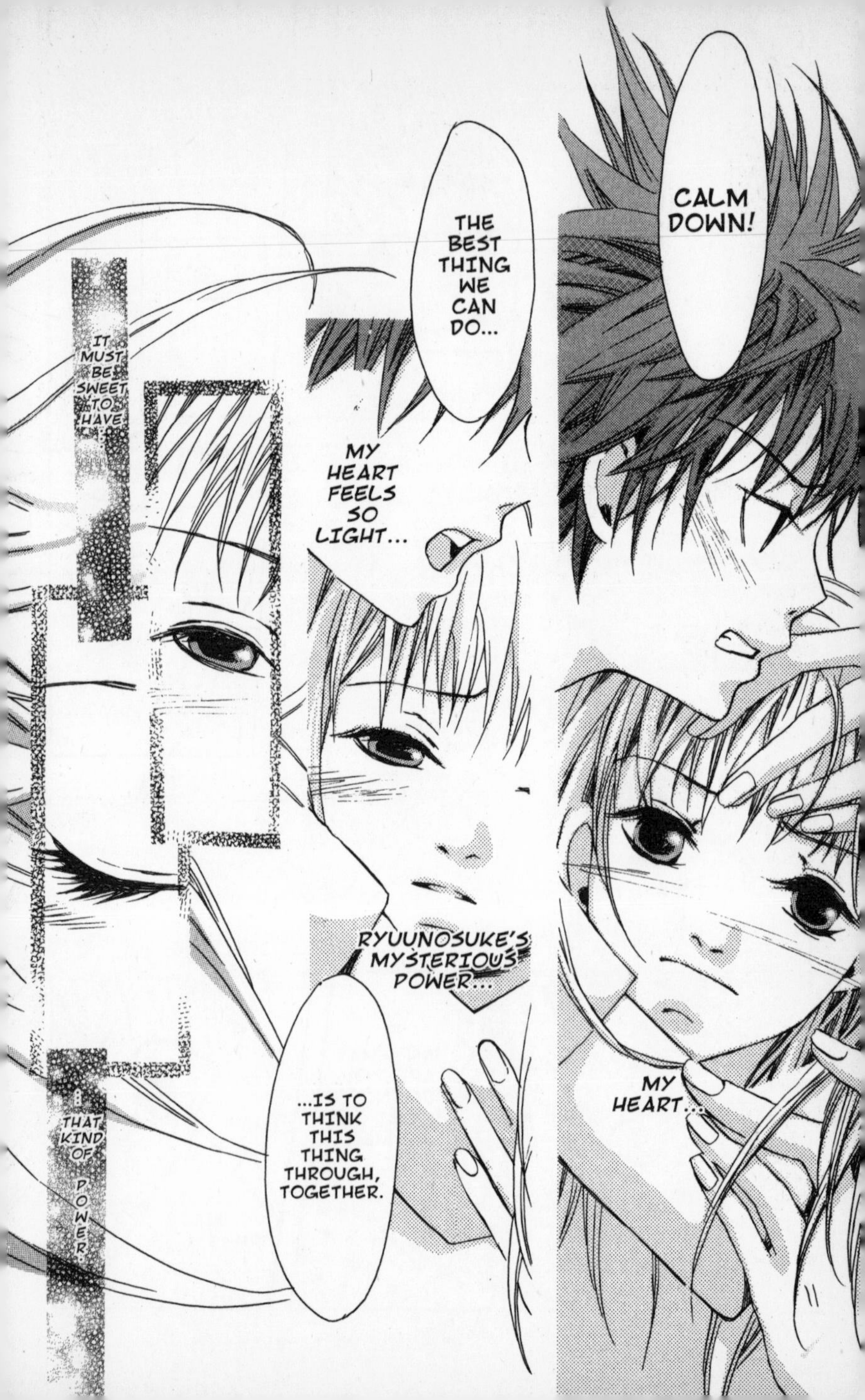
CALM DOWN!
MY HEART...
THE BEST THING WE CAN DO...
MY HEART FEELS SO LIGHT...
RYUUNOSUKE'S MYSTERIOUS POWER...
...IS TO THINK THIS THING THROUGH, TOGETHER.
IT MUST BE SWEET TO HAVE...
...THAT KIND OF POWER.

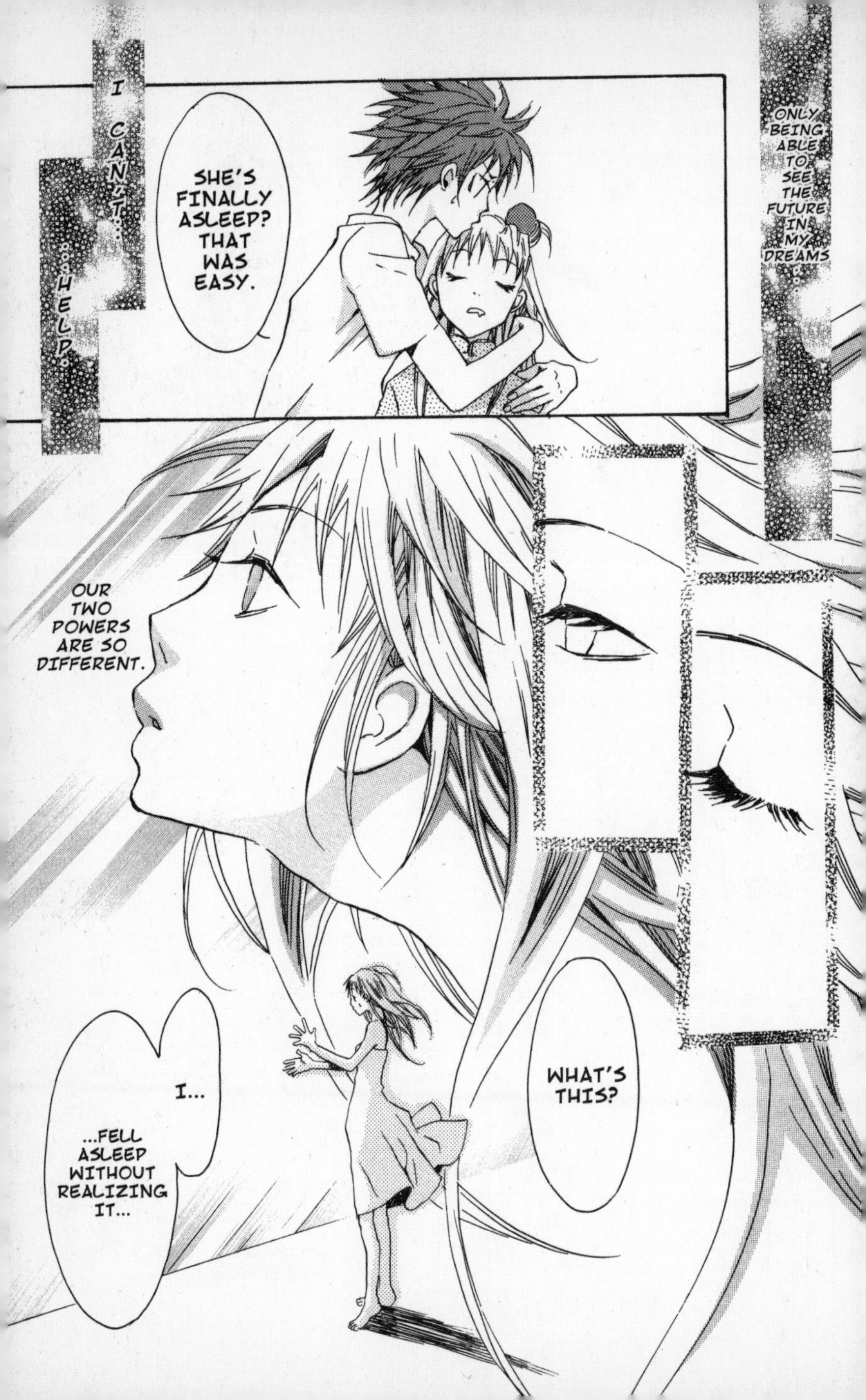
ONLY BEING ABLE TO SEE THE FUTURE IN MY DREAMS...
SHE'S FINALLY ASLEEP? THAT WAS EASY.
I CAN'T...
...HELP.
OUR TWO POWERS ARE SO DIFFERENT.
WHAT'S THIS?
I...
...FELL ASLEEP WITHOUT REALIZING IT...

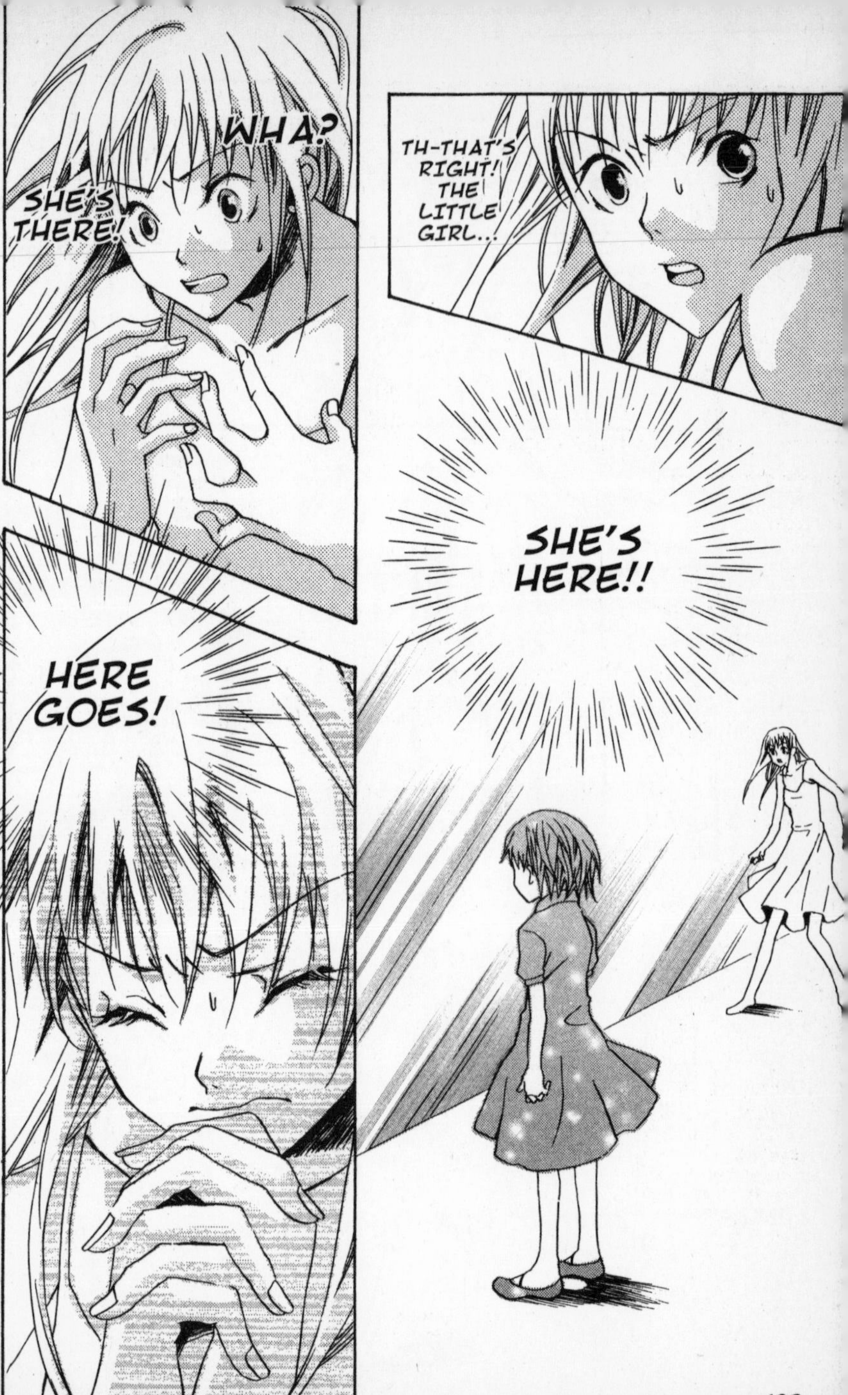
TH-THAT'S RIGHT! THE LITTLE GIRL...
WHA?
SHE'S THERE!
SHE'S HERE!!
HERE GOES!

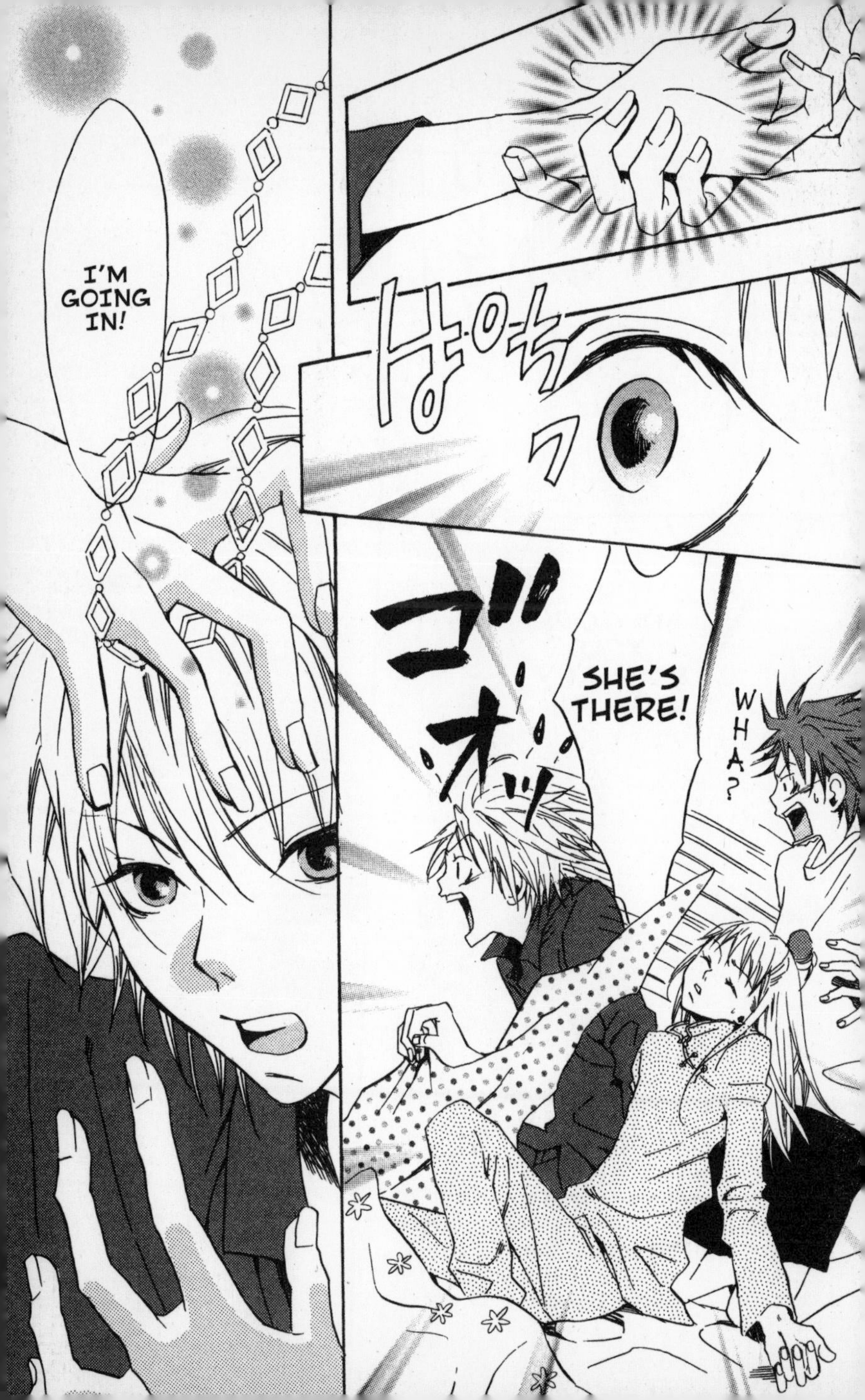
ゴオッ
SHE'S THERE!
WHA?
I'M GOING IN!

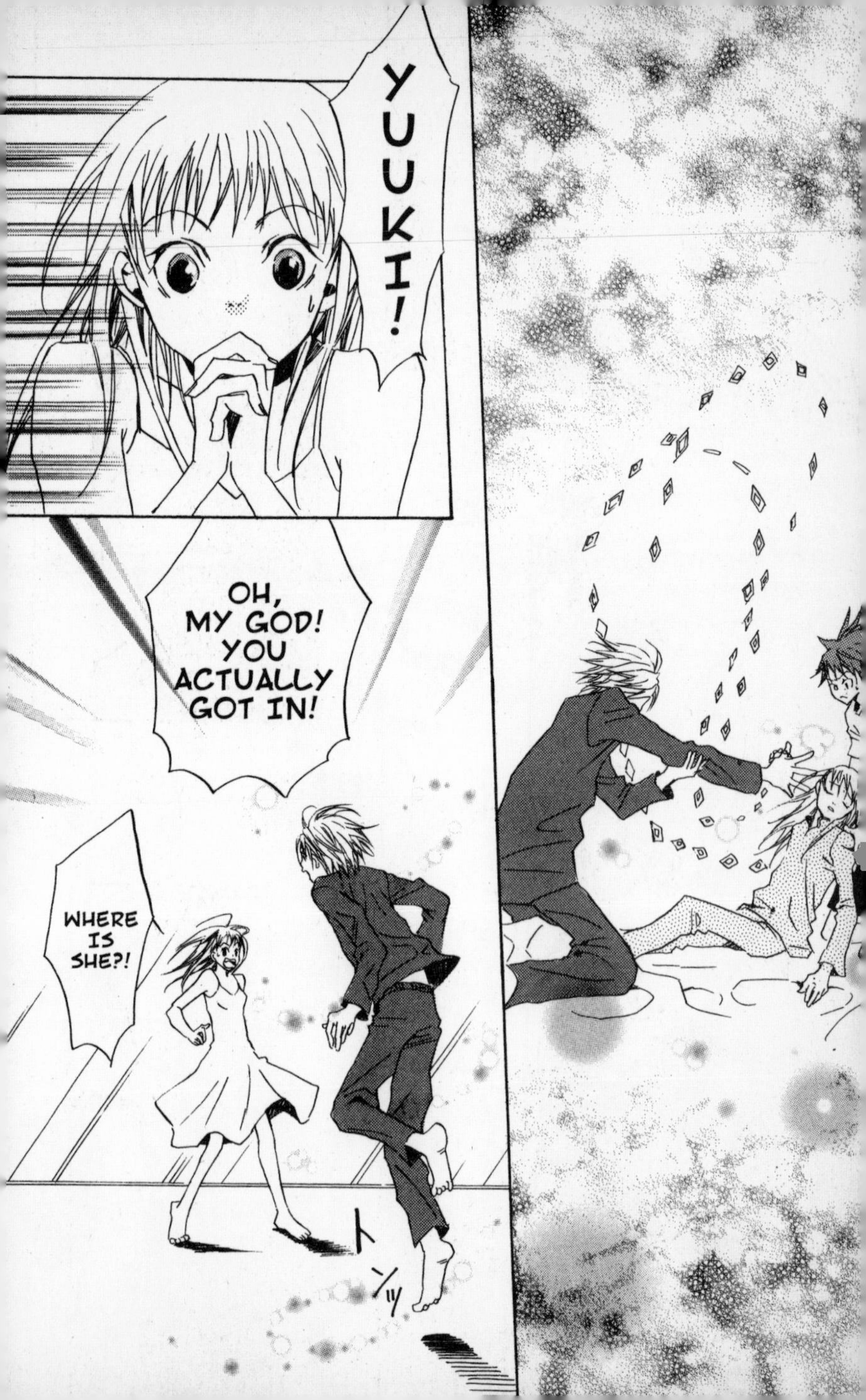
YUUKI!
OH, MY GOD! YOU ACTUALLY GOT IN!
WHERE IS SHE?!
トンッ

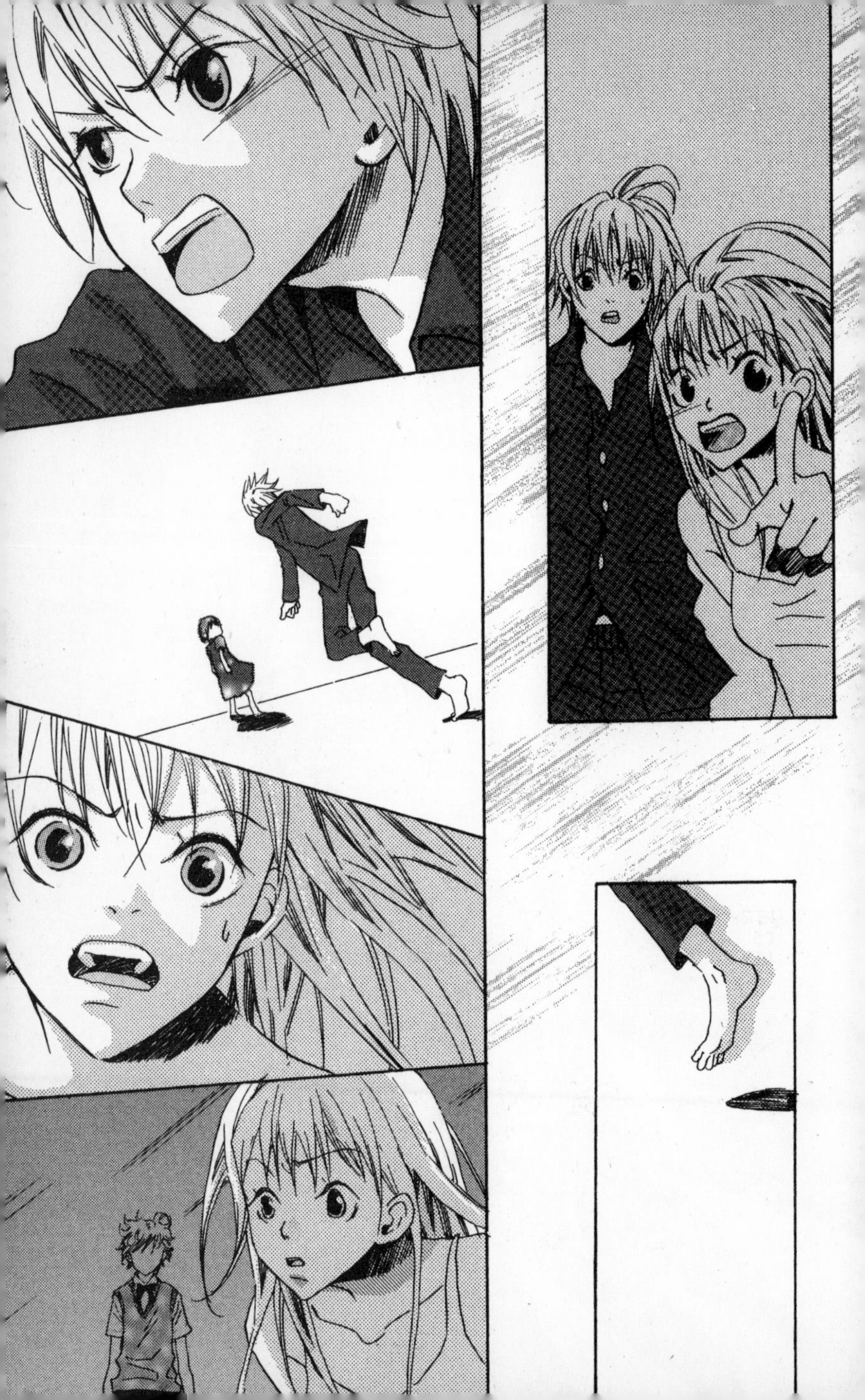

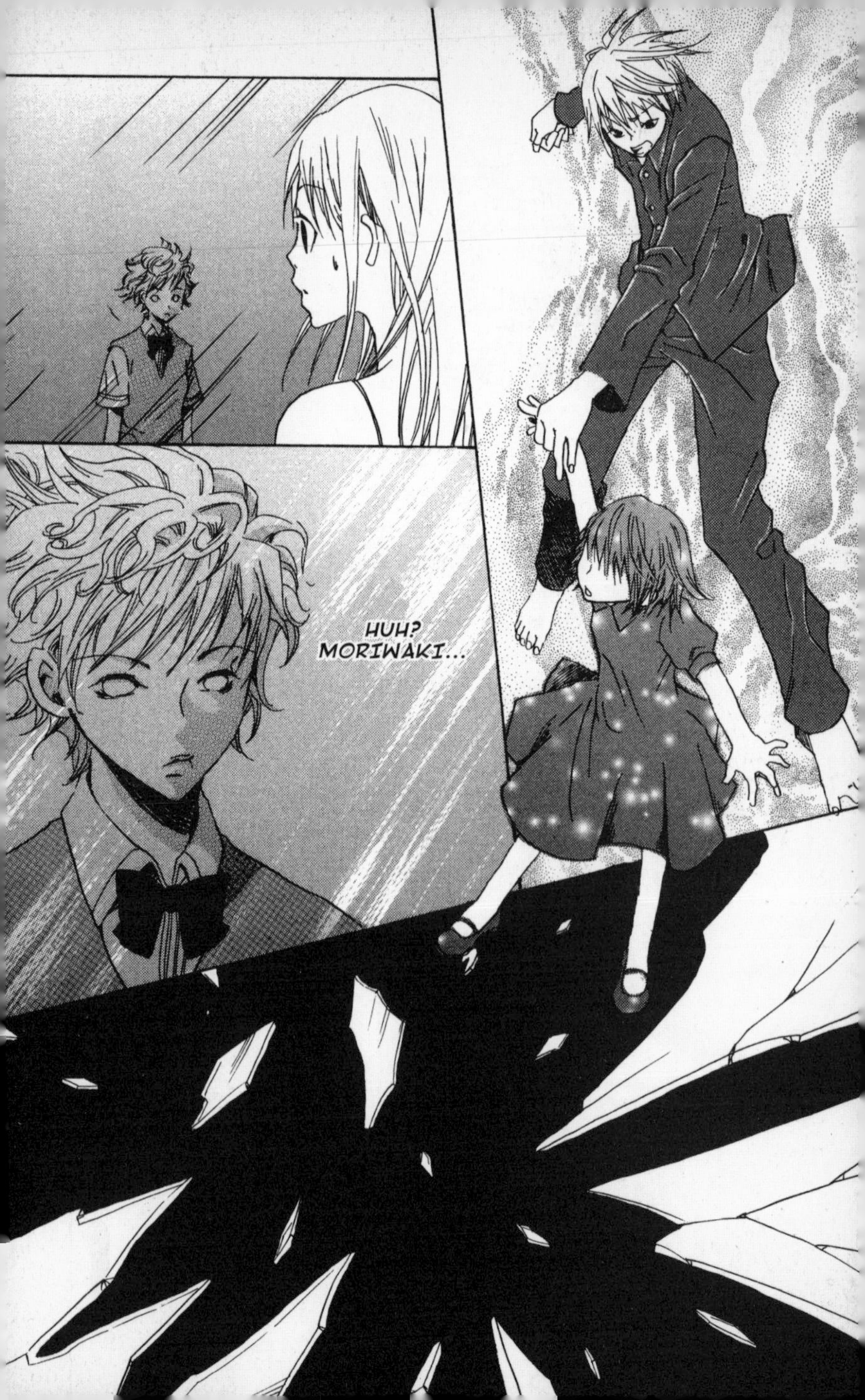
HUH? MORIWAKI...

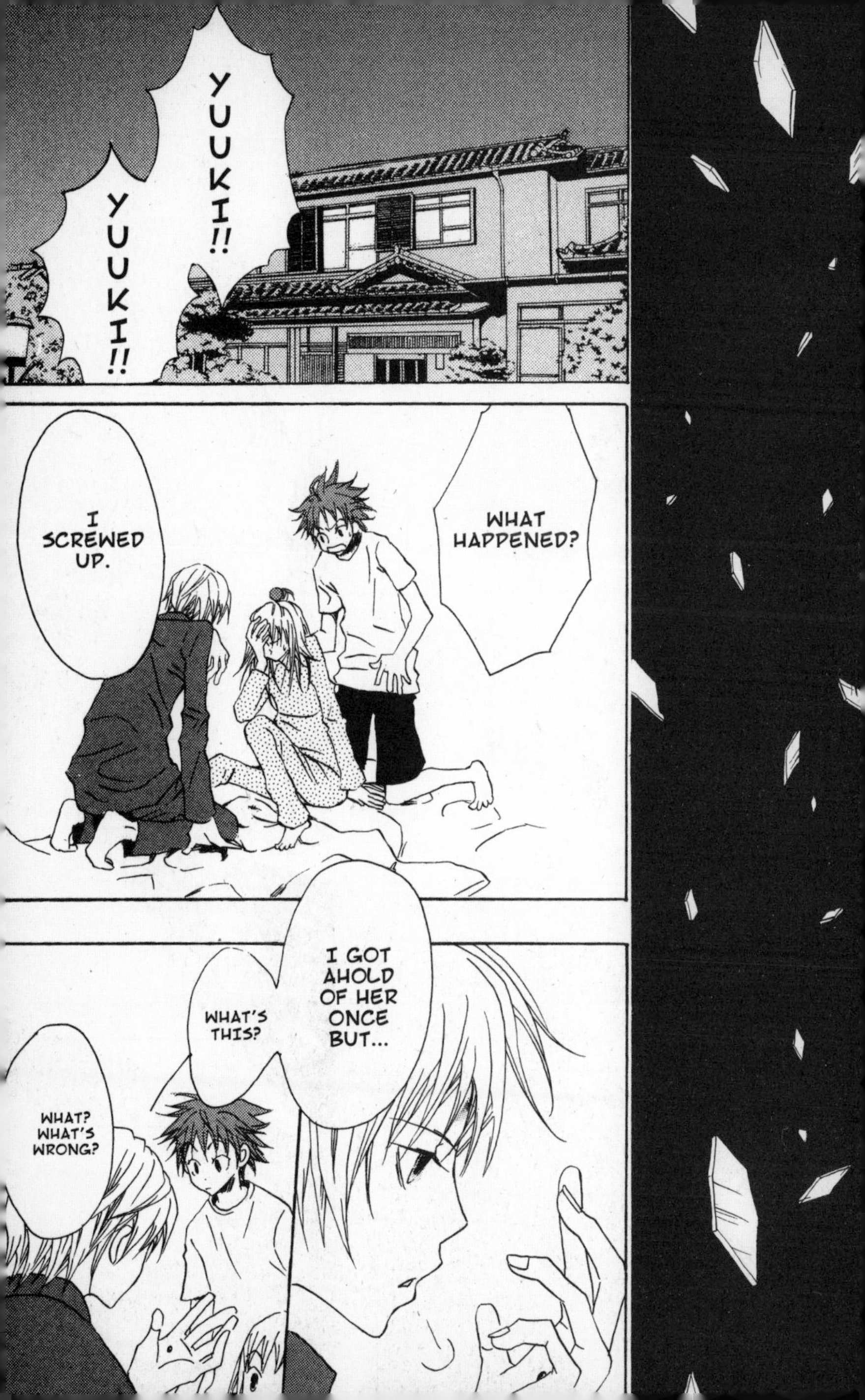
YUUKI!!
YUUKI!!
WHAT HAPPENED?
I SCREWED UP.
I GOT AHOLD OF HER ONCE BUT...
WHAT'S THIS?
WHAT? WHAT'S WRONG?

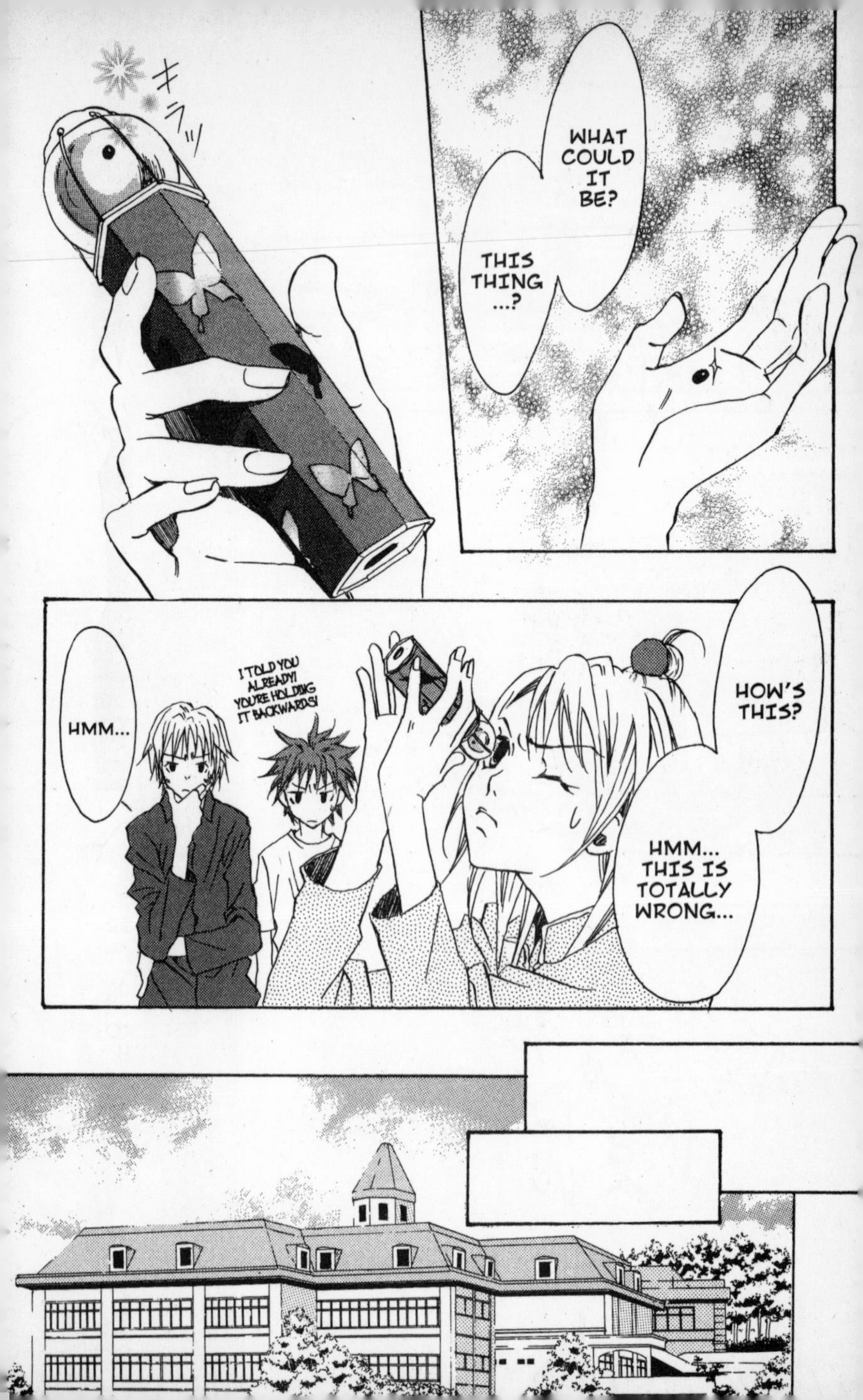
WHAT COULD IT BE?
THIS THING ...?
キラッ
HOW'S THIS?
HMM... THIS IS TOTALLY WRONG...
I TOLD YOU ALREADY! YOU'RE HOLDING IT BACKWARDS!
HMM...

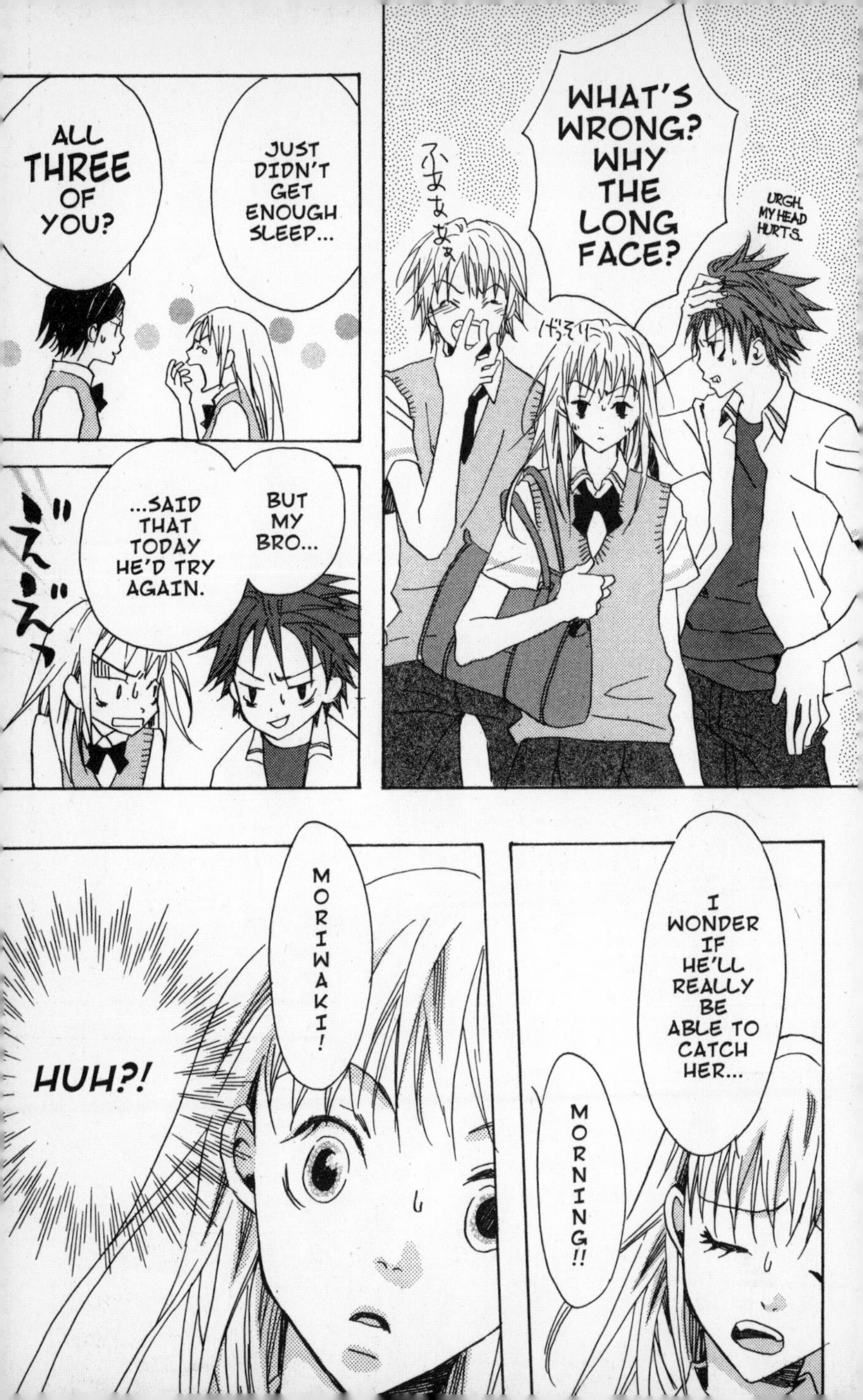
WHAT'S WRONG? WHY THE LONG FACE?
げっそり
URGH. MY HEAD HURTS.
JUST DIDN'T GET ENOUGH SLEEP...
ALL THREE OF YOU?
BUT MY BRO...
...SAID THAT TODAY HE'D TRY AGAIN.
I WONDER IF HE'LL REALLY BE ABLE TO CATCH HER...
MORNING!!
MORIWAKI!
HUH?!

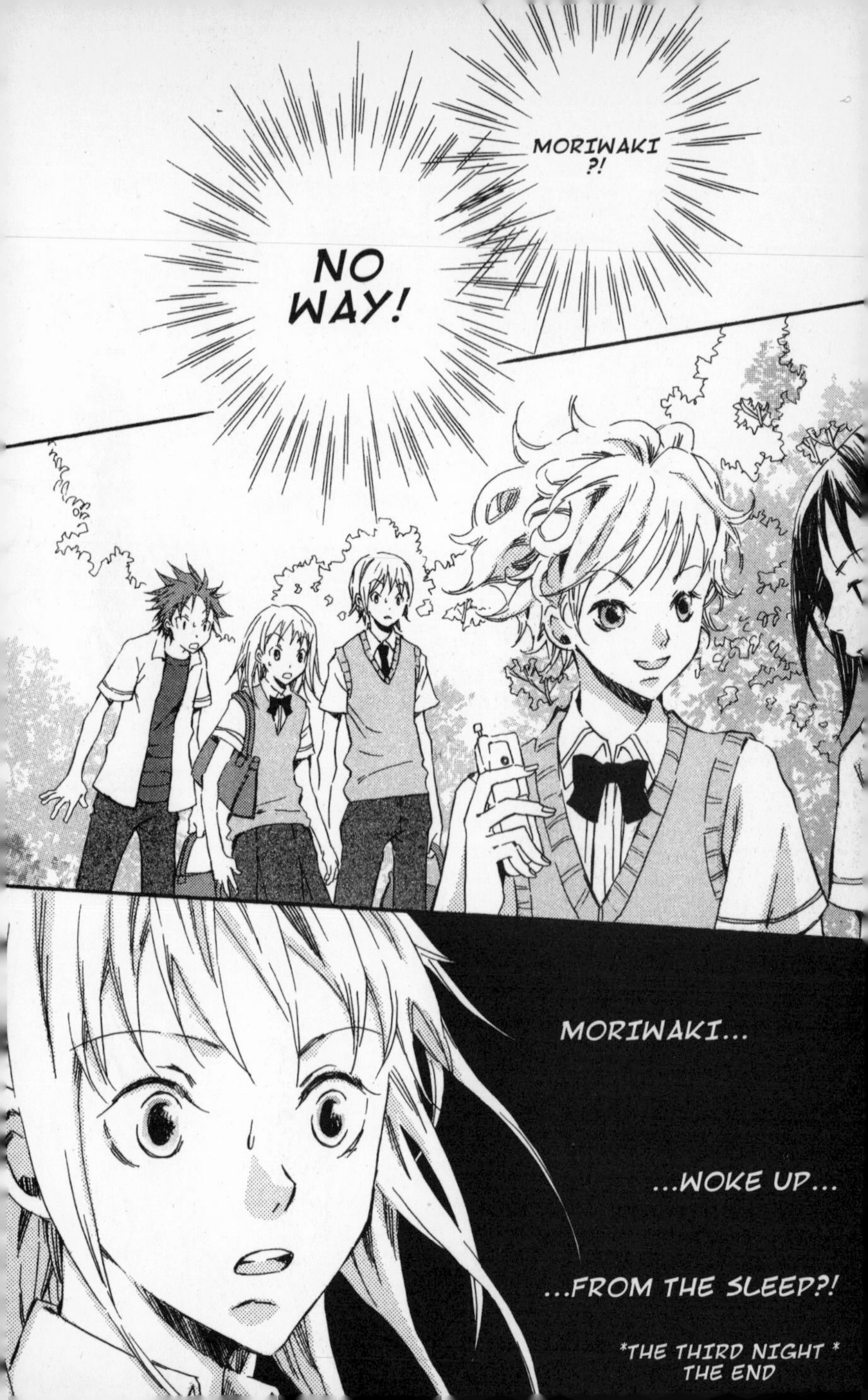
MORIWAKI ?!
NO WAY!
MORIWAKI...
...WOKE UP...
...FROM THE SLEEP?!
*THE THIRD NIGHT *
THE END

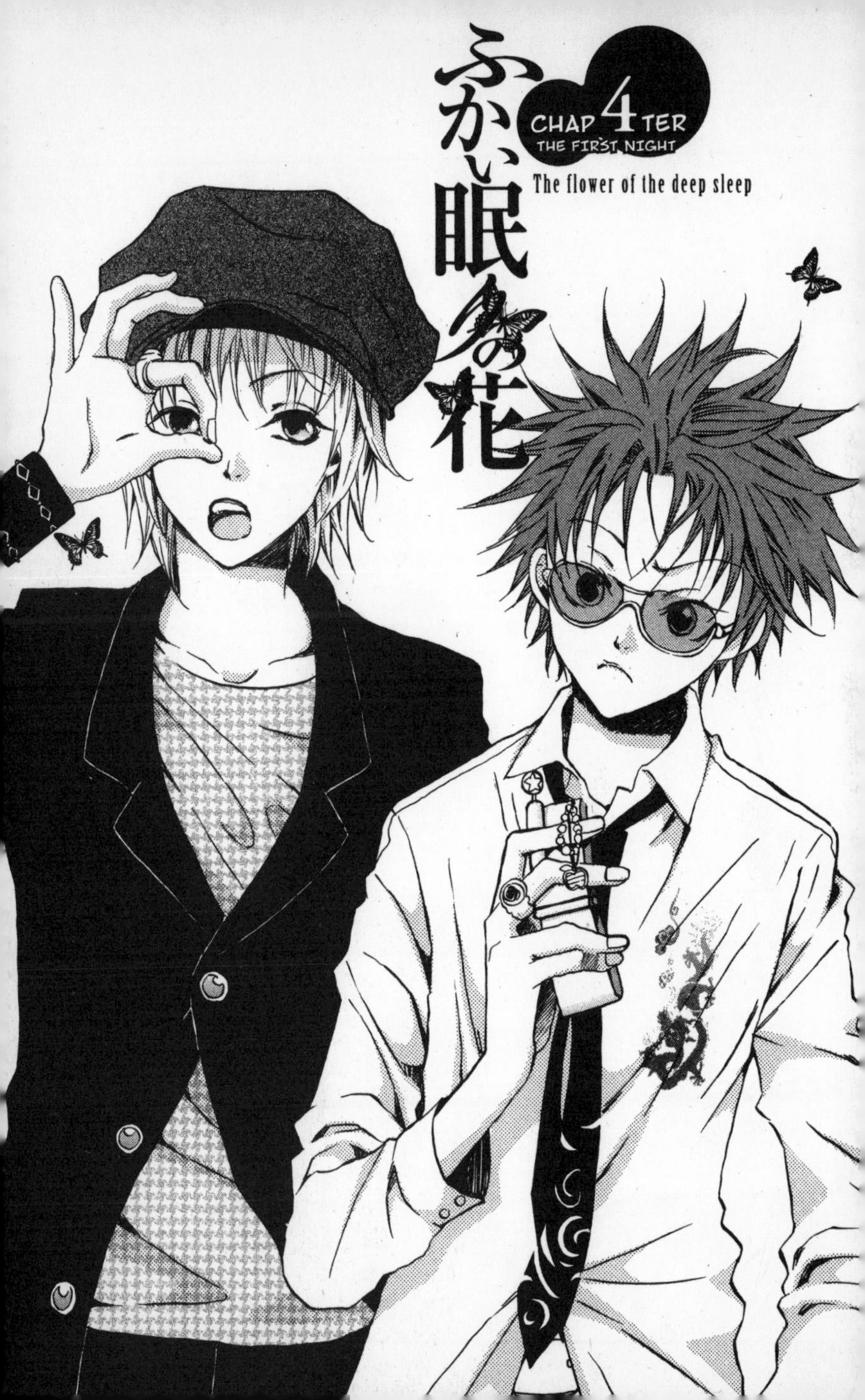
ふかい眠りの花
CHAP 4 TER
THE FIRST NIGHT
The flower of the deep sleep

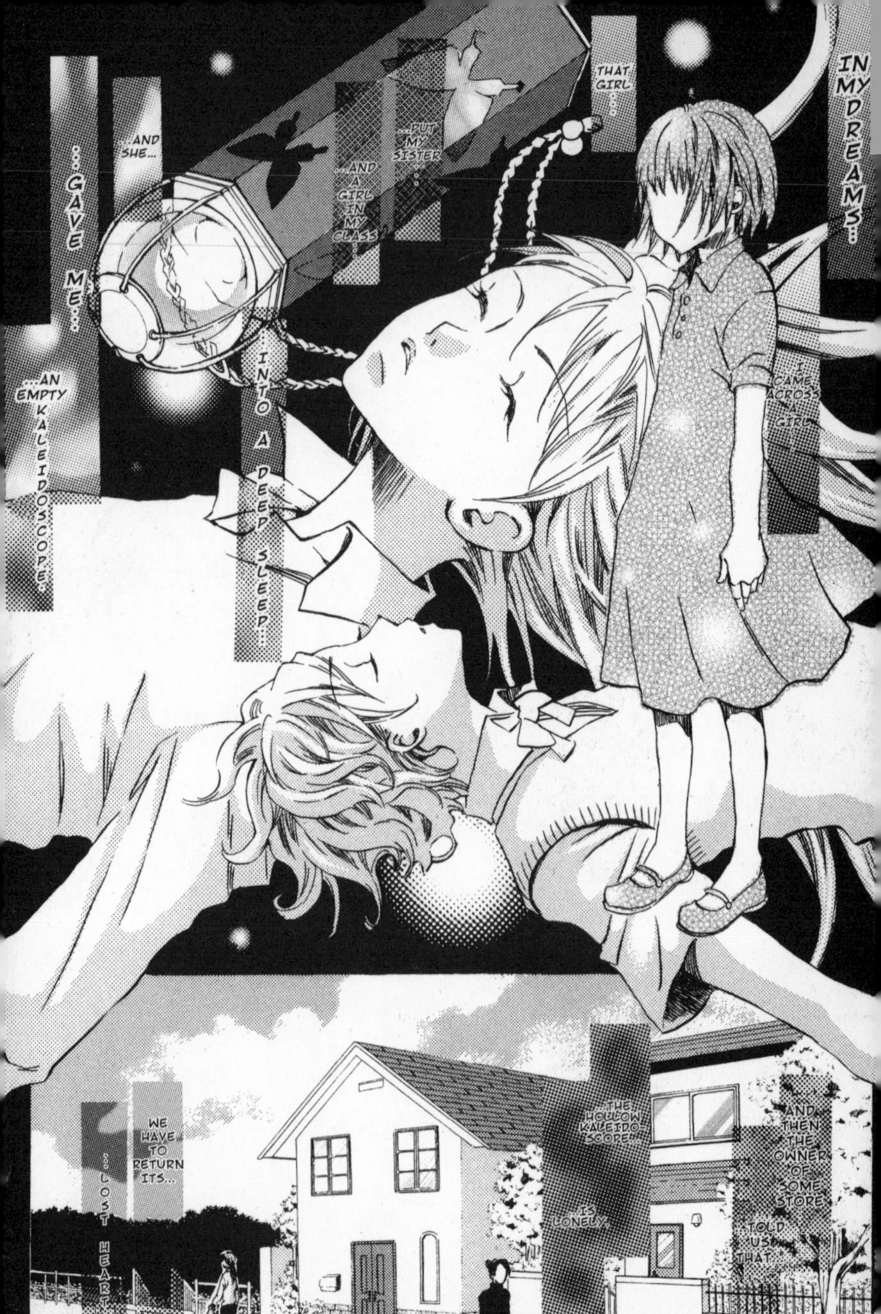
IN MY DREAMS...
I CAME ACROSS A GIRL
THAT GIRL...
...PUT MY SISTER...
...AND A GIRL IN MY CLASS...
INTO A DEEP SLEEP...
...AND SHE...
...GAVE ME...
...AN EMPTY KALEIDOSCOPE.
AND THEN THE OWNER OF SOME STORE
TOLD US THAT...
THE HOLLOW KALEIDOSCOPE
...IS LONELY.
WE HAVE TO RETURN ITS...
...LOST HEART.

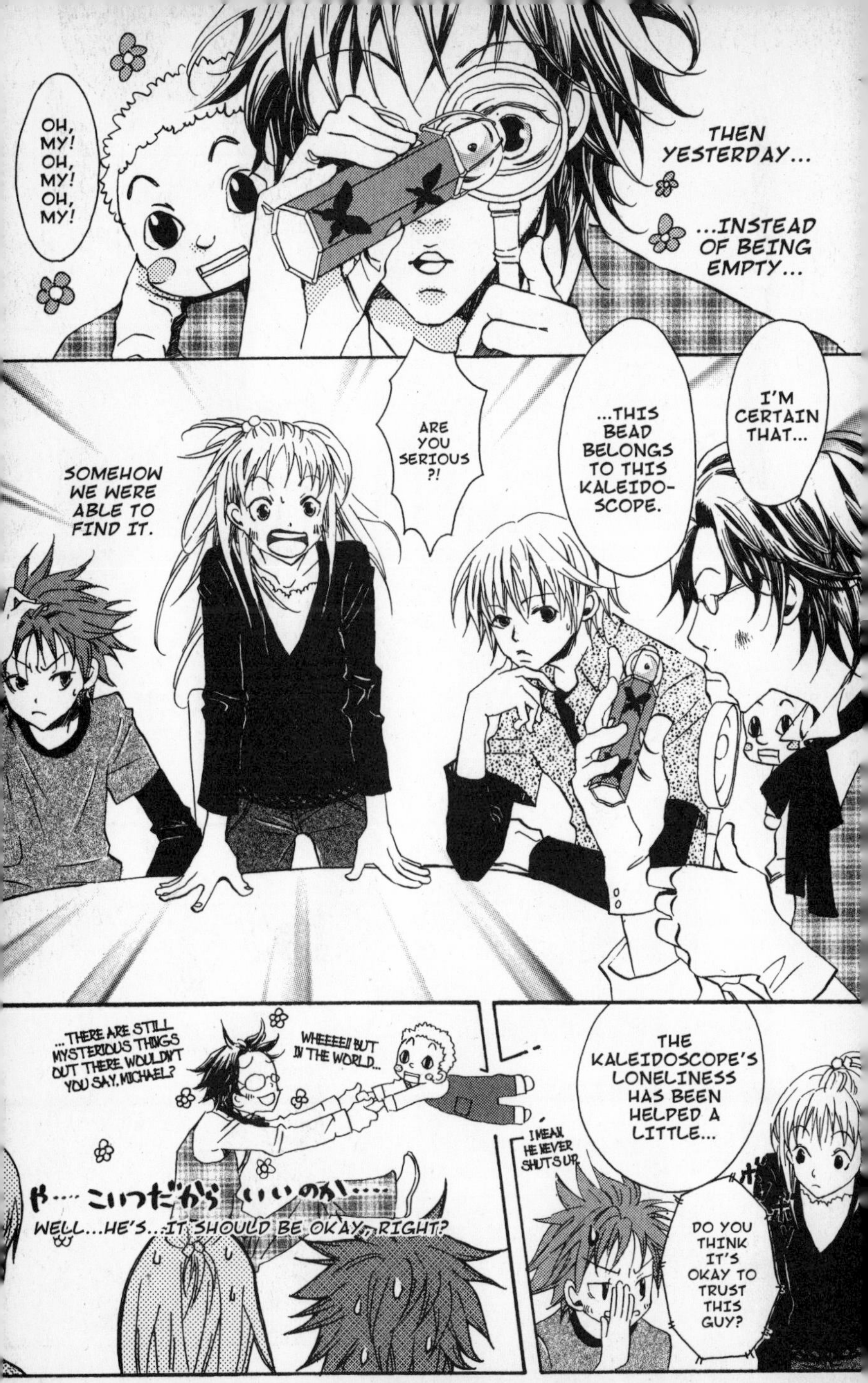

THEN YESTERDAY...
...INSTEAD OF BEING EMPTY...
OH, MY! OH, MY! OH, MY!
I'M CERTAIN THAT...
...THIS BEAD BELONGS TO THIS KALEIDO-SCOPE.
ARE YOU SERIOUS?!
SOMEHOW WE WERE ABLE TO FIND IT.
THE KALEIDOSCOPE'S LONELINESS HAS BEEN HELPED A LITTLE...
DO YOU THINK IT'S OKAY TO TRUST THIS GUY?
I MEAN, HE NEVER SHUTS UP.
...THERE ARE STILL MYSTERIOUS THINGS OUT THERE WOULDN'T YOU SAY, MICHAEL?
WHEEEE!! BUT IN THE WORLD...
や…こいつだから いいのか！…
WELL...HE'S...IT SHOULD BE OKAY, RIGHT?

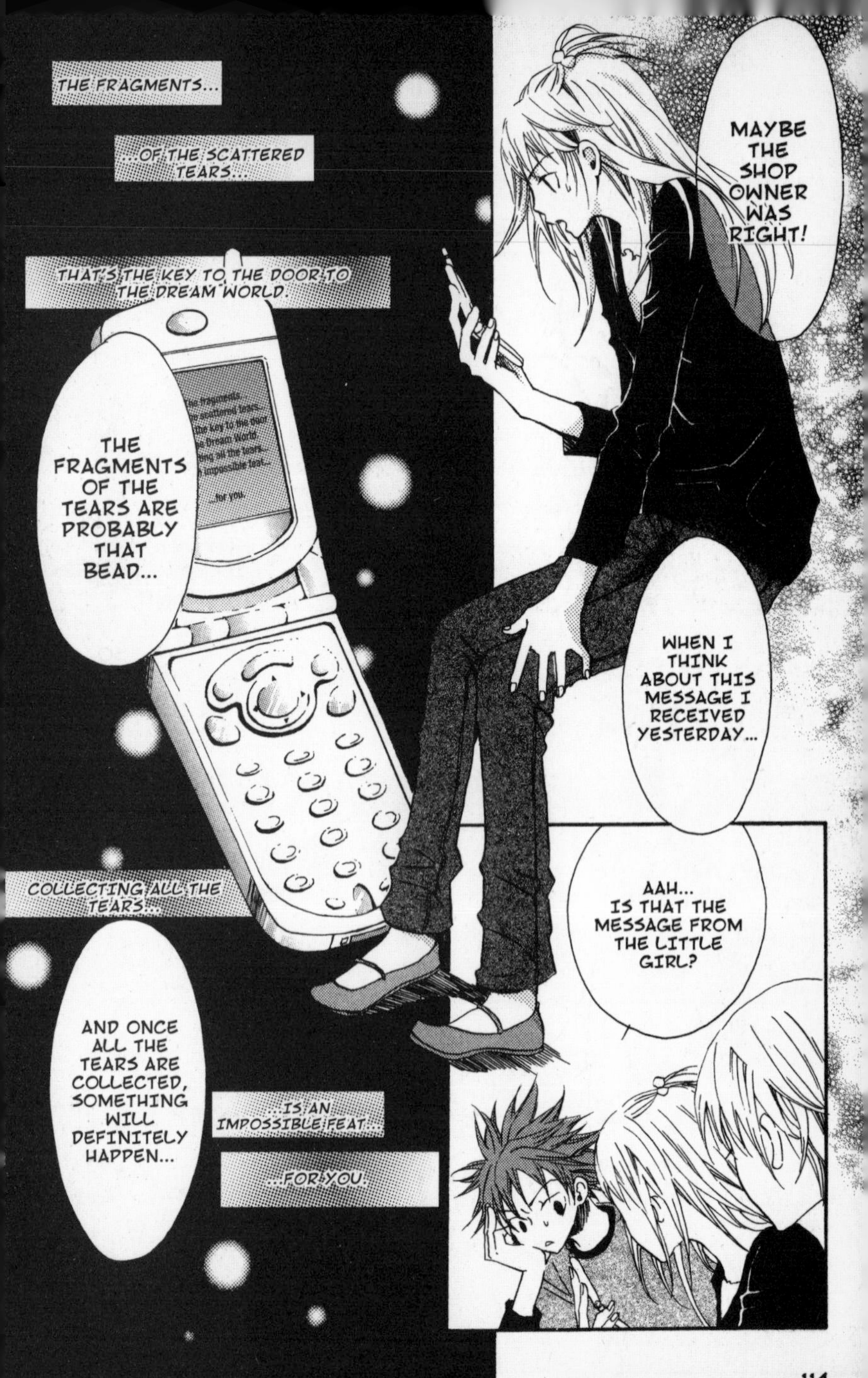
MAYBE THE SHOP OWNER WAS RIGHT!
WHEN I THINK ABOUT THIS MESSAGE I RECEIVED YESTERDAY...
AAH... IS THAT THE MESSAGE FROM THE LITTLE GIRL?
THE FRAGMENTS...
...OF THE SCATTERED TEARS...
THAT'S THE KEY TO THE DOOR TO THE DREAM WORLD.
THE FRAGMENTS OF THE TEARS ARE PROBABLY THAT BEAD...
COLLECTING ALL THE TEARS...
AND ONCE ALL THE TEARS ARE COLLECTED, SOMETHING WILL DEFINITELY HAPPEN...
...IS AN IMPOSSIBLE FEAT...
...FOR YOU.

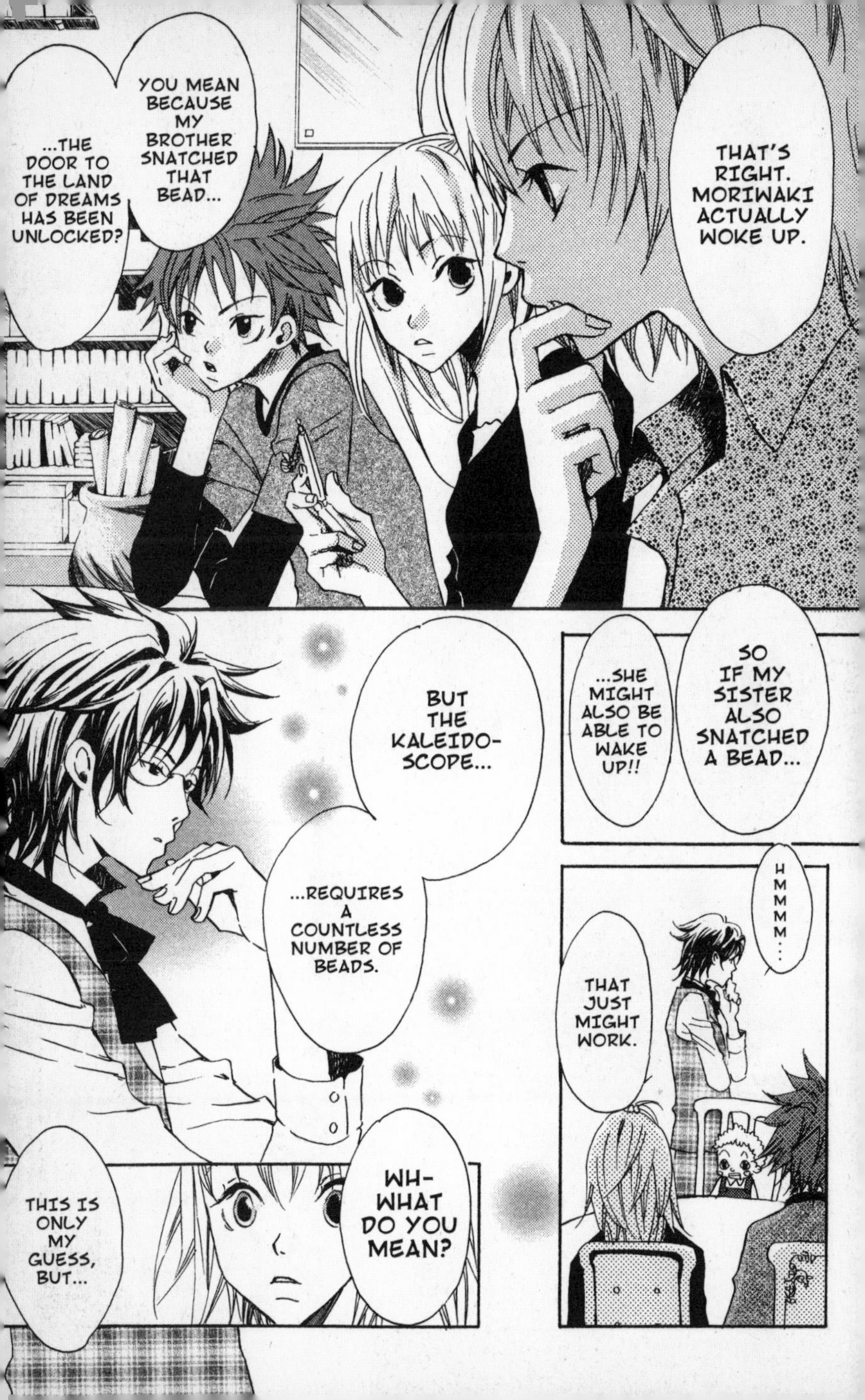
THAT'S RIGHT. MORIWAKI ACTUALLY WOKE UP.
YOU MEAN BECAUSE MY BROTHER SNATCHED THAT BEAD...
...THE DOOR TO THE LAND OF DREAMS HAS BEEN UNLOCKED?
SO IF MY SISTER ALSO SNATCHED A BEAD...
...SHE MIGHT ALSO BE ABLE TO WAKE UP!!
HMMMM...
THAT JUST MIGHT WORK.
BUT THE KALEIDO-SCOPE...
...REQUIRES A COUNTLESS NUMBER OF BEADS.
WH-WHAT DO YOU MEAN?
THIS IS ONLY MY GUESS, BUT...

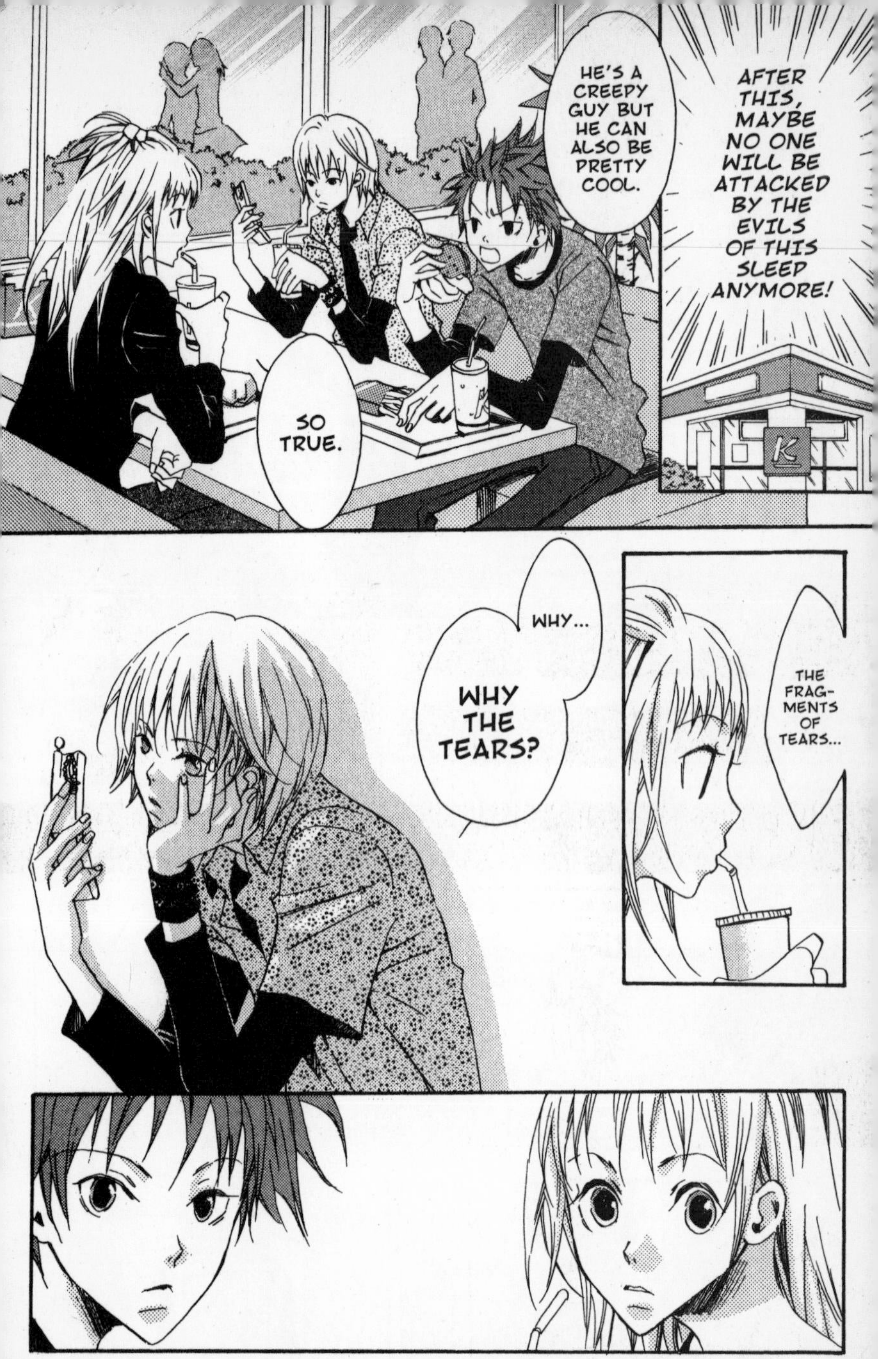
AFTER THIS, MAYBE NO ONE WILL BE ATTACKED BY THE EVILS OF THIS SLEEP ANYMORE!
HE'S A CREEPY GUY BUT HE CAN ALSO BE PRETTY COOL.
SO TRUE.
THE FRAG- MENTS OF TEARS...
WHY...
WHY THE TEARS?

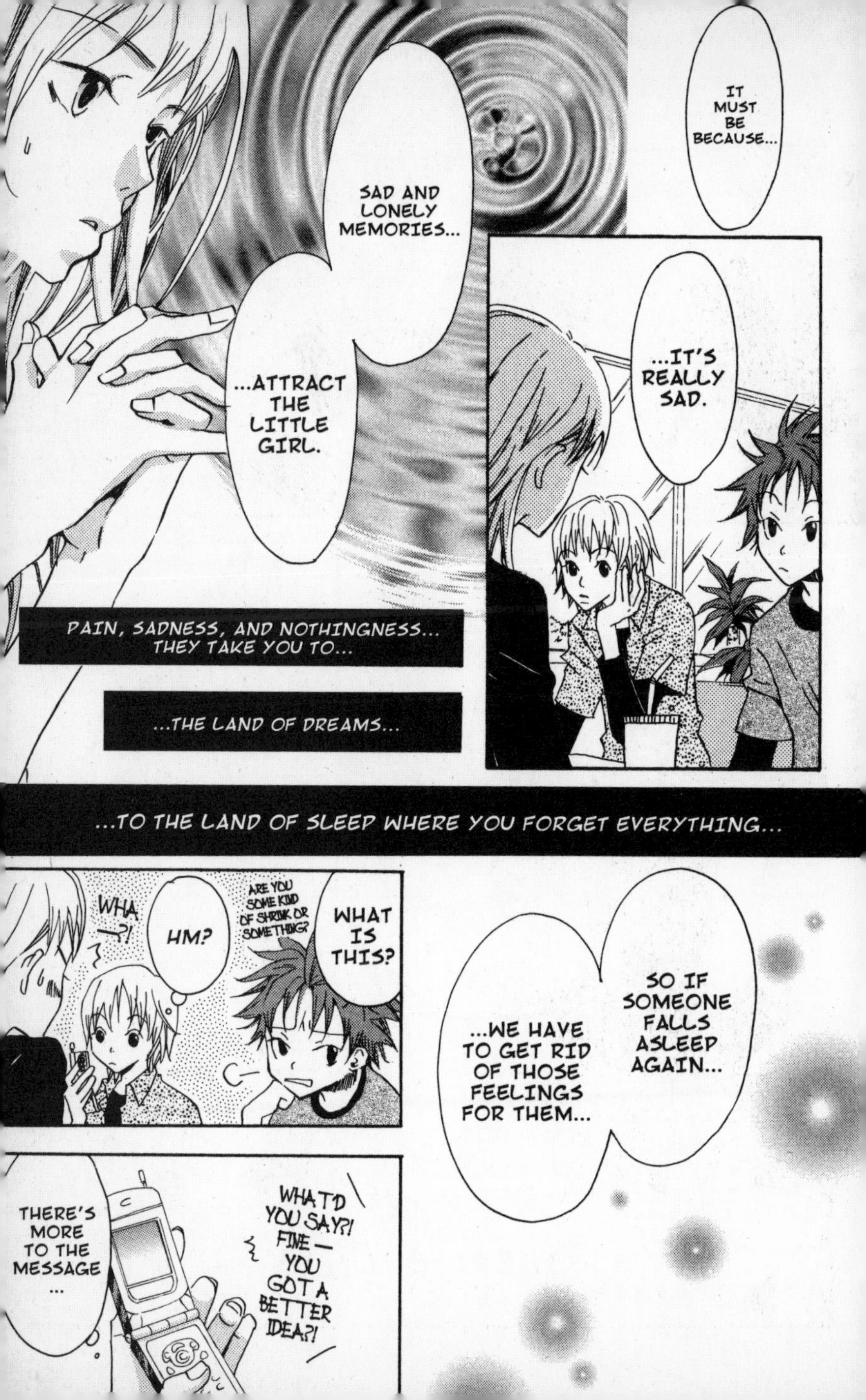

IT MUST BE BECAUSE...
SAD AND LONELY MEMORIES...
...ATTRACT THE LITTLE GIRL.
...IT'S REALLY SAD.
PAIN, SADNESS, AND NOTHINGNESS... THEY TAKE YOU TO...
...THE LAND OF DREAMS...
...TO THE LAND OF SLEEP WHERE YOU FORGET EVERYTHING...
SO IF SOMEONE FALLS ASLEEP AGAIN...
...WE HAVE TO GET RID OF THOSE FEELINGS FOR THEM...
WHAT IS THIS?
ARE YOU SOME KIND OF SHRINK OR SOMETHING?
HM?
WHA—?!
WHAT'D YOU SAY?! FINE— YOU GOT A BETTER IDEA?!
THERE'S MORE TO THE MESSAGE ...

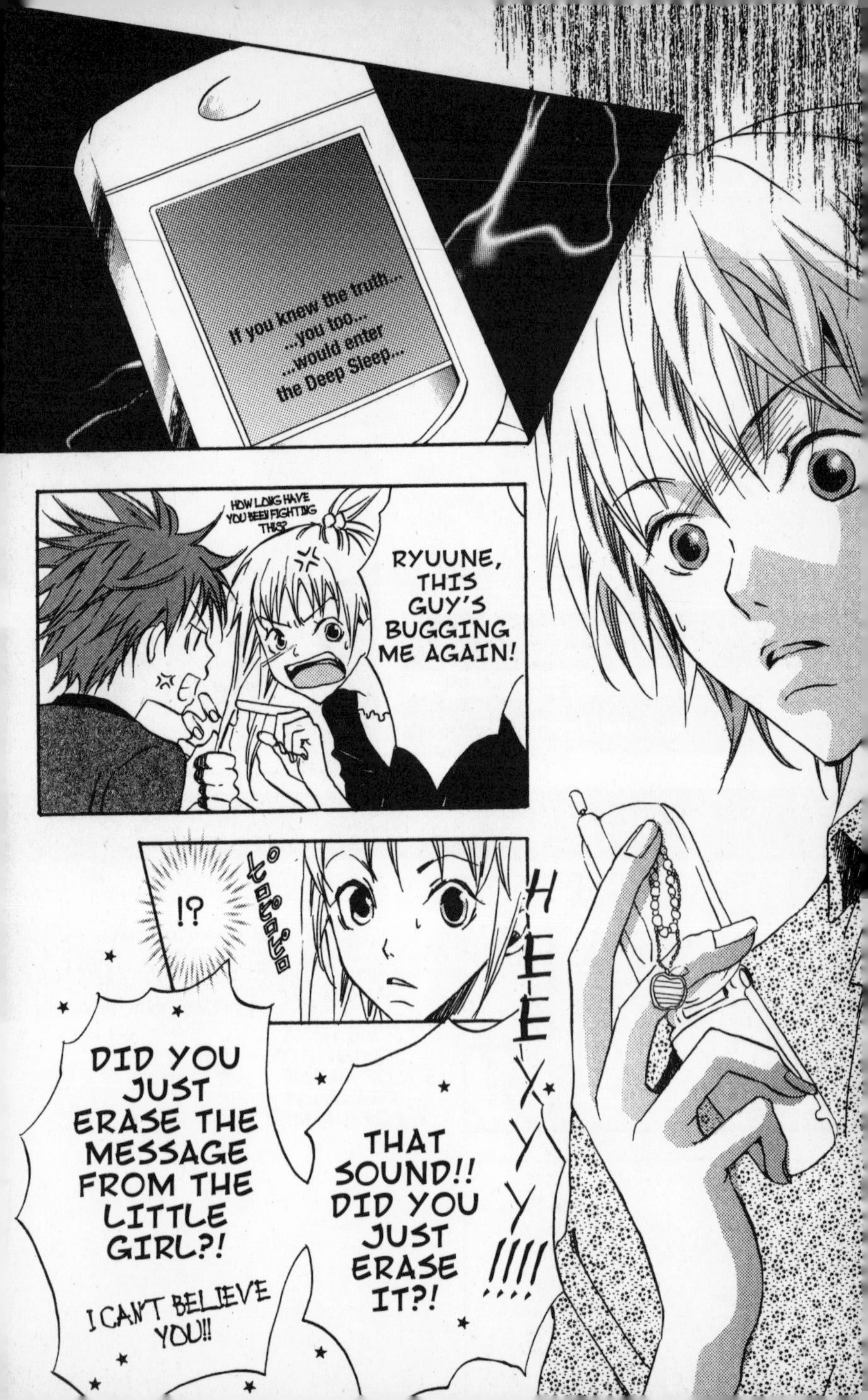
If you knew the truth...
...you too...
...would enter
the Deep Sleep...
HOW LONG HAVE YOU BEEN FIGHTING THIS?
RYUUNE, THIS GUY'S BUGGING ME AGAIN!
!?
HEEEXYY!!!!
THAT SOUND!! DID YOU JUST ERASE IT?!
DID YOU JUST ERASE THE MESSAGE FROM THE LITTLE GIRL?!
I CAN'T BELIEVE YOU!!

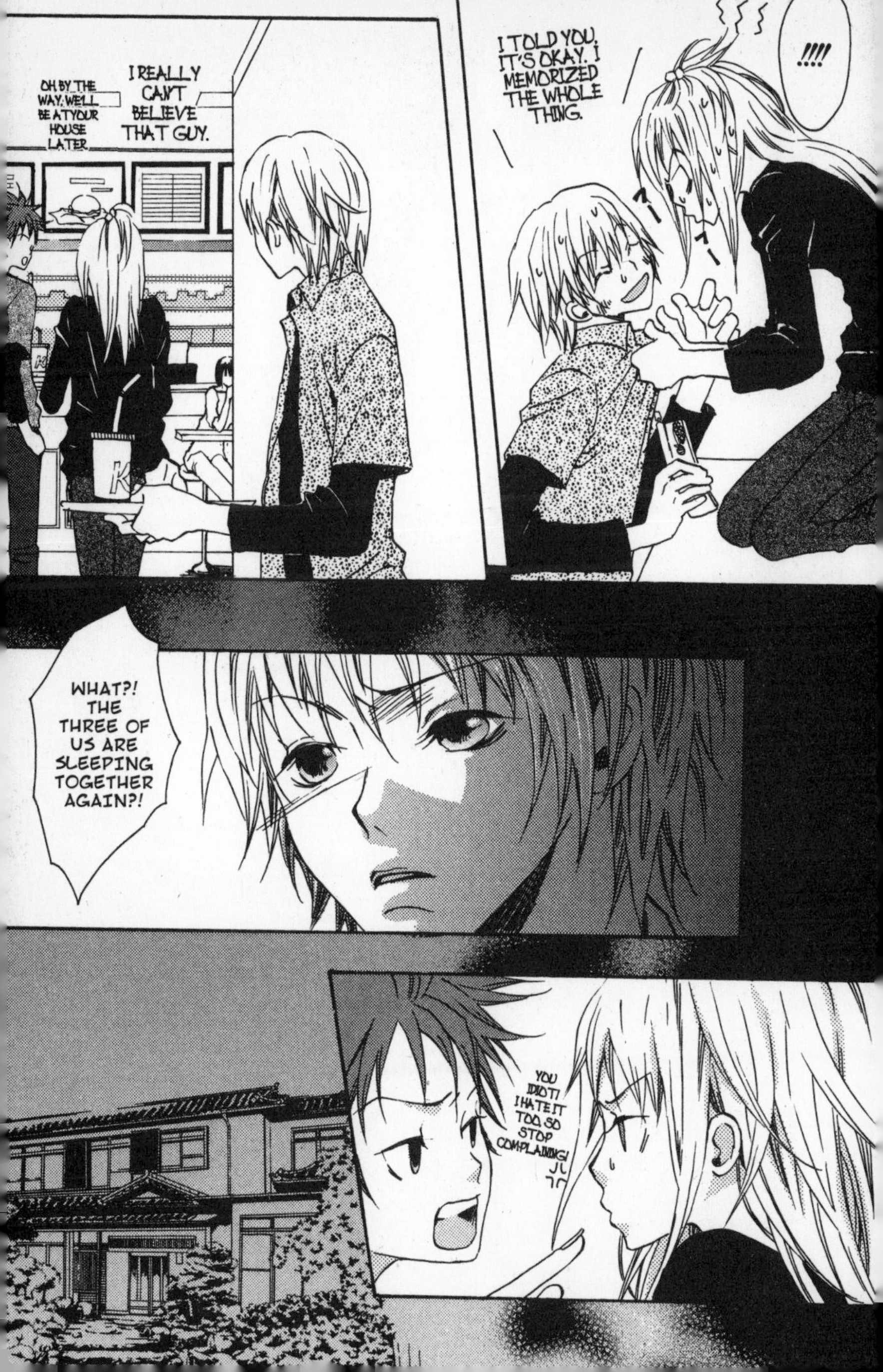
!!!!
I TOLD YOU. IT'S OKAY. I MEMORIZED THE WHOLE THING.
I REALLY CAN'T BELIEVE THAT GUY.
OH BY THE WAY, WE'LL BE AT YOUR HOUSE LATER.
WHAT?! THE THREE OF US ARE SLEEPING TOGETHER AGAIN?!
YOU IDIOT! I HATE IT TOO, SO STOP COMPLAINING!

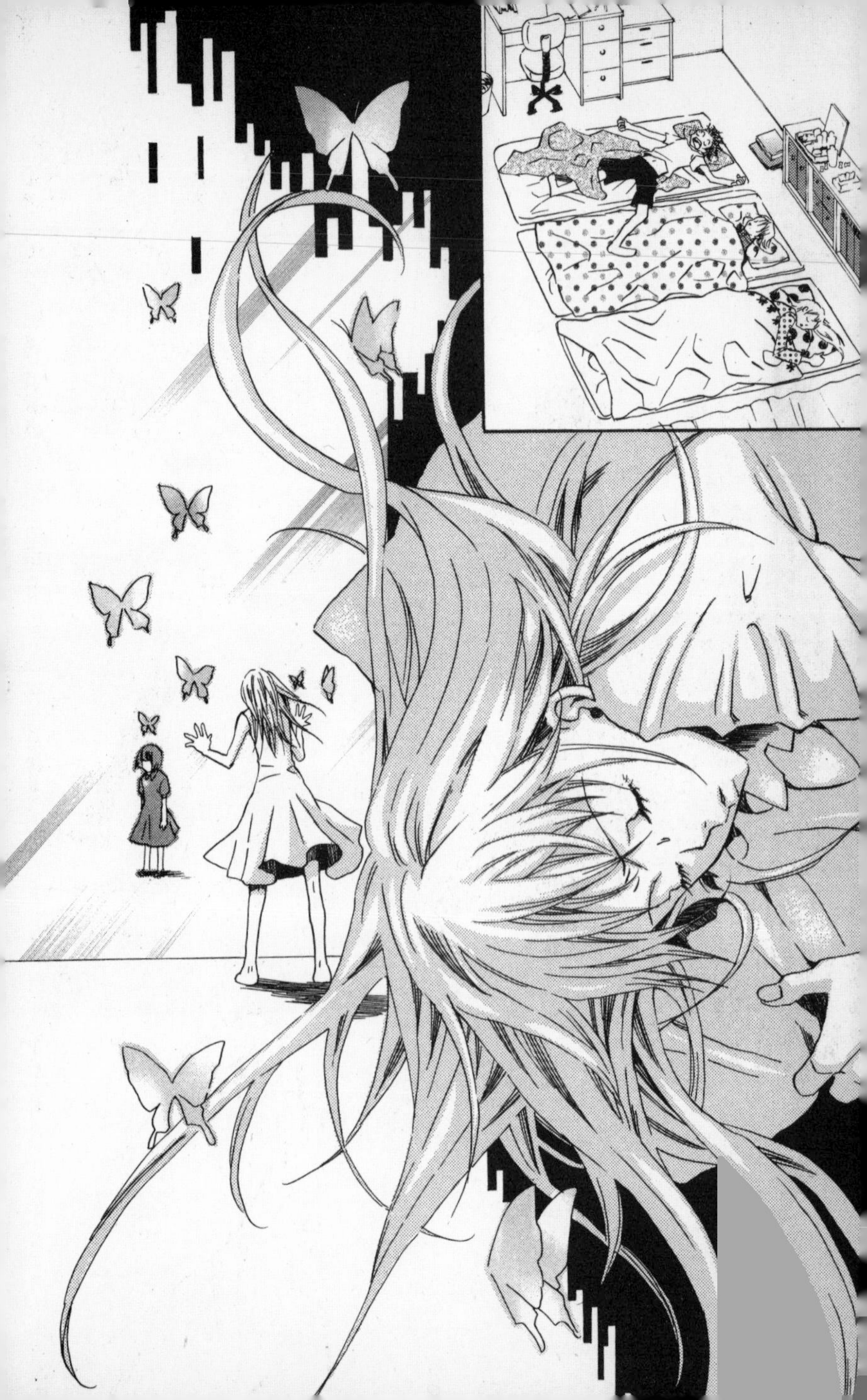

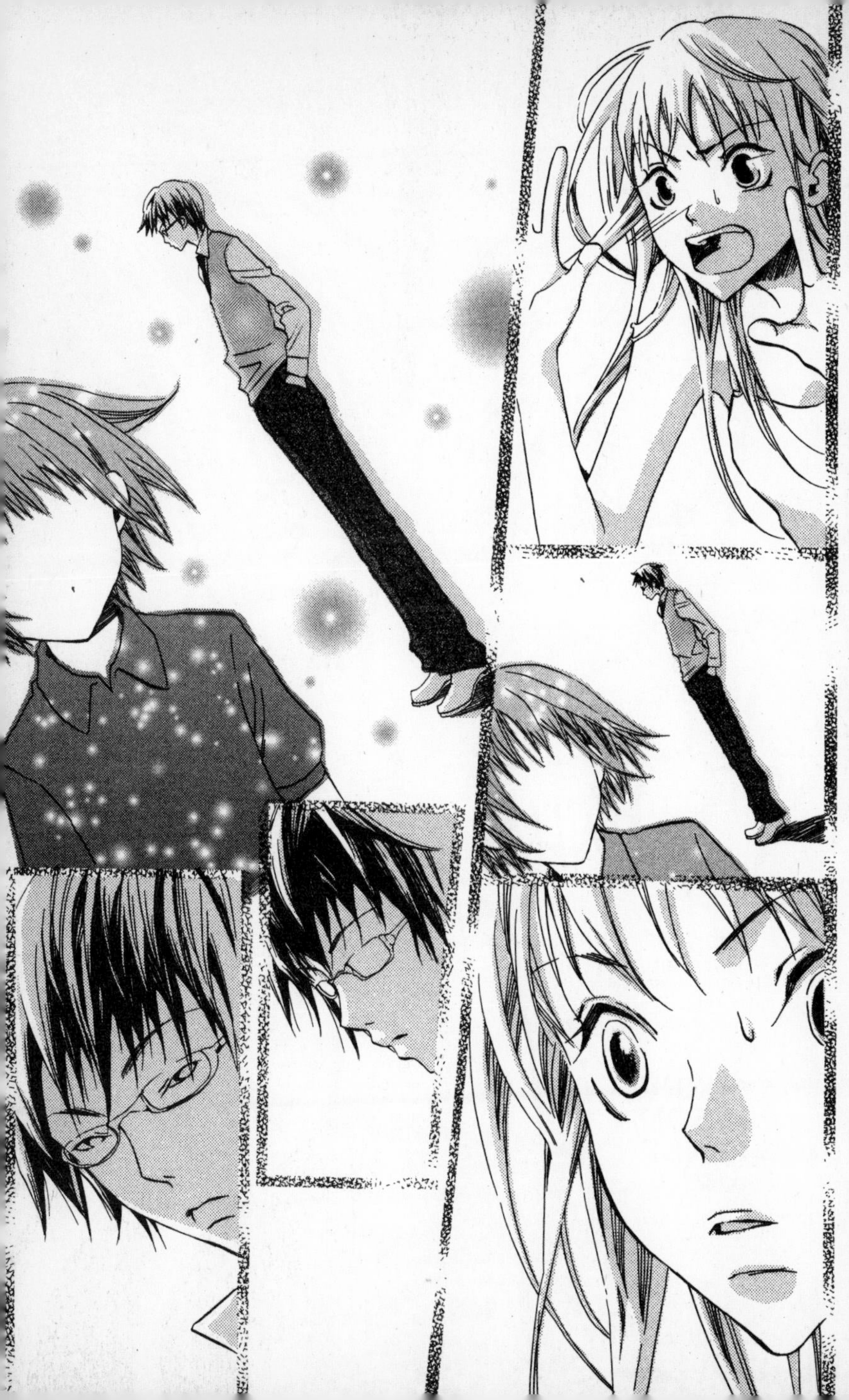

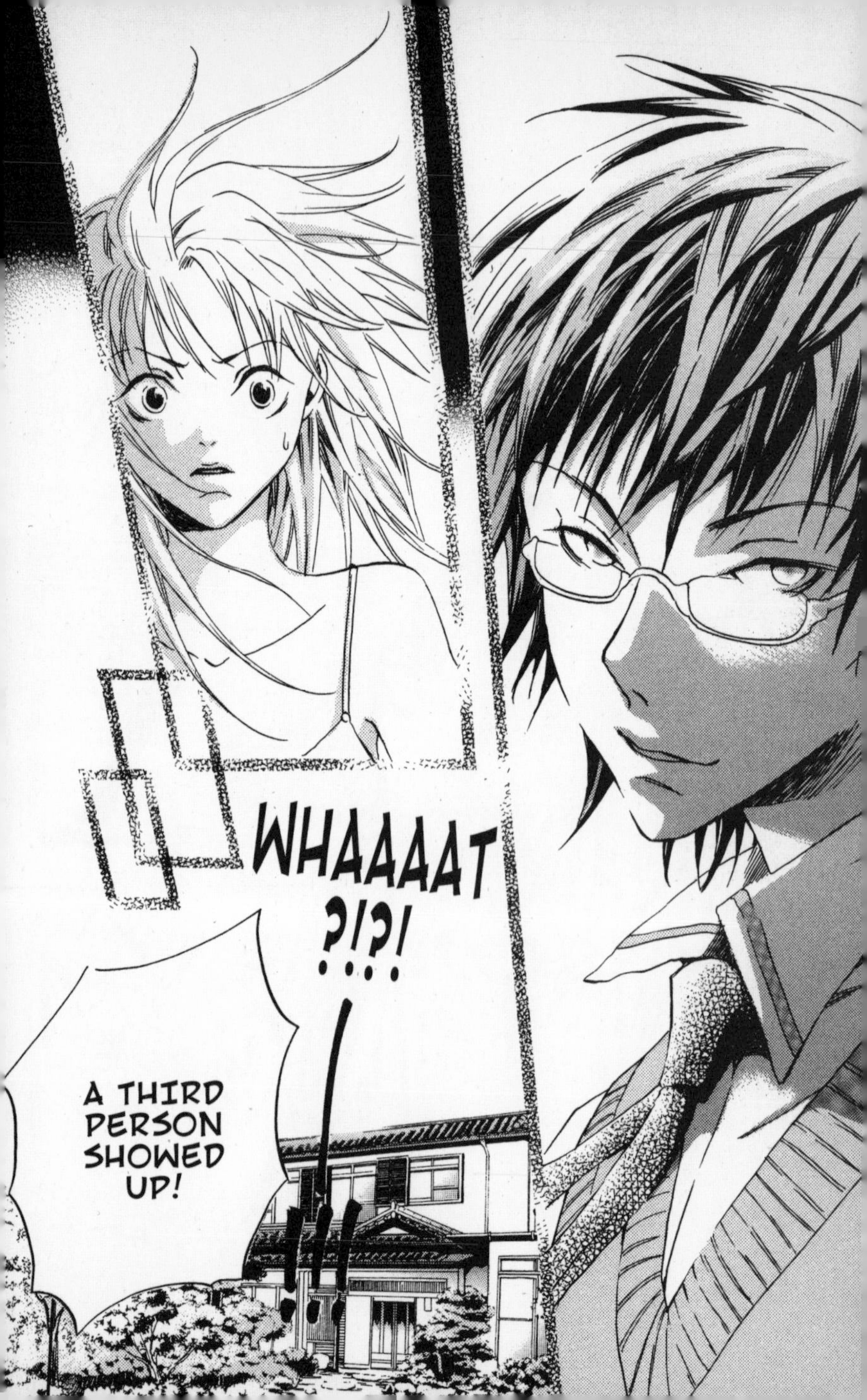
WHAAAAT ?!?!
A THIRD PERSON SHOWED UP!

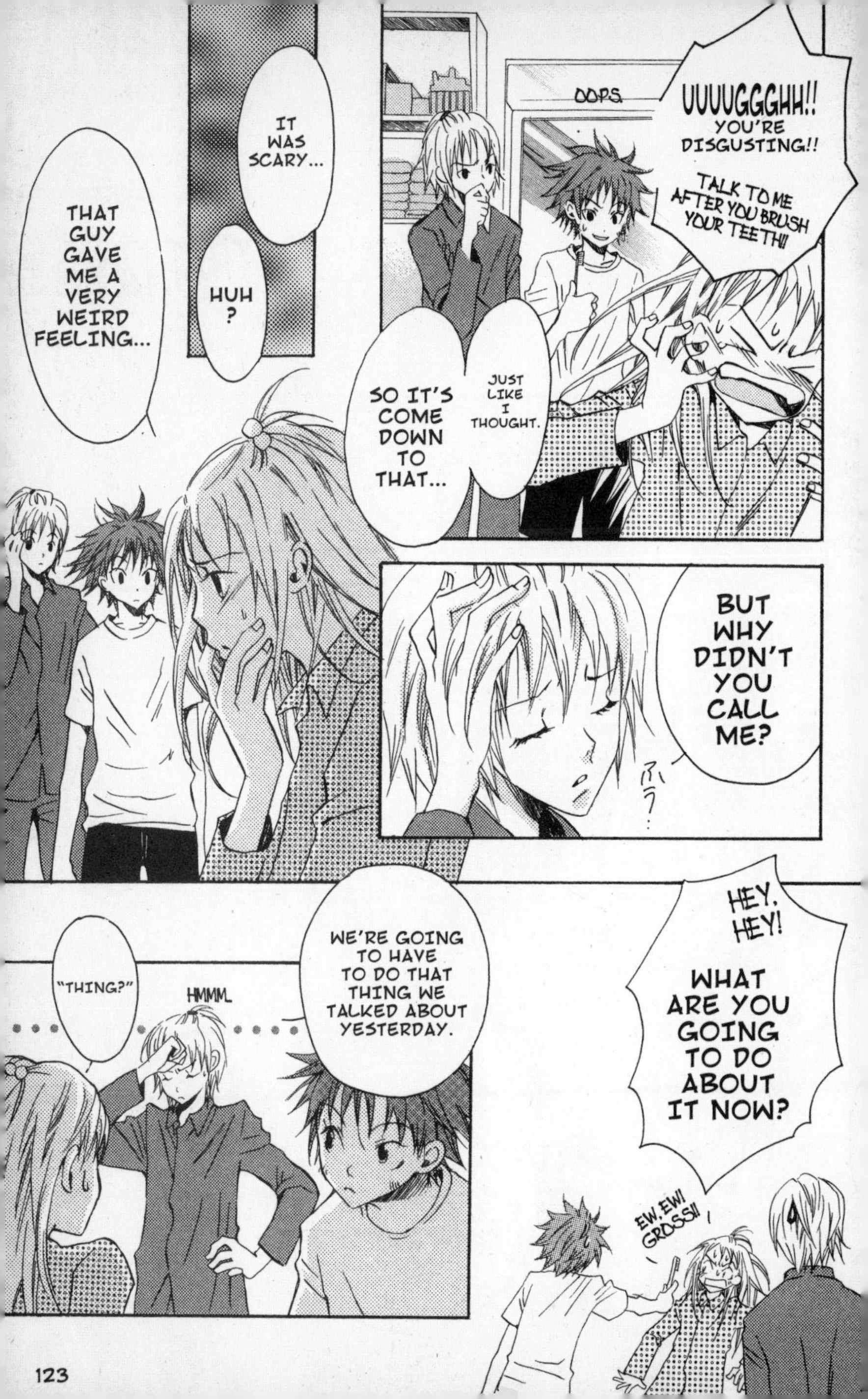
UUUUGGGHH!! YOU'RE DISGUSTING!!
TALK TO ME AFTER YOU BRUSH YOUR TEETH!!
OOPS.
BUT WHY DIDN'T YOU CALL ME?
フラ…
IT WAS SCARY...
HUH?
THAT GUY GAVE ME A VERY WEIRD FEELING...
JUST LIKE I THOUGHT.
SO IT'S COME DOWN TO THAT...
HEY, HEY!
WHAT ARE YOU GOING TO DO ABOUT IT NOW?
EW, EW! GROSS!!
WE'RE GOING TO HAVE TO DO THAT THING WE TALKED ABOUT YESTERDAY.
"THING?"
HMMM.

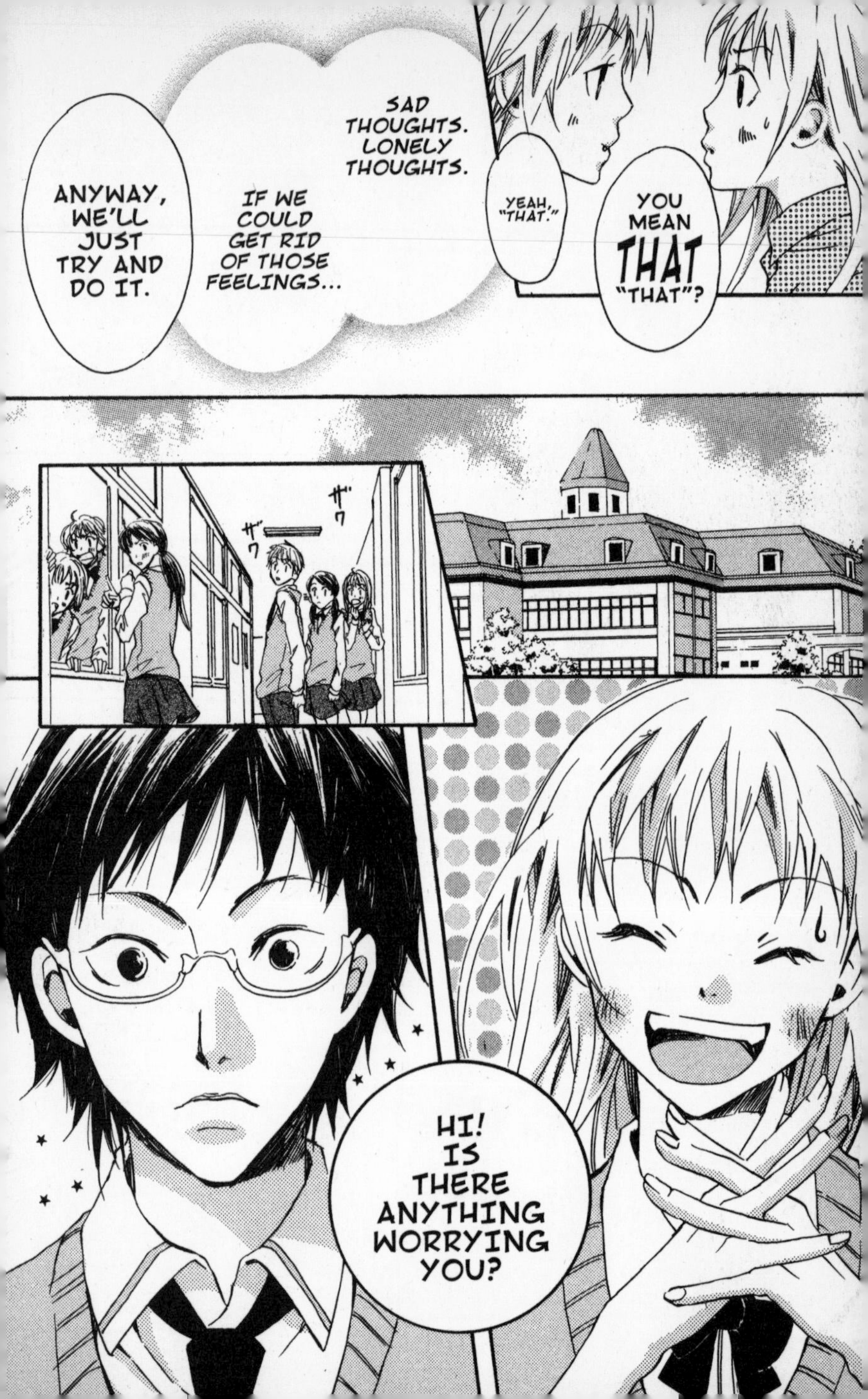
YOU MEAN THAT "THAT"?
YEAH, "THAT."
SAD THOUGHTS. LONELY THOUGHTS.
IF WE COULD GET RID OF THOSE FEELINGS...
ANYWAY, WE'LL JUST TRY AND DO IT.
ザワ
ザワ
HI! IS THERE ANYTHING WORRYING YOU?

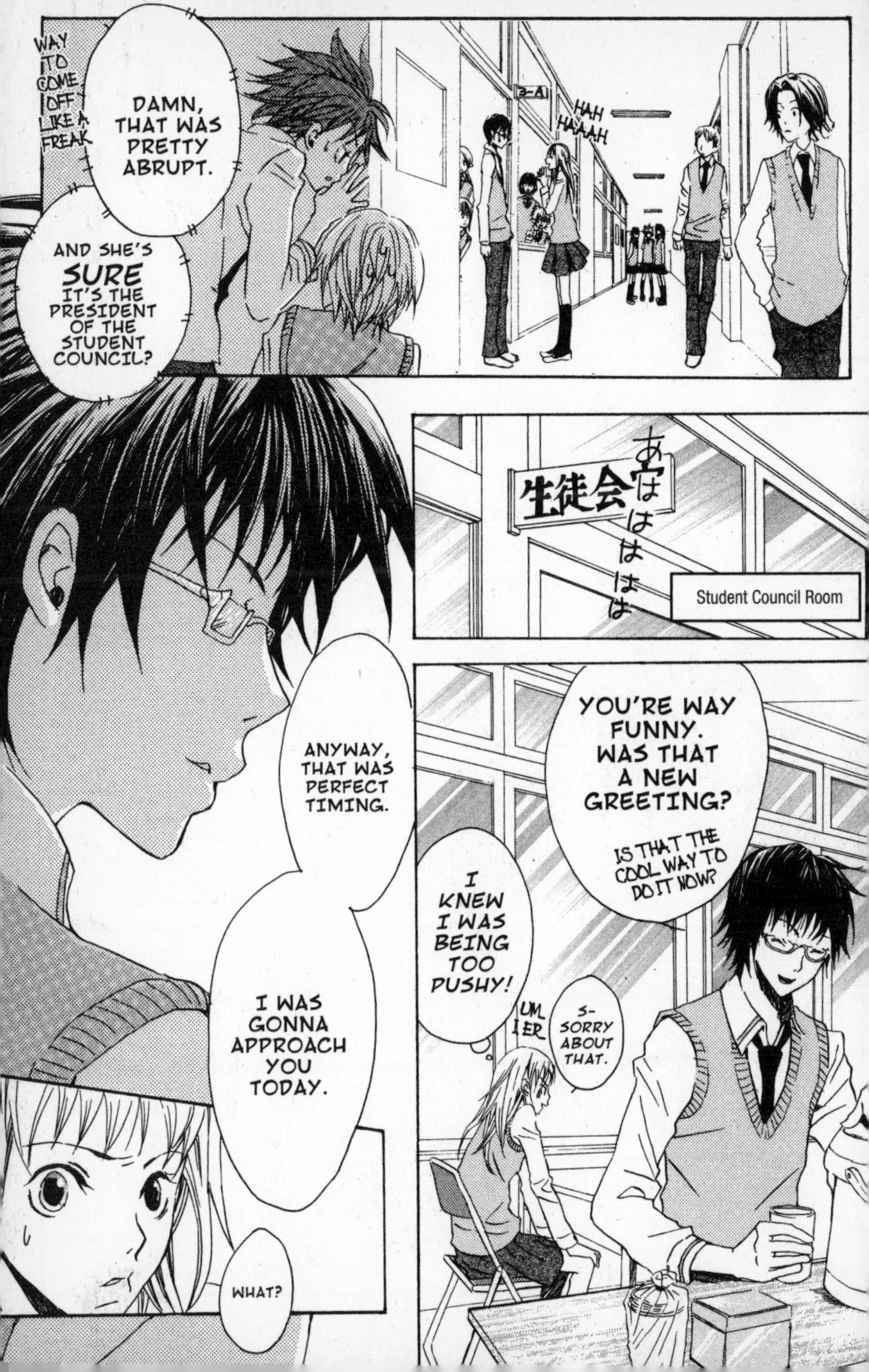
3-A
HAH HAAAH
DAMN, THAT WAS PRETTY ABRUPT.
WAY TO COME OFF LIKE A FREAK
AND SHE'S SURE IT'S THE PRESIDENT OF THE STUDENT COUNCIL?
生徒会
あははははは
Student Council Room
YOU'RE WAY FUNNY. WAS THAT A NEW GREETING?
IS THAT THE COOL WAY TO DO IT NOW?
I KNEW I WAS BEING TOO PUSHY!
UM ER
S-SORRY ABOUT THAT.
ANYWAY, THAT WAS PERFECT TIMING.
I WAS GONNA APPROACH YOU TODAY.
WHAT?

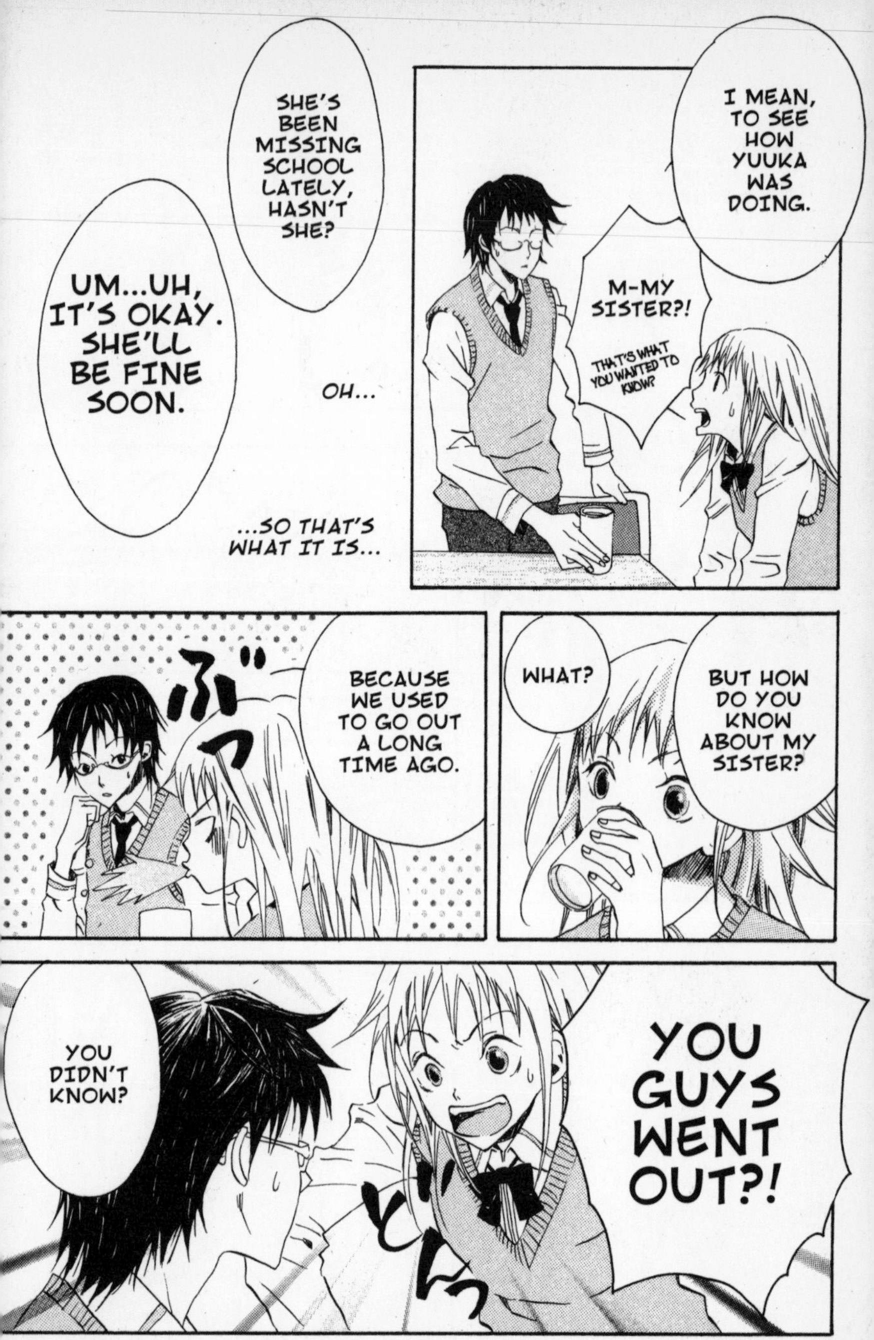
I MEAN, TO SEE HOW YUUKA WAS DOING.
M-MY SISTER?!
THAT'S WHAT YOU WANTED TO KNOW?
SHE'S BEEN MISSING SCHOOL LATELY, HASN'T SHE?
UM...UH, IT'S OKAY. SHE'LL BE FINE SOON.
OH...
...SO THAT'S WHAT IT IS...
BUT HOW DO YOU KNOW ABOUT MY SISTER?
WHAT?
BECAUSE WE USED TO GO OUT A LONG TIME AGO.
ぶっ
YOU GUYS WENT OUT?!
YOU DIDN'T KNOW?

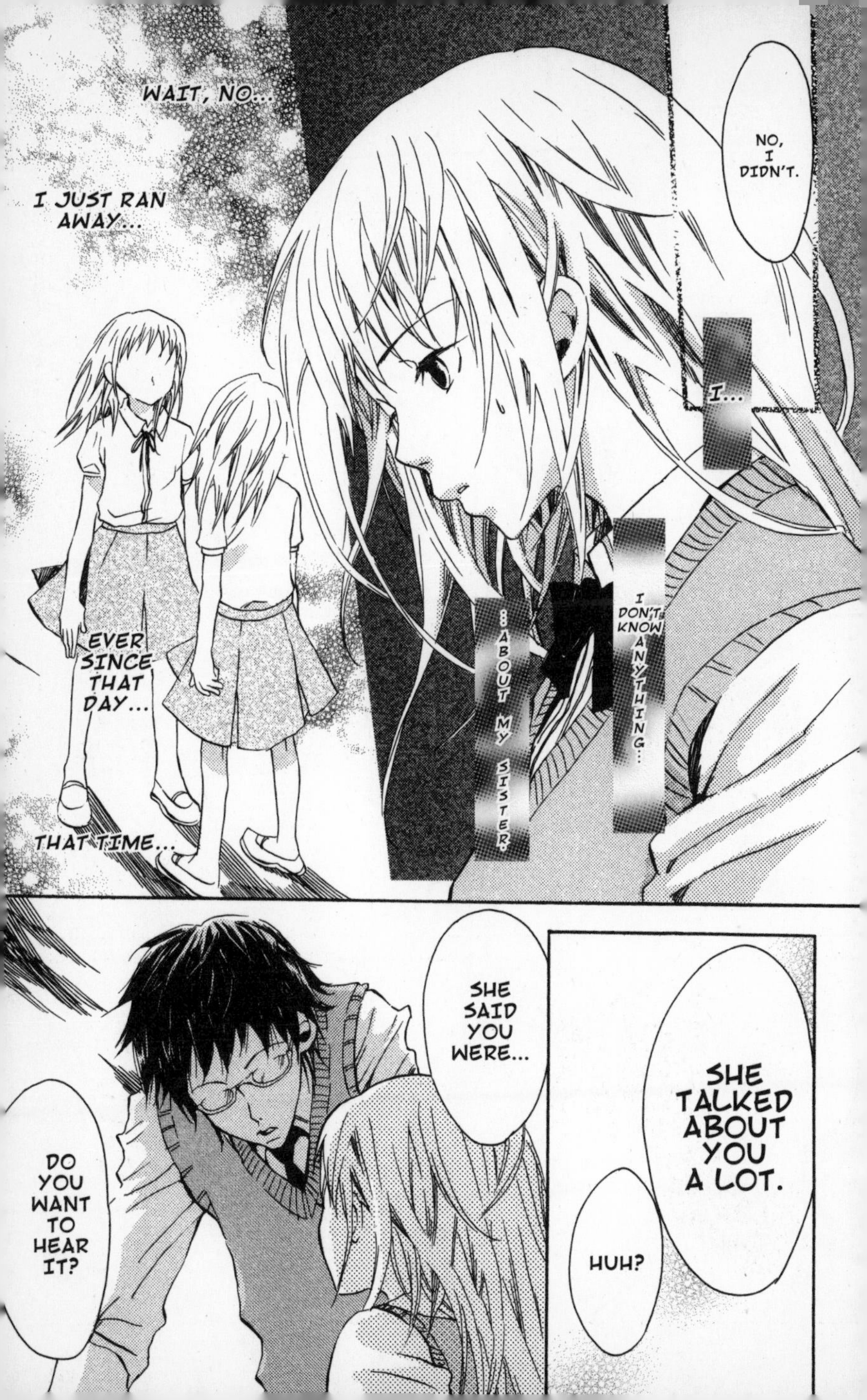
NO, I DIDN'T.
I...
I DON'T KNOW ANYTHING...
...ABOUT MY SISTER.
WAIT, NO...
I JUST RAN AWAY...
EVER SINCE THAT DAY...
THAT TIME...
SHE TALKED ABOUT YOU A LOT.
HUH?
SHE SAID YOU WERE...
DO YOU WANT TO HEAR IT?

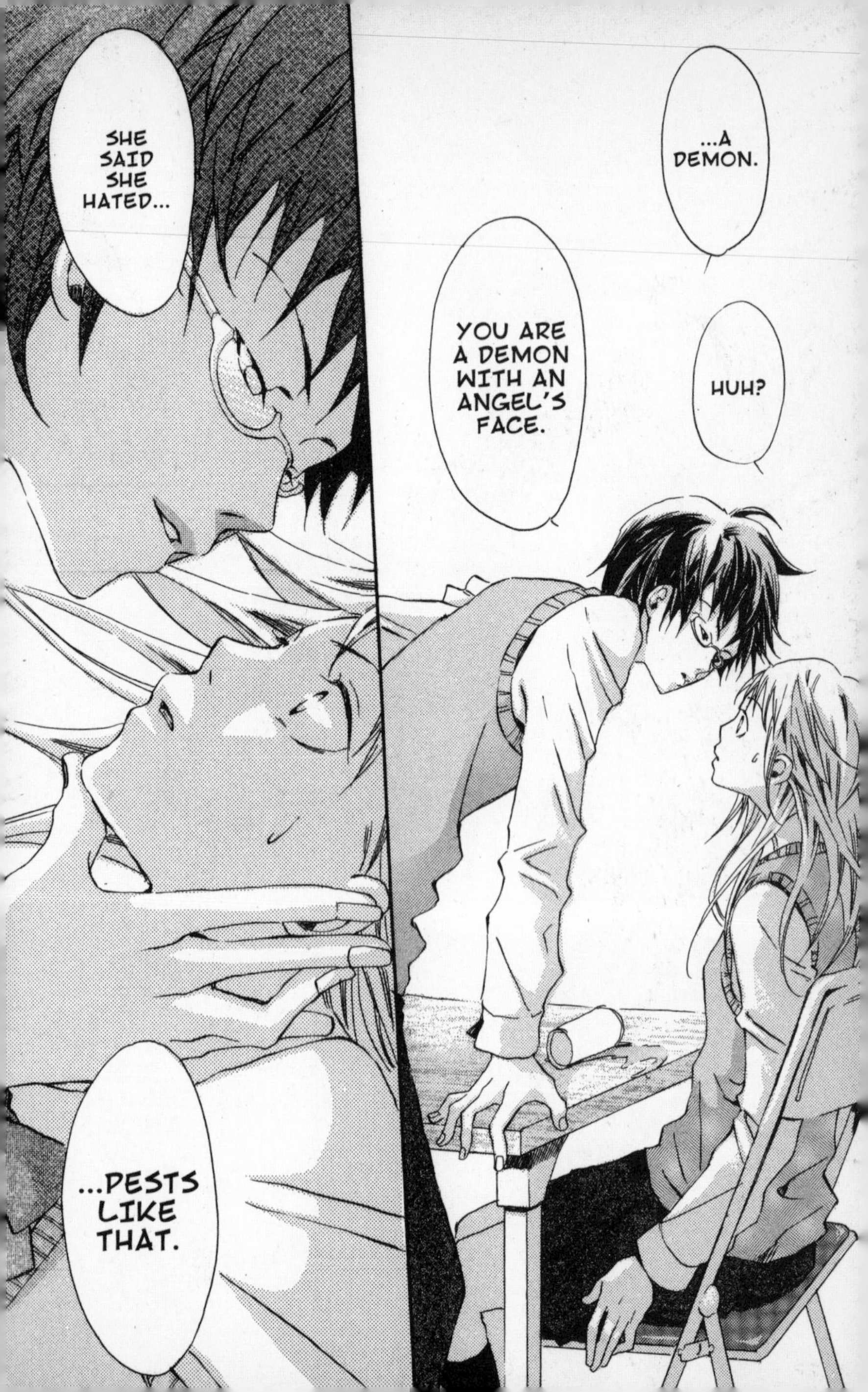
...A DEMON.
HUH?
YOU ARE A DEMON WITH AN ANGEL'S FACE.
SHE SAID SHE HATED...
...PESTS LIKE THAT.

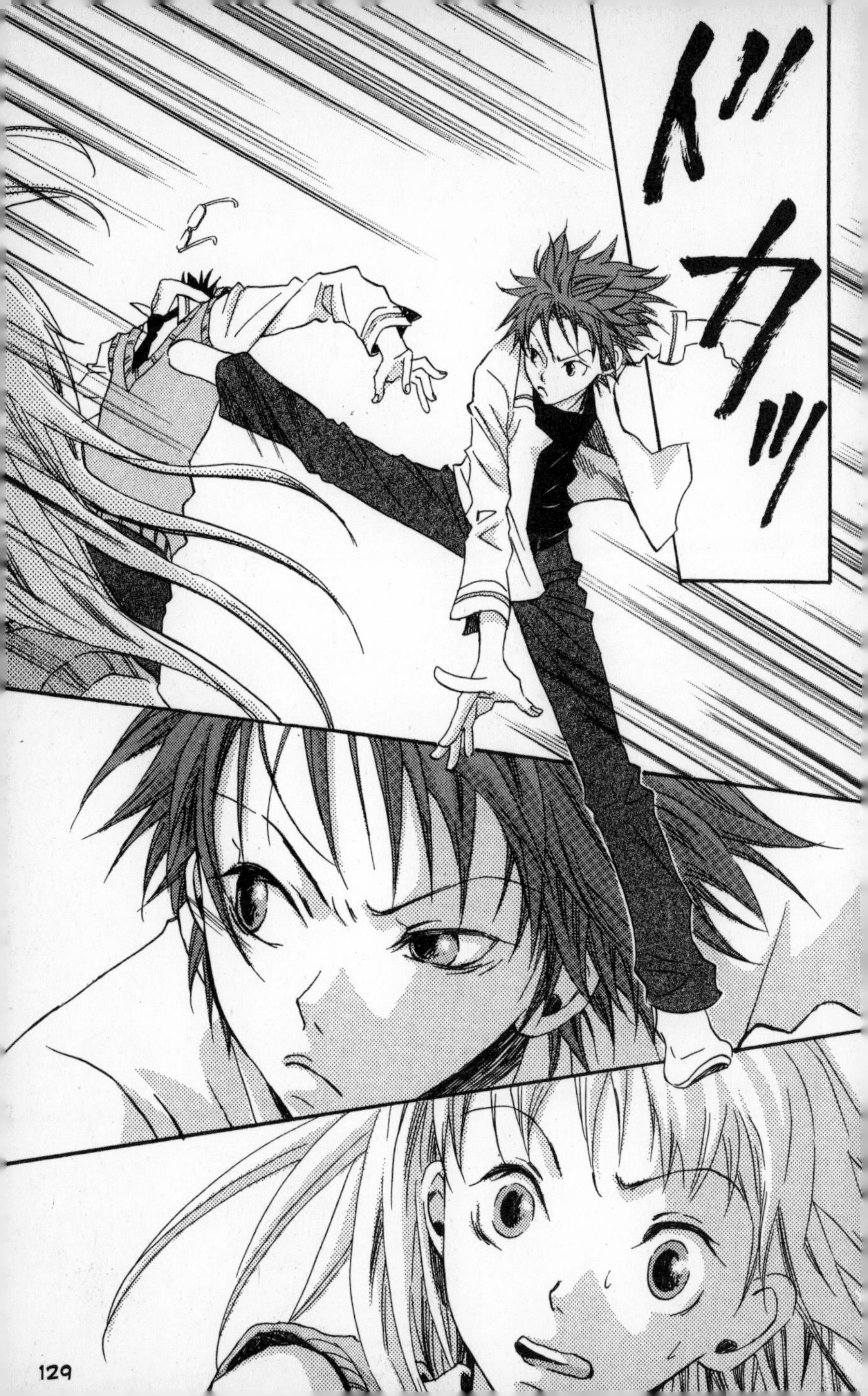
ドカッ

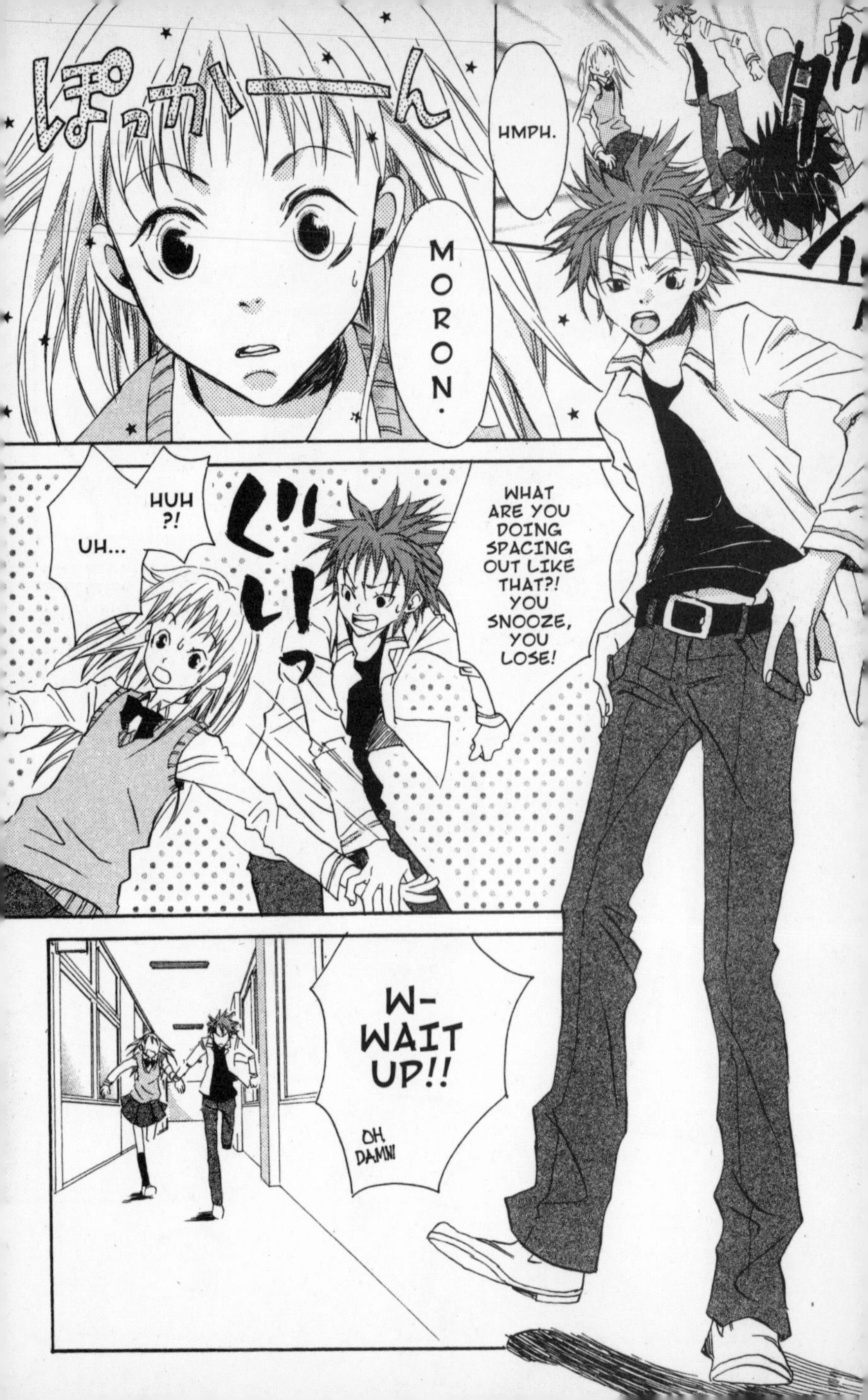
HMPH.
ぽっかーーん
MORON.
WHAT ARE YOU DOING SPACING OUT LIKE THAT?! YOU SNOOZE, YOU LOSE!
ぐいっ
HUH?!
UH...
W-WAIT UP!!
OH, DAMN!

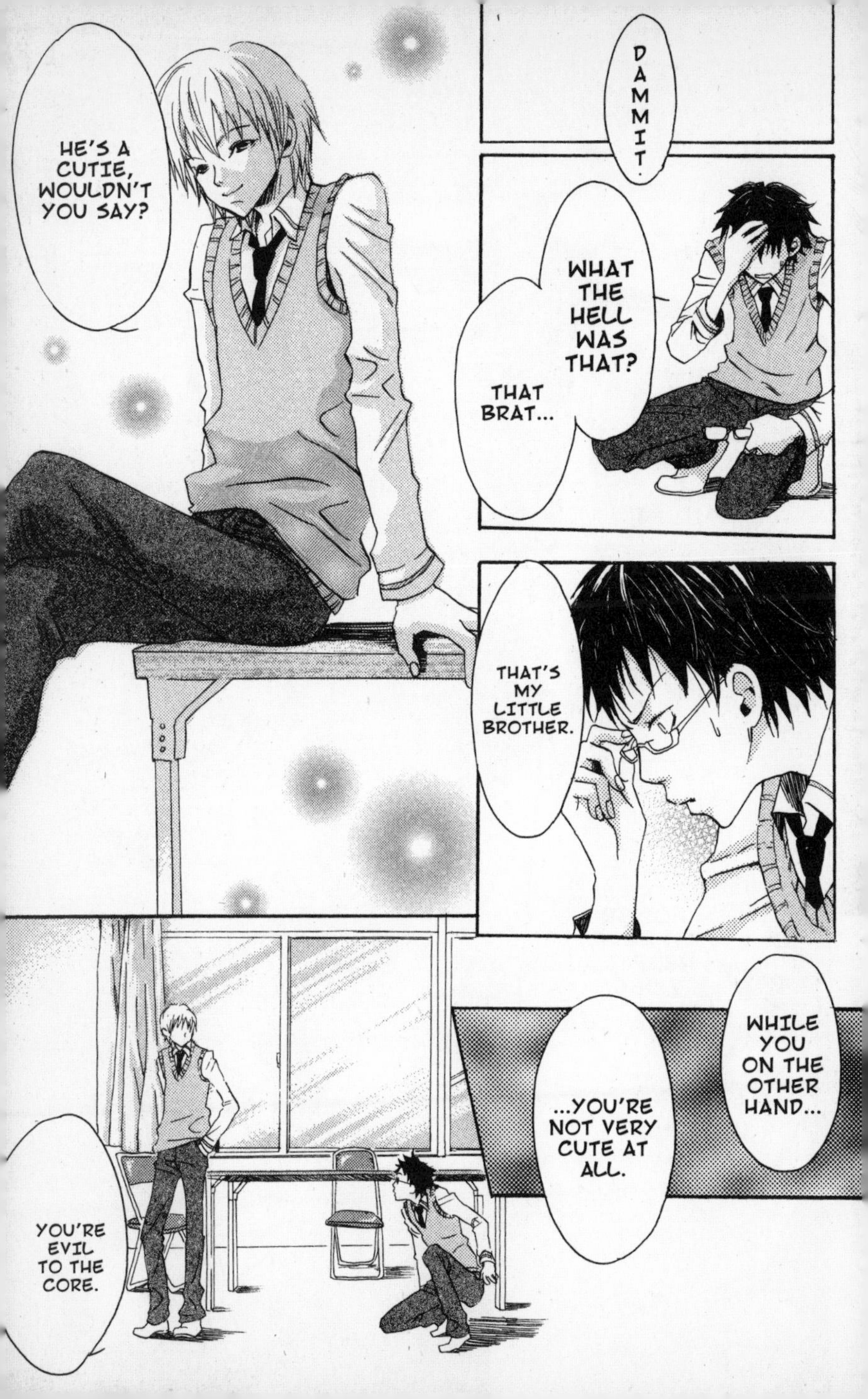
DAMMIT.
WHAT THE HELL WAS THAT?
THAT BRAT...
THAT'S MY LITTLE BROTHER.
HE'S A CUTIE, WOULDN'T YOU SAY?
WHILE YOU ON THE OTHER HAND...
...YOU'RE NOT VERY CUTE AT ALL.
YOU'RE EVIL TO THE CORE.

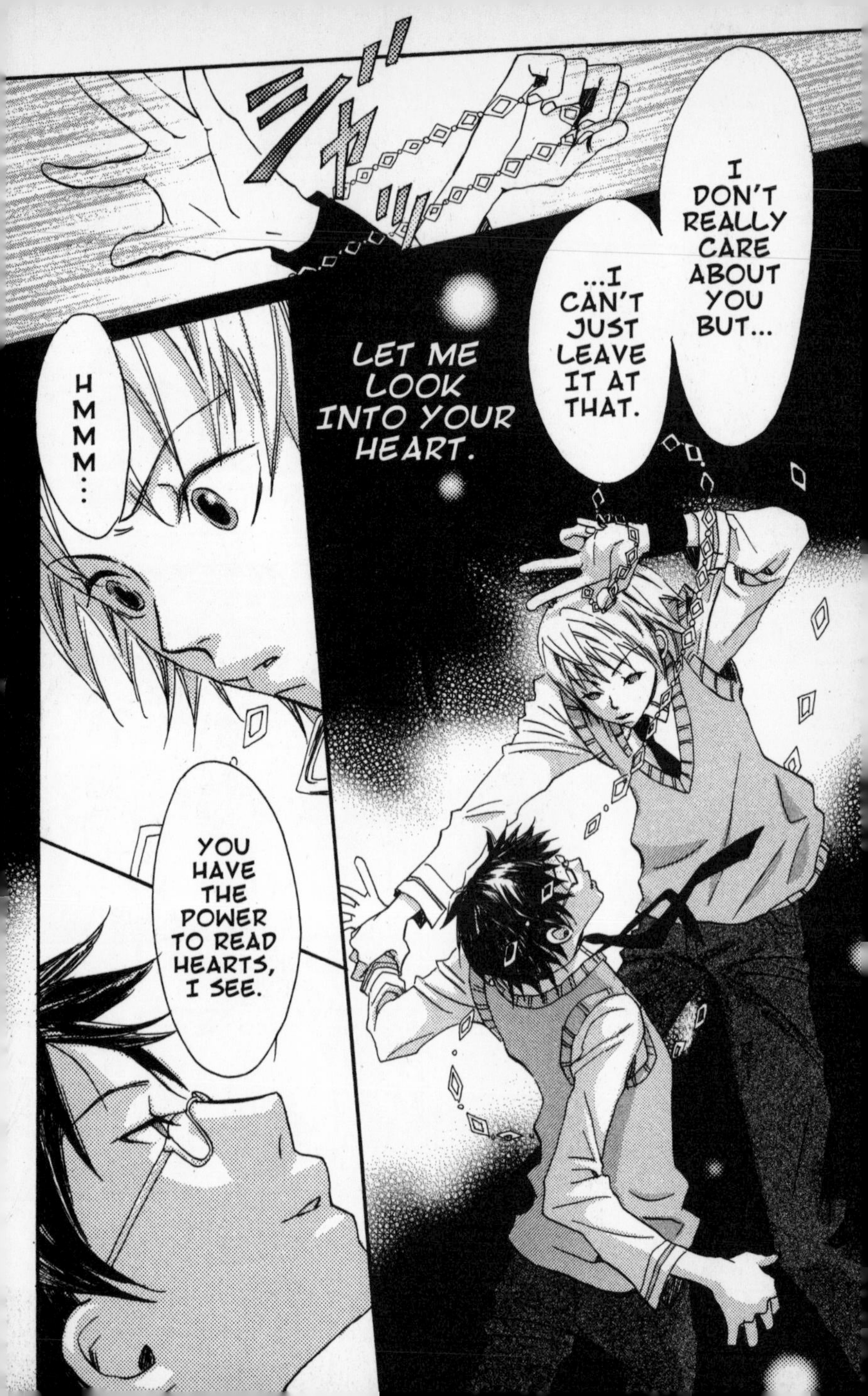
I DON'T REALLY CARE ABOUT YOU BUT...
...I CAN'T JUST LEAVE IT AT THAT.
LET ME LOOK INTO YOUR HEART.
HMMM...
YOU HAVE THE POWER TO READ HEARTS, I SEE.

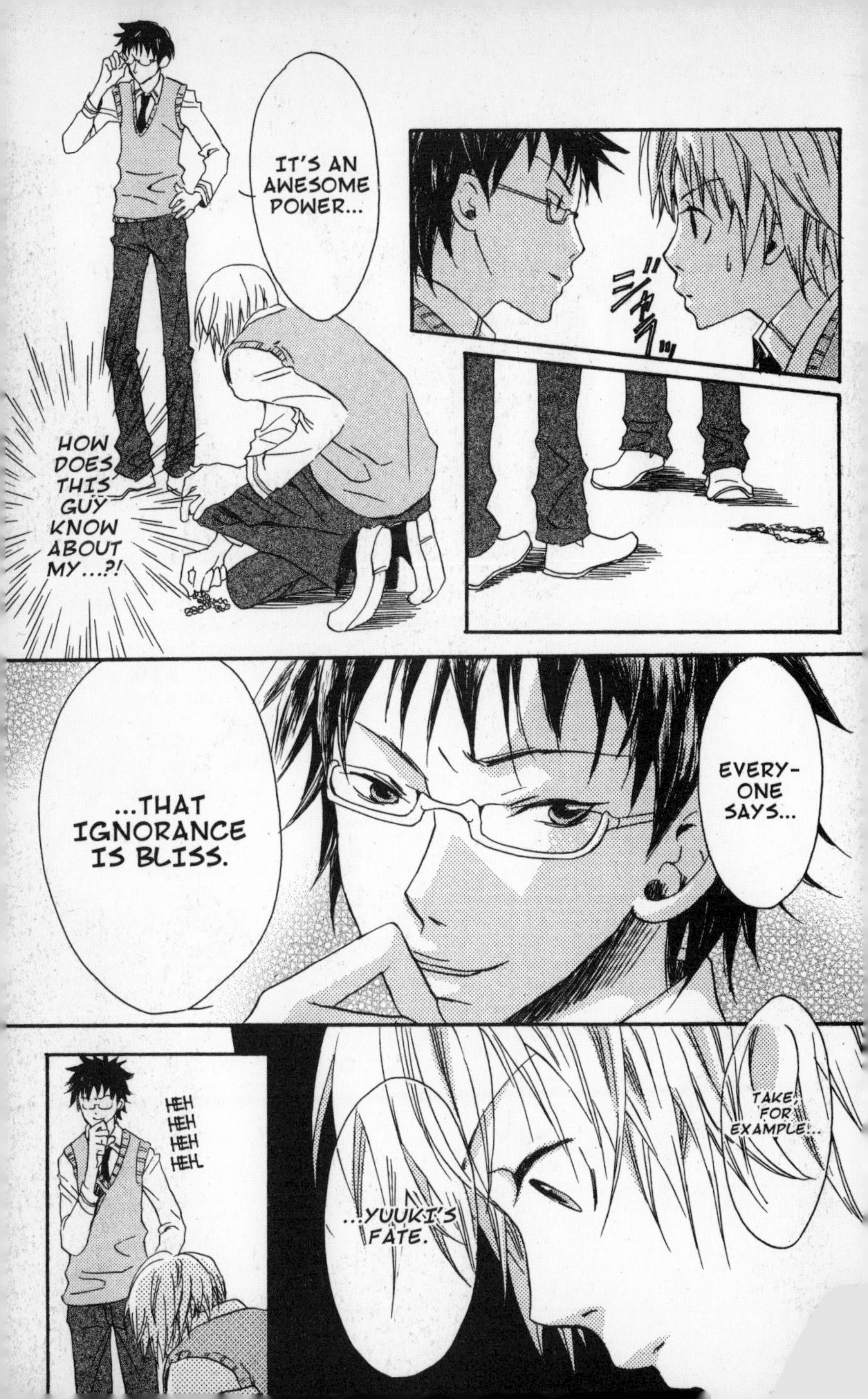
IT'S AN AWESOME POWER...
HOW DOES THIS GUY KNOW ABOUT MY...?!
EVERY-ONE SAYS...
...THAT IGNORANCE IS BLISS.
TAKE FOR EXAMPLE...
...YUUKI'S FATE.
HEH HEH HEH HEH

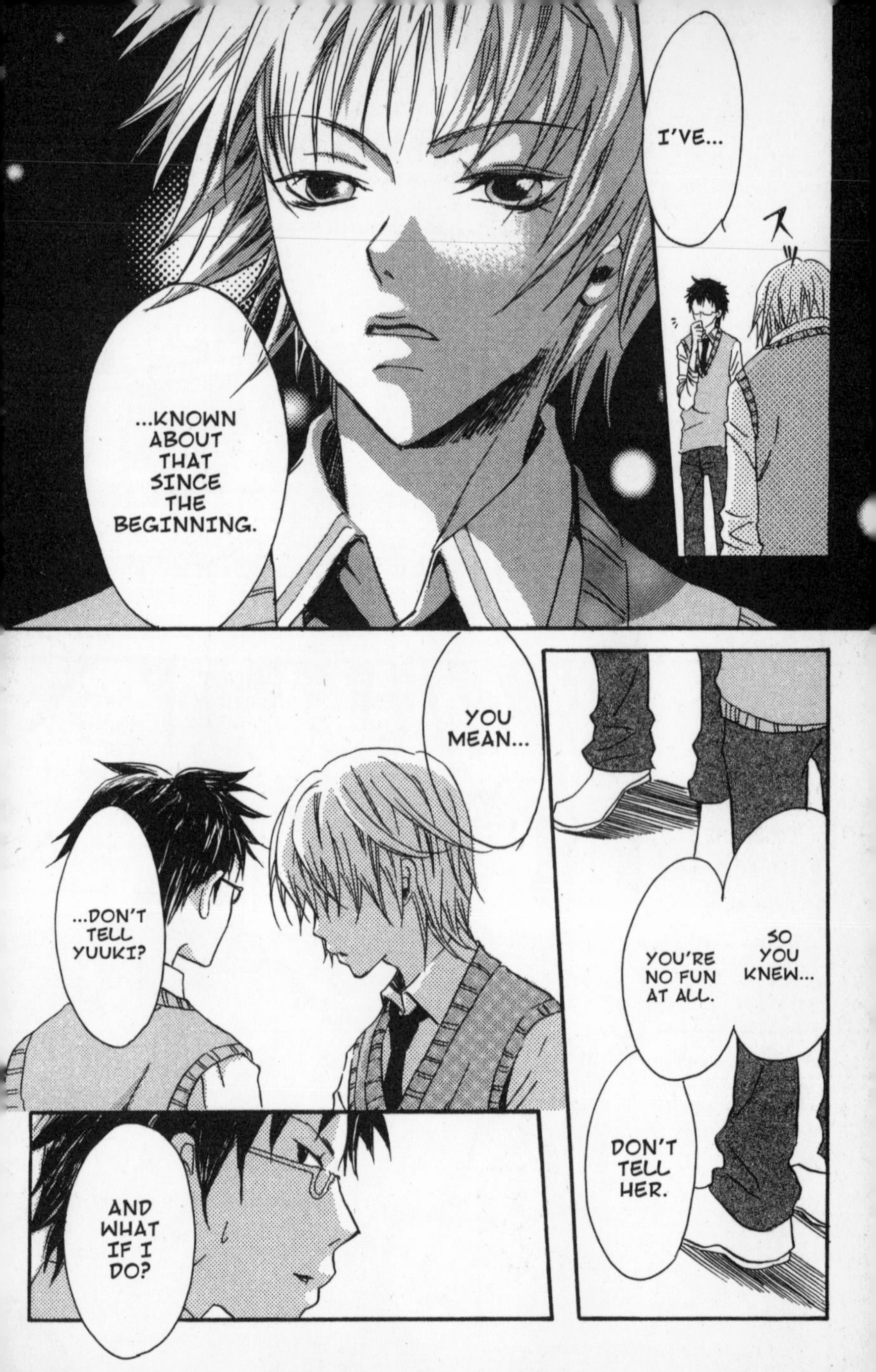
I'VE...
ス
...KNOWN ABOUT THAT SINCE THE BEGINNING.
SO YOU KNEW...
YOU'RE NO FUN AT ALL.
DON'T TELL HER.
YOU MEAN...
...DON'T TELL YUUKI?
AND WHAT IF I DO?

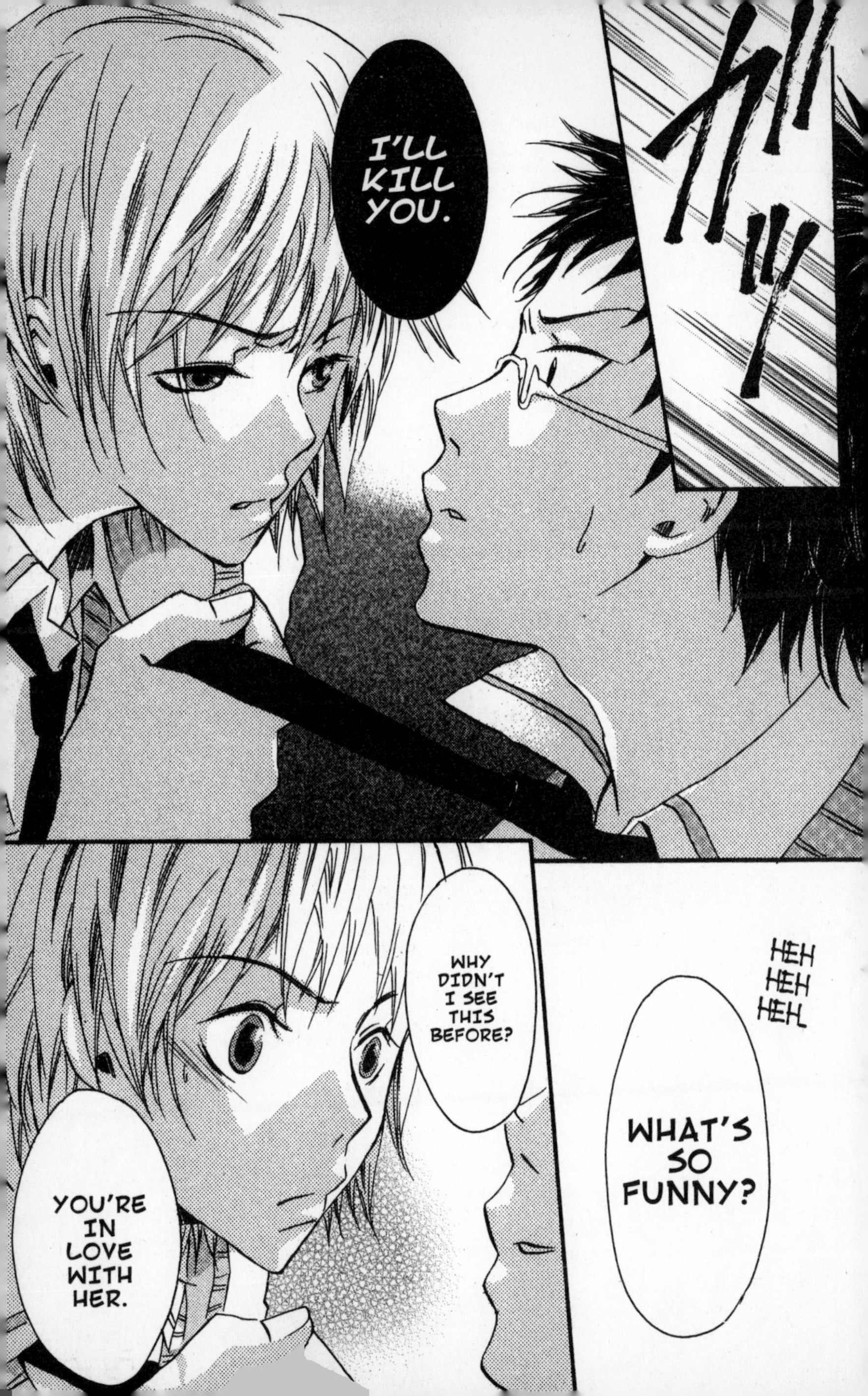
I'LL KILL YOU.
HEH HEH HEH
WHAT'S SO FUNNY?
WHY DIDN'T I SEE THIS BEFORE?
YOU'RE IN LOVE WITH HER.

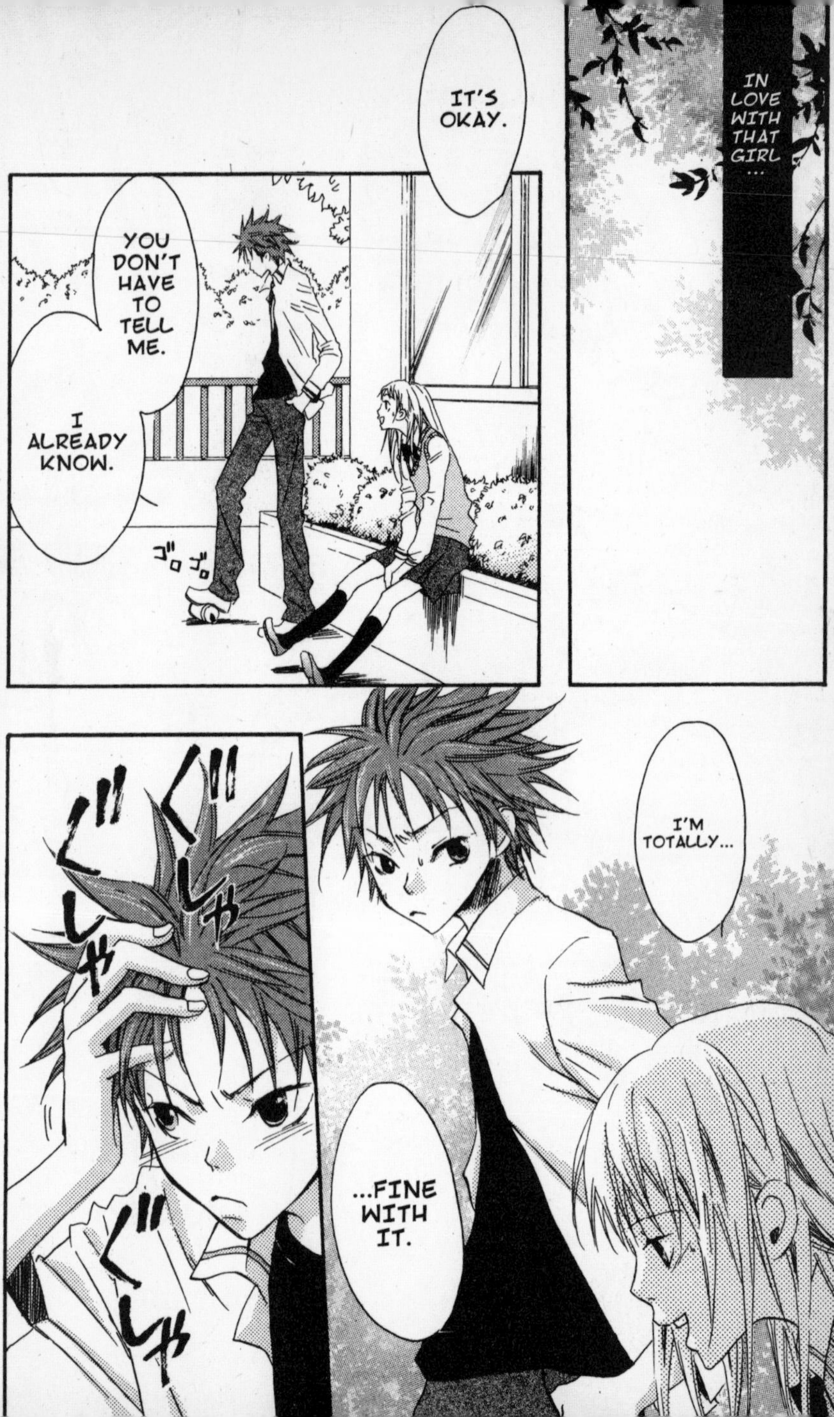
IN LOVE WITH THAT GIRL...
IT'S OKAY.
YOU DON'T HAVE TO TELL ME.
I ALREADY KNOW.
ゴロゴロ
I'M TOTALLY...
...FINE WITH IT.
ぐしゃぐしゃ
ぐしゃぐしゃ

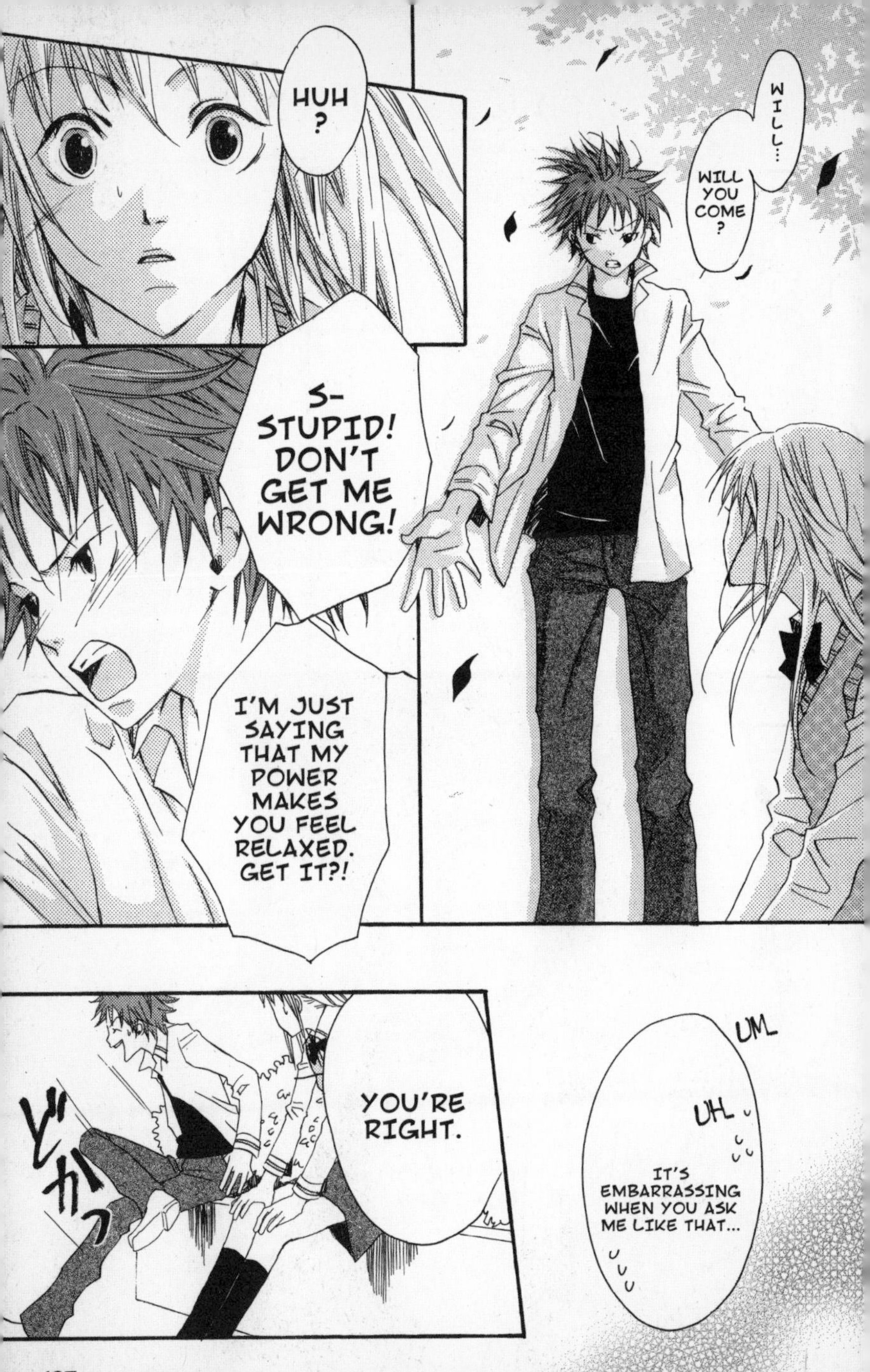
WILL...
WILL YOU COME?
HUH?
S-STUPID! DON'T GET ME WRONG!
I'M JUST SAYING THAT MY POWER MAKES YOU FEEL RELAXED. GET IT?!
UM
UH
IT'S EMBARRASSING WHEN YOU ASK ME LIKE THAT...
YOU'RE RIGHT.
どかっ

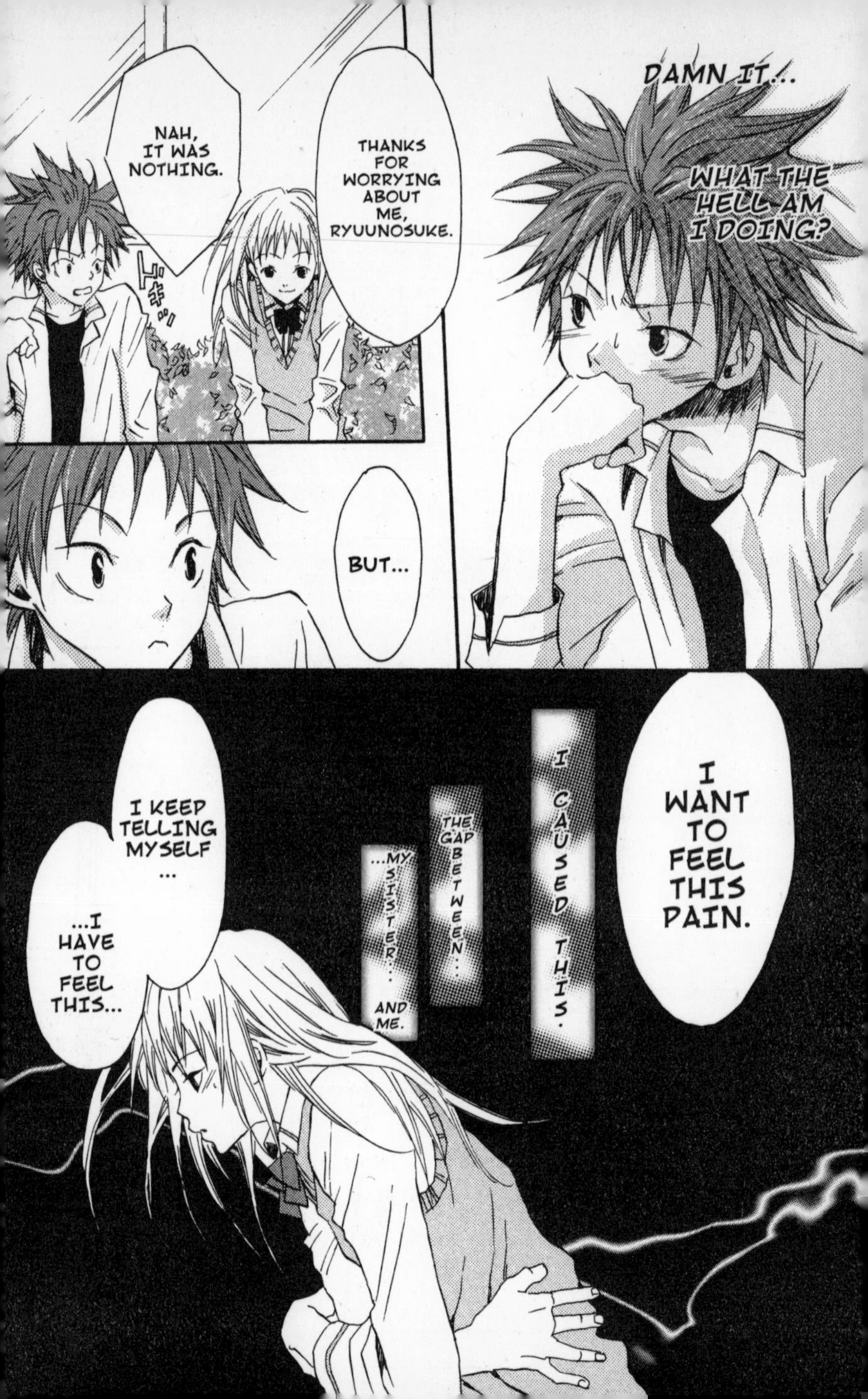
DAMN IT...
WHAT THE HELL AM I DOING?
THANKS FOR WORRYING ABOUT ME, RYUUNOSUKE.
NAH, IT WAS NOTHING.
BUT...
I WANT TO FEEL THIS PAIN.
I CAUSED THIS.
THE GAP BETWEEN...
...MY SISTER... AND ME.
I KEEP TELLING MYSELF ...
...I HAVE TO FEEL THIS...

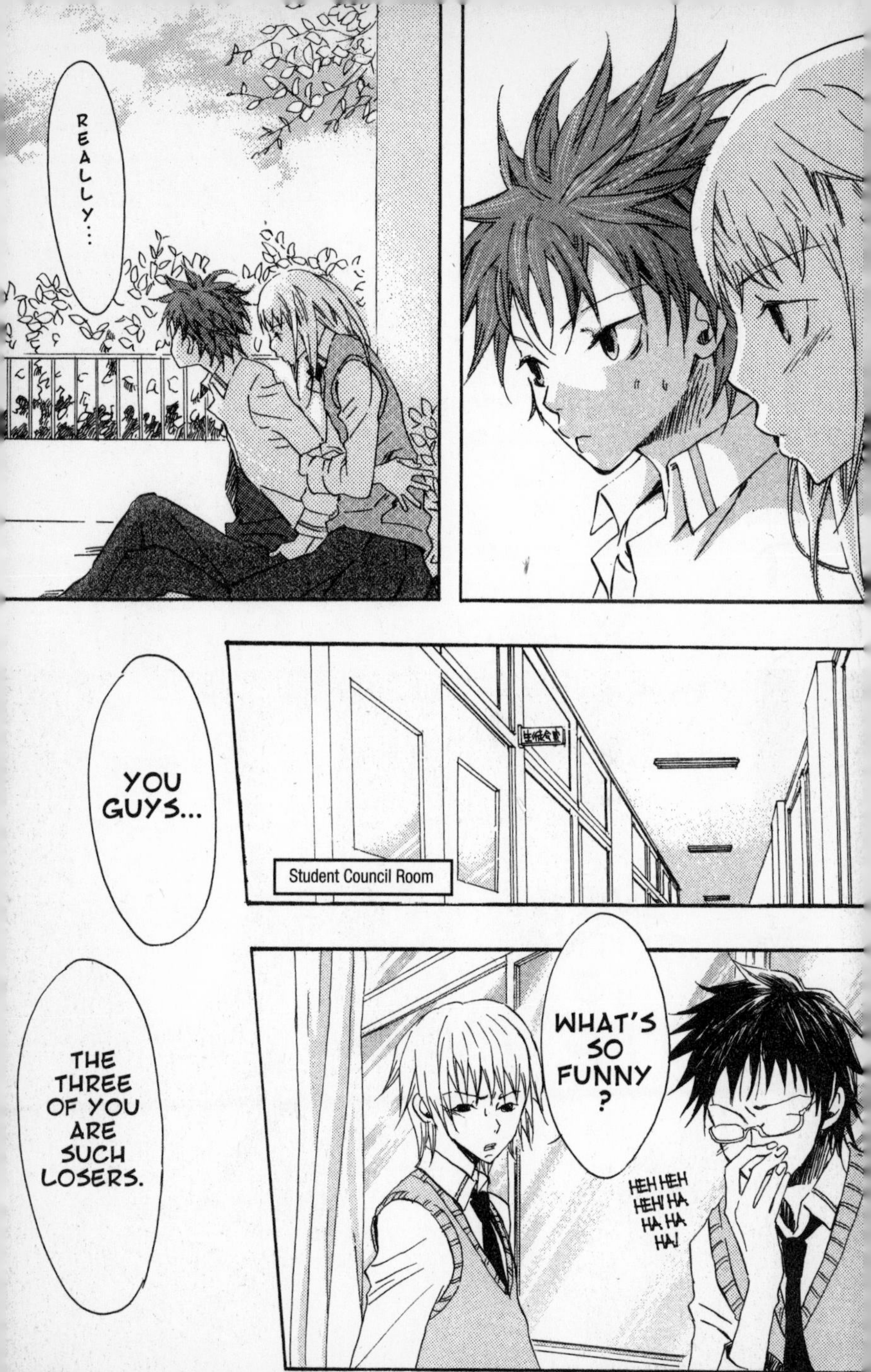
REALLY...
Student Council Room
WHAT'S SO FUNNY?
HEH HEH HEH! HA HA HA HA!
YOU GUYS...
THE THREE OF YOU ARE SUCH LOSERS.

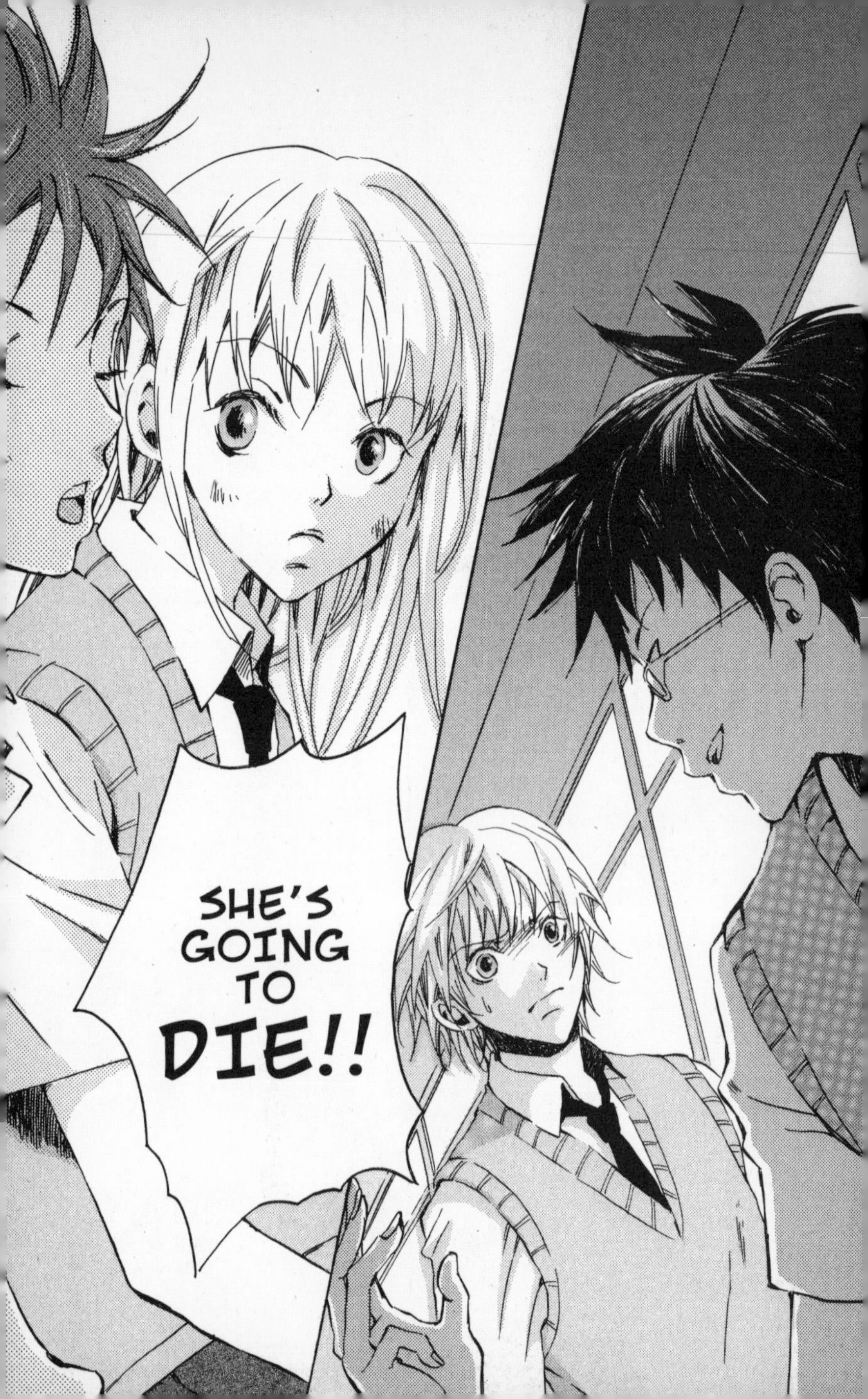
SHE'S GOING TO DIE!!

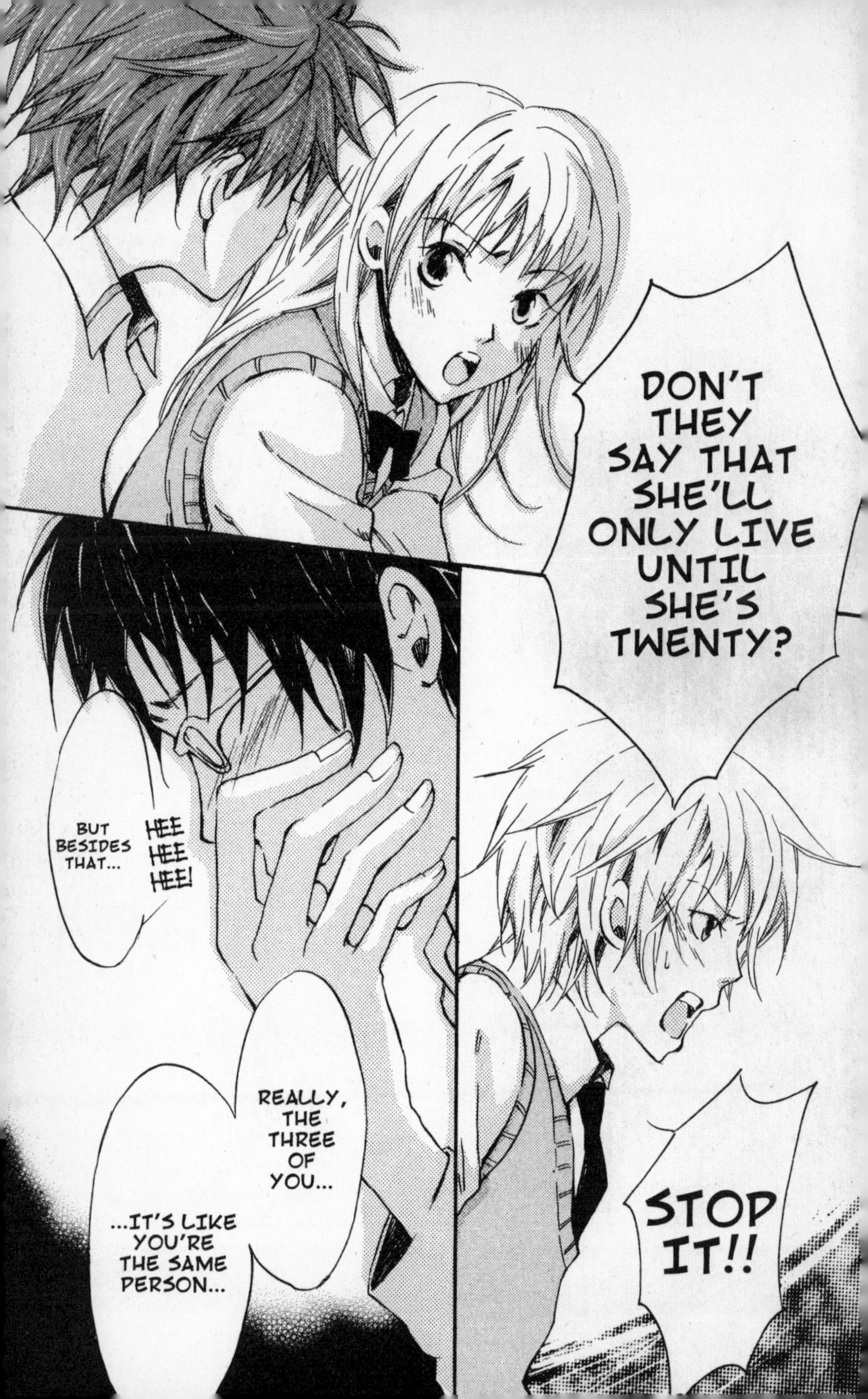
DON'T THEY SAY THAT SHE'LL ONLY LIVE UNTIL SHE'S TWENTY?
HEE HEE HEE!
BUT BESIDES THAT...
STOP IT!!
REALLY, THE THREE OF YOU...
...IT'S LIKE YOU'RE THE SAME PERSON...

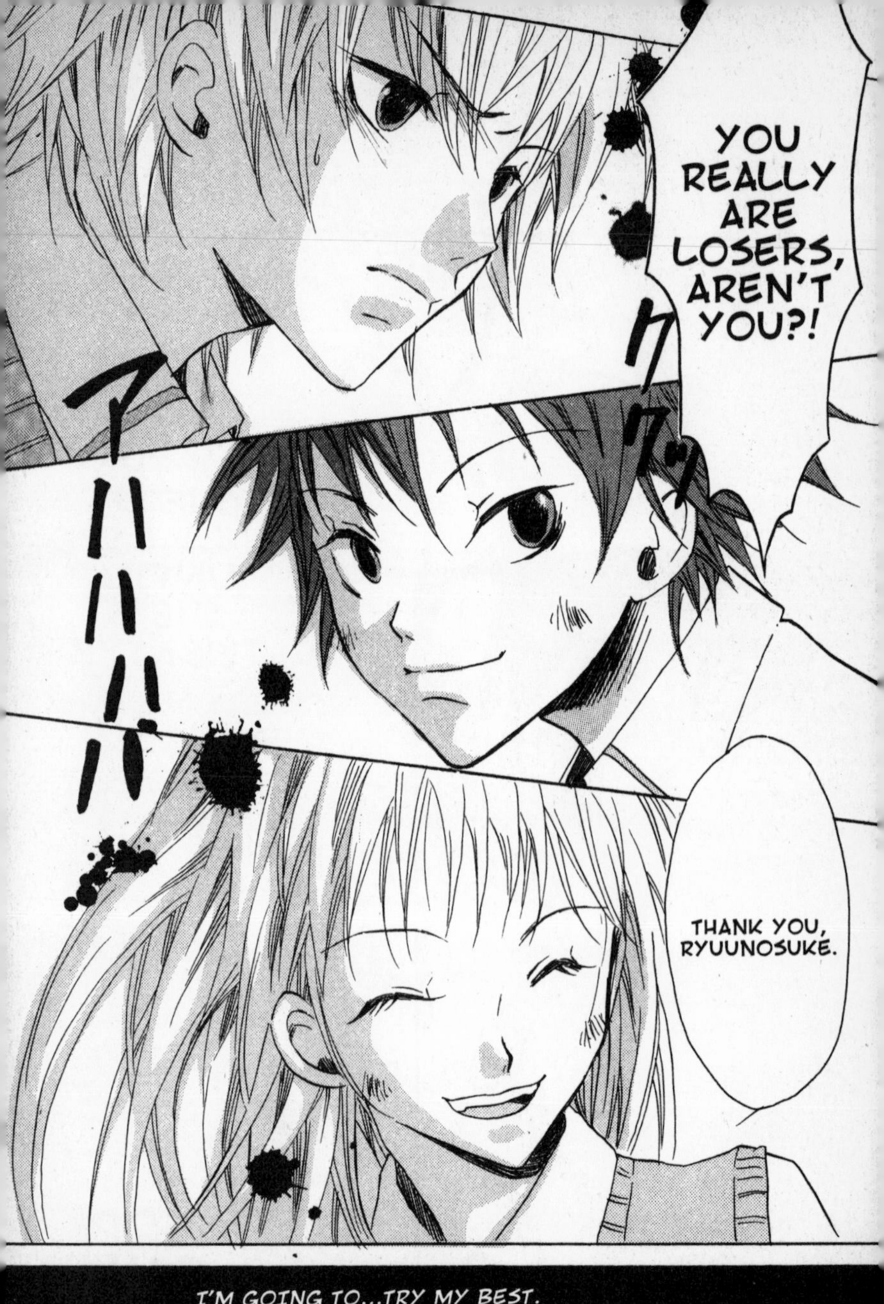
YOU REALLY ARE LOSERS, AREN'T YOU?!
アハハハ
THANK YOU, RYUUNOSUKE.
I'M GOING TO...TRY MY BEST.

* THE FOURTH NIGHT *
THE END

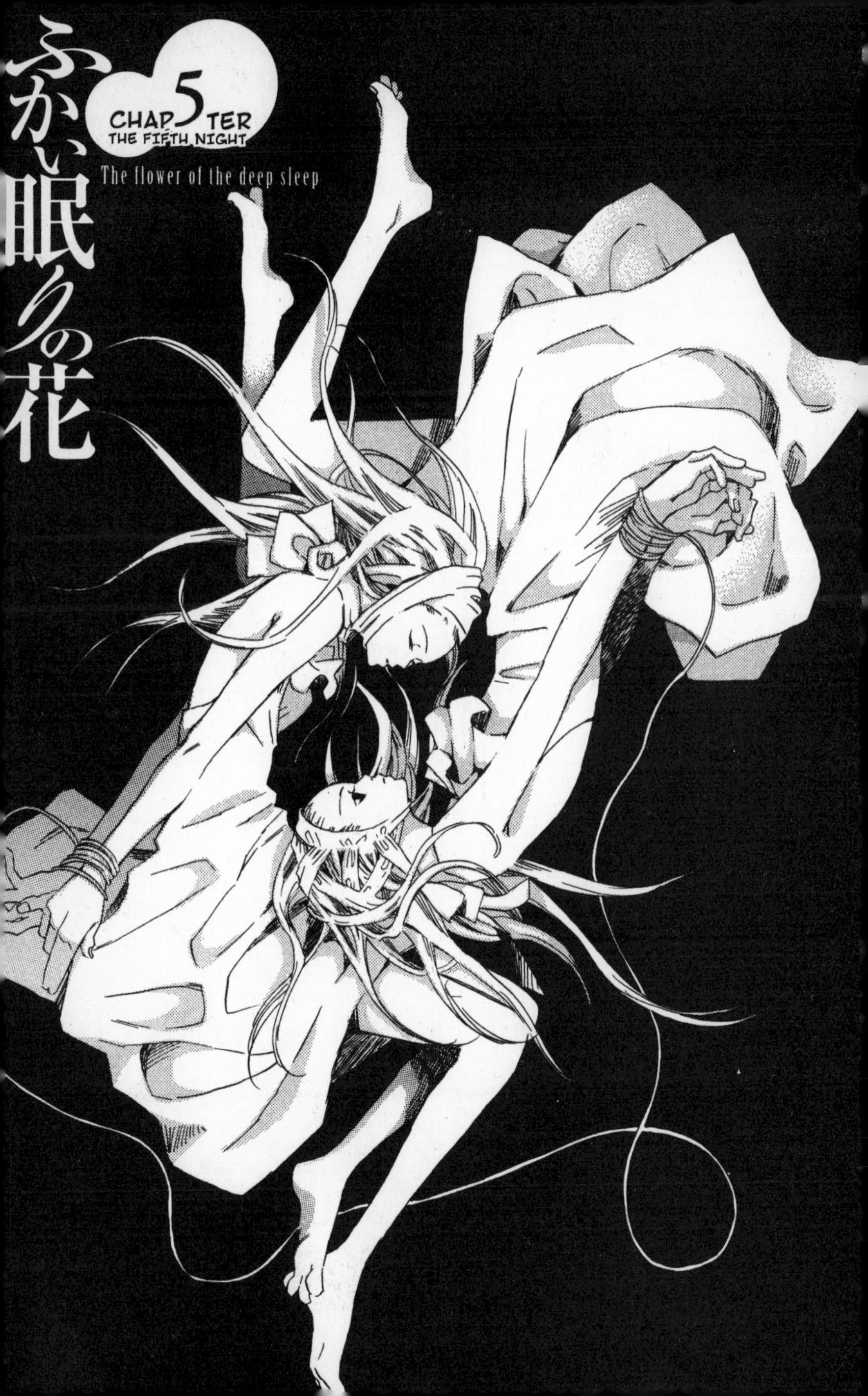
ふかい眠りの花
CHAPTER 5
THE FIFTH NIGHT
The flower of the deep sleep

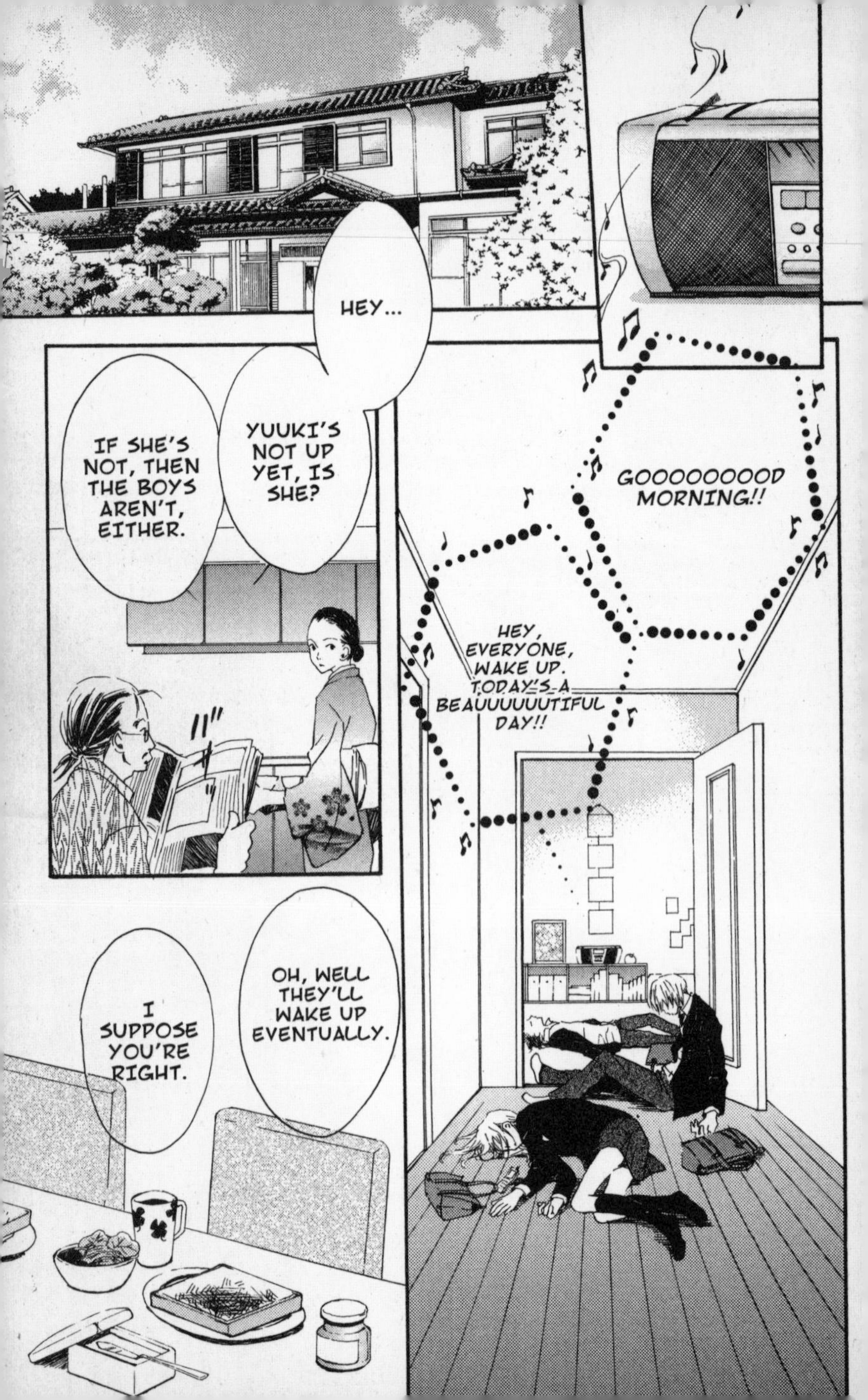
GOOOOOOOOD MORNING!!
HEY, EVERYONE, WAKE UP. TODAY'S A BEAUUUUUUTIFUL DAY!!
HEY...
YUUKI'S NOT UP YET, IS SHE?
IF SHE'S NOT, THEN THE BOYS AREN'T, EITHER.
OH, WELL THEY'LL WAKE UP EVENTUALLY.
I SUPPOSE YOU'RE RIGHT.

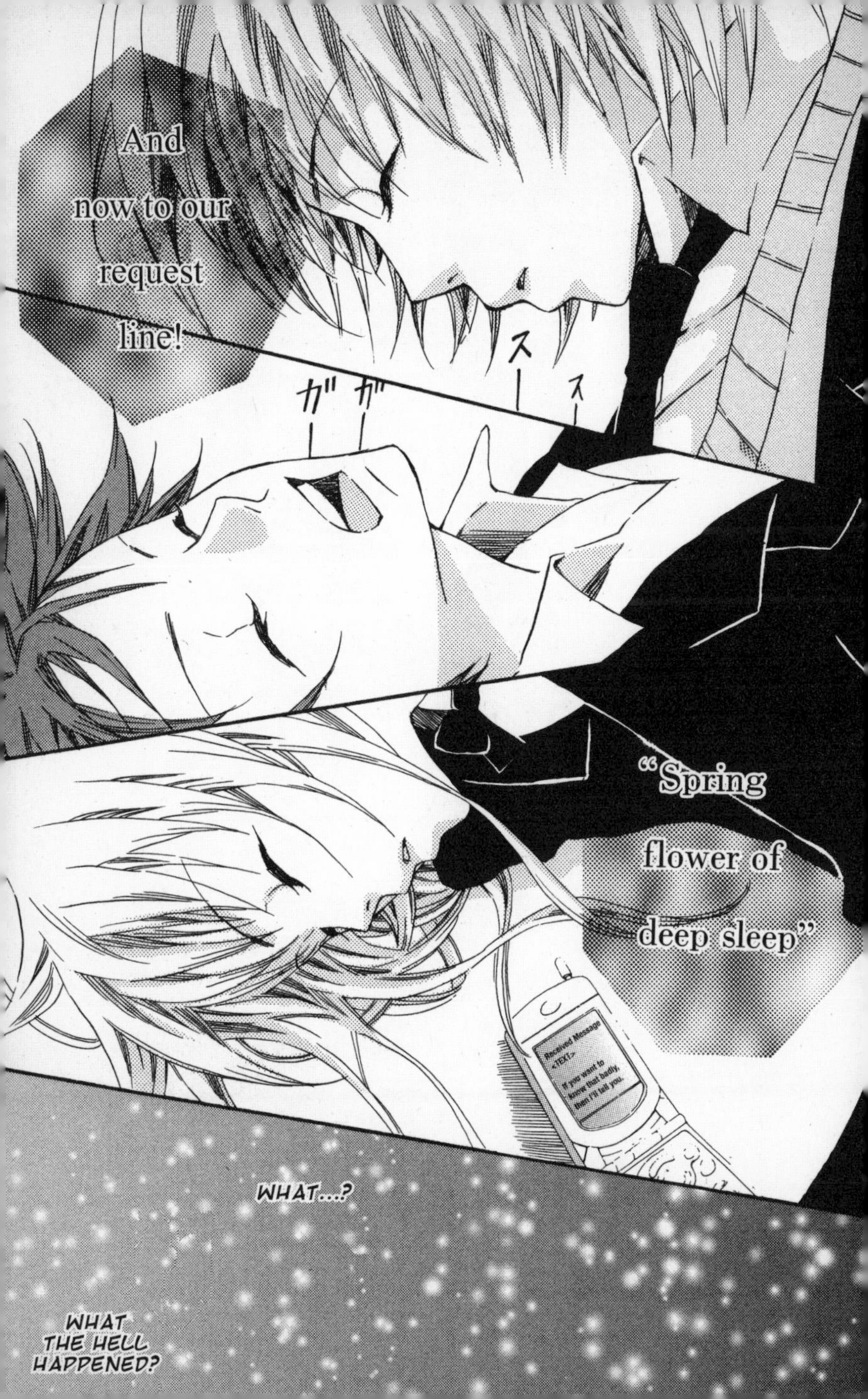
And now to our request line!
スー
スー
ガー
ガー
"Spring flower of deep sleep"
Received Message
<TEXT>
If you want to know that badly, then I'll tell you.
WHAT...?
WHAT THE HELL HAPPENED?

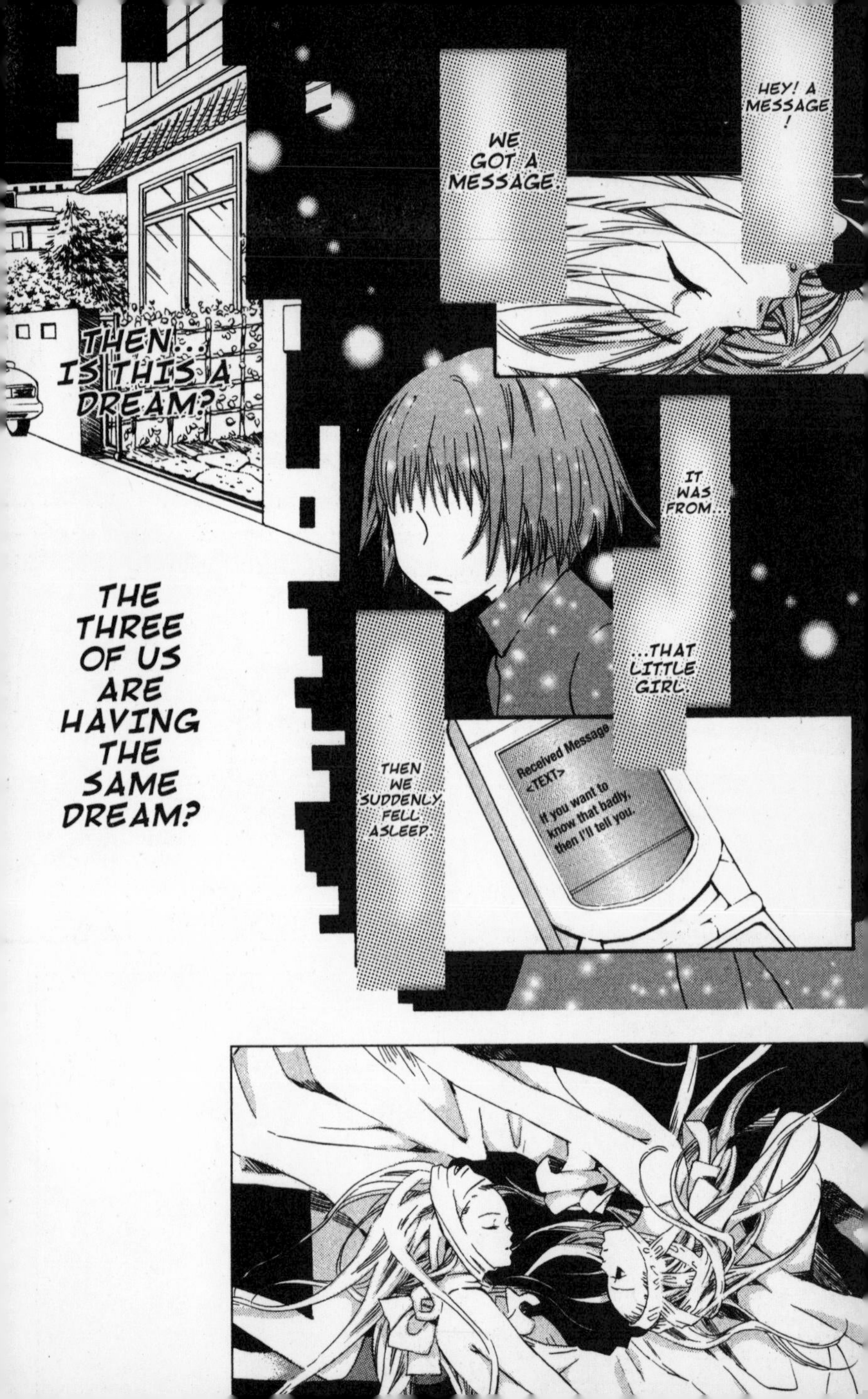
HEY! A MESSAGE!
WE GOT A MESSAGE.
IT WAS FROM...
...THAT LITTLE GIRL.
Received Message
<TEXT>
If you want to know that badly, then I'll tell you.
THEN WE SUDDENLY FELL ASLEEP.
THEN... IS THIS A DREAM?
THE THREE OF US ARE HAVING THE SAME DREAM?

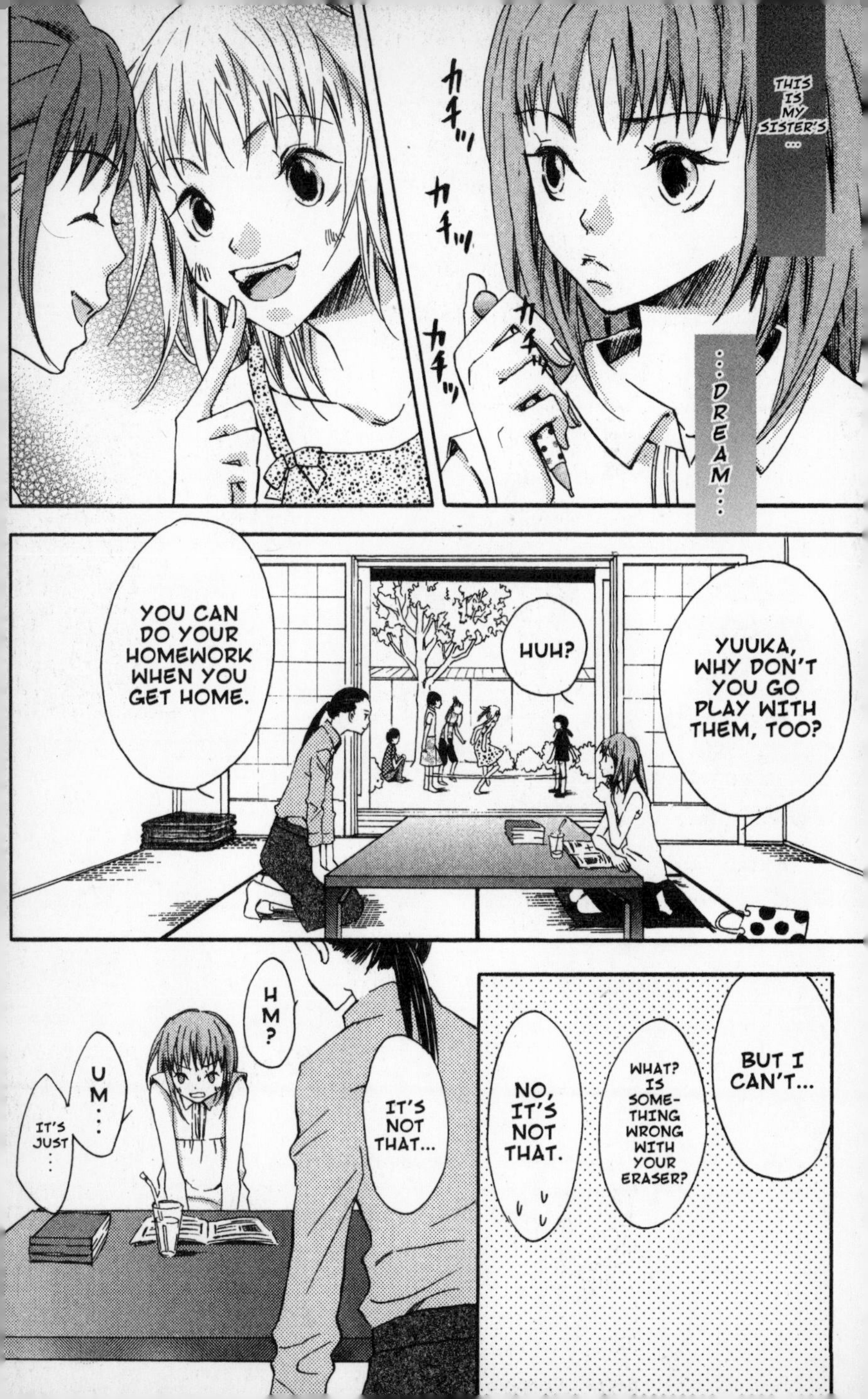
THIS IS MY SISTER'S...
...DREAM...
カチッ
カチッ
カチッ
カチッ
YUUKA, WHY DON'T YOU GO PLAY WITH THEM, TOO?
HUH?
YOU CAN DO YOUR HOMEWORK WHEN YOU GET HOME.
BUT I CAN'T...
WHAT? IS SOMETHING WRONG WITH YOUR ERASER?
NO, IT'S NOT THAT.
IT'S NOT THAT...
HM?
UM...
IT'S JUST...

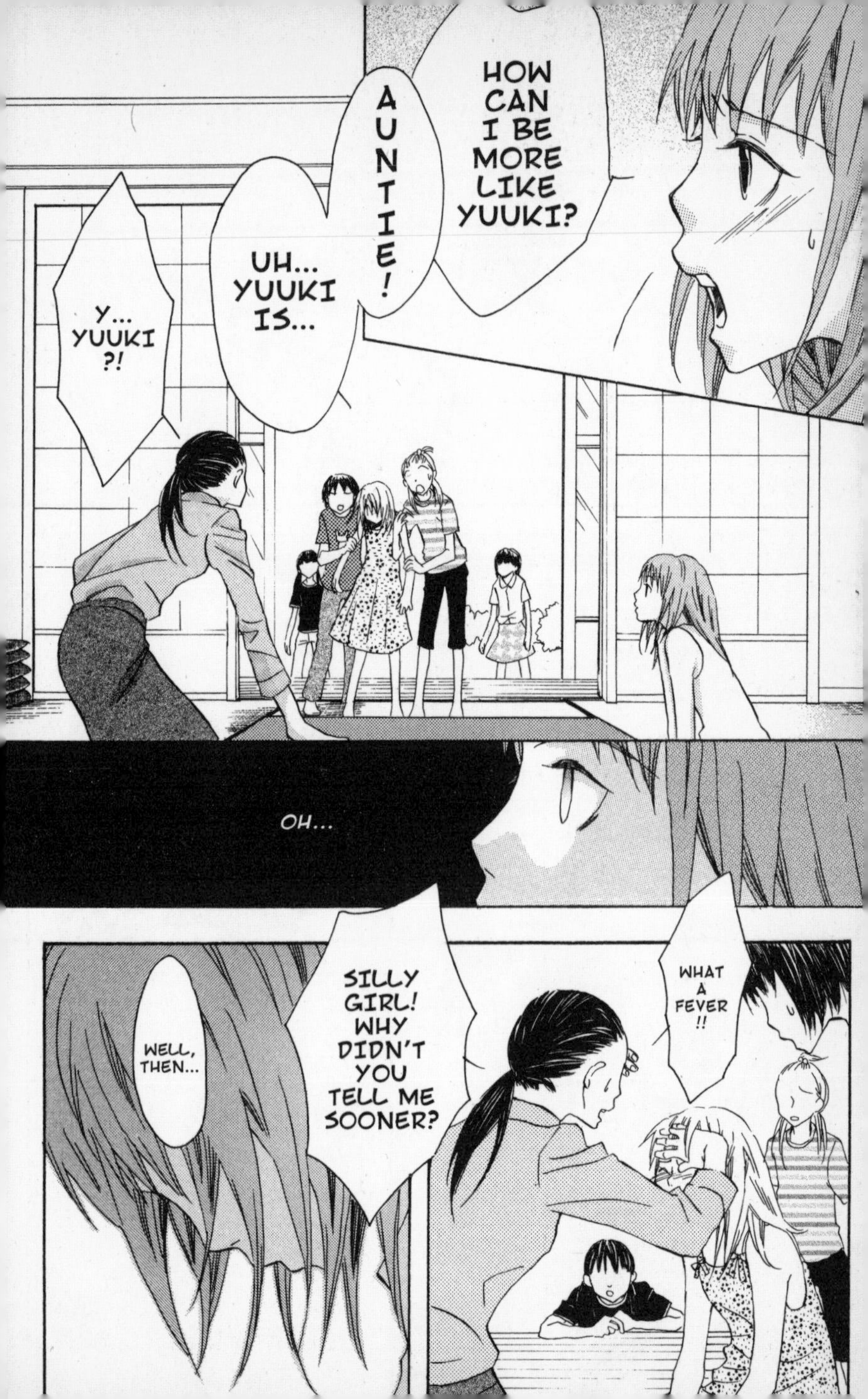
HOW CAN I BE MORE LIKE YUUKI?
AUNTIE!
UH... YUUKI IS...
Y... YUUKI ?!
OH...
WHAT A FEVER !!
SILLY GIRL! WHY DIDN'T YOU TELL ME SOONER?
WELL, THEN...

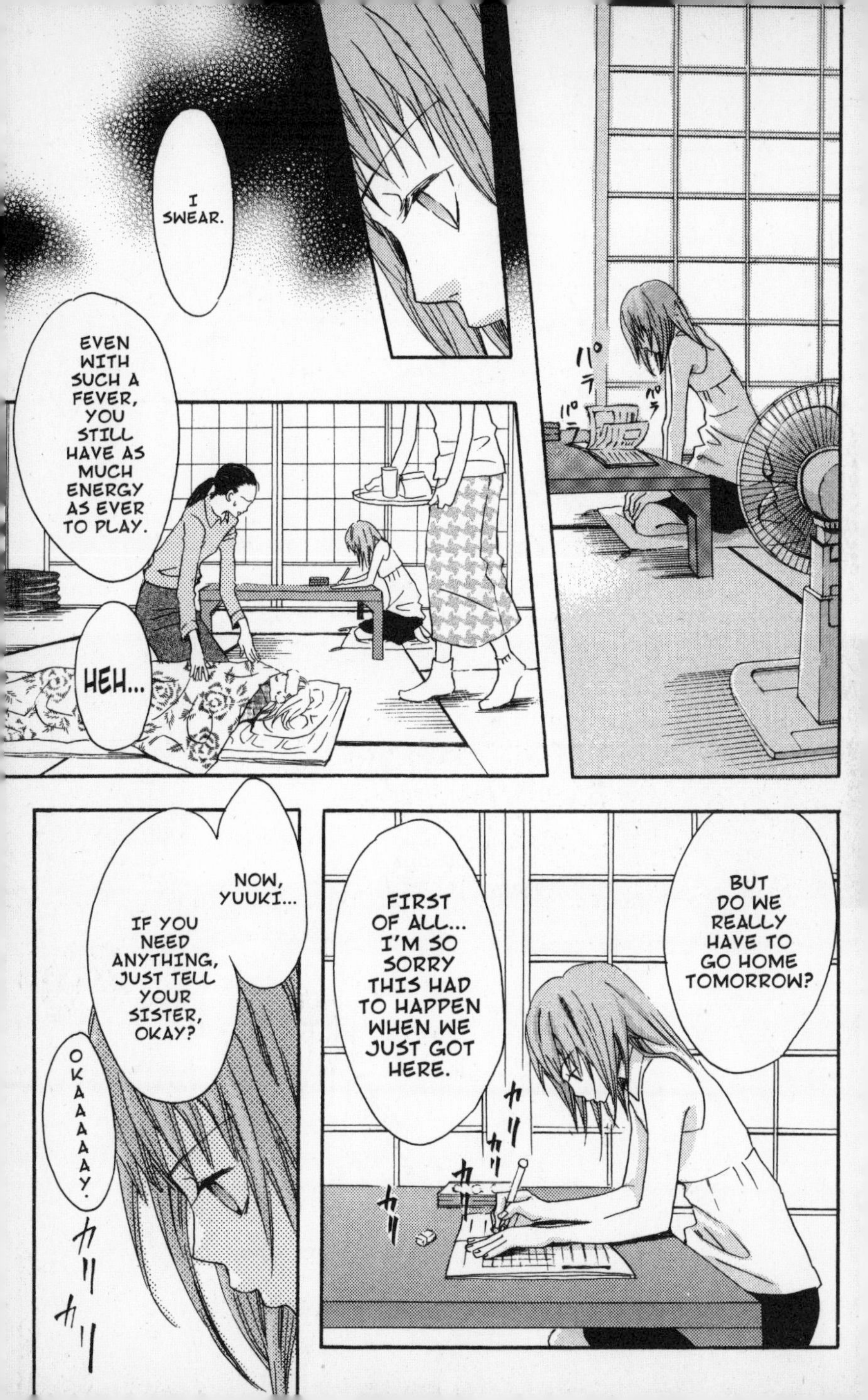

パラ
パラ
パラ
I SWEAR.
EVEN WITH SUCH A FEVER, YOU STILL HAVE AS MUCH ENERGY AS EVER TO PLAY.
HEH...
BUT DO WE REALLY HAVE TO GO HOME TOMORROW?
FIRST OF ALL... I'M SO SORRY THIS HAD TO HAPPEN WHEN WE JUST GOT HERE.
カリ
カリ
カリ
カリ
NOW, YUUKI...
IF YOU NEED ANYTHING, JUST TELL YOUR SISTER, OKAY?
OKAAAAAAY.
カリ
カリ

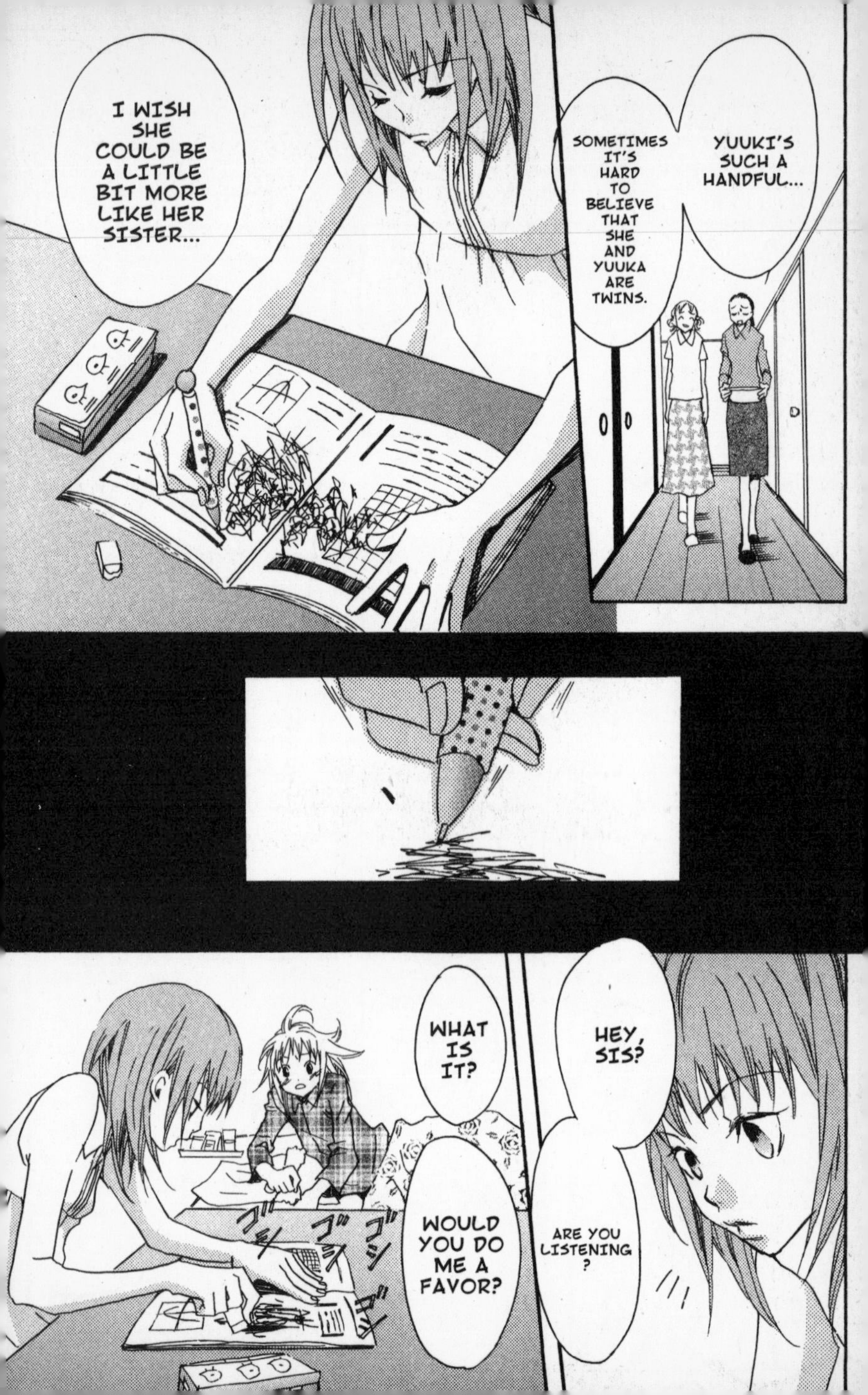
YUUKI'S SUCH A HANDFUL...
SOMETIMES IT'S HARD TO BELIEVE THAT SHE AND YUUKA ARE TWINS.
I WISH SHE COULD BE A LITTLE BIT MORE LIKE HER SISTER...
HEY, SIS?
ARE YOU LISTENING?
WHAT IS IT?
WOULD YOU DO ME A FAVOR?
ゴシ ゴシ ゴシ

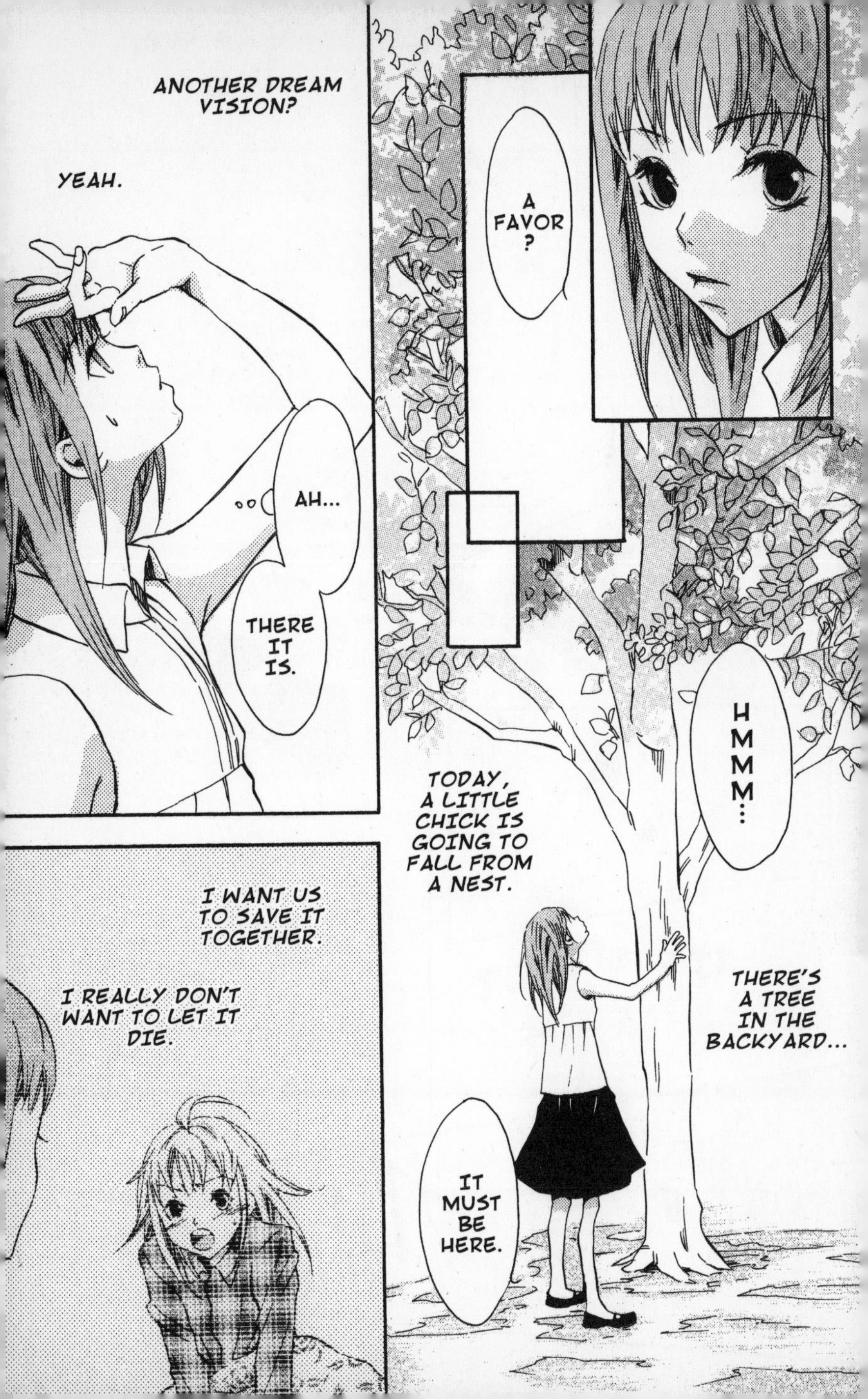
A FAVOR ?
HMMM...
TODAY, A LITTLE CHICK IS GOING TO FALL FROM A NEST.
THERE'S A TREE IN THE BACKYARD...
IT MUST BE HERE.
ANOTHER DREAM VISION?
YEAH.
AH...
THERE IT IS.
I WANT US TO SAVE IT TOGETHER.
I REALLY DON'T WANT TO LET IT DIE.

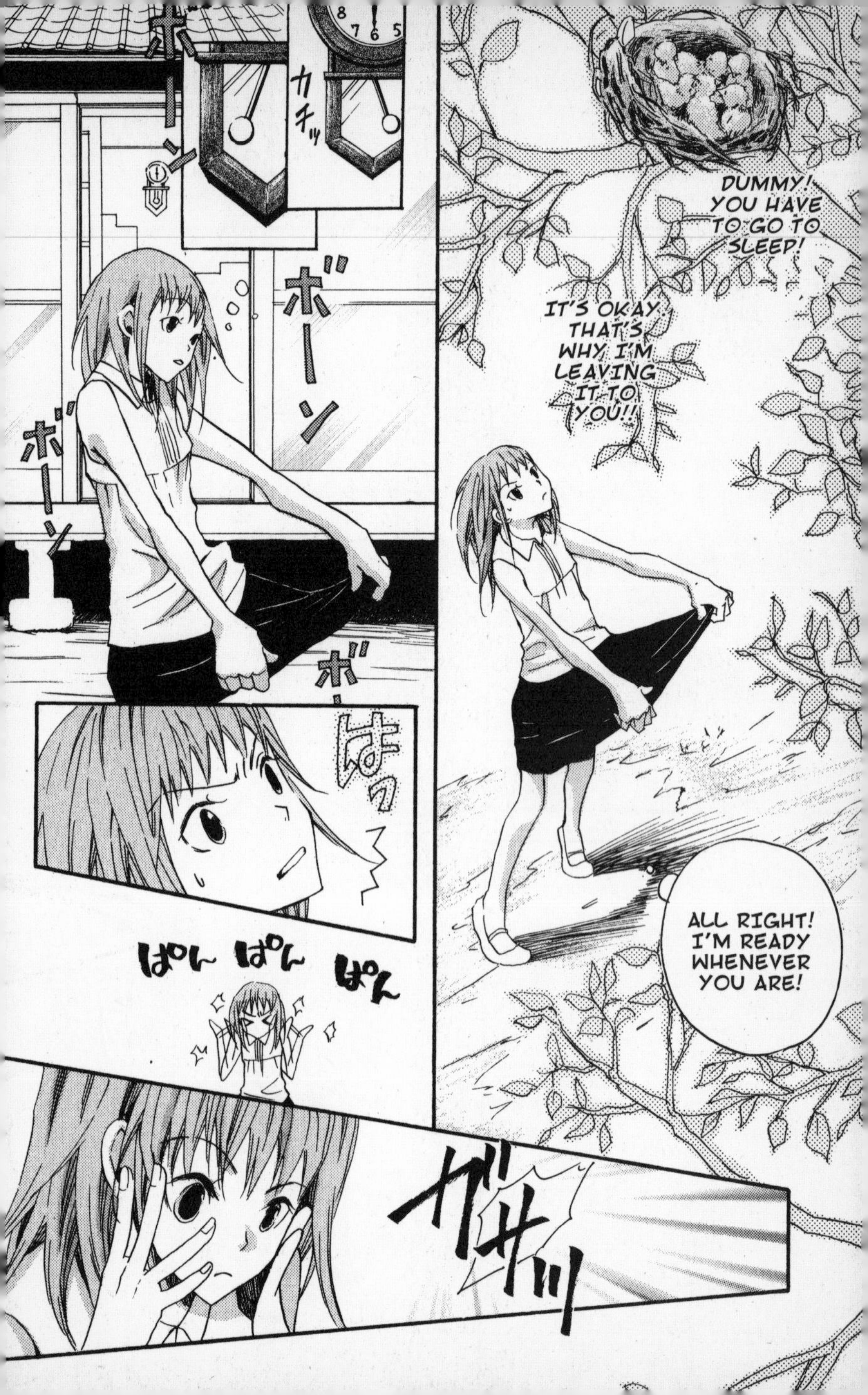
DUMMY! YOU HAVE TO GO TO SLEEP!
IT'S OKAY. THAT'S WHY I'M LEAVING IT TO YOU!!
ALL RIGHT! I'M READY WHENEVER YOU ARE!
ボーン
カチッ
ボーン
ボーン
ボ
はっ
ぱん ぱん ぱん
ザサッ

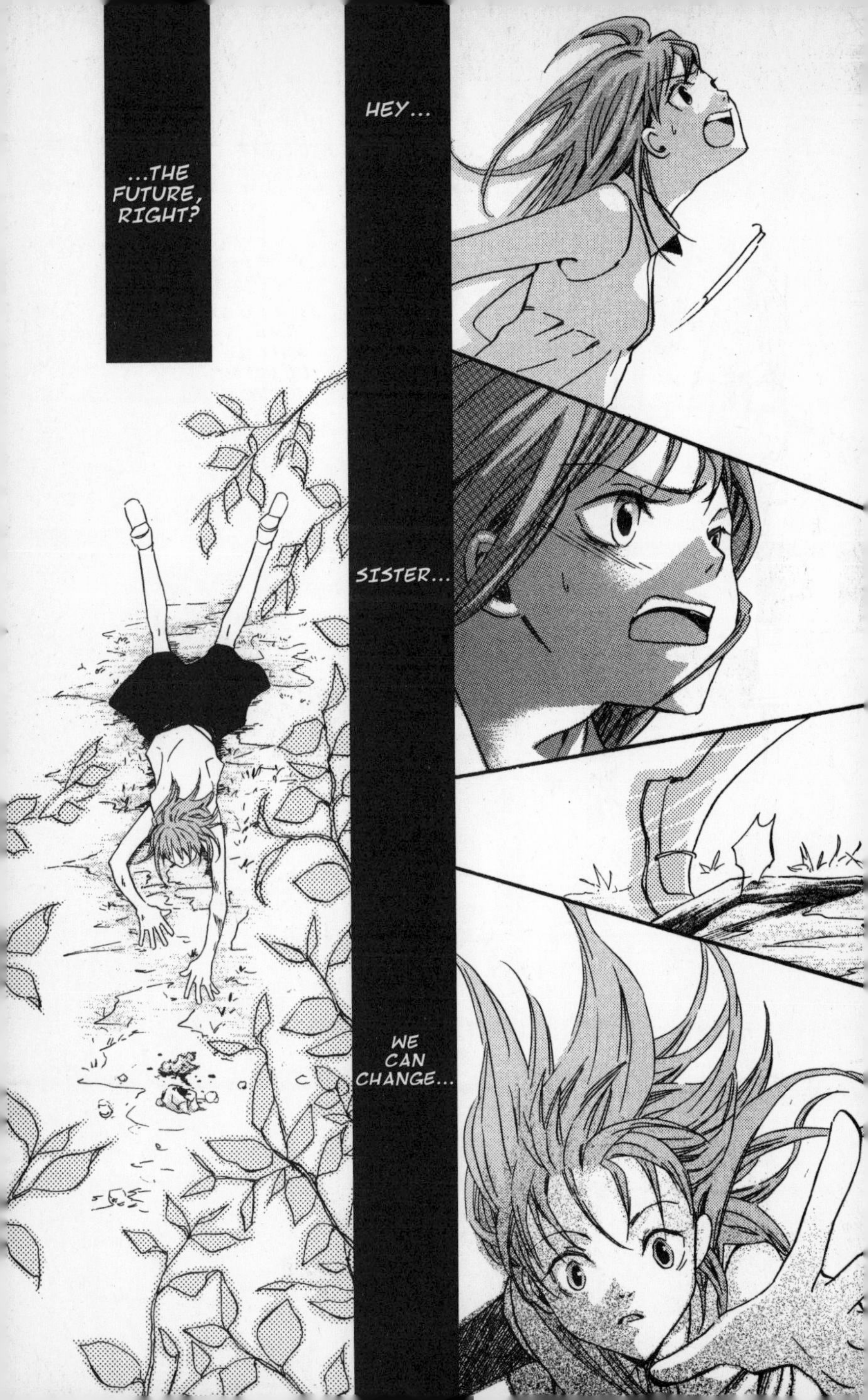
HEY...
SISTER...
WE CAN CHANGE...
...THE FUTURE, RIGHT?

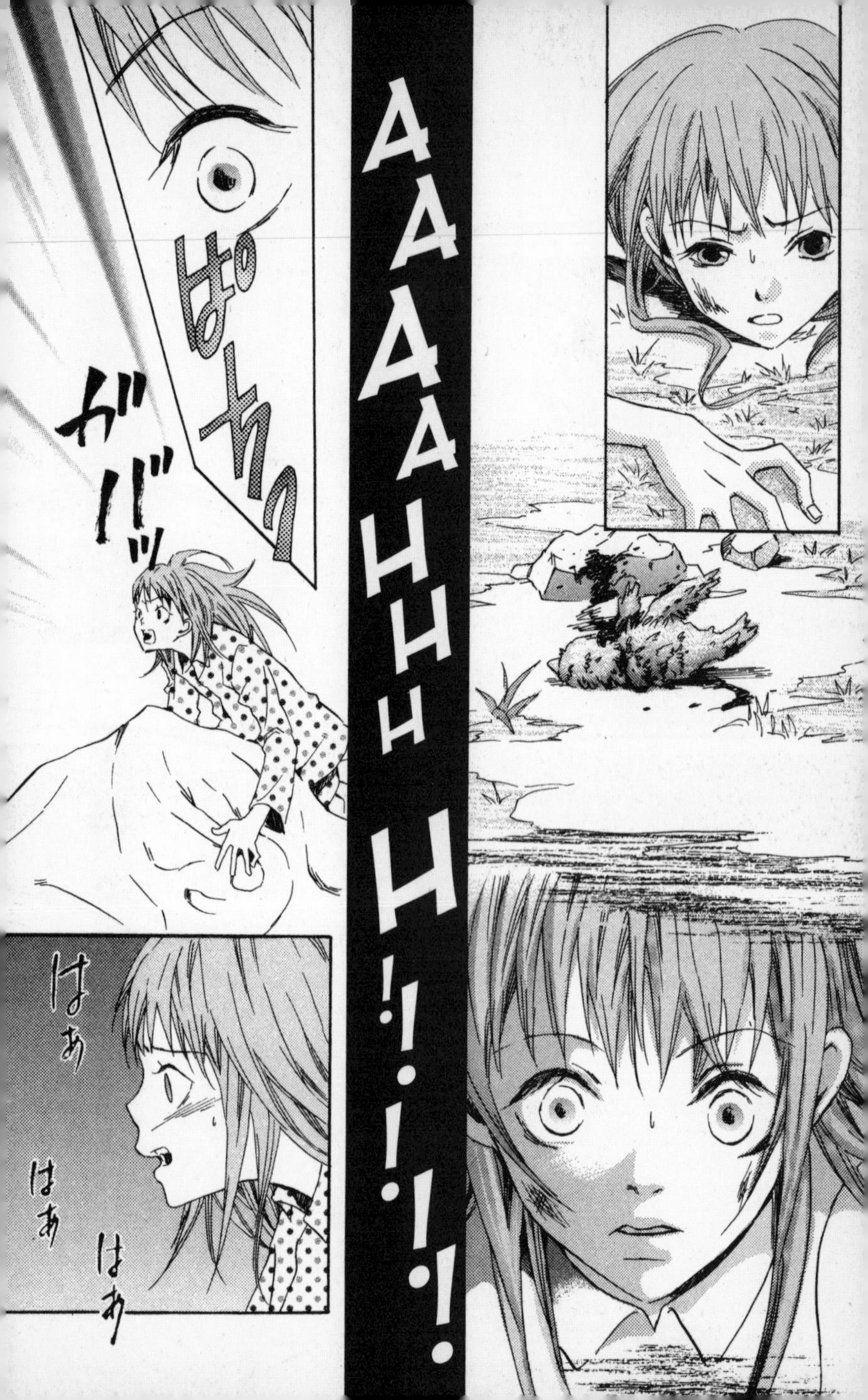
AAAAHHHH!!!!!
ぱちっ
がばっ
はあ
はあ
はあ

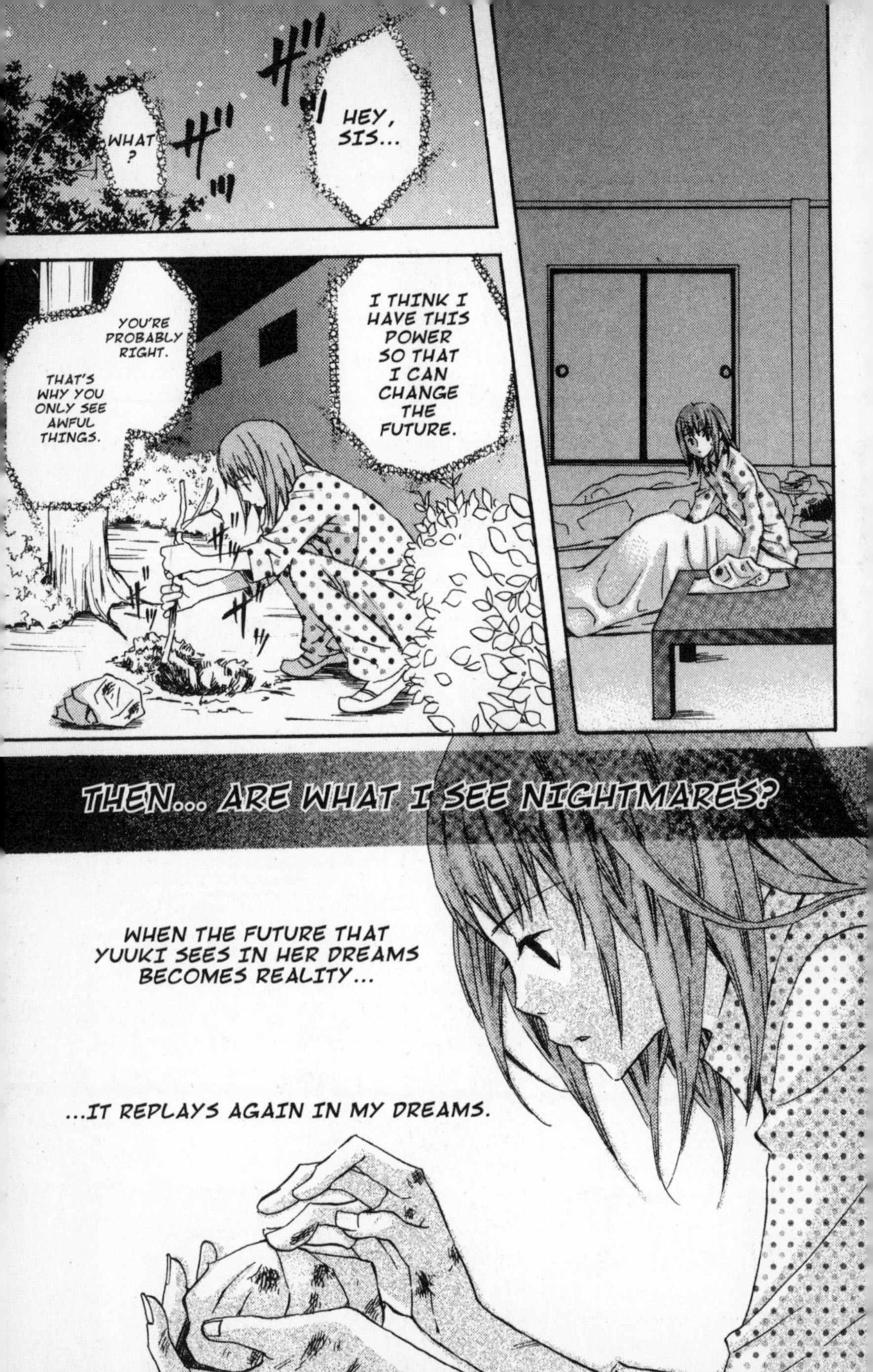
HEY, SIS...
WHAT?
I THINK I HAVE THIS POWER SO THAT I CAN CHANGE THE FUTURE.
YOU'RE PROBABLY RIGHT.
THAT'S WHY YOU ONLY SEE AWFUL THINGS.
THEN... ARE WHAT I SEE NIGHTMARES?
WHEN THE FUTURE THAT YUUKI SEES IN HER DREAMS BECOMES REALITY...
...IT REPLAYS AGAIN IN MY DREAMS.

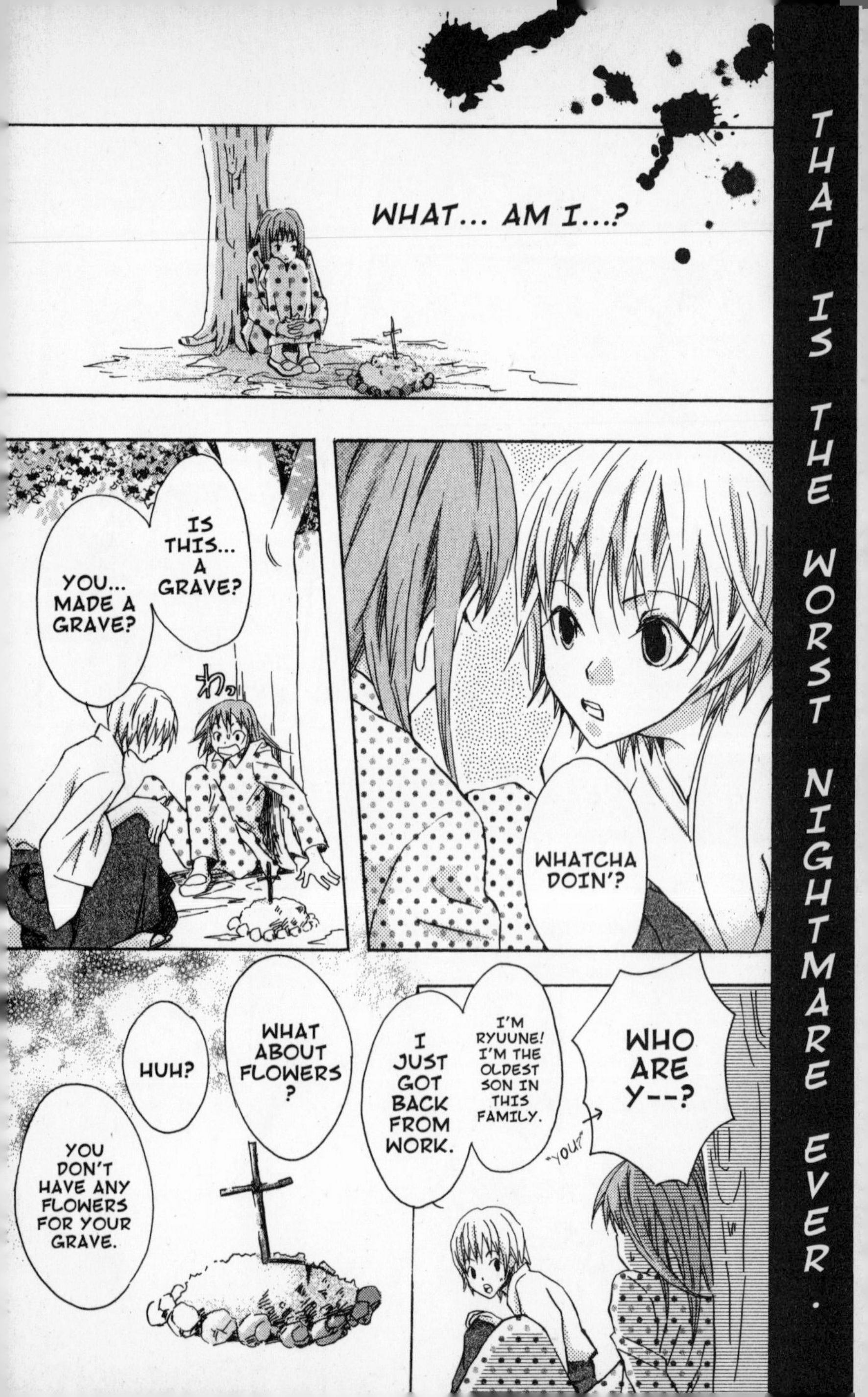
THAT IS THE WORST NIGHTMARE EVER.
WHAT... AM I...?
WHATCHA DOIN'?
IS THIS... A GRAVE?
YOU... MADE A GRAVE?
わっ
WHO ARE Y--?
"YOU?"
I'M RYUUNE! I'M THE OLDEST SON IN THIS FAMILY.
I JUST GOT BACK FROM WORK.
WHAT ABOUT FLOWERS?
HUH?
YOU DON'T HAVE ANY FLOWERS FOR YOUR GRAVE.

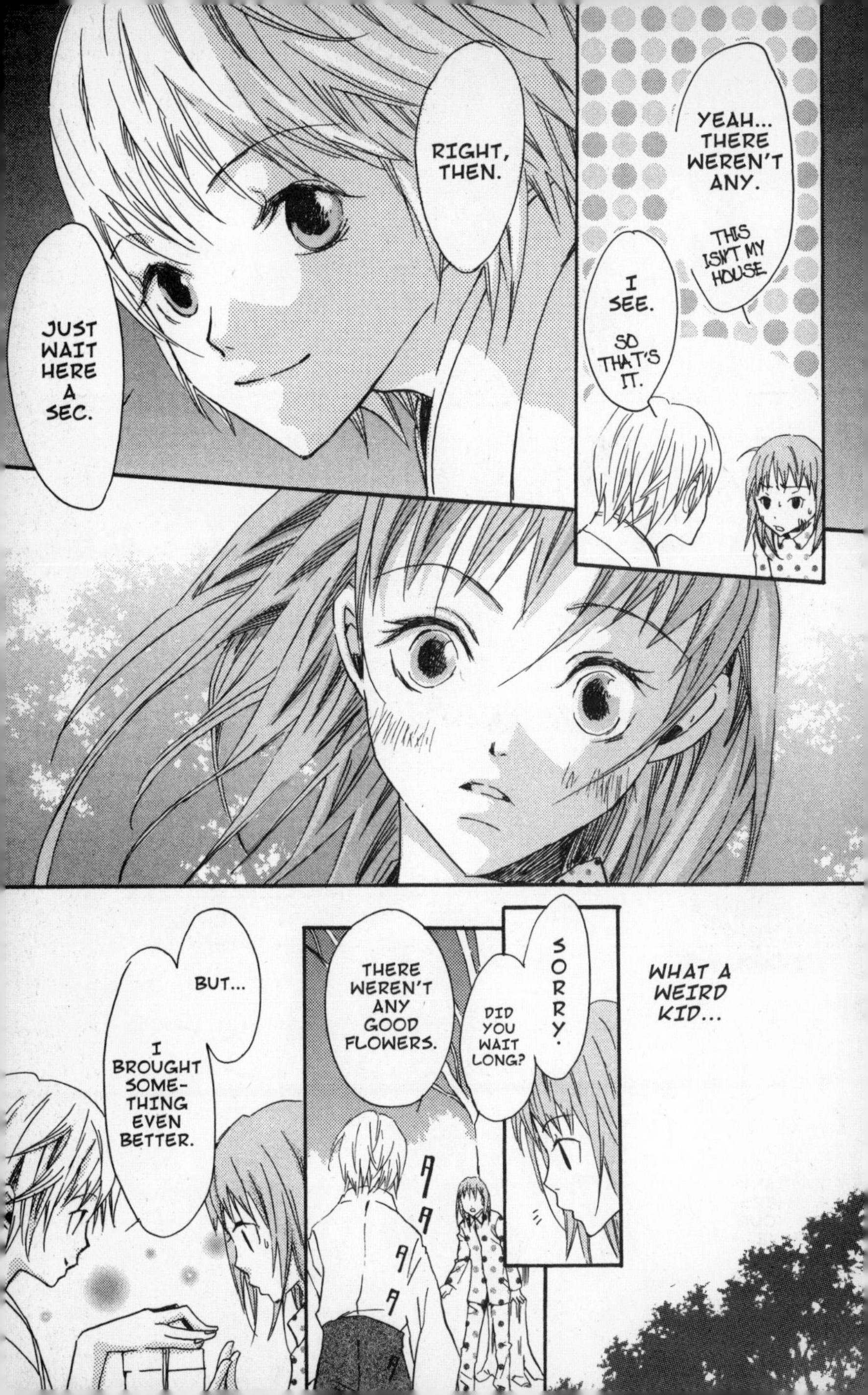
YEAH... THERE WEREN'T ANY.
THIS ISN'T MY HOUSE
I SEE.
SO THAT'S IT.
RIGHT, THEN.
JUST WAIT HERE A SEC.
WHAT A WEIRD KID...
SORRY.
DID YOU WAIT LONG?
THERE WEREN'T ANY GOOD FLOWERS.
BUT...
I BROUGHT SOME-THING EVEN BETTER.

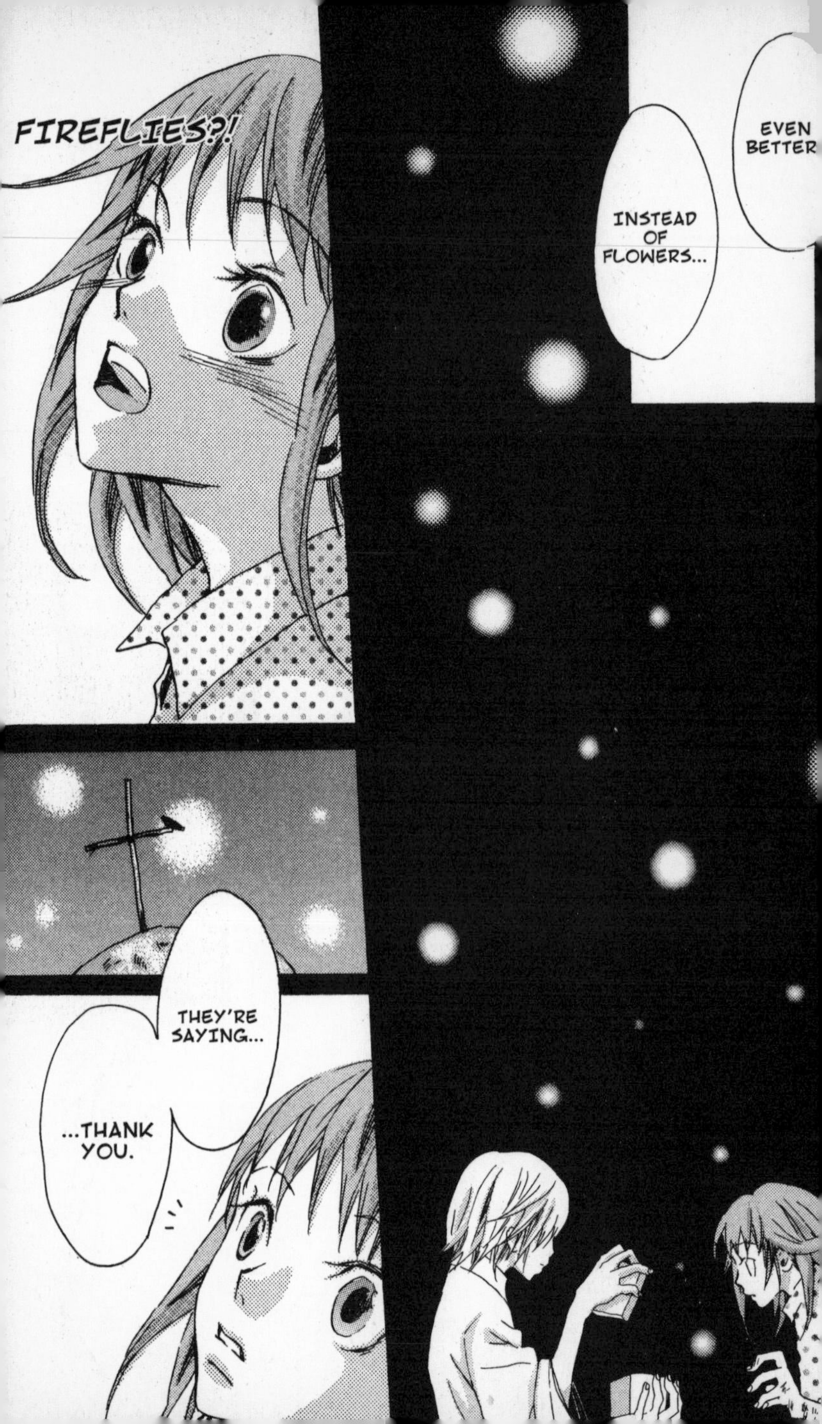
INSTEAD OF FLOWERS...
EVEN BETTER
FIREFLIES?!
THEY'RE SAYING...
...THANK YOU.

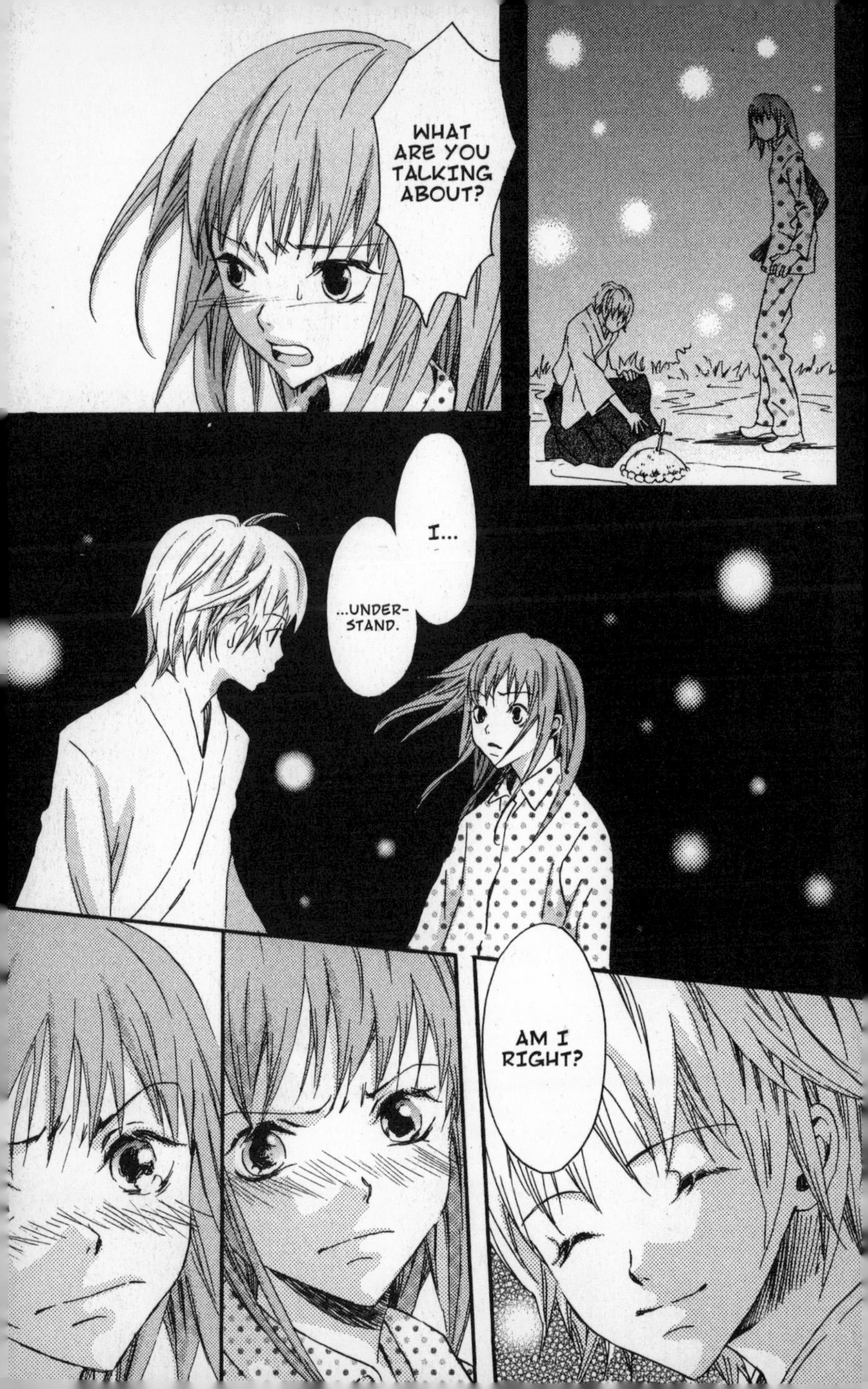
WHAT ARE YOU TALKING ABOUT?
I...
...UNDER-STAND.
AM I RIGHT?

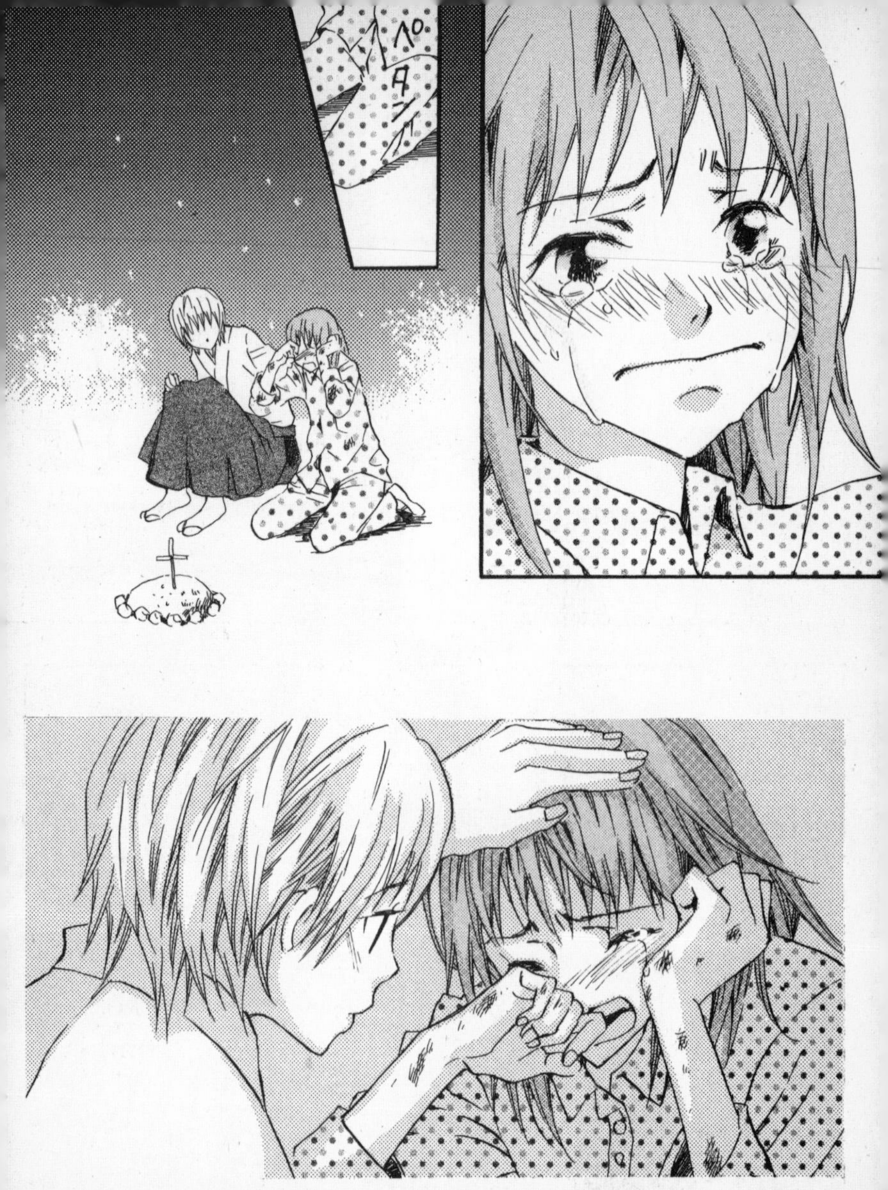
ペタン

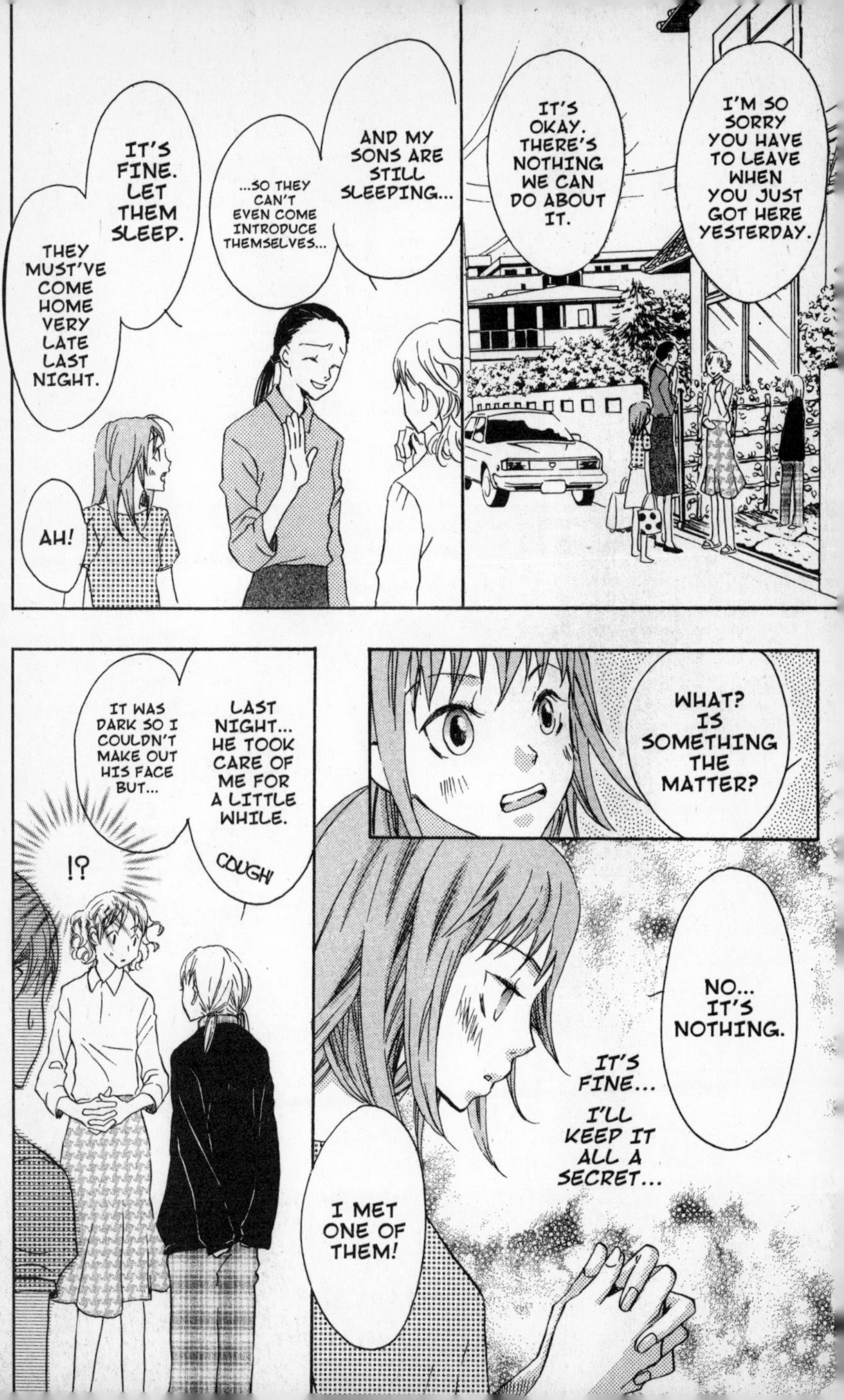
I'M SO SORRY YOU HAVE TO LEAVE WHEN YOU JUST GOT HERE YESTERDAY.
IT'S OKAY. THERE'S NOTHING WE CAN DO ABOUT IT.
AND MY SONS ARE STILL SLEEPING...
...SO THEY CAN'T EVEN COME INTRODUCE THEMSELVES...
IT'S FINE. LET THEM SLEEP.
THEY MUST'VE COME HOME VERY LATE LAST NIGHT.
AH!
I MET ONE OF THEM!
LAST NIGHT... HE TOOK CARE OF ME FOR A LITTLE WHILE.
IT WAS DARK SO I COULDN'T MAKE OUT HIS FACE BUT...
COUGH!
!?
WHAT? IS SOMETHING THE MATTER?
NO... IT'S NOTHING.
IT'S FINE...
I'LL KEEP IT ALL A SECRET...

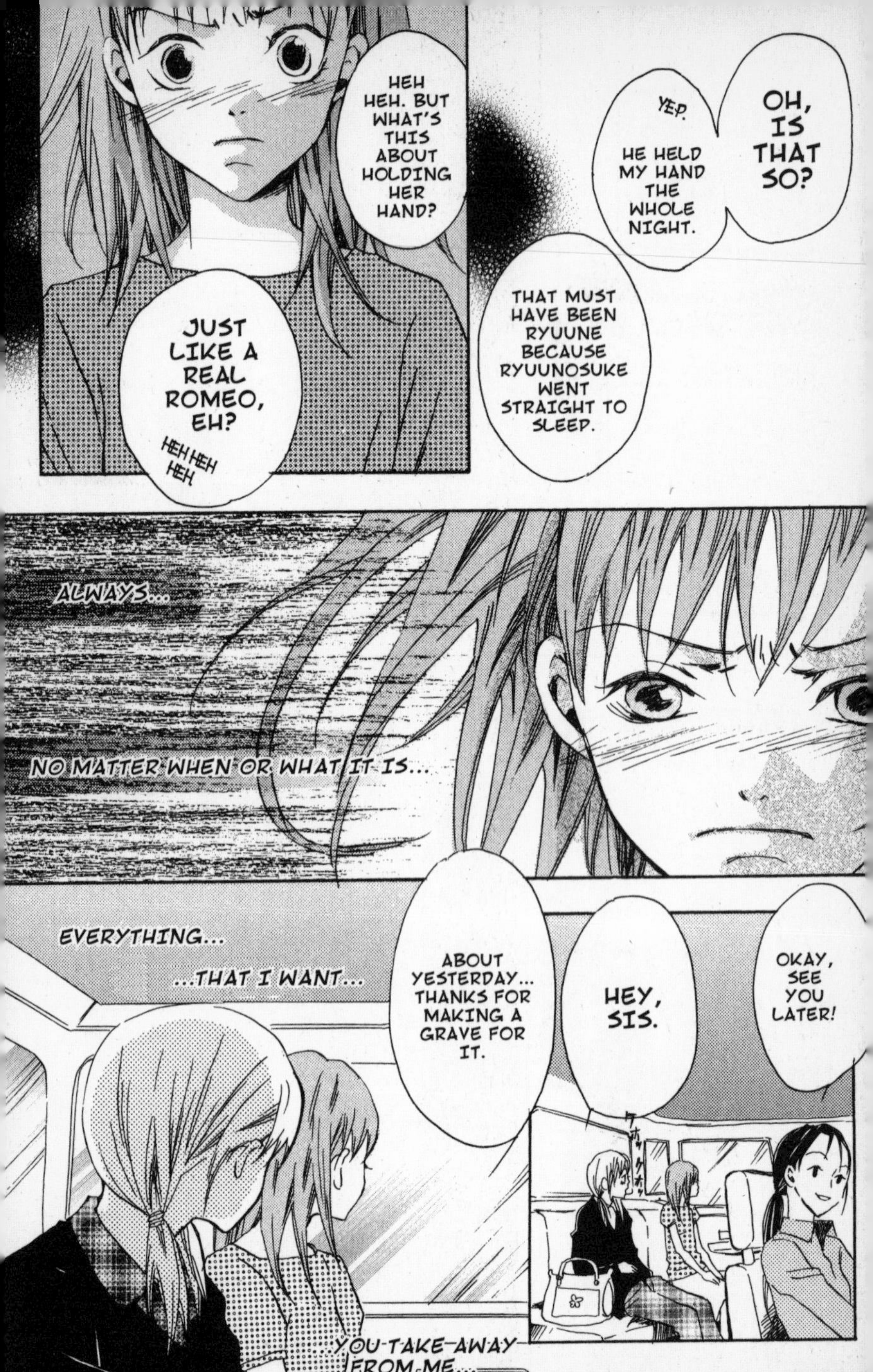
OH, IS THAT SO?
YEP.
HE HELD MY HAND THE WHOLE NIGHT.
HEH HEH. BUT WHAT'S THIS ABOUT HOLDING HER HAND?
THAT MUST HAVE BEEN RYUUNE BECAUSE RYUUNOSUKE WENT STRAIGHT TO SLEEP.
JUST LIKE A REAL ROMEO, EH?
HEH HEH HEH
ALWAYS...
NO MATTER WHEN OR WHAT IT IS...
OKAY, SEE YOU LATER!
HEY, SIS.
ABOUT YESTERDAY... THANKS FOR MAKING A GRAVE FOR IT.
EVERYTHING...
...THAT I WANT...
YOU TAKE AWAY FROM ME...

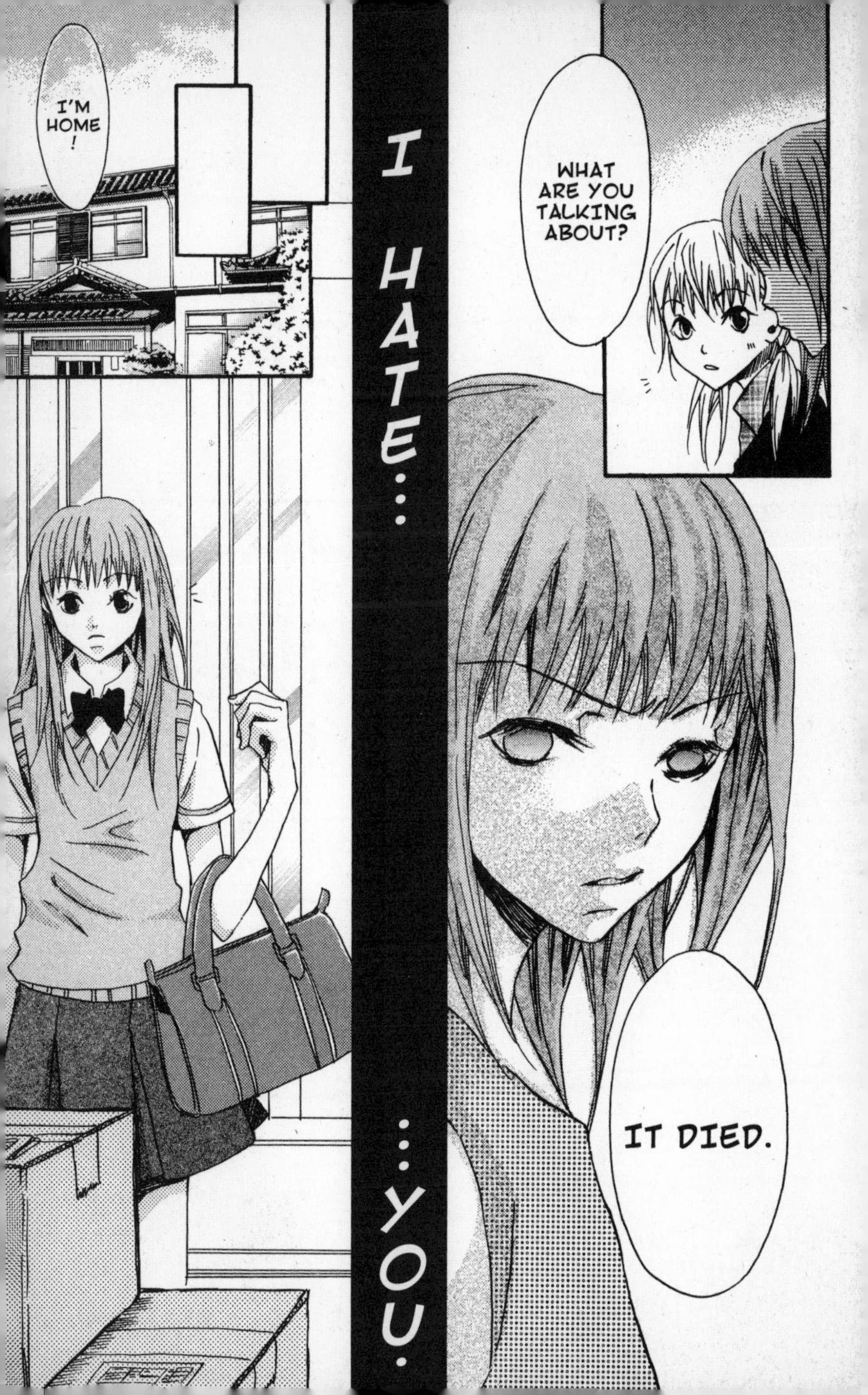
WHAT ARE YOU TALKING ABOUT?
IT DIED.
I HATE...
...YOU.
I'M HOME!

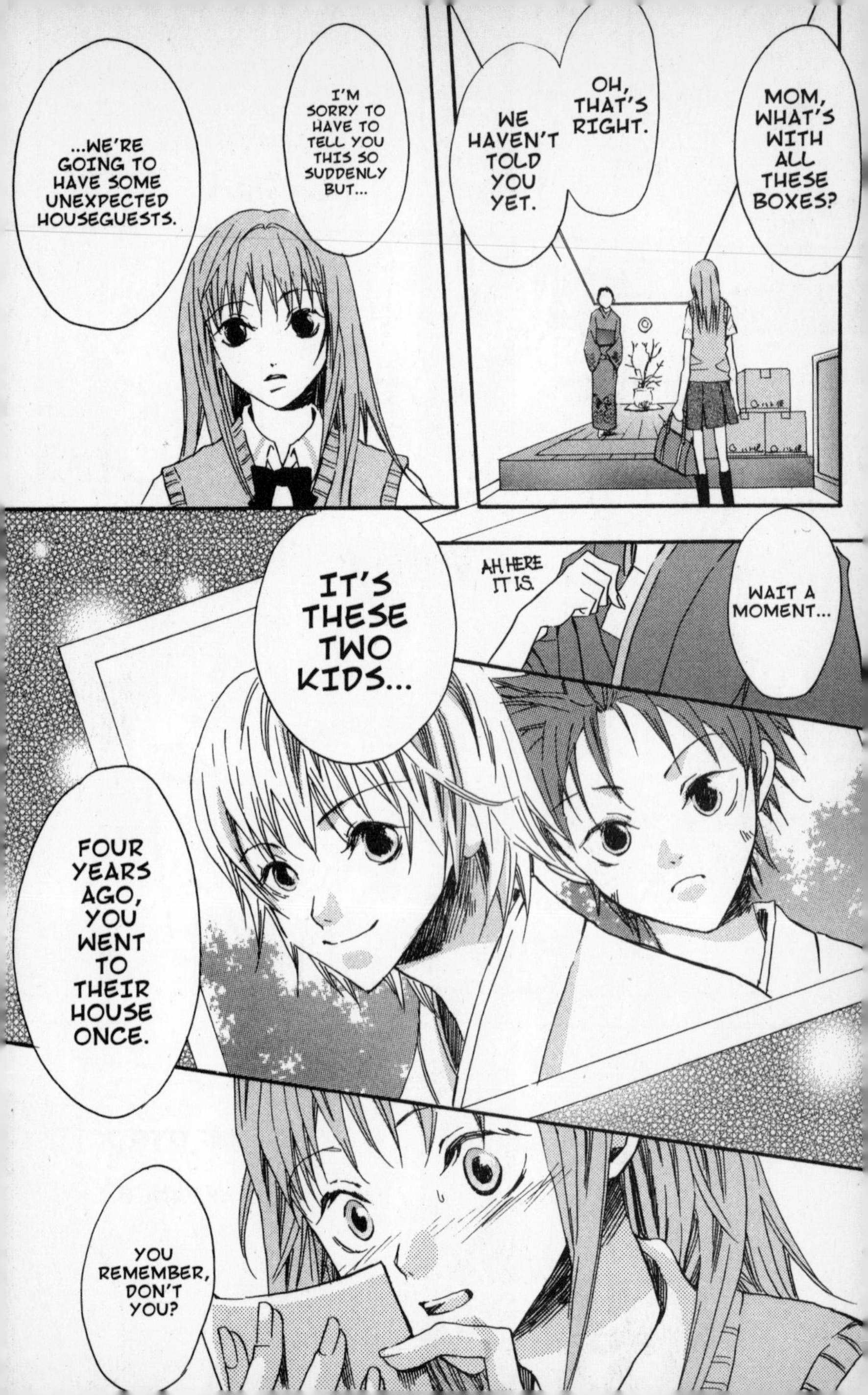
MOM, WHAT'S WITH ALL THESE BOXES?
OH, THAT'S RIGHT.
WE HAVEN'T TOLD YOU YET.
I'M SORRY TO HAVE TO TELL YOU THIS SO SUDDENLY BUT...
...WE'RE GOING TO HAVE SOME UNEXPECTED HOUSEGUESTS.
WAIT A MOMENT...
AH, HERE IT IS.
IT'S THESE TWO KIDS...
FOUR YEARS AGO, YOU WENT TO THEIR HOUSE ONCE.
YOU REMEMBER, DON'T YOU?

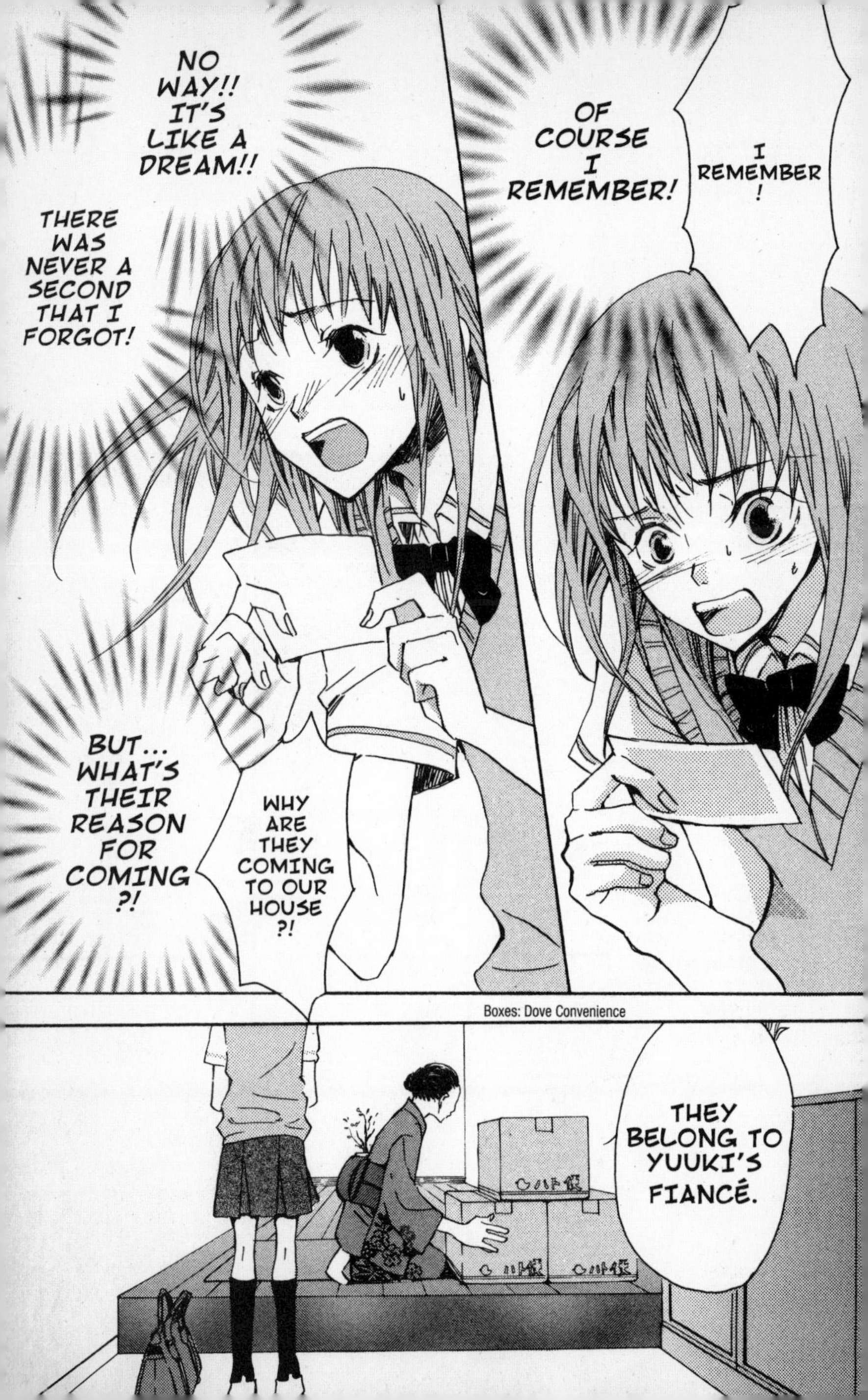
I REMEMBER!
OF COURSE I REMEMBER!
NO WAY!! IT'S LIKE A DREAM!!
THERE WAS NEVER A SECOND THAT I FORGOT!
WHY ARE THEY COMING TO OUR HOUSE ?!
BUT... WHAT'S THEIR REASON FOR COMING ?!
Boxes: Dove Convenience
THEY BELONG TO YUUKI'S FIANCÉ.

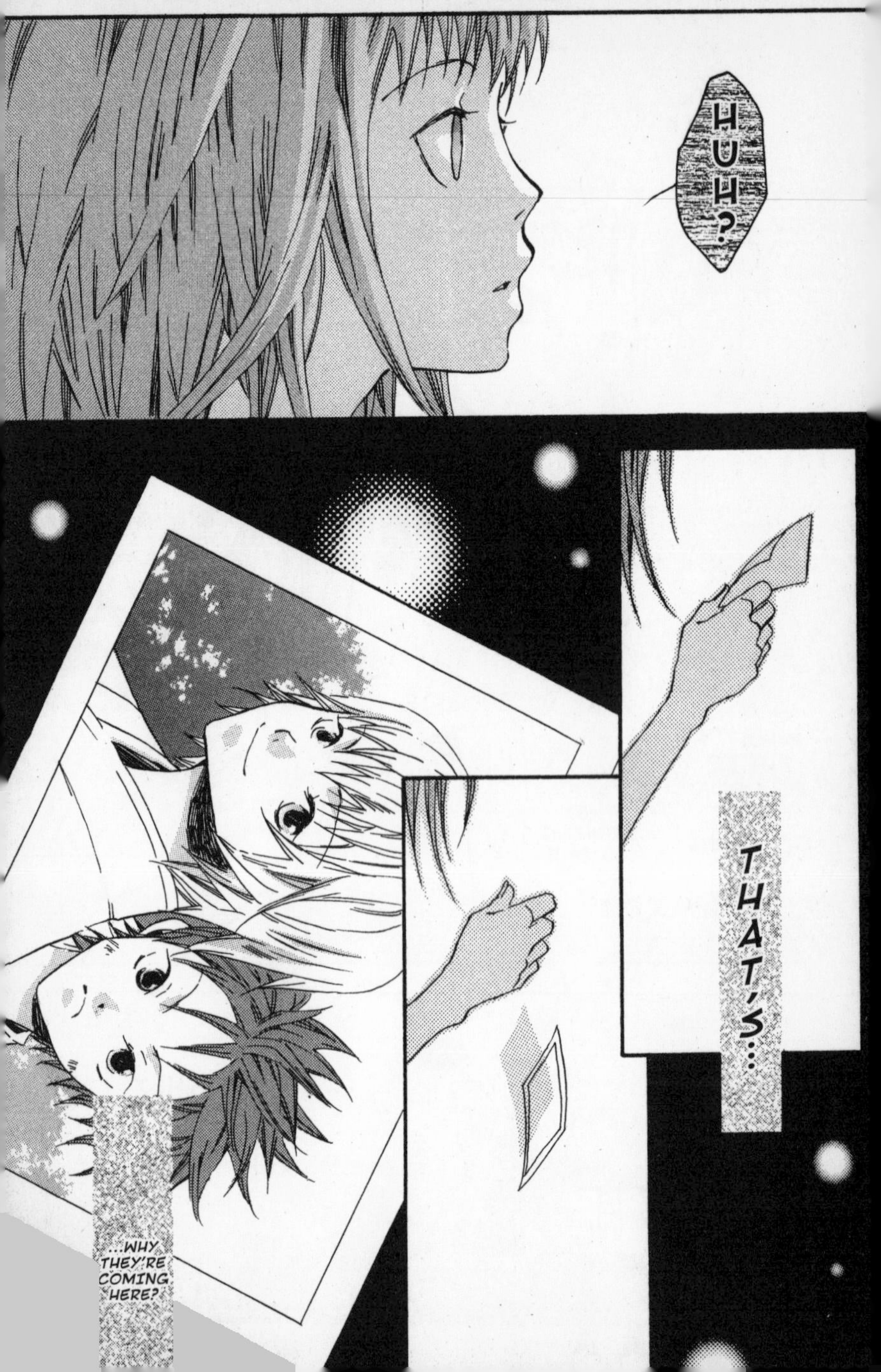
HUH?
THAT'S...
...WHY THEY'RE COMING HERE?

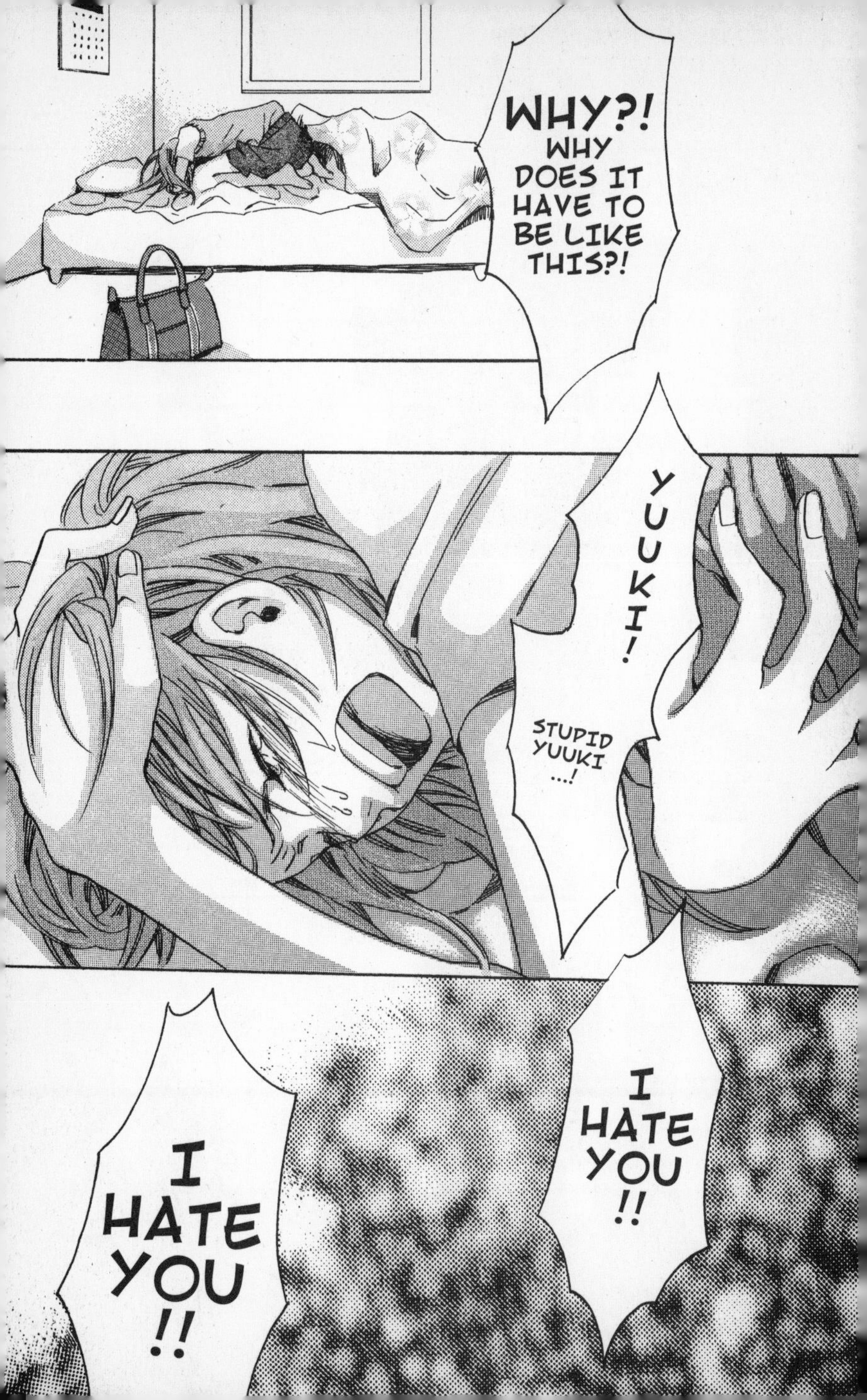
WHY?! WHY DOES IT HAVE TO BE LIKE THIS?!
YUUKI!
STUPID YUUKI ...!
I HATE YOU!!
I HATE YOU!!

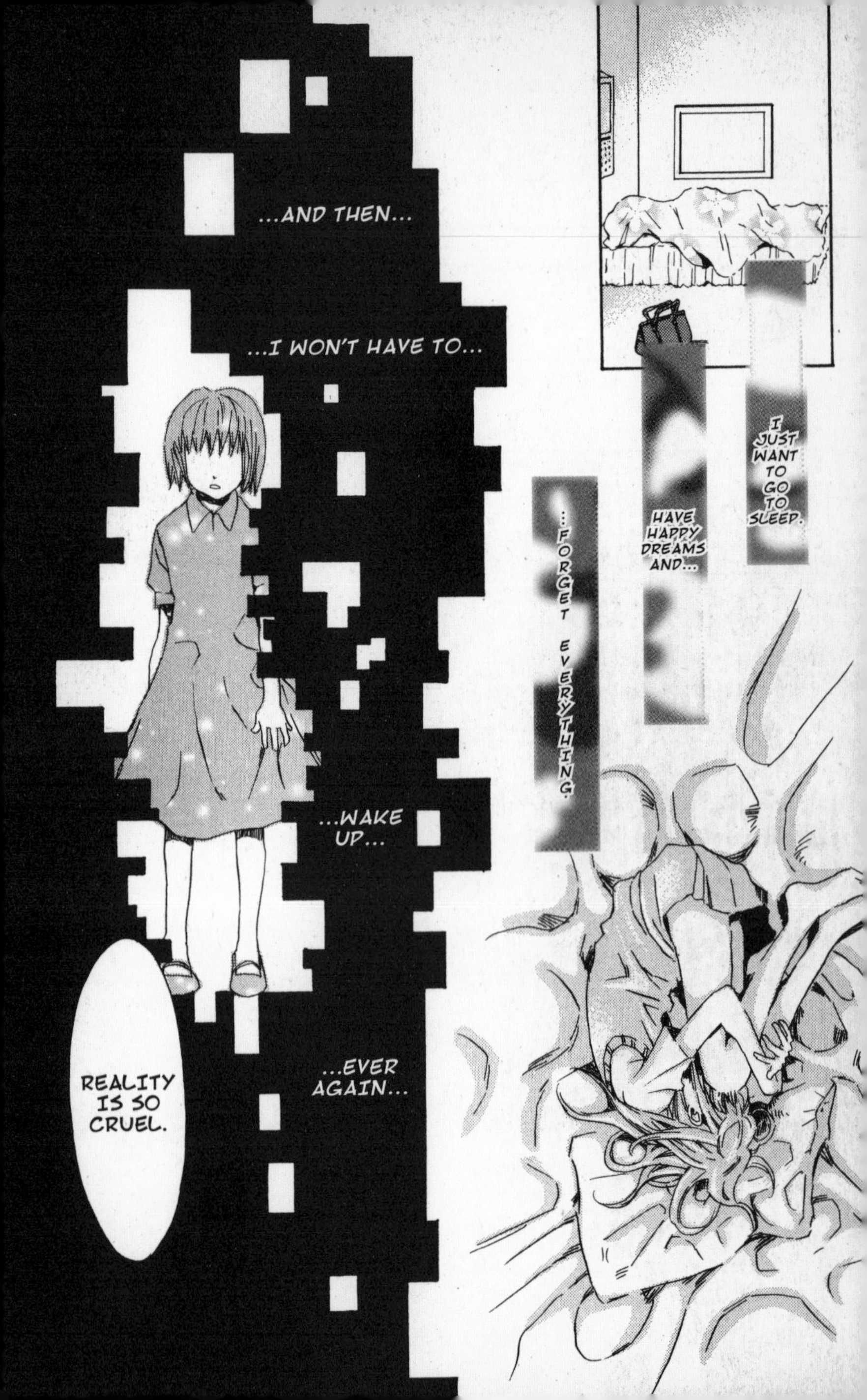
I JUST WANT TO GO TO SLEEP.
HAVE HAPPY DREAMS AND...
...FORGET EVERYTHING.
...AND THEN...
...I WON'T HAVE TO...
...WAKE UP...
...EVER AGAIN...
REALITY IS SO CRUEL.

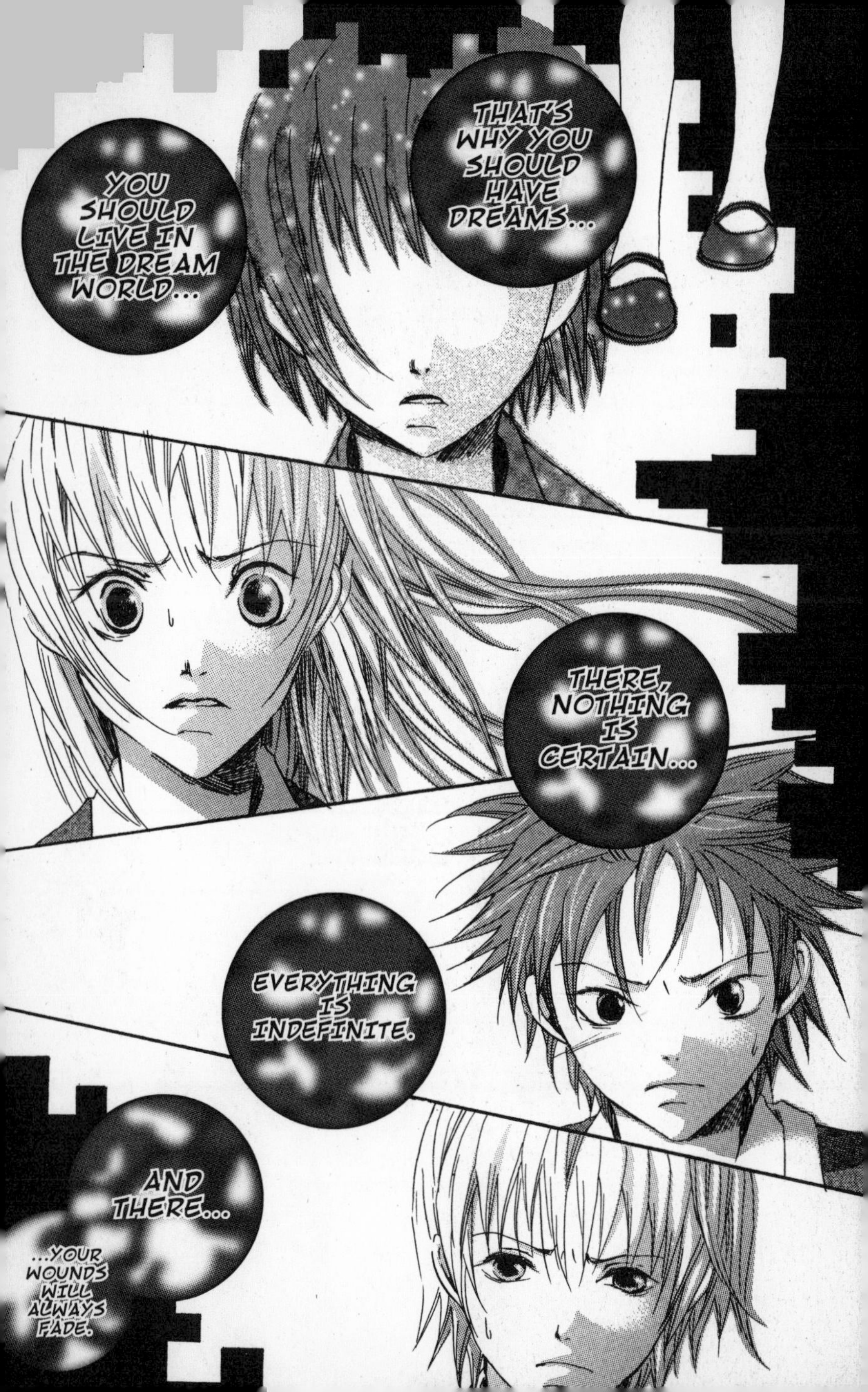
THAT'S WHY YOU SHOULD HAVE DREAMS...
YOU SHOULD LIVE IN THE DREAM WORLD...
THERE, NOTHING IS CERTAIN...
EVERYTHING IS INDEFINITE.
AND THERE...
...YOUR WOUNDS WILL ALWAYS FADE.

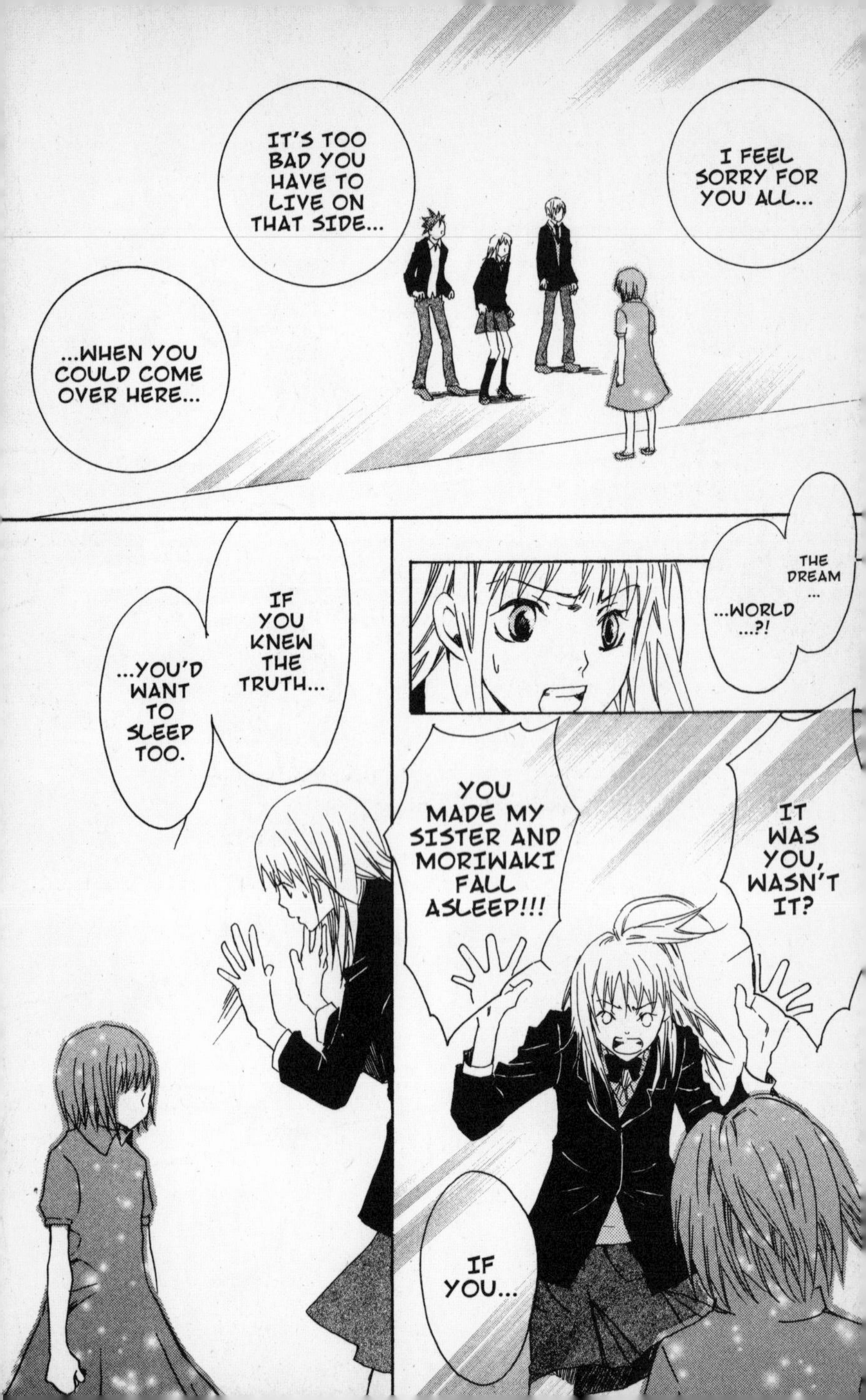
I FEEL SORRY FOR YOU ALL...
IT'S TOO BAD YOU HAVE TO LIVE ON THAT SIDE...
...WHEN YOU COULD COME OVER HERE...
THE DREAM ... ...WORLD ...?!
IT WAS YOU, WASN'T IT?
YOU MADE MY SISTER AND MORIWAKI FALL ASLEEP!!!
IF YOU...
IF YOU KNEW THE TRUTH...
...YOU'D WANT TO SLEEP TOO.

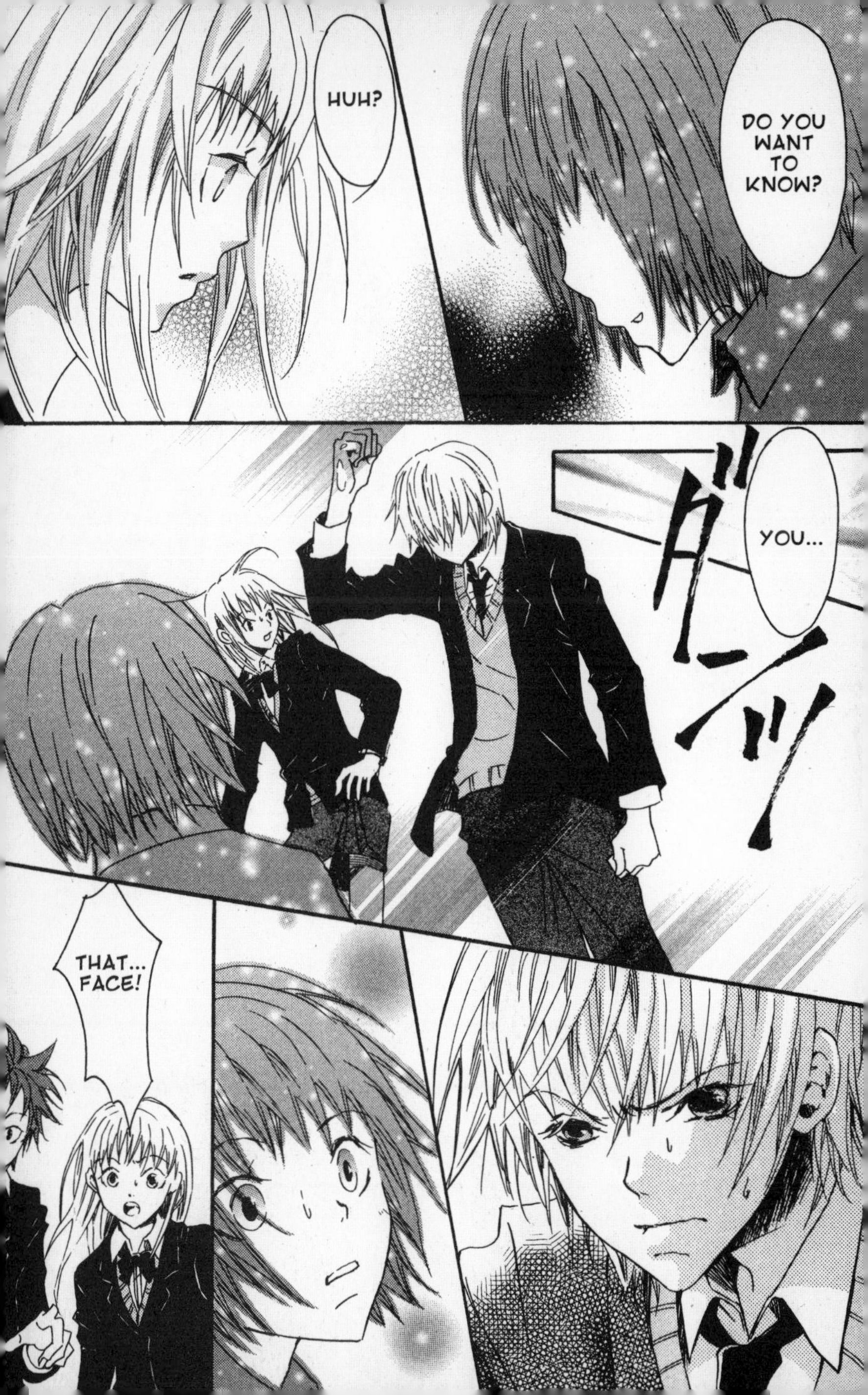
DO YOU WANT TO KNOW?
HUH?
YOU...
THAT... FACE!

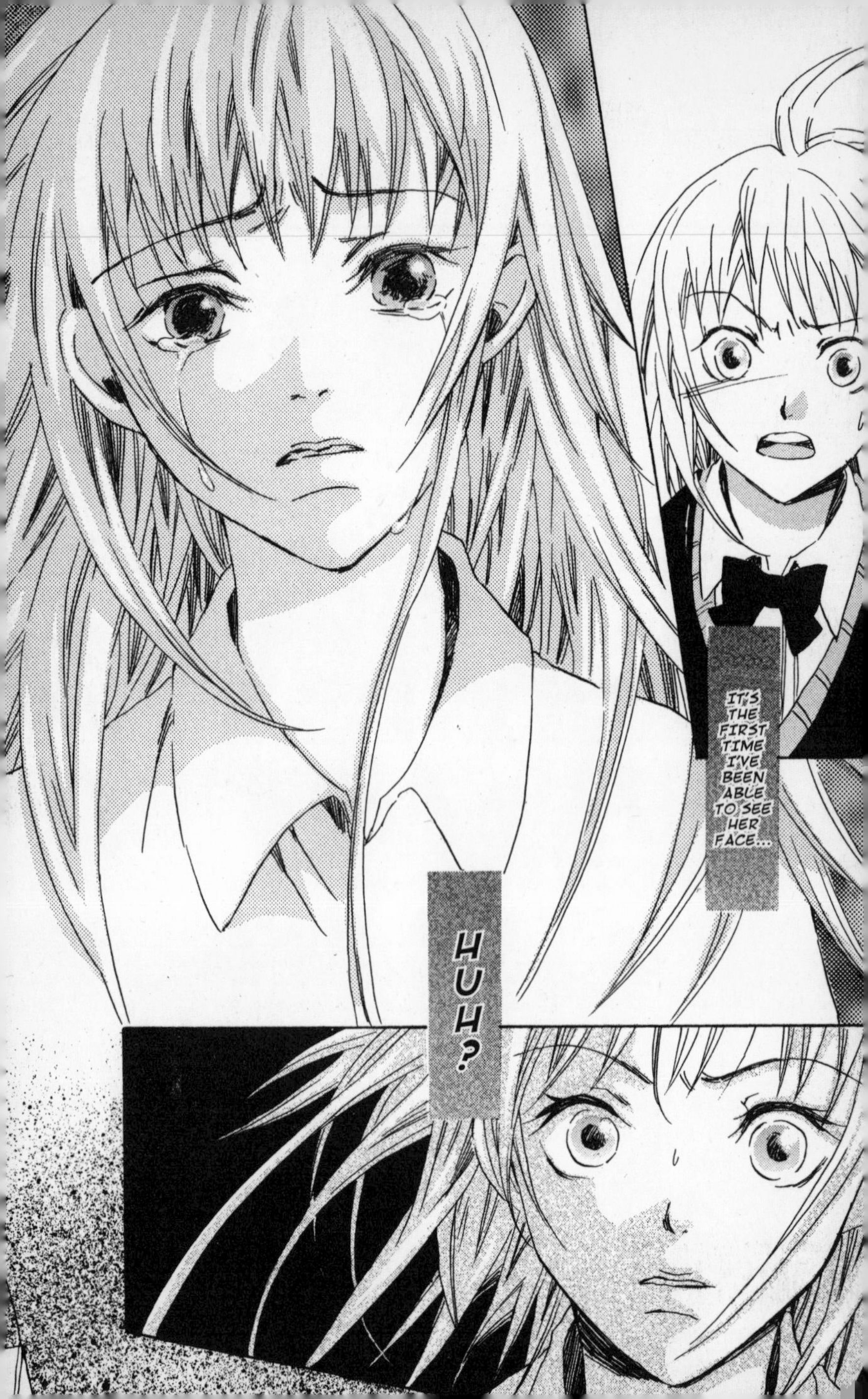
IT'S THE FIRST TIME I'VE BEEN ABLE TO SEE HER FACE...
HUH?

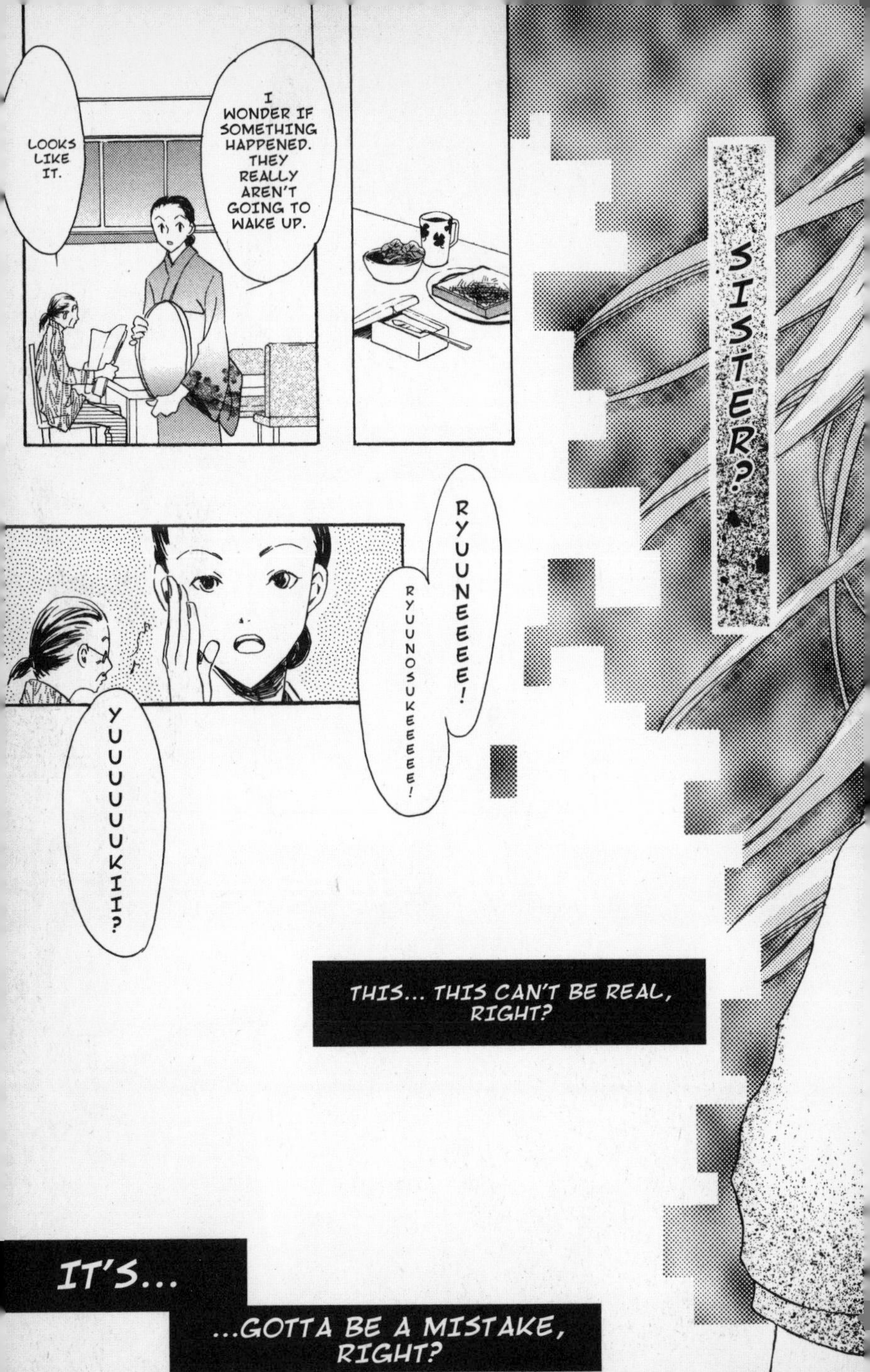
I WONDER IF SOMETHING HAPPENED. THEY REALLY AREN'T GOING TO WAKE UP.
LOOKS LIKE IT.
RYUUNEEEE!
RYUUNOSUKEEEEE!
YUUUUUUUKII?
SISTER?
THIS... THIS CAN'T BE REAL, RIGHT?
IT'S...
...GOTTA BE A MISTAKE, RIGHT?

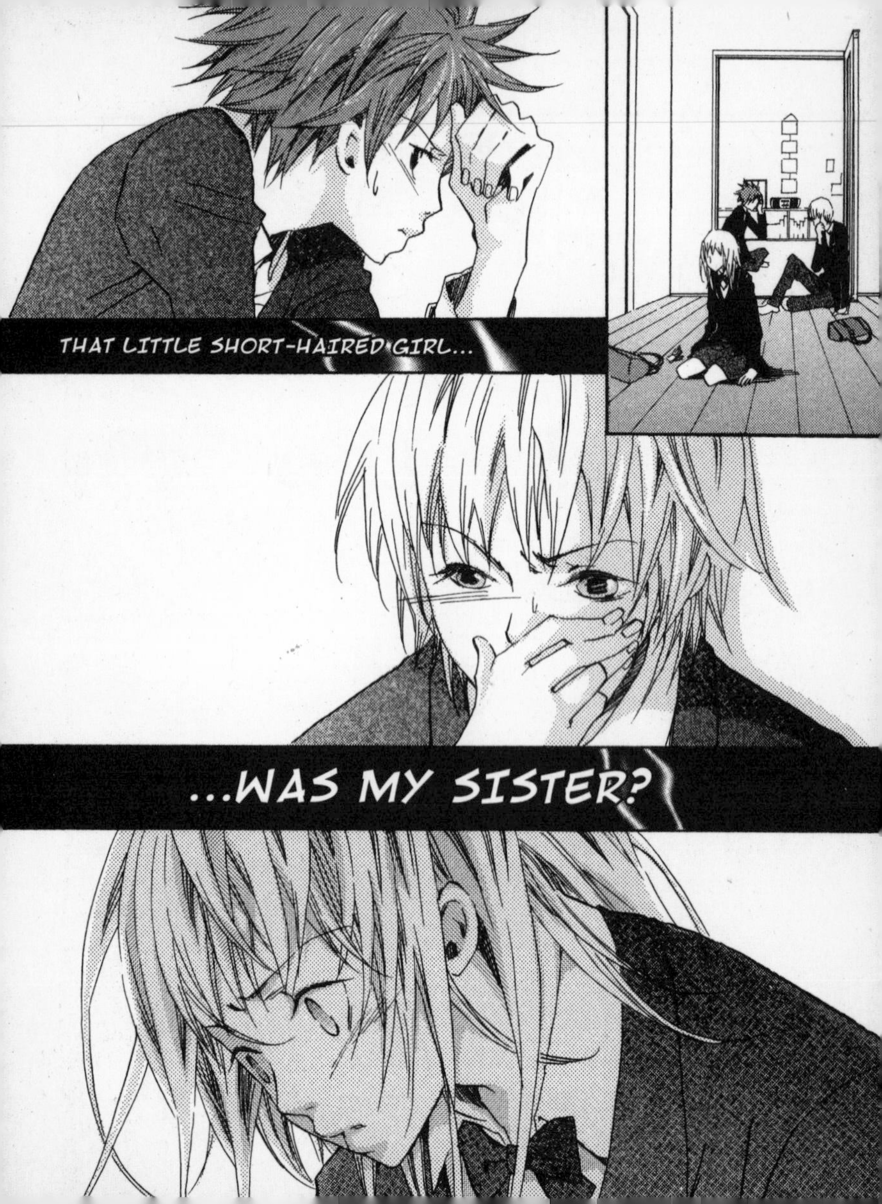
THAT LITTLE SHORT-HAIRED GIRL...
...WAS MY SISTER?

THE REAL SCARY STORY BEHIND IT ALL

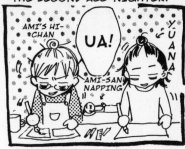

AFTERWORD

THANK YOU. THIS IS KAZUMI YUANA.
THANK YOU SOOOO MUCH FOR PICKING UP THIS BOOK!
OH, MAN...I'VE COMPLETED THREE BOOKS SINCE MY DEBUT BUT I JUST CAN'T GET USED TO IT. ALWAYS THE SAME OLD BEEEP

(‡ BITCHING AND COMPLAINING)

BUT I'M GONNA DO MY BEST. I WILL NOT BE DEFEATED.

ANYWAY, A SPECIAL THANKS TO THOSE WHO MADE TURNING MY WORK INTO A COMIC POSSIBLE: MY MANAGER, KAIJI; THE EDITORIAL DEPARTMENT; MY EVER-SUPPORTIVE READERS; ALL MY DEDICATED ASSISTANTS; TO FRIENDS AND FAMILY, AS ALWAYS. MANY THANKS TO YOU ALL!

AND LAST, SINCE I'M PLANNING ON CONTINUING TO DO MY BEST, PLEASE KEEP UP YOUR AWESOME SUPPORT!!

YUANA KAZUMI

OH, I'D LOVE TO RECEIVE YOUR ART AND LETTERS.

TOKYOPOP
5900 WILSHIRE BLVD.,
SUITE 2000
LOS ANGELES, CA 90036
HTTP://WWW.TOKYOPOP.COM

I ALSO HAVE A WEBSITE

URL > HTTP://WEB.FFN.NE.JP/YUANA

If my site gets taken down please try to find me.

THE SECOND ALL-NIGHTER:

YUANA
UA!
AMI'S HI-CHAN
AMI-SAN NAPPING
AAH!
びくっ
びくっ
RIGHT... WHAT WERE WE JUST TALKING ABOUT?
WHAT INDEED.

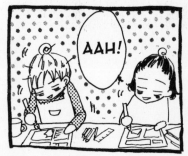

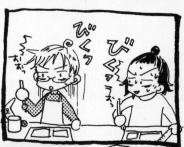

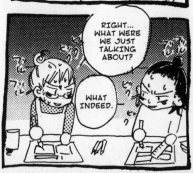

AAAH! HOW FREAKY! WE WERE TOTALLY HAVING A CONVERSATION IN OUR SLEEP! DOING MORE THAN A TWO-PANEL COMIC MAKES FOR A SLEEPY WORLD. YEP.

IN THE FINAL VOLUME OF

Flower *of the* Deep Sleep

YUUKI HAS THE POWER TO DREAM OF THE FUTURE, BUT WITH SUCH A GIFT COMES A GREAT BURDEN. CAN SHE MANIPULATE WHAT'S ABOUT TO HAPPEN? AND, MORE IMPORTANTLY, SHOULD SHE? IN A HAUNTING VISION, YUUKI SEES A MYSTERIOUS LITTLE GIRL WITH WHOM SHE SHARES A SECRET CONNECTION. WHO IS THIS GIRL? DOES SHE HAVE AN EVEN GREATER POWER TO INFLUENCE EVENTS? IN THIS HYPNOTICALLY GRIPPING TALE THAT BLURS THE LINE BETWEEN DREAMS AND REALITY, WILL YUUKI FIND THE ANSWERS IN TIME?

COMING SOON

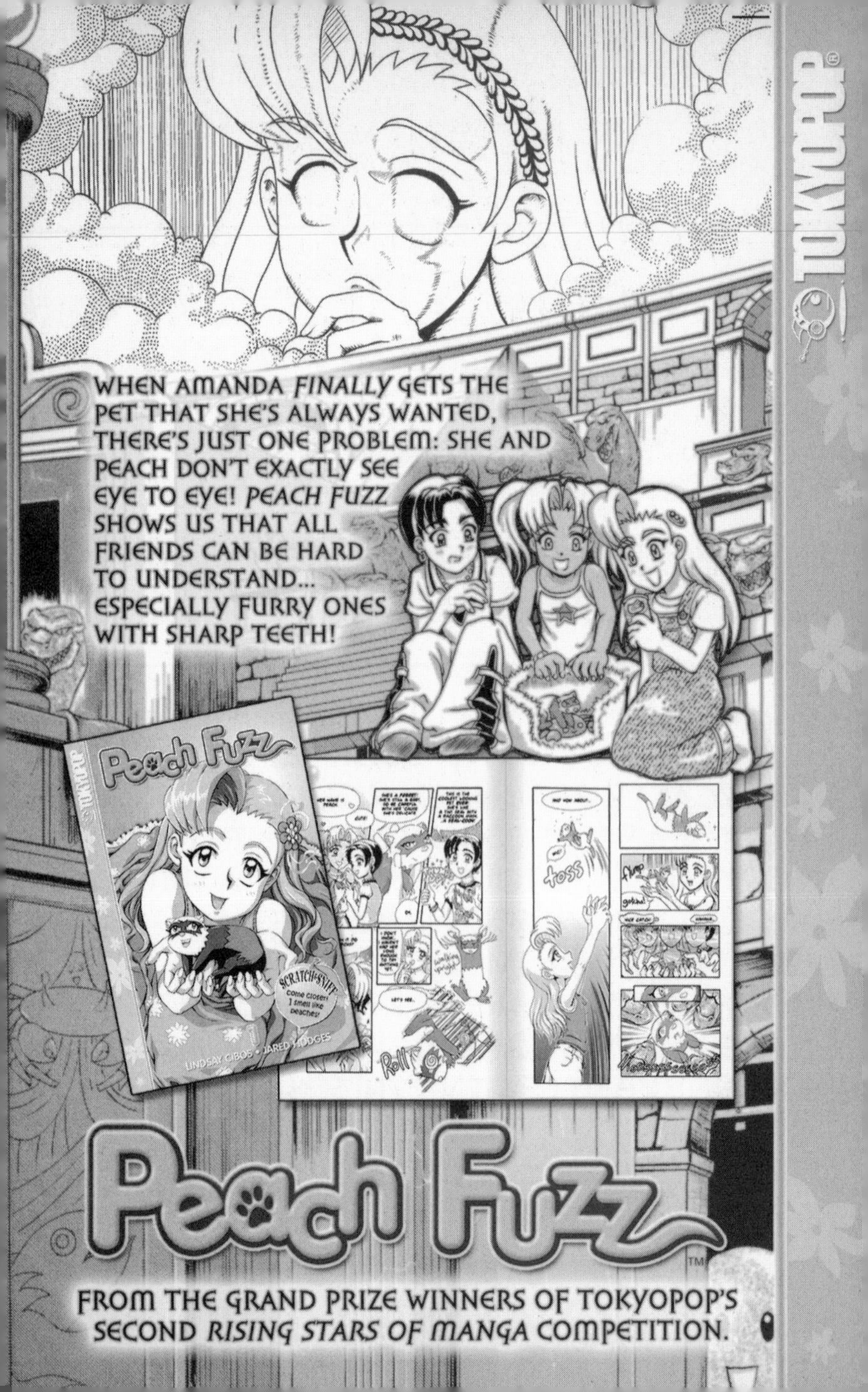
TOKYOPOP®
WHEN AMANDA FINALLY GETS THE PET THAT SHE'S ALWAYS WANTED, THERE'S JUST ONE PROBLEM: SHE AND PEACH DON'T EXACTLY SEE EYE TO EYE! PEACH FUZZ SHOWS US THAT ALL FRIENDS CAN BE HARD TO UNDERSTAND... ESPECIALLY FURRY ONES WITH SHARP TEETH!
Peach Fuzz
SCRATCH & SNIFF Come closer! I smell like peaches!
LINDSAY CIBOS • JARED HODGES
Peach Fuzz™
FROM THE GRAND PRIZE WINNERS OF TOKYOPOP'S SECOND RISING STARS OF MANGA COMPETITION.

THE EPIC STORY
OF A FERRET WHO
DEFIED HER CAGE.

I HEART HOLLYWOOD

Lindsey Kelk is a writer and children's book editor. When she isn't writing, reading, listening to music or watching more TV than is healthy, Lindsey likes to wear shoes, shop for shoes and judge the shoes of others. She loves living in New York but misses Sherbert Fountains, London and drinking Gin & Elderflower cocktails with her friends. Not necessarily in that order. Her first novel *I Heart New York* was published in 2009 and her third novel, *I Heart Paris* will be published in July 2010.

To find out more about the *I Heart* series, sign up for the newsletter, read exclusive extracts and much much more visit www.ihearthollywood.co.uk

By the same author

I Heart New York

Coming soon . . .

I Heart Paris

LINDSEY KELK

I Heart Hollywood

HARPER

This novel is entirely a work of fiction.
The names, characters and incidents portrayed in it are the work of the author's imagination. Any resemblance to actual persons, living or dead, events or localities is entirely coincidental.

Harper
An imprint of HarperCollins*Publishers*
77–85 Fulham Palace Road,
Hammersmith, London W6 8JB

www.harpercollins.co.uk

Special overseas edition 2010
1

First published in Great Britain by
HarperCollins*Publishers* 2010

ISBN: 978 0 00 734116 0

Set in Melior by Palimpsest Book Production Limited,
Grangemouth, Stirlingshire

Printed and bound in Great Britain by
Clays Ltd, St Ives plc

For Big Bear and Little Mouse
(not as nauseating as it sounds, honest)

So many thank yous to say – Lynne, Claire, Victoria and everyone at HC. When you come from inside the beast, you REALLY appreciate how much hard graft goes into making a book work. A million times, thank you.

Yo, Jimmy, LA wouldn't have been the same without you and I couldn't have 'researched' Hollywood half as well without Caterina (my favourite sassy blonde) Philipa and Squeaker. Thank you to Jane, Georgia, Keren, Catherine, Alison, Sam, Rich, Jimmy (again), Pete, Jenny, Ryan, Eric and Chris for abiding by the dress code, to James for going one better and coordinating completely and to Della, Lisa and Miss Aimee for distracting me to the point of almost not getting this done. I miss far too long phone calls, cocktails and boy-bashing with you.

Other than that, thank you to everyone that's emailed, Facebooked, tweeted and twittered at me about *I Heart New York*, you're all brilliant. Unless you said it was crap. I'm just going to ignore you. Mwah.

CHAPTER ONE

The wedding was perfect.

Just ten people at City Hall, no hymns, no readings, no fuss; and then over to Alta in the West Village for the reception. Tiny candles flickered in the faces of my favourite people: Jenny, Vanessa, Erin. And Alex. God, he looked pretty in a suit. I made a mental note to get that boy a three-piece more often. Like maybe at our wedding . . . no, bad Angela, too soon to even think it. Dum-dum-dee-dum . . .

'So you don't think I'm making a ridiculous mistake?' Erin whispered over my shoulder, bringing me back with a bump. 'I mean, it can't be six months since I was telling you I would never get married again.'

I shook my head. 'Not at all.' I glanced over at the new Mr Erin, or Thomas as he was known to his friends. Or 'that mad hot piece of ass' as he was known to Jenny. 'You wouldn't be doing this if it wasn't absolutely the right thing to do.'

'Uh, which it totally is. Hello?' Jenny Lopez swung in and planted a great big kiss on the bride, smudging Mac Ruby Woo lipstick all over her face. 'He's a super-hot,

1

super-rich lawyer and super in love with you. I'm pretty sure they are the main three factors to take into consideration before you hitch your wagon. Plus, wow, classiest wagon ever. Even better than your last wedding. And way better than the one before that.'

'My God, you are so rude,' Erin playfully slapped Jenny's mass of chocolate brown curls. 'But you're right. I couldn't *not* marry him. He's so sweet.'

'Yeah, sweet. I'm totally only getting married when the guy can rent out my favourite restaurant for an entire Saturday evening.' Jenny sighed and sank a full flute of champagne. 'Doesn't Thomas have any single friends? And I do mean, single, rich lawyer friends?'

I couldn't stop smiling. The last wedding I'd been to hadn't been such a roaring success. I had started the day as a blushing bridesmaid with a devoted fiancé and ended up a high-heel-wielding hand-breaker, whose devoted fiancé was at it with some tart in the back of their Range Rover.

After leaving everyone in the wedding party in tears and/or hospital, I had hotfooted it over to New York only to be taken in by Jenny: an entire family, best friend and therapist all in one. It hadn't been a walk in Central Park but I'd found my way eventually. A job blogging for *The Look* magazine, great friends, an actual life, all the things that had been missing for so long. As a hand slid around my waist and pulled me close, I was reminded of the other thing I'd found in New York: Alex Reid.

'So this is the nicest wedding I think I've ever been to,' he gently pressed his lips against my skin. 'And I have the hottest date here.'

'Firstly, there are only eight girls in the entire wedding and secondly, it's still not even true,' I said, turning to

2

brush Alex's long black fringe out of his eyes. 'Erin looks stunning, Jenny is ridiculously pretty in that dress and Vanessa—'

'Will you please just take the compliment?' Alex shook his head. 'And I don't care what you say, there's not a girl in the whole city that could compare with you right now.'

I wrinkled my nose and accepted a kiss, silently thanking my lucky stars. We'd met just after I had arrived in New York and got far too serious, far too quickly. He had put the brakes on and I had spent six months cooling my heels, pretending I wasn't ready to start dating but really wondering when it would be OK to call him. Eventually, I'd picked up the phone, cashed in all my karma chips and, thank God, Buddha and Marc Jacobs, he'd answered. Now I was just trying to have fun and ignore the constant burning feeling in my stomach, that this was it, that Alex was the one. There was no way I wanted a repeat performance of last time. I'd spent ten years with my ex and not once, not for a moment, had I felt so scared to lose him as I did when I lay wide awake at night, watching Alex sleep.

For the last two months, he had been the most attentive, thoughtful, heartbreakingly wonderful boyfriend I could ever have imagined. He bought me little gifts, like the beautiful sunflower, my favourite flower, he'd brought to pin to my olive green Cynthia Rowley shift for the wedding. He surprised me with indoor picnics when I was on deadline, ran out to pick up breakfast before I woke up and even trekked all the way over from Brooklyn to Manhattan with the handbag and keys I'd left at his apartment as well as a huge hangover-friendly pizza when Jenny and I had both managed to lock ourselves out of our place at three a.m. We never did find out where Jenny had left the keys . . . But, most impressively, when I'd drunk far too much at a wine tasting I was supposed to review for *The Look*, he'd held my hair back while I threw up. Outside a very fancy restaurant. While everyone was watching. On his shoes.

And it wasn't just that Alex was competing for the title of World's Best Boyfriend, there was also the little fact that he was also a total rock god to take into consideration. His band had released their third album while we were on our 'break' and, despite a little commercial and a lot of critical success, he was still being a complete angel. While Jenny was loudly insisting that he should be out snorting coke out of groupies' belly buttons, Alex was lying watching *America's Next Top Model*, eating Chinese takeout on our sofa.

I peered up and down the table as we sat down for dinner and couldn't remember a time I'd felt so happy or so at peace with myself. So what if these weren't the people I'd grown up with, or the people that had taught me to ride a bike? They were the people that had taught me to ride the subway and to stand on my own two feet. Or at least how to get back on them after I fell on my arse, drunk.

'Hey, how much does she make you want to puke?' Jenny nudged me. 'How come she's been married, like, seven times and I can't even get laid.'

'I was just having a lovely quiet moment, thinking how lucky I am to have found such amazing friends,' I tapped Jenny's hand. 'And then you go and ruin it.'

'Aww, you love me,' Jenny leaned her head on my shoulder and chucked me under the chin. 'And you know I love you too. But seriously, I'm going to cry. If you and Brooklyn over there think you're getting married before me you're so wrong.'

4

'Jenny!' I looked over at Alex but he was giving one of Thomas's investment banker friends his very best listening face. 'Shut it. We've been together for about two minutes. You'll jinx it.'

'Not possible honey.' Jenny swept her hand over the candle in front of her. 'How many nights have you spent apart since you got back together? Three? Four tops. He is totally into you. And I know you've got the wedding march on replay in your head. I will bet you anything that you have a ring on your finger inside the year. You want me to direct him to some of the more tasteful options? I know he's all, like, 'creative' but you have to get something you can wear for the rest of your life.'

I combed down my long light brown fringe nervously. 'Seriously, stop it. We're taking things slowly and you know it.'

Jenny smiled. 'I know but it's totally obvious. And you know that I'm really pleased for you, it's awesome. But Angie, we have to get *me* laid. It's been like six months, for crying out loud. Oh, thank God, food.'

'Yes, because I really feel like eating right now,' I muttered.

Dinner passed by altogether too quickly, the food amazing but not soaking up the champagne as quickly as I would have liked. A sausage roll and chicken drumstick would really have helped, but this was a classy New York function, not a Clark family knees-up. As dinner turned into speeches and speeches turned into drinks, I excused myself from a fascinating research analyst who almost passed out when I told him I didn't have a pension, and went to look for people I actually wanted to talk to. Erin and Vanessa were busy fulfilling bride and bridesmaid duties at the

5

door, Jenny was giving several of Thomas's friends her best nodding and smiling while Alex was presumably hiding from the same people in the bathroom. He could dress up in a suit and comb down his messy black hair but he couldn't hide the look in his eyes when Thomas and his friends started discussing stocks and shares. Without anyone to protect me from the same death by conversation, I vanished up to the balcony to hide.

'You planning on spying on people too?' Alex asked as I rounded the top of the stairs. He was leaning over the banister, nursing a champagne flute, his tie and collar loosened.

'So this is where you've been hiding,' I took a sip from his glass. Well, one more couldn't hurt. 'I thought maybe you'd left with your new boyfriend from dinner.'

'Yeah, I think we've hit it off. You know I've always been fascinated by high-yield bonds.'

'I knew the band was a front. So who are we spying on?'

He pointed down towards the makeshift bar at the back of the restaurant. 'Well, it was you but then you vanished, so mostly Jenny. Just trying to work out who her target is this evening.'

I spotted her immediately, leaning against the bar, all glossy curls and red pout. She sipped on a clear cocktail and checked her nails, ignoring the guy standing next to her, who was awkwardly trying to attract her attention with a weak cough and terrified smile.

'Looks like she's over Jeff at last,' Alex nodded.

'Looks like,' I frowned. 'But I don't really know. One minute she's all "I want to get laid, I want to get laid", but then she's sat at home every night watching *Nanny 911*. See? It's like he isn't even there.'

'Maybe she's just choosy?' Alex suggested as the

6

hapless banker gave up and moved on to Vanessa. 'Or maybe she just really likes *Nanny 911*?'

'Well, yes she does and she ought to be choosy, she's gorgeous, but it's more than that,' I said. 'I don't know. She goes out, she meets men, they give her their numbers and she never calls. And then at the same time she's rattling on all the time about how she's not getting any. I just don't know what to do for the best. I know she's hung up on Jeff still but it's the one thing she absolutely will not talk about. Sober.'

'Does she still think they'll get back together?' Alex leaned his head against mine.

I shrugged and pouted. The official line was that she was totally over her ex, but the unofficial, drunk-at-two-a.m. line was, 'I'll never get over him as long as I live, he's my soul mate.' But I had a feeling that wasn't something she wanted to share with Alex.

'So I don't tell her that some blonde moved in with him yesterday?' he asked. 'Sorry I didn't say anything earlier. I totally forgot.'

'Seriously?'

Alex nodded.

The fact that he had refused to sell his apartment just because it was in the same building as Jenny's ex was usually reason enough for her to decide she wasn't talking to him for days at a time, so it seemed to make sense to keep this little bit of information to myself. 'No, she cannot find out about that. She'd probably take to her bed for a month.'

'Sounds fun,' he smiled, one hand sliding up my back, the other holding fast to the balcony. 'Can we do that now please?'

I looked up into Alex's ridiculously green eyes, his fringe catching in my eyelashes as he dropped his face to mine for a long kiss. His body was warm against the thin silk of my dress and the balcony pressed into the small of my back. I felt my clutch slip out of my fingers and drop, not sure if it had fallen over the balcony, not sure if I cared.

'I should probably leave soon,' I said, my voice catching as Alex ran his hand down the back of my neck, curling the hair at the nape around his long fingers. 'I have a meeting with Mary at nine.'

'So my place is closer by subway, yours by cab.' Alex's eyes were dark and dilated, his breath quick. 'And I don't think people on the subway would be OK with what I have planned.'

'Cab then,' I smoothed down my dress and scooped up the bag. Thank God it hadn't actually gone over the edge and bashed anyone. I'd assaulted enough people at weddings in my time. 'Have to say, didn't think you'd be the sort of bloke to get turned on by weddings.'

'What sort of "bloke" did you think I was?' Alex smiled. 'And it's not so much weddings as you. Now get your ass in a cab.'

CHAPTER TWO

The next morning was grey and cold, just like every morning had been since the end of November. The hardwood floor in my bedroom felt like ice as I gingerly poked my toes out of the bed and felt around for my slippers. I knew it was stupid not to wear my giant bed socks when Alex stayed over, but we hadn't been together that long, I just didn't think he was ready for it and so I suffered. Like an idiot.

March was the opposite of July. I'd sweltered from the moment I stepped off the plane but now I sometimes wondered if I'd ever be warm again. Hot and sticky summer had given way to a cool and crisp autumn, which was all too quickly overtaken by subzero temperatures and snow storms. As pretty as three feet of snow was, I had learned already that it was a) not a rarity in the city and b) not a good thing. When it snowed at home, everything stopped. My mum waited until the gritter had been around the streets, then trekked up to the shops in her wellies, walking in the road, to buy unnecessary quantities of canned food and eight pints of milk that would go off before she could force my dad to drink them all to avoid them

9

going off. When it really snowed in New York, the roads jammed and the subway stopped but life didn't. And walking in the bitter winds with a face full of sleet did not make it easy to lead the glamorous life that my family in England might have imagined me living. Although that could also be because my emails and phone calls rarely mentioned the fact that I'd been walking around with a Rudolph-red nose, bundled up like the Michelin man for months.

I flicked at the curtain to check the state of the streets. At least it hadn't snowed in the night, but the sky looked grey and threatening and, below, people dashed backwards and forwards, bundled up for an arctic expedition.

'What time is it?' croaked Alex, rolling towards me and pulling the curtain back across the window.

'Seven-thirty,' I sighed, allowing him to pull me back into bed, my feet disappearing under the quilt. Alex was like my very own human hot-water bottle. No matter how cold the apartment was, he was always like a furnace. Aside from the obvious, it was one of my favourite reasons to have him in bed with me. 'And as much as I don't want to, I really do have to get up.'

'See, I go around telling people how awesome it is having a writer for a girlfriend,' Alex grumbled as I pulled away again, 'because she doesn't have to be in an office at nine a.m. every day. And here you are, at seven-thirty . . .'

'I can't help it,' I said, wriggling away from him and braving the icy floorboards again. I pulled on my giant fleecy dressing gown and looked back at him, his eyes squeezed tightly shut, the covers up around his nose. 'Do you really tell people your girlfriend is a writer?'

'Mmm,' Alex rolled himself over under the covers,

hiding his head as I flicked on a lamp. 'What else am I supposed to tell them? You're a British refugee who can't go home because you broke some guy's hand?'

'Arse,' I grabbed a towel off the radiator, heading into the bathroom. 'You can tell people whatever you want.' As long as you tell them I'm your girlfriend, I added silently with a great big smile.

The Spencer Media building was on Times Square, one of my least favourite places in all of Manhattan. Even today, on a frigid Monday in March at eight-fifty in the morning, the streets were pulsing with tourists, clutching their Starbucks and digital cameras with inadequate knitted mittens. I had never thought I'd consider a North Face padded coat a necessity, but then I'd never tried to live through January in New York with nothing but a pretty Marc by Marc Jacobs swing coat and a feeble H&M leather jacket. Never, ever in my entire life had I been so bloody cold. Now I understood the need to forgo my newfound interest in fashion and put on As Many Layers As Humanly Possible before I left the apartment. It was insane.

I pushed past a group of school kids taking it in turns to snap shots of the group, one switching in, one switching out to take over photographer duties, and wondered exactly how many tourists' pictures I had managed to land in since I started working for *The Look*. There were probably millions of shots of a disgruntled-looking girl tutting and sighing in the background all over Facebook.

The views from Mary's forty-second floor office almost made the trekking across Times Square worth it. The higher up I got, the more amazing New York looked to me. At ground level I could sometimes forget where I was – H&M here, HSBC there – but up in the office, surrounded by skyscrapers, watching the rivers sweeping around the island, I couldn't be anywhere else but Manhattan.

'Mary's been waiting for you,' an uninterested voice came from behind a huge computer monitor as I tried to locate the group of kids below.

'Aren't I early?' I asked the monitor. Mary's assistant, Cici, had never been my biggest fan but she usually gave me the courtesy of a dirty look. Unfortunately I was wearing so many layers, I couldn't find my watch, and Spencer Media was a little like Vegas, they didn't bother with clocks, presumably so their staff wouldn't realize how late they were working. Not many days went by when I didn't get emails from Mary and the other editors at nine, ten in the evening.

'Mary gets in at seven, your meeting was due to start at nine.' She stood up and swept around the desk. I couldn't help but hope she must have some really, really warm clothes to change into. Her teeny tiny bottom was squeezed into a skater skirt that just about covered her stocking tops and it didn't look as if she had any thermals on under the gauzy, pussy-bow blouse that topped it off. In fact, it didn't look as if she had anything under it. Oh my. 'It's now three after nine. You're late.'

Was it right for a PA to make me feel like a naughty sixth-former?

'Angela Clark is finally here,' Cici purred ahead of me as we passed though Mary's big glass doors. 'Can I get you anything, boss?'

'More coffee, and do you want anything?' Mary was wearing her standard uniform of skinny jeans, cashmere sweater and steely grey bob, but something about her was different. I realized she was smiling. This had to be a good start.

'I would love a coffee.' I tried a small smile at the assistant who huffed a little and flounced off. 'How are you, Mary?'

'Good, you?' She leaned across her desk and didn't wait for a reply. 'I have a treat for you. You're going to love me.'

'Sounds good.' I began to disrobe. Gloves, scarf, coat. 'I like treats.'

'Well, you know everyone here loves your blog.' Mary templed her fingers under her chin and smiled back. I had been writing an online diary for TheLook.com since I'd arrived in New York, thanks to Jenny's amazingly well-connected friend Erin and my complete lack of shame at spilling the details of my private life all over the internet. And to humour my journalistic ambitions, my editor occasionally threw me the odd book and music review for the magazine when they needed an extra hand. But the most exciting part of it all for me was my column in the UK edition, much to my mother's disgust. She didn't like that Susan in the post office knew what I was up to before she did. 'We have a new project for you. How do you feel about branching out?'

'Branching out?' I paused in my outerwear removal. This sounded an awful lot like a firing. 'Branching out from *The Look*?'

'No, not at all,' Mary nodded thanks as Cici arrived with her coffee. I looked up hopefully. No coffee for Angela. I was definitely being fired. 'This is it, Angela, your big break. An interview has come up and we want you to do it.'

'I've never interviewed anyone before,' I said slowly, not wanting to jinx anything.

'Sure you have, you interview people all the time.' The very fact that Mary couldn't look at me proved she didn't even believe herself. What was going on?

'I have asked questions of the fourth runner-up of *America's Next Top Model* cycle eight and waited in the queue for the toilets with an Olsen twin. They aren't interviews, Mary,' I said. 'Don't you have loads of writers that – you know – specialize in interviewing?'

'We do,' Mary said, looking up and staring me out. 'But this one is yours. Are you telling me you don't want to do it?'

Miraculously, a steaming coffee appeared in front of me, but Cici had turned on her heel before I could say thanks. Baby steps, I thought to myself.

I took a deep breath. Of course I wanted to do an interview. How hard could it be to ask some random a few questions? 'Of course I want to. It'll be great. I'll be great. I'll manage. I'll try.'

'No try here, Angela.' Mary pushed her frameless glasses up her nose. 'This is a biggie. One week in LA with James Jacobs.'

'James Jacobs? The actor?' I asked, sipping tiny scorching gulps. 'Me?'

'Yes you,' Mary leaned back a little in her chair. 'And yes, the actor. The very hot British actor.'

'You want me to interview him for the website?'

'Not quite,' she replied. 'It's for the magazine.'

'You want me to interview James Jacobs for the magazine?' I wondered if I'd slipped and cracked my head on the shower this morning. That would explain why I thought Mary was suggesting I should interview this very hot British actor.

'That's right,' she carried on. 'You go to LA, you bond over being British, talk about, I don't know tea and crumpets, and you get the inside scoop. He hasn't done an awful lot of press but apparently he really wants to do this. Let his female fans in on the "real him" or some other shit.'

'From what I've heard, he's already let rather a lot of female fans in.' I pulled off my last jumper, hot and flustered all of a sudden. 'Isn't he a bit of a slag?'

'If you mean, has he been "linked with several Hollywood starlets", then yes.' Mary made bunny ears around the quote. She typed something into her Mac at super speed, then swivelled the monitor to face me. 'But this is what we want to get past. His team are worried that all this "attention" could create a negative vibe with his female audience.'

The screen showed a Google image search. James Jacobs was tall, broad and athletic and there was no denying he looked good in a pair of swimming trunks. His dark blue eyes and damp, dark brown curls just added to the overall 'Abercrombie at play' look.

'Doesn't look very British to me,' I commented, taking the mouse and clicking through a few more pictures. 'Where's he from again?'

'Uh, his Wikipedia entry says London.' Mary took the mouse back and flicked through to what was obviously her favourite shot, halfway down the page, James staring directly at me, dark brown hair tickling his cheekbones, bow tie loose, top two buttons of his shirt undone. 'So you fly on Saturday.'

'Sorry, what?' I snapped back from the pretty pictures and looked at Mary. She had her, 'I'm really not kidding' face on. Not a favourite of mine. 'But, it's Monday?'

'Which gives you almost a whole week to prep.' Mary started to click at other things on her screen. A sure-fire sign that the meeting was all but over. 'So, Cici will book your flights, your car, hotel and organize all the other stuff. Cash, credit card, BlackBerry, whatever.'

'But, seriously, is this a good idea? Maybe I don't have the experience for this. I'm not a professional interviewer, I'm a talker at best – and, when I'm lucky, people talk back. That's really not a qualification.' I leaned over the desk. Was Mary not feeling well? 'And I've never been to LA before. What, I mean is, really, this doesn't make that much sense, surely?'

'Look, Angela,' Mary's eyes flickered across her screen. 'Here's the thing. I'm not supposed to tell you but they asked for you.'

'What?'

'Hey, I'm as surprised as anyone else.' Mary pulled a face. 'Not that I don't think you're great but, like you said, you're not a professional interviewer: we both know that. But James's people wouldn't have anyone else. It was the only condition of the interview.'

I didn't know what to say. What could I possibly have done that could attract the attention of James Jacobs's 'people'? I didn't think they would have been that impressed with my critically acclaimed series on which Manhattan department store was the best to hit for a free makeover before you went out (Bloomingdale's, Soho).

'If you're not going to do it, just say,' Mary went on. 'The entertainment team on the magazine are already incredibly pissed off. They can get someone else like that—'

'No!' I said quickly. 'It's not that. I absolutely want to do it. It's amazing. I just – I just don't get it.'

'Me either.' Mary really didn't believe in sugar-coating anything. Even when I would have preferred it. 'I can only tell you what they told me. James's team doesn't want a polished, super celebrity reporter who is going to stiff them with some horrible sordid Hollywood exposé. They want someone who is going to help show James as – you know – a fantasy guy. The whole point of the article is it needs to be fluffy,

16

not scandalous, sort of a "My Dream Week with James Jacobs". Almost like it was written by a reader.'

'So basically an amateur not experienced enough to weasel out the details of his secret love child?' I surmised, slightly relieved and slightly offended at the same time.

'Yeah, pretty much.' Mary had either missed or chosen to ignore the part where I was slightly offended. 'The entertainment editor thought it was maybe because, you know, you're British so he'll trust you.'

'Britain isn't just this little quaint village where everyone makes jam and says good morning to their neighbours, you know,' I grumbled half-heartedly. 'Margaret Thatcher was British and no one trusted her.'

'So, like I said, Cici will get you everything.' Mary pointed towards the door, where Cici stood, clipboard in her hand, hateful look on her face. 'And you'll blog from LA, OK? You can say you're doing an interview but it's probably best not to give too much away. Save it for the magazine. It'll be good for you.'

'And people weren't that mad on Tony Blair towards the end,' I added thoughtfully. 'And Sweeney Todd. Was he real?'

'No, Angela, he wasn't,' Mary looked back across the desk. 'Angela, they have asked for you. We are sending you. Against the wishes of the editorial team. Against the wishes of the publishing team. Do not fuck this up. You don't want to lose your visa, do you?'

I bit my bottom lip. It was like getting told off by my mum. 'Lose my visa?'

'This is a major interview for the magazine and, if you do it right, could even go international,' Mary explained. 'If this goes wrong, the publishers are hardly likely to want to continue with your blog, are they?'

'No,' I said, suddenly feeling very sick.

'Look, no one's expecting a Pulitzer prize-winning article, just go out there and talk to this man. There are a lot worse ways to spend a week in March. You're getting an all-expenses-paid trip to LA, plus you're getting paid. Suck it up, go buy a bikini and interview the handsome man.' She waved me out of my seat. 'I'll see you in two weeks. And don't screw it up.'

I felt a bony grip on my shoulder and rose tentatively out of my chair. Please let it be Death, I prayed silently, gathering up my sweaters, gloves and coat.

'Can we please hurry this up?' came the snide voice attached to the Vulcan death-grip. 'I have other things to do today.'

'Oh, Cici,' I said, trying not to be disappointed. She might be as bony as Death but Cici was a lot more dangerous.

'And then, as if I wasn't freaked out enough, she basically said they only want me because I'm an amateur.' I dropped my head onto the table in Scottie's Diner, across the street from our apartment, toppling the tomato sauce into Jenny's fries. 'Shouldn't I be insulted?'

'OK, firstly, you kinda are an amateur, aren't you?' Jenny gulped her Diet Pepsi and shrugged. 'I just mean you've never interviewed anyone before, right? And uh, hello, you're going to LA on Saturday?'

'Yes,' I started, 'but—'

'Shut. Up.' Jenny held out her hand. 'You're being paid to fly to sunny, hot LA from cold, fugly New York. In March. To interview one of the hottest men in the entire world. Who has specifically asked for you. And they're paying you for it. I see no bad here. It's a massive step for your career, you're interviewing one of the hottest men in the world. And you're going to LA. With one of the hottest men ever. In LA.'

18

'I can see that you've found a couple of positives.' I frowned, sipping my hot chocolate. 'But – and I know I sound like a whiny cow, but the more I think about it, it just doesn't feel like a good idea. I don't want to take on such an amazing opportunity and then cock it up because I don't know how to interview someone, let alone some Hollywood super-stud. Plus, I don't really want to disappear off to LA for a week on my own. Not at the moment . . .' I tailed off and looked into my hot chocolate, painfully aware that I had said absolutely the wrong thing.

Jenny shook her head. 'Uh-uh. You are not doing this: it could be my only chance to meet James Jacobs. And, you know, it would be nice to head out to LA again,' she pointed with a floppy fry. 'If you even suggest turning this down because you've just got back into Alex's shorts, I will be so angry with you.'

'Firstly, that's not what I meant,' I lied, pulling the fries across the table. Most days, I loved that Jenny knew exactly what I was really thinking, no matter what actual words made it out of my mouth, but some-times it was just irritating. 'And secondly, when were you last in LA? And thirdly, you're coming with me?'

'Firstly, yes I am, secondly a few years ago, I've so told you before and you never listen and, thirdly, that is exactly what you meant and it's bullshit.'

'It's not that I don't want to go, or at least not because of Alex. I–I don't know. I'll miss him. Is that the saddest thing ever?'

'Yes, it is.' Jenny gave me her best 'you're being ridicu-lous' look. 'You don't think he's going to cheat on you?'

'No, of course not,' I shrugged. The thought might have crossed my mind. 'Things are just going really well right now. But things were going really well before and look what happened.'

'Oh Angie,' Jenny said, 'it's different this time. Any idiot can see it's real between you two.'

'Wasn't it real before?' I asked. It had been everything I could do not to even think these things all day and now here I was, saying it all out loud. 'And he walked away. And did God-knows-what with God-knows-who. Who's to say I go away and he's out with his friends and, well, you know. Have you seen him? He's bloody gorgeous.'

'Yeah, so over that and hello? He won't cheat on you because he loves you.' Jenny stabbed at me with a fry loaded with ketchup.

'He hasn't said so.'

'Have you said it?'

'Nope.'

'Do you love him?'

'Yes.'

'Huh. So you've been thinking it but not saying it?'

'Er, yes.'

'So what makes you think he isn't thinking it but hasn't said it either?' Jenny reasoned.

'But what if I say it and he thinks I'm moving too fast and dumps me again?' I countered.

'So you don't say it,' Jenny held up her hands. 'Or you do. Whatever.'

'Hmm.' I nibbled a fry thoughtfully while Jenny wolfed down a whole handful. 'You were there on holiday?'

'Where, LA?' Jenny asked through a mouthful.

I nodded, trying not to look at the big potato-ey mess. For a very beautiful girl, Jenny could be foul sometimes.

'Way to change the subject. OK, don't laugh, but before I decided to become the new Oprah and before Tyra frickin' Banks beat me to it, I thought I might give acting

20

a shot. So I spent a while in LA, stayed out for the pilot season, but it wasn't for me so I came back to New York. It might be nice to go back out, see some friends. Maybe we could stay at The Hollywood. I could take a week's vacation and you know, you can introduce me to James Jacobs.'

'OK, OK, this is too much.' I couldn't help but grin at Jenny. 'And don't you dare try and change the subject – that's my thing. You went to Hollywood to be an actress?'

'And I'd have been a silver-screen goddess but the West Coast wasn't for me.' Jenny shook her head. 'Can we leave it?'

'Fine, I just – well, I can't imagine you playing anyone other than Jenny Lopez,' I said.

'It's the role of a lifetime.' Jenny gave me a quick flash of jazz hands. 'You do mean me and not the other one, right? Because I'd have to kick your ass.'

'You're more of a diva,' I agreed. 'So what's The Hollywood?'

Jenny waved at the old silver-haired man behind the counter. 'Sister hotel. It's The Union in New York and there's The Hollywood in LA, The Strip in Vegas and, uh, The Something Else in Paris. I can never remember. Scottie, could we get some more fries, please?'

'How many times do I tell you, my name it is not Scottie, it is Igor,' the guy behind the counter trundled over with more fries. 'I buy this place from Scottie, this is why it is called Scottie's Diner.'

'Thanks, Scottie,' Jenny gingerly picked up scalding hot chip and blew on it, 'you're good people.'

'Are you sure we could stay there? The magazine said they would put me up in an apartment some-where.' I couldn't believe the amount of crap Jenny could eat and never gain a pound. A true disciple of

WeightWatchers, I had forgone almost all foods with a calorie content higher than that of a carrot for a whole year to slim into my ill-fated bridesmaid dress. Walking the streets of New York City every single day helped, but I could never be one of those girls who scarfed ice cream, pizza and chocolate all day long without putting on weight. A girl like Jenny, who only ever put on a couple of pounds – tops; which went straight to her already curvy curves and never ever to her tiny waist. If she weren't such a great friend, I could really get around to hating her.

'We are totally staying there. Tell the magazine you're fixed,' Jenny was already halfway through the new plate of fries. 'As if I would let you stay in some skanktastic apartment. Who knows where you would end up. Besides, my friend Joe is managing the bar and I'm due a whole heap of vacation days. The hotel totally owes me. And Joe and I totally have history, he'll look after us.'

'By history, do you mean you shagged him? And by "us" do you mean "you"?'

'Well, yeah.' Jenny's eyes glazed over slightly. 'So if it doesn't work out with me and James Jacobs, I can always call on Joe. I need to get laid already.'

'Really? And Joe, this is Hot Joe who used to work at The Union?' I asked, testing the waters. 'You're sure you're up to seducing movie stars and bartenders?'

'I'm fine,' Jenny replied, without looking up at me. 'Seriously, I'm all shiny and new.'

'Good, because I've been worried.' I slapped her hand away from the fries. 'You haven't been your usual irritating self for ages.'

'It's just winter,' she said. 'I know I've been out of it a little. I've been thinking about taking a break, so well done on the perfect timing.'

I smiled. Going to Hollywood with Jenny could be fun. 'So, we're off to LA then?'

'Angie, honey, when have I ever steered you wrong? It will be awesome,' Jenny replied, scooping up the last fry. 'And I'm sure Alex is just delightful if you're into skinny hipsters, but Joe is almost, *almost* as hot as James Jacobs. You organize the flights, I'll organize the hotel and the booty call.'

'Ick,' I shook my head. 'Just ick.'

I hopped on the L train at Union Square after abandoning my overexcited best friend outside the hotel. As the train trundled over to Brooklyn, Jenny's giddiness started to wear off. I'd almost forgotten that this wasn't a girls' holiday, it was a job. It was a interview that, if I screwed it up, could cost me my job, my visa, everything. Climbing up the subway stairs, it just seemed like such a bad idea and, on top of everything, as tragic as it was, I really didn't want to leave Alex. I couldn't tell him I loved him in case he panicked and ditched me, but if I didn't tell him, how would he know not to cheat on me with every groupie in Brooklyn while I was away?

And the potential destruction of my personal and professional life aside, what was in LA anyway? A seven-hour flight, a whole city full of super-hot, super-bronzed beach bimbettes and, most terrifying of all, a week-long interview with a real-life, genuine movie star.

Writing my blog was easy: there was always something interesting to talk about, and anyone could review some books and even a few CDs – that just meant winging a couple of hundred words. But there was no way I could bluff my way through this. There was no denying that it could be a great opportunity for me as a writer, but it was also a fabulous opportunity for me to fall flat on my arse. I was just an 'amateur', after all. The vision of me throwing myself off the 'H' of the Hollywood sign clutching a signed photo of James Jacobs played over and over in my mind until I reached Alex's apartment.

'Hey.' He opened the door, pulled me in and pushed me backwards against the wall, kissing me hard on the lips.

'I am so cold,' I breathed, shaking my scarf, mittens and coat off onto the floor. 'Give me a good reason why I shouldn't go to LA on Saturday.'

'The pizza sucks?' Alex muttered, hoisting me up onto his kitchen counter, pulling off my top two sweaters in one swift move.

'That'll do,' I nodded, trying to kick my boots off behind his back but succeeding only in bashing him in the hip seven times.

'That actually really hurts.' Alex tugged the boots off for me.

I crossed my legs behind his back as he stumbled with me into the living room. 'Yeah, it's never like it is in films, is it?'

Alex's place was just as dishevelled as its owner, with books, guitar strings and worn T-shirts strewn everywhere. Luckily, the beautiful floor-to-ceiling windows that looked out over the East River to Manhattan made up for the disgusting kitchen. Lying full stretch on the sofa while Alex strummed something new on his acoustic guitar (and I pretended not to be watching *Gossip Girl* with the subtitles on) was officially my new favourite way to spend a Monday night. I yawned, gazing out at the skyline. When you weren't outside, New York was gorgeous in the snow. The sun, sea and sand could never compete.

The apartment was also about twenty degrees hotter

than mine and now, thoroughly warmed up, I was perfectly happy wearing nothing but Alex's T-shirt and my pants, moulding myself against his slowly rising and falling chest on the sofa, my bare legs tangled in his long, warm limbs. We hadn't quite made it into the bedroom, something I was always proud of. I'd come a long way from the Angela Clark who spent five or so years tucked up in her winceyette PJs before her ex came home so she wouldn't have to endure his huffing, puffing and generally uncomfortable fumblings.

'So, any reason in particular I should be trying to talk you out of going to LA on Saturday?' Alex asked, combing his fingers through my mussed-up hair. Between getting back together with Alex and the terrible weather, my do was very much a constant don't. 'That was a pretty random request, even for you.'

'The magazine wants me to go and interview this actor.' I waved a hand around, working very hard to come across as very casual about the whole thing. 'But they want me to go on Saturday and I've never really interviewed anyone before so I don't know. I'm sort of in two minds about it.'

'Sounds like a great opportunity,' he offered diplomatically. 'LA'll be warmer than New York.'

'Yeah,' I said, twisting my neck around to get a better look at him. 'I know, it could be amazing. It's just a long way and stuff.'

'It is,' he agreed. 'But you never know, you might like it?'

'Do you?' I asked. 'Like LA, I mean.'

'Mehh,' he held his hand up to mine. My small pale hands, with the nibbled-at fingernails filed down, palm to palm with his long, calloused, guitar-playing fingers. 'I don't love it.'

'So you wouldn't want to come with me?' I asked,

25

only briefly considering Jenny's wrath. 'It'll only be for a week or something.'

'However will I survive without you?' Alex kissed my hand.

I paused for a moment to feel his heartbeat. Perfectly even. 'I don't know. I just don't know if I should do it. Even if it could be incredible.'

'Then don't go.' Alex's heartbeat started to slow, I could tell he was about to drop off. That was my only bedroom-based problem with the boy. He always needed a post-shag nap whereas sex left me wide-awake. And since I overthought every situation at the best of times, his post-coital narcolepsy wasn't ideal for me. Depending on how the day had gone, I was either planning our wedding (I thought barefoot on the beach in Mexico; I'd never been but it sounded sort of fabulous) or panicking that the whole relationship was about to fall apart again.

I tried to toss and turn quietly, torn between running off to LA with Jenny and staying exactly where I was for ever and ever when my phone starting buzzing inside my beautiful bag. Slipping out of Alex's arms, I shuffled down the sofa and answered.

'Hello?' I whispered, creeping into the bathroom.

'Angela, it's me,' a voice crackled from a long way away. 'Are you there? You're so faint?'

'Louisa! How are you? Is everything OK? You never call my mobile.' Louisa was my best friend from for ever. We'd grown up together, gone to the same university, moved to London at the same time, basically done everything together – right up until I broke her husband's hand at their wedding. But since we had resolved that tiny issue, our regular weekly phone calls could go on for hours. She wouldn't mind if I had a wee while we chatted. I hoped.

'I know, but you weren't home and I couldn't wait, it's too exciting.' I hadn't heard her so giddy since she'd told me about her engagement. 'Tim's bank got taken over by some American bank this morning, did you see it on the news?'

'Louisa, given that I was engaged to a banker for five years and couldn't even tell you what his job title was, I think you're probably going to have to fill me in on the details. Is Tim's job OK?'

'Yes, better than OK!' Louisa was still gushing. 'They've asked him and his team to go meet the US operation. We're coming to New York for a week. Next week!'

I snapped upwards so quickly I almost toppled off the loo seat. 'Louisa, that's amazing! When do you get here? Do you know where you're staying? God, there are so many places I'm going to take you!'

'Angela, are you on the toilet?'

Yes. 'No?'

'Good, because that would be disgusting,' she said sternly. 'Anyway, we're all flying out on Friday night, I'm not sure where we're staying, Tim literally just called me to tell me. Oh, Angela, I can't wait to see you.'

'Oh I know, you too,' I said, trying to wash my hands and flush super quietly. 'And Tim. Oh, I can't believe it!'

'There's just one thing that might be . . . but well, it's nothing really,' Louisa's excitement faltered slightly. 'I mean, New York is a big city and everything, isn't it?'

'Louisa . . . ?'

'It's just, well, like I say, nothing. Forget I said it. I'm coming to New York!'

'Louisa Price!'

'Fine, well, it's not just Tim coming out.' Louisa finally sighed. 'It's his whole team.'

'So . . . Mark?'

'Erm, yes, and . . . well.'

'Mark and . . . her?'

Even six months after finding out my boyfriend had been cheating on me, I still couldn't actually say her name. As happy as I was with Alex, as pleased as I was to be out of that relationship, girl logic prevailed – he was an evil cheating scumbag and she was a nasty skank.

'Oh, Lou,' I massaged my temples. 'Seriously?'

'It'll be fine,' Louisa insisted. 'You won't have to see him, will you? Unless, I mean, unless you want to?'

'That's not even funny.' My brain was spinning. 'Why would I want to even see him?'

'Well, it has been ages and you two were together a long time,' Louisa said slowly. 'Maybe you'd feel better if you did see him?'

'Do you remember what happened the last time I saw him?' I could feel myself getting angry, and angry was not my best look. Hence the hand-breaking incident at Louisa's wedding. 'And what happened the last time you didn't tell me something? What's going on, since when were you Mark's biggest fan again?'

'All right, yes, Mark asked Tim to ask me if I would get you to meet him,' Louisa rushed. 'But I said he had to get in touch himself if he wanted to see you. Because if you don't want to see him then you don't have to and I said I wasn't going to try and trick you or guilt-trip you or anything. He's a tit.'

I stared at Alex's bathroom ceiling, feeling the entire last six months slip away. Of course it would make sense to meet with Mark. We had been together for ten years, grown up together really. And it would make me the bigger person; help prove to everyone that I had really changed in the last six months. And it would all be on my terms: New York was my home now, after all, and he'd never even been to America. And of course I really wouldn't want to but, if forced, I would be able to flaunt my beautiful new super-cool boyfriend. Nothing intimidated a money man like a guitar boy. They didn't understand them.

But of course none of that would matter if I wasn't in New York when Mark arrived . . .

'Angela, are you still there?'

'I am, lovely, but I have really bad news.' I took a deep breath. 'I'm actually going to LA on Saturday for work. I forgot.'

'You're what?' Louisa said.

'I'm going to LA to interview James Jacobs, so I won't be here.'

'And you forgot that?'

'Yes.'

'You forgot you were flying out to LA this Saturday and interviewing one of the most famous men in the world?'

'He's not that famous,' I protested. Wow, Louisa was pissed off.

'Is this because Mark is coming? Because you're better than that, you know.'

I paused before answering. 'Actually no, it's not just that,' I said. 'It's really something I have to do. It's an amazing opportunity, isn't it? I mean, I'm not going to lie, I'm a bit relieved that I'm not going to see him, it's not top of my list of things to do this weekend, but I do have to go to LA. I'm gutted that I'm not going to see you though.'

'Right.'

'Lou, please don't be mad?' I begged.

'I'm not mad,' she sighed eventually. 'I'm just sad that I won't get to see you. But yeah, it's no contest really, is it? I can see why you'd rather nip off to LA and meet James Jacobs than hang around in freezing New York for the week.'

And for the first time, so did I.

'You're amazing,' I smiled, excitement and relief bubbling up in my stomach. 'I'm going to email you with all the incredible places you have to go and you call me if you get stuck for anything to do at any time, OK?' We said goodbye and I hung up, breathed in deeply and then pressed speed-dial without even looking. 'Cici? Can I come in later and book my flights? I go on Saturday, right?'

CHAPTER THREE

Saturday came around altogether too quickly for me and not nearly quickly enough for Jenny. After calling in a few favours at work to get the week off, she had spent the entire week waxing, scrubbing and fake-tanning, in between sending increasingly indecent text messages to Joe at The Hollywood and throwing increasingly indecent bikinis into a tote bag. I took a more stressful approach to preparing for the trip.

After my not-so-fun phone call with Louisa, I'd headed back to bed to tell Alex I'd changed my mind about going LA. A sleepy smile and 'cool, bring me back something carb-free' wasn't strictly the response I'd been hoping for, but I wasn't going to let my hot boyfriend paranoia ruin LA for me. Admittedly, not so secretly, I had been hoping he would hate the idea of me taking off to interview the gorgeous man with an appalling reputation in sunny sparkly Hollywood and beg to come with me but not so much. He'd barely even acknowledged it.

And to make matters worse, he'd been 'working' all week and I'd hardly seen him. The band had just started writing their new record, which meant hours locked away in his apartment and a couple of unannounced arrivals at my place at random times in the night, with fevered eyes and a new song to play. And, well, everything else that came along with a two a.m. drop-in. Which wasn't *so* bad, but being with Alex all night and writing all day had not left me looking my best. By Friday evening, Jenny looked like a Playmate, all buffed, bronzed and big hair, while I looked more like an inmate, bedraggled, bloated and big bags under my eyes.

At eight in the bitter morning, Jenny stood impatiently on the corner of our street, huddled in her down-filled parka and even bigger sunglasses, while I lingered in my goodbye hug with Alex.

'So let me know when you get there.' He pulled at the slightly longer side of my bob, curling it around his finger. 'Just text or something.'

I nodded. 'If I'm not too busy bailing this one out for sexual harassment.' Jenny was reading her text messages with a wicked smile. 'Possibly literally bailing her out.'

'Well, as long as you're not sexually harassing anyone but me.' He leaned in for a warm kiss, his fringe brushing against my frozen nose, making me sneeze. 'How do you feel about phone sex?'

'You must be freezing,' I said, ignoring his question, 'and Jenny's about to get in a cab without me.' Oh, and I love you by the way, I added silently. 'Um, I'll call you later?'

'For the phone sex,' Alex nodded with deadly seriousness. 'Don't forget you're three hours behind me.'

'Well, you're always up three hours later than me anyway.' I nodded at Jenny to wave down a passing cab.

'This could be the perfect thing for us then.' Alex passed me my battered leather weekend bag. It looked

32

pitiful next to my (sigh, so pretty) Marc Jacobs handbag. Maybe it would find a new friend in LA. 'We could be the first couple to ever make a long-distance relationship work.'

'Yeah, whatever.' I tried to laugh. Trust a boy to say something stupid just before you got on a plane. God, I should just say it. 'Alex?'

'Angela?'

'I . . . I . . .' I paused, not really knowing what I was waiting for. Alex shivered expectantly, his breath fogging up between us, hands stuck deep into his jeans pockets. 'I'll be back next Monday. Don't get too used to being on your own.'

Congratulations on wimping out. What a great example of a strong, modern woman I was turning out to be.

'You're only going away for a week. I think I'll survive.' Alex kissed my frozen nose and shut the door. 'And again with the phone sex.'

'Bye, Alex.' I love you, I love you, I love you, I love you.

'You're not exactly down with the phone sex then?' Jenny asked as we pulled away.

'Shut up,' I replied pleasantly, watching our building – and Alex – vanish out of sight.

From the second we stepped out of the airport, it was completely obvious that California was going to be very different to New York. As we headed out onto the freeway, I couldn't quite believe we were in the same country. The city was wide open, cars streaming up and down the highways with their tops down, the skyscrapers of downtown sparkling in the distance rather than constantly pressing down on us and, bejesus, the sunshine.

Despite the bitching and moaning I'd done about the steamy New York summer at the time, one morning I had woken up and it had gone. The weather teased me with a couple of weeks of creamy, cardigan-appropriate autumn before dissolving into burns-your-nose-when-you-breathe winter. It wasn't like New York didn't try its best to win me over – the shops were soon full of cute jumpers, flattering opaque tights and massive quantities of delicious hot chocolate – but by Christmas, when I had been snowed in twice and lost a pair of suede shoe-boots to an unforeseen storm, I was dying for a little bit of sunshine. And here it was. Hiding away in LA all this time.

'Oh my God,' I blinked once. Twice.

'I know,' Jenny patted me reassuringly on the back.

'But it's sunny.' I looked up at the clear blue sky.

'I know,' Jenny sighed.

'In March?'

'Can we please just shush?'

'Jenny, look!' I pressed my nose up against the cab window, watching billboards and fast-food restaurants whizz by. At least taxi drivers still drove like psychos – London, New York, LA, all the same. It was oddly reassuring.

'Yeah,' Jenny muttered, touching up her make-up. A little Touche Eclat, some bronzer, a dash of lip gloss and, ta-da, she looked perfect.

I was avoiding even catching my reflection in the cab window. Even though I had spent the flight cleansing, moisturizing and then moisturizing some more, I knew I looked like crap. My skin felt like sandpaper and my hair hung around my cheeks, limp and lifeless. What was more annoying was that Jenny had done nothing for three hours but slump against the window, watch half a series of *America's Next Top*

Model and drink as many free glasses of wine as they would give her, occasionally slapping away my attempts to moisturize her against her will. And bless the man in the seat next to us for only complaining once when one of my misdirected paws full of Beauty Flash Balm accidentally landed slap in the centre of his forehead.

'Did you see that?' I pointed at a strip-mall. 'There's a shop called Condomania? Wow. And IHOP! I've heard of IHOP!'

'Angela, you've been living here for – like – nine months or something. Why are American stores and restaurants still a total revelation to you?' Jenny pointed with a mascara wand for emphasis. 'If this entire trip is going to be like the time you saw Twinkies in the corner store, then goddamn it, we are going home now.'

'Sorry,' I said, trying not to point out the Wal-Mart to our left, 'but it's exciting! You see this stuff on TV but then they don't have it in New York – I'm just a bit giddy. I can't believe I didn't want to come. Maybe it's the sun.'

'Yeah, whatever,' Jenny muttered. 'You know you have to interview a celebrity tomorrow, right?'

'It's just an interview; he's just a person, isn't he?' I wrinkled my nose at Jenny's incredulous head-shake. 'I mean, Alex is a bit famous, he's in a band and that doesn't bother me. They're just people, aren't they?'

'Yeah, that's what I said when I started at The Union,' Jenny sighed. 'Until Christian Bale checked in and I spent three days sneaking around his room and stealing his underwear.'

'Please tell me you're kidding.' I tore my eyes away from a Taco Bell.

'They're under my bedside table,' Jenny smiled happily. 'Thank God he never complained. I'd only been there a week; they would have fired me for sure. You're going to lose your mind when you actually see him.'

'Jenny, really, I'll be fine,' I said, trying not to doubt myself. What if she was right? 'He's just a person. I've talked to people before.'

'Good luck,' she said. 'Celebs aren't like normal people; it's impossible not to get fazed by them. They just have this, like, charisma.'

'But you see celebrities every day,' I argued. 'And you do nothing but slag off Angelina Jolie for wanting a special kind of tea.'

'Oh, yeah, I meant celeb boys,' Jenny conceded. 'I don't give a shit about the girls. You're going to lose it over James Jacobs, honey.'

I shook my head and smiled, turning to look back out the window. 'I've never even seen one of his films. I thought it would be better not to get caught up in the movie-star thing and just concentrate on getting to know him.'

'What's to know? He's super hot, he's a movie star so he must be super rich, and he's super talented. Jeff and I saw that one about the casino . . .' She trailed off for a moment. The 'J' word. 'He was pretty good.'

The rest of the cab ride was awkwardly silent but mercifully short. I was terrified of setting Jenny off with a mention of her ex: nine times out of ten it ended badly. Once I had tried to cheer her up after a shitty day at work (she'd mixed up Mischa Barton and Nicole Richie's dry cleaning – all hell broke loose) with a surprise Ben & Jerry's, only to get a weepy, slightly icky story about her, Jeff, the kitchen floor, a tub of Chunky Monkey and New Year's Eve 2007. Another time when she thought she'd seen him on the subway, I'd tried to distract her with several bottles of wine, but the evening had ended at four a.m. with Jenny in her PJs in a drunken rage, railing against all men. And then throwing up out of our third-floor window. Happy memories.

Soon we were off the freeway and passing stores and coffee shop chains I recognized. An American Apparel, a Starbucks, the Gap, a Starbucks and, eventually, actual people walking up and down the streets. Clutching Starbucks.

'We're here,' the driver barked, swerving sharply into a small circular driveway. 'Seventy-five bucks.'

'Seriously?' I whispered to Jenny, as I pulled out my wallet and handed over my precious 'expenses' cash from *The Look*.

'Cabs here are insane,' Jenny said, hauling herself out onto the street. 'Everyone in LA drives. Why do you think all the celebutards are always getting served with DUIs out here? No cabs.'

'Can't they walk if they know they're going out to get trashed?' I asked, crawling across the back seat after trying the door with no success. If it was possible, it was even sunnier at the hotel than at the airport.

Jenny looked at me as though I was completely backwards. 'This is not New York, Angela. Don't you know anything about LA?'

I didn't know anything about LA.

If it was possible, the lobby of The Hollywood was even swankier than The Union. The dim lighting was just as flattering, the dozens of candles were just as chokingly scented, but there was an extra layer of gloss on everything, from the shining gold surfaces to the hair of the girls behind the concierge desk. The only thing missing were the packs of well-to-do tourists huddled around their suitcases, mummified inside

North Face down jackets. In their place were what seemed to be half a dozen extras from *90210*. Tall, gorgeous and half naked, they lounged against furniture – not quite sitting on it, just against it. While Jenny checked us in I tried to remain staring at the floor to avoid mirrored surfaces, but I could see myself reflected in their gaze quite clearly. And no amount of flattering lighting was going to help.

'Come on Angie,' Jenny squealed over by the lift. 'We're on the fourteenth floor, amazing views. And we have adjoining rooms! You're just a door away from me.'

'Does that door lock?' I asked, trying to stop staring at the beautiful people in reception.

'Why on earth would you want to lock the door on me?' Jenny breezed into the lift and jabbed at the big round '14' button. 'Come *on*, the sooner we get unpacked, the sooner we can get in the pool.'

'The pool?' I dragged my wheeled case into the lift, while one of the girls in the world's shortest shorts lowered her sunglasses and checked me out with a genuine look of horror on her face. I was certain that she was visualising the horror of me in a bikini. Just like I was.

'Isn't it amazing, Angie?' Jenny squeezed my arm with slightly too much upper-body strength. 'We're in LA baby, woo!'

As the doors slid shut, the lift shot up and my stomach sank.

To make matters worse, I had not packed well. Or even vaguely appropriately. Standing by the bed, looking at my poor wardrobe choices in an American hotel room was familiar in the worst way. On top of the Egyptian cotton sheets were the entire contents of my weekend bag. Two pairs of Seven jeans, an assortment of American Apparel T-shirts (three-quarter-length sleeves), a couple of bargain cashmere cardigans I'd found at Century 21 and my long-sleeved, super-heavy Marc by Marc Jacobs shirt dress. Everyone had said it would be sunny in California, but it was still March, it couldn't be that warm, could it? Of course it could. Bugger.

And to make matters weirder, The Hollywood was absolutely identical to The Union. Same room layouts, same bed linens, Rapture Spa toiletries, same eight-dollar condoms in the 'intimacy kit' by my bed. Even the curtains were the same. I rubbed the heavy drapes between my fingers and peered out of the window. Down on the sunny side of the street, I could see people. Lots and lots of people. And every single one of them was strutting around in tiny shorts and even tinier tops. Shit.

'I'm coming in,' Jenny announced as she sailed through the adjoining door by my bed. At first she had been quite insistent that we should share a room, but she was equally insistent that she was going to give Joe a good seeing-to at his earliest convenience so, as much as I loved that girl, I really didn't want to have to sit in the bathroom with my headphones on while that happened. This was not the sixth-form trip to Belgium.

'What, you're not ready?'

Jenny's week-long grooming had proved completely worthwhile. She glowed from her hot pink toenails to her long chocolate curls. Usually, her hair was tethered in a ponytail for work, or at least restrained by an industrial-strength Alice band. Seeing it freed, fluffing out around her face and bouncing way past her shoulders, reminded me why I had been so in awe of this glamazon when we first met.

'Get your freaking ass into your swimsuit and get out this door,' Jenny demanded, snatching off her sunglasses and staring me down. Which reminded me why I had loved her five minutes later.

'Please don't kill me . . .' I slowly walked backwards to put a bed between us. I'd seen her motor in heels and so those flip-flops were not going to hold her back 'But I didn't actually bring a swimming costume. I didn't have one and, well, I forgot to buy one.'

'I knew this was going to happen. Didn't I tell you, you were completely unprepared for this?' She rummaged around in a giant metallic tote.

'You told me I was an idiot to pass up a trip to LA; you told me you were going to shag Joe until you broke something; and you told me you'd been waxed to a terrifying degree – but I don't remember you telling me I was underprepared.' I pawed through all my clothes again – not that it would achieve anything, I knew for a fact I didn't have a swimming costume. I hadn't possessed a swimming costume since I was seventeen. They were bad things that hated women.

'Yeah, I've definitely got it in there somewhere – but I'm pretty sure I didn't say "shag".' Jenny pulled a basic black two-piece out from the depths of the bag. 'What the hell are you going to do in that interview without me?'

Oh, she was so going to make me put that on.

Fifteen minutes and one very, very painful bikini-waxing incident later, involving an overenthusiastic Jenny, one pack of 'at home' waxing strips and a genuinely terrified me, backed into the corner of the bathroom, I finally found a difference between The Union and The Hollywood. The rooftop pool, the rooftop pool bar and the definitely-not-in-Manhattan view of the Hollywood sign, shouting out from the hills. I perched awkwardly on the edge of a sun lounger, frantically rubbing factor fifty into my English Rose-slash-pasty-pale skin, staring out at the bold white letters. But something didn't feel right.

'Mojitos.' Jenny sat two enormous cocktails on the tiny table between the two of us. 'Hooray for Hollywood, right?'

'I thought the sign would be, I don't know, bigger?' I squinted through my sunglasses. 'It just isn't what I thought it was going to be.'

'Hmm, I guess.' Jenny was busy staring at the bar. 'I suppose when you see it every day for a few months, you don't really see it any more, you know?'

'I guess,' I nodded. 'It's weird, though. When I saw the Statue of Liberty I couldn't believe it. It was amazing. This just feels weird.'

'That's because you're a native New Yorker now, honey.' Jenny passed me a mojito and clinked glasses. 'LA is cool, but if you're going to have fun, you're going to have to get past your idea of what you think it's going to be, because, honey, nothing ever really is.'

'Reassuring.' I pulled at the bandeau top of the bikini. I wondered if I had time for a quickie boob-job. 'At least tell me the shops are good. We have to go shopping; I can't fill this out like you.'

'The stores are fine, we'll get everything you need.' Jenny peeked over the top of her sunglasses as a tall, dark-haired man appeared behind the bar. 'Just as soon as I've got what I need.'

'Ick,' I shook my head and sipped my mojito. 'Go get 'em, tiger.'

Watching Jenny slink around the pool in her swimsuit, I leaned back into the padded sun lounger and concentrated on the Hollywood sign. It seemed so unreal, even though here I was with the sun on my face and a drink in my hand. It wasn't possible that just yesterday I'd been in snow boots and earmuffs just to go out and buy milk, the sun was too lovely. But I had a sneaking suspicion that it would have been even lovelier had Alex been lying beside me. God, I'd got so tragic so quickly.

Opening one eye, I peeked over to the bar. Jenny was already flipping her hair around and leaning backwards in her high-backed bar stool to give Joe a better look at her bikini. She wasn't wrong: he was incredibly good looking. He'd shaved off the thick black hair that Jenny had been raving about all week, but instead of it making him look like a convict, it only served to reveal an amazing bone structure and gorgeous brown eyes. Yep, I thought, he probably is worth travelling halfway across the country for a quickie. His black shirt did nothing to diminish his tan and I was fairly sure that trousers that tight were not conducive to a comfortable night's work. Huge tips, yes, but a fun night behind the bar? Not so much. Wouldn't it make him need to pee all the time? And how would he ever father a child?

It was only when Joe waved that I realized I was staring and it was only the filthy look on Jenny's face that alerted me to the fact that I was gazing in the general region of his crotch. I downed the remainder of the mojito, pulled a T-shirt over my borrowed bikini and padded over in Jenny's spare flip-flops, praying that I didn't have any mint in my teeth. A very sexy look.

'Hey, English!' Joe flashed a huge smile as I clambered onto the stool beside Jenny. They were too high for me to even attempt to be ladylike, not that I was fooling anyone. 'Great to see you.'

'Hi Joe.' I tried to give Jenny a subtle look to communicate his undeniable hotness. This was not possible.

'Joe was just tell me about all the cool places he's

going to take us,' Jenny chimed, winding a straw through her fingers. 'He knows all the cool places.'

'Sounds fun,' I said. 'You like it out here then?'

'Love it,' Joe said, mixing a second round of drinks. 'Sunshine, good living, hot girls, what's not to love?'

'Not as hot as New York though, right?' Jenny gave him a mock innocent look. Even after six months out of the game, Jenny's flirting was second to none.

'Not nearly,' Joe grinned, leaning across the bar to ruffle Jenny's hair. 'I already told you, you look good, Lopez.'

'I can always stand to be told again,' Jenny pouted. 'A girl's got to keep up her self-esteem. It isn't easy walking around in a bikini, honey.'

I ducked my head and smiled. There was clearly nothing wrong with Jenny's self-esteem.

'I don't know, you're doing pretty well,' Joe commented, passing over our drinks. 'And girls walking around in bikinis is as good a reason as any to stay out in LA for ever. Just let me know when the girls start walking around Union Square in their lingerie in January and I'll come running back, sugar.'

'Well, it depends whether or not you think it's worth the price of seeing all those people that really should never be wearing swimwear,' Jenny said in a low voice.

'Yeah, but they're the best tippers,' Joe countered.

For a horrifying split second, I wondered if they were talking about me. Was the bikini wax not good? But as I followed Jenny's gaze around the pool, I understood. It was true that not everyone looked quite as stunning as Jenny. There were a couple of other girls in bikinis with gleaming long limbs, perfect hair and full make-up. Clearly not about to take a dip. They lay together in silence, only moving to take a sip of an elaborate-looking cocktail and turn over, one after the other, every fifteen minutes or so. But looking along the line-up of loungers, it became very clear that not all bathing beauties were created equal.

On closer inspection, some of the women sunbathing were a lot older than I had first thought and their skin was slightly leathery under their sparkly make-up. Others wore strategically draped sarongs, positioned to conceal flabby thighs and chubby tummies, whereas other proudly flaunted their curves in horrifying neon yellow thongs and triangle bikini tops. This was going to make for all kinds of fun blogging.

Alongside the leather ladies were several solo men, either a tad overweight and straining in their Speedos, or incredibly skinny and pale, but all tapping away at laptops or BlackBerrys while sipping Coronas. There was just one fine figure of manhood, dozing opposite me, and I was fairly certain he was gay. Defined muscles, immaculately groomed and definitely waxed; all the signs were there. I tried not to think about my own less-than-worked-out figure. Yes, I had managed to keep my weight in check with lots of walking and the odd burst of WeightWatchers but I was nowhere near as toned and bronzed as the girls taking part in the competitive tanning over by the pool. I suddenly felt very pale and porky. And this was neither the time nor the place to suffer a crisis of confidence.

'I think I'm starting to burn,' I said loudly, inspecting a marble white arm, as one of the bikini girls turned over to display a tiny little bottom, tanning nicely in a silver thong. 'I'm going to head in. Remember, I have to be up to meet Mr Movie Star at eleven.'

'You sure?' Jenny asked, making no move to come with me. 'You don't want to go eat?'

'We have a great restaurant,' Joe bargained. 'I can get you a table.'

44

'No, really, I think I'm just going to get some sleep for tomorrow. And I have to blog, call Alex.' I kissed Jenny on the cheek and hopped off her stool. 'Big day.'

'OK, tell Alex hi,' Jenny called after me. 'And call me as soon as you're free tomorrow.'

I wandered along the corridor to the lift, slightly buzzed from the two mojitos. Tracing the pattern of the embossed wallpaper with my fingertips, I tried not to be weirded out by the fact that they were using the same air fresheners here as on the East Coast. It was like the hotel version of a Lush store. Different city, exactly the same overpowering smell.

Pausing in front of the huge wooden-framed mirror propped against the wall, I slipped the T-shirt up over my head, taking a deep breath before opening my eyes. Well, it wasn't that bad. I was never going to be a six-foot supermodel but I wasn't looking awful. Yes I was pale, but I had only been in LA for a day. My light brown bob was probably in need of a trim, but at least New York's miracle tap water kept it super soft. Leaving the hard water of London behind seemed to have cleared my skin up too, so that was OK and, joy of joys, working freelance meant No Early Mornings so my eyes, even though they might be suffering from some 'late-night lovin' bags, were super bright; even the fine lines I had pretended weren't there for the last two years seemed to have retraced their tracks. Seriously, if there was ever a case for girls not having to get up before ten a.m., I was it. The bikini still didn't exactly fill me with joy, but I would cope. At least nothing was technically hanging out or over, but I couldn't strictly claim to have abs of any kind. Unless maybe I shaded them in. I did have an awful lot of bronzer with me . . .

'Mirror, mirror on the wall,' I tutted at myself, scooping the T-shirt up off the floor and slipping it safely back over my head. I had never really been one that considered 'mirror time' time well spent, and I had a nagging feeling that LA wasn't the place or moment to change that if I didn't want to develop an eating disorder.

I pulled a tub chair, identical to the one that Jenny had hauled twenty blocks home from The Union, over to the floor-to-ceiling window, and collapsed into a warm and slightly tipsy heap. Hollywood Boulevard literally buzzed beneath me, dozens of tourists wandering up and down the star-lined pavement. I reached out to press my bare toes against the glass and stared out. I might only be able to see the tops of their baseball caps but I would have bet anything that they were all smiling. Why wouldn't they be, they were on holiday in Hollywood. And above them, past the world's biggest Gap ad on the opposite corner, were the famous Hollywood Hills. I wondered how many celebs were sitting in their own homes looking back out at me at that exact second. Which superstars were practically within touching distance? How many MTV reality shows could I feasibly get in the background of in the next seven years?

New York and London were both full of actors, musicians and writers, but it wasn't the same. For some reason, the idea of A-list celebrity was strictly Hollywood.

My phone vibrated quietly, snapping me out of a quickly developing bumping-into-Brad-Pitt fantasy. It was Louisa.

'Hey,' I said, and utched the chair right up to the glass to get better reception. 'Are you in New York? Are you OK?'

'Yes and yes,' she laughed down the line. 'We got in a couple of hours ago. Tim just went out to meet some people at the bar.'

'Some people? Right,' I smiled. Bless her for not

mentioning my scumbag ex's name. It actually pained me that he dared step foot in my New York. 'Where are you going now then?'

'I made Tim book that Balthazar place you were raving about for dinner,' she crackled down the line. 'And then I think I'm just going to have an early night. What are you up to? Met Tom Cruise yet?'

'Yeah, I'm having cocktails with him and Katie,' I said, happy that we were back on good terms. I hated falling out with anyone, dickhead ex-boyfriends aside. I couldn't help it, I was a Libra. And a wimp. 'We haven't been here very long, I'm actually in a bikini.'

'No way,' I could hear her laughing all the way across the country. 'I haven't seen you in a bikini since we were about six.'

'And you won't see it again. There will be no photographic evidence, believe me.'

'I'd give anything to be in a bikini,' Louisa moaned. 'It's bloody freezing here.'

'I did tell you,' I replied, thankful for the sun still shining through the window. The unseasonal warmth made me feel slightly less shitty for not being in New York with Louisa. I was not going to win World's Best Friend this year. 'But you'll be fine. Just stay in the shops and get lots of cabs. Seriously, cane Tim's expense account as much as humanly possible.'

'What expenses? He can't spend a penny these days. We're staying in a Hilton, for God's sake,' she sighed. 'I suppose I should be relieved he still has a job. Anyway, I've got to have a shower, I'm disgusting.'

'Never.' Louisa was never anything other than perfect, eight-hour plane journey or otherwise. 'But I do need to get some work done. Call me later.'

I ended the call, relieved at the lack of Mark-talk.

There's no way I would have avoided it in person. It was the first law of break-ups – the first time you saw someone, post-dumping, no matter how long ago it was or what had happened in the meantime, they wanted to rehash the whole event all over again. If I didn't ask about him, I would know they were thinking that I really wanted to but was still too upset about the whole thing. And if they didn't ask me about the break-up, I would know they were dying to tell me something, some fact or titbit to make me feel 'a bit better' and I really didn't want to know. But I would have to ask, complete girl that I was. And for 'girl', read 'masochist'.

I picked up my phone to dial Alex. It rang a few times before clicking off to his answer phone suggesting you not even bother to leave a message because he was pretty crappy at checking his voice-mail but that he hoped you'd call back soon. I hung up and stared at the phone for a moment. So he wasn't answering, I'd call back later. Just had to keep myself busy for an hour or so. Busy and awake. Glancing over at my laptop, I resigned myself to actually doing some work, crazy idea that it was. It wouldn't hurt to show Mary how serious I was about this, given how ridiculously ungrateful I'd been when she first told me about the interview. Logging on to my TheLook.com account, my fingers hovered above the keyboard for just a second.

The Adventures of Angela:
Hooray for Hollywood

So here I am in LA. Can you believe it? I'm such a jet-setter.
  Albeit a jet-setter hiding in her hotel room full

of two mojitos and no dinner. Not a good idea, just in case you were wondering. But, happier news, I'm staying in a gorgeous hotel, full of gorgeous people with gorgeous sunshine beaming down on me for the first time in what feels like for ever and I can't recommend it enough. I'm not recommending putting on a bikini for the first time in what feels like for ever, though – what a cruel and unusual punishment. It does seem to be curbing my appetite though . . .

Well, I hope you're having a fun weekend. I just wanted to check in and let you know that I have a super-exciting project while I'm out here in LA. Obviously I would never just hotfoot it to Hollywood to enjoy myself; everything thing I do is a massive sacrifice, as you know, but I'll tell you more about that tomorrow. For now I'll just turn up the A/C, roll into my giant hotel bed and get an early night before my big day.

Me? Smug? Never . . .

I pressed send and then rolled onto the bed. Even hinting at the interview made it feel all the more real. Picking up the remote, I decided to do a little research on James Jacobs. There was a chance I'd been taking the whole 'go in with no preconceptions' approach too far. What if he was a total diva and refused to talk to me because I hadn't even seen one of his movies? Couldn't hurt to watch one film, could it? I grabbed a ten-dollar bag of M&Ms and mixed a twenty-three-dollar vodka and Coke. Couldn't hurt to have one more drink, could it?

'Super-hot and super-talented James Jacobs . . .' I said to my reflection in the giant mirror, launching backwards onto the ridiculously comfortable pillow-top bed with the same deliciously soft bed linen I enjoyed, only ever so slightly illegally, every night. Flicking through the movies-on-demand menu, I eventually found the casino movie Jenny had mentioned. At least, if I fell asleep halfway through, she would be able to fill me in on the bits I'd missed.

But I didn't fall asleep. I sat up, staring at the screen, one hand clutching the comforter around me, the other systematically popping M&Ms into my mouth for two whole hours. I wasn't sure if it was that last vodka, Alex not answering his phone, or all the flesh on display at the pool, but by the end of the film I had a very serious, very unhealthy crush on James Jacobs.

Leaning on the triple pillars of journalistic integrity – IMDb, E! online and Perez Hilton, I learned every-thing there was to know, drama school, RADA, bit parts in various soaps and then the big Hollywood break. And then there were the hobbies: talented painter, keen hiker and, oh yes, he liked the ladies. Lots of them. A Google image search provided dozens upon dozens of pictures of a ridiculously beautiful young man in various states of drunkenness or undress from the last three years. Falling out of a club with Lindsay, lunching with Scarlett, frolicking on the beach with Paris and even attending the opera with Natalie. I clicked on a red carpet pic and enlarged it. Wow, he certainly knew how to work a tux. And a bra strap from the look of it.

'Angie?'

A dramatically loud hiss through the adjoining door made me jump.

'Angie, are you awake?'

'Yes, Jenny,' I said, dragging myself off the bed and over to the door that separated our rooms. I opened it up and watched Jenny fall through onto my feet. 'Fun evening?'

'I forgot to leave the air-con on in my room, can I sleep in with you?' she asked, crawling over to the bed and clambering in.

'Yes?' I rubbed my face and sighed, smiling. 'Just get off my side.' I pushed her bikini-clad body over to the other side of the bed but she was already asleep. 'So much for my good night's sleep.'

I'd had every intention of waking up for an early swim and a spot of tiny-dog watching before setting out to meet Mr Jacobs, but that was before Jenny decided to crash in my room and take up my entire bed. After rolling her back across to her side of the bed seventeen times in two hours, I'd climbed out of bed and made a den on the chaise longue and watched clips of James Jacobs on YouTube, transfixed by his pretty, pretty face. And after falling asleep at around three a.m., I woke up with the pillow glued to my face at ten. One hour before I was supposed to meet James Jacobs. *The* James Jacobs. Crap.

After a second's panic, I shook Jenny awake to enlist her services as my personal stylist. I scrambled around in the bathroom while she rolled out of bed, irritatingly hangover free, and disappeared into her wardrobe. Somehow I managed to be out of the hotel inside thirty minutes, wearing Jenny's jade green Velvet T-shirt dress, some pretty brown leather sandals and a matching wide leather belt. Three squirts of dry shampoo into my roots and approval for me to do my make-up in the cab; truly I had come a long way from when she wouldn't let me walk out of our apartment without a full makeover.

'Good luck, honey,' Jenny said, opening the cab door

and kissing my cheek. 'I'm gonna pick up the rental car so call me when you're through. And yes, I promise I'll get a nice safe car. I thought maybe we could meet my friend Daphne for dinner?'

'Yes, that would be lovely,' I said, raking through my handbag. Did I have everything? Did I have anything? 'And really, I'm not kidding. Don't come back with something ridiculous. We don't need a Mustang. And I wanted to ask last night, what happened with Joe?'

'He's making me work for it,' Jenny pulled a face. 'Did I get fat?'

'I don't even have time to answer that ridiculous question,' I yelled out of the car as we pulled away. 'You're gorgeous.'

'Tell that to James Jacobs,' she shouted back, causing everyone and their mother on the sidewalk to turn and look. But I didn't mind. Safe and sound in the back of the taxi, I was on my way to meet James Jacobs.

Without my Dictaphone.

I was so going to be late.

After the fantastically professional start to my morning, I made it to Toast with some dubiously applied blusher, a smudge of mascara and about three minutes to spare. According to my itinerary from the delightful Cici, Toast was a 'very LA brunch spot full of very cool people.' The implication of course being that I was very much not one of those people. And she was right. Fragile-looking waif girls dressed in skinny jeans, Ugg boots and The World's Biggest Sunglasses were stacked seven deep around a relatively ordinary looking café at the side of a relatively ordinary looking road. Maybe even slightly skanky road. It certainly wasn't the glamorous LA I was expecting. For the want of an approved outfit and a size zero figure, I stuck on my sunglasses and strode past the tables full of girls pushing food around their plates.

'Hi there, welcome to Toast. Do you have a reservation?'

There was a girl on the door with a clipboard. Of a café. On a Sunday morning.

'Hi, erm, yes, I do.' I scrabbled around in my beautiful handbag (at least that looked as if it belonged, even if I didn't) for the bit of paper that I'd rammed back in there during my scramble out of the cab. 'I'm a little bit early . . .'

'We're very busy, if you don't have a reservation . . .' Door Girl looked me up and down in a not particularly flattering fashion.

'No, I do, it's under someone else's name – James Jacobs, maybe? I'm meeting James Jacobs. It might be under *The Look*, as in the magazine?' I tried my most charming smile. It did not help.

'Sure, honey. James Jacobs,' she said. I really didn't like the extra-long pause between the words 'James' and 'Jacobs'. I waited until she took a grudging look at her list, then raised one perfectly plucked eyebrow so high that it was practically lost in her highlights. 'Oh. You're Angela Clark?'

I nodded and smiled again, trying not to look like a smug cow. Bwah ha ha ha.

'OK then, if you'd like to follow me? We've saved James's favourite table. He's not here yet but can I get you some coffee?' Scary Door Girl transformed into Lovely-Door-Girl-slash-helpful-waitress and I wondered if I hadn't just been a little bit paranoid. Maybe, just maybe, she was human after all.

'That would be great. Cream and sugar please,' I said, sitting down at James's favourite table, which was thankfully hidden away in a corner at the back of the café, inside and away from the crowds.

Door Girl frowned. 'Cream *and* sugar? Sure . . .'

Maybe I wasn't imagining it. Surely as the only person there that couldn't possibly be a relation of the Olsen twins, they ought to be welcoming me and my ability to 'do dairy' with open arms? Jesus, no one else sitting in that place had eaten in a month.

Everything on the menu looked delicious but my appetite had vanished. In just minutes, I'd be meeting James Jacobs. *The* James Jacobs. Who needed cinnamon pancakes and sliced bananas when you had six foot four of sex god coming to see you for breakfast? That was if he turned up. I had been three minutes early; he was now seven minutes late. I took out my newly acquired BlackBerry, playing the 'I'm waiting for someone' game for everyone to see. Scrolling through the messages, I looked for something from Alex. He hadn't called me back. And what was it, two in the afternoon in New York? That was so not on. Shouldn't he be pining for me by now? I tapped out a text message, deleted it, tapped out another, deleted it before settling on the perfect breezy 'missing you' message.

'Hey you, having brunch at Toast, yummy. Miss you A x'

I frowned at the sent message icon. Truly, I was a writer for a reason. Words were my tools. Tools that I wouldn't need to be using if my celeb didn't arrive soon. Nibbling on a piece of bread that the increasingly suspicious-looking Door Girl had set down in front of me, I weathered another forty minutes of sympathetic glances, not-so-subtle whispering and three cups of coffee before my phone rang.

'Hello?' I answered the unfamiliar mobile number in a heartbeat.

'Hello, Angela? This is Blake, James Jacobs's assistant?'

'Oh hi, I'm at Toast, am I in the wrong—' I started.

'Yeah, James isn't coming? His flight was delayed and he can't make it?' Blake continued.

'I – are you asking me or telling me?' I was a little confused by the way all of Blake's sentences ended in a question.

'He's totally sorry and we'll call you later with a new meet-up address? Bye.' And he hung up.

Door Girl was on me like a hawk. 'James isn't coming?'

'Ah, he can't make it.' I waved my hand airily, as though I was stood up by movie stars so often that it barely registered on my radar.

'So just the check?' The piece of paper was already in her hand and I could see she was itching to slap it down and fill my table with some Lauren Conrad-alike lettuce nibbler.

'Just the check,' I nodded. Bloody movie stars. I should have had the pancakes.

CHAPTER FOUR

'I can't believe that asshole didn't show,' Jenny said as we tore down West Third Street in the ridiculous red Mustang convertible that I had told her not to rent but now sort of secretly loved. What I most definitely did not love was Jenny's driving. She had chosen to confess that she hadn't been behind the wheel of a car since her last LA excursion years ago, and it showed. As if driving in LA wasn't scary enough.

'I called Mary and apparently it's not a big deal,' I said, clutching my seatbelt tightly. 'Apparently celebrity schedules are "fluid". I'll catch up with him later.'

'I can't believe James Jacobs is so unprofessional. I'm kind of heartbroken.' Jenny whirled around a corner and through a red light. No matter how many times she told me you could legally turn on a red signal, I still closed my eyes. 'I think you're in need of retail therapy, honey, and I am the Dr Laura of retail therapy. I'm taking you to the best shopping in LA.'

'I'm sure he had his reasons, but since you're offering,' I said, envisioning a *Pretty Woman*-style storm of Rodeo Drive, laden with stiff cardboard bags.

'Let's do some shopping. Show me some swank, Jenny Lopez.'

'OK, here we are,' she whooped, pulling into an underground car park.

'But we just left the café.' I was puzzled. We couldn't have been driving for more than two minutes.

'So?'

'Well, where are we?' I pushed up my sunglasses to take a look around in the dark. Rows and rows and rows of cars. I suppose it was Sunday, it made sense for people to be at their church. 'Wouldn't it have been faster to walk?'

'Jesus Christ, they ought to throw you out of the city.' Jenny squinted in the low light and swung the car reck-lessly across two empty spaces. 'What did I tell you about people never walking in LA?'

'And this is it? A shopping centre?' I just could not believe it.

'The Beverly Center, honey.' She scrabbled around in the glove compartment. 'This is *the* mall in LA.'

We could have been in Milton Keynes. 'A shopping centre?'

'Hey, did I rock up to LA with like, two T-shirts and a ski suit?' she asked me. 'No. But you did, so you need to do some shopping. So hush up and get your ass into Bloomingdale's.'

Once I'd got over the disappointment that was 'the mall' and had drunk my body weight in Jamba Juice, I started to focus on the task at hand.

'So tell me everything that happened with Joe,' I mumbled through the silk BCBG paisley maxi-dress that Jenny was trying to pull over my head in the Bloomingdale's changing rooms. I already had an olive green Roberto Rodriguez number, a yellow Phillip Lim

5.1 shift, black Kerrigan silk dress and half a dozen T-shirt dresses from Ella Moss, Splendid and James Perse hanging from the wall that Jenny had decreed were 'keepers'. So far I'd managed to distract her from the swimwear section.

'Nothing to tell,' she said, standing back, head cocked to one side, trying to work out what was wrong with the dress. 'Nothing happened.'

'The dress is about a foot too long, Jenny,' I explained, hoping to get that look off her face. She looked so disappointed in me. But that could be because she had already clocked my non-matching underwear, something Jenny and my mother felt very strongly about. 'And what do you mean "nothing"? He didn't make any sort of move?'

'Nothing, *nada*, zip,' Jenny pouted. 'I don't know, he just wasn't taking the hint. And the dress isn't too long, it's BCBG – you're too short. Try this. How's the phone sex going? I bet Brooklyn is really good at the dirty talk, right?'

'Shut up.' I blushed inside the column of silk that was being yanked up over my head. 'I actually haven't heard from him yet.'

'Really?' Jenny didn't even try to cover up the surprise in her voice as she zipped me into a very tight, very blue French Connection strapless mini-dress. 'But didn't you call him last night? You know, when you ditched me.'

'I didn't ditch you,' I squeaked – the dress was tight around the old rack. 'And no, I couldn't get through to him. It's fine, we've only been here for – what – a day? And he's working all hours on the new record. The record company are pushing them to get it out at the end of the year or something.'

'Yeah, I guess,' she replied, slipping on the BCBG

dress and looking like a goddess. Bitch. 'I just wish he wasn't so keen to talk to you every single time you're out and I'm in the tub.'

'Hmm,' I was officially not thinking about it. So far, my star-studded Hollywood adventure had been nothing but a disappointment, and wondering what Alex was doing two and a half thousand miles away was not going to help me have any more fun.

'Jenny, if I wanted to go somewhere really glam, where would you take me?'

'Seriously, would you get over it? I know this is a mall but it has the most stores, it's where everyone shops,' she said distractedly, holding out a Nanette Lepore petal pink number and a navy Theory shift. 'I mean, we'll totally hit Melrose, maybe The Grove before we go, but The Beverly Center has everything . . . I saw Britney here once. Before the whole head-shaving thing, when she was allowed out alone. And you can't afford Rodeo Drive, I know what you make.'

'No, I mean something really Hollywood?' I tried not to pull a face at the pink dress. 'A real, genuine LA experience.'

'Uh, maybe lunch at The Ivy? Drinks at La Deux?' she held up the pink for my approval. 'I guess maybe LAX or Hyde or somewhere if you wanted a club. I'm kinda out of the loop on where's hot.'

'Lunch actually sounds really good.' I held up a deep red Elizabeth & James number, Jenny nodded in agreement and stuck the pink dress back on the end of a random rail. If we had to discuss every shopping decision out loud, we would have no time to cover the other, almost equally important subjects in life. 'Is The Ivy nice?'

'Uh, I guess?' Jenny draped the red silk across herself, slipping her head between the hanger and the dress before heaving a pile of dresses into my arms. 'You should get these. Joe could probably get us a reservation. I'll get Daphne to meet us there.'

I clapped happily as Jenny wandered off to get better reception on her mobile, the red silk still swishing around her neck. So what if I'd been stood up by my movie star? What man could compare with Jenny Lopez, shopping and a super-swank restaurant for lunch?

'Can I set up a changing room for you?'

A helpful shop assistant appeared at my elbow and held her arms out to take the masses of silk and jersey that I was cradling. I paused for a second and thought of my feeble wardrobe back at the hotel. And then of my credit card limit. And then of my feeble wardrobe back at the hotel.

'Actually, could you just take them to the counter?' I asked. She nodded gleefully and literally ran across the shop floor. Sneaking a peek in my bag, I checked my mobile. Well, certainly not Alex, still nothing. I sighed and swung my bag around my back. I was going to need dessert.

It turned out that my interpretation of the real Hollywood and Jenny's interpretation of the real Hollywood were very different. I couldn't argue with the fact that The Ivy was exclusive and swanky, but unlike genuine A-list haunts in New York, there was no quiet dark entrance, designed to keep the undesirables away through sheer intimidation. Instead, it was slap-bang in the middle of a main road, nestled in between a row of shops and smothered by tourists and star-spotters. McDonald's on Oxford Street was less conspicuous.

Flashbulbs clicked and buzzed all around us as we pushed our way up the little footpath leading from the street into a pretty little country cottage. I paused on the patio and turned back towards the sidewalk – paparazzi waving, shouting and screaming. Blinking back towards the restaurant, I followed Jenny through the calm, quiet and unwaveringly beautiful diners, none of whom appeared to actually be eating; instead they were concentrating very hard on pretending that they weren't a living breathing version of the 'Spotted' page in *Heat* magazine. Trying to navigate a safe route through the wrought-iron tables and chairs and dozens of stiff cardboard carrier bags, I saw a hand shoot up at the back of the patio and wave us over.

'Jesus, why on earth did you want to meet here, J doll?' The hand belonged to Jenny's friend Daphne, who introduced herself and greeted us both with extravagant kisses. 'It's such a circus.'

'Angie wanted a real LA experience.' Jenny peered over the top of her sunglasses at me. 'And she got it.'

'This isn't really what I was expecting,' I said, switching my attention from the heaving crowds back on the pavement to Daphne. 'I was thinking, well, I don't know. Glamorous? Swanky? LA is weird.'

'Yeah, get used to it,' she said. 'I hope you don't mind, I ordered. I'm fucking starving.'

Given that the majority of The Ivy's clientele appeared to be the exact same group of blondes I'd seen at Toast that morning, who had just about had time to go home and get changed into little sundresses and rich old men instead of Ugg boots and gym boys, Daphne stood out a mile. Just like everyone else here, she was undeniably beautiful but, unlike anyone else, she was a vision of retro beauty. Her black shiny hair was coiffed into a Betty Paige bob and her porcelain skin made my English-rose-slash-pasty-Brit complexion look as though

I'd been in the Bahamas for six weeks. Teamed with the most precise eyeliner and perfect ruby red lips I'd ever had the privilege to behold, Daphne was an arresting sight. Jenny had told me she was an artist and a stylist, but I hadn't figured that her talent with a paint-brush would run to her eyeliner. Next to her polished perfection, I felt as if I'd turned up in my decorating clothes.

But weirdly, no one was giving Daphne so much as a second glance. Instead, every single person in the restaurant was pretending not to look at a tiny little brunette, skulking in the corner and wearing a ridicu-lous number of layers for such a sunny day, who was sitting with an incredibly average-looking man in a business suit.

'Who is that?' I asked quietly, joining in the pretending-not-to-notice game. 'I feel like I should know her.'

'You should,' Jenny said, sipping one of the gimlets Daphne had ordered for us. 'It's Tessa DiArmo, the singer? She stayed at The Union just before Christmas. Pain in my ass.'

'Everyone's a pain in your arse,' I said, giving in to curiosity and turning around for a good look. The girl was genuinely minuscule, with masses of wavy light brown hair and glowing tanned skin. Whatever 'it' was that celebs had, Tessa apparently bathed in it every morning. Without batting so much as an eyelash, she had the attention of every single person in the restau-rant. 'I never saw her in The Union. She's so pretty.'

'Wouldn't cut it with us, huh J?' Daphne said, sipping the fresh cocktail that had been silently replaced. 'You can't shake what ain't there.'

'Shake?' I tried to register the looks that were exchanging between the two girls, Jenny seeming slightly startled and Daphne smiling innocently into her drink.

'Jenny told you how we met, right?' she asked.

'No,' I turned to look at Jenny. 'She actually didn't.'

'Daphne,' Jenny let out a warning shot. I had a sneaking suspicion that Daphne wasn't going to be hushed by a stern tone of voice.

'Chill, J, it's so not a big deal.' She pressed her lips together, refreshing her pout. 'We used to work together. When J lived here last time?'

'When she was acting?' I asked.

'When she was dancing.'

I bit my lip and looked back at Jenny. Impossible. She was blushing.

'Dancing? You danced?' I really, really wanted Jenny to nod, smile and possibly demonstrate some tap moves.

'Oh baby doll, I do not believe Miss J never told you about our act?' Daphne pouted.

'You had an act?' This was too much.

'Sure,' Daphne said, as a waiter appeared with three giant salads. 'A burlesque act.'

Jenny's blush faded until her clear caramel skin paled to a sallow sea green. Even behind her giant sunglasses, I could see her eyes were as big as the huge salad plates in front of us. Simultaneously, we both reached for our gimlets and drained the glasses.

'Well,' I finally managed, 'Jenny Lopez, you dark horse. I should have known.'

'Excuse me?' Jenny reached across the table and finished Daphne's cocktail. 'What is that supposed to mean?'

'I just meant, you know, you carry yourself like a dancer,' I protested. Just one cocktail in and I'd already had too much to drink to lie convincingly. Daphne sat cackling across the table and making 'more drinks' signs at our waiter.

'And you've got good rhythm?' There was no way to dig my way out of this. 'No, I'm sorry, you're going to have to fess up about this one. Burlesque dancing, Jenny Lopez?'

'I'm going to the bathroom.' She pushed her chair backwards, straight into the person behind her. 'And when I get back, I really don't want to talk about it.'

'Of course,' I called as Jenny stormed across the patio, her massive tote bag bashing diners in the back of the head as she went. Waiting until she vanished inside the restaurant, I turned back to Daphne. 'I reckon we've got about three minutes: go.'

'OK.' She cleared her throat dramatically. 'Jenny and I met about seven years ago. She was out here waitressing, trying out at all these open auditions and shit, basically not getting anywhere. I was working in this vintage store on Melrose and, well, kind of stripping. But classy stripping, you know, not like "drunken bachelor parties" stripping.'

'Oh, of course,' I nodded, trying to think of an example of classy stripping. And failing.

'So we were both at this club one night,' Daphne went on, 'and we got to talking, got to dancing, got to some serious fucking drinking, and so I tell her that there's an open call for dancers on a new music show the next day. I kind of didn't think she would show, but I turn up and there she is. The full *Flashdance*, seriously: legwarmers, one-shoulder sweater, the whole outfit.

'But the problem is, Jenny can't really dance. I mean, she can move, right? But she's not a trained dancer. And look at me. I am so not what MTV are looking for. Anyways, we get up there, basically make asses out of ourselves, and just when we're about to go get real drunk and laugh about the whole thing, this chick comes up to us and asks if we've ever thought about doing burlesque.'

'And then what happened?' The vision of Jenny dressed as an extra from *Fame* was almost enough for me, but I had to get the rest of the story.

'What did I freaking say?' A firm slap on the back of my head heralded Jenny's return from the bathroom. 'We're so not talking about this.'

'Oh, we so are,' I pushed another gimlet at her. 'Get this down you.'

'Seriously,' Jenny necked the drink, 'we're not. We're also not going to be able to drive the Mustang back to the hotel. I'm wasted. I totally forgot how strong these were.'

'I'll drive, let's just have one more,' I said, tapping her hand. 'Go on, Daphne.'

'No, do not go on Daphne,' Jenny shook her head. 'And you cannot drive. Angie, honey, you're tanked. Can we just eat now please?'

For the want of knowing what else to do, I picked at my salad, smiling, nodding and accepting more drinks as they appeared. Jenny stared across the table at Daphne, her face like thunder. Dessert was looking more and more necessary to save the day. Or at least another gimlet.

'So where are we going next?' Daphne asked after the waiter had taken away our plates. 'You guys have a pool, right?'

'We're going to get the check and go back to the hotel,' Jenny said, looking at her watch.' Angie's on standby for Mr Movie star and you still need to call Alex, right?'

'I do need to call Alex,' I slapped Jenny's hand in agreement. Maybe I was a little bit tipsy. 'Can you hear something?'

'Angie, honey, it's your phone.' Jenny fished my BlackBerry out of my (divine) bag and held it up to my face. I leaned towards it, getting Jenny's finger in my ear.

'Yo,' I slurred.

'Hi, it's Blake?'

'Blake?' Did I know a Blake?

'James Jacobs's assistant?'

'Oh bollocks. I mean, oh yes, Blake, hi. How are y—'

'James wants you to come to the Chateau now?'

Crap crap crap crap crap.

'Now?' All together too many questions in this conversation.

'Call this number when you arrive?'

The phone chimed as Blake rang off.

'What's wrong?' she asked, tossing the phone back in my bag. 'Did he cancel the whole thing?'

'Oh my God, I wish.' I closed my eyes and willed myself to open them sober. 'Try the opposite. Right now.'

'They want to do the interview now?' Jenny winced. 'He's here?'

'He's here. And I have to go and meet him now. God, Jenny, I'm wasted! I'm going to get sacked, I'll lose my visa, I'll have to go back—'

'Jesus, overreact much?' Daphne stood up, leaving a huge wad of bills on the table (how expensive were those gimlets?) and held out her hand. 'Where's he staying?'

'Uh, at a chateau?' That didn't sound right even to me.

'Chateau Marmont, it's like, fifteen minutes from here.

66

J, take her into the bathroom and, fuck, I don't know, just do something with her. I'll order a cab.'

Daphne was, thank God, all business. Once in the bathroom, it became horribly apparent that I was in fact very, very drunk. And just as Jenny was trying to shuffle me out of her T-shirt dress, which was covered in salad dressing from where a tomato had escaped my fork, and into the new emerald green Robert Rodriguez silk dress that had charmed its way onto my credit card in Bloomingdale's, my BlackBerry began to chirp again.

'Answer it: it could be that gorgeous douche-bag cancelling,' Jenny puffed, fiddling with the black patent belt. 'And if it is, give me the goddamn phone so I can kick his ass. And give him my cell.'

'Can't reach it,' I said, trying to kick the phone out of my (poor) bag but only succeeded in booting it behind the loo.

Jenny looked up at me. 'This might be a nice restaurant, honey, but I won't forget crawling around on the floor of a public bathroom any time soon. You so owe me.' She grabbed my phone from behind the toilet and passed it up to me. 'Missed call from Alex.'

'Shit.' I pressed redial but it went straight to answer phone.

'No time, Angie, call him from the cab.' Jenny took my phone and my hand and led me through the packed tables out to the waiting cab that Daphne had summoned. 'You got everything you need?'

'I think so,' I nodded, gripping my bag tightly, hoping it might help the ground stopping spinning underneath me. 'Dictaphone, cash, room key. Call you when I'm on my way back?'

'Screw it, I'm clearly gonna have to make sure you get there OK.' Jenny pushed me into the back seat and hopped in after me. Daphne coughed loudly from the pavement, giving Jenny what I took to be her most apologetic pout. She leaned out the door and sighed. 'Fine. Get your ass in here, Pussycat Doll, let's go get a drink.'

Chateau Marmont was, as Daphne had promised, just fifteen minutes away, making it a straight thirty minutes between Blake's hanging up on me and my standing in front of the door of bungalow two. The girls had made up in record time and cackled off into Bar Marmont, leaving me to face the long walk up to the hotel alone. As much as I was trying to concentrate on just putting one foot in front of the other, I couldn't help but notice how beautiful the hotel was. Just how I imagined Old Hollywood to be. A beautiful turret sitting high up on the hillside, huge arched windows looking into lounges full of gorgeous high-backed chairs, palm trees, discreet but hot waiters everywhere. If it weren't for the ever-present BlackBerries, MacBooks and Lindsay Lohans lounging by the pool, I could almost believe I was back in the Fifties.

What I couldn't believe was how crap I felt. I couldn't decide if it was hot-even-for-LA-heat, the chaotic cab ride over, or my quickly building fear of meeting James Jacobs, jetlagged, drunk and made up in a taxi, that was making me feel sick to my stomach. I paused for a second and dialled Alex one last time. Just talking to him for a minute, a second, would be enough, then I could go in and do whatever it was the magazine were expecting me to do. But he still wasn't answering. As always in life, when my girlfriends were busy in the bar and I couldn't rely on a boy, I turned to my two constants, my handbag and lip gloss. A quick slick of Mac lip gloss and I was as ready as I'd ever be.

One quick knock and the door opened.

'Hi, I'm . . .' I looked up with my biggest brightest smile and lost the ability to speak. James Jacobs opened the door.

'Angela Clark?' he finished for me with a smile that put mine in the shade. 'Hi, I'm James.'

'I . . . I . . .' I reached out, grabbing something hard, spinning away from the door and puking into some very pretty bushes just before everything went very, very dark.

Waking up in a strange place to the sound of a strange man laughing was not something I was incredibly experienced at, and so, when I opened my eyes in a bedroom that was most definitely not my own, wearing something that was not my dress, I panicked slightly. In that I rolled off the bed, cracked my elbow on the bedside table and screamed. Before I could locate an open window and make an escape, a shadowy figure appeared in the doorway. Oh, I had seen *Misery*, I knew what was happening.

'Hello? Can I help you?' Since there was no time to escape from the scary stranger holding a blunt weapon and blocking my escape, why not be polite? My mother would be very proud.

'Doubtful, at least not before you put your dress back on,' A deep BBC British accent came out of the dark and then the curtains opened. From my vantage point on the floor, I could see a very tall, very handsome man holding out my beautiful new green dress and a huge glass of water. Ha, like I was about to drink his drug-laden cocktail. Unless it wasn't a drug-laden cocktail and the very handsome man holding my dress was in fact James Jacobs. Oh, balls.

'James . . . Jacobs?' I pulled the hem of the T-shirt I found myself in down over my knees.

'Angela Clark?' He set down the glass and held out a hand to pull me up. 'I hope you're feeling better.'

'Oh, erm, yes.' This wasn't happening. This couldn't be happening. The six-foot-something Greek God standing in front of me holding out a freshly pressed dress with a gorgeously lopsided grin couldn't possibly be James Jacobs. 'I am so sorry. I just don't know what happened.'

'Food poisoning, I'm sure,' he said smoothly, laying the dress out on the bed. 'There's a shower just through there and I had this cleaned so it's puke free. When you're done, I'll be in the living room.'

'Thank you?' There was such a serious chance I was still dreaming that I just decided to go with it. 'Was I sick on your shoes?'

'Little bit,' he said, luckily still smiling. 'Don't worry, I've got more shoes knocking around here than a Footlocker. I'll live.'

A quick shower, a long session with my Touche Eclat and I was dressed, ready to face my fate. Mary was going to go insane. It was one thing for me to blow the biggest chance of my career but, mid-shower, I realized it wasn't just me: I'd blown the magazine's shot at a major interview. They'd told me numerous times in the last week that James Jacobs hardly ever did press and I had just thrown up on his shoes, passed out in his hotel room and, oh my God, had he undressed me? This humungous Abercrombie & Fitch T-shirt certainly wasn't what I'd arrived in. I wasn't sure if that was supposed to go in the ticks or crosses column.

'Hi.' He stood as I sloped into the living room, all six gorgeous feet and four beautiful inches of him, clutching loose pages of something in his tanned hands.

'Hi.' I didn't know where to look.

Seriously, my Alex was so incredibly sexy, just the thought of him made my stomach curl up and purr, but this giant chunk of man was something else. His curly dark brown hair was longer than it had been in any of the photos I'd seen online and his blue eyes were so dark they were almost black. Even in a slightly scuzzy T-shirt, I could see broad shoulders tapering into a slender waist and, oh my, his great big thighs were just itching to get out of those jeans and into a hot tub. With me. And a bottle of baby oil.

Bad Angela: time to be professional. Plus, even if I was interested, I had a feeling that James Jacobs didn't go for girls that introduced themselves by vomming on his shoes. Perhaps I could give 'friends' a go.

'You're feeling better? I can give my assistant a ring and ask him to get us some coffee or something if you want,' he said, gesturing for me to take a seat on the sofa. 'I thought you were out for the count, to be honest.'

'How long was I passed – asleep?' I asked, looking around the bungalow. Anything to avoid looking directly at The Hottest Man Ever. It was all very cool, very *LA Confidential*, the total opposite of The Ivy.

'Couple of hours. I didn't know if there was someone I should call or anything, so I thought it was better to just let you sleep it off.' James folded himself back into the easy chair as I took the sofa. His legs were so long. Long enough to wrap themselves around a girl with a good shin to spare. Hypothetically speaking.

'The only thing is, I'm actually going to have to get off quite soon – I've got a meeting with a director this evening.'

Fantastic. I had actually blown it. How lovely of him to give me a couple of seconds to check him out before dropping the bomb. 'Oh, of course. I'm really sorry about, well, everything. It has been great to meet you. I'll let the magazine know what happened. Sorry.'

'Really? I can't imagine they'd find it as funny as I did, to be honest. Wouldn't you rather just crack on tomorrow and pretend this never happened?' James put down the pages of the script he was holding and held out his hand. 'I love your writing. Really bloody funny. Can't wait to see how the interview is going to work out.'

Which was when I realized it wasn't a script that he'd been holding, they were printouts of my blog. Pages and pages from 'The Adventures of Angela', photocopies of articles I'd written for the US and UK editions of the *The Look* scattered all over the coffee table. Wow. Beautiful and prepared.

'Thank you, but well, it's difficult to take a compliment when you've just been sick on someone's shoes,' I said, eyes firmly on his bare feet. He even had sexy feet. Eyes on the carpet. 'So you still want to do the interview?'

'Absolutely,' the voice attached to the beautiful man replied. 'Stop stressing about it. It'll be a great story to tell the grandkids.'

I snorted a tiny bit of water through my nose. 'Won't it?' I managed eventually. 'Anyway, if you have a meeting, I should let you get on. What time do you want to start tomorrow?'

'Ten?' He stood up again to get the door. 'I'll get Blake to send a car for you. Where are you staying?'

'I'm at The Hollywood,' I said, concentrating on putting one foot in front of the other. 'Uh, my friend works at The Union in New York, so we're staying there.'

'I love The Union. I haven't stayed there yet but I, uh, visited a friend when she was staying there last year.'

72

James pulled out the big guns, a little shy smile with the big blue eyes peering out from behind his hair. 'I'll have to come and see you at The Hollywood. See if it's as swish.'

'Swish,' I echoed. Then I actually giggled. 'So tomorrow at ten.'

'Tomorrow at ten.' He kissed me on the cheek as I stumbled backwards out through the door. 'Bye then.'

As the door closed, my sanity began to trickle back. I needed a cab. I needed to call Jenny. I needed to call Alex. God, that man was good looking.

As the cab travelled along Hollywood Boulevard, taking me further away from James Jacobs geographically, the further away I felt from reality. Surely none of that had just happened. The only thing that was certain was that Jenny did not appreciate my turning in early again.

'This is the second night in a row you've ditched me, Angie,' she yelled over the row of the bar. 'Seriously, come on. You've already thrown up, you may as well get back on it.'

'Jenny, I really wish I could,' I lied through my back teeth. All I wanted was my bed. 'I have to meet James tomorrow morning and I just need to call Alex and get some sleep.'

'Call Alex?'

Apparently that was the wrong thing to say.

'You're going to go back to the hotel and call Alex instead of coming to meet me?' Jenny wasn't amused. 'You get your ass out here and tell me every single thing that happened with James Jacobs.'

'She's blowing you out for a guy?' I heard Daphne crow over her shoulder. 'What an asshole.'

'No, I . . . Jenny, I just need to sleep,' I sighed. 'Seriously. We'll go out tomorrow.'

'Yeah, whatever,' she hiccuped. 'Until you decide you have to stay in and wait around for a boy to call. Just don't bother calling me in the day when Mr Movie Star stands you up again. I have plans.'

'Doing what?' I asked but she'd already hung up. Jenny was so much fun when she was drunk and grumpy. Why did I have a feeling Daphne was not going to be a good influence?

Back at the hotel, I stripped off my new dress and pulled on the ancient Blondie T-shirt I had 'borrowed' from Alex before I left. It must have been washed a thousand times but it still smelt of Alex's apartment, of home. I dialled his number again.

'Hello?'

'Alex? It's me.' I had never been so happy to hear his voice.

'I tried to call you earlier.'

'I know, I'm sorry.' OK, so we weren't starting with 'I love you, I miss you, I'm going mad without you'. 'It's been such a ridiculous day.'

'Yeah, I've been busy too. We were in the studio until – like – three this morning,' Alex replied through a yawn. 'Shouldn't you be interviewing your movie star?'

'That all got off to a bit of a dodgy start but it'll be all right, I think. James is really, really nice,' I said, smiling at the thought of Alex with his black hair all ruffled on the pillow, my head resting against his chest as he fell asleep, his fingers curled around my wrist. 'You sound sleepy. Are you OK?'

'I guess I was asleep,' he yawned again. 'And just how nice is this James? Should I be worried?'

'No,' I slipped into bed and set my alarm for eight a.m. 'I think you'll be OK. Especially since I . . .'

'Since you?'

'Since I just babbled like an idiot. I'm sure he thinks I'm the worst interviewer he's ever met.' I decided not to share the shoe puking until I got back to New York. It felt more like an 'in-person' story. 'You should go back to bed. I don't want to be the reason the world has to go without a new Stills album this year.'

'You're the reason there's going to be another album at all,' Alex said softly. I curled up against the pillows and smiled. No six-foot sex god could compete with that. 'So, about that phone sex we talked about?'

I was sure what he really meant to say was 'I love you and I can't live with you.' But he didn't.

'Goodnight, Alex. Get some sleep.'

'What are you wearing?'

'Goodnight, Alex.' I hung up and flicked off the lights. Boys.

CHAPTER FIVE

When James had said he'd send a car, I really wasn't expecting a limo. And I really wasn't expecting him to be inside it. Thankfully, I'd managed to prise myself out of bed at a reasonable hour and was fully prepped. Well, made-up and blow-dried. I had tried to come as far away from yesterday's vomit incident as possible in a cute inky blue Ella Moss jersey dress, evidence of my credit card abuse in Bloomingdale's. Nothing pukey about this little number. I just couldn't bend over at all. Fingers crossed the superstar could be distracted enough by legs so as not to notice my lack of stellar interviewing skills . . .

'Good morning, Miss Clark,' James utched across the back seat of the limo, as though there wasn't enough room in there. Or possibly because he was confused by my size 12 backside. Given most of the girls I'd seen at Chateau Marmont would struggle to tip the scales at 100 pounds, I could understand why he'd be concerned about my girth. 'You're looking very refreshed.'

I took that as code for 'not about to vomit'.

'Well, thank you very much, Mr Jacobs,' I replied with a winning smile. For God's sake, I'd already puked in front of the man, where was the point in being star-struck?

'Let me introduce my assistant, Blake.' James gestured towards a very stressed-looking, but very cute blond sitting in the opposite corner of the limo. For shame, I hadn't even noticed him; I was way too busy checking out James's huge thighs in his teeny tiny workout shorts. For my interview, of course. 'We were just running in the hills. Well, I was, Blake was reading Perez Hilton on his BlackBerry.'

'Shut up,' Blake held out his hand. 'Sorry I missed you yesterday?'

'Oh, really, don't be. The fewer people involved in yesterday, the better,' I said, shaking his hand and my head politely. Blake was actually very good looking, exactly how I would describe a Californian All-American Boy: rumpled blond hair, incredibly tanned and athletic looking in his workout gear. If it weren't for the fact that he was seriously setting off my gadar, I would have been absolutely warming him up for one Miss Jenny Lopez.

Well, if one Miss Jenny Lopez had actually made it home the night before. A quick peek in her room on the way down to meet James presented a still-made-up-from-the-morning-before bed. I looked down into my (suffering slightly from being on the floor of the toilets in The Ivy) Marc Jacobs handbag to see if she'd replied to my text. Nothing yet.

'Yeah, anyway, I'm basically here to make sure you stick to the approved topics and if at any time I say stop, we stop and the interview is over, OK?' Blake barked. 'You did get the list of approved topics?'

Approved topics . . . I tried not to pull the 'was that one of the pieces of paper Cici gave me and I've left in the hotel?' face.

'Absolutely.'

Absolutely certain it *was* one of the pieces of paper Cici gave me that I'd left in the hotel.

'Fantastic,' Blake continued, as though James wasn't even in the car. I was trying to pay attention but how can anyone listen to instructions when James Jacobs is sitting just a couple of feet away and pulling a very cute 'aren't all these rules so silly?' face. Concentrate. Concentrate. 'The idea of the interview is for you to introduce your readers to "the real James Jacobs". So really we want you to focus on his movies, his hobbies, his ambitions for the future. And you know what we don't want to focus on.'

'He's talking about the sex, drugs and rock and roll,' James whispered theatrically. Cue my first ridiculously loud and faintly hysterical cackle of the day.

'Hilarious, James, just hilarious.' Blake raised a well-groomed eyebrow. 'Let's make jokes in front of the reporter. Don't write that down.'

'Oh, really, I'm not . . .' I paused, took a deep breath and started again. 'I'm here to work with you, not to try and trip you up or anything.' Wow. How professional did *I* sound?

'We know, Angela,' James reached over and took my hand. Be still my thumping, thudding heart. 'Blake is just a little bit over-cautious. Some reporters are just out for as scandalous a story as they can get. I'm just worried that you'll be a little bit let down – if only my life was exciting as it looks in the papers.'

Blake smiled tensely at me and nodded to James. Hmm. It hadn't actually occurred to me that this might be hard work. How much media training had this man had? If James wasn't going to give me anything, then what was I going to write about?

'I'm sure it'll be great,' I said, pulling my all-new

78

superstar interviewing pad, pen and Dictaphone out of my bag. 'So, what is the plan for today?'

'Terribly exciting.' James stretched over to the minifridge (limos are awesome) and passed me a bottle of water before tossing one at Blake and opening a third for himself. 'I have rehearsals at the studio this morning. I thought you might want to come and see the set, meet the rest of the cast?'

'Sounds fun,' I said casually. I was going on set! I was meeting the cast!

'And then I thought maybe we'd get some lunch. I could show you some of my favourite Hollywood hang-outs.'

'That would be great,' My head heard Hollywood hang-outs but my stomach only heard lunch. I'd spent so long sorting myself out that breakfast had been completely forgotten, and since everything I'd eaten yesterday had ended up in the bushes outside James's bungalow, I was starving. I would have given my right arm for a Jaffa Cake. 'Really keen to see your favourite bits of town. I have to say, I'm not loving LA yet.'

'You're not?' James looked surprised but ignored Blake's loud tutting. 'Haven't been completely seduced by the sunshine? Most Brits love it out here.'

'The sunshine's great,' I agreed, 'but I think my expat loyalties are already spoken for. I live in New York.' I did so enjoy saying that.

'I like New York too, but LA is just fantastic,' he insisted. 'Where have you been so far?'

'Uh, The Beverly Center, The Ivy and Toast. Where you stood me up.'

'Yeah, sorry about that.' James slipped in another small smile. Seriously, how did anyone ever get mad at him? 'My flight was delayed. Serves me right for agreeing to do a movie in Canada. And no wonder you don't love it here. You've been to a shopping center and a tourist trap. Trust me, I'll show you some good places. Now tell me how you ended up in New York.'

All the way from Hollywood to Century City, I told James the tale of how I had fallen in love with New York, starting with my journey from hand-breaking bridesmaid to magazine columnist and blogger, via new handbag, new BFF and new super-sexy boyfriend. And when I put it all together, it even sounded pretty cool to me. But then, I missed quite a lot out.

'So you're dating the lead singer of Stills?' James seemed impressed. 'They're really good. Do you think they'd be interested in working on soundtracks at all? They would be perfect for my next film.'

'Alex really wants to work on films,' I said excitedly. Get me, well-connected girlfriend of the year. 'You should definitely talk to him.'

'Why don't you call him?' James said, snatching Blake's BlackBerry from his hands and passing it to me. 'Go on, I would love to talk to him. I'm a massive fan.'

Since the pretty man asked so nicely and since Blake looked so pissed off, I dialled. And predictably Alex did not answer.

'Oh well.' James threw the BlackBerry back at Blake and laughed. 'We'll try him later. Looks like we're here. Did you know Fox's headquarters were the Nakatomi building from *Die Hard*?'

'No way!' I yelled, hanging out of the window like an overexcited Labrador.

'Yep,' James yanked me back in as we drove straight through security. 'They were in *Alvin and the Chipmunks* too but the less said about that the better.'

'Were you in *Alvin and the Chipmunks*?' I asked, narrowing my eyes.

James stared straight back at me. 'The less said about that the better.'

Hooray for Hollywood indeed.

For some reason, I'd thought I would be able to swank around the studio without a single bat of an eyelid, as if I always hung out on movie sets, as if watching Adam Sandler whizz past me on a little golf cart was just an average Monday; but I turned out to be a little bit more of a slack-jawed yokel than I had hoped. Wandering around with James wasn't helping. Almost every other person we passed wanted to speak to him or at least find some feeble excuse to stop him and stroke his arm, slap him on the back or give his forearm an affectionate squeeze or an altogether slutty gaze. I tried not to be jealous but I couldn't help but feel completely invisible.

'This is where I'm filming today,' James said, after the seventh assistant to the assistant's assistant of the day had finished blathering on about how privileged she was to be working with him.

From outside, it just looked like a massive warehouse, sandy coloured and sun-bleached, like everything else I'd seen in LA, but once James opened the door and I stepped inside, something crazy happened. We were back in London. I turned to look out through the door. Outside, sunny, shiny LA. Inside, London at sunset. Trafalgar Square, to be exact.

'No way,' I said, stepping lightly, completely disoriented. 'This is bizarre.'

'It stops me getting homesick,' James said, taking my hand and leading me through a maze of wires and cameras. 'Have you ever climbed on a lion in Trafalgar Square?'

'No.' I stared all around me. 'I actually never have. Isn't that sad?'

'You can do it now if you want,' James said, pointing across the floor to a perfect replica of a Trafalgar Square lion, beside a Nelson-less half-column. 'Give me your phone, I'll take a picture.'

It was madness. Once we were inside the walls, away from the miles and miles of cables and lamps, my brain just couldn't register the fact that we were still in LA. I couldn't even really believe I was inside. The things they can do with lighting these days . . . At James's insistence, I clambered up on top of the lion, a little bit shocked to find it wasn't actually bronze but something slightly less solid and warm.

'Is this going to break?' I asked, trying to throw my leg over without flashing my pants. 'It doesn't feel very solid.'

'It's fine,' James insisted, squaring me up in the viewfinder of my crappy phone camera. 'Just try not to kick it or anything. Jessica Alba was on it the other day and it was fine.'

I clung to the lion's neck, trying not to think about how many Jessica Albas I weighed and praying to the prop gods that this lion was built to take the weight of real people as well as Hollywood waifs. A quiet creak was enough to convince me that it wasn't.

'I don't think I can get down,' I said, trying not to panic. This was not going to be my finest moment. 'Seriously?'

James laughed, stuck my phone in the back pocket of his jeans and held out his hands. 'Come on then, jump.'

'I can't,' I said, gripping the lion slightly too tightly with my thighs. 'I'm stuck.'

'You're not going to be able to do the interview from up there, are you?' he pointed out. 'And I have a scene in here in about an hour. I've read my script: you're not in it. Jump.'

I pursed my lips and closed my eyes. This wasn't going to be flattering, however I hard I tried. Folding my leg underneath me and almost dislocating it in the process, I inched along the lion as far as I could before I felt myself sliding down its backside much faster than I had anticipated.

'Shit!' I wailed, collapsing into James's outstretched arms.

'This is going to be the best interview ever, isn't it?' James asked.

With massive quantities of self-restraint, I shook myself out of his broad, hard chest and coughed, not knowing whether to brush my hair or my skirt down first.

'I'm probably not going to mention this part,' I said, accepting my phone back. It was warm from his pocket. 'But this set is amazing.'

'Yeah,' he nodded, looking around. 'Always seems crazy to me when they spend a fortune on a set, though. Although I suppose they can't go around blowing up parts of the real Trafalgar Square.'

'You're blowing bits of it up?' I asked, hoping it wouldn't be my lion.

'Shit, I'm supposed to be sworn to script secrecy.' James pulled an imaginary zip across his mouth. 'You didn't hear that from me.'

'Of course,' I said. 'Are you blowing it up today? Can I watch?'

'Bloodthirsty, aren't you? Nope, sorry, Trafalgar Square doesn't get it until next week.'

'James!' Blake yelled from the steps of the National Gallery and tapped his watch. 'Trailer!'

'Want to see my trailer?' James raised a perfect eyebrow.

I raised mine. 'I bet you say that to all the girls.'

'Maybe a couple,' he admitted, putting an arm around my shoulder and walking me off into a Waterloo Sunset.

If walking onto the set had been like walking into London, walking into James's trailer was like walking into heaven. I'd never, ever seen anything so plush. It made The Union and The Hollywood look like a youth hostel.

'This place is amazing. Why would you even have a house?' I charged up the steps and into the lounge. Three massive plush sofas dominated the space, all pointing at a huge flatscreen TV with a beautiful low coffee table set in the centre. Under the TV was a DVD player, a Blu-ray player and several games consoles. It was basically boy heaven.

'Gets boring after a while,' James said, his hand hovering over a fruit platter on the coffee table before he skipped over onto a bowl of M&Ms. 'Sometimes I just really want to fuck off back to my mum's. You can fly direct to Sheffield now, can't you? I could be there in a day.'

'Sheffield?' I gave James a questioning look. 'I thought you were from London?'

'Not approved!' Blake called from the kitchen. He stuck his head around the door. 'We're not talking about James's past, Miss Clark.'

'OK.' I launched myself into one of the squishy sofas and filed it away.

'So, James has to go do some actual work. We'll be, like, two hours. You'll stay here?' Blake pushed James through the door as he threw me a helpless shrug and disarming wink.

'Perfect,' I said to myself, pulling my laptop out of my bag. It was almost twelve already and my blog wasn't about to write itself. Couldn't hurt to at least attempt to get it in on time . . .

The Adventures of Angela: LA Story

So finally, I can let you in on my secret . . . right now, as in right this second, I'm blogging to you from the trailer of a very cool, very talented and, well, gorgeous movie star. Seriously, we're talking A-list, super-hot, 100% amazing Ac-Tor-type person.

What's great for me (but possibly a little bit rubbish for you), is that I'm actually interviewing him for The Look – my first-ever proper interview! But that's not the most rubbish bit (unless I do a really shoddy job, that would be a bit tragic): what's really sad is that I'm not allowed to tell you who it is.

I know, what a tease.

What I can do is tell you all about LA and all the adventures I'm having . . . Which have so far totalled a bit of shopping and puking outside a bungalow at Chateau Marmont. I am all class, I know. But seriously, what gives? Why am I not loving this place? I was so excited to leave the New York snow but LA just seems a bit empty and impersonal instead of glamorous and exciting. Am I doing something wrong? If you have any recom- mendations, please email me and let me know where I should be going. And yes, before you ask, I have a car.

Course, things might pick up when Mr Movie Star takes me out this afternoon . . . I do this all for you, you know.

Blog written and emailed to Mary back in New York, I popped in the earphones from my Dictaphone and prepared to type up my notes. Hmm. Me telling James how I ended up in New York. James laughing. Me telling James how much I disliked LA. James laughing. Blake telling me I had to stick to approved topics. James laughing. So far, all I had for the interview was: *James Jacobs loves to laugh.*

Before I could even start to panic, I heard my phone buzzing in my bag. Mary – Office. Meep.

'Hi Mary,' I said, shuffling onto the edge of the chair and actively not biting my nails. 'You got my blog?'

'I did, you were sick outside his bungalow?' Mary wasn't one for pleasantries.

'Er, yeah, food poisoning,' I bluffed. 'James didn't know anything about it, I just thought it sounded funny on the blog.'

'Right.' I know she didn't believe me for a second. 'Is everything OK? Have you got some good stuff?'

'Yes?'

'Do you want to send it to me?'

I stopped actively not biting my nails. 'It's not ready.'

'It's not ready?'

'And I'm a perfectionist.'

'Right. Send me something tomorrow.'

I didn't know if it was a good or bad thing that she hung up without absolutely kicking my arse, but I was fairly sure that it was not good. Mary might have agreed to let me do the interview, but if things looked as though they might be going badly, she would pull me off in a heartbeat, and I was absolutely not going to let that happen. This was my chance; I really wanted it to work. Somewhere along the line, I'd got it into my head that if I could do this, then I could do anything. That maybe Mary would send me more exciting assignments than reviewing the new Christina Aguilera album. I just *had* to do a good job. Even if I had absolutely no experience, precedent or genuine reason to believe that I might be able to. Shit.

So what had I really learned about James Jacobs? He liked to run in the hills, he had just filmed a movie in Canada and he may or may not be from Sheffield. Hmm. Not even enough to warrant a ten-second interview on Facebook let alone a magazine interview.

OK, Angela, I told myself, as soon as James comes back to the trailer, you will be a hard-hitting journo. You will be the world's most investigative interviewer. You will check your make-up and hope that you are still looking human. And then, of course, James will walk back in while you have two giant rings of Touche Eclat highlighting your impressive eye bags. He was shadowed, of course, by Blake.

'Well, you, Angela Clark, are a rare beauty.' He gave me one of his most dazzling smiles. It was a wonder he didn't think everyone in the universe was mentally challenged, it was so difficult to actually give a coherent response when he really turned it on.

'It's a terrible load to bear,' I agreed. 'So what are we up to?'

'I'm all done here for today.' James stretched, touching the tips of his fingers to the ceiling of the trailer. 'Just let me get changed and then I thought we could head out into town.'

'Sounds like a plan,' I agreed, watching him vanish into the other room, giving me a chance to pat (never rub) the magical make-up into my skin and check my phone. Nothing from Jenny still; nothing from Alex. It was nice to feel loved. I sent a quick text to Jenny to check she was alive, but didn't have time to put together an Alex-appropriate message before James reappeared, car keys in hand, Blake by his side. It took time to be breezy.

'So, where are we going?' I asked, dropping my phone into my bag.

James held out a hand and hoisted me up. 'We're going to show you LA. Ready?'

Outside the trailer, James's limo had mysteriously vanished and in its place was a huge, petrol blue truck. Oh dear.

'A Hummer?' I tried not to raise an eyebrow at the cliché. Very *Entourage*.

'An H2H – hydrogen-powered Hummer. Don't judge a book by its cover, Angela.' James held open the door.

'You are a long way from home right now, James Jacobs,' I tested, shaking my head and clambering up inside.

'Not approved.' Blake 'helped' me into the cab with a firm shove to the arse. 'Seriously, Miss Clark, we are not talking about James's past in any way—' But before he could climb into the car after me, James leaned over, slammed the door shut and ran around to the driver's side. Sliding in and gunning the engine, he gave his assistant a hearty salute as we pulled out of the parking space.

'Bye Blake, I'll keep her on the approved topics, don't worry,' James called as we drove off, making an overly dramatic 'I can't hear you' gesture at his furious assistant as he revved the engine ever louder and peeled out of the car park. 'Now, I love that guy, but seriously, how are we supposed to do an interview with him barking "not approved" every ten seconds?'

'Couldn't agree more.' I wound the window down, trying to ignore the giddy butterflies building up in my stomach as we pulled out of the studio lot and onto the Avenue of the Stars. It wasn't just the ridiculous street name, it was cruising at high speed in a great big shiny truck. It was looking out of the window and up into the sunshine. It was the great big genuine grin on James's face. 'But aren't you afraid I'll ask you some horribly inappropriate questions and print some scandalous filth in the magazine?'

'Here's hoping,' he grinned.

'What do you think?' James asked as we screeched to a halt.

For the second time that day, my eyes turned to fall on something impossibly beautiful. I'd been so busy fiddling with James's iPod in the truck, trying to work him out by his song selections (impossible: he had everything ever recorded from Strauss to The Stones – and Stills, of course) that I hadn't even looked out of the window once we pulled onto the freeway.

Why bother? The streets weren't interesting like in New York or London. No one walked anywhere, the strips of shops were ugly or run down; there was literally nothing to look at. But while I'd been busy not paying attention, the ocean had appeared from nowhere. The Hummer was surrounded by people laughing, running, Rollerblading. We were at the beach.

Practically falling out of the truck, I ran towards the sand, leaving a sandal behind me. 'It's amazing,' I said, more to myself than anyone else. 'Look at it.'

'So this is Malibu. Beats Skegness, doesn't it?' James said quietly, presenting me with my abandoned shoe. He knelt down and cradled my bare foot in his hand, slipping on the sandal. Instinctively, I caught my breath and my balance, holding onto James's shoulders. Which was fine until my balance and my breath decided they didn't want to be caught and I toppled forward in slow mo, right on top of James.

'Beats Skegness,' I muttered.

I was only vaguely aware of the fact that my skirt had ridden up well clear of my knickers, but I was intensely aware of the tiny flecks of green in James's blue eyes, the scar in his eyebrow from a long-departed piercing and how ridiculously shiny every single strand of his hair was. Somewhere not that deeply hidden, my biological clock set itself to Pacific Standard Time and I felt a very strong urge to have all of James's babies. As soon as possible.

'That's twice you've fallen for me today.' James stared up at me for a moment, then brushed my hair off my face. 'You know your eyes are really beautiful.'

'What?'

'Your eyes, they're really pretty.' James gently pushed me off and sat up. 'So, blue. Have you ever thought about going darker with your hair?'

'Muh?' Seriously, I was dry-humping him on the beach and he was asking me if I'd thought about cracking out a bottle of Nice 'N Easy?

'I'm sorry,' he said, gently pushing me up and averting his eyes while I put myself away. 'I spend far too much time with make-up artists. They're always telling me if my hair was darker it would make my eyes look bluer. Apparently.'

'Make-up artists,' I nodded. 'So not all those hot women you're forever being pictured with?'

'Not approved,' James smirked, taking my hand and pulling me up onto the sand. 'Shut up and come on.'

The endless ocean melted between the cloudless blue sky and golden beach, but it just couldn't compete with the skin-on-skin contact. I was sure that the tiny thrills that kept tickling up and down my back would go away if I could just speak to Alex. But my phone had only had the decency to buzz once and that was to remind me that the repeat of *Gossip Girl* was starting. Or it would be if I had been in New York and not Malibu. I gave myself a mental shake and breathed out. Either I was just going to have to put Alex out of my mind and get on with the interview, or I was going to have a week's worth of embarrassing anecdotes and an empty Dictaphone.

'Shall we sit down for a while?' I asked, kicking off my sandals and pulling out my 'I'm a professional' paraphernalia.

'Jesus, I suppose so,' James screwed up his face. 'I know you're a journo and everything, but can we at least attempt to keep it fun? I'll let you in on a secret, I'm not a very good celebrity.'

'I'll try,' I said wryly. 'And I can let you in on a secret too: I'm not a very good journalist.'

'Don't be daft,' he said. 'I've read your stuff, you're great.'

'Don't you have people to do that sort of thing for you?' I asked, trying not to be too flattered. 'Surely you don't actually read for yourself?'

'There's actually just my manager, an accountant somewhere who makes sure I don't go broke – and Blake. When I first moved here, I had dozens of people, but it just didn't work. I've never been great at letting people think for me and talk for me, and I hate having dozens of people around me when I don't know if they're genuine or not. That's one of the reasons we're doing this.' He tilted his head and looked squarely at me. 'Blake is . . . Blake is great at running my life but I don't think he's the best person to put in front of journalists. All the media people out here are just, well, just too much. They have to know every single thing that you ever did or might do. There was just no privacy, ever. This, by the way, is off the record.'

I held up the Dictaphone. 'You want me to turn this off?'

Instead of answering, he took it from my hand, turned it over a couple of times and gave it a considered look. Before throwing it hard and far into the sea. 'Don't worry about it.'

'Don't ever ask to borrow my phone,' I said, wondering how I would write that off as expenses. Shit. 'So let's just sort this out. The magazine told me we were trying to do a piece to explain to all your adoring female fans that you're not some heartbreaking Hollywood lothario but just a misunderstood artist looking for your perfect woman. What was it that you were expecting?'

'Well, that sounds good, let's do that one. What do you need from me?' he asked, concentrating on running streams of sand through his fingers. 'I'm literally yours between now and the weekend.'

I tried not to think about what 'literally yours' could amount to and concentrate on the job at hand. Ish. 'I have a billion questions but, to be honest, I've never had to work off questions before. How about if we chat, I'll check the topics we're supposed to cover every so often, and when I write stuff up at night, you can check it before I send it to my boss?'

'You'll never work for *Vanity Fair*, you know that, don't you?' he shook his head. 'But that sounds perfect.'

'OK,' I nodded. 'Before we start properly, though, I have to ask you one thing. And yes, I know I can already hear Blake giving it some "not approved", but since you just chucked my Dictaphone in the ocean, I'm asking it anyway. Where are you from?'

'Well, Angela Clark, I went to drama school in London—'

'Not the biog, thank you very much. Where were you born?' I pressed. I was getting the honest answer to this if it killed me.

'Fine, fine, I'm surprised it's not common knowledge anyway,' he shrugged. 'I'm from South Yorkshire. Near Sheffield actually.'

'No way,' I laughed out loud. 'My grandparents lived in Sheffield; I spent every summer there for years. I could hear you had an accent but I couldn't quite place it.'

'What did you expect? They don't really go in for "it's grim oop north" at RADA,' he said, flicking a handful of sand at me. 'Where's your Yorkshire accent?'

'Didn't say I was from there, I just spent a lot of time throwing a tantrum on the floor of Redgates toy shop as a child,' I said. 'Happy memories.'

'Ahh, Redgates. I got all my *Star Wars* figures there. That's how I knew I wanted to be an actor, I wanted a little plastic figure of me, just like my Luke Skywalker.' He made a little pile of sand between us, then pressed it flat with the palm of his hand. 'I thought they made figures of everyone, you know? And when my mum said they only made them of people in films, I decided that was it. I'd have to be in films. God, I haven't thought about Redgates for years. My mum would take me there on my birthday and then we'd go to the Wimpy on The Moor. How mad is that?'

'Mad,' I agreed. 'Who would have thought: James Jacobs, the toast of Hollywood, Yorkshire born and bred.'

'Well, I wasn't James Jacobs then,' James grinned. 'Just plain old Jim.'

'Jim?' I tried not to laugh. 'Jim Jacobs?'

'What's your problem with Jim? My dad is Scottish.'

'Nothing, I can just see why you changed it,' I said, composing myself. 'You don't really hear people talking about Sexy Jim or Hot Jim, do you?'

'I suppose not,' he said, laughing at something he clearly wasn't going to share. 'It's more of an Old Jim or Pervy Jim.'

'Or Fat Jim,' I added.

'Did you just call me fat?' He pushed me sideways, knocking me off my balance, back into the scorching sand.

'No,' I said, trying not to count up how many times he had already seen my knickers. 'I called you Fat Jim.'

'Come on, fat or not, just thinking about a Wimpy is making me hungry,' he said, jumping up and pulling me with him. 'Let's go and get something to eat.'

I nodded and followed, trying not to be distracted by his denim-clad rear as we strode across the sand. He was like a walking, talking Levis ad. There was no possible way he could have spent his formative years anywhere other than an Abercrombie & Fitch catalogue. 'So when did you leave Sheffield?'

'Eighteen. I went to study drama in London and never went back,' he said, beeping the car's alarm. 'My parents moved away and there wasn't much opportunity for an actor up there. Well, there was panto at the Crucible but the less said about that, the better.'

'Panto?'

'The less said about panto the better,' he repeated sternly. 'It is weird people don't know where I'm from, I suppose. I got my break here and everyone just assumes I'm from London. Are you going to out me as a northerner?'

'Can I?' I asked, hopeful that I would have something to write.

'I'll do you a deal,' he replied. 'You can have that if

94

you promise not to mention the word panto in relation to me – ever.'

I thought carefully for a moment. 'Hmm, well . . .'

'Angela . . .' It was more of a warning than anything
else, but I did like hearing him say my name.

'Fair enough.'

Back at the car park, I quickly checked my phone
to find a couple of missed calls from Jenny. I bit my
lip, my phone must have been buzzing all the time we
were sitting on the sand and it hadn't even occurred
to me to check it.

'Boyfriend?' James asked, looking from my phone to
my slightly strained expression. 'If you need to give
him a ring, I can amuse myself for a minute.'

'No,' I said, dropping the phone back in my bag. I
was working, after all; Jenny would understand that.
'It's fine. Should you call Blake? I bet he's going
mental.'

'I bet he is.' James looked away and smiled. You
could almost mistake him for normal people until he
cracked out the teeth. Talk about a Hollywood smile.
'Huh, just the twenty missed calls from Blake.'

'Really?'

James nodded. 'He worries constantly. It's his job.'

'Shouldn't you call?'

'He'll wait. Now strap yourself in, I drive like a
maniac. Apparently.'

'You don't say,' I clicked my seatbelt. 'Where are
we off to now?'

'Honestly? You've got me completely worked up,'
he said, gunning the ridiculously loud engine. 'So
there's only one thing to do . . .'

'Oh my God,' I moaned. 'I think I'm in heaven.'

'You're amazing.' James looked so shocked. 'I can't

tell you the last time I had a meal with a girl that ate the bread. Or even the burger.'

'Well you might want to prepare yourself,' I warned him, reaching across the table for a giant handful of fries. 'I'm about to go into carb overload.'

There appeared to be several perks to hanging around with a movie star. You could leave work and go straight to the beach in the middle of the afternoon; you could talk your way out of a speeding fine by signing an autograph for the policeman's fourteen-year-old daughter; and you could get a table at 25 Degrees, the most amazing burger restaurant in the entire world, just by smiling at the waiter. I had tried not to feel smug as we cruised past all the people waiting for a table, but it was hard. Yes, it was the James Jacobs, and yes, he was with me. I knew that he was only with me because it was sort of his job but it was still a little bit lovely.

What wasn't as lovely was panicking about what kind of state I was in when all these people were staring. I hadn't so much as touched up my lip gloss since we left the studio. And while I wasn't completely unused to people whispering behind their hands about the man I was with, this was on another level. Loads of people knew who Alex was in Brooklyn, but the difference was that you could be standing in line for coffee in the Starbucks nearest to Alex's apartment and three of the five people in front of you would also be in bands. While here, as far as I could see, no one else in the restaurant had been nominated for the Best Fight, Best Kiss and Best Actor at the MTV Movie Awards last year. And I was absolutely certain there wasn't another contender for *Heat*'s Torso of the Week within a hundred-foot radius.

'I just have to . . .' I couldn't quite finish the sentence; nothing seemed particularly appropriate. So I just shuffled along the leather banquette clutching my (beloved but now slightly sandy) handbag. James nodded, blissfully lost in his giant burger. The restaurant was long and narrow, making it impossible to hide from the dozens of pairs of eyes that followed me all the way out to the toilets. And I couldn't really blame them: I would have stared too.

'Are you *seriously* James Jacobs's girlfriend?'

What I wouldn't have done was follow me out, grab my arm and ask a really rude question. But then I wasn't a huge, angry-looking girl with bright red dyed hair and a bum-bag.

'What? Are you retarded or something?' she demanded, arms now folded, her face absolutely enraged.

'Sorry, no, I'm . . .' I paused and looked back. James was still scarfing his dinner, absolutely oblivious to the attention he was receiving. 'No, I'm not his girlfriend.'

'Yeah, I totally said there was no way you were his girlfriend,' the girl looked visibly relieved. 'But my sister . . .' she paused to point over at a skinny girl with matching dyed hair waving from a small table opposite the bar. 'She said you were because she heard you talk and you were British. Are you his sister? You don't look like his sister.'

'I'm interviewing him,' I said, completely flustered. Now I just really needed a wee. 'So no, I'm not related to him or going out with him. Excuse me, I'm just off to the bathroom.'

'I'll wait here, you totally have to introduce me,' the girl yelled after me. I couldn't believe it, did Blake have to put up with this all the time? I couldn't help but wonder what that girl would have done if I *had* been his girlfriend. I'd dealt with the fact that there must be girls that had crushes on Alex (and the less pleasant fact that, before we'd met, he'd been a bit of a slag), but that was all ancient history. The threat from Alex's groupie following was incredibly limited compared to that of an actor. And James was something else altogether; every woman with eyes knew who he was. And once you combined his celebrity with his looks and the hateful fact that he was actually really, really nice, it was difficult not to have a bit of a crush on him. Not that I did. Honestly. Well, not that I'd ever cheat on Alex.

And I knew Alex would never cheat on me. Would he. Would he? No, of course not. Not even if I was away in LA and he was back in New York without me, writing his new album, getting all excited out and about in Brooklyn, maybe having a drink with the rest of his band who were all single and surrounded by that limited but not inconsiderable number of groupies I was just thinking about.

Couldn't hurt to give him a call.

I sank into one of the velvet couches in the gorgeous lobby. 25 Degrees was nestled inside The Roosevelt; it was such a gorgeous hotel and I felt as though I was letting it down in my simple jersey dress, even in the middle of the afternoon. Glancing around, I counted no less than eight people making calls around me. No need to worry about a tut and a sigh, then. In fact, I couldn't think of a venue I'd been to yet where people weren't on their phones. I speed-dialled Alex and let it ring. It was almost five in LA, so almost eight in New York, too late for him to be asleep, way too early for him to be writing. Maybe he was just out. Maybe he was surrounded by groupies. Hot skinny blonde groupies plying him with compliments.

And drugs. Oh God, they're definitely giving him drugs—

'Angela?'

'Hey, I just wanted to . . .' Check you weren't in the middle of a drug-fuelled orgy with a bunch of groupies. Or Kate Moss. 'Are you OK?'

'Yeah, sorry, I can't talk,' Alex sounded as if he was outside and I was instantly homesick for the sound of sirens and honking horns. Groupies honking their horns at my Alex . . . 'I'm just getting on the subway.'

'Going anywhere nice?' Like Kate Moss's hotel room?

'We're gonna try out some new stuff at an open mic night in the city,' he said. 'See what it sounds like live.'

'Really?' I was surprised at how upset I was. He was going to try out new songs without me? 'Wish I was there.'

'Did you want me to wait until you got back?'

'Yes. Will you?'

'No.'

'Oh.'

'You were kidding, right?'

No, I thought. 'Yes,' I said, 'of course. Let me know how it goes?'

'OK, talk later.' And he hung up.

'Yes, the interview's going great. No, I'm not going to have an affair with James but it's sweet that you're worried,' I muttered to myself as I redialled Jenny.

'Angie?' she answered.

'You're all right then?' I asked, faking annoyance. 'Where were you last night? With Joe?'

'No,' she sniffed. 'Sorry Angie, I can't talk, I'm busy. And you don't want to get in trouble with your movie star.'

I didn't know what to say, she sounded slightly

peeved. 'Everything is fine with the interview. I wanted to check you were OK. I was worried when you didn't come back to the hotel last night.'

'Not worried enough to call before this afternoon or come out last night though, huh?' she countered.

'Miss J, come *on*!' I heard Daphne yelling in the background. 'Are you talking to that British chick?'

'Sorry Jenny, I was so ill and I knew I was going to have to actually be able to think today. Can't we go for dinner tonight?' I asked. Moody Jenny was not fun.

'I don't think I'll make dinner, we're out,' she said, vaguely. 'I'm sorry, I know you're working. I just hoped we were going to get to spend more time together. Where are you?'

'The Roosevelt.' I looked around at the beautiful interiors. 'It's so gorgeous here.'

'Is James with you?' Jenny asked, slightly more interested. 'Could he get us on the list for Teddy's?'

'If I knew what that was, maybe.'

'It's the club in the Roosevelt.' She sounded excited for the first time since she'd picked up the phone. 'Go ask him and then call me back.'

'I might have finished your burger,' James said, not at all apologetically as I dropped back into my seat. 'But if you wanted to order something else, I could absolutely help you with it.'

'I'm fine,' I said, idly picking at a tasty chip. 'Suppose we should really crack on with the interview.'

James frowned. 'Actually, I'm a bit knackered. How would you feel if we held off until tomorrow? I could do with an early night.'

'Fair enough,' I nodded. An early night? Not very Hollywood hell-raiser. 'I ought to get one myself but I have a horrible feeling I'm going to end up out with my friend.'

'Do you know where you're going?' he asked, polishing off the last bit of my bun and starting on the fries. 'There are some right shit-tips around here if you're not careful.'

'She said something about Teddy's? That's here, isn't it?' I really couldn't bring myself to ask him to get us in. It was just too embarrassing.

'Yeah, Teddy's is fun,' James chewed thoughtfully, 'but – and don't take this the wrong way – it's really hard to get in. What time were you thinking of going?'

I shrugged. 'Don't know – late, I think. Jenny is out doing . . . something.' It bothered me that I didn't know what that something was.

'There's no point really getting there before eleven. Tell you what, I'm going to go back to the hotel and then why don't I come back and meet you here? I'm sure I'll feel better later, and if I'm with the enemy, I'm less likely to get into trouble,' he said before draining his Diet Coke.

'The enemy?' I was completely confused.

'Journo,' he nodded towards me.

'Oh,' I almost laughed out loud. 'Sorry, I feel like I'm letting you down.'

James set down his glass and pushed my hair back behind my ear, his hand lingering against my flushed cheek. 'It *is* a shame,' he agreed.

His thumb traced my cheek, his fingers twisting themselves into my hair. His dark blue eyes found mine, searching them with something like a smile that just made it to the very corners of his mouth. I breathed out slowly, thinking what a good job it was that I hadn't finished my burger, when my stomach did a triple somersault and my heart was catapulted to somewhere in my throat.

'Well, I'd better let you go,' I mumbled against his cool palm.

'Sorry,' James said, dropping his hand and his eyes. 'I'd better let you go.'

This was absolutely, definitely going to be harder than I'd hoped, I thought as I staggered out of the restaurant. But maybe for completely different reasons than I had imagined.

CHAPTER SIX

The short walk from The Roosevelt to The Hollywood was just enough time to convince myself that the whole cheek-stroking incident hadn't actually happened. And if it had, it was just because, as I had expected, James Jacobs couldn't communicate with a girl unless he was trying to get in her pants. Except it hadn't been that way all day. Looks aside, he was exactly the opposite of what I had expected. He wasn't arrogant, he wasn't rude and, irritatingly for Angela Clark, interviewer extraordinaire, he didn't seem to want to talk about himself at all. Hmm. I'd been completely ready to fall in love with his beautiful face and expecting to grit my teeth and tolerate him being a total arse, but I wasn't at all prepared for him to be nice. Even nicer than nice maybe. I needed a drink.

Standing by the barrier in The Hollywood's rooftop bar, mojito in hand, the big white letters nestling in the hills didn't seem any more real than they did on Saturday. If living in New York was like walking into a living movie, arriving in LA was like walking onto the set. It all seemed slightly artificial, as though the sky and the hills and the Hollywood sign could just pull away to make way for a more successful city if this one didn't test well. I leaned over the balcony, and tried to take it all in. Nope, still not buying it.

'Hey, English. Where's Lopez at?'

'Hi Joe,' I smiled as he leaned against the barrier, his tight black shirt pulling against his arms. I didn't remember them being so massive, but I guessed that was one of the perks of shaking cocktails all day. Insta-biceps. 'I've been out all day, no idea where she is.'

'Yeah,' he held his hand up to shield the sun out of his eyes. 'Jenny said you were interviewing James Jacobs. How's it going?'

He stroked my cheek and I think he was going to kiss me and I really wanted him to and that makes me a horrible person because I have a lovely boyfriend but he hasn't called me or texted me and isn't it OK anyway because he's a movie star? I thought.

'OK, I suppose,' I said.

Joe snorted. 'Guy's a douche. I'd love to hear what shit he's spinning you.'

'No really.' I was actually a little bit surprised. I didn't know Joe well but he didn't seem like the kind of person to be jealous. 'He's not like you'd think. Not like he is in all the magazines.'

'Please, I don't read that kind of trash.' Joe turned around, resting his back against the barrier. 'I've met him and I'm telling you, he's an asshole.'

'Really?' I asked. 'Where? When? What did he do?'

'You're like a proper reporter now, huh?' Joe laughed. 'Who, where, what, why, when? You really have changed, English.'

'I don't know about that,' I said, resting the chilled glass against my forehead. 'Still haven't got a blind clue what I'm doing.'

'You seem to be doing pretty good to me.' Joe draped an arm over my shoulders and gave me a half-hug. 'You've been here, what, six months? And from nowhere, here you are, interviewing douche-bags in Hollywood. And, I might add, looking totally hot. I bet Lopez is pissed that she gave you such a great makeover.'

'Thank you?' It seemed like at least half a compliment. 'But I think Jenny's safe. She's totally incredible anyway. And so ridiculously gorgeous,' I added, marking it up mentally to score some points with Jenny if she was still mad later on.

'Yeah, Lopez has always had it. But living with her looks good on you,' he squeezed my shoulder. 'Hey, whatever happened with you and that guy in Brooklyn? Is that still through?'

'Alex?' I was surprised Joe remembered. He'd moved to LA about a month after Alex and I had failed miserably the first time around and I hadn't mentioned his name once after he broke it off. 'We actually got back together.'

'Too bad.' Joe held my gaze a second too long before I broke off to stare back out at the hills. What was going on today? Did I have an 'I'm easy and desperate' sign taped to my back? Or was my dress still tucked in my knickers?

'So tell me how you know James. Did he stay here?' I asked. I might not be an amazing interviewer but I was very experienced in changing the subject.

'Nah, I've met him out a couple of times.' Joe frowned. 'Guy's got an attitude. He's just kinda off. Thinks he's something special, I guess.'

'That's so weird.' I couldn't quite believe we were talking about the same person. 'He's been such a gentleman to me.'

'Maybe he's different with the ladies,' Joe shrugged. 'And that fag he hangs out with. What an ass.'

'Blake might be a bit highly strung,' I said tightly, 'but I don't see how his being gay makes him an ass.'

'Don't get me wrong,' Joe held out his hands, 'I got no issue with that, man. This is Hollywood, more than half the guys out here are gay. He's just, well . . . He doesn't play well with others.'

'Why don't you come out with us tonight?' Two birds, one stone, I thought. Jenny will forgive me if I bring Joe and Joe gets to see that James isn't, well, whatever he thinks he is. 'We're going to Teddy's.'

'With James Jacobs?'

'And Jenny,' I offered. 'Come on, I'm sure we'll hardly see James. He's just going to get us in.'

'I could have got you in,' Joe sniffed.

'Well, I'd really like it if you came. Jenny too,' I said, squeezing his arm.

Joe paused, looked back at the bar he had been tending all day and then back at me. 'What time?'

Since she'd blown back into my room around eight, Jenny had been in a much better mood than when we'd last spoke. But she hadn't breathed a word about her whereabouts, waving me off with an insincere 'just doing stuff' in reply to any and all of my questions. Not too irritating. After what felt like a lifetime in the shower, she emerged a goddess, her masses of curls bouncing around her face like a halo, skin glowing with two days of sunshine and the most infectious smile I'd seen on her in months.

'LA suits you then?' I asked, as we jostled for space at the make-up mirror. I couldn't help but feel as though she should have to apply her make-up blindfolded as a handicap. Where the sun had given her a golden sheen, the beach had left me blotchy and my hair was just an unmanageable mess.

'I'd forgotten how much fun it was,' she admitted. 'Makes me feel like doing crazy stuff. Makes me feel – I don't know – alive? Is that too cheesy?'

'No. I know exactly how you feel,' I said, sketching around my eyes with a jet-black Mac pencil. The aim was to draw attention away from my riotous mane and flaky nose. Not too big an ask, then. 'Not about here, admittedly, but that's how I feel about New York. Maybe you needed to get away, give yourself a bit of a kick-start.'

'And now I need something else.' She gave me a wink and started on her fourth coat of mascara. 'Seriously, I know you can't make a move on James Jacobs, but what's the protocol on me taking him for a test drive? I'll give you all the details. Now that would be an exclusive worth reading.'

'Jenny,' I warned, slipping into my new bright yellow Phillip Lim mini-dress. I'd hoped the sunshiny colour would lift me into an LA frame of mind. So far, all it had lifted was my credit limit, but it was beautiful. 'I don't think it's the best idea you've ever had. What about Joe?'

'What about Joe?' She pulled on what I recognized immediately as her lucky dress. A beautiful red, purple and gold Alice + Olivia silk number with a deep V-neck slashed to an empire line. The crossed straps on the back emphasized her flawless tanned skin and tiny waist while the flared skirt whirled around her as she moved. My God, she meant business. 'If I'm not totally mistaken, Joe had his chance already. You should always aim for the top, Angie. If you don't believe you're worth the best, why will anyone else?'

'Oh dear, Oprah Lopez is back,' I said, slicking on

some clear lip gloss and hoping for the best. 'You know I am just as keen as the next man for you to have some empty, meaningless, hopefully utterly demeaning sex, but does "the best" have to be the man I'm interviewing?'

'Of course not,' Jenny took my shoulders and looked at me closely, assessing my make-up. 'I mean, if James knows Jake Gyllenhaal I'll be more than happy to trade up.'

'That so wouldn't be trading up,' I said quietly, taking the new lip gloss she held out. 'James is definitely hotter than Jake. And nicer too, I bet. And a better actor.'

'Uh-oh, someone has a crush,' Jenny nodded at the peachy gloss. 'And what does Alex think about you trading up?'

'Please . . .' I blushed. I was so happy that she was talking to me again, it just didn't seem necessary to tell her about the cheek stroking. 'Not even a movie star would be trading up from Alex. You can't compare hotness with love, can you?'

'Wait, he's said he loves you?' Jenny stopped in her nose-powdering tracks. 'When did this happen and why am I only finding out now?'

'Well, no,' I admitted. 'He still hasn't actually said it. I just meant that I wouldn't swap what we have for anything.'

'Angie, I wish you would just pick up the phone and say it,' Jenny said. 'What are you waiting for? You can say it first, you know.'

'I hate it when you flip into Oprah mode,' I mumbled, slipping on my ever-ready Louboutins. How did a simple red sole transform a strappy gold sandal from 'nice shoe' to 'spend-a-month's-rent-on-me-and-I-will-complete-you'? Those shoes and I had been through a lot together, including breaking someone's hand; and even though they should remind me of some not-so-good times, the effect they had on my legs was magical. And therefore they would always be forgiven everything.

'So that's it? You just don't want to say it first?' Jenny pressed on. I knew she wouldn't rest until she got an answer. And the cow could always tell when I was lying.

'No,' I sighed, perching on the end of the bed to fasten my shoes. 'I don't want to say it first, OK?'

'It's more than OK,' she said, sitting down next to me. 'But really, I already know you love him, honey. Everyone knows. Erin knows, Vanessa knows, I think even Scottie in the diner knows. So I'm pretty certain Alex knows.'

'His name isn't Scottie,' I sighed. 'So you think I should say it?'

'No, what I'm saying is, you wear your heart on your sleeve, Angie, and maybe this time you wait him out.' Jenny combed my hair back off my face. 'Let him do the running. If he loves you, he'll say it.'

'If.' It was hours since we'd spoken and I was starting to get really annoyed that he hadn't called back.

'Anything else you want to tell me, doll?' Jenny asked. 'Because if he has done anything wrong—'

'No, no.' I breathed in deeply and stood up. 'Just me being paranoid. He's just been hard to get hold of the last couple of days. Come on, let's go and get you some.'

'Hell, yeah.' She kicked on her sandals. 'But he can't say he wasn't warned. If I see so much as a tear out of you because of him, I will kick his ass all the way across the Brooklyn Bridge.'

'I'll have to get you back to Brooklyn first,' I said,

linking arms and pulling her out of the room. 'You seem awfully at home here.'

'Well, let's see how I get on with your movie star,' Jenny said cheerfully. 'I can always fly back in his private jet if I really have to.'

Joe was waiting in reception, propped against the desk in tight black jeans and second-skin grey T-shirt, artfully stretched at the deep V-neck. He was clearly taking his rivalry with James very seriously. Even if James didn't know anything about it. Jenny literally leapt out of the lift and scooted over, curling herself into the crook of his arm, her dreams of private jets and Malibu mansions forgotten for at least the length of time it took us to walk from reception to James's waiting car outside.

I wasn't sure whether to be happy or not, but he'd swapped the Hummer for the limo, much to Jenny's delight. But nothing could compare to the look on her face once she was safely positioned between a slightly terrified-looking James and a slightly territorial-looking Joe. I hopped in next to Blake for the five-minute ride down to The Roosevelt, trying to pretend the awkward moments with both James and Joe had not happened. Trying and failing.

'How come we have to drive five minutes down the road?' I asked after the introductions were done. 'It's not terribly environmentally friendly, is it?'

'Want to see what happens when I hang around Hollywood Boulevard at eleven at night?' James asked, pressing the button to let down the blacked-out window. 'Hi ladies,' he called at a group of girls hovering outside Gap.

'Omigod, are you . . . ?' The tall brunette closest to the limo dropped her drink, spilling Coke all over the pavement.

110

They peered inside at James and, honestly, even if he hadn't been a megastar, I don't think I would have been able to keep it together. His tight black shirt stretched over his 'just finished a movie' six-pack and his loose, straight-cut jeans couldn't conceal his fantastic thighs. And even though he was sitting on it, I'd already had a sneak peek at his backside when he climbed across the limo seat. Not that I was looking.

'Yeah, James Jacobs,' he nodded, holding up a hand in a short wave. 'Have a great evening.'

All three of the girls paled and stood open-mouthed for a split second as James buzzed the window back up. Then they broke out into an ear-piercing, glass-shattering scream. Before I could lean back into my seat, they were on the car. Actually on it.

'Enough games, James?' Blake sighed, as the limo began to move at a crawl, leaving the girls behind us. 'This is all going to end up in her freaking magazine. Is that what you want?'

'Does that happen everywhere you go?' I asked, staring back at the girls standing in the middle of the street, clutching at each other just to stay vertical.

'More or less everywhere,' James laughed. 'You didn't notice it today?'

'Only in the restaurant,' I said, thinking back over the day. It was quite possible that people had been collapsing left, right and centre, but I had been so busy trying not to fall in love with James myself that my own mother could probably have passed out in front of us and I wouldn't have noticed. 'Wow. That must be a nightmare.'

'You learn to live with it,' he said, smiling at Jenny, who had been silent (for the first time in her life) for the whole journey but sat staring at James with the

111

most ridiculous grin I had ever seen etched into her face. Joe, however, had a face like thunder. Maybe this wasn't my best idea ever. 'Shall we go in?'

Teddy's really was fun, if not completely surreal. Like the rest of The Roosevelt, it was gloriously old Hollywood, and wandering through the darkened bar, past the subdued booths lined with wine-coloured velvet and mahogany-coloured people, I felt just like Elizabeth Taylor. If Elizabeth Taylor had been incredibly self-conscious about weighing at least as much as two of every other woman in the room. Whilst having to restrain her best friend from physically attacking every man in the room. But then maybe Elizabeth Taylor did have to do that, how would I know?

'Jesus, Angie, I think I've died and gone to heaven,' Jenny whispered as we were escorted through to a VIP table. 'This is totally where I belong.'

'Well, don't rely on me hanging out with you when you're here,' I whispered back. 'I feel like someone stuffed an Olsen twin down my dress. How thin are these girls? And I think Joe is going to deck James. Or Blake. Or both.'

Despite James's attempt at conversation, Joe had maintained an impressive stony silence, except for when he was addressed by me or Jenny. Plus he and Blake had been exchanging stares ever since we got in the limo and it had only got worse since we arrived at the club.

'So, Joe,' I started with my quickly formulated plan of distraction. 'Do you come here a lot?'

'Mmmm,' Joe nodded, swirling the beer he had insisted on buying himself at the bar, 'with some of the guys from the hotel. And you know, sometimes

I model a little. I actually did a job at the Tropicana a couple of weeks ago, the roof bar here.' He sat down in between me and Jenny, sliding an arm around each of us. It might have looked casual, but the firm grip on my shoulder said it was anything but.

Jenny idly caught his fingers and entwined them with her own, even though her eyes were firmly locked on James. I was working extra hard at not making eye contact with anyone other than myself in the mirror behind the bar. And someone that looked just Kristen Stewart. Oh. And Kristen Stewart.

'Have you ever thought about acting?' James asked, pouring everyone a generous measure of vodka from the bottle that had just been brought to our table.

'Whatever,' Joe replied, looking away. 'Modelling is one thing but dancing around in tights for a living? I don't think so.'

'Hey,' Blake turned sharply.

James laughed, seemingly oblivious to Joe's enormous attitude problem. 'It's just one of the perils of superhero movies. But you know what, tights are surprisingly comfortable. You do get used to them.'

'Tights, really?' Jenny mooned, dropping Joe's hand and giving James's knee a quick squeeze. 'Are you wearing them now?'

'Seriously?' Joe narrowed his eyes at Jenny as she let out her most impressive flirty laugh. 'Everyone knows actors are just delusional egotists. They all end up in rehab sooner or later.'

'Are you taking Jenny on for title of the next Oprah or what?' I forced out a laugh but this was all getting a little bit too tense and I really wasn't one for confrontation.

'I'm gonna take a walk.' Joe measured his breathing

and draped his arm possessively around my shoulders. 'You coming, English?'

James looked over at me but I really wasn't sure what his dark blue eyes were trying to say. I opened my mouth to stall but Blake beat me to it.

'Maybe that's not a bad idea,' he challenged Joe, taking a swig straight out of the vodka bottle. 'Maybe you should both just go.'

'Me?' I asked, snapping to surprise. 'What did I do?'

'You brought this asshole,' Blake replied. 'As far as I'm concerned, the interview is over. In fact, James, we're leaving.'

'Great, why don't you just move on, fag?' Joe said into his beer bottle.

'What did you just call me?' Blake stood up suddenly, followed in a heartbeat by Joe and then James.

'Hey, guys, come on.' James pushed himself in between the two as they squared up. 'This isn't happening.'

'No, this is bullshit.' Joe pushed his way past the two of them, knocking Jenny off the edge of her seat and into me as he left. The weight of the Lopez wasn't ever going to cause me trouble but the vodka soda she spilled all down my dress wasn't exactly ideal.

'Oh, shit,' I said, leaping up, right into James's waiting arms.

'We have to get out of here,' Blake said, pulling at James's shoulder. I froze for a second, pressed against James's chest, my wet dress soaking through against his shirt, until it was warmed by the heat of his skin. It wasn't until he'd scooped me up, as if I weighed nothing, as if I was half an Olsen, let alone three strapped together, that I realized we were moving out of the club.

'Angie?' Jenny yelled over the music, still on the floor beside the wreckage of our table. 'Wait!'

'Jenny,' I protested, preferring the view of James's dark brown curls to the stares and whispers all around us. And, oh dear God, the camera flashes.

'Blake, go back for her,' James commanded, striding into the lift, leaving an incensed Blake standing stock-still. 'Now I remember why I stopped going out.'

I didn't know what to say. On one hand I felt awful about leaving Jenny – sick, actually – but on the other, I knew that the second James put me down, the inter-view, my job, possibly my visa and then more or less my entire life was over. I had to try and get this back on track somehow, otherwise Jenny wouldn't have a roommate to be mad at.

'James, I am so incredibly sorry,' I said as we scram-bled into the limo and tore off up Hollywood Boulevard. 'I–I should just go back to my hotel and—'

'That's not a good idea,' James said quietly. 'Have a look out of the back window.'

Twisting against my seatbelt, I turned to look back, trying not to get dizzy at the speeds we were travel-ling. I don't know what I was expecting to see but, whatever it was, the sea of bright lights and industrial-strength flashes was not it. True, I still had an issue with what side of the road we were supposed to be driving on, but these cars were literally all over the road. The honking, the screeching, even the screaming was so loud, so intense. It made a wander down our block in New York sound like an episode of *Songs of Praise*.

'What's happening?' I asked, slightly dazed and very nauseous.

'Paparazzi,' James sighed. 'My good friends, the paparazzi.'

'How did they know where you were?'

'Who knows? Maybe someone overheard us this afternoon and tipped them off. Maybe they were already outside Teddy's on the off-chance someone would show up. Maybe someone called them when we arrived.'

'But we were only there for half an hour?' I couldn't believe it, no matter how fast we went, they came at us faster until they were swarming all around the car.

'Get away from the window.' James pulled me into the centre of the limo, on the floor between the seats. 'Some of the flashes are bright enough to see you through the tinted glass.'

'Wow, this is glamorous,' I said, trying to shuffle my dress around my thighs to avoid any further pant revelation.

'Yes, the rock-and-roll life of a movie star.' He held out an arm to steady me as we skidded around a tight corner. 'But you're all-over rock and roll, surely?'

'Me?' I squirmed across the floor of the car, trying not to nestle against his broad, warm and still slightly damp chest.

'Your boyfriend, the rock star? Alan?'

Oh. 'Alex. His name is Alex. He's so not a rock star. There's a pretty big difference between him and Bono.' I fumbled around on the floor of the car looking for my bag. 'What time is it?'

'Not even twelve, what's up?'

'Just wondered.' I pulled out my phone. Twelve here, three in New York. And a missed call from Alex. Just one. Twenty minutes earlier and no message. 'Bugger.' Just as I was about to redial, James snatched the phone out of my hand.

'If you throw that out of the window, I will freak out.'

'Sorry,' he said, turning the phone off. 'They'll hack it.'

'They'll what?' Could this get any more bizarre?

James nodded slowly. 'They can hack your phone if you use it near enough. I don't know how.'

'But how do you call anyone, ever?' I asked.

'I don't. It's like living in Nineteen ninety-five.' He shrugged. 'If I really need to get hold of someone, Blake goes out and calls them for me.'

'So you can't text your friend to see what flavour muffin they want?'

'Can't go out and buy muffins. Can't really eat muffins.'

'And you can't call a taxi when you're hammered?'

'To be fair I have a driver.'

'What if you need to extend your credit limit to buy something amazing?'

'Yeah, that's not really a massive problem right now. Unless that something is a Bentley.'

'I might be able to live with not having a mobile phone if I was you,' I said, feeling less sympathetic by the second.

James nodded. 'But if I wasn't me, we wouldn't be running away from the club now. The paparazzi wouldn't be chasing us. And you wouldn't be sitting on the floor of a car ruining your beautiful dress, not able to call your boyfriend.'

'But if you weren't you, I wouldn't be in LA at all, I wouldn't have met you and, well, I wouldn't have been able to wear my beautiful dress in March anyway.' I shuffled back up onto the seat as the limo twisted around some invisible corners and then slowed to a stop. The din from the paparazzi got quieter and quieter until I couldn't hear anything but the ticking of the cooling engine as we climbed out.

James ran his hands down my sides, smoothing down the creased-up skirt. I breathed in sharply as they ran

117

back up my bare arms. 'It's a great dress, did I tell you that already?' he asked, towering above me. He was awfully tall. I hadn't noticed how awfully tall. 'Phillip Lim, right?'

'Every so often, you throw me off completely, you know?' I said, cricking my neck to get a better look at him. 'If you weren't all Hollywood, I'd think you were gay. Which would just about break Jenny's heart.'

'Good to know,' he said, fumbling for keys in his jeans pocket. I was right, his backside did look great. 'We should have just stayed here. You know what they say, if you're going to get into trouble, do it at the Chateau.'

He wanted to get into trouble? Meep. 'I really should go back to my hotel,' I choked. 'It's late and I was supposed to be conducting an interview with someone tomorrow.'

'I heard he's a delusional egotist who likes to prance around in tights,' James said, opening the door and pulling me inside. 'So I think you'll be fine. Besides, I can get that dress dry cleaned inside twenty minutes and then get you a car home once the paps have moved on outside. Come on, I'm dying for a cup of tea.'

Following him into the bungalow, I shrugged. I couldn't argue with a well-thought-out plan.

'Can I use my phone in here?' I called from the bathroom, peeling off my damp yellow dress. The bathroom was full of products: Clinique, Anthony Logistics, Peter Thomas Roth. Sent over by PRs, I figured, but still, men with more moisturizer than me made me edgy.

'The landline should be OK, but I'm keeping your mobile hostage until you leave.' James knocked once on the door and then came in. Giving me just enough time to grab one of the robes hanging from the back of the door. But not enough time to put it on. 'Nice knickers, Calvin Klein?'

'Erm, yes,' I said, trying to slide into the robe without revealing an inch of flesh or white lace. Not an easy task at the best of times, and even more difficult when you were a) ridiculous clumsy and b) in the hotel bathroom of a stupidly hot actor. A stupidly hot actor who had taken off his shirt. Oh. It was pretty.

'Don't tell your model friend, but I did a campaign for them last year.' He took one arm of the robe, in theory to help me put it on, but in practice just to help me get even more wound up in the acres of jersey. 'I think that's the set Eva wore.'

Perfect. Who didn't want to be compared to Eva Mendes in their underwear?

'I'm so sorry about that,' I said again. 'I don't know what his problem is. It's just . . . God, Jenny is going to kill me.'

'I'm sure she'll be fine.' James pushed his hair back off his face. Had his cheekbones always been so high? What else were those brown curls hiding? 'And please stop apologizing for that knobhead. I'm just surprised you're friends with him, to be honest. You did realize he was all over you? Do you know, I haven't called anyone a knobhead for ages. You really do bring out the English in me.'

'Thanks, I think.' I pushed past him, moving very quickly through the bedroom, accidentally glancing at the rumpled bedsheets and settling in the living room. In an armchair. Made for one. Could he please just put a shirt back on? I was only human, for God's sake. 'And, just for the record, he's absolutely not interested in me. I don't even really know him; we're not really

119

friends. He and Jenny used to work in the same hotel in New York, that's all.'

'So they're friends?'

'Sort of,' I wrinkled my nose. There was no way Jenny would be exploring their 'friendship' now. I was going to suffer for this one.

'I see, friends with benefits?'

Before I could clarify, there was a knock at the door. James opened up and swapped my dress for a tray of drinks. 'Thanks,' he said to someone I couldn't see. 'Tea?'

'Yes please,' I sighed, realizing suddenly how tired I was. 'I'd kill for a cup right now.'

'I don't want to know how you're going to react to my HobNobs then,' he said, producing a full packet of biscuits. 'This really is the best hotel in the world.'

'Don't say that in front of Jenny,' I said, taking a handful of crumbly biscuity goodness. 'She's all about The Union. Or at least she was; she hasn't stolen anything in ages.'

'So we've got twenty minutes to fill,' James said, nursing his steaming mug. 'What do you want to do?'

What did I want to do? Now there was a question. My head wanted to call Jenny, make sure she was OK and actually going to speak to me again. My heart wanted to call Alex and see how his gig went, hear his soft sleepy voice and have him put the phone on his pillow until he fell asleep so I could just listen to him breathe. But another, slightly less poetic part of me was absolutely burning to stand up, take that cup of tea out of James Jacobs's hand and put all of his flirting to the test. To trace a finger up his abs, his sharply cut chest and over his full bottom lip. Just press it, just to see if it was as firm and plush as it looked. And then possibly nibble on it a little bit. And then—

'You've got such a strange look on your face,' James interrupted. 'What are you thinking about?'

Pushing you backwards against the sofa and doing lots of very dirty things until my passport expires.

'Nothing really.'

'There's something I wanted to say, actually,' he carried on. 'About this afternoon, at the burger place.'

Maybe just a quick nibble. 'No need, really.'

'Yes, there is. I'm sorry, I just get caught up easily. Really, it's pathetic. I spend so much time spouting crap that's written for me, I start coming out with it when they haven't even given me a script.' He rested on the arm of my chair. And smelt delicious. 'I suppose that's why Blake gets so angry. I get myself into so much trouble with all those photos.'

'Photos?'

'Of me. Well, if they were just of me it wouldn't be a problem.'

'Oh.'

'They're just photos, Angela,' he said, looking down at me.

'You don't have to explain anything to me.' I stared straight ahead. Trying not to be jealous.

'Well, I do, you are the reporter,' he said. 'But I'm just saying. Although I can't help but wonder what that interview is going to come out like.'

'The interview.' I covered my face. 'I'm really not doing well, am I? I'm so going to get fired and then I'll be deported. And homeless. And someone's going to have to tell my mother . . .'

'What are you talking about?' James pulled away my hands with his own, warmed through by his hot tea. 'Why are you going to get fired?'

'Because Blake cancelled the interview.' I looked at him as though he was slightly stupid. Very pretty but slightly stupid.

James looked back at me the exact same way. 'Blake can't cancel the interview.'

'He can't?' I asked, puzzled. 'I thought he did everything?'

'Well he didn't set it up,' James explained.

'He didn't?'

'No, Angela. I did.'

'OK, I know I'm not very clever at the best of times, but I don't understand . . .'

'The interview, you, it was my idea,' James said, looking really rather pleased with himself. 'I'm not stupid, I know what people must think when they see all those photos of me and, well, every woman I've ever met. So I read some women's magazines, checked out some of the writers and that's how I came across you.'

'You asked for me?' I was confused. Not unusual, admittedly. 'It was actually you?'

'I asked for you. I loved your writing,' he nodded. 'But once I'd chosen you, I had to put everything through Blake, after I'd picked a magazine, otherwise it would have been weird. Actors don't usually set up their own press. To be honest, Blake wasn't completely convinced you were the right pick, so I would really, really appreciate it if you could at least attempt to prove him wrong.'

'So the interview isn't off?'

'Well, you threw up on me yesterday, got me and my assistant into a fight today, I can't wait to see what you come up with tomorrow.' He shook his head and looked out of the window. 'I'll call for your car, you should be safe now.'

I sat back in the chair and watched the muscles in his back leave the room. James Jacobs had chosen me. The interview wasn't off. Maybe I wouldn't have to leave the country after all. Which meant Alex and I probably wouldn't be breaking up because I had to go back to England. Which was a really, really good thing.

Unless Alex was still so busy getting it on with his groupies he didn't even have three minutes to spare to leave me a voicemail. The battery indicator on my silent phone flickered in the bottom of my clutch. Obviously it wasn't as though he was desperate to get in touch and tell me he loved me or anything. How come he couldn't even tell me how he couldn't bear to live a single second of his life without me when a global superstar – no, megastar – had handpicked me out of every single journalist in the entire world to interview him? I'd now been in his hotel twice. And twice I'd been out of my frock. That had to be a sign. Another knock on the door interrupted my entirely unhelpful thoughts.

'That'll be your dress,' James called from the other room. 'Your car's going to be about five minutes.'

I wrapped myself up in the dressing gown, trying not to trip over the hem and opened the door. There was my dress, all pristine, wrapped in shiny plastic. Twenty-minute dry cleaning had revolutionized my life. 'Thank you,' I said, taking the hanger.

'No . . . thank *you*,' said a voice behind a huge camera.

'What the . . . ?' I stumbled backwards, holding my dress out in front of the rapid fire-flashes.

'Angela!' James yelled, sprinting across the living room. 'Close the door, get away from the door!'

I slammed the door into the camera, heard a dull

123

thud, a quiet 'shit' and then the sound of quickly retreating footsteps. Dazed, I looked at James, but he was already on the phone, yelling incoherently. For the want of something to do, I staggered into the bathroom and got changed. I checked myself in the mirror: nope, my skirt wasn't tucked in my pants, not even a bra strap was on show. Impeccable. For me. And if you went for the 'startled deer in headlights' thing, I actually looked pretty good.

'OK,' I said, teetering back into the lounge and grabbing my handbag. 'I think it's best if I just go, I've caused enough chaos tonight.'

'You can't go out there now.' James looked at me as if I was stupid. He and Jenny would actually get on really well. 'I've just called security but they haven't caught him yet. You can't go anywhere until they've got that camera.'

I wanted to laugh but had a feeling that it wouldn't go down well. 'Seriously? James, all they've got is a picture of me holding some dry cleaning.'

'Yes, maybe,' James mused. 'Or, they've got a picture of you, without your dress on, standing in the doorway of my bungalow at one a.m. What's that going to be worth to your boyfriend? Or your editor? Or your mum?'

'My mum would probably be quite impressed actually,' I said, feeling a little bit sick. 'But I see your point. I really can't stay here, though. I have to see Jenny; I have to go back. Is there no way out without those arses getting a photo?'

All six-foot-something of James Jacobs stood squarely between me and the door, staring me down with an intensity I usually saved for the person in the queue between me and the last espresso brownie in Starbucks. And I wasn't sure if I was the person or the brownie. 'Do you really want to leave?'

No no no no no no no no no no.

'Yes.' Wow, who knew I was so strong?

'Then I'll call a car to come to the back of the bungalow,' he said, breathing out and letting his shoulders drop. 'They should have something that won't attract attention. I left the phone in the bedroom.'

I realized I hadn't breathed out since I'd said I wanted to leave and the zip on my bag was cutting into my hand, I was clutching it so tightly. This was horrible. How could I even be thinking these things about James when Alex was at home in New York, just waiting for me to call. Probably. He just wasn't desperate to call me. Or tell me he loved me. Or even come to LA with me. Whereas James seemed relatively keen for me not to leave for one reason or another. Surely ninety-nine out of a hundred girls in this situation would stay, boyfriend be damned. Maybe if I talked to the boyfriend quickly, it would be easier.

I released my vice-like grip on my bag and pulled out my mobile. Yes, it was four a.m. in New York, but he wouldn't mind a quick call. And tough luck if he did.

'Hello?'

'Alex, it's me,' I gushed. 'I'm sorry; I suppose I didn't expect you to answer. I'm just having the most chaotic night and—'

'Angela?'

'Yes?'

'It's four in the morning.'

'I know.'

'What do you want?'

I bit my lip. 'I just wanted to speak to you. Tell you I missed you.'

'Are you drunk?'

'No,' I frowned. 'I'm just having a bit of a nightmare

125

evening. We were out and James got into a fight and then there were loads of paparazzi—'

'Seriously, Angela, I'm sleeping. Call me tomorrow, OK?' Alex sighed.

I tried not to be stung. He was perfectly within his rights to be a bit peeved but I had been hoping he might have thought my spontaneous call was cute. He certainly seemed to think it was acceptable to turn up on my doorstep at all hours of the night. Surely just calling to tell someone you missed them at four a.m. was romantic?

'OK,' I muttered into the phone, 'go back to sleep. I just wanted to say – I just thought I'd call and . . . well, I love you.'

'What?' he suddenly sounded considerably more awake.

'I'll call you tomorrow, go back to sleep. Bye.' I hung up, threw my phone back into my bag as if it was on fire and clapped a hand over my mouth. How had that snuck out?

'Did you say something?' James asked, appearing back at my side.

Before I could answer, the hotel phone rang once and then stopped. 'That's your car,' James said, taking my arm and leading me towards the back door of the bungalow. 'So, we're not meeting tomorrow, right? Unless you want to come and watch me in make-up testing?'

I shrugged. I had been known to enjoy a touch of guyliner. Had I really just told Alex I loved him?

'So I'll collect you Wednesday morning. Eleven OK?'

'Fine,' I said, stumbling the short distance between the back door and the open crack of the waiting car's back door.

'And don't worry about anything,' James said, closing the door behind me. 'Tonight was just a standard Monday, as depressing as that is. Get some sleep.' He leaned in the window, gave me a soft, warm kiss on the cheek and then slapped the top of the car.

If all my Mondays were this eventful, I thought drowsily as we pulled out of the hotel and onto Sunset Boulevard, I'd need to get more than 'some' sleep to make it through my week.

CHAPTER SEVEN

Without the paparazzi chasing me, the ride back to The Hollywood seemed to take for ever. Eventually, we rolled up to the door and I rolled through the lobby and up to my room, dog-tired and desperate for sleep.

'Where the fuck have you been?'

Sleep, I was apparently not going to get. Jenny was standing in the middle of my room, looking absolutely wild.

'Jenny.'

'Don't you fucking "Jenny" me,' she ranted, stamping her tiny foot. 'You left me in that club! Left me on the *floor* to run off with that *asshole*. I cannot believe you.'

'I didn't run off, I was carried off,' I started, afraid to get too close. Jenny was holding her shoes in one hand, which made her both quicker than me and in possession of a deadly weapon. I'd done enough damage with a pair of stilettos in my own time to know how dangerous they could be. 'Jenny, I feel horrible, I'm so sorry. But James said you'd be OK and honestly, you didn't want to be with us—'

'Oh "James said"?' she yelled, throwing one of the shoes at me. I dodged; at least she was one weapon down.

'Well, if James said, then I'm sure it was fine that you left me on the floor of a club, soaked through with some dick's drink. I don't believe this. You spend one day with some sonofabitch movie star and you're acting like a total bitch?'

'OK, that's not too harsh? I didn't have any choice in the matter of leaving you. Unless you didn't notice, I didn't exactly swan out of there on my own feet. And I think you're mistaking James for that dickhead, Joe. He was the one throwing drinks around.'

'Only because that Blake asshole was getting in his face.' Jenny brandished the other shoe. It was not fun being on the other end of this. 'They were both being totally rude to Joe the whole evening. They were totally looking down on him because he's a barman, even though it's so obvious they're just jealous. Joe could so be bigger than James Jacobs if he wanted.'

'How are you coming up with this stuff?' I asked, throwing my bag down on the bed and kicking off my own shoes . . . but keeping them close in case we ended up duelling with them later. 'Joe had a problem with James and Blake, especially Blake, from the second he got in the car. Before then, even. He was being weird about them this afternoon; I only invited him for your sake.'

'You think I need you to get me pity dates? Like, Joe only came because you asked him? Oh my God, who do you think you are?'

'Jenny,' I shook my head. 'I can't do this. I'm tired and you're being ridiculous. Why don't we just go to bed and talk about this tomorrow?'

'Now I'm ridiculous?' The other shoe flew past my head and hit the door. 'What's ridiculous is you. We've been in LA two days; you've blown me off twice and then you left me on the *floor* of a club in front of dozens of people. That is ridiculous. You are ridiculous.'

'Jenny, I'm sorry,' I really, really wanted to sleep. 'I'm sorry I blew you out but I was tired and a bit drunk. And I'm sorry I didn't come back for you but we got chased by the paparazzi and I was stuck in the hotel. And I'm sorry you think I'm blowing you off for James – I'm absolutely not, but it's my job to interview him. That's why we're here, remember? So I do have to spend time with him. I wish I could just hang out with you instead. I really do.'

'Whatever,' she bristled, hands planted on her hips. 'I cannot believe you left me. That Blake guy is an ass-hat.'

'And Joe was totally out of order with Blake.' I stood my ground. Hurricane Jenny just needed a slap sometimes. 'And he got you back OK, didn't he?'

'If you mean, he dragged me up by my wrist and tossed me in a lift to find my own way back here, then yes,' she pouted. 'If you're asking if he apologized for his pig-headed behaviour and then brought me back to the hotel, then no.'

'I'm sorry, Jen, but Joe was being a bit of an idiot. But I know Blake can be difficult too. I'm sorry. I should have . . . I don't know what I should have done. But I shouldn't have left you.'

'No, you shouldn't.' She dropped her arms to her sides. 'I'm sorry, I shouldn't have blown up. I'm tired, I guess. And cranky.'

'Me too,' I said, slowly crossing the room and sitting on the bed. Jenny collapsed backwards beside me. 'Seriously, though, you need to sort out your temper. Do you think Oprah kicks off like this?'

'Yeah, whatever,' she said, wriggling out of her dress

and under my covers. I was forgiven then. 'But I'm telling you, Blake is a total asshole. And James should so ditch him. Joe says—'

'Please, can we not?' I sighed, pushing myself up and slipping off the dress to hang it. 'Don't go mental, but have you thought that Joe might be a bit jealous of James and was just taking it out on Blake?'

'Whatever,' Jenny yawned. 'I'm still pissed but I'm also super-tired. Let's talk about this tomorrow. Let's do something fun.'

'Uh, yes?'

'Damn straight, yes,' Jenny muttered into her pillow, flicking out the light without asking.

'Night Jenny,' I whispered, asleep before my head had even hit the pillow.

My alarm was set for nine, so I was completely confused as to what was making all the noise when the little alarm clock next to my bed said eight-twenty.

'Turn off your freaking phone,' Jenny mumbled into her pillow.

'Who would be calling?' I croaked, still shattered.

'Meh? Alex?'

Oh shit, Alex.

I rolled out of bed and grabbed my bag from the floor. It was a 212 number but not Alex's landline.

'Hello?'

'Angela Clark, would you like to explain to me what is happening over there?' It was Mary. 'Angela? Are you there? Or are you still too tired from your night of fucking up our lives to talk to me?'

'Mary, I don't know what you're talking about.' I rubbed my eyes. Ew, last night's mascara.

'I suggest you check, oh I don't know, Perez Hilton, TMZ, maybe any other website in the entire world and then call me back with a really good excuse as to why I shouldn't fire your ass.'

I blinked at the dead phone. What was she talking about? Crawling across to my computer, I quickly logged on and flipped to Perez. Which I may or may not have added to my bookmarks during my bout of James Jacobs research/worship.

And there it was. Or rather there they were. A picture of me and James sitting on the beach in Santa Monica. A shot of us eating at 25 Degrees. Him carrying me out of Teddy's. James putting me in the car at Chateau by the supposed secret exit. Well, it turned out James was right: the pictures did look pretty bad. Especially when built into a completely fictitious photo-story of our alleged affair.

Sigh, Hollywood's favourite British export, James Jacobs, is breaking our heart again! It must be at least a week since he was pictured getting hot and heavy with some skank in Hyde, but no, despite popular opinion, it hasn't shrivelled up and fallen off. Looks like James is in love! The Casino Night *star hit up several romantic LA hotspots with a new lady love yesterday. Word of advice, James – when you've gone to all the trouble of wooing a girl all day long, it's not cool to get her in and out of your Chateau Marmont bungalow within an hour. Word on the set of his new movie,* The Big Time, *is that James takes longer to get his scenes in the can than anyone else on the film. At least he's taking time to make sure the job is done better in at least one area of his life. Sorry, honey, James is all about his 'craft'.*

Oh shit. At least they hadn't got the photo of me in James's dressing gown. Yet. Scrambling into the bathroom,

I dialled *The Look* and waited to be put through to Mary, not having a clue what to say.

'This had better be good,' she answered.

'Mary, look, I've seen the pictures,' I breathed in deeply, 'and they're not what it looks like at all. Honestly.'

'That's the best you can do?'

'It's the truth.' I pulled a towel down from the rail and wrapped it around my legs. 'Everything was above-board, it's just how it looks on the internet. I don't know what else to tell you. It's rubbish, total rubbish.'

'And I'm supposed to believe that?'

'Yes?' I pulled my shoulders up around my ears.

'Well,' Mary said after a long moment's pause. 'I guess this is what happens when we put inexperienced reporters on important assignments. What were you thinking going on a date with the story, Angela?'

'A date? Me and James Jacobs? Come on, Mary,' I tried to laugh. 'The beach thing was part of the interview, James wanted to go do it there – do the interview there – and there were three other people with us at Teddy's. Mary, I really don't want you to think I'm mucking this up. The interview has been going great, honestly.'

'Adding "honestly" to the end of every sentence isn't going to stop me having to work my ass off to keep you on the interview. The only reason you're not on a plane back right now is because we had an email from James's people reiterating the fact that he wouldn't speak to anyone else from the magazine.'

'Seriously?' I was surprised. When had he done that? Why had he done that?

'So you can see why everyone in the entire office thinks that you're, well, more than interviewing him.'

Mary did not sound at all impressed. Or convinced. 'Angela, whatever's happening over there, just be incredibly careful. This has not helped you here.'

'Hones . . . Mary,' I really couldn't believe this was happening, 'I am going to deliver the best interview you ever read. I promise. And there is nothing happening with James. You know me, I would never.'

'Fine, just don't let me down, Angela,' Mary warned before hanging up.

Well, wasn't this just perfect? I rested my suddenly thumping head against the cool glass screen of the shower and closed my eyes. And there was me worrying that I'd get fired because I'd upset James. But instead, every single person at *The Look* thought I'd boffed him and they wanted to sack me for that instead. What was I supposed to do? Before I could make a decision, my phone beeped into life again. Please don't let Mary have changed her mind . . .

'Hello?'

'So, there are some real interesting photos online this morning,' Alex said.

'Yes, yes there are . . .' This was so not the best-ever start to my day. I really hadn't had time to think about how to broach this with Alex. I was still trying to work out what I was going to do about the 'three little words' situation. So I went for three different ones. 'Isn't it stupid?'

'I don't know, is it?' He wasn't exactly giving me a belly laugh.

'Alex, you know those photos aren't what they look like. It's all just been part of the interview, that's all, but I suppose that doesn't make a very good story and God, I don't know, maybe there isn't enough news in the world this morning.'

'I suppose not,' he said without any emotion. It was

horrible: he could at least have the decency to shout or call me a slag or something.

'Seriously, it's ridiculous. The magazine just called to say we might sue.' OK, so not entirely true but I couldn't stand this. 'The whole thing is ridiculous. James got into a big fight with Jenny's friend Joe in the club and that's why we had to run out. And I got a drink spilt all over me and so James got my dress dry cleaned. This is what was happening when I called you last night. This is what I was trying to tell you about.'

'That would be the phone call at four this morning?'

'That would be the one,' I said slowly. 'I was having a horrible evening; I just wanted to talk to you. Sorry.'

No response.

'How was your open mic thing?'

'It was good.' His voice was still measured and flat. 'So what are the plans for today? Shopping for engagement rings? Quickie wedding in Vegas?'

'Alex, there's nothing going on with me and James. I know those stupid photos look like . . . something, but really there is nothing going on. All that I've done since I've got here is fail miserably as a interviewer, row with Jenny and try to call you. And to top it off, I'm this close to getting sacked.' I felt sick saying it all out loud.

'Just a tip on the interviewing thing – I'm pretty sure you don't have to go back to the guy's hotel room at one a.m.,' Alex replied evenly. 'I've always managed to keep my pants on in interviews.'

'Really? Because I didn't think you had such a great history at keeping your pants on.' It was out before I'd thought about it. Such were the perils of being so bloody quick.

'Right, there are pictures of you on the internet,

whoring yourself all over LA with some asshole actor you just met, and *you're* bringing up *my* past?' At least I'd got his attention now. Shit. 'Is this where I mention the part where you were dating someone else behind my back when we met?'

'No, this is the point where you calm down and realize that this is all really stupid and that I wouldn't ever cheat on you and that sometimes, just sometimes, trashy websites print things that aren't true.' How dare he be on the other side of the country for our first row. I could practically hear him thinking down the line but he still didn't say anything.

'Look, Alex, all I'm asking is for you to trust me and not the internet. That shouldn't be too hard, should it?' I was not happy. These kinds of conversations had not gone well for me in the past. Plus, it wasn't as if I hadn't considered crossing a very unprofessional line with James, which wasn't exactly helping my argument ring true.

'I'm sorry, this is all just too weird,' Alex said, finally. 'I don't know what to say.'

'I'm sorry too, I didn't mean to say that stuff,' I sniffed. 'I'm just being all paranoid because we haven't really spoken since I got here and then all the pictures and stuff and then Mary called and now you're freaking out—'

'Angela, hey, hold up,' Alex interrupted. 'I meant, I'm sorry I can't really talk about this over the phone. We'll only end up saying dumb stuff. More dumb stuff.'

'So what, we're not going to talk until I get back?'

'You're back on Sunday.'

'But it's Tuesday . . .' I bit my lip. 'Can't I just call you later?'

He sighed loudly. 'I'm sorry. Just, well, let me call you, OK? Bye.'

I looked at my phone, just to check. Yes, he had hung up. This really was the perfect start to the perfect day. If I'd known I was going to get into such a mess anyway, I would have just shagged James senseless when I had the chance. Bloody stupid bloody conscience.

'Angela, you're on the internet!' Jenny shrieked from the bedroom. 'You're freakin' famous!'

Brilliant, just brilliant.

It took me far too long to convince Jenny to back away from the laptop and not email my details directly to Perez Hilton. She felt very strongly that I should be making the most of my potential new-found fame, or at the very least sign up for reality TV shows and get us both into gifting lounges. I, however, felt very strongly that I should go back to bed and sleep until everyone in the world stopped reading celebrity gossip or the internet broke down, whichever came first. But I couldn't. I had things to do. I had a blog to write, and tomorrow, assuming James was still on for it, I had to drag my arse out of the hotel and carry on with the interview. He might have emailed the magazine but he wasn't answering his phone to me. Swearing I would meet her for brunch as promised, I sent a still slightly pissed-off Jenny on her way and settled down at my laptop.

The Adventures of Angela: Valley of the Woes

Hmmm. So my LA adventure isn't exactly going according to plan. Since you're reading this, I'm assuming you're fairly familiar with the internet and the pages full of wonderful, wonderful things it contains. Like net-a-porter.com. Unfortunately, it turns out there are some pages of not-so-wonderful things and lots of those pages are made right here, in LA.

Now, I did sort of know that before I got here because who hasn't whiled away a few harmless minutes/hours/entire working days on Perez Hilton or WWTDD? Come on, there isn't a person alive who doesn't want to see the private mobile phone pictures of a Disney starlet, right? But what I didn't know was, despite all the evidence out there, sometimes not only are the things on these websites not entirely truthful, sometimes they are as familiar with reality as I am with Brad Pitt. That is, not familiar at all. Goddamn it.

I guess a lot of people think it would fun to be on one of these websites, to be pictured hanging out with celebs in some swanky Hollywood night-club but, well, just like the websites themselves, sometimes things aren't what they seem.

Hopefully, I'm still in for a Hollywood ending . . . and I'm still waiting for your recommendations as to where to get one. Email me at notacompleteslapperhonest@thelook.com

After emailing the blog to Mary (and praying to every conceivable deity I could think of, including the genie from Aladdin), I searched through mine and Jenny's wardrobes twice, searching for a 'I really haven't done it with James Jacobs' outfit; but now, for some reason, everything looked as if it was right out of the Playboy Mansion.

Who in their right mind would believe I was sleeping with an A-list movie star? This was me we were talking about: mismatched underwear, not capable of curling my eyelashes without catching my eyelid, dodgy muffin top in all but one pair of my jeans, Angela Clark. Slightly useless, can't even change a plug at twenty-seven, not a seducer of superstars, dress-shedding über-minx, Angela Clark, international super-slag. I settled on my jeans (sadly not the non-muffin-top pair) and stripy Splendid rugby top. Buttoned up. Every wanton inch of me covered. Sweating like a bee-hatch in the seventy-five-degree weather but covered from head to toe.

'So I get that you didn't love The Beverly Center,' Jenny said, adjusting her sunglasses and spinning out of The Hollywood's valet parking lot. 'And I'm guessing that you're gonna be freaking out about those photos for pretty much the whole day, right?'

'Probably,' I agreed sombrely. I was still so numb from my conversation with Alex, I didn't even have the energy to be scared of Jenny's driving.

'So what can we do to get you out of your funk?'

'Mmm-hmm.' I traced a finger along the edge of the car door. At least since we were in the convertible my hair would look like crap whether I'd done anything with it or not. Which I hadn't. And, joy, the sun was out. If I was really lucky, I could get burnt again.

'God, you're going to make this hard work, aren't you?' Jenny slapped the steering wheel. 'I know, Angela, if someone said "LA" to you, what would you think of?'

'What?'

'What would you think of? What would you associate with Hollywood?' she pressed on.

Paparazzi. Blonde hair. Breast implants. 'Sunshine?'

'Anything else?' she asked.

Feeling completely out of place. Missing Alex. Worrying about James. 'Movies?'

'Which movies?'

'Jenny,' I really wanted to just go back to bed. 'Are you getting at something?'

'Honey, I'm just trying to distract you. This is all gonna be over by tomorrow. Sometimes life throws you a curveball and you've just got to run with it.' Jenny pulled up outside a row of shops. Sparkly, shiny, lovely looking shops.' Or shop for it.'

'Where are we?' I asked, blinking up at the prettiness. Everything was so white. And big. 'What are we doing?'

'We're about to spend an obscene amount of money,' Jenny grinned.

Once the car had been safely handed over to the valet parking assistant (I would never get used to that), Jenny pulled me along the wide, sunny street past designer store after designer store.

'Never before in my life have I wanted to be a hooker so badly,' I clutched at Jenny's hand, my mouth wide open. 'But oh, would you look at that bag?'

'I know, hello *Pretty Woman*,' Jenny squeezed my hand back. 'Even I would sleep with Richard Gere for that dress and, hello, so old now?'

'So this is Rodeo Drive?' I marvelled. 'Why on earth did you take me to a mall yesterday?'

'Because we can't actually afford anything here.' She pulled me away from the Louis Vuitton window, leaving my sticky paw prints all over it. 'But I thought it might distract you for a while.'

'We can't afford anything?' I fought the urge to go into the closest shop and buy a giant hat. And gloves. 'Really?'

'Angie, when we go shopping in New York, where do we go?' Jenny asked.

'Bloomingdale's? Bergdorf's?' I couldn't stop staring at the pretty things. Things I'd seen in magazines, in

The Look, but that were now right here in front of me! In a shop! To buy!

'Not where do we go to try things on but never buy them unless they're in the sales. Where do we actually go shopping?'

'Um, Century 21 and Filene's,' I admitted. 'When you're not there to stop me, Gap.'

'Exactly. And I killed my credit card at The Beverly Center yesterday, so no, we really can't afford anything.' Jenny fished around in her handbag for some lip gloss, slicked a completely unnecessary layer on top of her already shiny lips and then added a desperately needed pop of colour to mine. 'But no one needs to know that, right? There's nothing like trying on thousands of dollars' worth of couture to take your mind off your problems.'

If my only issue with LA was still that it wasn't nearly as glossy and glamorous as I'd been expecting, then Rodeo Drive would have solved all my problems. From the dramatic white marble store fronts, the palm trees sprouting up out of the glossy pavement, right through to the serious-looking doormen that stood sentry outside each designer destination, this was everything I'd been expecting.

Yes, the Ugg boot girls were still everywhere, but they had been watered down by a new breed of LA woman. I couldn't help but stare. They were tiny, just like the platinum blondes, but they seemed so much glossier, so much more expensive, and I could not tell you how old a single one of them was. You couldn't actually see any discernible designer labels on anything they wore, unless you checked out the shop assistant carrying the stiff paper bags out behind them, but they reeked of money. One of them stepped right out in front of us without looking, making me jump back. She paused, looking at me and Jenny in the same way I sometimes looked at the puppies in the window of the pet store near Bloomingdale's, as if we were cute but she really didn't want to get too close in case we slobbered on her. Or worse.

'So what do you want to try first?' Jenny asked, completely oblivious. 'Dior? D&G?'

'Oh, there.' I pointed across the road to a gorgeous window display, full of beautiful ballerina-style dresses in pretty petal colours. 'Miu Miu me up.'

After my second glass of champagne, I was more than ready to accept that Hollywood had its charms after all. Jenny was head to toe in couture, a gorgeous bronze dirndl skirt cinching in her tiny waist and five-inch platforms forcing her onto her tippy-toes.

'How do they feel?' The inordinately attractive salesman cupped my foot in his hand and slipped the ankle strap of a beautiful, sequin-covered sandal through the little tiny silver buckle.

'They feel lovely.' I was almost too afraid to stand on the delicate little heels. When would I feel more like Kylie and less like Lily Savage when I tried on a girlie outfit?

'You know, I think we just got one of the matching purses in today. It's in the back,' he whispered. 'I have to see how it looks with the shoes.'

'Me too,' I agreed, staring at my feet. Why would anyone ever put their foot inside an Ugg in LA? In New York, it snowed, it was cold, you needed their sheepskin-lined goodness; but here, you could feasibly walk around in nothing but fairy-spun Miu Miu creations all year round. In fact, you didn't even have to walk; this was the perfect place for Limo

Shoes. Maybe that was why everyone drove everywhere.

I flicked around my BlackBerry, while my New Best Friend, the shoe salesman, was bag hunting. The BlackBerry was still a bit of a mystery to me. I'd got into enough trouble with just a mobile, without being able to respond to work emails whilst out and about. Out and about meaning drunk. Before I could cast it back into the bottom of my (very jealous to be surrounded by all these younger Miu Mius) handbag, it started to buzz in my hand.

'Hello?' I answered automatically.

'Angela, it's James.'

Oh, James. Bugger. I'd been so distracted by the prettiness, for fifteen minutes I'd managed to forget all about everything.

'Angela, are you there?'

'I am.' I waved manically at Jenny. I couldn't do this alone. Even in eight-hundred-dollar sandals. Especially in eight-hundred-dollar sandals.

'I wanted to say I'm so sorry about the photos. Blake is trying to get them taken down right now.' He sounded genuinely worried. But then he was an actor. 'Are you OK? And we've spoken to the magazine. It'll all be fine.'

'Well, it was a bit of a shock—' But before I could finish, Jenny snatched the phone out of my hand and sprinted down the shop.

'James? Jenny,' I heard her begin before she vanished out of hearing range. I fumbled with the teeny tiny buckles on my sandals but apparently they had been crafted by elves and my lumbering sausage fingers (swollen from the LA heat, surely?) couldn't unfasten them quickly enough.

'I don't know, she's kind of messed up,' she said,

slinking back up the store. 'But I'm trying to take care of her. We're shopping.'

'Jenny,' I hissed, 'give me the bloody phone.'

'We're in Miu Miu,' she winked, holding me at arm's length. 'Yes, I think she'd love that. OK, I'll put you on to someone.'

By the time I'd found my way out of the shoes, my BlackBerry was in the hands of my lovely sales assistant who had returned holding something long and disarmingly sparkly. 'But of course Mr Jacobs,' he gushed, hanging up and giving me the phone. And the pretty sparkly thing. I felt like a kitten with a ping-pong ball. BlackBerry or shiny bag. BlackBerry or shiny bag.

'What was that all about?' I asked Jenny, unable to take my eyes off the bag. It was long and slender and round, like a pencil case I'd had in Year Eight. But, unlike the pencil case I'd had in Year Eight, it had a tiny five-hundred-dollar price tag, hidden discreetly inside the beautiful lining, and was covered in glittering, golden iridescent sparkles. Oh, and a little leather strap to slip around my wrist so that I would never, ever, ever lose it. Even in my sleep. 'Jenny?'

'We'll take the bag and the shoes, thanks,' she said, snatching the bag out of my hands and passing it back to the assistant. His eyes were shining almost as much as the sequins. 'And ring up these bad boys.' She pointed at the yellow and black Mary Janes on her feet and dropped onto the padded bench beside me.

'You should get your photo taken with some more famous people.' She slung her arm around my shoulders. 'James wants to pay for your shoes. Actually, our shoes. But if he asks, both pairs are yours. He said to charge them to his account and he'll see you tomorrow.'

'Are you kidding me?' I asked, watching the bag and

the shoes being whisked away behind the counter while the staff whispered intensely amongst themselves. 'He can't do that. We can't let him do that.'

I pouted, wondering just for a second what Mary would have to say about me accepting handbags and shoes from James. And right up until the assistant replaced my empty champagne glass with two huge, ribbon-tied cardboard carrier bags, I really thought about refusing to accept them. Sort of.

'Oh Angie, Angie, Angie.' Jenny ruffled my hair and gave me a huge grin. 'He can and we can. And I could not be happier. Where next?'

Jenny's talent for shopping was matched only by her talent for eating, so after Miu Miu, after Dolce & Gabbana, Cavalli and Gucci, she finally gave in. I couldn't enjoy even La Perla on an empty stomach.

'Tiffany's shouldn't be part of a shopping centre,' I said, spearing the omnipresent lettuce leaf on my plate. 'I don't care how posh a shopping centre. It's just not right.'

'Yeah, whatever . . .' Jenny leaned back, smiling up at the sunshine with her eyes closed. 'Eat your crab cakes and stop bagging on LA.'

'I'll leave LA alone if you'll tell me about the last time you were here,' I gambled. 'I want to here all about your dancing. And how on earth the Pussycat Dolls managed to let you slip through their fingers.'

'Shut up,' Jenny carried on staring upwards. 'Is that a humming bird?'

'It is and even though that might be the coolest thing I've ever seen,' I replied, watching the tiny bird as it darted by our table and hovered by a floral display beside us, 'you're not going to distract me. Did you really dance?'

'Yes.'

'Did you strip?'

'It wasn't stripping, it was burlesque.'

'So you did strip?'

She sighed and looked back at me. 'There was no nudity in my routine.'

'So how come you came back to New York so quickly,' I stirred my Diet Coke with my straw, 'if you and Daphne were so amazing? Couldn't the dancing have led to other stuff?'

'Probably,' she laughed quietly. 'It led to Daphne doing other stuff. Other stuff for guys who came to see us dance. Other stuff for money.'

'Daphne did it for money?' I asked. According to the people at the next table who dropped their cutlery, altogether too loudly. 'Daphne was a prostitute?' I added quietly.

'I don't think she would say that,' Jenny said diplomatically. 'Maybe a private call girl. She seemed to think it was pretty glamorous at the time.'

'But you didn't?' I asked. 'Think it was glamorous, I mean? I know you would never do that. Would you?'

'Trust me, there was nothing glamorous about those guys,' she said.

'So you didn't, right?' A dozen humming birds doing a synchronized dance routine couldn't have got my attention at that moment.

'Of course I didn't,' Jenny said, 'but it was tempting. Suddenly Daphne had all this money, she stopped doing auditions, started missing gigs. Eventually, she stopped dancing altogether and I felt weird doing it alone. Especially since Daphne had kind of gotten us a reputation. I guess it would have been easier to just do it, but I couldn't.'

'So you came home?' I wasn't used to watching Jenny

squirm. It wasn't nearly as much fun as I'd thought it might be.

'I went back to New York, yeah.' She looked up and gave me her brightest smile. 'And thank God I did, or you would have been screwed.'

'She's not still doing it, is she?' I couldn't help myself, even if Jenny was clearly trying to change the subject. 'Not still, you know . . .'

'Angie, it scares me that you can't even say the words at your age. And no, she isn't. She quit, like, right after I left. She started seeing some rich old guy and I guess she didn't need the cash any more. And she's making good money as a stylist now so . . .' She trailed off.

'Do you miss living here?' I asked, even though I didn't want to. She was my Jenny, my 'I'm walkin' here' New Yorker Jenny, not Daphne's LA private dancer.

'It's different now; it was so long ago. I'm not twenty-two any more; everything is so different.' She gave me a little smile. 'It is nice to be out in the sunshine again, though. I don't know, I don't want the same things I wanted the last time I was here. I don't know what I want.'

'You'll work it out,' I said, watching her pretend not to be bothered. 'You always do.'

'Yeah.' Jenny pulled out her bright yellow Miu Miu shoe. It was all sorts of beautiful. 'I always do, don't I?'

'I can't believe you had this big crazy life.' I was always amazed by Jenny. I'd never ever known anyone like her in my life. It didn't matter how long we spent together or how long we talked, one way or another, she surprised me every single day. Some days it was with a packet of peanut butter M&Ms, others it was with the fact that she used to be a burlesque dancer while her friend was a high-class hooker. 'How do you stand behind that concierge desk every day without going mad?'

'I don't know.' She pulled a couple of curls out from her ponytail and held them out to inspect for split ends. 'I guess I had Jeff to keep my mind busy for a while but sometimes, yeah. I don't know.'

We ate in silence for a few minutes, Jenny concentrating on her salad, me painfully aware that the waiter was still judging me for asking if the crab cakes came with fries. They didn't.

'What are you going to do about James?' Jenny asked eventually.

'What do you mean?' I stalled, not actually knowing the answer.

'Seems to me that if your boyfriend already thinks you're sleeping with a super-hot guy who is so clearly into you, you may as well,' she reasoned.

'He's not clearly into me,' I replied sternly, but I couldn't help a tiny internal smile at the thought that he might be. 'Just because he got a couple of shops to give us some free stuff. It's nothing to him, Jenny; it's like you letting your friend crash in an empty room at the hotel or something. A perk of the job.'

'I could totally get used to these kinds of perks,' she held up the shoe again. 'But honey, I'm telling you, just from what I saw last night. He likes you.'

'No, he doesn't and, even if he did, which he doesn't . . .' I fished around in my handbag for my wallet. Expenses be damned, this was going on the work credit card. '. . . I wouldn't be interested.'

'Yeah you would. If you didn't have a boyfriend,' Jenny said, stealing a bite of crab cake from my plate.

I considered my answer carefully, knowing she would jump on whatever I said. 'If I didn't have a boyfriend and I wasn't working and he wasn't this ridiculous actor. Maybe.'

'Oh my God, you're totally hot for him.' Jenny clapped her hands together. 'I knew it! I could so tell last night. Angie, how often do you get a chance like this? How often does *anyone* get a chance like this?'

'That doesn't matter.' I blushed from my cheeks down to my toes. 'And it doesn't matter how hot he is or if he likes me. It's just work. Even if it doesn't feel like it right now, it's work.'

'You forgot the "I already have a boyfriend" bit.' Jenny raised an eyebrow. 'I'd have thought Alex was quite enough of a reason. That's interesting.'

'No it isn't interesting,' I corrected. 'That just goes without saying.'

'So things are OK? He hasn't freaked out about the pictures?'

There was no point hiding this stuff from Jenny. It would only come back to bite me on the arse when I needed her help later, which I always did. 'He wasn't best pleased about them,' I admitted. 'But it'll be fine.'

'I figured as much,' Jenny nodded. 'He's totally the jealous type.'

'No, he so isn't. Is he?' I asked. 'What makes you say that?'

'Come on, Angie.' She wiped her hands on a napkin and then redid her ponytail. 'Alex is all deep and meaningful muso boy. You don't get the love songs, the random three a.m. booty calls because "he just had to see you" without a touch of possessiveness. I just can't see him being OK with you running around Hollywood with a some hot, slutty guy with all the world watching. Can you?'

'I said he wasn't best pleased about it,' I mumbled,

giving the waiter my credit card without even looking at the bill. 'But it'll be OK, won't it?'

'He's your boyfriend, I don't know,' she said, passing me her lip gloss. She really was a stickler for detail. 'What do you think?'

'I think we should stop talking about boys, go and get the car, then go for a swim.' I took my card and the receipt back from the waiter. 'And if there's a spa or something, we should get massages. This is still your vacation, after all, and I don't have to be anywhere until eleven a.m. tomorrow.'

'Got to say, Angie,' Jenny stood up and started grabbing our many bags, 'I have always loved the way you think.'

CHAPTER EIGHT

Right up until the moment James's limo pulled up outside The Hollywood at four minutes passed eleven the next morning, I'd been waiting for the phone call from Blake to say that they weren't coming and the interview was off. But there they were and there I was, Jenny's giant sunglasses on, Starbucks in hand, and (beautiful but looking more battered by the day) Marc Jacobs bag over my shoulder. Taking a deep breath, I sucked it up and opened the car door. If I thought Alex had been upset and Mary was angry yesterday, then I needed a new word for Blake.

'This is why these fucking "day in the life" interviews never, ever work,' he ranted as the limo pulled away from the hotel, staring me down. 'You don't speak until we're back in the hotel. This is why we should have met for one hour in a hotel suite with a publicist and a security guard and this would never ever have happened.'

I couldn't argue with his logic.

'Would there have been bottled water?' James asked.

'Of course.' Blake seethed in my general direction.

'And those tiny pastries?'

'No because you're carb-free this month.' He folded his arms and gave me an intensely filthy look.

'Blake, calm down, it's not Angela's fault.' James placed a careful hand on his assistant's shoulder. I slid off my sunglasses and tried my hardest to look innocent.

'No, the pictures were your fucking fault, I already told you that,' Blake replied, not taking his eyes off me. 'And it's your fault that she's still here. But I'm telling you both, this is it. I'm not leaving your side from now on.'

'I get it, Blake,' James smiled easily. 'We're absolutely going to play by your rules. But if we're going to be doing a full hour's talking, I'm going to need a coffee. Coffee Bean is just round the corner, can we get something? You know I hate the coffee at the hotel.'

'Fine,' Blake said, eyes still locked on me. I thought about putting my sunglasses back on. 'She can go get your coffee.'

'You want Angela to get out of a limo and order my favourite coffee at my regular coffee shop?' James reached across the seat and took my hand. I resisted the urge to giggle. Nerves, just nerves. 'Really, Blake, you'd just be fuelling the fire. This place is always crawling with paps.'

'Crawling,' I croaked.

'I said not a word out of you until we get to the hotel,' Blake shot back, climbing out of the limo.

I held my breath until the door slammed shut. 'I'm so sorry,' I choked. 'I know it's not funny.'

'Angela, just a sec. Hey, Jack,' James squeezed my hand then pressed the mic button to speak to the driver. 'I think I saw some photographers as we pulled in. Can we make a move? Uh, Pinkberry on Beverly Drive?'

A shadowy nod through the tinted glass and we were off.

'Well, that's a relief, isn't it?' James sighed, stretching his arms out along the back of the seat. 'Honestly, Blake's been going crazy since those pictures were posted.'

'And he's not going to go even more crazy now?' I panicked. 'We have to go back for him! He's going to call the magazine, honestly, James, I'm so close to getting fired right now. If he calls them—'

'He's not going to call them.' James picked some nonexistent fluff from his dark blue shirt. 'How many times do you need telling? Blake can't cancel anything. And the magazine can't fire you. I emailed them as soon as the pictures were posted yesterday. I'm only doing this interview with you and they know that.'

'You just don't make any sense.' I rubbed my temples and tried not to think about how his shirt was exactly the same colour as his eyes. 'All I've done is cause you trouble. You could have a real interviewer; you could just do that one-hour hotel room thing Blake was talking about and save yourself all this hassle. And the photos, aren't you upset? Or at least annoyed?'

'Did you do no research before you met me?' James shook his head. 'There have been much worse pictures of me leaked online. Pictures, videos. God, things I could never show my mother. And why would I want to sit in a room giving the same old spiel about my next movie, what I like about living in LA, what I miss about the UK, blah, blah, blah, when I could be eating burgers and talking about actual real things with you?'

'Fair point,' I conceded. 'But you're not even a little bit bothered by the photos?'

'I'm only bothered that they bother you,' he shrugged.

'I'm used to them. The women that are in them with me are usually used to them.'

He didn't even blush. So I blushed for the both of us.

'And I'm sorry, I should have said something at the time. Once you've spotted the photographers, it's usually too late,' he said, peering out the window. I looked past him, onto the Beverley Hills sign set against a spotlessly manicured lawn. Not quite the Hollywood sign but still, terribly glam. 'How was your friend when you got back?'

'Jenny? Not amused with me in the slightest,' I admitted, 'but she was more or less calmed down by the shopping. Thank you, by the way. That was, well, madness. You really didn't have to do that.'

'Don't even mention it,' James waved away my thanks. 'And what about your other friend, Joe?'

'I haven't seen him. I'm so sorry, he was totally out of order.' I still couldn't quite believe how pathetic Joe's behaviour had been. 'And, like I said the other night, he's really not my friend.'

'Yeah, he was a bit . . .' James paused. 'Well, never mind. There's nothing in life that can't be solved by frozen yoghurt.'

'Oh my God, you're such a woman,' I said. 'I'd like to hear you say that in Sheffield.'

''Shut up and get your wallet out,' he said, as we pulled up at the side of the road. 'You're buying.'

'Frozen yoghurt?' I climbed out of the limo after him. 'That sounds like a fair exchange for everything we bought yesterday.'

'Yeah, but I won't have to pay for that stuff; this is pricey frozen yoghurt.'

'You have forgotten where you've come from, Jim Jacobs,' I tutted.

*　　*　　*

It turned out that Pinkberry frozen yoghurt was ever so slightly magical. As James loaded his with pineapple and strawberries, I packed mine with Coco Pebbles cereal and chocolate chips. And I got change out of ten dollars. Just.

'This is amazing,' I raved through a mouthful of yoghurty goodness. 'Shouldn't this be all tasteless and healthy?'

'It is healthy, or it was until you shovelled all that crap on to it,' James teased. The street outside was packed with tanned, good-looking men in workout gear and more of the ever-present Ugg girls.

'So I thought we'd crack on with your tour of my favourite bits of LA,' James carried on, striding down the road, past all the girls that stared and all the men that pretended not to. The only difference today was they were staring at me as much as him. 'So how about The Grove, do some more shopping? What do you think? That should cheer you up.'

'Sorry, James,' I hugged myself tightly. Why was everywhere in LA so open? What I wouldn't give for a shadowy side street or a subway station. 'I know you don't want to do the usual sit-down thing, but could we maybe go somewhere slightly less, I don't know, somewhere less open?'

'Maybe The Beverly Center?' James finished up his yogurt and dropped it in the rubbish bin. 'Or Melrose? There will probably be paps on Melrose though.'

'Are there going to be photographers everywhere you go?' I asked, actively ignoring two girls clutching tiny dogs and huge coffees, staring at us from across the road.

'Maybe,' James shrugged. 'Seriously, I told you, it's not a problem.'

'It is a problem,' I said, spotting a group of pre-teens,

head to toe in Juicy Couture, blatantly comparing the real-life James Jacobs and 'mystery girl' to the images on their Sidekicks. 'I'm sorry, but it's going to be a problem for me.'

'Not at all.' James threw his arm around my shoulders. I could practically hear everyone in the street breathe in. 'If it's a problem for you then it's a problem for me. If you could go anywhere in the world right now, where would you go?'

'New York?'

James smiled. 'Well, I can't get you across the country in half and hour but I can do the next best thing.'

Back in the limo, we drove out of Beverly Hills, through Hollywood, and kept going until James tapped on the glass partition to stop Jack, his driver. As soon as we stepped outside, I felt as though I was home. Gone were the tans, the big boots and the teeny-tiny shorts and in their place were beards, battered Converses and vintage plaid shirts. Starbucks were replaced by corner cafes run by slacker hipsters, Urban Outfitters taken over by vintage stores and the huge cineplexes swapped for a tiny art-house cinema. And while I couldn't see the ocean, the beautiful blue sky was framed by the hills and mountains that surrounded us.

'You like?' James asked, leaning against the ridiculously conspicuous limo. I couldn't believe we were only ten minutes out of Hollywood.

'I like,' I nodded, slipping my (beloved) bag over my head and across my body. 'Where are we?'

'Los Feliz,' he said. 'It's as close as I can get you to home without using the jet.'

'I bet the pizza isn't as good as in Brooklyn,' I said, looking around. Not one single person was looking at us.

'So let's get down to business. Where are we doing the interview?'

'In here,' he pointed to a small dark doorway behind me. 'After you.'

James opened the door from the sunny street into a small, dark bar. I passed through a beaded curtain, blinking. Like Teddy's the night before, it was lined with red booths, but they were cracked vinyl instead of velvet. The high-gloss sheen of bought-in Old Hollywood glamour, accessorized by Jessica Simpson, was completely blown out of the water by actual, genuine old-school class, accessorized by the slightly stale smell of a couple of decades of debauched nights. The tiny stage in the centre of the room was set up with a drum kit, several guitars and an upright piano.

'Hey, James,' came a voice from behind the bar that lined the back wall, lit by vintage-looking lampshades. Except I had a feeling they weren't vintage-looking so much as so genuinely old that they might fall apart if I touched them. The girl talking to James had gorgeous flame-red hair and winged black eyeliner. 'Just get whatever you need, I'll be out back.'

'Thanks, Marina,' James sat down behind the piano. 'Welcome to The Dresden. It's my favourite club in all of LA. No paps.'

'You play?' I asked, sitting down beside him.

'I do.' James lifted the lid and played a few soft chords. In the darkened room, watching James play the piano, I felt a million miles away from all of it. From the pictures on the website, from Alex, from Mary. I placed my fingers on the cool piano keys and stared at the keyboard.

'You play?'

'No,' I said. 'I can't even play the recorder.'

'You sing?' he asked.

I looked up into his dark blue eyes and laughed out loud. 'No, I can't sing,' I spluttered. 'Oh my God, stop it. Didn't we come here to do an interview?'

'Yes.' He closed the piano lid. 'I just feel a bit of a fraud doing the whole "ac-tor" interview thing with you. It's the journos that create the persona, you know. It's their questions that bring on the whole "I love the smell of the ocean at midnight" bollocks.'

'Can I quote you on that?' I asked. 'Because I don't have any questions about the smell of the ocean at any time and that sounded pretty good to me.'

'OK, let's do it this way,' James said. 'You ask me a question and then I'll ask you a question. That should take the pressure off?'

'And give me some ideas for more questions,' I agreed, rummaging in the bottom of my (full of rubbish but never a pen when you needed it) bag. 'Since you threw my Dictaphone in the Pacific Ocean, I have been reduced to shorthand, so go slow.'

'I'll go however fast or slow you want me to go.'

I refused to blush. Refused.

'So, old Jim Jacobs,' I cleared my throat and put on my most professional face. '*Desert Island Discs* time. Your three favourite albums?'

'Easy and, I'm sorry to say it, not that original.' James gave me a mock yawn. 'The Smiths, *The Smiths*, Nirvana, *Nevermind* and Pulp, *Different Class*. Because I know you're going to make a big deal of me being from Sheffield.'

'You could have gone for Def Leppard,' I replied, scribbling down his answers and wondering whether or not they would actually be on his 'most played' list if I checked out his iPod. Like they would be on mine.

'My turn,' James stretched his arms out above his

head, stretching out his moment. 'Angela Clark, why are you so bothered about what other people think?'

'You could just ask me my three favourite films,' I stalled.

'Answer, please.'

'Easy and, I'm sorry to say, not that original,' I mirrored his stretch and pulled my hair back into a ponytail before letting it fall back down. 'I'm not bothered. My turn.'

'I don't think so.' James shook his head. 'Do you think I didn't notice you freaking out when those girls were looking at us outside the yoghurt place? And even though I've told you about a million times that your job is safe, you're still worrying about the interview, about the magazine. So don't tell me you're not bothered.'

'You didn't tell me I had to be honest.' I pulled a stray strand of hair out of my lip gloss. I would never be a lady. 'You just said I had to answer your question and I answered.'

'OK then. Your turn.'

'Right,' I said, surprised. I hadn't really expected to get off that lightly but I wasn't about to push my luck. 'Three things you can't be without when you're travelling.'

'A small donkey, Michael Caine and toenail clippers.' James stared back at me, completely serious. 'My turn.'

'You're not funny.'

'The fifty million people that saw my last movie would disagree with you.'

'I'm writing that down if you don't give me a serious answer.'

'You give me one then.'

I sighed. 'Fine. I am a little bit bothered.'

159

'Thank you. Now tell me why?'

'Why? It would be easier for you to tell me why you *aren't* more bothered. How does the whole thing not faze you? Even if this happens to you every single day, twice a day even, I don't understand how you can just laugh it all off and expect everyone else to do the same.'

James leaned over, brushing my hair behind my ear.

'Because it's not real,' he said quietly. 'I know those photos aren't real, the people I love know they're not real; it's all just another character. Even this interview, as much fun as it is and as much as I'm loving hanging out with you, what goes in the magazine will end up being an interview with a character we create. The questions you ask me aren't supposed to find out about the real me, not the cold, hard facts. They're supposed to find out things your readers want to know, about the James Jacobs they've seen in all those stupid romcoms I've done.'

I didn't really know what to say. He wasn't wrong.

'Angela, it doesn't matter if everyone outside this club thinks we're at it like rabbits in here, we know we're not and that's what matters. And no one with half a brain believes what they see on celebrity websites.'

'Yeah, that's what I thought too.' I chewed on the end of my pen, looking back at the bar. 'Can we get a drink?'

'Someone thinks the photos are real.'

Despite the fact it would mortify my mother, I clambered underneath the bar and poured myself a drink. 'Yeah.'

'Is it your mum?'

Oh my God, I hadn't even thought about that. I doubled the shot. 'Not yet.'

'The boyfriend?'

'The boyfriend.' I poured a Diet Coke on top of the vodka but there was only room for a third of the bottle.

'I can't believe he called you a liar.' James followed me over to the bar.

'What?' I mixed my drink without a straw. 'He didn't say that.'

'He thinks the photos are real,' he said. 'And you said they weren't, so I'm fairly sure that means he called you a liar.'

'Not exactly.' I took a long swig, pulled a face and added some more Coke. 'He was just a bit — well, not very happy about it. Which is completely understandable.'

'But you told him nothing was happening and he didn't believe you?' James pressed on, settling on a bar stool. 'Beer for me, please.'

'Great, now I'm a barmaid,' I muttered, grabbing a Corona from the fridge. 'I told him they weren't what they looked like. That doesn't mean he didn't believe me. He was just a bit annoyed. His ex cheated on him so, you know, it's hard for him to trust people sometimes.'

'But you're not his ex,' James squeezed a chunk of lime into his beer. 'And you haven't cheated on him.'

'No but, well, I was dating someone else when we met, but no I haven't cheated on him. On anyone. Ever.' I slipped a napkin under his bottle. At least I'd have experience in bar work for when I lost my job at *The Look*. 'I would never cheat on Alex.' I looked up confidently. 'I would never cheat on him.'

'Then he's got no right to make you feel bad about some paparazzi shots,' James reasoned. 'He should just take your word for it and think himself lucky that he has such an amazing girlfriend.'

'I wouldn't go so far as amazing.' I sipped my drink. 'Just common or garden perfect would do it.'

'Do you always make jokes about yourself?' James set his bottle back on the bar. 'Because you are amazing, you know. And your boyfriend should never make you doubt that.'

'I don't make jokes about myself and I'm not amazing.' The bar was so quiet, I could hear my heart thudding. This didn't feel as though it was essential to the interview. 'Really. Anyway, I have more questions for you.'

'You're cute, you're clever, you're funny, you clearly love this idiot even though he doesn't deserve it,' James carried on, pushing the lime right down the neck of the bottle. 'If you were my girlfriend, I would never let you be miserable. Ever.'

'I don't know,' I said, examining my fingernails. 'I don't think anyone can make me feel better about the fact that I'll never be *America's Next Top Model*.'

'Yeah, you don't ever make jokes about yourself,' James replied.

The longer we sat in silence, the more awkward it became.

'Has he ever cheated on you?' he asked. 'The boyfriend?'

'No. Of course not,' I said quickly. 'He wouldn't.'

James studied me silently while he drank his beer.

'Can we get back to the interview?' I asked, my stomach dropping.

'Because if you were my girlfriend—' James started again.

'The interview?' I interrupted. Too much. This was just too much.

'My video iPod, running shoes and a copy of *The Great Gatsby*.' He knocked back the rest of his beer.

I looked up.

'The three things I can't be without when I'm travelling,' he shrugged. 'What else have you got?'

We passed another hour discussing James's favourite designers, his favourite holiday spots, his favourite restaurants, and everything else a *Look* reader could feasibly want to know about her favourite actor, until my hand was cramping and my pad was full.

'Do you know what?' I said, jotting down his favourite place to buy bagels. 'I think we're done. You are released.'

'You mean I have to go back to Blake?' James asked, with mock horror. At least it seemed like mock horror; I would have been genuinely terrified. 'You don't want to do something this evening? I cleared my schedule.'

I smiled and shook my head. 'I actually just want to go back to the hotel and sleep. The last few nights have been late ones and I really should go and write all this up, send it over to the magazine. Prove we're actually working.'

'Fair enough. I can wait until tomorrow,' James stood up and stretched. He really was very tall. 'As long as you are going to be working and not just going into hiding. Promise me you won't let anyone make you feel shit about those pictures?'

'Brownie Guide promise,' I saluted. 'You're right. I'm sure I'm just overreacting.'

'Good. And if your boyfriend hasn't sent a dozen roses to your hotel when you get back, he'll have me to answer to.' He opened the door back into the bustling sunshine. 'I'm not having him making you feel rubbish for no reason.'

'If I didn't know you were a hateful, ego-driven movie star, I could be fooled into thinking you were actually quite nice,' I said, shielding my eyes and looking up into his. 'You must be a very good actor.'

'Make sure you put that in the interview,' James said, dialling his driver. 'I am good but I mean it. You should never let anyone make you feel crap. I don't have those people around me any more.'

'No, you only have really positive people like Blake,' I said, watching the limo appear around the corner. 'He really makes your life easier?'

'I know he seems like hard work to everyone else,' he said, 'but I don't know what I'd do without him. Even if he is going to lose his mind after we binned him off again today.'

'It's fine, I'm sure he'll just blame me,' I replied. 'Again.'

'I'm sure he will,' James agreed. 'I'm sorry. Thank you for putting up with him. And me.'

'Thank you for making this so easy for me,' I slid on my sunglasses to get a better, slightly hidden peek at him.

'I know you won't believe it,' he said, pulling out his own shades. 'But I'm having fun. Hanging out with you reminds me of something I don't have any more.'

'What's that?' More than three per cent body fat?

'I don't really know,' James said, pushing my sunglasses up onto the top of my head and looking down at me. I could feel his stare right in the pit of my stomach. 'But it's there.'

'Then I'm choosing to believe it's a good thing,' I said, pushing them back down as the limo pulled up beside us. How was him being an absolute angel as well as all kinds of gorgeous, while Alex was being a total arse, helping me anyway?

CHAPTER NINE

Jenny was nowhere to be found back at the hotel, which left me free for the world's longest nap. But after an hour of staring at the ceiling, I was forced to accept that sleep wasn't coming. There was just too much on my mind and, to be honest, the vodka I'd necked at The Dresden hadn't helped me clear it up.

If I could just sort out one of the dramas in my mind, maybe I'd be able to get half an hour's sleep. OK, first, Alex. Staring at my phone, I tried to replay our conversation but it all sounded so much worse in my head. If he would just call, if he would just tell me it was all right. If he would just bloody say that he loved me. But that wasn't about to happen any time soon. And hello? How sad was I that I needed my boyfriend to tell me he loved me to make me feel better? OK, very, but it didn't stop it being true.

I added another pillow to the stack already behind my head and grabbed my BlackBerry from the nightstand. No missed calls, no new emails. Nothing from Mary about the blog entry I'd sent over that morning. No matter what James said, my job was still on the line. Once the interview was over, he wouldn't have any pull at the magazine and if Mary thought I was going to shag every person I worked with, there wouldn't be any more work. Plus Jenny was still in such a strange mood, she wasn't exactly helping me out.

And if that wasn't enough, I had the most unexpected problem of them all to deal with. James was definitely flirting with me. Definitely. What was I supposed to do? My job was hanging by a thread, my boyfriend wasn't talking to me, my best friend was one missed call away from kicking my arse and here was this insanely beautiful man – not even a man, a movie star – telling me I'm amazing, stroking my hair and asking me to stay the night. It wasn't fair. I was only human, unlike him. Stupid Greek God of a man, how dare he try it on with me? Seriously, what was a girl supposed to do?

It had taken me six months to sort my life out after arriving in New York, amazing friends, wonderful boyfriend, the perfect job. And it had only taken me four days in LA to screw it all up. Wow, that must be some sort of record. Really, there was only one thing to do.

'Hello?'

'Hello, Dad, it's Angela.'

'Angela, love, it's midnight, what's wrong?' Dad yawned. At least they clearly hadn't seen the photos.

'Sorry, I hadn't thought about the time difference,' I apologized, looking at the blinking clock on my nightstand. 'Nothing's wrong, I just wanted to have a quick word with Mum, is she up?'

'She is now,' he muttered.

'What's wrong? Angela, are you coming home?' The classic motherly panic. 'What's happened?'

'No, Mum,' I said. 'I just wanted to have a bit of a chat. I'm working in LA this week, aren't I?'

'I never know where you are from one day to the next,' she sighed. 'And you haven't wanted a bit of a chat for months, let alone at midnight. So what's wrong?'

'It's only four here, sorry, I wasn't thinking,' I said. How true was that?

'No, thinking hasn't been your strong point since you moved away, love,' Mum agreed. 'What's wrong now?'

She'd been awake for four minutes and she was already having a go at me. Why hadn't I called her earlier?

'Nothing really, I just wanted to call you about, well, some pictures,' I tried to work out how to rephrase 'the internet is crawling with suggestive photographs of your only child' for my fifty-nine-year-old mother, but it just wouldn't come out. Couldn't think why. 'I'm in some pictures.'

'You're in the pictures? Is that why you're in LA; you're going to be in a film?'

'No, Mum, I'm interviewing someone, I'm not in a film.' I closed my eyes. 'It's just someone took some photos of me and the person I'm interviewing, he's an actor, and they're saying that we're . . . going out together.'

'You're going out with an actor?' I heard running water and opening cupboards. If she was making tea, this could go on for a while. 'I thought you were going out with that man with the guitar?'

'I am going out with that man with the . . . oh, his name is Alex, Mum,' I could actually really use a cup of tea. Or something stronger. 'I'm not going out with the actor, I just wanted to let you know that the photos make it look like I am going out with him. But I'm not.'

'Just a minute love, I'm making tea. I suppose all you drink is coffee now. Can't beat a good cup of tea though, can you? Those Americans might make more sense if they all had a cup of tea for a change. Coffee gives me the jitters.'

'Of course I still drink tea,' I sighed. 'And you can get tea here.'

'Coffee gives your dad the runs, of course,' she went on. 'Now what's all this about you going out with an actor?'

'OK, let me start again.' I sat up in bed. 'I'm not going out with an actor but there are some photos on the internet that make it look like I am. And I don't want you to get upset when you see them.'

'Why would I get upset? And where on the internet, let me have a look,' she slurped her tea. 'Where are my glasses?'

'You've got the internet?' I crossed the room to my laptop. 'When did you get a computer?'

'Your dad's been doing a course. I thought I'd be able to send you emails but I haven't quite worked that out yet. Your dad's been doing that Facebook thing though. All the pictures from Louisa's weddings are up there, you know.'

'Dad's on Facebook?' I asked, logging on and searching. Oh my, there he was. Not a good picture.

'That's the one. Now what's the name of this website?' she asked.

'Mum, I don't think you need to look at the pictures. I just wanted to let you—'

'If I just Goggle you, will they come up?' she interrupted.

'If you what?'

'Goggle, oh, it's wonderful Angela, you just type in anything and it comes up,' she went on. 'I got this really lovely recipe for an apple crumble. It's so much better than your Auntie Susan's one. Oh, here you are, here's your picture.'

'No, that'll be my blog, Mum.' I was talking so quickly, I wasn't sure what I was saying. I just could not cope with her seeing those pictures. 'The pictures didn't have my name on but I thought someone might see them and recognize me and tell—'

'Well, it says it's you,' she carried on talking over me. 'You and James Jacobs? I'm sure I've seen him in something; he's very good looking, Angela.'

'Wait, what website are you on?' The photos had my name on them now? I typed my name into Google Images. And there I was. There we were.

'They're on lots of websites, Angela. Well, you do make a very good-looking couple.' She sounded oddly proud. 'When do we get to meet him?'

'Mum, I'm not going out with James Jacobs,' I repeated. 'These photos aren't real.'

'That's not you being carried into that big black car then?'

'Well, yes, it is but not—'

'And that's not you coming out of the hotel?'

'Yes but—'

'That's a lovely dress, Angela. If you'd dressed like that when you were living with Mark, he might never have left you for that tart from the tennis club. All those bloody jeans and sloppy jumpers . . .'

'Mum!' Really. Why did I call her?

'Never mind, I dare say Mark will be feeling pretty silly when he sees that you're going out with a film star, won't he? Malcolm, what was that film we saw about the casino? Angela's new boyfriend was in it,' she shouted without taking the phone away from her mouth.

Suitably deafened, I turned my attention to the first website that came up.

Updated: We finally *have confirmation on the identity of James Jacobs's new lady love! She is none other than Angela Clark, fellow Brit, journo and, according to our sources, currently dating lead singer of New York rockers, Stills, Alex Reid. Way to trade up, journo girl. That said, we always thought Alex Reid was kind of a cutie; obviously no James Jacobs, but if he's looking for someone to help him through the heartache, we are available . . .*

There, beside a new shot of James carrying me out of Teddy's, this one showcasing my pants fabulously, was a picture of Alex, all bundled up, heading into Bedford Avenue subway station. I didn't know if it was new or if it was old, but he looked gutted. 'Oh shit,' I breathed.

'Angela, language.'

'Mum, I'm sorry for waking you up,' I said, rubbing my eyes. No time for a nap now. 'I've got to make some calls. I'll give you a ring later.'

'OK love. And I shouldn't worry about those pictures. You know what they say, today's newspaper is tomorrow's fish and chip wrapping. Just try not to show your pants in the next ones. Speak to you soon.'

'There had better not be any next ones,' I muttered to myself, hanging up and redialling. I hated it when my mother was right.

'Alex, it's me . . .' Seriously, would I never ever learn to think about what I was going to say on voicemail before I called? 'I know you said not to call but I had to. Can you call me please? I just want to speak to you; these photos are just stupid. I spoke to my mum and, yeah, you don't care that I spoke to my mum, do you? Anyway, please just call me back?'

Not my finest work but far from my worst. That accolade was firmly attached to the photo of my pants that was currently circulating the internet.

I spent the next couple of hours dutifully writing up my interview with James. As someone who had never ever interviewed an A-list celebrity before, it didn't read half bad. If I hadn't met him, this interview would totally make me fall in love with him. Unfortunately, I had met him and, as much as I was trying to pretend otherwise, my feelings definitely weren't entirely professional. I would probably leave that out of the interview.

Just as I was considering ordering the entire room-service menu, my phone buzzed into life. I snatched it up, praying it would be Alex. My lovely boyfriend Alex, whom I would not be cheating on. Ever. Honest.

'Yo, Angie, you still with James?' Jenny yelled down the line.

'Nope,' I looked at the clock. Where had she been all day?

'Whatever, we're at The Grove, Daphne had to pick some pieces up from Nordstrom – she's styling Rachel Bilson tomorrow, can you believe it? She's so hot. Tiny but hot,' Jenny carried on. 'But I'll be in the lobby in twenty minutes and then we're going out for dinner. And then we're going *out*. Daphne, where did you get a rez?'

The sound of honking horns drowned out the name of the restaurant. 'Jenny, are you on the phone while you're driving?' I asked, holding my head in my hands.

'Uh, no?'

'Please just be careful,' I said. Jenny wasn't completely concerned with her personal safety at the best of times and the idea of her behind the wheel of a car terrified me. 'I don't know about going out for dinner. It was really weird out this morning, loads of people just kept staring.'

'Yeah, but you were with James though, right? Well, tonight you'll be with us. No one will look, I swear. Well, they will, but only because of our collective hotness. Just go get ready. Oh shit, we needed to turn there, right?'

Before I could argue, she hung up. Or at least I hoped she had hung up and not just caused a six-car pile-up.

Despite really not wanting to leave my hotel room, I really didn't want to get into another row with Jenny. Instead of taking to my bed, I went to my wardrobe and pulled out my black Kerrigan silk dress. Jenny was probably right. Surely a real celebrity would have cocked up by now and taken my place on Perez's front page? The dress was perfect: slouchy black silk with pink sash that loosely tied around my waist. It was pretty but certainly not sexy and if I teamed it with flats instead of the skyscraper heels that Jenny had bullied me into getting when I'd bought it, it was positively demure. I combed out my hair, added a big old sweep of blusher and a quick flick of mascara. Passably presentable but in no way attention-seeking.

Which I could not say about Jenny and Daphne. I wasn't sure if it was them waiting for me in the lobby or if they were holding auditions for new Pussycat Dolls in the bar. Jenny's hair was huge, either from overenthusiastic teasing or driving with the top down all day, and her gorgeous tan was accessorized with bright red lips, five-inch heels and a skin-tight, funnel-neck black leather mini-dress. And Daphne was hardly letting the side down. Her black hair was carefully curled and pinned (and lacquered within an inch of its life), her make-up flawless and Fifties. Seamed stockings, a ridiculously tight black pencil skirt and fitted white shirt with a red patent-leather belt wrapped around her teeny-tiny waist completed a look I could never even hope to replicate. It was all I could do to apply eyeliner without blinding myself – how did she walk around looking like that?

'You both look nice,' I choked, feeling as though I had turned up to a school disco in my pyjamas. 'I didn't realize we were doing dressy?'

'Isn't this awesome?' Jenny span for me. 'I knew you'd love it; it's Marc Jacobs. Daphne borrowed it for her shoot tomorrow. You're not wearing your Miu Mius?'

I shook my head, looking doubtfully at my battered ballet pumps.

'Kerrigan dress?' Daphne asked, looking me up and down. 'Nice.'

I nodded, trying not to be totally in awe of Daphne. Again. Oh yes, I could throw up in front of a movie star and then straddle him on the beach, but put me in front of a proper grown-up girl and I lost it. I'd always wanted to be one of those girls who was completely put together, who glided through life in sky-high heels with nothing but a tiny clutch bag rather than the girl clumping around in biker boots, dropping her satchel on the subway and scattering tampons everywhere. It just wasn't on the cards. And then I remembered that Daphne Did It With Boys For Money and I didn't know where to look any more.

'So where are we going?' I asked, following the glamazons out to the car. 'Should I go and get changed?'

'We have heels in the car.' Jenny took my hand and smiled.

'A simple, "you look nice as you are" would have done,' I frowned.

Dominick's was a cool little restaurant on Beverly Boulevard, full of pretty people, but at least here they seemed to be actually eating their meals rather than pushing their food around their plates. I took that to be a good sign.

'See,' Jenny gestured around with a fork full of spaghetti carbonara. 'No one is looking at you.'

'No, but they are looking at you spilling sauce all down your borrowed dress,' I said, passing her a napkin. Against all the odds, we were actually having a great night. I had got over my nerves, Jenny had got over her tantrum and, once I'd got over the urge to ask Daphne how much she charged for what, she turned out to be a fabulous source of Hollywood gossip. And since I'd served as that day's tabloid fodder, I figured I was allowed to find out the dress sizes of the cast of *Desperate Housewives*. 'So what are the plans for later?'

'On a Tuesday night?' Daphne pursed her perfectly lined lips. 'LAX? Hyde? Bar Marmont would be OK but we were only there on Sunday.'

'If Bar Marmont is anything to do with Chateau Marmont, I don't think so.' I scarfed a giant mouthful of steak. 'Will Hyde be crawling with photographers too?'

'Honey, it's LA,' Daphne shrugged. 'Anywhere worth going to will be crawling with photographers.'

'I could really get to hate LA,' I said to my steak. 'Honestly, how do you relax if you can't just go out and get drunk with your friends?'

'Don't you take your problems out on LA,' Daphne warned. 'That's my baby you're bad-mouthing.'

'Yeah, it's not LA's fault you're having a shit time,'

Jenny chimed. 'LA is beautiful. Awesome sunshine, shopping, beaches, clubs and hot, hot men. And that's before we even get onto all that nature stuff, like hiking in the hills, because we would never go hiking in the hills if we're honest. But you get my point, right?'

'And aren't you supposed to be writer girl?' Daphne asked. 'Everything here is a story, everyone. New York is so boring and practical. Everything here is cooler than in New York.'

'I don't think so,' I smiled, shaking my head. 'Not even.'

'She's right, Angie,' Jenny butted in. 'If you would just try and have a good time, you might enjoy yourself out here.'

'You, Jenny Lopez, are cheating on New York,' I tutted, but maybe she was right. Maybe it wasn't entirely the city's fault that I was having a shitty time. But I would not be miserable if I was still in New York. 'James took me to this place today, The Dresden? He said there are never any photographers there.'

'And so it's not worth going there,' Jenny repeated slowly. 'Don't sweat it Angie, honey. But you know, if you really want this to go away, you should go out and get photographed.'

'How do you work that out?' I asked, trying not to be distracted by the stupidly good-looking waiter who was taking away our plates. I really was turning into a big ho. And why was everyone in LA gorgeous? It was incredibly off-putting.

'You go out, the paparazzi recognize you and you get your chance to give them a quote. Looking awesome, of course,' she winked. 'And flanked by your hot girlfriends.'

'It's not a bad idea,' Daphne agreed. 'You can tell them you're working together or just tell them you and

James are old friends or something. Even if they don't buy it, they'll probably still publish it and that might get you off the hook with the magazine.'

'Maybe,' I said doubtfully. Talking to the paparazzi just didn't seem like a good idea. 'I don't know.'

'Did you speak to Alex yet?' Jenny asked. 'What did he say?'

'Not since yesterday,' I admitted, carefully studying the dessert menu to avoid Jenny's glare. 'He isn't answering his phone.'

'Tell me you're joking?' She slapped the menu down onto the table. 'He hasn't called you?'

'Don't,' I said. I really didn't want to get into this again.

'If that asshole doesn't call you in the next ten seconds to say anything other than "I know everything I read online is bullshit and I'm so lucky to have a girlfriend like you", I'm on the next flight back to New York to kick his ass.' She stared me down.

'Jenny, look at it from his point of view,' I said, taking back the menu. If only because there was a tiramisu on there I desperately wanted to get involved with. 'I'm away in Hollywood, interviewing this actor with a horrible reputation, and after two days there are pictures all over the internet of him carrying me into a limo and me hanging around his hotel room in a dressing gown.'

'There weren't any pictures of you in a dressing gown,' Daphne raised a perfectly pencilled eyebrow, 'were there?'

'He's just been so perfect since we got back together.' I changed the subject quickly. 'And then I get here and it all goes tits up. It'll be fine when I get home.'

'Out of sight, out of mind.' Daphne offered a saccharine smile, which did not help matters.

176

'Or maybe he's missing you so much, he can't bear even to speak to you.' Jenny clasped her hands to her heart. 'Oh, Angie, it's all too romantic. And bullshit. He's being a dick. His boy genes have kicked in again.'

'Thanks for making me feel so much better, both of you.' I frowned. 'It doesn't really matter now, does it? Whatever the problem was before I was branded an international super-slag by Perez Hilton, as far as he's concerned, he's got a solid-gold reason to be pissed off with me. And you know his ex cheated on him; he's not the world's most instantly trusting man. Once I'm back in New York, he'll be fine. I'm sure.'

'So what, you can't leave the city without him freaking out that you're cheating on him? Sounds like a dream relationship,' Daphne said into her wine glass. 'And if he's going to give you shit for something you didn't do, you may as well do it, is all I'm saying.'

'You're not being fair,' I said, sinking half a glass of red wine. 'And, God, I'm not entirely innocent, am I? I suppose I have sort of been . . . well, James has been . . . I can hardly say it . . . maybe we've been flirting a bit. And I haven't done anything but I have to admit, I've seriously thought about it.'

'Angela, first of all, I don't care if you blew the entire cast of *Gossip Girl*. If you told Alex you didn't, and he didn't believe you, he's getting his ass kicked when we get back.' Jenny took my hand. 'And second of all, you need to elaborate on "flirting".'

'Oh, it's nothing.' I tried to backtrack, quickly. 'It's just brushing my hair away from my face, holding my hand, saying stuff.' Daphne was staring with wide-open eyes while Jenny toyed with her dessert spoon. 'And after that thing at Teddy's, he sort of suggested I stay at the hotel.'

'And you didn't?' Daphne looked impressed. 'Angela,

you deserve some sort of award, not some asshole boyfriend who believes everything he reads.'

'He probably just meant because of the paparazzi,' I said, knowing full well that wasn't what he'd meant at all. 'I'm just reading too much into everything because the Alex thing is messing with my head. I'm completely rubbish at boys, I never know what they're thinking.'

'Not one girl on this planet does.' Jenny shook her head at me. 'But I still cannot believe you came home on Monday night. You had James Jacobs, *People* magazine's fifth sexiest person in the world, and my personal third, throwing himself at you and you said no. Angela Clark, you are stronger than strong.'

'Who's first and second?' I asked, filling up my glass from the bottle of red in the centre of the table.

'Christian Bale at one, Jake Gyllenhaal at two. The ranking is fluid depending on whichever's doing the tough guy movie at the time.' Jenny opened up the menu. 'You're the one that likes guys skinnier than you. Which I'm guessing is the only reason you passed up James Jacobs. God, even after that whole scene in Teddy's I would struggle to pass that up. And don't try and change the subject on me again.'

I finished the wine by topping up Jenny's glass. 'What's it going to take to shut you up?'

'Come out after dinner,' Jenny bargained. 'Out out. Dancing, drinking out. And enjoy it.'

'I refuse to commit to enjoying it,' I shrugged. 'But a drink wouldn't hurt right now.'

'Score.' Jenny and Daphne high-fived. If people weren't looking at us before, they certainly were now.

One hour, two desserts and three martinis later, our car was still sitting in the valet parking lot at Dominick's and we were in a cab on our way to Bar Marmont. Everything in me (aside from the martinis) said it was a bad idea, but I was having so much fun with Jenny and Daphne, it was starting to seem silly to go back to the hotel just because some photographers might be out and they might recognize me. Besides, I was just about drunk enough to feel a dance coming on.

'So, Jenny,' I clung to the hanging strap in the back of the cab as we motored around an uneven corner, 'where's Joe this evening?'

'Working.' She gave me a stern look. 'Obviously, he would be here with me if he weren't.'

'But you haven't . . .?' Surely I would have had every nasty detail if she'd finally done the deed.

'No, we haven't,' she pouted and reapplied her lip gloss. 'I think maybe he's sick. But we will. He must be sick, right?"

'You've only got four more days,' I reminded her. 'Better work fast, Lopez.'

'Unless you stay longer,' Daphne said quietly as we stopped suddenly.

'Not now,' Jenny said, pushing her out of the door.

I looked from Daphne to Jenny. What was that supposed to mean?

'You've only got four more days,' Daphne sang as we started up the stairs to the door of the bar. I wasn't sure what to be more concerned about, the weird tension that had just shot up all around Jenny, the photographers lining the street below or the huge man with the clipboard staring at us. And, quite frankly, if I didn't get to a toilet very soon, we were about to have a very embarrassing incident at the door. Just not the one that the man with the clipboard was expecting.

'Good evening ladies.' He looked us up and down

and blocked the door. 'We're real busy tonight. You staying at the hotel?'

I panicked, the velvet rope was not my friend. Daphne, however, seemed very well acquainted with it.

'We're with James Jacobs,' she said smoothly. 'He's staying here.'

'You're with James Jacobs?' He didn't even bother to raise an eyebrow.

'Well, I'm not "with him",' Daphne said, stepping to one side. 'But she is.'

The doorman looked at me, presumably not having noticed me hiding behind Jenny's enormous hair, and a slight flicker of recognition passed over his face. But not in a particularly good way. I gave him my biggest please-let-me-in-so-I-can-pee smile, but it seemed to be lost in translation. Or possibly I just looked drunk.

'Mr Jacobs is already inside, maybe I'll go ask him if he's expecting guests.' He stared at me, then passed the clipboard to a lesser, slightly smaller door-boy behind him.

'Please do,' Daphne smiled, as sweet as sugar. I felt myself starting to sway a little, from the martinis, the beat I felt through the floor and the implausible height of the heels Jenny had made me trade with her in the cab. Apparently she was quite hot enough in flats but I needed the help. And about twenty coats of mascara and enough eyeliner to embarrass a raccoon. Before the bouncer could leave his post, a familiar face appeared at the door.

'Angela!' James yelled over the music that was pulsing inside. 'What happened to your early night?'

'Hello!' I squeaked, pushing past the doorman (ha!) and letting James pull me into a very short hug before I squirmed free, scanning the place for the bathrooms.

The relief was immense, we were in and I was moments away from being able to pee.

'James, this is Daphne and you remember my friend, Jenny? Back in a minute.' I waved behind me before pelting off down a narrow hallway to join a short queue of girls. As far as I could tell, girls only queued for two things in the US, sample sales and the bathroom, so unless someone was hawking Jimmy Choos in the back, this was where the toilets were.

For a fancy club, the toilets were not classy, I thought as I slammed the stiff door of the shabby cubicle closed behind me, but the bar was painfully hip. From the pretty butterfly wallpaper to the red-fringed lampshades, Bar Marmont reeked of understated glamour. And the crowds milling around the bar were hardly letting the side down. I wondered if we'd accidentally wandered into the auditions for *America's Next Top Model*. If *America's Next Top Model* started accepting male models. And not-so-model males with black Amex cards. But above all, it felt safe. And I didn't just mean the bolt on the toilet door. The bar felt comfortably exclusive.

Maybe James was right; maybe the Chateau and its shabby chic bar were safe. Safe enough for me to drink myself into not thinking about Alex for a couple of hours at least. Except there he was, in the corner of my mind, smiling, brushing my hair out of my eyes while his fell across his cheek. I could smell his deodorant, his sweaty post-gig T-shirt, and I could hear his soft lullabies in my ear over the buzzing bass of the bar. Maybe I should just send a text. Just to remind him I was still here. My oversized clutch seemed like the Tardis. Where was my phone? I washed my hands then leaned against the wall, frantically searching through my bag and spilling lip gloss after lip gloss on to the floor as the cubicle started to spin slightly. Who needed so many lip glosses? Was I even wearing lip gloss? Ah-ha, there was my phone, hiding under the reams of toilet roll I'd stuck in my bag in case there wasn't any left later. Before I could second-guess myself, I tapped out a quick message.

'I know you're angry but it's all bollocks. Miss you. A x'

I stared at the screen as the send icon blinked a couple of times. Sending. Sending. Sent. Another couple of seconds to see if he was going to text back. And a couple more.

'Come on, I'm dying out here,' a not very ladylike voice yelled from outside. The lock on the toilet door wouldn't hold up to more than one good kick, and if she felt anything like I had two minutes ago, she would do that in about thirteen seconds. I tossed the phone back into the bottom of my bag. There was only one thing for it. More drinks. It was going to take a couple more mojitos to get me into a dancing mood now, but I was quite committed to making sure that happened.

I shuffled back through the bar without getting so much as a second glance from the gorgeous people all around me. Which was oddly nice. Jenny and Daphne had already set up shop with James, Blake and a small crowd of hangers-on, but even they didn't turn to wave as I walked over. I was invisible. I had thought that the only way to become anonymous in LA would be to adopt the uniform – blonde hair, big boobs and a super-tanned, size zero stick figure – but apparently I could just hang out in a very cool bar full of beautiful, beautiful women and then no one would even bat an eyelid. Might still be worth getting the boob job, though.

No one in the entire place even batted a heavily made-up eyelid as I sat down, except for James who immediately pushed Blake up from the seat next to him to make room for me. Either he really wanted to sit next to me or he thought my arse was too big to fit in the tiny space between him and Jenny. He would have been right, of course. I squeezed in and raised my hand to everyone around the table. Jenny gave me a blinding smile over the rim of her martini glass and Daphne winked over the shoulder of a tall, skinny guy with the most impressive afro I had ever seen. And glowering in the corner was my old friend Blake, offering me his welcoming grimace.

'Good evening, madam.' James sported his usual uniform of indecently tight jeans, fitted black shirt and matinee idol eyes. 'Jenny tells me she lured you out against your will.'

'Hmm.' I eyed Jenny to my left. She raised her glass in return, before turning back to the beautiful Joe-a-like sitting opposite her. 'There was some coercion involved.'

'And some martinis?'

'She mentioned that, did she?'

'Well, I didn't know what you wanted to drink.' James passed me a very full martini glass. 'And I don't know what you like.'

'Thanks,' I smiled and sipped.

'Apart from me, of course,' he added.

I frowned and chugged.

'So did you get hold of that boyfriend of yours or what?' James asked, leaning in close so I could hear him over the music.

'Nope.' I finished my drink, and carefully placed the empty glass on the table in front of us. 'But it's fine.'

'If he's still being a knob about the photos, I could call him,' James offered. 'Although I'm guessing I'm the last person he'd want to speak to.'

'If I thought he'd answer the phone, I would love you to call him.' I closed my eyes and found James's arm draped casually across my back instead of the wooden frame of the booth. A hot hand curled around my shoulder in a half-hug.

'Well, if I'm honest, I'm not sure anything I have to say to him would make him feel better,' James said into my hair. 'I'm really glad you came here tonight.'

I turned too quickly to look at James but his face was altogether too close and I bumped my nose against his. He brushed his lips over mine, almost too gently to even feel.

'Don't,' I coloured up. 'I mean, I'm sorry, but no.'

James gave me a half-smile and pushed up off the booth, striding down the bar. The beautiful people instinctively cleared a path and stared after him. It was funny how they recognized one of their own.

Watching his denim-clad backside vanish in the crowd as they melded back together, I desperately tried to clear my mind. Daphne was knocking back shots of vodka straight from the bottle, and I wondered how she was going to manage her Rachel Bilson shoot tomorrow. And how Jenny was hoping to get all the different stains out of that leather dress. And just when was Blake going to actually get up out of his seat and kick the living crap out of me rather than just stare at me. Oh, about now.

'What exactly do you think you're doing?' he demanded, throwing himself across the table and almost pushing Jenny out of her seat at the side of me.

'Hi, Blake.' I hoped that if I refused to argue, surely he'd give up eventually. 'So sorry about this morning. James thought—'

'That's the problem, James doesn't think,' Blake said. He might have been quiet but he was clearly furious.

'*I* think. That's my job. He acts, I think, you ask questions and then you go home.'

Apparently he would argue regardless.

'And while you might not care about your job, your boyfriend and all that other crap, it is also my job to ensure that James keeps the things that important to him.' He paused. 'Don't make it my job to ensure that you lose the things that are important to you.'

Meep. 'Blake I—'

'No,' he went on. 'I said from the beginning that this was a bad idea, and if Monday night wasn't bad enough, here you are again with your slutty friends, all over James. It's pathetic.'

OK, now I was annoyed. 'Firstly, it was never my intention to end up splashed all over the internet with my knickers on show, you know; and secondly, please don't call my friends slutty. You don't know them, how dare you call them slutty?'

Blake leaned his head to the left to look around me and laughed.

I span around. Jenny was safely positioned within an inch of the Joe-a-like's lips and Daphne was dancing with her man. Well, she was dancing; he was sitting. She was dancing in his lap. Oh my God, she was giving him a lap dance.

'No, not slutty at all. You've been here, what? Twenty minutes?' Blake curled his lip. 'Yeah, I know you. I know all of you. Do you think you're the first nobody to ever make a play for James?'

'Blake, this is really boring. I'm getting very tired of repeating myself.' I turned my back on my slutty friends. Couldn't really fight him on that front. 'No one is making a play for James.'

Trying not to wobble in my five-inch heels, I stood up quickly. 'Jenny,' I barked, not taking my eyes off

185

Blake's smug face. He wasn't quite so handsome in the middle of a row. 'Jenny, can I please have a word?'

She looked up, eyebrows knitted together in a silent plea to stay where she was.

'Jenny. Bar. Now.' I turned and marched. Perhaps it was a bit slow and, well, very uneven, but it was still a march.

'Angie, honey, what are you doing to me?' Jenny groaned, straightening her hemline as I dragged her through the crowd. For some reason, it didn't magically part for us.

'What are you doing?' I asked, wrestling for an inch of the bar. 'I'm there having a screaming row with Blake, he's calling us a bunch of slags and I turn around and you're practically at it with a stranger. And Daphne actually is.'

'Damn,' Jenny whistled, looking back at Daphne. A small crowd was forming around her, obscuring my view. Thank God. 'She's so sexy. It's such a shame she didn't keep up the burlesque.'

'Jenny, pay attention, that is not the point I was getting at,' I said, ordering a Diet Coke but knowing full well I was past the ability to sober up with the help of one soft drink. 'I'm going to find James and say goodbye, then I'm leaving. I've got enough on my plate at the moment with Blake actively trying to ruin my life.'

'Angie, I'm really sorry but I'm gonna have to go Oprah on your ass.' Jenny pressed her lips into a thin line. 'What the hell is wrong with you?'

I stared, a little bit shocked. 'What's wrong with me? I'm not the one getting off with a stranger in the middle of a bar—'

'And I am, so what's the problem?' she asked, hands on hips. 'And that's not where I'm going so shut up and listen. Yeah, I get that those photos of you and James were hard to see but they weren't real and everyone will get that. Your magazine, your mom, Alex. And I will not get into an argument about this, but if he *doesn't* get it, if he never speaks to you again, then he is not worth getting this upset about, honey. Fact.'

'But—'

'No, I'm not done,' she grabbed my Diet Coke and took a swig.'I have two more very important points to make. Firstly, what the hell has happened to my Angie? Why are you walking around whining and snivelling because your boyfriend is being an ass and a hot movie star is trying to get in your pants? Where's the girl who broke a guy's hand when she found out her boyfriend was cheating on her? Who got on a plane to New York without even giving it a second thought?'

'Don't know.' I always had been very eloquent.

'And secondly – and it is very, very important that you think about what I'm about to say.' Jenny grasped my shoulders a little too tightly. 'Your mom lives a long way away so she's not here to explain one of life's fundamental lessons to you. When a real-life hunk of a man makes a move on you, you let him. You know I like Alex, when he's not being an asshole at least, but Angie, this is a genuine movie star. A drop-dead-gorgeous, prime specimen of a man. And he obviously wants you. What is wrong with you?'

'Jenny . . .' I protested feebly.

'Has Alex called you?' she asked.

'No,' I said.

'And have you called him since I last asked you?'

'No,' I sipped the Diet Coke innocently.

'Have you texted him?'

'Yes,' I admitted to the floor.

'Then you have no excuses. You have to do this

for me.' She looked as though she meant it. I couldn't think of a time I'd seen her look so committed to a cause. 'OK, so you don't have to sleep with him, but where's the harm in dancing with him? Maybe making out a little? Alex will never find out. And besides, you're in the middle of an argument, you're practically on a break.'

'Jenny, if I learned anything from *Friends*, and I did, it's that being on a break doesn't mean anything.' I pulled my left foot out of my ridiculously high shoe and rested it on the cold floor for a moment. Ahh, sweet relief. 'And besides, I told you, I'm going home. I have had far too much to drink tonight.'

'Just dance with the man and let me watch,' she pleaded. 'If you're going to guilt-trip me about making out with that guy back at the table, at least let me live vicariously through you.'

'If you can tell me the name of that man, I will book you the honeymoon suite at The Hollywood.' I gave her a moment.

'John?' she shrugged.

'Not even close.'

'Whatever, Angie.' Jenny pointed to James as he wandered through the bar, looking for us back at the table. Looking for me. 'Just one dance. And then you can leave. I'll even take you home myself.'

'Maybe that's the problem though,' I said, feeling a familiar tickle in my stomach. 'If I dance with him, I don't know if I'll be able to go home.'

'Awesome,' Jenny grinned, pushing me away from the bar and pulling me back over to the table; in these heels, I was in no position to try and stop her.

Either the music was getting louder in the bar or I was getting steadily drunker, Diet Coke be damned. The bass pounded through the floor and up the slender stems of my heels. I really wanted to dance with James. Or go home to bed and conduct the rest of my interview with James over the phone. Or dance with James. Which was how I knew it was definitely time to go home. But Jenny dragged me onwards, back to Blake, 'John' and some random tiny brunette sat awfully close to my James. Not my James. Just James.

'Angela,' James held out a hand and pulled me down into the seat next to him with a bump. Jenny sashayed past Blake and set herself down, returning his filthy look with her own killer stare. I loved that girl. 'Angela, Jenny, this is my friend, Tessa.'

The new girl, clad in denim hot pants, big boots and a baggy white T-shirt held out her hand, but it was so tiny, I hardly dared to take it. I felt like Jabba the Hut shaking hands with Tinker Bell.

'Hi,' she said, shaking hands with Jenny. 'Have we met?'

'Yeah, it's Tessa DiArmo, right?' Jenny shook her hand smoothly. 'We met at The Union last year.'

I watched Jenny schmooze Tessa like a pro, in complete awe. She really ought to be the one interviewing celebrities, no one fazed her. And no wonder I didn't remember Tessa; everything about The Ivy was a bit of a blur, except for the toilet floor. Living in London with Mark, I'd barely been able to open a bottle of wine on my own, but since I'd moved out to New York, I could get a cork out with a pair of eyelash curlers in under a minute if needs be. The privileges and perils of being freelance.

'Right, The Union. I don't stay anywhere else in New York. Except The Grammercy. And maybe The Bowery. Or The Hotel on Rivington.' Tessa nodded thoughtfully, clearly not registering that Jenny actually worked at The Union. 'I should go back soon – it's been like,

189

weeks. Maybe the Soho Grand. We should hang out. I love your outfits. I so need a new stylist. Your dress is awesome.'

I realized Tessa's wide-eyed stare was aimed at me.

'Well, no one styles me except for Jenny,' I joked, looking down at my black dress. Well, she had picked it. 'She's a miracle worker.'

'Yeah? Maybe you could help me out. I have this awards thing tomorrow night,' Tessa went on, oblivious. 'And I don't know, nothing anyone brings me is like, interesting?'

I started to laugh but a sharp elbow to the ribs from Jenny turned my giggle into a cough. Then a squeeze from James's hand turned the cough into a squeak. And then a hiccup. I was getting more drunk by the second.

'Well, why don't we go shopping tomorrow?' Jenny suggested carefully in her I'm-so-casual-about-this-it-hurts voice. 'I could pull a few things together for you, I'm sure.'

'Sure,' Tessa beamed. Apparently she'd been to the same charm school as James. Her grin practically knocked me back against the chair. 'Where?'

'Melrose maybe? I would love to see you in some Betsey Johnson,' Jenny started, grasping Tessa's hands in hers. 'Something short, flirty, maybe a puffball?'

'Wow, that's totally not me,' Tessa looked at Jenny with a mixture of awe and fear. 'You don't think that's going too far?'

'Honey, I'm so over the Uggs.' Jenny patted her hand. 'Trust me. I never get it wrong. So, for shoes, I'm thinking maybe Choos? Something metallic?'

'As fascinating as this is,' James whispered into my ear, snapping my trance, 'How about a dance?'

On the other side of the table, Blake and the former object of Jenny's affections looked equally pissed off.

It seemed that Jenny's man was not amused at having lost his conquest to a discussion about designer shoes, and Blake was just burning up, watching James lead me across the room. I looked back at Jenny and Tessa, both waving their arms around, enthusiastically debating the merits of Giuseppe Zanotti heeled glads over Roger Vivier platform peep-toes. They wouldn't miss me for a moment. And I really did want to dance, however bad a feeling I had about dancing with James. A distinctly inappropriate warm, tingly feeling. Sod it, I thought, letting myself be pulled along. One dance wouldn't hurt anyone. Well, it might hurt Blake and, right now, that was actually a total plus.

The music seemed to get just a tiny bit louder, a tiny bit faster, as James pulled me in towards him and began moving with the beat. He pressed his hands palm to palm against mine for a second, then pushed his fingers through mine, entwining our hands and pulling me closer. Happily, he was a great dancer, moving with ease and taking me with him, constantly swaying, spinning, not giving me a second to think. My head rested against his chest at heart height, my warm cheek against his shirt. As we settled into our rhythm, James span me around, pressing my back up against him, and wrapped his arms tightly around my waist. Which was just as well or I would have fallen over. Five-inch heels were not conducive to speedy dance moves or speedy getaways. He slid his hands down across my stomach, leaving a trail of butterflies in their wake, and then twirled me around, pulling my arms up above my head.

I'd been in LA for such a short time, but it felt like I'd already forgotten how to have fun. And wasn't that what LA should be? Fun? I'd been so busy worrying about the interview, panicking about things Alex, freaking out over those stupid photos. I'd got so stressed so quickly. But I was fairly certain that this was what fun felt like. Being with people that weren't judging me or kicking my arse for something that hadn't even happened. This was what it felt like to be with someone who wanted to be with me. I stretched my hands high above my head, then let them run through my hair, tipping my head upwards to look back at James. His eyes were closed and he was singing along to the music. And good God he looked amazing.

I turned back around in his hands and reached my arms around his neck, my fingertips tracing his collar. James's eyes opened and he looked down at me, pausing for a moment and then suddenly dipping me low, almost to the ground. I felt like Baby, and nobody puts Baby in a corner. There were only two things I could possibly do, totally off balance, completely helpless in his arms, his face barely inches from mine. Laugh out loud or kiss him.

So I laughed.

Then he kissed me.

CHAPTER TEN

'Sorry,' James whispered, pulling me back upright. I clung to his shoulders while the blood rushed back around my body. 'Should I have asked first?'

Too many things were going through my head for me to reply. If it had just been a quick kiss, just a peck, I might have been able to laugh it off, but it would seem that practice really did make perfect. It had been a real Hollywood kiss. My lips were still tingling but I didn't have a trace of stubble burn. No wonder James had made his way through half of Hollywood; every part of me was burning up.

'Angela?'

'Sorry,' I blinked, let go of my grip on his shirt and pressed my fingers to my lips, 'what?'

'Are you OK? You're not going to throw up, are you?' Given my previous, it was a legitimate question. I felt like a fourteen year old in front of my movie-star crush. I had literally lost the power of speech.

'Angela, really, are you OK?'

'I'm probably going to go now,' I managed, finally. 'Away.'

'Away?' James frowned.

'I mean home,' I mumbled.

He slipped one hand around my waist and brushed my hair out of my eyes with the other. 'Do you want to come back to my bungalow?'

Yes.

'No.'

Wow, I said no.

'Really?' James looked a little bit surprised. 'I thought, maybe, you would want to, you know, come back?'

He wasn't nearly as surprised as I was. 'But I can't. It's just really not a good idea.' I looked back to the table. Tessa had left and Daphne was nowhere to be seen. Jenny, however, was sitting staring at me, her mouth wide open and clapping excitedly. 'I think I'm going to grab Jenny and go home.'

'OK.' He squeezed my hand and nodded at Blake back at the table. I couldn't help but notice that he did not look pleased. To say the least. 'Let me get you a car at least. Don't go anywhere.'

Before I had chance to escape, Jenny was at my side. 'Angela. Clark. Oh. My. God.'

'Shut up, I know.'

'You just made out with a movie star.' Jenny's smile was so wide, she had to be in pain.

'I don't think one kiss is making out,' I said.

'Who says you have to stop at one kiss?'

'Jenny, if you're so desperate for someone to shag a movie star, why don't you do it?' I closed my eyes and tried not to think about James's offer.

'Angie, if I could, I would,' Jenny said. 'And it would be amazing. For him.'

'Whatever.' I needed to get out of there. 'Honestly, if you don't stop talking about sex instead of doing it, I'm going to have to sleep with you. It's getting really boring.'

'You should have just said.' Jenny looked stung. 'I didn't realize I was boring you.'

'I'm sorry,' I said quickly. 'I didn't mean that. Ignore me.'

'No, please go on,' Jenny's mood flipped. 'Tell me more about my problems.'

'No, I'm not saying what I mean,' I sighed, my brain too messy to make sense. 'It's just that, well, you do keep talking about it an awful lot without actually doing it. And it's not like you can't just pull someone, is it?'

'Did it occur to you that maybe I don't actually want to sleep with some random guys?' Jenny asked. With me in her heels and her in my flats, I towered over her, but clearly she could kick my ass at any height.

I paused for a moment. 'No?'

'Well maybe it should.'

'But everything you said?' I rubbed my forehead.

'Jesus, Angie, for someone so smart, you really are so dumb when it comes to guy stuff.' She folded her arms tightly. 'Do you honestly expect me to stand here making you feel better because some hot guy is throwing himself at you while your devoted boyfriend breaks his heart over you back at home? You want me to make you feel better because you have two guys after you while I can't even keep one?'

Jenny pushed past me and threw herself into the crowd, towards the door. She was right, I was incredibly stupid, but not just at boy stuff. I wasn't terribly good at girl stuff either. The bar was so busy, I could only just see the top of her hair weaving through the crowd on the way to the door before she vanished.

'Genius, Angela,' I muttered to myself, all alone in the middle of the packed bar. I didn't know what to do. There was only one thought that was crystal clear and that was my growing need to pee. I pushed my way through to the toilet and rapped on the closed door.

'Hello,' I shouted over the music, 'is anyone in there?' No one was answering but the door was stuck and my last martini was not prepared to hang around and see if anyone came out in a couple of minutes. Better to be embarrassed at seeing someone else having a wee rather than have everyone in the bar see me wet myself, I figured. I looked around quickly before grabbing the handle and giving the door a quick bash with my hip. For the first time since I walked into Bar Marmont, I thanked the lord that I was a size 12.

The door gave more easily than I had expected and I tumbled through backside first, losing my balance. I closed my eyes and held my hands out to avoid spending any more time face first on a toilet floor, but instead of hitting the wall, I felt something warm. And human.

'What the fuck are you doing?' demanded a gruff voice as I span and smacked my eye straight into the door handle.

'OhmygodImsosorry,' I squealed, trying to get out but my stupid heels wouldn't let me move fast enough. My eye throbbed as I fumbled for the handle but the door had got stuck shut again. I just had to get out of there.

'Angela?'

I froze on the spot and wondered if there was any chance I could actually will myself backwards in time. Of course it wasn't a stranger that I had just busted getting hot and heavy in a toilet, that would be too easy. Of course it was James. And of course everyone would assume I'd come in here to join in. But if he

196

wasn't in here with me, who the hell did he have pressed up against the wall?

'Oh shit.'

I opened my eyes slowly. Standing close to James, hands lost in his brown curls, the same curls I'd been twirling around my fingers minutes ago, was a very flustered-looking Blake. And while James had managed not to give me stubble burn when he kissed me, Blake wasn't quite so talented. James's smooth tanned jaw line was red raw, his eyes wide and dark.

'I–I have to pee,' I said, stunned. Without words, Blake's arms dropped to his sides. He looked from me to James and then back again before shoving me out of his way (which really only left into the wall) and yanking the toilet door open.

'Angela, I can explain,' James said quietly. 'It's not what it looks like.'

'I really need to pee,' I repeated, staring at the floor.

'Right, OK.' James wiped his mouth hastily. 'I've, erm, called the car for you. And I'll wait outside. I should explain or something. I want to explain. I'll just wait outside.'

James closed the door carefully behind him but I still couldn't move. As if I needed more evidence that Jenny was right. I really was stupid when it came to boys.

Eventually I snapped out of my trance, peed and washed my hands, but I really didn't want to go back out into the bar. What was I going to say? What was James going to say? And was Blake actually going to be done with it and murder me now? I just couldn't quite believe what I'd seen.

I stared at myself in the mirror. Not a good sight. My hair was a total mess, my eyeliner was smudged halfway down my face and apparently shock did nothing for my complexion. I'd never seen myself look so pale. I took my Stila convertible colour out of my bag. Perhaps if I looked better, I'd feel better. I smudged the fuchsia pink onto my cheeks and lips. Or perhaps I'd look like a very surprised clown. I felt so stupid. How could I not have seen this?

Opening the toilet door and crossing everything I could in the hope that James and Blake had left, I headed back into the bar. There they were, standing opposite me, James looking absolutely terrified, Blake with a surprisingly blasé look on his face. He raised an eyebrow at me, whispered something to James and then left.

'So,' James pressed his lips into a thin line. The lips I'd kissed. The lips that had kissed Blake.

I stood and stared at the floor.

'Angela, we have to talk about this,' he went on.

'No, really, we don't,' I replied. I just wanted to be away from him. I wanted to be back at home, wrapped up in my duvet with Alex.

'Angela, please.' He stepped forward and held out his hand, but I shot back. It was too much, I needed to leave.

'James, please, I just want to go home,' I said, shrinking away from his hands and starting out through the bar. I'd got as far as the door before he came after me.

'Wait!' James shouted. Everyone between him, me and the door stopped everything they were doing and stared. He made the space up between us in moments. 'We have to talk about what you – what you think you saw,' he added quietly.

'You mean you kissing Blake?' I asked.

James went slightly grey and pushed me out through the door.

'Please, don't,' he said, putting a firm arm around my shoulders.

'What? You weren't kissing Blake?' I tried to shake him off. 'Let me guess, you were giving him mouth to mouth?'

'Angela, honestly, there are people, paps, everywhere.' James gestured to the street below us and tried to steer me towards a parked Lexus at the side of the road. 'Just get in your car and I'll explain.'

'Explain that you were kissing Blake?' I asked.

The pack of paps at the bottom of the stairs all turned together.

'James, over here!' one of them sniped behind a sea of popping flashbulbs. 'Give us a smile?'

'Well?' I stopped on the steps and shrugged. 'Are you going to tell them or am I?'

'Why don't you tell us, honey?' he called back. 'We've heard James's side of the story a whole bunch of times before.'

'Angela, please,' James held on to my hand and squeezed. 'Don't.'

I paused and looked back at him. He really was disgustingly beautiful. But I had never ever been so angry with someone in my entire life.

'No. No way, you're completely out of order and—'

Before I could finish, James grabbed my face in his hands and planted a deep kiss on my lips. Well that was one way to shut someone up. My traitor eyes closed instinctively; I knew the flashbulbs were going into overdrive all around us, but he suddenly dipped me so low that there was no way I could wriggle free. Before I could think of anything, James pulled back, scooped me up and dived into the waiting car. The shock of the freezing cold air-con, the soft leather seat and the speed at which the car tore off from the pavement shocked me into silence.

'Angela, I'm really sorry.'

I stared at the back of the seat in front of me.

'It's just . . . it's complicated.'

Absolute silence.

'I didn't mean to lead you on or anything. Not really.'

I turned to face him.

'You didn't mean to lead me on?'

'No.'

'So you didn't mean to kiss me when we were dancing?'

'Well . . .'

'And you didn't mean to flirt with me all week?'

'No, that's not what I meant.'

'So you haven't been flirting with me all week?'

'This isn't what was supposed to happen.'

I turned back to stare at the seat. 'I didn't realize there was a plan.'

James's phone chirped into life.

'Blake?' I asked, trying to make out something familiar beyond the darkened windows. I had no idea where we were.

'Blake,' James sighed.

'He must be pissing himself laughing at me.' I ran my fingers through the ends of my hair. The sun was really drying it out; I'd need to get the split ends sorted out when I got home. Shocker; another shitty thing about LA. 'So what was supposed to happen?'

'What do you mean?'

'If this wasn't supposed to happen, what was?' I asked, looking at my reflection in the tinted glass. The girl looking back looked so pathetic, I didn't recognize her.

'Angela, I didn't mean to embarrass you,' James said quietly.

I just couldn't get over how tragic I'd been. Jenny

was right, what was wrong with me? I'd lost my grip on myself so easily.

'James, did I ever tell you what happened with my ex?' I asked, finally.

'Alex?' James asked.

'No, I don't think he's technically my ex yet.' The Angela in the window looked back at me. I wiped away the lip gloss that was smudged around her mouth and fluffed her hair. She was starting to look a little bit more familiar. Familiar and really, really pissed off. 'My ex-boyfriend in London. He was cheating on me with this girl from his tennis club. I found him having sex with her in the back seat of our car at my best friend's wedding.'

'Oh,' James sounded more than a little bit confused. 'Sorry.'

'Mmm. It was the most embarrassing moment of my entire life.' I traced my reflection's features in the steamed-up glass of the window. 'It was awful ... horrible. Being embarrassed like that in front of all my friends, my family. Being betrayed by someone I trusted. Honestly, I thought I'd never get over it.'

'I can imagine,' he said cautiously.

'But once I'd pissed in his shaving bag and vanished halfway around the world, I felt a lot better.' I reached across the seat and took James's hand.

'Really?' he breathed out.

'Yeah. Oh, and I might have broken the groom's hand during his first dance.' I gave James's impossibly clammy hand a quick squeeze. 'He knew about the affair and didn't tell me. Don't you think that was a really shitty thing to do?'

'Yes?' James's tan had faded to a slightly sickly green colour.

'I can't begin to imagine what I would do to someone

if they embarrassed me in front of – oh, I don't know – the entire celebrity-obsessed Western hemisphere?'

'Angela, seriously—'

I squeezed his hand tighter. 'God, I don't know. I'd have to pay some tramps to shit in his car or something.'

'Really, I'll sort it all out,' James squeaked.

'Or I could go back, have a chat with the paps about his secret gay lover?' I shrugged.

For a moment, James fell silent. 'They wouldn't believe you.'

'I reckon there're two schools of thought there, James.' I dug my fingernails into his palm before throwing his hand back in his lap. 'The first one, which I was really clinging to until tonight, is that yeah, no one really believes what they read on celebrity websites. But the other one is the one that has really stood the test of time.'

His gorgeous blue eyes were completely blank. It was quite depressing.

'You know how they say there's no smoke without fire,' I pursed my lips. 'It would be excellent gossip, wouldn't it? Even if no one believed it. Definitely worth printing.'

'No one would print it,' James shook his head. 'It's too dangerous. They'd think I'd sue. And you wouldn't do that.'

The car suddenly pulled to a stop. I opened the door to see a row of stars stretching out along the pavement. We were in front of The Hollywood. Thank God.

'Angela, please. We have to talk.' James reached out to pull me back into the car.

'Do you really want to piss me off any more this evening?' I asked, shaking off his hand. 'I was serious about the tramps.'

He let go of my hand, launching me out onto the pavement. I stumbled forward, catching my balance between Greta Garbo and Julie Andrews. Great, a nun and a recluse. Also known as my future.

CHAPTER ELEVEN

'Pick up the phone, pick up the phone,' I chanted, pacing up and down my room waiting for Alex to answer. My laptop lay open on the bedroom table, pictures of me and James kissing, him throwing me in the car, the look of shock and anger on my face already mistaken all over the internet for impatience and passion. Of course he wasn't picking up the phone.

It was probably for the best, I thought, throwing my phone across the room. For a shocking change, I really hadn't worked out what I was going to say to him. 'Alex, the world-famous movie star that the entire world knows has done it with dozens of gorgeous women, is actually super gay. Only it's a secret so please don't tell anyone.' Nope, it just didn't have a ring of truth to it. I had to think about how I was going to explain before he called back.

Unless he called back right away.

'Alex?'

'Angela.'

'Alex,' I took a deep breath, 'I had to speak to you before you saw the pictures.'

'Angela, I already saw the pictures, remember?'

Alex said slowly. 'And we were going to talk about it when you get back.'

'Well, yes, but,' I looked back at the computer, 'they were the ones from yesterday.'

'Meaning?'

'There might be some more?'

I sat down on the bed and stared at my toenails. Given that I was only a couple of floors above Hollywood Boulevard at midnight, the room was very quiet. They really should mention that on their website. Total selling point.

'From the same night?'

'No, but I can explain.'

'What site are they on?' Alex asked, his voice completely flat. 'Or is it just all of them again?'

'Alex, please don't look, just let me explain.' I winced at the sound of clicking keys down the line. Of course he was by his computer.

'Gotta say, you look good,' he said eventually. 'And how many guys actually get to see their girlfriends cheat on them in real time? God bless the internet.'

'Alex, just stop.' I stood up; drama always felt more manageable when I was vertical. The carpet was also very soft. Maybe I could get a job as The Hollywood's copywriter after Mary fired me. 'It's not like it looks. James is—'

'Totally out of your league? Yeah, you've done really well there, Angela.' He didn't even sound like my Alex.

'Please stop it and just let me explain.' I tried to find the right words but my head was totally empty.

'What do you want me to say?' At least he was starting to sound a little bit angry now. But it turned out that wasn't as much consolation as I had hoped.

'First there are all these photos of you practically dry-humping the first celebrity you ever meet, then you're not answering your phone, then you're calling me at four in the morning and saying, well, whatever. What am I supposed to think? What do you want me to say?'

'Don't make out like I'm the one who's been ignoring you! I've been trying to talk to you since I got here,' I protested. 'You were the one who didn't want to talk to me. You were the one who wasn't answering his phone.'

'And the fact that I actually have things to do here without you holding my hand means you get to fuck around behind my back?' he yelled.

I almost dropped my phone. 'What?'

'What do you mean what?' he asked. 'One day you're holding hands on the beach, leaving his hotel room in the middle of the night, and the next you're kissing him outside a club? You're gonna tell me there's nothing happening there at all?'

There weren't many times in my life I'd been stunned into silence but they were racking up tonight.

'Tell me you haven't slept with him.' Alex's voice was rough and low. 'Say it. Now.'

'I–I haven't slept with him,' I stuttered. He hadn't asked if I'd thought about it; he'd asked if I'd actually done it. I heard a sigh and more keystrokes. 'Please stop looking at the pictures. I haven't done anything, Alex, I would never. Please just believe me.'

'And that's where we have a problem,' he said quietly. 'I don't think I do believe you.'

My phone was burning hot against my ear but I couldn't put it down. Long after Alex had hung up, I was still standing in the middle of the hotel room, clutching the tiny piece of plastic as it cooled slowly. Did he really just say that? After what seemed like a lifetime, my brain flicked back on and I redialled. There was no way I was leaving it like that. But Alex's phone didn't even ring; instead I got a 'cannot be connected message' right away. I tried again from my room phone just to make sure but it wasn't happening. He must have taken the battery out or something.

I sat down at the desk and flicked through the pictures online. I scrolled through the galleries that had already sprung up across the gossip sites, dedicated to me and James. It was so weird. And not just because most of them were slaughtering my outfits and the size of my arse, although they were all taken from extraordinarily bad angles. Honest. The strangest thing was that to hundreds – if not thousands – of girls around the world, it must look like a dream come true. Ordinary girl is sent to interview hot movie star, hot movie star falls for ordinary girl and whirlwind romance ensues.

It certainly was far more romantic than the truth: ordinary girl is sent to interview hot movie star, falls for hot movie star's clichéd fake flirting, lets hot movie star kiss her then discovers he's gay but is plastered all over the internet, gets dumped by actual love of her life and ends up with no one. Yeah, who was going to pay to read that? Flipping down the lid of my laptop, I wondered if anyone was going to pay to read anything I wrote ever again. Surely this was going to push Mary over the edge. If ever I needed Jenny Lopez, it was now, but she was nowhere to be found. Again. Probably still pissed off after our face-off in Bar Marmont. I stared at my mobile, frustrated. And then almost crapped myself when it started to ring. It was Louisa.

'Hello?' I answered cautiously. A lecture was absolutely guaranteed. Louisa loved to make a drama out of a crisis.

'Hey, Angela!' she chirped. 'I just had to call you. We had the most amazing meal ever last night. We went to that Alta place you told us about, oh my God. I had to call you. There were these prawns, God, honestly.'

I listened to her rapturous restaurant review, silently confused. She wasn't going to even ask about the photos?

'And then we had this cheese thing for dessert. Honestly. Wow. I don't think I can ever eat again. Are you having fun in LA, babe?'

I really didn't know what to say. She didn't know. Louisa had never been much of a one for celebrity gossip, but then before I moved to New York, neither had I. It was hard to avoid it in America.

'Ah, not really,' I said slowly. It was actually very nice not to be shouted at for two minutes. 'I'm having a bit of trouble with the interview. And Alex and I are having a row.'

'Oh honey,' Louisa said down the crackly line. 'What about?'

'He thinks I've cheated on him.' With James Jacobs, I added silently.

'But of course you haven't! You would never do that. Why on earth would he think it?' It was reassuring that, after everything, Louisa would automatically believe I was the wronged party without even getting half the story. But then, she hadn't seen the photos. Or the video on TMZ. Or the E! News bulletin.

'No, I haven't,' I agreed. 'But he's seen a photo that sort of makes it look like I did. And he just doesn't want to listen to me.'

'Oh babe, just let him calm down and then talk to him,' she reasoned. 'I'm sure it will blow over once you're back in New York. Just concentrate on getting your job sorted out.'

'You're probably right,' I said, wishing the issues weren't quite so interwoven. 'Anyway, you didn't call to listen to my problems. I'm really glad you liked Alta.'

'Loved Alta,' she corrected. 'We should definitely go when I come back to visit you.'

'Definitely,' I agreed. Unless I lost my job and my visa and then we'd be going for dinner in Nandos in Wimbledon.

'Call me if you need me, babe, got to run. Love you.' She blew me a kiss down the phone.

'I will, love you too.' I hung up. Well that was weird. But just as weirdly, what she said made sense. I had to concentrate on getting things back on track.

Tomorrow wasn't going to be fun and even less so with the hangover I'd just guaranteed. Flicking on the TV (was *Friends* ever off television?), I pulled my worse-for-wear-but-still-the-best-thing-I'd-ever-owned bag up onto the bed. When everything else was going wrong, at least a girl could still rely on Marc Jacobs to make her smile. Dredging through the crap in the bottom, I eventually found a pen and notepad, scowling at my BlackBerry as it blinked at me.

'Sometimes I just want to write things down, OK?' I told it. Before looking around to check that no one had just seen me go completely insane and talk to a phone. Just Ross and Rachel, thank goodness.

1. Call Mary
2. Call Alex or Alex's friends

That would prove trickier, since the only phone number of any of Alex's friends I had ever had was Jenny's ex, Jeff, and Jenny had made me delete it after a healthy night in our apartment of Ben & Jerry's, red wine, and burning everything he had ever come into contact with, including an old brush they had used to tease their hair for a hilarious Eighties fancy dress party. The brush nearly took the entire apartment block with it when Jenny tossed it in the burning bin. It turned out to be not only disgusting but also a very dangerous fire hazard. But there was a chance I'd written it in the back of my diary – I was just too drunk to work that out at that exact moment.

3. Speak to James

As much as I wanted to just call *The Sun* and tell them that James was as gay as a goose, I just couldn't do it. Damn that stupid misguided sense of dignity. Or was it pride? Or maybe just the idea of me stretched across the front page of the *News of the World* in a pair of La Senza lace shorts with everything padded, pushed and teased under the headline 'James Jacobs's Beard Tells All!' was just too much. Actually, the *News of the World* wouldn't say beard, they'd probably go straight to 'Pathetic fag hag, Angela Clark spills the beans on James Jacobs's late-night gay orgies in Hollywood's public bathrooms . . .' My mother would be so proud.

4. Sort things out with Jenny

It was just too much that things were weird between us, especially with everything else going on, but I had a horrible feeling that things were going to get weirder before they got better. Or was that just a horrible feeling that I was about to throw up? Dropping the pen and pad, I raced to the bathroom to double up over the toilet just in time.

When would I learn?

'Jesus Christ, Angie, what the hell happened to you?'

I woke up slowly, my face cold and seemingly stuck to something hard, a flip-flopped foot in my blurry eye-line. Trying to move my head hurt far too much, and for some reason my left arm was completely paralysed.

'Angie, can you hear me? Did you take something?' The voice carried on but it sounded so far away. 'How long have you been on the bathroom floor?'

Ahh, that made sense, I was still on the bathroom floor. Which was why it was cold. Which was why I couldn't move my arm. Which was why Jenny's feet were almost touching my nose.

'For Christ's sake, Angie, are you thinking your answers instead of saying them again?'

Yes, I thought.

'Mmhuh,' I said.

With the help of Jenny and a towel rail not meant to be used to hoist ten stone of incredibly hungover girl up off the floor, I was soon sitting, or slumped, on the toilet seat. I readily accepted the glass of water she held out to me, not bothering that it came from the bathroom tap, and glugged it down. Which was my first mistake.

After I'd thrown the first glass of water up, I slowly sipped a second, Jenny shaking her head at me from the edge of the bath.

'I cannot believe you, Angie.' She pushed my hair back off my face. 'What happened after I left?'

'What happened?' I closed my eyes again. It didn't help. 'You want to know what happened?'

'Yeah,' Jenny said, taking my empty glass and refilling it from the bath tap. Was it weird that it tasted like heaven? 'I mean last night. What happened to "I would never cheat on Alex, even if we're on a break?"'

'I remember, I wasn't that drunk,' I replied, despite the fact that that was clearly a lie. 'What are you talking about?'

'The photos of you and James?' Jenny gave me her 'duh' face. 'The ones that Erin and Vanessa and Gina all emailed over today? I kinda didn't expect you to be here. Did he leave already or did you just come back to the hotel after you did the deed?'

'Oh my God.' I suddenly felt very, very sick again. 'It's so not what you think.'

'You didn't, did you?' Jenny asked, her annoyingly healthy face lit up like Christmas.

'Jenny, he's gay,' I said into the palms of my hands. She scoffed. 'If he said no, you can just say so.'

I looked up, my attractive white pallor apparently adding to my serious face.

'No. Way.'

'Yes.'

'No. Way.'

'With Blake.'

'Really? That's hot.'

'Missing the point entirely, Jenny.' I pulled a flannel from the towel rail, ran it under the cold water and pressed it against my face. 'What am I going to do?'

'Well, you're gonna take a shower first,' Jenny said, standing up and pulling the shower curtain across behind her. 'Then you're going to explain to me every last little detail of how you uncovered this juicy, potentially financially rewarding piece of gossip, and then you're coming with me to go shopping for Tessa DiArmo's award show tonight.'

'You're seriously doing that?' I asked, peeling off my sweaty dress and stepping into the shower. Ahh, the sweet relief of running water.

'Don't ever doubt me, Angela Clark,' Jenny called, closing the bathroom door. 'Get your ass clean and be downstairs in ten minutes.'

Ten minutes was always going to be a stretch but, fifteen minutes later, I emerged from the lift with a very roughly blow-dried bob, hastily applied make-up and my satchel thrown across my body. Jenny looked my jeans and T-shirt up and down and sighed.

'That's so not the ensemble to be photographed in, honey,' she said, wrapping her arm around my shoulders and guiding me out to the car. 'Where's the big hat? The dark glasses?'

I pulled my sunglasses triumphantly out of my handbag. 'I'm wearing the exact same outfit as you,' I protested. But of course I wasn't. My baggy boyfriend jeans and little pink American Apparel T-shirt couldn't compare with Jenny's skintight Sevens and clingy, white, deep V-neck. At least our black Havaianas were identical.

We picked up iced coffees en route, me thankful for any reason to get out of the car-slash-death-trap, Jenny ecstatic to be able to demonstrate her ability to sip a Frapuccino whilst driving, and I filled Jenny in on the James/Blake situation. Once I'd finished the story for the third time, I tilted my head back and stared up at the beautiful blue, cloudless sky. At least if I looked up there, I couldn't see Jenny running red lights.

'So what are you going to do?' Jenny asked, swerving around a tight corner onto Melrose Avenue. 'Did you make everything OK with Alex? Did you speak to Mary?'

'I spoke to Alex but it didn't go that well.' And that's putting it mildly, I added to myself. 'I have to call Mary but I've been sort of putting it off. I'm guessing the fact that she hasn't called me yet is not a good sign.'

'It all sounds pretty clear to me, honey,' Jenny said, swinging the car into a car park beside a building that seemed to be covered in grass. 'You just have to tell her the truth. It's just gonna sort this whole thing out.'

'I know but, well, actually, I don't know . . .' I pulled my frizzy hair into a loose ponytail and wrapped a band around it. 'I can't just out him, can I? Obviously he's hiding it all for a reason.'

Jenny stopped the car with a jolt. 'Are you fucking with me?'

'Jenny—'

'This ass-hat makes out with you in public, allows photos of the two of you to be published all over the internet, effectively destroys your relationship and costs you your job and you don't want to casually drop into conversation that he's the new Clay Aiken?'

I wrinkled my nose. 'Yeah, well.'

'Great argument,' she climbed out over the locked car door.

'They do open, you know,' I grumbled. 'Where are we anyway?'

'And I thought I'd made a shopper out of you.' Jenny held her arms out in a flourish. 'This, my British friend, is Fred Segal. Fashion emporium and Los Angeles institution. And where we're meeting Teresa inside in a half-hour, so we need to get our shit together.'

'Tessa's really coming?' I asked, pulling off my sunglasses and following Jenny past a row of tables and chairs, already packed with pretty people. 'Jenny, that's incredible.'

'I know, crazy right?' Jenny smiled and nodded at the man holding open the door for us. 'She texted me this morning to say she'd meet us here. Daphne is going to freak out when she finds out. Tessa DiArmo is a big get for a stylist.'

'I'm sure she'll be happy for you,' I lied. 'Where did she go, anyway?'

'Uh, she went home with that guy she was . . . talking to,' she muttered into a clothes rail.

The store appeared to be split into lots of different little sections but, unsurprisingly, Jenny knew exactly where she was going. It was as if she had inbuilt shopping GPS: I was fairly sure I could drop her in any major shopping capital in the world and she'd be able to find the nearest Starbucks, bathroom and Marc Jacobs concession. It was a talent I very much hoped to develop when I grew up.

'Well, if she'd stayed maybe she would be styling Tessa,' I said in my least judgemental voice. Which was still fairly judgey. 'But anyway, I wanted to talk about last night. About what you said before you . . . left.'

'I called ahead to set up a room for Tessa DiArmo?' Jenny confidently accosted a passing salesgirl. 'Can you please make sure that it's ready? We're going to be sending things over soon. Thanks.'

The girl looked us up and down once, nodded and then rushed off to the back of the store. Jenny kept her back to me.

'Do you think this would suit Tessa?' She held out a Twenty8Twelve T-shirt dress. 'Too casual for an awards show, though, right? But maybe with heels and the right jacket . . .'

'Jenny, you realize I'm not going to let this go, don't you?' I said, pushing the dress away. 'What you said last night? And no, it wouldn't suit Tessa. It would suit me though.'

She tossed the dress towards me. 'I have to find like ten outfits before Tessa gets here, so can we not do this now?'

'We are doing it now; you do your clearest thinking when you're shopping.' I passed the dress on to the assistant that had appeared back at Jenny's side. 'I thought this trip was all about you getting laid. What's happened with Joe?'

'Turns out maybe it wasn't as easy as I'd thought.

215

Or at least he isn't any more,' she said, turning her attention to a grey strapless Hache mini-dress. 'The folds on this are really interesting. This could look gorgeous with – like – a little leather jacket and some chunky heels?'

'Yes, it would,' I agreed, passing it to the assistant at her elbow. 'So that's the problem? Joe? Because you could get men loads better than Joe, you know.'

'Yeah, for sure. Except it turns out maybe I don't want to. What about this?' She pulled out a gold sequined tank dress.

'Jeff?'

'Jeff.'

'Oh, Jenny.'

I watched her lips press into thin, colourless lines as she systematically flicked through the rail of clothes in front of her, from left to right.

'I'm gonna get you guys some water,' the salesgirl said eventually, backing away from the awkward silence. I nodded and smiled as she scuttled away.

'You know, I'm not the best person to be giving out relationship advice, but you will get over it eventually. That is actually a fact. And I'm pretty sure one you told me once,' I picked out a red Hervé Léger number and held it up to Jenny. 'I wish you'd just talked to me about this. Practise what you preach and all that?'

'Yeah, except I'm not that good at taking my own advice,' she said, nodding at the red dress. 'He's moving in with his new girlfriend, you know? He called me to tell me in case I found out from Alex. I guess, even after everything, I really thought we were supposed to end up together. Now I'm not so sure.'

'This new girlfriend could be a total rebound thing,' I suggested. 'You don't know.'

'I'm not sure any more.' She finally turned around.

Silent tears tracked down her face. 'Maybe I need to get away for a while. Jeff is everywhere at home, I just can't move on.'

'You're thinking about leaving? New York?' I didn't know what to do.

'Maybe. For a while. I don't know.' She took my hand. 'Angie, I really want today to go good. Can we just talk about this later? I don't want to be all blah when Tessa gets here.'

'Of course,' I said, giving her a quick but tight hug. 'But as soon as you're done and you're ready, we'll talk. Dinner?'

She nodded quickly. 'Definitely dinner; but please don't freak out, honey, there isn't anything to talk about yet. And we've still got a world of trouble to get you out of.'

I pulled a face. 'Do you know, for five very short minutes, I'd almost forgotten about all that?'

Jenny laughed. 'Good luck with that.'

'I'm going to try and give Alex another call.' I pulled a silver puffball dress off the rail and passed it to her. 'Get her to try this on. I'll be back in a minute.'

Fred Segal was like a very fashionable labyrinth. Each little salon led into another dead end, a cul-de-sac of couture. Eventually, I followed the sunlight out to the door we'd come in and managed to snag a table in the café. Holding my phone to my ear, I closed my eyes. All I needed to do was press one button. Instead I ordered a smoothie. And checked my emails. And looked at Perez Hilton on my BlackBerry. I just didn't know what to say to him. Last night's call was so awful, I didn't see how I could salvage things over the phone and, after seeing the look in Jenny's eyes, seeing how broken she was at the realization that she'd never be able to make it work with Jeff, the prospect of losing Alex for good was painfully real.

When my phone actually rang, I answered automatically, and even though I must have pressed a button to connect it, I was still surprised.

'Angela? It's James.'

And immediately I wished I hadn't.

'Angela, are you there?' He did not sound good.

'Clearly I am,' I replied, frozen to the spot.

'Are you OK? Where are you?'

'I'm fine actually,' I said. 'I'm just waiting to go on the Ryan Seacrest show to out you. Then I'm going on E! News.'

'Please, I really want to sort this out,' he said hurriedly. 'Please don't go on air.'

I sat and looked around the café. I was getting the odd look but most people were trying very hard to look as interested as possible in nothing at all.

'As much as that's what you deserve, you can calm down,' I sighed. 'I'm not going on the radio to out you. I'm just wandering up and down Melrose handing out flyers. I like the personal touch. Much more effective.'

'You're on Melrose? Will you come to the hotel? We really need to talk,' he rushed.

'We really don't,' I replied evenly. I was so incredibly angry with him; just hearing his voice focused my mind completely. It was a much easier emotion to manage than the big ball of blah that took over when I tried to think about Alex. 'There's no way on God's green earth I'm coming over to your hotel.'

'But if we meet outside the hotel, we're going to get photographed,' James said. 'I thought—'

'I've been told that you're not good at thinking.' I slurped my smoothie. It really was delicious. 'I'm not

218

coming to your hotel. I'm calling my editor and telling her everything and then I'm going back to New York to attempt to salvage my relationship.'

'Angela, please, if you say anything to your editor they'll out me.'

'I really don't give a shit.'

'Please Angela,' he whined. 'It's everything. Everything I've ever worked for. Please don't do it.'

'It's not my problem, James.' No time to be weak now. So what if I outed him? And destroyed his career? And ruined his life? Meh. 'I've got my own concerns. I'm going to have to make my money somehow given that you've probably cost me my job.'

'Come off it, you're not a kiss-and-tell girl,' James stammered. 'Just come and meet me. Please? We'll meet anywhere you like. We'll work out how to save your job and everything, but please just don't say anything to the magazine. Not yet.'

I should have just hung up. I should have direct-dialled the *News of the World* and told them to get the La Senza matching set out. But I didn't. 'Where?'

'Definitely not the hotel?'

'Definitely not the hotel. The opposite of a hotel. As far away from a bed as humanly possible. The most public place on earth would be preferable.'

'Disneyland?'

'You're not kidding, are you?' I realized I was holding my empty smoothie glass against the edge of the table at a dangerously smash-and-slash angle. And the couple sitting next to me were looking awfully nervous. 'No, I don't think The Magic Kingdom is going to be able to sort this, James.'

'It is the happiest place on earth.' I could hear a hint of a smile in his voice. How dare he think he was off the hook with this?

'And I would hate to get blood on those character costumes. I bet they're a bitch to get dry cleaned.'

'Right, OK,' he said, considerably less pleased with himself. 'You're on Melrose? And you want to meet somewhere without any even vaguely sexual connotations. Where are you exactly? I'm sending a car.'

'Fred Segal.' I placed the glass back on the table and put my hands in my lap, offering an 'I'm not crazy, honest' smile to the people beside me, but they were too busy tapping away on their BlackBerrys and Sidekicks to acknowledge my sanity.

'Because that's the place to keep a low profile,' he said. 'Bumped into Paris yet?'

'Do you want me to come or not?' I snapped. Seriously, how come no one looked over when I was trying to be nice but as soon as I raised my voice, I had everyone's undivided attention? 'And there's no way it's just me and you. Blake comes too.'

'Oh, Angela, I don't think so,' James said quickly. 'He's really not in a very good mood.'

'And he'll be in a better mood if I out the pair of you?'

Silence.

Sighing.

'Fine. Just stay there and I'll send the car.'

Hanging up, I pulled out my make-up bag. Wherever James went, so went the paps. Things were already bad enough without my under-eye circles making the news. I stared at myself in the mirror of my powder compact. How bizarre was this? How did I manage to go from not being able to get served in the Slug and Lettuce in Wimbledon without shouting at a barmaid, to having to worry about whether or not I was going to end up on the gossip page of some tabloid with big red circles drawn all over my many, many imperfections? All I wanted was to crawl into bed and not come back out until all this had gone away. Maybe I'd come out for Christmas dinner but then I'd be going right back in.

Bags banished and blusher blended, I took a deep breath. Time to bite the bullet.

'Mary Stein's office.'

'Hi Cici,' I said bravely. 'Is Mary about?'

'Oh, Angela,' Cici managed to stretch out my name to last about three minutes. She must have been loving this. 'I'm not sure she's gonna be able to speak to you right now. She's on a conference call with the publisher. You know, because of you.'

'Right, well, it's really important,' I said through gritted teeth. This bit was even worse than actually talking to Mary. 'Can you try and put me through?'

'Uh-huh.' The glee in her voice was unbearable. 'But if she can't talk to you right now, I can fill you in on what I've heard so far. You know, about you.'

'Appreciated. Can you please just try and put me through?'

The hold music kicked in for what felt like forever.

'Well?'

'Oh, Mary,' I was a little bit surprised. Mainly because I didn't think Cici was even going to try and put me through, since she clearly really wanted to tell me all the lovely things that were being said about me in the office. 'Hi.'

'No, not hi, well?' Mary sounded livid. Even though I couldn't see her, I knew I'd got her full attention, which wasn't ever a good thing. Mary was much less frightening if she was clicking away on her giant Mac while she was talking to you. 'You realize you have fucked up on a massive, massive scale?'

'Mary, please just let me get this out. I know it looks bad—' I started.

'Looks bad?' she interrupted before I'd even finished my first sentence. 'It is bad. You're absolutely over.'

'Mary, please,' There wasn't enough blusher in the world to put the colour back in my cheeks. 'Let me finish. I know exactly what it looks like, but it isn't. There's nothing going on with James. And seriously, I have the best interview. I'm sure once you get my copy . . . once everyone sees my copy, they're going to love it. And James is going to do the photo shoot. It can be saved, can't it?'

'Angela, I think the sun has fried your brain. Do you really think the magazine wants to publish your interview right now? You're splashed all over the internet as a two-timing star-fucker. We'd get more readers for an interview with your ex right now.'

'Jesus, will everyone stop saying he's my ex?' I groaned. 'I haven't bloody done anything.'

'Unless you're gonna take an internal exam live on TV to prove you're still a virgin, I don't think anyone's going to believe that,' Mary replied. 'Or maybe you could do it on the radio. I'm pretty sure they did that on the *Howard Stern Show* once.'

'Mary, honestly, you work in the media. How can you believe the internet over me?' I was determined not to cry. Not here.

'I learned not to believe everything I read a long time ago.' Mary relented slightly. 'But it doesn't matter what I believe. People don't care about what's true and what isn't; they care about being entertained, they care about who has the best story. And your interview with James isn't the best story any more. You are.'

'I'm not a story,' I said quietly. 'I'm just me.'

'Well, I'm telling you what the publisher told me,'

she went on. 'So don't flip out on me. It's like this. The blog is suspended for a couple of days. We're not taking it down; we just need to decide what direction we're going in.'

'I don't understand, direction?' I wasn't quick on the uptake at the best of times. 'It's just my blog. My diary.'

'It is right now,' Mary agreed. 'But there's been a massive spike in traffic since yesterday, and obviously the new readers want all the details about you and James. But the publishers don't want to give that away for free online.'

'And there aren't any details for them,' I said.

'OK, Pollyanna, have you finished?' She didn't wait for a response. 'The publishers want your exclusive story – either you and James or just you in next week's issue of *Icon* – and then they want to change the direction of the blog to fit your new . . . status.'

'But Mary, it's not like that.' This wasn't happening.

'This is the best offer you're going to get, Angela,' Mary said. 'If you don't play it their way, you're out.'

'What am I supposed to do? It's not true. And what about Alex? I have to sort things out with him, Mary, and there's no hope in hell of that if I'm mincing around in a magazine declaring my love for James.'

'How are you going to sort things out with him from the UK?' Mary asked. 'Because if you lose your job here, you know you lose your visa.'

'You're blackmailing me?'

'Angela, honey,' Mary sighed. 'This isn't a game. If you say you're not with James, I believe you, but this has happened now. It's not about the truth, it's not about you; right now it's about what sells magazines. An interview with you and James in *Icon* will sell more magazines than an interview with James in *The Look*. And a blog about you as a celebrity's girlfriend will be

223

more popular than a blog about your life in New York. You're not stupid, you must be able to understand that.'

I paused. It was everything I could do not to be sick on the spot. Maybe losing my visa was the best option. I could just go home. Pretend none of this had ever happened.

Unless I had another story. One that was far more interesting and a whole lot more exclusive.

'Mary, I can prove that I'm not sleeping with James,' I started slowly. 'But I can't tell you why just yet. How long do I have to sort something out?'

'For fuck's sake, Angela, I know this is shitty but will you just get over this? They're going to run something whether you're part of it or not,' Mary barked. 'I'm trying to help you out by giving you some control.'

'Fine,' I breathed out for the first time in what felt like hours. 'If I can't sort this out I'll do the interview. Please, Mary, please just hold it off until the end of today, and if I can't work it out, I'll do whatever you want. Photos, interviews; everything. Me and James.'

'You've got until the end of today,' Mary said quietly. 'I'll be in my office. Call me when you've got the loaves and the fishes.'

'Loaves and fishes?'

'Angela, you're going to need a miracle.'

224

CHAPTER TWELVE

It took me fifteen minutes to find Jenny, and that was with the help of three assistants. Seriously, that shop was designed solely to keep the uninitiated out. Eventually, I spotted her holding up a tiny leather tuxedo-style jacket next to a silver sequined shrug. Her face fell when she saw me coming towards her.

'I like the leather,' I pointed.

'You look like living shit, what happened?' she asked, dropping both jackets on the floor and gently taking my shoulders. 'You OK?'

'Thanks,' I breathed. It was still a struggle not to vomit on the spot. 'I just spoke to Mary.'

'That bad?' Jenny winced. 'Angie, you gotta just tell them the truth.'

'Who would believe it? Really?' I shook my head. 'I'm going to sort it out though, don't worry. Just meet me for dinner tonight.'

'Yeah, sure,' Jenny agreed, scooping up the discarded jackets. 'Where are you going?'

'I'm meeting James,' I said.

Jenny stared at me. 'Have you lost your mind? Give me that frickin' phone. I'm calling your editor right now.

No, I'm calling Erin, she's in PR and has hooked up with just about everyone. She'll know what to do.'

'Jenny, please, don't. Just let me have today to sort this all out. Please let me try? If I can't, we'll do it your way.' And Mary's way and James's way and everyone's way but mine, I thought.

Jenny stood pouting, not even slightly convinced.

'You've got Tessa to worry about,' I reminded her.

'Who's worrying about me – why?' asked a little tiny voice behind me. I turned to see Tessa DiArmo in the gold sequined dress I'd given Jenny, huge chunky leather heeled shoes and a studded cuff. She looked amazing.

'Wow.' I was stunned. Her legs seemed to go on forever and the gold brought out highlights in her hair that I hadn't seen before. 'Tessa, you look incredible.'

'Put this on,' Jenny said, passing her the leather jacket. 'It'll give the *paillettes* a tougher edge.'

'*Paillettes?*' I mouthed.

'Big-ass sequins,' Jenny explained. 'It's fashion-speak, designed to make you feel dumb.'

'I love it,' Tessa said, spinning around and making the sequins or, *paillettes*, dance in the sunlight. 'I'm absolutely wearing this tonight.'

'Fantastic.' Jenny's face lit up. I hadn't seen her look that happy since Ryan Phillippe had checked into The Union last October and she'd 'accidentally' taken his unrequested complimentary welcome basket up while he was in the shower. 'Now go try on the Léger.'

'I'm too skinny for Léger,' Tessa whined, heading back into the tiny room. 'He makes me look like a toothpick.'

'That's why you're trying on the bustier style, it'll give you the illusion of curves,' Jenny yelled through the door. 'No jewellery and go with the strappy

Louboutins. Oh, and try the leather jacket with that one too.'

'Jenny, you're really good at this,' I said, catching her off guard with a side hug. 'She looks amazing.'

'I know, right?' She flushed and hugged me back. 'And it's so much fun. I'm shopping with someone else's credit card, telling them what to do and they're listening *and* paying me for it. I think they call it "living the dream".'

'Yay you.' I felt my phone vibrate in my pocket. The car must have arrived. 'Look, I'm going to go. You have fun and I'll call you later.'

'As long as you know I'm not happy about this,' she yelled as I walked away. 'You tell that dick that I'm going to beat his ass when I next see him.'

James had clearly decided it wasn't safe to be in the car with me and had sent his driver alone. I couldn't help but wonder about all the things he had seen, all the things he must know. James must be paying him a fortune not to spill it all. That, or he was actually a decent person. Wow, I did not love the fact that the idea of him just being a good person was my second thought.

We drove south in silence for about ten minutes before pulling up outside what looked like a park. A park with an animatronic mammoth sinking into a pool of stinking black goo.

'Here?' I asked the driver, trying to spot James and Blake. And there they were, sitting on a bench just inside the gate.

'Here,' he confirmed, turning off the engine. 'Try not to push them in.'

The pair of them stood when they saw me walking across the grass. I stopped short of the hug that James offered and folded my arms, mirroring Blake's barely restrained fury. Who thought we would ever have something in common?

'Tar pits?' I asked, looking around at the groups of tiny school children running around us. They were too tiny and high on being out of the classroom to recognize or care about James, but their teachers were all trying very hard not to stare.

'No one's going to think we're shagging round the back of a museum, are they?' James shrugged. 'There are children everywhere and, you know, tar isn't exactly an aphrodisiac.'

'Whatever.' I tried to prepare myself. This wasn't going to be easy and I hadn't reckoned on my resolve weakening on seeing how awful James looked. Well, awful for James. His hair was rumpled and his dark circles were as pronounced as mine, but he still looked as though he was just playing the part of heartbreak, while I looked more like Amy Winehouse after a particularly bad night out. And even if he looked like shit, he still smelt awfully pretty. 'Can we just get this over with?'

Blake led the way and past the tar pits to a large deserted expanse of park around the back of the museum. He leaned against what was, according to a small inscription on its base, a plastic sculpture of a giant prehistoric sloth and looked the other way. James sighed and sat down on the grass a few feet from him. I looked from one to the other. Blake's face was frozen, impossible to read. Maybe James's lack of sleep was down to more than just worrying about what I might say or do.

'Angela,' James started, pulling at my hand. I sat down beside him, not really knowing what else to do. 'First, can I just say I'm sorry?'

'You've actually said that a couple of times already,' I said, my eyes still trained on Blake. 'And I think it's best if I talk first. Sorry if you'd been rehearsing.'

'Go for it,' he said, squeezing the hand I'd forgotten he was holding.

'I spoke to my editor this morning.' I pulled my hand away and paused to see his reaction. Stupid bloody actor didn't bloody have one. He should absolutely play professional poker. 'The magazine doesn't want to run your interview any more.'

'What?' He looked shocked. 'What did you say?'

'Calm down, I didn't tell them anything. Yet . . .' I noticed we'd almost got Blake's attention. 'They want us to do a "we're so in love" interview in *Icon* next week instead. Apparently, I'm no good as an interviewer any more because everyone thinks I'm a great big slag who came out here solely to seduce you.'

'Seriously?' James shook his head.

'Seriously.'

'Well, thank fuck for that,' he laughed, pushing me back in a giant bear hug. Too shocked to do anything but worry about grass stains on my T-shirt, I lay staring helplessly up at Blake.

'That's brilliant!' James roared. 'This is going to solve all our problems. We'll do the interview, you'll move here, everyone will think we're dating. This is perfect. We'll get an apartment – how about Los Feliz? You liked it there, didn't you? Or would you rather be near the beach? Oh, Angela, this is fantastic. Why didn't you tell me on the phone?'

Finally finding some strength, I pushed him off me and shot up to my feet. 'Because we're not doing it! I have a life and a job and a boyfriend and I'm not giving that up to cover up for you.'

'But it'll be perfect.' James looked confused. 'I'll pay

for everything. And you'll have your own room in the apartment and everything. It's not like we'll really be dating after all, is it?'

'Can you hear yourself? I'm not doing this, James. You have to tell the magazine the truth.' I span round to Blake. 'And you, you can't seriously be OK with this?'

He shrugged but his face was ashen, eyes burning. And, oh my God, were they red around the edges? Had he been crying?

'Angela, do you think this is the first time this has happened?' James jumped to his feet, his hands on my shoulders. 'We get on well, don't we? We're friends? And it would be great for your career. Think of how cool it will be, living in LA, in the sun, going to parties, premieres – it would be a dream.'

'But not mine,' I shrugged off his hands. 'James, listen to me. I have a life. I have a boyfriend. And if you don't come out, tell the truth, I'm going to lose it all. If we're really friends, you'll do it.'

James rubbed his hands down his face. 'You don't even know what you're asking. You're being so bloody selfish.'

'*I'm* being selfish? You don't actually know anything about women, do you?' I snapped.

'Doesn't know much about men either,' Blake muttered.

I carried on regardless. 'All I'm asking you to do is to tell the truth and you're asking me to lie and give up absolutely everything. Which sounds more reasonable to you?'

James threw his hands up in the air. 'But think about what I'm offering you. You'd pass all that up for some arsehole that thinks you're shagging about behind his back and a crappy job writing for a website?'

I'd been angry before. I was pretty pissed off when my mum boil-washed my Bay Trading angora sweater dress the night before the Year Ten disco. I was fairly annoyed when Peter Jenson told everyone in the sixth form that I was a lesbian after he walked into the bathroom at Louisa's sixteenth birthday party and we were in there chatting while I had a wee. And, of course, I wasn't overly pleased when I found my boyfriend shagging his mistress in the back of our car at my best friend's wedding. But none of that was anything to how I felt at that exact second.

There he was, this ridiculously beautiful man who had everything going right for him in the world, standing in front of me waving around what he genuinely thought was the perfect life, like the moon on a stick, while his secret boyfriend stood six feet away, leaning against a giant brown plastic mammal. And *I* was being selfish? No wonder Blake was such a twat all the time. His boyfriend was the biggest arsehole in the universe and he couldn't complain about him to anyone.

'Do you love Blake?' I asked.

'What?' James looked past me to where Blake was staring at us from the arms of the sloth.

'Do you love him?' I asked again.

'Angela, just stop playing games. Are you going to fuck me over or what?'

I ignored him and carried on. 'Because I actually love my boyfriend and the idea of him not knowing that for sure is actually worse than any of this bollocks right now.'

As soon as I'd said it, I knew it was absolutely true. I couldn't get the look on Jenny's face when she talked about Jeff out of my head, and I didn't want to ever feel that way about me and Alex. 'I don't believe that you two are in love. If you were, you wouldn't care who knew, you'd just want to be together.'

'As if it's that easy,' James snapped back. 'I'm not some random guy that can just do whatever he wants when I want, Angela. My career depends on my reputation. It's all a character, everything I do.'

'Oh shut up. It's not the Fifties any more, you idiot.' I took my turn to push him; unfortunately his six-foot-plus frame didn't actually budge. 'No one cares if you're gay.'

'It wasn't the Fifties when I was growing up either, but they cared then,' he fumed quietly. 'I'm not doing it, so just pack it in. Blake understands why we have to do things the way we do.'

'Do I?'

For the first time I realized Blake wasn't leaning against the (actually hilarious in any other situation) giant sloth because he was too cool to stand up, he actually couldn't stand on his own. His eyes were no longer a little bit red around the edges but wet with real tears.

'Do I, James?' he asked again. I suddenly felt extraordinarily uncomfortable. Oh bugger.

'We talked about this last night,' James said, in a considerably softer tone of voice than the one he'd been using with me. 'You said—'

'No, you talked about it last night.' Blake's voice got louder as James's got quieter. 'And I didn't say anything, but I'm saying something now. Bitch's right. There's no need for all this bullshit any more. I know you had a hard time when you were younger but it's over. You're here now and you've got me. If you felt the same way I did, none of the rest of it would matter.'

I paused in my steady backtracking out of the way. Did Blake just call me a bitch? Arse, I was on his side!

'Blake, don't.' James's pretty face was dangerously close to crumpling. I swapped positions with Blake, him holding James's shoulders, me clutching the oversized paw of the sloth. He looked fascinated by the proceedings. For a giant, infamously lazy plastic creature.

'Don't what? You remember when you asked me not to make you choose and I said I never would?' Blake placed a hand against James's cheek. 'Well, I changed my mind. I'm asking. In fact I'm telling. If you do this interview with her, I'm gone. Call me when you've made up your mind. Or don't. I won't be at the hotel when you get back.'

We watched Blake stalk across the park and out of sight before James turned to me.

'Drama,' I said, raising my eyebrows.

'Is it too early for a drink?' James asked, holding out his hand.

I hesitated before I took it. He looked exactly how I felt. He looked exactly like Jenny had that morning. He looked heartbroken.

'It's a bit early,' I said, slapping his hand away and walking on ahead. 'But that's never stopped me before.'

After our third block of driving in silence, I fished my phone out of my bag and willed it to ring.

'Oh, just call him,' James said without turning to look at me. 'It's like looking at puppies in the window of a pet shop. I can see your reflection in the window.'

I smiled tightly and speed-dialled Alex, but it still didn't connect, no answer phone, no anything.

'Hold this,' I said, passing James my phone and emptying my handbag out onto the car seat. I knew it was in there somewhere.

'Good God woman, how much crap have you got in

that handbag?' he asked as I sifted through Post-it notes, loose dollar bills and chewing gum wrappers. 'I've seen apartments with less stuff in them.'

'I know, I know,' I said, shaking out an address book for loose entries. 'I promised myself when I got this bag that I'd look after it but, well, I'm just a bit rubbish.'

'Wait until I see Marc next and tell him what you've done to his bag,' James tutted, sorting through assorted tampons and lip glosses. 'He'll be disgusted.'

'You know Marc Jacobs?' I froze mid-dig. 'You actually know him?'

'I did some ads for him,' James nodded. 'He's cool.'

'Keeping that from me until now is officially the shittiest thing you've done,' I said, unfurling a screwed-up bit of old receipt from the back of my diary. 'Got it.'

Before I could regret it, I dialled.

'Jeff, it's Angela. Clark. Alex's girlfriend? Jenny's friend?' I said quickly before he could even speak.

'Yeah, I actually had you at Angela,' Jeff replied. 'What's up?'

'Uh, well, I was wondering if you knew if Alex was in?' I stammered. 'He's not answering his phone and well, I'm not in the city. Is he about?'

'He's not, no. He didn't tell you where he went?' Jeff sounded surprised. At least it seemed as if there was one person in the world who hadn't heard all about my 'Angela's Adventures in Hollywoodland'. It was just unfortunate that it was my best friend's ex-boyfriend who I was absolutely forbidden to speak to ever again. 'Hey, uh, how's Jenny doing?'

'He went somewhere?' I leaned forward, resting my forehead on my knees.

'Yeah,' Jeff replied. 'He came over last night and asked me to keep an eye on his place. He had a bag, seemed in a rush to get someplace. So, she's OK?'

'What? Oh, Jenny, yes,' I lied. 'She's fantastic actually.'

'Cool, tell her I said hi,' Jeff said. 'OK, well, when he comes back, I'll tell him you called? Bye.'

'Shit,' I said, sinking back against the car seat. I felt as though I'd been kicked.

'Bad news?' James asked.

'Until you say "Angela, I'd like you to organize my coming out interview in as public a forum as possible," I think everything is going to be bad news.' I frowned at him. 'Don't think you're forgiven because your boyfriend dumped you. We're not even yet.'

'Tell me about Alex,' James said, sliding his arm around my shoulders. It was weird how quickly that had gone from stomach-flippingly exciting to stomach-churningly irritating. 'Tell me why he's worth all this.'

'This isn't all about him,' I said. 'This is about you not being an arse and giving me my life back. I only just got one, for God's sake, it's hardly bloody fair that I should lose it so quickly.'

'Just shut up and tell me about him.'

'Fine. Alex is . . .' I didn't know where to start. 'He's kind, intelligent, he's sweet, he's thoughtful, creative—'

'You haven't mentioned hot yet. Or good in bed. Come on, you're not describing him to your mum.' James slapped my knee. 'Sorry, carry on.'

I gave him as filthy a look as I could muster. 'He's just . . . he's passionate about things. About his music, about me. That's what was missing from my life for so long. Passion. Passion for something, anything really.'

'I know this isn't going to make me popular,' James said. 'But you know they say passion doesn't last? They say that for a reason. You can't seriously be asking me to throw my entire career down the shitter because you really like doing it with a boy in a band.'

Just when I thought we were making headway.

'Passionate, not passion – there's a difference; and besides, that's not everything. I love him because he makes me feel like I can do anything. He makes me feel like the person I want to be.' I tilted my head to one side. 'I feel so sorry for Blake.'

'What's that supposed to mean?'

'Don't you feel the same way about him?' I asked.

James didn't say anything.

'Excuse me,' I leaned forward to speak to James's driver, 'could we please head back to The Hollywood?'

'Yes ma'am,' he nodded curtly.

James gave me a sideways glance and sighed.

'So are you going to do it or not?' I asked finally, as we pulled up outside my hotel.

'You still don't get what you're asking me,' James shook his head. 'There's so much more riding on this than your boyfriend.'

'I know,' I said. 'There's my job, my visa, my apartment, my reputation, the respect of my family and friends. Oh, and your boyfriend.'

'Don't think this is easy for me,' he closed his big blue eyes, the hollows underneath looking more pronounced in the dim light of the limo. 'But, I'm sorry, I can't do it.'

It took all my strength to push open the car door and step out on to the pavement. I really had thought he would come through, if not for me then for Blake. The limo pulled away quickly before I could get back in and beg James to change his mind, leaving me standing alone in the street.

Not knowing what else to do, I dialled Jenny. When it went straight through to her voicemail for the fourth time, I gave up. There was no point calling Alex again and Mary didn't want to hear anything I had to say unless it was 'can't wait to whore myself all over *Icon* next week'. And as much as that was looking pretty inevitable, I just couldn't bring myself to make the call.

I forced myself through the twilight of The Hollwood's lobby and into the lift. The gold-tinted walls softened my reflection, but even the tiny security camera in the ceiling could see how pathetic I looked. My hair had frizzed out in the humidity and all the make-up I'd plastered on in Fred Segal had melted or been silently cried off in the last three minutes. I wasn't sure it would be good or bad to see Alex at that exact second. He'd see what a mess I was in, but he'd also see what a mess I was. Not exactly love-of-his-life material. Why hadn't I just told him I loved him? Why hadn't I said it at Erin's wedding? Or befo   re I left for the airport? There had been so many opportunities.

Exhausted, I crashed through my bedroom door, pulled the curtains closed on the Hollywood Hills and rolled onto my bed. Nothing to do now but wait for Mary to call with the bad news.

CHAPTER THIRTEEN

I woke up a little bit disoriented, the seams of my jeans sticking into my legs, but it only took a couple of seconds and a quick look at the bedside clock to remind me why I was in bed on a Wednesday afternoon. It was six in LA, nine in New York. Time was up. There was no way now to sort things out before Mary agreed to the *Icon* interview and Jenny took over as my personal kiss-and-tell stylist. At least I might look half decent in the photos that would be ruining my life next Tuesday. I did need a new Facebook profile picture.

One of my favourite things about staying in good hotels was their 'don't ask, don't tell' policies. Even though housekeeping had replaced several vomit-tinged towels from the bathroom floor, they had happily restocked the mini-bar. In fact, there might have actually been more vodka in there than yesterday. Clutching my mobile, I sat cross-legged in front of the fridge. For the want of a better plan, I mixed a vodka Diet Coke and drank it down in one. And mixed another. And drank it down.

After making it through the rest of the vodka, the gin and the white wine, I grabbed hold of the counter and pulled myself up. Hmm. Too drunk to stand up easily without support, but not drunk enough to move on to the Jack Daniel's miniatures. I slicked on some lip gloss and changed my T-shirt quickly before grabbing my room key and barrelling through the door. There really was only one place to go in times of trouble. The place where everybody knew your name.

'Angela?'

Of course, in this instance, there was only one person who knew my name and that was Joe. But a bar was a bar and a drink was a drink.

'Hey,' I said, dropping onto a stool in front of him. The pool bar was practically empty, sun-worshipping hotel guests gone in to get ready for the night ahead, local party-ers not even nearly ready to come out yet. 'How are you?'

'Uh, I'm OK,' Joe replied, not looking convinced that the same could be said for me. 'So what's going on with you?'

'Fucking. Nothing,' I said, bashing my hand on the bar with each word. 'He's a knob, Joe. Everything on the internet, it's all shit.'

'I'm gonna go out on a limb and say you're talking about my good buddy James Jacobs,' Joe said, passing me a cocktail menu and some nuts. 'So you're not, you know?'

'Mojito please.' I scarfed a handful of nuts. How long was it since I'd eaten? 'And ew, not even. I'm too good for him anyway. Not that he could, anyway. He wouldn't know what to do with me if he had the chance. What's that all about?'

'I'm pretty sure I don't know,' Joe said with a grin. 'But you are right, you're too good for him.'

'Yeah I am,' I nodded enthusiastically, while Joe

pounded away at the mint, sugar and lime. He really did have great arms. At least as good as James's. 'Are you OK, Joe? We haven't seen you since Monday.'

'I'm fine,' he nodded passing the drink across the bar. 'You get used to dealing with assholes in this town, Angela. But I guess you get used to dealing with assholes everywhere, right?'

'Mmm-hmm,' I agreed. It was a good mojito. 'Everywhere.'

'So, is there any chance I can convert you to LA?' he asked. 'Since the assholes are pretty much a global epidemic?'

I shook my head so violently, I had to grip the edge of the bar to keep from falling off my stool. 'Nuh-uh.'

'Still in love with New York, huh?' Joe slipped another straw into my drink and took a long sip. 'There's nothing you like about LA?'

'I don't hate this,' I said, bumping foreheads with him as I leaned in for another sip.

'Me either,' Joe said, holding my gaze for a moment. Nose to nose, eye to eye, I felt myself flush from head to toe.

'I'm having dinner with Jenny later. You should come along.' I pulled away, losing my balance again. 'Or are you working?'

'I actually get off at seven but you guys don't want me along.' Joe took out a pair of shot glasses and a bottle of tequila. 'You're gonna be talking about your boyfriends and shoes and shit. What am I gonna add to that?'

'Shut up,' I slapped his arm, spilling the tequila as he poured. 'We would totally want you there. And trust me when I say there will be no boyfriend talk. Jenny doesn't have one, you know.'

Joe held out my hand and kissed it. After an

240

impossibly long second, he sprinkled salt along the damp lip print. 'On three?'

'Three?' I whispered.

'The tequila?' Joe put a full-to-spilling shot glass in my free hand.

'If I do the shot, will you come to dinner with Jenny?' I stared at the gold liquid. I had some sense of awareness that this was a really bad idea but the salt was on my hand now, what was I supposed to do? I had been brought up not to waste food. Or drink. Or condiments.

'I'll come to dinner,' Joe nodded. 'One, two, three.'

'Eurgh.' Ignoring the sting of the tequila in the back of my throat and the instant urge to retch, I bit down on the lemon wedge Joe held out for me. 'I hate tequila.'

'But you did it like a pro,' Joe said, refilling the glasses. 'One more and then I figure I can get out of here.'

I nodded, taking the glass. The sun was starting to set behind the Hollywood Hills, the lights on the hidden homes of the rich and famous starting to twinkle. If I were to sit on the roof of The Union at seven in the evening, in March, in jeans and a T-shirt and, oh, I'd forgotten to put on shoes, I would actually freeze to death.

'Angela?'

'Yu-huh?' I snapped back. Joe held up his own shot glass.

'I said three, like, five times.'

'OK then.' I necked the shot, shuddered and slammed down the glass. 'Where should we go for dinner? I'm starving.'

'You might want to change first,' Joe said, logging out the till and handing over to a tall blonde girl in a matching black collarless shirt.

'We're going somewhere posh?' I asked.

'No, but your shirt is inside out and there's make-up all over it.' Joe scooped me up off my stool and carried me over to the door.

I giggled, slight hysterics overtaking me at being held off the ground. 'What? This is what all the hipsters are wearing in New York.'

'Well in that case . . .' Joe set me down and peeled off his own shirt, turning it inside out and slipping his arms back through the sleeves. Thank the lord, he didn't fasten it back up. '. . . Better?'

'Much,' I agreed, falling into the lift as the doors opened.

'You so can't come in my room,' I said, fighting with the key card and lock. 'I'll be two minutes.'

'I'll behave myself,' Joe said, pushing in close behind me before I could shut the door, 'I swear.'

'Yeah you will,' I said, stepping over the pile of bottles, glasses and dirty T-shirts I'd created by the mini-bar. 'But my main concern was you seeing what a shit-tip I'd left this place.'

'Angela, this is a hotel, I have seen much worse.' He stooped down and retrieved my mobile from the sticky mess of discarded bottles. 'You have missed calls.'

I took the phone and scanned down the list, holding my breath. Mary, twice, Jenny, once. No James. No Alex. I tossed it on the bed and turned back to the wardrobe, determined not to cry. Or fall over.

'Not the right person, huh?' Joe said. I screwed up my face.

'Angela, I don't know exactly what's been going down but I do know that you would never do anything to hurt anyone,' Joe said softly, crossing the room and pulling me into a warm hug. 'So whatever you're beating yourself up over, you can stop it now.'

'Nyuh,' I agreed into his shirt, arms hanging helpless by my sides.

'Do you remember when you first came to New York and we went out to karaoke?' Joe asked, stroking my back, catching the very ends of my hair. 'And Jenny sent me up to bring you breakfast. I remember her telling me all about your ex, about how he cheated on you and you caught him. You seemed so devastated.'

'I was.' My voice was muffled by Joe's chest. 'And I wouldn't ever cheat.'

'I know,' Joe said. 'You're just not that kind of a girl. I know that.'

'But Alex thinks I did,' I said quietly. God, he smelled even better than James, if that was possible. 'He's gone away.'

'Then he's even more of a dick than I thought he was.' Joe pushed me back slightly and tilted my chin up to face him. 'I would never have let you come out to LA on your own. I would never let you out of my sight.'

'He won't even take my calls,' I said weakly. I eyed the bed behind us. I really needed to be in it, alone. But surely I wasn't supposed to be alone in such a time of crisis?

'He isn't taking your calls?' Joe asked. 'He doesn't believe you?'

'I would never cheat on him.' I shook my head, my fingers curling around the open edges of his shirt. 'His friend said he left. I . . . he . . . I tried to explain but . . . I think he's finished with me.'

'Then this isn't cheating.' Joe's hands slid up my back and into my hair, pulling my face into his. His kiss was soft, warm and gentle, his chest hot and hard. I knew it was a bad idea, a much worse idea than the tequila but equally comforting. No, I was a bad, bad, bad person.

'I was going to change my T-shirt,' I mumbled, breaking away from the kiss. Woah. Dizzy. 'For dinner.'

'Let me help,' Joe said, slipping his hands under the thin material of my shirt and guiding it up over my head and then hooking it back around my waist, holding me close to him. 'You want to change your jeans too?'

My skin burned where he had touched me and my lips were desperate for more kisses but, really, my primary concern was just staying upright. Kisses were bad. Even if they felt delicious, they were bad. 'I'm all right in my jeans actually,' I managed eventually. Joe released his grip around my waist only for me to fall forwards into him. Stupid traitor legs.

'You should definitely change.' Joe dropped my T-shirt and found the waistband of my jeans. Why did I wear slouchy jeans today? If I'd have been in my skinnies, he wouldn't have been able to get a toothpick down there, let alone an entire hand down the back of the waistband. Oh, and now down the back of my knickers. If the room would just stop spinning for a moment, I'd be able to sort myself out.

'Nope, no, I'm fine,' I insisted, pushing him away. Or at least I hoped I was pushing him away. There was every chance I was actually just thrusting myself into him. Everything was starting to get a little bit confusing. 'I think I should go to bed.'

'I think so too,' he said, his breath hot on my neck, followed by his lips, followed by his fingers, all wrapped up in my hair. I tried not to close my eyes but it was hard. I tried not to let Joe push me back on the bed but with one slightly graceless shuffle, my resolve and my balance caved in.

'Where were we with your jeans?'

'I think I should call Alex,' I whispered against the

weight of Joe on top of me. Why was a big heavy man so much more preferable than a quilt when you'd had a drink? 'This is not good.'

'Not good?' he whispered in my ear, planting a string of kisses from my throat up to my lips. Where was my T-shirt? Why was I in my bra? 'Doesn't it feel good?'

'No?' I protested weakly by holding my hands out in front of me. Apparently this was also a come-on. Someone laced their fingers through mine and pushed my hands up above my head. I was so tired and so warm and so . . . no, something wasn't right. And it wasn't just the fact that I couldn't really see any more. 'I have to speak to Alex.'

'How about I be Alex?' said the low voice in my ear. 'And you just do what you're doing.'

'You're Alex?' I closed my eyes just for a moment. When did that happen? But yay, Alex. 'Oh, I love you.'

'Yeah, I love you too,' the voice whispered back. 'You're not going to fall asleep, are you?'

'Nope,' I replied, closing them for a moment more. 'I don't think so.' And it was true: passing out wasn't exactly the same as falling asleep, was it?

Waking up with a throbbing head, a mouth like Gandhi's flip-flop and the overwhelming urge to turn my stomach inside out was not something I'd ever planned on turning into a hobby, but here I was, the second day in a row, getting ever so good at it. As well as drinking enough to put an elephant down, I'd also apparently forgotten to close the curtains, and the painfully bright LA sun beamed through the floor-to-ceiling glass. Not nice.

I peeled my face off the pillowcase (drool was an amazing natural adhesive) and pushed myself into a semi-vertical sitting position. Which was when I realized that there was someone else in the bed. And I was in my bra. And, a quick shuffle confirmed, my pants. Thank Christ for that at least. Not that there was any guarantee that they had been on all night long.

As my heart dropped into my stomach, I felt it start to race, apparently in competition with my brain. But there was nothing. Complete blank. I leaned over the edge of the bed, trying not to disturb the clearly rumpled bedclothes, and groped around on the floor for my T-shirt. Whoever this was and whatever I'd done, I didn't want to deal with it in my underwear. Even if he had already seen me in it. Apparently.

Walking my fingers along the floor until the tips just reached my top, I noticed another larger, darker shirt beside it. A black, collarless shirt looking just like the millions of work shirts from The Union that Jenny left lying around our apartment. Oh shit. Oh shit shit shit shit shit. Really not wanting to confirm what was already coming rushing back to me, I turned my head slowly. Lying beside me, completely out of it, was Joe. I didn't dare peek under the covers but next to his shirt were his shoes. And next to them, his trousers. Oh shit shit shit shit. Without thinking, I bolted out of the bed as fast as my wobbly legs would carry me, grabbed my phone from the bedside table and made for the door.

'Jenny!' I yelled, hammering her door down, while pulling on my T-shirt in the hallway. I nodded at a passing couple, too stressed to be embarrassed about being busted in my underwear in a hotel hallway. This was the walk of shame in the extreme. 'Jenny, for fuck's sake, open the door.'

A couple of seconds later, I heard the latch click and

the door gave way to reveal a mighty pissed-off-looking Jenny. 'Angela, it's really, really freaking early. What the fuck?'

'Just let me in,' I pushed past her into the identical hotel room. Unsurprisingly for Jenny, it was a complete shit-tip. Clothes, carrier bags, shoes and towels everywhere. 'I need your help.'

'What else am I here for?' she muttered, closing the door behind me. 'It's not like I have a hangover or anything.'

'Where were you last night?' I asked, surveying the bombsite that was her room. From the four-inch heels and slinky dress lying in a silky, spiky pool by her bed, I guessed she'd been out.

'I told you, Tessa invited me to the awards thing she was doing. You got my message, right?' Jenny yawned and grabbed the hotel phone. 'Hi, could I get coffee and uh, I don't know, toast?' She paused and gave me a questioning look. I nodded back, knowing for a fact that I wouldn't be eating anything for a good couple of hours yet. 'Yeah, coffee and toast sent up? Thanks.' She threw herself backwards on the bed and started popping M&Ms from an open pack on the bedside table. 'I love being on the other end of that phone. So what's up? You look like shit.'

Gingerly, I joined her on the bed, trying not to make it bounce for fear of vomming. 'Uh, I think I've done something really stupid?'

'So what's new?' Jenny raised an eyebrow. 'I told you not to go meet James yesterday. What did you do now?'

'It's kind of a "who did I do?" problem.'

'What?'

I knew she was paying attention when the M&Ms she was throwing down her throat missed her mouth

247

and clattered against the window. 'Angie, what the hell?'

'Well, things didn't go well with James and so I came back and had a couple of drinks.' I really hadn't thought this through. How could I phrase this? 'A lot of drinks, actually. And then I went upstairs for more drinks.'

'When we get back to New York, I swear I'm putting you in AA,' Jenny muttered. 'Or at least getting you one of those Lindsay Lohan ankle monitors. You picked up a guy in the bar?'

'Mm-hmm,' I traced the edge of my big toenail and wondered when I'd chipped my pedicure. 'Jenny, I'm such an idiot.'

'Angie,' Jenny scooted across the bed and put an arm around my shoulders. 'People do stuff when they're stressed, calm down. What was it your mom said to me when I lost Kirsten Dunst's dry cleaning? Worse things happen at sea?'

'I think in this instance my mum would say, "Angela you great big dirty slag, I can't believe you shagged the barman",' I took a deep breath and looked up. This time Jenny couldn't even pick up the M&Ms; her hand was frozen in mid-air.

'Joe?'

'Joe.'

I wrinkled my nose, trying to force my prickling tears back into my eyes.

'You slept with Joe?'

The arm around my shoulders had got very tense all of a sudden.

'I think so.' I picked out a red M&M and passed it to her. 'I just woke up and, I don't remember, but he's in my bed and his clothes are not.'

'He's still there now?' Suddenly she was on her feet. 'He's in your room?'

'Yes, hence my being in here,' I replied, steadying myself on the bed. Fast movement, queasy stomach. Badness. 'What are you doing?'

'Angie, you were so drunk you don't even remember what happened, right?' she bolted towards the door. I followed as quickly as I could. Not that quickly. 'And he was working so he was sober, at least he should have been. And I hardly think you threw yourself at him, you don't exactly have any precedent for one-night stands. I'm gonna kill him.'

'Jenny, wait,' I chased her down the corridor, pulling my T-shirt as far over my pants as I could. 'I don't even know what happened, please don't—'

But it was too late: she'd swiped her key card and thrown open my room door before I could catch her.

'OK assface,' I heard her yell as I staggered through the door.

'Jenny, please.'

But aside from the wild-eyed brunette slamming into the bathroom, it was empty. No barmen in the bed; no closeted gay movie stars in the bathroom: no one.

'Jenny, will you please calm down and talk to me?' I closed the door behind me, giving the same couple that had passed me in my pants earlier a polite wave. 'Please?'

'Angie, I just can't believe he would do this,' she said, dropping to her knees and checking under the bed.

'I don't think he's under there.' I stepped around the pile of bottles by the mini-bar and retrieved the last standing Diet Coke. 'As embarrassed as he might be about waking up in my bed.'

'He had better be on a plane to Mexico,' Jenny said, clambering back to her feet.

'I'm not that bad.' I closed the curtains, still feeling a little mogwai-ish. Turned out bright lights and eating-slash-drinking after midnight were bad for me too. 'Although I'm guessing it wasn't my best performance.'

'Oh shit, Angie,' Jenny stopped for a split second. 'That's so not what I mean. Don't you even feel bad about this for a second. He *totally* took advantage of you and for that I'm going to end him.'

'You're not pissed off?'

'Why would I be pissed?'

'Because I'm a big slag who can't remember doing it with the boy you were planning on doing it with?'

Jenny laughed. 'Honey, I think we already agreed that I'm so not ready to do it with anyone. Of course I'm not pissed – not with you, anyway. You're my best friend. You do stupid stuff. I sort it out. This is our thing, it's the thing that we do.'

'This is true,' I agreed, starting to sip the water. At least the drama had taken my mind off my hangover. Until now. 'I just can't believe I'm so stupid. What am I going to tell Alex?'

'You're not going to tell Alex anything,'

'But I can't lie to him.'

'And what's going to happen? Assuming he comes to his senses over all this James Jacobs shit and I allow him to get back with you, if you tell him he'll break up with you all over again.' Jenny pulled me over to the bed. 'It's not like you're getting a free pass, you still have to feel like a piece of crap, but telling Alex is the stupidest thing you can do. Yeah, you'll clear your conscience but he'll never ever forgive you. You want to lose him over a drunk one-night stand?'

'Not really. Not if I haven't already lost him over a nonexistent affair. I can't believe this has happened.' I buried my face in a pillow. 'As if things weren't shitty enough.'

'So, you keeping your mouth shut and my kicking Joe's ass off the continent aside, what happened with James yesterday?' Jenny softened for a moment. 'He wouldn't speak to Mary?'

I shook my head. 'He wouldn't risk it. To be honest, I can completely understand. He doesn't really know me; it's not like we're lifelong besties, is it? And I'm asking him to risk everything he's worked for by confessing this huge secret that will completely change his life. I suppose there's a bit of difference between him losing his job and me losing mine. Who am I compared to him, really?'

'You're someone who's telling the truth. That counts for something.' Jenny picked up my phone and flicked through my messages.

'Not enough,' I said. 'Mary said she was going to give the *Icon* interview the go-ahead if I didn't get back to her last night. I didn't get back to her last night. God, how have I managed to get myself into this state?'

'The state where we're two hot single girls.' She gave me my phone back. "And you're about to make a ton of money from selling a sordid sex story? Awesome.'

'I do love that you always find a bright side,' I said, giving her a squeeze.

'That's my job,' she replied. 'Alongside my new stellar styling career. Tell me I can style the shoot?'

'If there has to be a shoot, you can style the shoot,' I choked. And then burst into tears.

Jenny pulled me in for a full-on, nose-squishing, tear-choking hug. 'Angela Clark, what am I going to do with you?'

251

CHAPTER FOURTEEN

Once she'd run me a bath, removed all sharp edges and laid out a comfortably noncontroversial outfit on the bed, Jenny left the room, allegedly to call Tessa about a styling meeting that afternoon, but I had a sneaking suspicion that it was to go and find, beat and kill Joe. Luckily, there was altogether too much going off in my head for me to process any of it – James, Alex, Mary and – not least of all – my very first-ever one-night stand, which had been so incredibly fantastic that I couldn't remember any of it and he had vanished off the face of the earth. I stripped off, dropping my T-shirt and underwear straight in the bin. I was in no rush to remember anything that had happened in them ever again.

The bath was reassuringly hot, taking my breath away as my legs turned tomato red under the water. I breathed out slowly, slipping the rest of my body under the water, feeling the scorching heat turn to comforting warmth. I pulled my arm up out of the water and considered how the bottom half had already gone fully lobster, while the top was still pale pink. And that was as about as intellectual as I felt like being.

After the third failed attempt at turning the cold tap on with my left foot, I realized the insistent chirping coming from the bedroom was my phone. I let it ring through three times, before I realized whoever was calling was not giving up easily. Sloshing out of the bath, I padded through the bedroom, to see who wanted to speak to me so desperately. Three missed calls: two from Mary, one from a strange 818 number but no messages. Before I could take a look at the 818 number again, the phone buzzed into life in my hands. Mary again.

'Hi, Mary.' I had to bite the bullet sooner or later so it might as well be while I was dripping wet and naked.

'Why the hell aren't you answering your hotel phone?' she yelled. I glanced over to see the receiver hanging off the bedside table. Clearly a casualty of my night of passion. 'Or the ten thousand emails I've sent you?'

'Sorry.' I looked around for my handbag. Had I taken it with me to the bar? 'Slightly mad night.' All I wanted to ask was whether or not I was fired, but I was so scared that she'd say yes.

'You had a mad night? Were you on a conference call until eleven with the publishers, trying to convince them to hold your James Jacobs story? They're convinced it's going to leak before we publish next week. Tell me you've got him sitting tight?'

'Well he's hardly going to go and brag about me elsewhere, is he?' I grumbled, looking around for something to wear. The air-con in The Hollywood was not conducive to solo nudity.

'Angela, I don't think you understand,' Mary carried on. 'Once someone's made a decision like this, there's usually not a lot of time to capitalize on it. The last thing we want is for him to change his mind or, even worse, decide that he's so happy with the world knowing he's gay that he runs around the city making out with God knows who before the issue breaks.'

I froze on my hands and knees, pulling open the bottom drawer of the wardrobe. 'What?'

'What do you mean what?' Mary sounded as confused as I was. 'Tell me you've booked in the new interview time?'

'New interview?'

'With James and his boyfriend?'

I sat back on my knees. 'You know?'

'Of course I know. Are you OK? Have you been drinking?' She started talking very slowly. 'I spoke to James yesterday. He said it was all organized, that you were going to do the interview and that he wanted it to run in this week's *Icon*. Angela, I need your copy by tomorrow. We're booking the photo shoot for Sunday but you don't need to be there for that, I need you back here. Tell me you're going to pull this off.'

'He told you?' I asked, dazed. 'He told you everything?'

'He told me he prefers kissing boys to girls if that's what you mean?'

I felt as if the room was shaking beneath me and peered over the bed like a meercat, checking that Los Angeles wasn't being swallowed up by The Big One outside.

'Angela, this is not a game,' Mary said. 'And if you thought the publishers didn't want you on original interview, you can't even imagine what they think about you covering this. I need your copy filed by tomorrow lunchtime – one p.m. your time – for subbing and then I need you back here. We'll have to release the story Monday before the magazine comes out Tuesday. Cici is booking your flight back Sunday afternoon.'

'I don't know what to say.' I stared into the glass, not even out at the hills, just at the glass. 'I actually don't.'

'You'd better have something worked out for first thing Monday morning,' she said. 'Because I want the whole story in my office at nine a.m.'

Putting the phone down, I finally came to my senses long enough to pull on a pair of knickers and a T-shirt and sat with my back against the bedside table, my legs stretched out in front of me. James had called Mary. He was going to do the interview. I pulled my feet upwards, feeling the stretch in my calves. Why hadn't he called me to tell me? I fumbled behind me for the hotel phone receiver.

'Hi, this is Angela Clark in room six-oh-eight . . . do I have any messages?'

I heard the breathy girl on the front desk click on a keyboard. 'Good morning Miss Clark, I think we do. Actually, you have quite a few. Should I send someone up or would you like me to read them to you now?'

I paused. 'Could you get them sent up? Thanks so much.' Probably best not to get them read out loud. I scrambled to my feet and attempted to make myself presentable. My mother would die if she thought I was opening the door to – well, anyone, looking like this. It was the same logic as cleaning the house from top to toe before she went on holiday in case she had burglars. Hair in a ponytail, teeth very quickly and not at all thoroughly cleaned, followed by mascara and lip balm. I was scouting for an appropriate bottom half to my inappropriately short T-shirt and stripy pink pants ensemble when I heard the knock at the door. Damn, they were fast in this hotel.

'Come in,' I called from the wardrobe but, instead

of hearing the door click and sweep open, there was another knock. Fine, they would just have to see my pants. Again. Figuring half the hotel had seen me in my underwear already, and what difference did one more bellboy make?, I opened the door.

'Hi.'

It wasn't a bellboy.

It was Alex.

'I know LA is a little more dressed down than New York but, Angela, that's ridiculous.' He tucked a pair of tiny white earphones down the front of his T-shirt and shook his head.

I hung onto the door for fear of falling over. It was really him.

'Can I come in?' he asked, his long dark fringe dropping into tired-looking eyes. I nodded and moved backwards with the door to make room for him and his rucksack. 'So you trashed the room already?'

I nodded again, still not letting go of the door. It was really him. Standing in front of me, in my hotel room in his creased-to-death jeans, holey green T-shirt and battered black Cons, looking so ridiculously anti-LA that my mind refused to compute the image of him against the window, against the backdrop of the Hollywood sign.

'Angela, please say something,' he said after another minute of silence. 'Or at least close the door?'

I prised my fingers from the wood and allowed the door to swing itself shut but I couldn't cross the room. What if I touched him and he disappeared? What if I said the wrong thing and he walked out for ever?

'OK, one thing at a time.' Alex set his bag down on the table by my laptop. 'I have to use the bathroom and then maybe we can talk?' He walked towards me but I couldn't read his face as he slipped by into the bathroom. He looked tired, that was for sure, but tired because he'd just got off a plane, tired because he hadn't been sleeping? And he definitely didn't look happy.

When the bathroom door opened, I was still frozen to the spot. Alex looked at me, looked down at the pile of bottles Jenny had moved from the floor into the bin and then back up at me. His face was damp and slightly pink from where he'd splashed it with water and a few strands of his long fringe clung to his cheek. I reached out slowly to brush them away but Alex caught my hand and held it to his cheek.

'Hi,' he said softly.

'Hi,' I replied.

'Should I go out and come back in again?'

I shook my head slowly. He really was here. I was touching him and everything.

'I am so sorry for everything I said,' he bit down on his full bottom lip, 'on the phone. I just, I don't know, I freaked out.'

'That's OK,' I mumbled. His hand was so hot.

'No, it's not.' His green eyes were so bloodshot, I could barely stand to look at them. I knew he wasn't someone that slept a lot at the best of times. 'I didn't even start to listen to you. I didn't even try.'

'That's OK,' I repeated. It really wasn't but then that was before I shagged the barman.

'Angela, stop saying it's OK. It isn't.' He pulled me towards him gently. 'I sat staring at the phone for something like three hours after we spoke. I was so completely wrong to have said what I did.'

'That's – I mean, you could have called?' I said, painfully aware that a) I looked like absolute shit and b) my room stank of booze. 'Why didn't you call? Why didn't you answer when I called you?'

'I thought a grand romantic gesture would be better?'

Alex took my other hand in his to stop me pulling at the hem of my T-shirt. 'Or, after we talked and I saw the pictures of you online, I threw my phone out the window. Which made calling you kind of tricky.'

'Right,' I replied.

'I know you must still be angry,' he went on. 'But can I just explain? Just let me say what I've spent the last ten hours practising and then if you still want me to go, I will.'

'Want you to go?' I wasn't sure what parallel universe I'd been pulled into where Alex thought my inability to string a sentence together was because I was angry with him. I was angry – furious in fact – but only with myself.

'OK, the last time we spoke I was a complete asshole but that was only because I was so insanely jealous. I knew that you would never . . . you know. I did know that. You're not my ex or – well – me.' He tried to draw me across the room but I couldn't be moved. 'But my head was kinda messed up. I guess I didn't want you to go to LA.'

'You could have said that before I left.' Finally I started to get the feeling back in my feet and allowed myself to be pulled along the carpet. 'You could have come with me.'

'I didn't think I should. And everything's been happening so quickly again, I thought maybe some time apart would be a good thing. But hey, I have been wrong before.'

'True,' I whispered.

Alex was backing slowly towards the bed. The bed that was still messed up from whatever happened the night before with Joe.

'And I guess that's why I wasn't answering my phone.' He slid his hands up my arms, resting them on my shoulders. 'I wanted to prove that I wasn't missing you. That I wouldn't fall apart again without you. Tragic, huh?'

'Tragic.'

'Turns out I was wrong, so I guess you're stuck with me now. If you still want me?'

'Of course I do,' I said, a tiny little tear sneaking out of the corner of my eye. 'But there's still stuff we have to talk about, I have to explain. It's not as easy as—'

'It's as easy as we make it.' Still with both my hands in his, Alex pulled me sharply towards him and I crashed into his chest. He smelled like sleep and the deodorant that sat on his bathroom windowsill. 'You don't have to explain a thing. You said nothing happened with that guy and I should have just believed you. There should never have been a question for you to answer. I am so sorry. But I'm here and I want to make it right. Tell me what to do.'

I had never felt like more of a shit in my entire life. Here he was, this beautiful boy that had flown thousands of miles to apologize for believing photographs that thousands of other people all around the world, including my bloody mother, were taking as gospel. He was here to tell me that he didn't believe them, that he was the one in the wrong, and now he was trying to pull me into a bed that had until very, very recently contained a very naked barman and a very stupid me.

'Angela, are you OK?' He held my tear-streaked face in his hands. 'I know things aren't going to be OK right away. I don't expect you to forgive me now. I just want to know that you might be able to later.'

'I–I can't believe you came,' I stuttered. 'I can't believe you're here.'

'There was nowhere else I could be.' He pressed his forehead to mine, my tears running against his cheeks. 'So these are happy tears that I'm here, not sad tears because you hate me?'

'I don't hate you. You should hate me,' I faltered. I had to tell him. It was one thing to keep it to myself when I thought things were over, it was another to lie flat out when the man had flown all the way across the country to see me. 'I'm so sorry, Alex.'

'Stop talking.' His lips found my cheeks and kissed away the tear tracks. 'You always talk too much.' Without thinking, I tilted my face upwards and kissed him back, his lips salty from my crying and dry from his flight. I wasn't sure how something that made me melt so completely could make me feel sick to my very stomach at the same time.

Alex drew me down on top of him on the bed. I awkwardly straddled his lap, my shins against the edge of the bed frame. His lips softened as they turned to my throat, to the ribbed neckline of my T-shirt. I let him pull me closer and push me backwards against the pillows as I tried to concentrate on his half-closed eyes, his shortness of breath; but every time I tried to let go, I could feel Joe in the bed with us.

'Alex, I can't,' I choked, reaching out for his hand before he could go too far. 'I'm sorry, I need to sort some stuff out and we need to talk.'

He brushed his hair out of his eyes and sighed softly. 'I'm sorry, I shouldn't have.' He pushed up and sat on the edge of the bed with his head in his hands. 'You want me to go?'

'God, no.' I sat up too quickly and threw my arms around him. What if he left and never came back? 'I just can't do this. Yet. But will you stay with me?'

'I'll never leave again unless you ask.' He leant in

and kissed me again, deep and warm. 'Do you have stuff to do today?'

I went through the list in my head: call James, sort out the interview, find Jenny, gag Joe, sew a scarlet A to the front of all my clothes. Nothing that couldn't wait. 'Not right now. Can we just lie here for a while?'

Alex nodded and kissed the tip of my nose before kicking off his Converses and crawling across the bed. Silently, I lay back against him, pressing myself against his chest, curling my legs through his. I clutched the arm he draped across me tightly and listened to his steady breathing, felt his breath on the back of my neck as it slowed down. He was asleep inside minutes but I just couldn't close my eyes without seeing Joe's naked back in front of me.

What had I done?

Once I was certain I wasn't about to wake up from my dream-slash-nightmare and find my bed had been completely empty for the last twenty-four hours and not taken on a revolving-door policy when it came to hot boys, I crawled out of Alex's grip and pulled on some long overdue jeans. I padded as quietly as I could into the bathroom and stared at my phone. Whom should I speak to first? What should I say to any of them? Better to just make that call than to sit on the toilet staring at a mobile phone, surely that wasn't overly hygienic.

'I've been wondering when you'd call.' James didn't sound as happy as I was hoping he would be. 'Left it a bit late, haven't you?'

'Well, you won't believe this but there's this rumour going round my office that you're gay.' I stretched my toes out to rest on the heated towel rail. Ooh, damn it, too hot. 'Isn't that shocking?'

'Very funny,' he echoed. Apparently the bathroom wasn't the best place to have a mobile phone conversation. 'So when are you coming over to do this? I'd really like to get it over with.'

'Oh, thanks,' I heard Blake call down the line. 'I'm so glad you're excited about this.'

'Shut up,' James countered, but I could hear a smile in his voice. 'Seriously though, there is — according to your terrifying editor — some urgency in the matter.'

'I know,' I said, pressing my toes against the cold tiled floor. 'She has been quite insistent on the urgency. The only thing is, Alex just turned up here and I sort of can't leave him right now.' What I failed to add was 'because I'm terrified that if I leave him alone in this hotel room for even a moment, he'll find some shred of evidence that I shagged the barman last night.'

'He showed up, did he? To apologize?'

'Mm-hm.'

'Any diamonds accessorizing that apology?'

'No.' I couldn't imagine how I could feel worse than I did right then, but possibly diamonds would have pushed me over the edge. Of the roof. 'Things are a bit complicated. I have to submit my copy by tomorrow lunchtime so if I came to you about nine, would that be OK? That gives us a couple of hours to talk and then I've got another couple to sort it all out.'

'Are you that good a writer or just that desperate for a seeing-to that you can't leave your man?' James asked. 'And I expect an honest answer, given that I'm about to out myself for you.'

'Oh, so you're doing this for her now?' Blake again.

'Do I have to bring him on the interview?' James asked. 'He's been bloody intolerable since I agreed to all of this. There's still time to change my mind, isn't there?'

'No there isn't,' I said quickly. 'So we'll do it at your hotel?'

'Fine, it's where all the best scandal goes down.' I heard a scuffling in the background and then giggling. 'Sorry, Blake's freaking out that I'm actually organizing something myself. Piss off; you're supposed to be organizing the photo shoot, not listening in on my conversation. Have to say, Miss Clark, I'm a bit gutted you're not going to be in the pics.'

'I've been in quite enough pictures with you,' I replied. 'See you tomorrow at nine, then?'

'OK,' he said. 'And Angela, I am really sorry for all the hassle. Hopefully it's all going to work out for the best. For both of us.'

I tried to smile as I ended the call, happy for James and Blake that they were together, but I was still pissed about the fact that if those photos of James and me had never leaked, I would probably never have ended up in bed with Joe in the first place. I paused between phone calls to wash and moisturize, my skin had got so dried out here. Smoothing on an inch-think layer of Beauty Flash Balm, I stared back at myself in the mirror.

I didn't look any different for having had a skanky one-night stand, so why did I feel so different? Same blue eyes, same light brown hair, same 'not bad really but would definitely get veneers if I ever got mega-rich' teeth. If only I could remember what had happened, maybe I could stop imagining the worst. Unless it had been the worst and my brain was trying to protect what little self-esteem I had left. And the worst thing was, as much as I could complain about James and the photos, about Joe taking advantage, there really was no one to blame for all this but myself. I was going to sort it out myself. With a little help from Jenny.

I dialled her mobile and got her answer phone. The first time that girl answered her phone herself, the world would end. 'Hi Jenny, it's me. So I don't know where you are but I really need to talk to you. Alex just turned up – he's here in my room and I don't know what to do. I'm totally freaking out about the whole . . . situation. Help? Please?'

'Hey,' Alex said, curling his long body around the door, 'you OK?'

'I thought you were asleep,' I said, quickly wiping away the smears of moisturizer all over my face. 'I was just sorting out some stuff.'

'That's cool, you don't need to tell me.' He stretched up, gripping the top of the frame, his T-shirt pulling up over the waistband of his jeans and revealing his tight, pale abs. Good job I was holding on to the sink. 'So my body clock is totally wrecked and now I'm starving. You want to eat?'

'I am actually really hungry.' I couldn't remember when I'd last eaten. 'Do you want to go out?'

Alex let go of the doorframe and stepped tentatively into the bathroom. He smiled and wiped away a little leftover moisturizer from my cheek, making me flush from head to toe.

'Do you?'

I shook my head. 'Not really.'

'Me either.' He pulled off his shirt and unfastened his belt buckle. 'But I do need to take a shower. You coming in?'

I looked at the floor. Why was he making this so difficult for me? The empty sick feeling in my stomach eased into tickling butterflies. Before I could say anything, Alex was right there, kissing me so hard, my lips felt bruised and my breath was knocked clean out of me. As he hooked his hands under my arms and pushed me up against the sink, I wrapped my legs around his waist, kissing him back. Maybe this was the best way to clear my head. It certainly felt like a good idea. Not that I could really use that as an indicator of good ideas, given my previous.

I was vaguely aware that I'd knocked on the tap as a startling stream of cold water ran down my lower back, but I was so busy helping Alex yank my T-shirt up and over my head that I didn't really mind. Instead of trying to turn it off, I let myself twist my fingers into his hair, just like I'd wanted to ever since he'd walked through my door. I held on tightly around his neck as Alex staggered backwards, sliding me off the sink and clattering into the towel rail.

'Is this OK?' He breathed hard in between kisses that made my knees weak. So weak that getting to the floor as soon as possible was really the only solution.

'I thought I was the one who talked too much,' I replied, pulling him down onto the cold, hard tiles.

CHAPTER FIFTEEN

'I can't believe that guy is gay,' Alex said afterwards as we lay on the bathroom floor, draped in The Hollywood's fluffy towels. I wasn't sure my legs were up to making it across the room anyway, and it seemed as if it would be unflattering to crawl. Not to mention the fact that having two men in my bed in one day was really just too skanky.

'I know.' I shuffled slightly closer against Alex's chest. The closer I was, the safer I felt. 'It's mad, isn't it?'

Even though Alex was trying really hard with his whole 'you don't need to explain yourself to me' routine, I had really wanted to give him the whole story, or at least the whole James Jacobs story, as soon as was post-coitally appropriate.

'I guess you never really know about this stuff.' Alex idly stroked at strands of my hair, holding them up and let them fall gently back to my head. 'People believe what they want to believe. It's kinda depressing that he didn't think he could just be who he is from the beginning.'

'I'm just so sorry you got dragged into it all,' I said

266

quietly, utterly blissed out from the hair stroking. 'I nearly died when they had that picture of you online.'

'Yeah, how weird was that?' His voice sounded deep and sandpapery in the confines of the tiny hotel bathroom. 'I don't know where they got that picture. Good to know internet gossips think I'm cute, though. The guys haven't stopped laughing.'

'Jealous,' I said.

'Totally,' he agreed. 'The sick thing is, record sales are up.'

'Do I get commission?' I asked, manoeuvring my towel to make sure any dodgy bits were covered. It was one thing to be naked in the throes of passion, it was quite another to be totally starkers under the harsh bathroom lighting once your boyfriend had already got some.

'Can I work off my debt?' he whispered into my ear. A shiver ran down my spine that had nothing to do with the temperature of the floor tiles.

'I thought you were hungry.' I pushed his hair back out of my face as Alex positioned himself over me. 'They won't bring room service up if we're at it on the bathroom floor.'

'Don't tell me you haven't got a secret stash of snacks in this room.' His breath was hot on my neck and I felt my back arch upwards towards him. 'You're never more than fifteen feet from a packet of M&Ms.'

'I'm sure I don't know what you mean,' I said, hoping he wouldn't find the giant bag of peanut butter M&Ms before I could hide them.

The day drifted away from me before I was really able to do anything with it aside from intermittently reaching out to make sure Alex was still there and drifting in and out of my first non-alcohol-induced sleep for days. Eventually, Alex and I managed to put on just enough clothes to make ourselves decent and we wandered out to the closest McDonald's for sustenance – and to give housekeeping enough time to change the bed. I was just watching Alex tuck into his second Big Mac when my phone trilled to announce a text message. It was Jenny.

'Hey, things ok with Alex? U didn't tell him about Joe? Am with Tessa, let me no if u need me xoxo'

I looked up, watching Alex devour his burger as though someone was going to take it off him. I didn't know whether to smile or cry. I knew that Joe could appear at any second and completely mess this up.

'Haven't said anything, ok at mo. Have fun, cu tomorrow? A x x x'

I pushed my chicken sandwich away, suddenly not quite so hungry as I was desperate to get back in the hotel room with a 'Do Not Disturb' sign on the door.

'Not hungry?' Alex asked, eyeing my leftovers.

I shook my head. 'Full of M&Ms.' I sipped my Diet Coke while Alex made short work of the McChicken Sandwich. 'How's your jet lag?'

'Hmm,' Alex replied, holding his hand up to hide a mouthful of fast food. 'I don't even know what time it is. It's getting dark though.' He nodded towards the street outside. The sun had almost completely set and all of Hollywood Boulevard's tourists, costume characters and general crazies were lit up. I tried not to stare as Spider Man and Jack Sparrow wandered in off the street and ordered up a couple of Happy Meals. 'Are you sure you don't have anything you have to do today? Isn't this interview thing going to be really difficult?'

'Yes and no.' I pulled my hair back into a tight

ponytail and then let it go. 'I'm assuming the magazine is going to rewrite whatever I do but, you know, I don't want to turn in some rubbish. My plan is to get as much information as possible, pull it into the best shape I can and then at least there's material for the editors to work with. I've got tonnes of background stuff from the last week, so tomorrow I need the "We Love Each Other" stuff to add to that. Which is what's going to be difficult. I can't imagine they're actually going to be overly sharey even now, to be honest. Blake hates me.'

'Cool, I guess I should be looking into flights home. You know what you and Jenny are doing yet?' He started on the fries.

'Nope,' I said, fiddling with the bendy straw in my Coke. Couldn't he just hurry up and finish already? 'It'll be some time on Sunday though. Cici is supposed to be booking them tomorrow. Shall I see if she can get you on the same flight?'

Alex nodded. 'My grand romantic gesture wasn't well planned.'

'I don't think they're supposed to be.' I reached across the table and squeezed his hand. Which was stupid because it slowed down his eating even more.

'So what's going on with Jenny?' Alex finally flattened out the empty fries box. And started on his Coke. 'Did she hook up with that waiter guy?'

I felt myself turn a little bit green. 'Turns out she wasn't ready to be hooking up with anyone.' I moved the subject on from Joe as quickly as possible. 'She's just so burned out over Jeff, I really don't know what it's going to take to shake her out of this mood she's in. I mean, it's not like she's been short of men throwing themselves at her and she's still going out and everything.' I willed Alex to neck his drink so we could get back to the safety of my room. 'I don't know, maybe the break will do her good. She's been hanging around with one of her old friends who does some styling stuff. They've been sort of playing at that while I've been working. Jenny's pretty good at it.'

'Jenny good at telling people what to do?' Alex shook his paper cup and took one last slurp. 'I don't believe it for a second.'

I didn't sleep a wink Friday night and it had nothing (or at least not as much as you might think) to do with Alex being naked beside me. As relieved as I was to find the hotel room restored to its former pre-worst-night-of-my-life glory, I was still uneasy. How could I lie here with Alex and pretend everything was OK when I had cheated on him in this very bed? I almost put my ex's face through the windscreen when I busted him cheating on me.

The next morning, I was up, showered and dressed before Alex had even flickered an eyelid. My new plan was simple: get the interview with James out of the way, get Alex out of the hotel, and get everyone out of LA. I was certain Jenny was right: it was better not to tell Alex anything and, had I been able to leave my regrettable/forgettable one-night stand behind me in another city, a very, very long way away, that might have been easier. Now he was here, at the scene of the crime, I just felt like an absolute skank.

I grabbed my lovely, trustworthy handbag and made for the door, leaving a note for Alex. I wasn't due at James's hotel for hours, but Jenny had left me the car keys and there was no way I could hang about in the room, driving myself mad. After awkwardly navigating the valet parking system, I prepared myself for the fabled LA traffic as best I could (putting on sunscreen, lipstick and sunglasses) and flicked on the convertible's sat-nav. I'd never driven an automatic before – well, I hadn't actually driven a car since I'd been in America – but it was just like riding a bike. Apparently. Unfortunately, even at six-thirty on a Saturday morning, LA's roads were neither bike- nor international-driver-friendly. I got the hang of driving on the wrong side of the road fairly quickly, but turning right on red just wouldn't sink in. Luckily, there were lots of straight roads for me to pootle along until I could steel myself to pull into an open Starbucks, grab a coffee and a muffin and set the sat-nav for Griffith Park.

The park was beautiful: so different to everything I'd seen of LA so far, wilder than Central Park and a million miles away from London's carefully tended open spaces. Parking up by a huge open-air theatre, I picked up my coffee, plugged in my iPod and wandered out into the park, following the runners and dog walkers. After twenty minutes of drowning out my thoughts with the loudest music I could find, I found myself outside the Griffith Observatory. Sipping my cooled coffee, I sat down on the grass and stared down at the city as the sun came up slowly. Well, wasn't I a long way from home?

LA looked very different from up here; for the first time I felt as though I was Away. New York was so tight and tall, a thin sliver of an island, breathing in and stretching up high, as if it was holding its hand up to the world for attention. New York made me walk fast, made me want to be as tall and glossy as its skyscrapers, twenty-four seven. For all its glamour and celebrity, up here in the hills, LA looked more like a city that had just breathed out, kicked off its heels and opened a window. The buildings were a little lower, a little sun-bleached and more spread apart, not pressed up against each other, racing up into the clouds. It was a city so sure of itself that it just didn't need to fight for attention. And besides, it was so sunny and warm, why not relax a little?

But of course I'd spoken too soon. Inside my bag, my phone chirped into life. Who could be missing me at this time? The screen flashed over and over with Mum Home.

'Hello?'

'Angela?'

'Mum?'

'Hello, love! I was just talking about you. Are you with your movie star?'

'Mum, why are you using your posh voice?' I asked, instantly regretting answering the call.

'I don't know what you mean, dear.' Mum went on in the same voice she had used for my teachers and the engineer who came round to install Sky+. 'Anyway, Sheila's been round, you remember Sheila from the library? Well, she says that your boyfriend used to go out with that girl from that film you like . . . you know, the one about that man out of *Ghostbusters*, when he goes to China and she's ever so pretty, Angela.'

I survive my first drive in LA and this was how I rewarded myself? When did I become a masochist? 'Mum, he's not my boyfriend. Alex is my boyfriend. We have been through this.'

'I know it's all the rage going out with two people at once these days but, honestly Angela, it'll end in tears,' she rattled on. 'Don't think I don't know. I was seeing another man when I met your father and yes, I admit there might have even been a bit of an overlap but—'

'Mum!' I shouted, attracting the attention of several labradors and a chihuahua. 'There's nothing going on with me and James at all. I'm just going out with Alex.'

272

'Oh.' She sounded ridiculously disappointed given that she had never met either man. 'Well, that's a shame. He seemed lovely.'

'Well, I'm very sorry.'

'Are you trying to tell me you're not going to marry that actor or was there something else? I'm just about to do your dad a sandwich.'

I breathed in and out slowly, watching the sun spread across the city. See how different it could be? If I hadn't salvaged my job at *The Look*, I would most likely be having a sandwich with Dad as well.

'I just wanted to give you a ring,' I said, trying to be patient. "Let you know I was all right. That I wasn't shacked up with James Jacobs.'

'Don't feel bad, that blonde girl is ever so pretty. Not that you're not, Angela love, but you know. So, how long are you in Los Angeles for? Have you booked your flights home?'

I tried not to be offended that my mother didn't think I was as pretty as Scarlett Johansson. I mean, surely your mum was the only person in the world that might think that about you? Unless you were Scarlett Johansson's mum and then I suppose you'd have to think her sister was fairly pretty too. If she has a sister.

'Do you have to ask me that every time I call you?' I asked, draining my freezing cold coffee. Ick. 'I don't know, Mum. I suppose I might come home for Christmas this year if you're not on a cruise again.'

'I didn't mean here,' she tutted, as if I was the stupid one. Which, given the last week of my life, was probably fair. 'I meant when are you going back to New York?'

'Oh.' I smiled at my flip-flops. Home. 'Sunday.'

'Don't worry, Angela,' Mum sighed dramatically.

'We've quite got used to the idea that you've abandoned us. You've got your new life now with your boyfriends and your friends. How is Jenny? Now she's a beautiful girl.'

'She's fine.' I don't know what I was expecting, really. 'Mum, can I ask you something?'

'What a silly question, of course you can.'

'Have you ever kept a secret from Dad?'

She was silent for a moment.

'A secret as in, what he doesn't know won't hurt him, or a secret as in, he still thinks I make my own Yorkshire puddings and don't buy in Aunt Bessie's?'

'The first one.' I was disgusted. Fancy buying in frozen Yorkshire puddings.

'Then yes, of course I have,' she said. 'All relationships have their little secrets.'

'Really?' I had to admit to being a little bit curious about my mother's secrets. As long as they weren't dirty. Ew. 'Like what?'

'Well, obviously there're the little white lies, like the Yorkshire puddings. And the roast potatoes. And once I used that powdered mashed potato for Sunday dinner because I'd been on the Blue Nun with your Auntie Les and he was none the wiser,' she said. 'But, well, there have been a few things that I'm fairly sure he'd rather not know about. You have to use your judgement, Angela – it's part of making a relationship work.'

'But don't you think he deserves to know?' I asked. 'Shouldn't you be honest about everything?'

'Would you rather know?' She was still speaking slowly, as if she was choosing every single word very carefully. Which was extremely weird for my mother. 'Imagine if that fella of yours had – I don't know – got a bit tipsy and kissed the girl from the bakery under the mistletoe at a Christmas party and maybe she'd thought it was a proper kiss and he hadn't but maybe she'd kissed him on the lips instead of the cheek and—'

'Mum, did you kiss Mr Owens from the bakery?' I shouted down the phone.

'And that reaction is why your dad doesn't know about it,' Mum said primly. 'And so, whatever you've done, I suggest you don't go telling that boyfriend of yours unless you want to peel him off the ceiling. Calm down, Angela.'

She was right. I hated when that happened.

'I'm going to go, Mum. I've got some work to do before I go back to New York. We fly tomorrow; yes, I'll call when we've landed,' I promised, knowing full well I wouldn't and that she'd have forgotten I'd even said that I would before she got back to Dad's sandwich.

'All right love.' At least she was using her own voice again. 'And just think about what I said. And don't ever tell your dad about the Yorkshire puddings. I think he'd be more likely to forgive a kiss than using frozen Yorkshires.'

Hoovering down my muffin, I took one long last look at LA as the morning sunshine tickled it awake, stroking the rooftops of the city from Los Feliz below me, shining down on Hollywood, skipping over Beverly Hills and bouncing off the waves and the beaches of Venice and Santa Monica. I heaved myself up, dusted off my jeans and wandered off back to the car with something of a smile starting on my face. Surely if Mum could keep her frozen Yorkshires to herself, then there was no reason why I couldn't just forget the Joe incident ever happened.

Forty hairy minutes later, I was pulling in at a Coffee Bean to pick up more coffees and muffins as a goodwill

275

gesture for James and Blake and to break up the terrifying drive through LA. Once I'd prised my fingers off the steering wheel, I spotted my phone flashing in the bottom of my bag. Unlike everyone else on the roads of LA, I couldn't drive and talk at the same time. I could barely even drive and think. There were two texts. One from James.

'Couldn't remember what we were doing so we're coming to you. See you @ pool bar 9?'

Shit. What time was it?
8.40.
Shit.
And another from Alex.

'Can't believe you snuck out, I feel so used. Will hang out here till you're back, got my swimsuit somewhere . . .'

Shit shit shit.
I threw my bag and phone into the back seat and turned on the engine. Never again would I take issue with Blake's anal-retentive management of James's schedule. And never again would I make arrangements with the monkey instead of the organ-grinder. I took a quick moment to think about how inappropriate that thought was and then rolled out into traffic.

I couldn't get to the roof of the hotel soon enough. Jabbing the roof terrace button in the lift, I felt my newly acquired sense of calm slip away, picturing James confronting Joe. Alex confronting James. Blake confronting Alex. Joe telling Alex everything.

Tearing out of the lift as fast as my flip-flops would

carry me, I could hardly bear to look. There they were, James, Blake and Alex, sitting at one of the tables, drinking coffee and, oh my God, laughing.

'Hey!' Alex stood up and leaned in for a quick kiss. I stared from one to the other, resting on Blake, who stared back with the smile of an angel. An angel that knew something I didn't. 'So I met James and Blake.'

'So I see,' I said, sitting down cautiously and accepting the coffee that James poured for me. On closer inspection of the bar, there was no sign of Joe. Phew. 'And how's that working out for you?'

'Uh, I kicked his ass for upsetting you with the photo stuff, then he kicked my ass for being a dick about the photos, and then he said he really liked my band and now we're having coffee.' Alex squinted against the sunshine. 'I think that's about where you came in.'

'Really? And now you're best mates?' I couldn't stop staring at Blake. He looked so horribly pleased with himself. And uh, hello? Shouldn't Alex still be angry on my behalf?

'I believe you mean BFFs,' James said. 'We are in Hollywood, darling.'

'And honestly, I'm not sure I could win in an actual fight,' Alex whispered theatrically. 'But I'll take him on if you want?'

'Oh, she'd love that,' Blake said. 'Get the two of you stripped to the waist and bare-knuckle boxing.'

'Right. Well, this is lovely. Given that we were supposed to meet at your hotel,' I glugged down the coffee, worrying about my dangerously high levels of caffeination. Worrying about what else Blake might decide to throw into the conversation. 'But I suppose at least you've all met and I'd rather there wasn't any violence.'

'Yeah, lucky escape,' Blake piped up. 'There is usually

violence involved when we meet your friends, huh, Angela?'

'Did Jenny hit him?' Alex asked.

'No,' I said quickly, cutting Blake off. Ooh, I knew he was still going to give me grief. 'Long story which we don't have time for right now. I don't know if you remember but we have an interview to do and I don't think it's a very good idea to discuss such a sensitive subject out here where everyone can hear, do you?'

'Let's go back to the Chateau then.' James sank his espresso. 'Car's downstairs.'

'There isn't time,' I sighed. Stupid boys not doing what they're told. 'We're going to have to do it in my room. Sorry Alex, are you OK up here for a while? We'll just be a couple of hours.'

'Sure,' he nodded. 'I was joking about my swimsuit, though. But there's a pretty good record store not far from here; maybe I'll go check it out.'

'OK.' As far as I was concerned, getting Alex out of the hotel was a great idea. Joe was nowhere to be seen right then, but still. 'I'll call you when we're all done.'

'Why don't we all go for dinner tonight?' James suggested. 'It's the least I can do, really. Let me take us all somewhere really nice.'

'Sounds great,' Alex agreed. 'We don't have plans, do we?'

'What plans could you have?' Blake asked, beaming at me again.

'None.' I pursed my lips. He was loving this. 'Dinner sounds lovely.'

'And you'll bring Jenny, right?' Blake put his arm around my shoulders as we headed back to the lift.

'If she's free.' I didn't want to seem too tense. It wouldn't do any good to have Alex be suspicious of

Blake and I didn't want to piss James off before I got the interview logged.

'And you know who else you should bring?' Blake squeezed me in a half-hug. 'That Joe guy. You know, prove there's no hard feelings.'

'Oh, Blake, really?' James pulled a pained expression and slumped against the wall of the lift.

'Do you want him selling a story on the back of the interview next week?' Blake asked. James shook his head. 'Then we should invite him. Angela?'

I felt like a hobbit in the middle of three six-footers, packed into such a tiny space, all staring at me. 'Mmm-hmm.'

'Great, we'll make a res for six then.' Blake smiled as the lift pinged at our floor. 'Maybe Dolce?'

'Whatever,' I said, shepherding them out of the lift and turning back to Alex, who yawned noisily, oblivious to Blake's meddling. Not that he could even know how much trouble he was causing. 'I'll see you later?'

'Later,' he replied in the deep, dark voice that made my stomach flip. Another quick kiss and then he was gone.

'All right,' James said, barely suppressing a big fat grin. 'So I see what you see in him.'

'Oh shut up,' I said, marching off towards my room. 'We're so not doing boy talk.'

'Then what's the point in being out?' James moaned, trailing along behind.

Four hours later, I stared at my final draft of the James Jacobs Coming Out interview. There were probably a few too many 'I was so confused' and 'I went through some dark times' quotes, but peppered liberally with James's sense of humour and, as much as it pained me, his genuine love for Blake. Plus Blake's carefully crafted, 'I never thought of myself as gay, I just fell in love with a man; I think anyone can fall in love with anyone' line. I had to admit, he was good at his job. Even when reading his coming out interview, thanks to Blake, James Jacobs's legions of female fans would be able to cling to the hope that they could turn him back.

I attached it to an email and sent it through to Mary, crossing everything. Once it was gone from my sent box, I picked up the phone and dialled Cici.

'Mary Stein's office,' she answered tightly.

'Hi, Cici. It's Angela.'

'Oh, the girl who turned James Jacobs gay,' she replied flatly. 'I just want to say thank you so much for fucking your job up so royally that I have to work on Saturday.'

'Oh, sorry.' I didn't really know what else to say. Apart from "HA", which wouldn't be very nice. 'Erm, I just called to confirm my flights for tomorrow.'

'Three-thirty out of LAX. And Mary wants you in the office at nine on Monday morning. And she said she'd call you once she'd looked at your interview. Which we only just got.'

'It wasn't late,' I protested. 'Mary said to get it to her for four o'clock your time.'

'And we've all loved sitting in the office all day waiting for it,' Cici replied. 'I can't believe you turned him gay.'

'You know, he was actually gay before I got here.'

'Sure he was.'

'You do know there's no Father Christmas, don't you?'

'Whatever, I'm emailing you the flight details now.'

'Same deal with the tooth fairy.'

'Bye girl who turned James Jacobs gay. Try not to bump into Jake Gyllenhaal on your way home.'

Hanging up, I re-read the article once more. It was sweet. I was happy. Flipping down my laptop, I moved over to the wardrobe and pulled out my travel bag. Packing would mean leaving. Leaving would mean never seeing Joe again. Never seeing Joe again would mean Alex could never find out what had happened. And that made me even happier.

Just dinner to get through, but what was I going to wear? Certainly not the jeans I'd filthied in the park, I noticed as I walked by the mirror. Seriously, was no one going to tell me I'd been walking around with dirt all up the backs of my legs all day? I pulled out the green Robert Rodriguez dress I'd worn to meet James. And put it away. No matter how beautiful it was, I didn't really need to prompt James to tell hilarious stories about me throwing up outside his cottage. Hmm, probably better not wear the yellow Phillip Lim either. One by one, I packed up my new dresses, trying not to think about my credit card bill, until I was left with nothing but a couple of T-shirts and Jenny's bikini. Not ideal for a sit-down dinner.

Without a better idea, I picked up the phone and called Jenny.

'Hey honey, everything OK?' She answered on the first ring for the first time in for ever.

'Almost,' I said, throwing unworn underwear in my bag. 'James and Blake want to take us for dinner tonight. Will you come?'

'Oh Angie, I don't know,' she crackled down the line. 'Is that a good idea?'

'Probably not,' I admitted. 'But James wants to apologize or something by buying us dinner. And Alex sort of accepted for me and I sort of accepted for you.'

'So you're actually calling to tell me I'm coming to dinner?'

'Yes. But you know, it might be fun?' I tried. 'I'm sure we'll end up somewhere nice and it'll be good to have a proper night out before we leave LA. One where no one ends up on the front page of Perez Hilton.'

'Hmm, yeah,' she said vaguely. 'It's just . . . I was kinda hoping we could do dinner tonight, just me and you. I really need to talk to you.'

'I know, I feel like I haven't seen you properly in ages.' I sniffed my black Kerrigan dress. Nope, couldn't get another wear out of that. 'Why don't we have a goodbye LA drink before dinner. I'm sure Alex won't miss us for an hour. I don't suppose you have anything I could borrow to wear, do you, stylist·extraordinaire?'

'I'll bring you something.' I could hear a smile in her voice but she still didn't sound too chipper. 'What time's dinner?'

'Uh, eight?' I looked at the clock. It was only just after one. 'Jenny, are you OK?'

'Let's just talk later, OK?' The line was breaking up. 'I'll come by your room at six? We'll get you all hot and then grab that drink.'

'And you promise not to beat James to death?'

'I do.'

'And Alex?'

'Maybe.'

'Jenny.'

'OK, I'll behave,' she relented. 'I just wish we could just do dinner on our own.'

'You can bring Daphne if she's about?' I bargained, even if the thought of adding Daphne to the mix didn't exactly fill me with joy. I hadn't seen her since she vanished with a stranger on our big night out at Bar

Marmont, and I didn't feel as though she had been missing me.

'Yeah, I don't think so,' Jenny let me off. 'Let's just get that drink.'

'Well, if you change your mind, Blake is going for a "more the merrier" vibe.' I took off my flip-flops and dropped them in the travel bag. 'He wants me to invite Joe.'

'Oh shit, what did you say?' she asked. 'Don't think I've forgotten about that ass-hat. I can beat him to death, right?'

'I'm sort of relying on not seeing him between now and tomorrow.' I wandered over to the bed and considered a nap. 'But if we ever come back to LA, you have my full permission to kick him hard in his face. More than once.'

'Awesome,' Jenny cackled. 'See you at six.'

As Jenny rang off, I heard the door click open.

'Hey, you done in there or should I go away?' Alex called through the door.

I smiled. 'I'm done, you can come in.'

He opened the door fully and held up a plastic bag. 'Good, I'm all shopped out.'

'That's pathetic.' I took the bag from him and flipped through the CDs. I hadn't heard of any of the bands but I was sure they were all very cool. 'You call one carrier bag shopped out. Jenny would laugh in your face.'

'Jenny laughs in my face all the time.' He took the CDs from me and placed them on the bedside table. 'What are the plans for this afternoon, Scoop?'

'Hmm, I think I have a very important nap to take,' I said, falling back onto the bed and taking his hands in mine. His pale New York skin had turned pink in the sun. Too cute. 'You?'

'I could get behind a nap.' Alex climbed over me, leaving one leg thrown over mine. 'But I'm not that tired.'

'I don't know what to tell you,' I said, relaxing back against him. It wasn't just his face that had caught the sun; he was warm all over. 'I'm knackered.'

'You'd better let me do all the work, huh?' I felt his lips on the back of my neck and closed my eyes. We did have a few hours to kill and it would be a terrible waste of a hotel room if we didn't, wouldn't it? As Alex's hands slid around my waist, I could only think that we should fall out all the time.

CHAPTER SIXTEEN

'Knock-knock, the fashion fairy is here,' Jenny declared, sailing into my room without actually knocking. 'Oh jeez, I'm supposed to be pissed with you, Brooklyn, could you at least put your pants on?'

I opened my eyes to see Alex sitting at my laptop in his boxers. Bless.

'OK Lopez,' he said, grabbing his jeans from the floor. 'But she's in my T-shirt so I'm gonna have to take whatever you've got in that bag.'

'Ooh, is that for me?' I was suddenly very awake. Jenny was holding a very large, stiff bag from – oh, be still my beating heart – Marc Jacobs.

'It is unless anyone asks, then it's for Tessa DiArmo.' With a flourish, Jenny produced a stunning vibrant purple silk shirtdress. 'What do you think?'

'Jenny, it's beautiful,' I breathed, bounding across the room to get closer to the pretty, pretty dress. 'I don't think I've ever seen anything so amazing.'

'Uh, boyfriend in the room?' Alex coughed from the table.

'I know, I'm amazing and, besides, I wanted you to look awesome for your last night with the paps.' Jenny hung the dress on the front of the wardrobe. 'So shower fast, wear your Louboutins and get your ass upstairs to the bar. You've got thirty minutes.'

Forty minutes later, I was wearing the most expensive outfit that had ever graced my body, the highest heels I'd ever attempted to walk in, and mismatched underwear, as usual. Hopefully Jenny wouldn't check; she would be so disappointed. I also hoped she'd let me off with the extra ten minutes I'd spent on my smoky-gold eye make-up since it matched the ensemble.

'You look amazing,' Alex said, adjusting the delicate gold belt around my waist. 'Like you forgot your pants and you don't even care.'

'I'm wearing my pants,' I said, confused. Was it too short? Could you see my arse?

'Language barrier.' He tugged lightly at the hemline. 'I meant trousers.'

'Fashion barrier,' I said, slapping his fingers. 'It's supposed to look like this. See you downstairs later.' A quick kiss and I was gone. The dress needed to be out where everyone could see it.

Stepping onto the balcony felt different, knowing that it would be the last time I'd see the view, judge the lingering sunbathers. And knowing that I was wearing a fifteen-hundred-dollar dress instead of Jenny's bikini and a post-wax rash felt pretty good too. Jenny was already at one of the tables, gazing out at the hills and sipping on what looked like her second mojito. For God's sake, I was only ten minutes late.

'You started without me?' I pulled out a chair and sat down very carefully. As much as I loved the dress, I knew it was going to have to go back tomorrow. Sob.

'You're late,' Jenny passed a full glass over to me. 'But you're hot. Damn, I'm good.'

'You are. You're looking pretty good yourself,' I agreed, leaning across the table so as not to spill even a drop of condensation on my dress and getting an eyeful of Jenny's amazing cleavage in her deeply slashed scarlet dress. 'If I didn't know better, I'd think you'd been styling for years. All that spending my money has been totally worth it. Are you going to try and do it when we get back? Because the free clothes would be amazing.'

'Yeah,' she looked at her nails. 'Drink your drink.'

'Oh no.' I tried not to look at my nails. Damn it, chipped to buggery. I was destined never to be completely put together. 'I'm not getting wasted tonight. I very much enjoyed waking up without throwing up this morning and I'm hoping to give it another try tomorrow. Although I'm probably going to need a drink over dinner, Blake is going to be a right pain in the arse, I can just tell.'

'You don't need to be that intuitive to work that out. Blake is an ass, period,' she slurped on her straw noisily.

'Jenny.' For the first time in what I realized was a good couple of days, I looked at my best friend. She did not look happy. 'Jenny, what's wrong?'

She smiled up at me. 'Actually nothing. For the first time in for ever, nothing is wrong.'

'Explain please?'

'Aw, Angie.' Jenny pushed her masses of chocolate curls back off her face then placed her hands flat on the table. 'I'm just gonna say this. I'm staying in LA.'

'Huh?'

She unwrapped my icy hands from around my mojito and held them in hers. 'I'm staying. With Daphne. I'm not coming back to New York.'

'You're staying?' I asked, squeezing her hands lightly. 'For how long?'

'I don't know,' she squeezed back. 'A while?'

'I don't understand, you're not coming back with me?'

'No.'

'You're not coming back with me tomorrow?'

'Nope.'

'Or next week?'

Jenny sighed and then smiled. 'I need some time out from New York, from work. I need some time to breathe.'

'But you can't just decide you're not coming back,' I said, panicking. 'You can't just say "oh I'm staying in LA for a bit". People don't.'

'You did,' Jenny reminded me, completely unnecessarily. 'And it worked out OK.'

'Only because I had you.' I hated it when people used facts to prove their point. They were so difficult to argue against. 'You can't just go making rash decisions: that's my job. The balance of our friendship will be completely thrown off and then, God, I don't know, the universe might end or something. Talk to me. What's really wrong?'

'You so already know.'

'Jeff?'

'Jeff.'

I gave her my very best Oprah look. 'You're going to uproot your entire life because of a boy?'

'Like you did?'

'Will you stop using me as an example?' I frowned. 'I am not a good example.'

'Honey, you're the best example.' Jenny squeezed my hands back, harder. 'You're the only example. I told you once that you were my personal hero and it's true. I haven't been myself for a really long time, you

288

know that. You're not going to sit there and pretend you haven't noticed?'

'I might be.'

'And I need to get away. I have loved living with you and if I thought I could get you to move to LA, I would – but I have to do this, Angie, I have to.'

I really didn't want to hear this. The idea of going back to New York without Jenny was terrifying. 'And your job?'

'They've actually been amazing,' she smiled. 'They're gonna let me work out my notice here while I set up the styling thing. And yeah, I know it's a flakey thing to do, but it's not forever. If it doesn't work out, I can go back to hotel stuff.'

'And you're going to live with Daphne?' I asked, making a mental note never to talk to Jenny's manager at The Union ever again.

'Yeah.' She released her grip on my hands and went back to her mojito. 'I'm sorry I didn't talk to you about it. You've just had so much going on, I didn't want you to be stressing over me.'

'Oh, Jenny.' I felt like crap. Even crappier than when I'd woken up next to Joe, if that were possible. 'I wish you'd said something. Why didn't you tell me it was this bad when we were at home?'

'I guess I didn't know it was this bad until I got here.' She looked out off the roof terrace. 'Yeah, I was down about Jeff, work was pretty crappy, but I just thought, you know, it was winter, and I don't mean to sound like a bitch but I was kinda jealous of you and Alex getting back together. I figured I'd get over it after a while.'

'And now you don't?'

'Now I feel like being here will be better for me for a while.'

I sat quietly for a moment. How could Jenny, my Jenny, think that being here would make her feel better?

'LA is different for me, Angie,' she said, reading my mind. Irritating. 'I know you've had a pretty shitty time so far but that's nothing compared to all the shit I've been through in New York for the last ten years. You know how you felt when you turned up? That's how I feel here. Like I could do anything, like there are a million new things to try. The only sucky thing is that you won't be here.'

'There's nothing I could say to get you to come home with me?' I asked, recognizing a losing battle when I saw it. 'Because I am about a minute away from freaking out.'

'I'm sorry.'

There was no way I was going to cry. There was more than my eye make-up at stake here. I didn't know if you could get tears out of a Marc Jacobs.

'Don't be sorry. If you need a bit of time away . . .' I felt a tiny tear trickle down past my mascara and make a tiny dark purple spot on my knee. Bugger. 'I just feel like I've let you down.'

'Honestly, Angie, I've been killing myself over this but I don't know what else to do.' She reached out and pressed away the tear track with a napkin. 'No tears. I don't have time to redo your make-up and I hate when you look like shit.'

'You're not going to like what's coming then,' I bleated as another tear followed the first. And then another and another until I was a blubbering, sobbing mess.

'Oh for Christ's sake,' Jenny groaned, scooting around the table and holding two new napkins under my eyes. 'Stop crying or I'm gonna throw you over the edge. And press these under your eyes. Don't rub.'

'Thank you,' I sniffed, pathetically. 'I'm sorry. You have to do what's best for you, I know, and I want you to. I'm happy for you, I promise. I'm miserable for me. Because you know, it's all about me.'

'Yeah, I know.' Jenny scooted up and gave me a hug. I tried to stop crying but all I could think was how much I would miss her hugs, all fluffy hair tickling my nose and coconut and candyfloss perfume. It wasn't fair.

'It'll be worth it when I'm a mega-stylist and we can actually keep these clothes,' she promised, breaking off the hug.

'That is true,' I agreed. 'So do we have time for one more girlie drink or do we have to—'

'You, asshole!'

Before I could finish, Jenny was on her feet and tearing over to the bar. It took me a couple of seconds to work out what was happening and before I could even stand up, Jenny was clambering up onto a stool and leaping over the bar, fluffy hair flying, arms windmilling into, oh God, Joe.

'You absolutely asshole,' she shouted, battering him backwards into a row of bottles. There weren't many people loitering around the pool but if she hadn't had their full attention before half a dozen bottles clattered and smashed on the floor, she had it now.

'Jenny!' I yelled, stumbling over as quickly as I could in my high, high heels. She certainly knew how to cap an emotional moment. 'Jenny, stop it!'

'What the fuck is wrong with you?' Joe yelled, eventually gathering his wits and folding Jenny's tiny fists up inside his bigger ones and holding her at arm's length. 'Lopez, chill the fuck out.'

'Don't you dare tell me to chill out,' she screeched. 'How could you?

'How could I what?' he barked back, his eyes darting around the bar until they rested on me. And then he smiled. 'You jealous, Lopez?'

Once I'd resisted the urge to throw up, I let Jenny beat him around the head for a couple more minutes before stepping in.

'Jenny, stop it, you'll break a nail,' I said, pulling her backwards slightly. Men never knew how to deal with aggressive women. Seriously, he just had to look at her heels: any challenge to her balance and she was over.

'Hey, English, call off your dogs.' He gave me a smile. 'I'm sorry I didn't call, but when I woke up and you'd vamoosed, I figured you'd come find me. When you wanted me.'

He paused to smile. I paused to gag.

'Where'd you get to anyway? You could have called Lopez from the room if you'd wanted to brag.'

'Oh, ew, Angie, can I get back to kicking his ass now?' Jenny bristled behind.

'Jenny,' I warned, even though I really did want to let her. How much of an arse was he?

'The reason I vamoosed was . . . because I was . . . well, a bit confused. To be honest, I don't strictly remember what happened.'

'Honestly?' Joe looked a little crestfallen. 'Wow.'

'So help me God, Joe,' Jenny started up again. 'You want to check your ego before I beat the living shit out of you for taking advantage of my best friend when she was out of it.'

I felt myself blush from head to toe. The few remaining people around the pool murmured to each other. What else did they expect but a bit of drama? They were in Hollywood, after all.

'Calm down, Lopez.' Joe folded his arms. 'I didn't do anything she didn't want. Right, English?'

'I don't remember,' I said, not knowing where to look.

'Well, he can't have been very good, so I'd say that's a blessing,' surmised a voice on the other side of the bar. Looking up, I saw Blake and James standing across from us. James had his arms folded, while Blake went for a slightly less concerned hands in pockets combined with a 'ha, I knew you were a big slag' expression.

'I don't think anyone was talking to you, man.' Joe turned to face the boys. I really want to say I wasn't a little bit excited. But I was.

'Doesn't sound like anyone particularly wants to talk to you, either,' James shrugged. 'And yet here you are. Maybe you should apologize to Angela and then just go away.'

'Apologize for what?' Joe walked around the bar. 'For sealing the deal when you couldn't?'

'Please can we just not?' My voice sounded awfully high to me. 'James, Blake, let's just go to dinner and Joe, I don't remember what happened the other night but whatever it was, I regret it massively and I don't want to talk about it ever again.'

'Whatever.' He looked me up and down. 'Just don't come back begging for more when this fag can't get the job done later on.'

'Right, that's it.'

In one swift move, James was in front of Joe, his arm up in his throat, pushing him back until his head cracked against the bar. It didn't look comfortable.

'James,' Blake shouted a short warning. 'Think.'

James nodded but didn't take his eyes off Joe. 'Apologize to Angela and then, if she's happy, we'll pretend this never happened. All of this.'

'I'm not apologizing,' he coughed. 'Nothing even happened – she was too wasted.'

'I was? Then why were your clothes on the . . .' I flushed an even deeper shade of red. 'Why were you still there in the morning?'

James rammed his forearm into his throat again. 'You might want to think really carefully before you answer.'

'I thought you might sober up a little?' Joe croaked. 'But you just talked about your ex, threw up and went back to sleep. It was too late to go home, I had a shift in the morning.'

'So we didn't?' I could barely breathe.

'We didn't,' Joe replied.

'But you let her think you did? You are all class.' James let him go with one last shove. 'Well, at least we'll all sleep better tonight. You're not even nearly good enough for her.'

'Jesus Christ, you can fucking have her,' Joe coughed and righted himself. 'Bitch.'

Which was about the point when James turned around and knocked Joe flat on his back with one almighty punch.

'I really feel like I've missed something here.'

I span around to see Alex staring at the sorry scene.

'Alex, it's uh, it's . . . this is Joe,' I pointed at the bloody, groaning pile on the floor. It was impossible to tell from his expression what he'd seen. Or heard.

'I waited downstairs but no one showed so I came up to find you.' He hadn't moved from the entry of the lift. 'I didn't realize you were . . . rumbling?'

'All right, Alex,' James said, stepping over Joe, who was sobbing loudly. 'We had a bit of trouble with this one but we really should get off. Reservations are in about half an hour and we have to get all the way up to the Mondrian. Nice shirt.'

Blake and Jenny followed James into the lift, Blake smirking at me, Jenny holding in nervous giggles, while I stepped awkwardly over Joe and took Alex's hand.

'What was that all about?' he asked, accepting my light kiss on the lips.

'Uh, I don't really know,' I said, pulling him along behind me. 'I told you they had a bit of a fight on Monday. I think it was the same thing.'

'Right,' Alex looked back at Joe while I silently prayed for him to keep sobbing long enough for me to get Alex safely into the next lift. 'Man, how glad am I that James didn't decide to kick the crap yesterday?'

'Very?' I asked, jabbing at the button.

If it was possible, the evening only got worse after we left the hotel. Luckily the manager set us away from the rest of the diners in the restaurant so at least we couldn't ruin anyone else's evening with the massive cloud of awkwardness that hung over us. Knowing my talent for saying the worst possible thing at the worse possible time, I ate in silence, keeping my leg pressed up against Alex, occasionally trying to distract him with a gentle squeeze of the thigh. And, if his responsive back-stroking was anything to go by, it was working.

In between ordering masses of food and many, many bottles of wine, James kept the conversation going for everyone, volleying questions at Alex about the band, about New York and, most dangerous of all, about me. Alex handled the grilling well, smiling, nodding, only occasionally kicking me lightly under the table and trying to divert the conversation to Jenny and Blake, but Jenny was too busy doing her bit by drinking as much of the wine that James kept ordering as possible.

By the time her too-little-too-late duck arrived, she was on her second bottle and veering wildly between overexcitedly discussing her new LA life with Blake and choking up over leaving me behind in New York. And when Blake wasn't getting Jenny all worked up about the celebrities he could introduce her to, he was asking me increasingly awkward questions, preferably while Alex was listening. By the time the waiter came to ask if we wanted dessert, it was a relief to say no, get the bill and call for a cab. I couldn't remember a time when I'd felt more tense.

'Well, have a safe flight back to New York.' James shook Alex's hand and pulled him into an acceptable one-armed man hug. 'Good to meet you, take care of her. I'm guessing that one gets herself into trouble fairly easily.'

'Yes, she does, and she isn't going to have me to get her out of it any more.' Jenny threw herself on me. 'Seriously, Brooklyn, I'm giving you my number before you go tomorrow and I expect you to call me the first time she falls down an open hatch in the sidewalk or something.'

'I'm not going to fall into a hatch in the sidewalk,' I mumbled into a mouthful of hair. 'Honestly Jenny, I'll be OK.' I was so going to fall into a hatch in the sidewalk.

'Yes you are,' Jenny insisted, flinging herself from me to Alex, who held his arms out, terrified. 'And I'll have to accessorize your cast or something. You promise you'll call me whenever you need me.'

'I promise,' Alex said, peeling her off him. 'And so does Angela.'

They climbed into our cab, leaving me, Blake and James outside the restaurant.

'So, Blake, I know it's been a bit weird—'

'We so don't need to do this.' He cut me off and walked off towards his and James's car, holding up a hand in something of a wave. 'Bye, Angela.'

'At least that wasn't awkward,' I breathed out, letting James draw me into a big hug.

'Yeah, thank heaven for small mercies,' he said. Even now, after everything, I couldn't help but notice how delicious that man smelled. 'I'm sorry this week was so difficult but I'm really glad I met you. I think everything's going to be better though. Even though you can't tell, Blake is so happy and that's because of you.'

'Well, I'm very glad I made him happy,' I lied. 'And you promise you'll take care of Jenny?'

'Cub scout's promise,' he saluted. 'And you promise you'll invite me to your wedding?'

'Baby steps,' I gave him a stern look. 'I just hope we can get through all this when we get home.'

'You'll be fine.' James kissed me on the cheek and pushed me towards the cab. 'You're so clearly horribly in love.'

'Yeah,' I said, peering into the back seat. Alex was cradling a sobbing, slightly worse-for-wear Jenny and mouthing 'help?' in the darkness. 'I hope so.'

'I think so,' James said as I slid into the back seat and Alex's free arm.

'Don't come too close, I'll cry on your dress,' Jenny sniffed. 'If I fuck it up, I can't take it back.'

'Then James will have to pay for it.' I wrapped her into a hug across Alex's lap as James shut the cab door, laughing.

CHAPTER SEVENTEEN

I hadn't expected to be sad to be checking out of The Hollywood, but after Jenny and I had bundled all of our bags into the back of the Mustang, I felt strange walking out of the doors for the last time.

'Are you sure you've got everything?' I asked a very hungover Jenny, who nodded back and draped herself delicately across the back seat, in between her cases.

'Angie, I'm only moving, like, ten minutes up the road,' she said from behind her hair. 'If I forgot something, I think I can come and get it when I turn up for work here tomorrow.'

'Did you speak to anyone about last night? Is everything still OK about you working here?'

'Everything's fine for me,' she said, sipping from a bottle of water. 'Joe got his ass fired so I don't imagine I'm gonna have any hassle.'

'He got fired?' I hissed, watching Alex wander outside, looking around for us. 'How come?'

'I don't think the management really like it when the staff get into a bar brawl with really famous movie stars. Or when they sleep with the guests.'

'But he didn't sleep with the guests,' I said quickly as

Alex waved and started over to the car. 'And it was James that hit Joe. Not that I'm defending him, obviously.'

'Obviously,' Jenny said. 'And, don't get mad, but they think that because I told them he did. And it really doesn't matter who started or finished the fight, this is Hollywood: celebrities are never guilty. He deserved it, Angie. Don't start feeling all guilty now.'

'I don't.' I was as surprised as she was. 'He's a complete shit.'

'Yeah, he is.' Jenny gave me a feeble high five. 'Hey, Alex.'

'Hey.' He stood by the driver's door. 'Am I driving?'

'Well she's not.' I looked back at Jenny, who was getting greener by the second. 'And if I'm being totally honest, I don't really fancy it. I have no idea where we're going.'

'Then I'm driving.' He opened the door and dropped in beside me. I hadn't ever really thought about it, but living in New York, I'd never seen Alex drive. I didn't even know that he could, but as if he wasn't amazing enough, he put on a pair of Ray-Bans, turned over the engine and pulled out onto Hollywood Boulevard.

'What?'

'Nothing,' I smiled happily. 'I just didn't know you could drive.'

'I guess there are still lots of things you don't know about me,' he said, slowing down for a red light. 'And I guess there are lots of things I don't know about you.'

'Guys, pull over,' Jenny groaned, batting me on the back of the head. 'I'm gonna be sick.'

'Well there's one less thing not to know about, Jenny,' I said, stroking her hair while she threw up into her handbag, trying not to think about what Alex could mean.

* * *

'So, I'll call you when we get back?' I said to Jenny, carrying her bags into the living room. Daphne's place was beautiful, all open plan, big windows and a terrace with a view out over LA. Maybe there was something to be said for having a sugar daddy.

'Yeah, call me when you're back at the apartment.' Jenny propped herself up against the doorframe. 'I guess I might need you to send some stuff.'

'I suppose so,' I said, thinking how weird it would be to walk in without her, not knowing when she would be home. If she would be home.

Jenny slipped down the frame, buzzing her own door bell. 'I have to be sick again.'

'Do you want me to stay for a bit?' I risked her puking down my back and went in for a hug. 'I can stay if you want?'

'I'm cool, go get your flight,' Jenny said, falling on the bell again. 'What is that noise? Angie, say you don't hate me for staying here?'

'Of course not, I do get it,' I said reluctantly. 'I just wish you didn't have to be so far away to sort your head out.'

'You could always move here with me for a while?'

I looked back out at the car. Alex's head was bobbing along to whatever he was listening to on the radio.

'Or you could stay in New York with him.'

'If he still wants me to after all of this,' I said.

'Jesus, Angie,' Jenny let go of the doorframe long enough to slap me round the side of the head. 'I'm gonna have to get more minutes on my call plan if I have to talk you out of this every time you guys have a row. You're just gonna get in the car, fly back home, maybe fool around a little on the plane and then pretend that none of this ever happened.'

'Sounds like a plan,' I said, letting her out of the hug. 'I love you, Jenny, you always know what to say.'

'Yeah, well, that's my thing,' she said. 'Love you too, Angie. You always know how to mess up and make me feel needed.'

Walking back to the car, I tried not to cry but I couldn't help it. When everything else had gone wrong in my life, Jenny had always been there to help me make sense of myself. What would happen now? And why was it so easy for us to throw around the reasons why we loved each other when I couldn't say to the person who needed to hear it the most?

'She OK?' Alex asked, turning down the radio.

I nodded. 'She will be.'

'You OK?' he asked, wiping away the tears that were rolling down my cheeks.

'I will be.' I ran my fingers under my eyes to pick up any stray mascara streaks and smiled. 'Airport?'

'We've actually got a couple of hours,' he said, rolling out into the street. 'And I'm not desperate to spend any more time than we have to in LAX.'

'What do you want to do?' I asked, suddenly nervous to be alone with him, even though he was smiling.

'I know this is going sound weird, but I was kind of thinking the beach? Who knows when I'm going to be back in LA, right? I feel like I should at least see the Pacific Ocean.'

'Alex Reid, beach bum,' I shrugged off my cardigan, getting my last few rays of LA sunshine. 'Who would have thought it?'

I paused on the boardwalk to kick off my sandals while Alex strode on across the beach. Seeing him silhouetted against the sky and the ocean was so surreal, I hardly dared to follow, in case he disappeared like a mirage. Except instead of a palm tree and a sparkling spring, there was a pair of black jeans and an un-ironed Kellogg's Corn Flakes T-shirt hanging from his wide shoulders and slim hips. He turned and smiled, interrupting my shameless ogling.

'You checking me out?' he held his hand over his eyes, the Santa Monica sun too much for his Brooklyn-bred eyesight, even with his Ray-Bans.

'Maybe?' I said, stepping into the sand. Good God it was hot. Good God he was hot. So much hotter than James Jacobs. Anyone could spend half their life in the gym and get a two-hundred-dollar haircut. Only Alex could pull off that too-long-on-one-side fringe that hadn't seen a comb in — well, how long could it be since he'd had it cut? A month? But it was still so soft when I tiptoed across the sand towards him and cautiously brushed it away from his face. 'You're going to burn even faster than me. Do you have any sunscreen?'

'I'll be fine,' he said, taking my hand from his face and holding it in his. 'Don't tell anyone but I actually tan pretty well. I just don't see that much sun at home.'

'I suppose you don't get many tanned rock stars,' I said, happy to be talking about nothing. 'It's not very hipster, is it? Not very—'

'Angela, I love you.'

I knew that my mouth was hanging open in a slightly unattractive fashion but I couldn't move a muscle.

'Angela?'

I blinked. Nope, he was still there. I wasn't asleep. Maybe I had sunstroke from not wearing a hat in the car on the way to the beach. Or maybe I was still drunk from, well, the whole week.

'Are you OK?'

'Yes,' I said finally. 'What did you say?'

'Something I should have said before you left but I didn't want you to freak out and then be too far away to do anything about it. I love you, Angela.'

'Why?'

'What?'

'Why do you love me?'

Well, why not try and ruin this perfect moment? Well done, Angela.

'Sit down,' Alex sighed, pulling me down onto the sand beside him. It really was red hot; fine for him in his jeans but more than uncomfortable on the backs of my legs. 'Of all the responses you could have given me, I wasn't expecting that. You want me to tell you why I love you?'

'Yes please,' I said quietly, not quite able to meet his eyes. It wasn't that I didn't believe him – well, it was; but more that this scene was so surreal – Alex sitting there next to me in his skinny jeans, his crumpled T-shirt, all pale skin and black hair clashing against the sun and the sand – that it genuinely felt as though I was dreaming.

'OK, I love you because you have that knee-high stack of books at the side of your bath that are all curling up at the corners because you spend hours in that tub when you should be working. I love you because you put my socks on the radiator if you get up before me, which you always do. I love you because you make me want to do things that I would never have done six months ago.' He shook his head. 'I love you because you make me want to come out to LA and tell you I love you.'

'Oh,' I pushed my hair behind my ears and tried to smile at the sand, 'really? Even after all this week's nonsense?'

'Any particular bit of nonsense you're referring to?' he asked.

I actually wasn't sure if there was. 'No?'

'So no four a.m. phone calls you want to elaborate on?'

Well, that could have been worse. 'Oh. Yes. There was one of those,' I nodded, looking away again. 'That would be the one when I said I love you.'

'That was the one I was thinking of, yeah,' Alex replied evenly. 'Why, what did you think I meant?'

I shrugged, drawing a figure eight in the sand with my finger. 'Just been such a mad week. I wasn't thinking of anything in particular.'

'So you weren't thinking about you spending the night with that guy James knocked out last night?' he asked.

I paused my circling, paused my breathing for a moment. 'Not especially.'

'You know that trust is really important to me, Angela,' Alex said, putting his hands over mine. 'It's not like we didn't have this conversation already.'

Oh God, I thought, squeezing my eyes closed tight. Don't let this be happening again; don't let him do this again.

'I would really appreciate you telling me what happened instead of me having to piece it together from what I heard last night. I'm guessing whatever I dream up will actually be way worse than what actually happened.'

'I didn't know you were there,' I said. 'You heard all of it?'

'I don't know. Why don't you tell me?'

'OK,' I started, trying to run through the story in my head before it all came spilling out. Was there any way for me to tell him the whole story without him getting up and walking away at the end of it? Probably not.

'Right, short version? I thought I'd lost my job, I thought I'd lost you, James was refusing to sort everything out and so I got totally wasted at the hotel bar. Joe helped me get back down to my room, he kissed me and I passed out. The next thing I knew, I woke up, he was there, I freaked out and that was that. And I only really found out what happened last night. Which was nothing. Nothing at all. It was just so stupid. I was just so stupid.'

'So you weren't going to tell me?' he asked.

'I didn't know what there was to tell.' I looked up but Alex was leaning back on his elbows, staring out at the sea. His nose was bright pink. 'OK, no I wasn't going to tell you.'

'Even when you thought you'd slept with him?'

Was there even a right answer? 'I think I would have told you when we got home. But when it turned out nothing had happened, no, I don't think I would have said anything.'

He didn't move, didn't speak.

'I couldn't see the point in making things worse than they were. Nothing happened; I didn't think it made sense to hurt you for no reason.'

After what felt like for ever, he breathed out and nodded. 'Makes sense.'

'And the rest of it is all sorted, right?' After being almost scared to make eye contact with him all morning, now all I wanted was for him to look at me. 'All the stupid photo internet stuff.'

'Did you know James was gay when you were in his hotel room that night?' he asked.

What happened to 'you don't have to explain anything to me'?, I thought, puffing out my cheeks in concentration. 'No, but there was nothing going on,' I said. That wasn't a lie. Nothing actually went on.

'I don't want to come off as paranoid, but it seemed kind of strange that you would call me at four in the morning and tell me you love me hours before the pictures of you and James came out.' He turned his head to look at me and took off his Ray-Bans. 'Why do you love me, Angela?'

Arsehole. Turning my question back on myself. 'Why do I love you?'

'It's really easy to say I love you, it's another altogether to explain why,' he said. 'As you know.'

'Yeah, OK,' I closed my eyes again. It wasn't that bloody easy, was it, or I would have told him weeks ago and we wouldn't even be having this conversation. Why was this so tricky? I was for ever telling other people why I loved him.

'I love you because you always have a T-shirt under your pillow for me, even if you don't know I'm coming to stay. I love you because you know I want sugar in my tea in the morning but not at night and because you always pretend you forgot I wanted a skinny hot chocolate in Starbucks because you know I really prefer full fat but don't like to order it in case the girl behind the counter thinks I'm fat.'

Alex started to smile. So I carried on.

'I love you because when I get out of the subway and I see you in the coffee shop by your place or I'm coming back home and you're in the deli buying me Lucky Charms, I actually get butterflies in my stomach. Every time. Or when I'm knocking on your door, just before you answer, I can feel them bubbling up inside me. And when I wake up, I look for you, even if you're not there. It's like my brain just thinks you should always be there, like waking up with you is my default setting.' I copied his pose and leaned back on my elbows. Damn, the sand was still hot. 'Is that OK? Did I pass?'

He leaned over and kissed me gently on the lips, his skin warm against mine. For the longest moment, no one said anything.

'I'm sorry, it wasn't a test for you,' he said, pulling away slightly. 'It was a test for me. I didn't mean to make you feel shitty, I never wanted to be one of those asshole boyfriends who doesn't trust his girlfriend but, there's no excuse, I guess I'm not totally over what happened with my ex. But you're not my ex. I know that. I promise I'll never ever question you, ever. I was totally being that asshole.'

'Is that it?'

'That's not enough?'

'I mean, you're not going to say you love me but you can't be with me?' I pressed my forehead against his, wondering why I couldn't just shut my mouth.

'I was just going to stop at I love you,' he said, pushing me back into the sand and kissing me again.

'I can work with that,' I said, rolling on top of him. The sand was still awfully hot.

CHAPTER EIGHTEEN

'Jenny, it's me,' I mumbled into my mobile. 'Pick up if you're there?'

Nothing. And I was trapped in a pitch-black apartment with none of the lights working. No matter how many times I flicked the light switch by my bed on and off. My mum would have been very proud.

'Shit,' I sighed. 'Well, if you get this, can you call me back and tell me where the fuse box is? Seriously, what were you thinking, moving to LA?'

I pressed the red button to cancel the call and waved the light from my phone around the room, wandering out into the hallway. Surely it would be somewhere around here? I'd been living in the apartment on my own for a week and so far I'd had to call a plumber in when I dropped my Tiffany necklace down the plughole in the kitchen, call an exterminator in when I mistook one of Jenny's old clip-in hair extensions for a mouse, and call some random stranger in off the street when a massive spider decided it wanted to share the shower. I was determined to conquer this crisis on my own.

Stupid Alex and his stupid three a.m. phone call.

I squinted up above the doorframe, was that big white thing a fuse box? But as much as I appreciated his semi-drunken declaration of love at all hours of the night, if he hadn't called this time, I wouldn't have woken up, then I wouldn't have had to go for a wee and found out the electricity was off. Which would have meant I wouldn't have worked myself up into a panic that there was a blackout, which would have meant I wouldn't have called him back and he wouldn't have worried me even more by saying it was just my electric that was out. Living on my own was not working out well.

I bit down on my bottom lip and pressed my hand to my forehead, not knowing quite what to do. I glanced around, looking for inspiration, and found it sparkling through the window. The city skyline lit up the living room, the Chrysler building outlined in white light down the street. I felt my way across the room, success-fully only stubbing my big toe twice.

Leaning against the windowsill, I stared out onto the still busy street below and I breathed out, slightly calmer. How could Jenny leave this? How could year-round sunshine and a convertible compete with New York City? Even now, in the middle of the night, the streets were alive with people. Could Jenny pop on her Uggs right now and be eating chow mein within five minutes? Not likely. Well, it was possible but I was pretty certain she'd have to at least get in that convertible and drive ten miles to find it. I watched a stream of yellow cabs and police cruisers rolling past, couples holding hands and running across the street, trying to beat the light; a general assortment of characters wandering around, ridiculously early on a Tuesday morning, not freaking out because they couldn't reset their electricity.

'Come on, Angela,' I said to myself, 'this is stupid.'

For a second, I considered just going back to bed and worrying about it in the morning, but I knew it would keep me awake. I was going to beat this. I padded back through the living room, bashing my knee as I went.

On closer, tiptoe, inspection, the white thing over the door did look an awful lot like a fuse box. Only one of the switches was down and, from my feeble recollection, that meant a fuse had tripped. Of course, I didn't have a stepladder. Or a step. Or anything that could feasibly be used to climb on to reach. I looked at the phone in my hand – I could call Alex? He could probably reach but that would feel a tiny bit like admitting defeat. And I had to be in the office at nine. If he came over now, half cut, there was no way I'd be getting to sleep anytime soon. Which wasn't a horrible thought, I smiled to myself, but no, I had to do this. I refused to be such a rubbish girl. Unless being a rubbish girl might be just the thing . . . I dashed back into the bedroom, looking for my highest heels. Two minutes later, I'd accessorized my hot pink Victoria's Secret pyjama top and American Apparel hot pink boy shorts with my gold Christian Louboutin stilettoes. Very sexy.

I grabbed a can of hairspray from the side of the sink on my way back into the hall and reached up as high as I could, bashing at the cover of the fuse box until it flipped down.

'Come on,' I puffed, extraordinarily pleased with myself. I pushed up onto my toes, trying to flip the tripped switch without spraying myself in the eyes with Elnett. Every part of me strained. If I could do this, I could do anything. I could sort out all the bills I had to transfer into my name. I could work out what the 401k thing was on my wage slip from *The Look*. I could work out what the equivalent to Night Nurse was in the chemist – how many variations on a cold medicine did one city need?

On my seventh little leap, I bashed the lid of the can against the switch, clattering backwards into the door.

'Angela?' yelled a voice on the other side.

I jumped up, my heart pounding from the shock of my late-night caller and my admittedly surprising (even to me) success at resetting the fuses.

'Angela, are you OK? I heard a bang?'

I pushed myself up out of the pile of shoes I'd landed in (Jenny had always been on at me to put them away) and peered through the peephole. It was Alex.

'Ange, let me in.' He was standing with one arm against the wall, staring at the floor. 'I'm not drunk. Well, not really.'

I opened the door slowly, so happy that my heart still skipped a little when I laid eyes on him, even with his flushed cheeks and wide eyes.

'Very sexy,' he slid through the door, taking me around the waist. 'Promise you'll always be waiting for me in heels at three in the morning?'

'Oh,' I blushed, trying to kick my way out of the shoes. 'I'll see what I can do.' I'd spent months trying to maintain an illusion of sleeping exclusively in sexy nightdresses or Alex's old T-shirts. This was not a look I'd have chosen for an impromptu sleepover.

'So this blackout thing, just a ruse to get me over?' he asked, pushing me gently backwards towards the bedroom.

'No,' I protested, albeit not very strongly. 'The fuses tripped but I fixed it. Are you proud?'

'Absolutely,' he smiled glassily, flicking lights out as we went. 'I think we should turn the lights out though, just in case.'

'Just in case,' I agreed. So I'd be going into the office knackered in the morning. Again.

'Morning Cici,' I yawned, sailing past her desk, bright and early and absolutely shattered. 'Is Mary in yet?'

'Morning girl-who-turned-James-Jacobs-gay,' she sang back. 'Of course she is. Gonna try and turn her too?'

'It's been a week. You're not even starting to get tired of that joke yet, are you?'

She shook her head and smiled sweetly. 'It's so not a joke. You turned one of the hottest guys on the planet gay. I should kick your ass. You turned that hipster boyfriend of yours yet?'

'Not as far as I know.' I was fairly certain he wasn't gay after last night. And this morning. And hopefully later this evening.

'Good, he's kind of hot. For a hipster,' she shrugged. 'Don't come any closer, I'm dating someone who doesn't seem to be a complete loser at last and I don't want you turning me gay either.'

'I'll try to keep my distance,' I promised. Shouldn't be too bloody hard.

Mary sat at her computer, as always, sharp grey bob swinging as she tapped away at the keyboard, little square glasses halfway down her nose. 'Angela, honey!'

I froze. Honey? What was wrong?

'Sit down, honey,' she said, looking up and switching off her monitor.

Double honey? Something was definitely wrong. And she had never, ever turned off her computer in my presence. I hoped she wasn't ill.

'Circulation figures are in for the James Jacobs issue of *Icon*,' Mary said. 'And they're good.'

'What's good?' I held my breath.

'Two and a half million good. Up from one and a half.' She could hardly sit still. 'There are a lot of very happy faces on the exec floor this morning, Angela Clark.'

I bit my lip a little bit too hard. Two and a half million people were reading my interview? OK, really two and a half million people were reading about James Jacobs being gay, but still, it was my interview.

'And that's without factoring in the website hits, the uplift in traffic to your blog, even subscriptions are up. To *Icon* and *The Look*.' Mary broke out into what could only be described as a grin. 'Angela, I'm so, so proud. And so, so sorry about how hard it was to get here. I know I was kind of an asshole when you were out in LA.'

'Not at all,' I said, thinking quite the contrary but being far too English to agree with her. 'So I'm not in trouble with anyone?'

'Hardly,' she beamed. 'As of the second those numbers came in, you are the A-number-one golden girl of Spencer Media. I think you could march up there and demand your own magazine right now if you wanted it.'

'Might be a bit ambitious,' I said, feeling myself colour up. It was now or never. 'I was thinking, though . . .'

'Dangerous pastime.' Mary raised an eyebrow.

'What do you reckon the chances would be of me writing more stuff for *The Look*. I mean, the magazine.'

'Like?'

'Like maybe a column? Or some features?' I sat on my hands to try and avoid biting at my nails. 'Or anything really?'

'You know I was joking about your own magazine,

313

right?' Mary pressed her finger against her lips and shook her bob. 'You want to write a column in *The Look*?'

I pushed out my bottom lip and nodded. 'Any chance of that?'

'You know I don't work on the magazine, Angela. It's not as though I can commission a column for the magazine, just like that.'

'But you could speak to someone?' That golden girl status had dropped pretty bloody quickly.

'Yeah, I could speak to someone. But so could you.'

'I know I could speak to my editor on the magazine but I really don't know her as well as you. She just sends me CDs and stuff to review but I don't see her, hardly ever, and—'

'That's not what I meant, Angela,' she said. 'I meant, given the position you're in right now – and I do mean right now as in today – you could go and talk to some other magazines. Your profile is very, very high, but that won't last long.'

'But I don't want to go elsewhere,' I protested. 'I love working with you and I don't—'

'Yes, but imagine you'd come in here this morning and told me that you'd been approached by another publisher, maybe one of our rivals, and they'd offered you a blog and a column and that you were considering it . . .'

'I'm imagining,' I said slowly.

'And if you'd told me that, I can't see that we'd want to let you go, so I would offer you a raise on your blog and offer to speak to the magazine editor right away . . . So, anything you want to tell me . . .?'

'I've been approached by another publisher?'

'And?'

'They've offered me a blog and a column?'

314

'Right.'

'So . . .'

'So, I can offer you a raise on the blog and I'll speak to the magazine editors today.' Mary flicked her computer screen back on. 'I'll call you later.'

'Thanks, Mary,' I said, standing up to leave, not entirely certain of what had happened. 'I'll speak to you later?'

'Yes you will,' she said without looking up. 'And really good work on the interview, Angela. All the bull-shit that went along with it aside, you did great work.'

'Thanks?' I was fairly certain it was a compliment. 'Bye Cici.'

'Bye girl-who-turned-James-Jacobs-gay.'

Yes, of course I wanted to spend more time here.

'So you fixed the fuses?'

'Yes, Jenny,' I sighed, hustling along Forty-Second Street towards Bryant Park. Already the little square of green was full of busy Midtown workers trying to snatch five minutes in the spring sunshine. The weather had broken in the last week and the streets of New York were suddenly somewhere I wanted to be again and not the subzero enemy of the ballet pump, friend only to the ugly Ugg. The last time I'd been sitting in the park, (trying unsuccessfully to mend a broken heel), it had been so cold, I could barely breath. 'But seri-ously, you shouldn't leave me alone. I'm sure I broke the oven.'

'You have an oven?'

'We. We have an oven,' I practically shouted down my mobile phone. 'It's still very much our oven. And yes, it's definitely there. I found some old cereal boxes in there; you've been using it as a cupboard.'

'You didn't find a roommate yet?' she crackled.

'It's only been a week,' Through sheer force of habit, I looked both ways up and down the road, even though the traffic only went north, before sprinting across Sixth Avenue. 'I haven't even been looking for a flatmate. I've been so busy.'

Which wasn't entirely untrue. I'd had an entire week of TiVo to catch up on and, well, I was still hoping I would open the door at any second to find Jenny on the doorstep, bag in hand, sobbing that LA was a big bag of crap and she was home for good.

'Busy turning more hot guys gay?'

'Don't you start,' I muttered. 'Anyway, how are you? Bored? Missing me? Coming home?'

'Uh, real answer or answer that will make you feel better?'

'The second one.'

'It sucks. It's been raining every day; I'm not getting to do any sort of styling; totally didn't meet Ryan Phillippe yesterday and I hate it.'

'Just as well,' I said over the swishing and cursing in the background. 'Jenny Lopez, tell me you are not driving while you're talking to me.'

'I'm not driving while I'm talking to you?'

Well, I had asked her to lie.

'How's Alex? Everything OK?' she yelled, but not over her own horn because she wasn't driving.

'Yeah,' I said. 'I think so. I mean, we had the talk before we left but we haven't really discussed it since. Any of it.'

'You two using the L word?'

'Hmm. Kind of.'

'You using the L word when you're not drunk or in bed? Or drunk in bed?'

'Not really. I feel a bit like the whole LA thing never happened.'

316

She went quiet for a moment. 'Doesn't mean a thing, Angie.'

'Hmm.'

'It's not like he was totally gushing with the emotion before, is it?'

'Yeah, he sort of was.'

'Yeah?'

'Yeah.'

'But you don't think there's anything wrong?' she asked. 'Maybe he's just, you know, expressing his feelings without words. Baby.'

'He writes songs for a living, Jenny,' I replied. 'I think he's fairly comfortable with words. I don't know. I'm just getting so tired of trying to second-guess him, but I don't want to say anything and risk getting into another deep and meaningful. What if something is wrong and he starts thinking it's all just too much like hard work?'

'It does sound a little like hard work, honey,' she said. 'You should dump his ass and get back over to LA. You could totally blog from here. Ooh, you and James could do an internet show! It would be awesome.'

'Maybe,' I smiled at the thought. It would be awesome. 'Have you seen him?'

'Uh, no, because he wasn't there when I did not met Ryan Phillippe last night. And he did not say to say hi.'

'Right. I'm going to ignore the Ryan Phillippe thing until you manage to fit it in a third time. He's OK?'

'He's totally OK,' she confirmed. 'He's so out, it's not even funny. He and Blake are making out all over town. You haven't seen the pictures?'

'Strangely enough, I haven't really been keeping up with the gossip blogs,' I said. 'I'm glad everything's all right for him, though. Blake not so much.'

'Yeah, right.' She broke off to launch a series of impressive expletives at whoever was in the next car. 'You know how I'm not driving? Well, I didn't just turn the wrong way down a one-way street so I'm just gonna go because I'm . . . busy.'

'Just be careful,' I tried not to tut. How was I supposed to take care of her if she was living two and a half thousand miles away? 'I'll speak to you later. Love you.'

'Well fuck you too asshole! Love you, Angela,' she called back and hung up.

After stocking up on too many boxes of cereal and cartons of milk, I ambled upstairs, struggling with my keys. I juggled a box of Lucky Charms, a half-empty Starbucks and my beloved, but now quite frankly knackered handbag, managing to wedge my cereal between the door, my cheek and shoulder while I fumbled my key into the lock, waiting for a click.

'I could just hold that for you?'

'Oh God, Alex,' I gasped, throwing my shopping across the landing, narrowly avoiding blinding him with a box of Cap'n Crunch. 'I didn't hear you behind me.'

'That would be because you were talking to your shopping the whole way up the stairs.' He took a couple of boxes from me and kissed me on the forehead.

'I don't have a flatmate any more, OK?' I muttered, pushing the door open. 'I have to talk to someone.'

'Yeah, I've kind of been wanting to talk about that,' Alex said behind me. But I wasn't really listening. The apartment was full of flowers. Not just a couple of bouquets on the windowsill and the kitchen counter but actually full. Every surface was groaning with hand-tied bouquets of roses, boxes of lilies, vases spilling over with gerberas and every single arrangement was a different colour. It was so beautiful that the fact a complete stranger had broken into my apartment escaped me for a second. I turned and looked at Alex. Unless it wasn't a complete stranger. Maybe it was someone who just so happened to be hiding out at the top of my stairs.

'Did you do this?' I asked, dropping the rest of my shopping. 'It's incredible.'

'I really want to say yes,' he said, following me into the apartment. 'But all I did was this.'

He took my hand and covered it in both of his, leaving something small and hot in my palm. It was a key.

'You borrowed the spare key?' I asked, still disoriented by the flowers; the sweet smell of the roses was almost unbearable. I put the key down on the side and went to open a window. 'Is that how you let the flower man in?'

'I didn't let anyone in,' Alex said. 'I was waiting across the road in the diner for you. Like I said, I didn't do this. Starting to wish I had: sure as hell would make this easier.'

'Make what easier?' I asked, hunting for a card. There had to be something in one of the baskets. Eventually I spotted a big white envelope peeking out of one of the cardboard bags packed with freesias and baby's breath. 'Oh my God, it's from James.'

'Great,' Alex said flatly.

'"Dear Angela,"' I read aloud. '"Hope this isn't too OTT. I can't help it, I'm gay you know. Jenny lent me her key, I've asked the courier to leave it in the bedroom. She says you can bring it back when you come back out to visit us VERY SOON. Love James x." Isn't that so lovely?'

'Lovely,' Alex repeated, still standing in the doorway,

framed by two giant three-foot vases packed with towering lilies.

'Just let me find the key and I'll make a drink,' I called from the bedroom. 'Did you want to do something? Sorry, I haven't even said hello, this is just mad, sorry. Oh my God.'

'What is it now?'

'I don't know but it's from Marc Jacobs,' I squealed, ripping open a second white envelope that rested on top of a large, stiff white carrier bag. Jenny's key fell on to my floor, vanishing under my bed. 'From my friend Marc. He says look after this one.'

Inside the carrier bag was a huge white dust bag and inside the dust bag was an enormous royal blue leather satchel. I dropped my old beloved bag on the floor and slipped the slender strap over my head, letting the bag rest against my hip. I span to show Alex, beaming from ear to ear. He gave me a tight smile and bent down to pick up my spare key.

'Isn't it beautiful?' I stretched 'beautiful' out for about a minute before turning back to my mirror to admire the bag. 'Isn't James so amazing?'

'Yeah,' Alex said, one hand behind his head, ruffling his short choppy hair while his long fringe flopped down over a distinctly unhappy expression. 'Where should I put this key?'

'Well actually, I was thinking.' I felt my face flush and started to stumble over my words. 'I was thinking that you should maybe hang on to it.'

'You were?' he asked, half a smile starting on his face.

'I was going to get one cut for you,' I nodded, excited that he wasn't freaking out. 'After last night's fuse-box fiasco, I think it would make sense. I mean, Erin has one but she's all the way up town and it makes more sense for you to have it, doesn't it?'

'Oh. OK. You want me to hold on to this for emergencies.' His smile dissolved into a thin line.

'And you know, to let yourself in and stuff. So you don't have to wait for me in the diner,' I added quickly, squeezing the skinny strap of my bag. Why did I feel like I'd messed up? 'I want you to have a key to my apartment.'

'Thanks.'

I looked back at the tiny silver key sparkling amongst all the flowers on the kitchen top.

'Alex, if that key you gave me wasn't my spare, then what was it?'

He sighed, his shoulders dropping. 'It's the key to my place.'

'You were going to give me a spare key?' I asked. If he was giving me his spare key, why was he being so funny about me giving him mine? 'How weird is that?'

'It wasn't supposed to be a spare,' he said, sitting down on the edge of my bed. 'I know you don't really want to get another roommate and I guess Jenny isn't coming back anytime soon, so I was kind of going to suggest that you move in with me.'

I sat down next to him on the bed.

'All the shit we went through last week, Angela, it's all because we're still playing stupid games. I know we got it all wrong the first time, that it was all too much too soon, but I know that I love you so what are we waiting for? As soon as you left for the airport, I missed you. As soon as I saw those pictures online I freaked out, I was so jealous. I hated the thought of losing you so much that I got on a plane to come and see you.'

'Right.' I said.

'The more I think about it, the thought of not having to go further than the next room to see you just makes

321

me really, really happy,' he held a hand above my knee then dropped in on the bed. 'So if I've been a little weird this week, it's because I've had a lot on my mind.'

'Right.'

I ran my finger along the gold zipper on my bag. Lovely bit of craftsmanship.

'I'm not asking you to pack a suitcase and come with me right away,' Alex said. 'But I'll leave you the key, OK?'

'OK,' I said, pulling the zip backwards and forwards.

'I know I can't compete with your Hollywood boyfriend but I picked this up on the way.' He lifted up the flap on his battered satchel and pulled out a single sunflower and placed it on my lap. 'I guess I thought it would be romantic or something. Angela, are you going to say anything?'

I tugged the zip all the way closed and carefully pulled the strap over my head, placing the bag back inside its dust bag. I had no idea where the dust bag was for my first bag. Really, I shouldn't be allowed to have nice things if I couldn't look after them. Even if I really wanted them.

'I don't really know what to say,' I offered, still not quite able to look at him and gripping the end of the bed with both hands. 'Not because I don't want to live with you. I'm just a bit surprised.'

'Yeah, me too,' he breathed out, placing one of his hands over mine. It was warm and covered my hand completely. 'So, you'll think about it?'

'I will,' I promised, finally breaking my staring contest with the carpet and stealing a sneak peek at his deep green eyes. They were big and wide and hopeful. 'I will. Everything you said, it was right. I will think about it.'

'Then that's enough for now,' he said, putting the

sunflower in my hand. 'I have to go – I have terrible pollen allergies and this place is worse than a florist's.'

'You big girl,' I said, following him out to the hallway. 'Do you want to do something later?'

'I have practice, could go on,' he said, wrinkling up his nose at the roses on the counter. 'See you tomorrow?'

I nodded, kissed him once more and then watched him jog down the stairs. Closing the door, I leaned back against it, his sunflower still in my hand. Putting it in the only vase I had in the house, I set it on the windowsill, clearing James's flowers to give it some space.

I dropped to the sofa and yawned. It was reassuring to be back on New York time, blogging from my own living room; comforting, even. For as long as it was my own living room. God, this moving in thing was going to take some thinking about. Maybe living with Alex could be amazing. Waking up with him, going to sleep with him, not going to sleep with him . . . but I couldn't make a decision based on that, could I? There was that racing heartbeat again.

'Blog first, life-changing decisions later,' I said to my laptop, logging on.

The Adventures of Angela: I want to be a part of it . . .
So it looks like my interview with James Jacobs was a hit! I hope you all enjoyed it; you have no idea what I went through to get it for you. Well, actually, I imagine you have a fairly clear idea. As much as I'd love to think otherwise, I'm guessing you check in on blogs other than mine from time to time . . . In hindsight, it was all worth it. And that only has a tiny bit to do with the handbag that was just delivered. Thanks James.

While I have you here, I'd just like to clear some-thing up once and for all. I have never actually made anyone gay (as far as I know?), I just sort of brought it to the world's attention, so anyone worried about my magical ability to 'turn' hot boys can sleep easy in their beds tonight.

Back to the blog. Have you noticed how pretty it is outside today? I'm not sure if it's because spring is around the corner or just because I didn't lose a toe to frostbite today but I'm so happy to be back in New York. Don't get me wrong, Hollywood was fun and it has successfully stolen away my best friend, so I know I'll be going back soon, but is there anywhere on earth that compares to New York City? I don't have to worry about the paparazzi because, let's face it, I'm just not New York news. I don't have to worry about getting in the car just to go out and buy milk because the deli on the corner is open twenty-four hours a day. And I don't have to worry about the constant re-application of sunscreen twelve months of the year; although I can't stress enough that we should all be wearing a moisturizer with sunscreen and, to be honest, waking up to sunshine was absolutely not the worst part of last week. Especially when you've been rolling yourself up in two hoodies, a dressing gown and four pairs of socks just to get from the bed to the bathroom every morning from December until March. Anyway, looks like I'm not going anywhere soon. At least not anywhere too far away . . .

I mailed the blog to Mary and curled up on the sofa. The flat really did stink. Thousands of dollars' worth of flowers might sound like a great idea but in reality it was like living on the perfume counter in Bloomingdale's. Too much. Alex's apartment always smelled the same. Strong coffee in the kitchen, his fresh, soapy shower gel in the bathroom and, if he had the window open, a soft sweetness in the bedroom from the nearby sugar factory.

I got up and wrestled with the window to let in some air but it wouldn't budge. Jenny had always been the only one who'd been able to get it open. Sighing, I gave up and tried the kitchen window. Alex's sunflower sat in the middle of all the other ornate arrangements. Maybe I wasn't designed to live alone, but was that a good enough reason to move in with someone? Where was Jenny when I bloody needed her. I knew she'd say I should just call her but it was early in LA and she had taken to sleeping in as late as possible since she'd stopped working shifts. Before I could turn to the only people I knew would be able to give me good advice, the cast of *Friends*, I heard something in the hallway.

Popping up over the back of the sofa, like a meerkat, I watched the front door swing open to reveal Alex, holding a box of Cheerios.

'I found these downstairs, you must have dropped them,' he said sheepishly.

'Didn't you leave like, half an hour ago?' I asked, climbing over the back of the sofa and taking the cereal.

'Yeah, I've kind of been sitting on your front step,' he admitted, slipping his key back in his hip pocket. 'I was thinking.'

'Thinking?' That was never good.

'I know you need time to think about moving in,' he said, taking my hands in his. 'So I wanted to give you something to think about.'

He pulled me into a gentle kiss that grew stronger and stronger until I was short of breath and pressed backwards up against the fridge door.

'Well that doesn't really help,' I said, pushing him away. 'How am I supposed to think clearly now?'

'You're not,' he grinned, moving back in for another kiss. 'You're supposed to move in with me.'

'You want to come over later?' I asked as Alex pushed my hair back and held my face in both of his hands. 'After practice?'

'It'll be late,' he whispered in between kisses.

'You have a key,' I breathed hard. 'Let yourself in.'

'Sounds good.' He kissed me once more and then slipped back out the door. 'See you later.'

I locked the door and hugged myself tightly. Oh, this was not going to be an easy decision. But then, where was the fun in easy decisions?

Angela's Guide to LA

First things first, as a born-again New Yorker, I was most upset to realize that if you're going to be in LA for any length of time, you absolutely, one hundred per cent need a car. Preferably a very cool convertible, although a less sexy hybrid will score you more eco-points if you bump into Leo DiCaprio. It goes completely against the grain but you'll struggle if you're relying on public transport, pay through the nose if you want to take taxis and never leave your hotel if you're planning on walking everywhere. Bear in mind that people drive like crazies in LA and, while it's obviously incredibly illegal, a lot of people drive drunk, so just be really, really careful, especially at night.

Book ahead online to get the best deals. You can pick up hire cars at various places around the city and at some hotels if you don't fancy hitting the highway straight off the plane. Just be brave and as ballsy as you can be. Double points if you can text, drink coffee and swear at the car next to you all at the same time by the end of your holiday…

My other piece of advice is to wear SUNSCREEN. I'm not a massive sun worshipper at the best of times and I basically had to baste myself from head to toe every time I went outside. In March. Take a bottle of factor 40, buy more while you're there.

SHOPPING

I think my favourite thing about LA was the amazing shop names.
Everything is that little bit more theatrical. Want a tennis racket?
You need to head to The Merchant of Tennis. Black-tie event at short notice?
Hit Friar's Tux Shop. It's classic. The sense of humour of Los Angeleans isn't
always immediately apparent, but are you telling me that the manager of
The Merchant of Tennis isn't going to be a giggle?

Melrose Avenue

Melrose is great. It's got a really
eclectic mix of shops, handily
appointed coffee shops and
restaurants and lots of opportunity for
star-spotting.

Marc by Marc Jacobs

www.marcjacobs.com
8410 MELROSE AVE, LOS ANGELES, CA 90069
On the west side of Fairfax Avenue,
Melrose is dominated by fabulous
designer boutiques, including my
beloved Marc by Marc. It carries the
men's and women's lines as well as
some of the bargainous special
collection items that can be hard to
find. And if that isn't enough for you
and you're feeling flush, the main
collection Marc Jacobs store is directly
opposite. Yay!

Betsey Johnson

www.betseyjohnson.com
8050 MELROSE AVE, LOS ANGELES, CA 90046
Love Betsey Johnson. Can't fit into
Betsey Johnson but LOVE Betsey
Johnson. Definitely pop in and check
out her beautiful girlie designs. Hands
up if you can't live without a polka-
dot puffball strapless mini-dress. I
only see my hand. Put up your hand!

Fred Segal

www.fredsegal.com
8100 MELROSE AVE, LOS ANGELES CA 90046
Fred Segal is a complete institution in
LA. It's also covered in grass. No,
really: all the exterior walls. And the
interior is like a labyrinth, so if you
manage to get in, find something you
like, buy it before David Bowie
appears in Lycra leggings and tries to
distract you with a crystal ball.
Also, the café here is legend so book
ahead and stop in for breakfast or a
mid-shop snack.

Wasteland

www.wastelandclothing.com
7428 MELROSE AVE, LOS ANGELES, CA 90046
If you like your shops to make a little
bit more effort with their frontage,
then you should probably pop along.
Honestly, the front of Wasteland looks
like an explosion in a pop art factory.
I loved it. I also loved their mix of
second-hand high-end designer and
genuinely quirky vintage finds. Don't
go here if you don't have a lot of time.
You will need time. And cash. But
once you've visited, you won't need
new shoes for a while.

Japan LA
www.japanla.com
648 N. FULLER AVE, LOS ANGELES, CA 90036

Hello Kitty, Hello kitsch. This is such a great shop, just off Melrose. It's tiny and full of all things cute and tiny. Strangely enough given the name, there's a high percentage of Japanese goods for sale here, but who doesn't like to know where you can get a Godzilla Kewpie Doll or giant clip-on Gloomy Bear Claws?

Rodeo Drive
www.rodeodrive-bh.com

You know you need your Pretty Woman experience. Who wouldn't feel amazing strutting down this ridiculously clean street, armed with stiff, crisp paper bags. I would recommend you don't try the hooker thing, though: the police do not look kindly upon it and nothing for sale on Rodeo Drive is worth that... Well, maybe Miu Miu. Or Tiffany. And La Perla is nice... I mean, nothing.

The Grove
www.thegrovela.com
189 THE GROVE DRIVE
LOS ANGELES, CA 90036

The one place I don't love is The Beverly Center. It's literally just a shopping centre. If you really must do a mall, go to The Grove. There might not be quite as many shops but it's outdoor, there's a cinema, a lovely French restaurant and a lot of my favourite stores. They've got a Nordstrom, which is a really great department store stocking most of the top brands, an Anthropologie, a Victoria's Secret, an Abercrombie and, if you're really missing New York, a tiny little Barney's.

Plus you can walk through to the Farmer's Market and eat yourself stupid. And, if this isn't enough, you can actually get a cab here, if you can imagine that.

Kitson on Robertson
www.shopkitson.com
115 S. ROBERTSON BLVD
LOS ANGELES, CA 90048

Kitson is famous for attracting the Paris Hiltons of this world and I honestly didn't want to like it but what can I say? I'm easily led. They have pretty things and the staff are nice, which is more or less all it takes to get a sale out of me.

Squaresville
1800 N. Vermont Avenue
Los Angeles, CA 90027
If you venture as far east as Los Feliz (and you should), make sure you pop into Squaresville. It's honestly one of the best vintage stores I've ever, ever, ever been to – and I've been to loads. There's everything from 1970s sundresses and 1950s wedding frocks right through to seriously distressed denim and vintage Joan Jett and the Blackhearts tour T-shirts. Loads of good bags, shoes and – well – interesting hats too. What's not to love?

Nordstrom Rack
www.shop.nordstrom.com
227 N. Glendale Ave
Glendale, CA 91206
and
300 The Promenade N.
Long Beach, CA 90802
If you have a car, and you most probably will have, you should absolutely try and check out a couple of LA's outlet malls or, at the very least, a Nordstrom Rack. Carrying all of Nordstrom's overstock and factory seconds, you can bag the best bargains here. Elbows at the ready, breathe in deep and go for it…

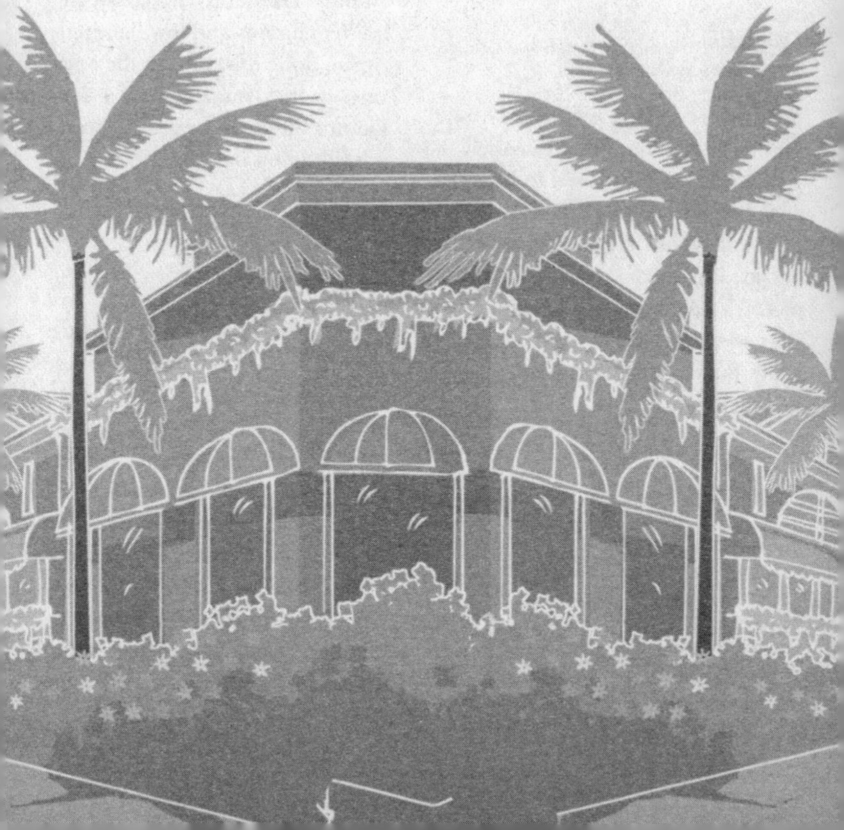

EATING

The Ivy on Robertson

Tel: (+1) 310 274 8303
113 N. ROBERTSON BLVD
LOS ANGELES, CA 90048

It's a total cliché but the food at The Ivy really is delicious. I can't quite believe that people will genuinely order and then not eat it but I have seen it with my own two eyes. Get a table on the patio for lunch, wear huge sunglasses and keep your head down. Everyone will think you're a celeb. And whatever you do, leave room for ice cream: delish.

Dominick's

www.dominicksrestaurant.com
8715 BEVERLY BLVD
WEST HOLLYWOOD, CA 90048

Not far from The Ivy and insanely yummy. Dominick's used to be a rat pack hangout and it feels reassuringly old Hollywood. Try and get a table outside if it's nice (and of course it's nice, it's LA), order the artichoke to start and enjoy the hot waiters. No really. Super, super hot. Not that I was looking.

25 Degrees/Dakota at The Roosevelt

www.25degreesrestaurant.com
www.dakota-restaurant.com
7000 HOLLYWOOD BLVD
HOLLYWOOD, CA 90028

Ridiculously good food. 25 Degrees for delicious burgers and Dakota if you want to upgrade to steak. I am greedy so I need fries and onion rings with my burger but a) the portions are pretty huge so it's good to share if you can and b) the waiting staff do get a little bit confused by girls that eat. The milkshakes are also very yummy. Dakota is very classy, all leather curtains and low lighting. Again, don't miss out on the onion rings or fries, but the steak is the star. Do not fill up on bread. I repeat, do not fill up on bread…

The Farmers Market

www.farmersmarketla.com
6333 WEST THIRD STREET
LOS ANGELES, CA 90036

OMG. Never have I seen so much yummy food in one place. Honestly, for a city that doesn't eat, LA has a lot of delicious things on offer. Choose from Bryan's Pit Barbecue, China Depot, Deano's Gourmet Pizza, The Gumbo Pot and, well, more or less any other food stuff you can think of. I opted for The Gumbo Pot and was not disappointed. Get the hush puppies. I don't know what they are but they're deep fried, delicious and not shoes…

DRINKS

The Dresden Room in Los Feliz

www.thedresden.com
1760 N. VERMONT AVE (AT KINGSWELL AVENUE)
HOLLYWOOD, CA 90027

Not only is The Dresden super-cool in a retro style, it was also the star of Swingers (besides Jon Favreau and The Double V). Prepare to rack up some top girlfriend points if you take your boy. Order the Blood and Sand cocktail and have the number of a taxi company to hand.

Skybar at The Mondrian

www.mondrianhotel.com
8440 SUNSET BLVD
WEST HOLLYWOOD, CA 90069

Now I'm told the Skybar isn't what it used to be in the cool stakes, but it is pretty spectacular. The view is amazing, the people are still pretty and it can still be a bit difficult to get in. Worth it, though, seriously: the view is gorgeous and the open-air cabanas and impromptu late-night dancing in the bar is all sorts of fun.

Bar Marmont

www.chateaumarmont.com
8171 W. SUNSET BLVD
WEST HOLLYWOOD, CA 90046

If you really want to spot a celeb, or at least a black American Express card, try Bar Marmont. As part of Chateau Marmont, home away from home to Hollywood's elite for decades, it prides itself on its discretion. Plus, it's bloody beautiful – all red lamplight, butterflies on the walls and gorgeous people wall to wall.

Not that it's relevant, but the toilet in the lobby of the actual hotel is insanely massive. Seriously, there is a little waiting room before you get to the actual toilet (slash shower room…) with a sofa and a massive TV that is bigger than my entire apartment.

HOTELS

The Renaissance at The Hollywood and Highland

www.renaissancehollywood.com
1755 N. HIGHLAND AVE
HOLLYWOOD, CA 90028

If you're looking for somewhere central, The Renaissance is perfect. The rooms are clean and spacious, there's a rooftop pool with a view of the Hollywood sign, there are giant elephant statues (no, really) and, most exciting of all, it's part of the Hollywood and Highland complex – a mini-mall with some great shops and yummy restaurants. I always find it easier to sleep knowing I'm only five minutes from Sephora. Actually, the most important factor here is that the boot camp sessions for the last series of American Idol were held at The Renaissance.

The W

www.starwoodhotels.com
930 HILGARD AVE (AT LE CONTE AVENUE)
LOS ANGELES, CA 90024

Everyone loves a W and this bad boy is all beautiful little-bungalow-style suites. Gorgeous. The beds are insanely comfortable, every last aspect of the place is flawlessly designed and the staff are ridiculously helpful. Obviously this all comes at a price but you're in LA, right? It's probably a price worth paying.

The Roosevelt

www.hollywoodroosevelt.com
7000 HOLLYWOOD BLVD
HOLLYWOOD, CA 90028

This is a genuine piece of old Hollywood history. The first-ever Academy Awards ceremony was even held here and the outdoor pool features an underwater mural by David Hockney – oooh. Slap bang in the middle of Hollywood, this is a great hotel for business or pleasure. But mainly pleasure, with Teddy's Nightclub, Library bar, The Tropicana Pool Bar (notoriously difficult to get in to but easier for residents) and the Dakota and 25 Degrees restaurants. The Roosevelt is forever popping up on TV and in movies, crawling with hot young things.

The Tower Beverly Hills

www.thetowerbeverlyhills.com
1224 BEVERWIL DR
LOS ANGELES, CA 90035

The Tower isn't the most super-cool hotel in all of LA but it is lovely, it has a great little pool, there are two computers in the lounge with free internet access and all the rooms have little balconies. Plus it's ten minutes' walk from Pinkbery, fifteen minutes' walk from Rodeo Drive and, if you're feeling brave, about half an hour's bus ride away from Santa Monica beach. Most importantly, it isn't ridiculously expensive, either, which leaves all the more money for all that lovely, lovely shopping you're going to do.

Log onto
www.iheartholllywood.co.uk
to find out more about
the *I heart* series and read
an exclusive extract from
I heart Paris

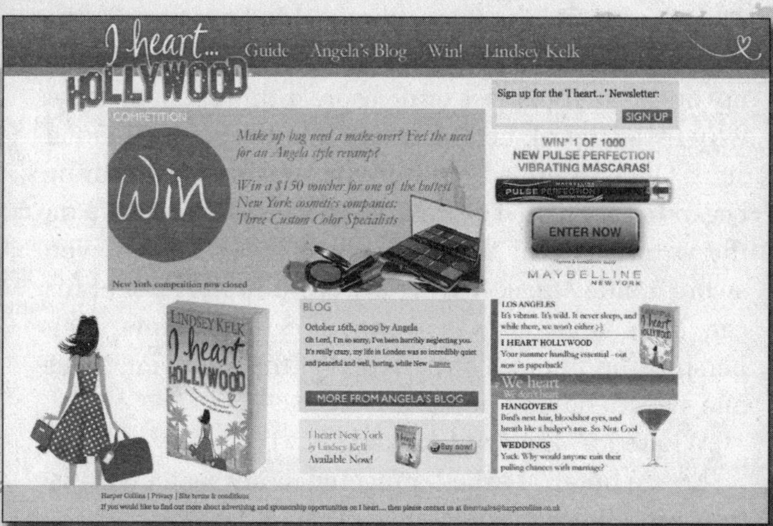
I heart...
HOLLYWOOD
Guide
Angela's Blog
Win!
Lindsey Kelk
Sign up for the 'I heart...' Newsletter:
SIGN UP
COMPETITION
Make up bag need a make-over? Feel the need for an Angela style revamp?
Win
Win a $150 voucher for one of the hottest New York cosmetics companies: Three Custom Color Specialists
New York competition now closed
WIN* 1 OF 1000 NEW PULSE PERFECTION VIBRATING MASCARAS!
ENTER NOW
MAYBELLINE NEW YORK
LINDSEY KELK
I heart HOLLYWOOD
BLOG
October 16th, 2009 by Angela
Oh Lord, I'm so sorry, I've been horribly neglecting you. It's really crazy, my life in London was so incredibly quiet and peaceful and well, boring, while New ...more
MORE FROM ANGELA'S BLOG
I heart New York by Lindsey Kelk Available Now!
Buy now!
LOS ANGELES
It's vibrant. It's wild. It never sleeps, and while there, we won't either ;-)
I HEART HOLLYWOOD
Your summer handbag essential - out now in paperback!
We heart
HANGOVERS
Bird's nest hair, bloodshot eyes, and breath like a badger's arse. So. Not. Cool
WEDDINGS
Yuck. Why would anyone ruin their pulling chances with marriage?
Harper Collins | Privacy | Site terms & conditions

You'll also have a chance to enter
competitions, keep up-to-date
with Angela's adventures through
her blog, read top tips
for where to eat, drink,
shop and sleep in LA,
and much much more!

In case you missed the start of Angela's
fabulous adventures, here's a taster from

I heart New York ♥

The plane landed at JFK without a hitch and, while the homeland security guard didn't seem that interested in my break-up (business or pleasure didn't seem to cover why I was there), he did let me into the country. Good start. Once I stepped out into the sunshine, everything began to feel real. The cabs were yellow, they were on the wrong side of the road, and my taxi driver even swore a blue streak tossing my bag into the boot of his car. Man alive, it was warm. If women glow, men perspire, and horses sweat, right at that moment, I was one sweaty bloody horse.

'Where to?' the driver asked.

'Erm, a hotel?' I asked, plugging in my seatbelt as we took off. 'I need a hotel.'

'You fuckin' serious?' he asked, swerving onto the highway before I could even reply. 'Which fuckin' hotel? There are fuckin' millions of hotels.'

'Oh, yeah, I – well – I—' before I could finish my sentence, I started to tear up. 'I don't know anywhere. I just sort of got here.'

'Well, guess what lady?' the driver yelled back at me, 'I'm a fuckin' taxi driver, not tourist information.

You want me to fuckin' drop you here in the middle of Queens or you want to give me the name of a hotel?'

In response, I burst into tears. Witty comeback, thy name is Angela.

'Jesus fuckin' Christ. I'm dropping you off at the first fuckin' hotel we pass,' he muttered, turning the radio all the way up.

Twenty minutes of talk radio later, I was hanging out of the window like a dog in a bandana, and I had *just* about stopped crying when I spotted it.

The New York City skyline. Manhattan. The Empire State Building. The beautiful, beautiful Chrysler Building. The Woolworth Building with its big old churchy steeple. And I fell in love. It hit me so hard that I stopped crying, stopped thinking, stopped breathing. I felt as if I'd been winded. Winding the cab window all the way down, I breathed in the skyscrapers, the giant billboards, the industrial riverside stretches and the sweaty, steamy air. I was in New York. Not at home in London, not at Louisa's wedding, and nowhere near my filthy, cheating fiancé. And so, for the want of something else to do, as we disappeared down into the midtown tunnel, I burst into tears again.

The first hotel we passed turned out to be the last hotel the cabbie had dropped off at, and it was beautiful. The Union was set just off Union Square Park, with a lobby dimly lit to the point of a power cut, and filled with the overpowering scent of Diptyque candles that smelled like fresh washing on the line. Overstuffed sofas and ancient leather armchairs filled the space, and the reception was picked out in fairylights. Suddenly finding myself in such perfect surroundings, I was very aware of the state of my hair, my dehydrated skin and my rumpled clothes. I really, really did look like complete crap, but this place couldn't be further from a two-bedroomed terrace in south west London. It was just what I needed.

'Welcome to The Union,' said the incredibly beautiful woman behind the counter. 'My name is Jennifer, how can we help you today?'

'Hi,' I said, pulling my handbag high up on my shoulder and kicking my travel bag towards the reception desk. 'I was wondering if you had a room available?'

She smiled serenely and began clicking away on a keyboard. As she tapped, her glossy spiral curls bounced away behind her. 'OK, we are a little busy but . . . I have a junior suite at $800 a night?' She looked up. My expression apparently suggested that was a little bit out of my price range. 'Or I have a single at $350. But it only sleeps one.'

'Oh, OK,' I fished around in my battered old bag for a credit card and tried not to work out the cost of the room in real money, 'it's just me. Well, I just found out my boyfriend was cheating on me and we broke up and I had to leave home and I thought, well, where's better to get away to than New York? And,' I paused and looked up. She was still smiling at me, but with a healthy dose of terror in her eyes. 'Sorry, I'm sorry. A single would be fine.'

'And how long would you be staying with us?' she asked, tapping away again. I guessed she was alerting everyone to the fact that there was a desperate woman checking in. My photo was probably being distributed to the whole staff with a 'do not engage in conversation' note.

'Sorry?' I hadn't thought that far ahead.

'When will you be going home?' she said slowly.

'I – I don't have a home,' I said, equally slowly. 'So, I don't know.' I was dangerously close to tears and really didn't want to let them go in the reception of the swankiest hotel I'd ever stepped in. But, wow, I really didn't have a home.

'Well, I kinda just wanted to know when you would be checking out, but the room is free for the next week, shall I put you in for seven nights and see where we go from there?' she suggested. I nodded and handed over my credit card. Jennifer exchanged it for a sexy black room pass key, emblazoned with a silver U. 'Room 1126 on floor eleven, take the elevator and then turn left. It's at the end of the corridor.'

I nodded numbly and took the key, tripping over my own bag as I turned.

'Do you need anything at all, Miss Clark?' Jennifer asked. I turned and tried to smile, shaking my head.

'Head check?' I could only make jokes for so long before I evaporated.

'Just phone down if you want anything at all,' I heard her call. Hopefully, she wouldn't send up a therapist, I had always been warned that Americans didn't always get sarcasm.

If the room was a single, Mark's house was a mansion. A huge, white bed dominated the tastefully painted cream bedroom, topped off by a dramatic brown leather headboard. Past the bed, a floor to ceiling window with beautiful views of Union Square Park below. A walk-in wardrobe was tucked away to my left, and to my right was the bathroom. I dropped my travel bag and opened the door. It was beautiful. White tiled walls, black slate floor. The toilet and sink were tucked neatly away against the wall, while the rest of the room was completely taken over by a glass encased bath and shower. Two chrome showerheads jutted out from opposite walls, and a glass shelf held small but perfectly formed designer toiletries. A chrome shelf by the sink groaned under the weight of fluffy towels, and a thick waffle robe hung behind the bathroom door.

I backed back into the bedroom and looked out at the window, but paused before I got there. This was just what I'd been looking for, but between being completely exhausted and suddenly incredibly hungry, I just couldn't bring myself to look outside and see a strange city. Instead, I headed back into the bathroom, via the well-stocked mini bar, and ran a bath, using the whole bottle of bubbles. Stripping off my clothes, I stepped into the bath, wishing that my brain would stop ticking over for just a second. Using the edge of the bath as a makeshift bar, I mixed a $15 vodka and coke in the toothbrush glass and poured half a packet of $8 peanut butter M&Ms into my mouth. It was less than twenty-four hours since I was in that shower back in the UK, thinking how badly I needed to get away, and here I was. Away.

I lay back and sighed deeply, letting the ends of my hair soak through. Gradually the sigh turned into a whimper, and the whimper became a sob. I was allowed to cry, wasn't I? I'd been cheated on by my fiancé, deceived by my best friend, and humiliated in front of all my friends and family. Reaching for the M&Ms, I managed to polish them off in one go, washing them down with a large swig of my drink. What was I thinking, coming all the way to New York on my own? I wasn't being brave, I was being stupid. There was no one here to help me, to talk to me, to watch *Pretty Woman*, *Dirty Dancing* and *Breakfast at Tiffany's* with me. I should towel off, call my mum and get a plane home. This wasn't impulsive and exciting, it was immature and cowardly. Just a really, really elaborate version of hiding in my room and getting wasted. I'd made my point, and more or less paid a grand for a bath and a bag of sweets, now it was time to face reality.

I heart New York

It's official. Angela Clark is in love –
with the most fabulous city in the world.

Fleeing her cheating boyfriend and clutching little
more than a crumpled bridesmaid dress, a pair of
Louboutins and her passport, Angela jumps on
a plane – destination NYC.

Holed up in a cute hotel room, Angela gets a
New York makeover from her NBF Jenny and
a whirlwind tour of the city that never sleeps.
Before she knows it, Angela is dating two sexy guys.
And, best of all, she gets to write about it in her
new blog (Carrie Bradshaw eat your heart out).
But there's one thing telling readers about your romantic
dilemmas, it's another figuring them out for yourself…

Angela has fallen head over heels for the big apple,
but does she heart New York more than home?

I heart Paris

July 2010

Angela Clark is a British girl living the life dreams are made of in fabulous New York. But she's never been to the romantic capital of the world: Paris. So when boyfriend Alex suggests a romantic trip there, tying in with his band's tour and Angela writing an insider's guide to the hip city for a glossy fashion mag, Belle, she jumps at the chance.

Soon Angela finds herself meandering along charming streets lined with designer shops, sipping creamy hot chocolate and eating croissants. It's a world away from New York but she could get used to the joie de vivre of Paris.

But when Louisa, Angela's best friend shows up from London, it's not quite the happy, girly catch up she'd hoped for and everything in Paris seems to be going from bad to worse. Louisa reminds Angela that her old life is only a train journey away. With Alex spending so much time partying with the band and meeting up with his ex, for the first time in ages, Angela is homesick.

Suddenly Angela is questioning her new life in New York and wondering – is it make or break for her and Alex?